2495
p

COMMENTARY
ON THE

CATECHISM
OF THE
CATHOLIC
CHURCH

COMMENTARY ON THE

CATECHISM OF THE CATHOLIC CHURCH

Edited by

MICHAEL J. WALSH

A Liturgical Press Book

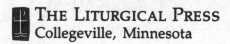

THE LITURGICAL PRESS
Collegeville, Minnesota

Published in the United States of America,
its dependencies, and Canada by
The Liturgical Press
Collegeville, Minnesota 56321

Published in Great Britain by Geoffrey Chapman,
a Cassell imprint

First published 1994

Library of Congress Cataloging-in-Publication Data
The Catechism of the Catholic Church : a commentary / edited by
Michael J. Walsh.
   p.   cm.
Includes bibliographical references and indexes.
ISBN 0-8146-2305-0
1. Catholic Church. Catechismus Ecclesiae Catholicae.
2. Catholic Church—Catechisms.   I. Walsh, Michael J., 1937–
BX1959.5. C384   1994   93-37440
238′.2—dc20   CIP

Typeset by Litho Link Ltd, Welshpool, Powys, Wales
Printed and bound in Great Britain by
Mackays of Chatham PLC

CONTENTS

Acknowledgements   vii

Abbreviations   viii

Introduction: Apostolic Constitution *Fidei Depositum* **and the**   1
     Prologue (paragraphs 1–25)
     Michael J. Walsh

The human capacity for God, and God's initiative   6
     (paragraphs 26–141)
     Excursus on magisterium and 'Magisterium'   34
     Robert Murray SJ

The doctrine of faith (paragraphs 142–197)   36
     Dermot A. Lane ₁ ¹⁹⁴¹⁻

The doctrine on God (paragraphs 198–231)   50
     Brian Davies OP

The doctrine of the Trinity (paragraphs 232–267)   66
     Catherine Mowry LaCugna ₁ ¹⁹⁵²⁻

Creation and original sin (paragraphs 268–421)   82
     Gabriel Daly OSA

The incarnation of the Son of God (paragraphs 422–511)   112
     Jacques Dupuis SJ

The mysteries of Christ's life (paragraphs 512–570)   127
     Gerard O'Hanlon SJ

The death of Christ, his descent among the dead,   143
     and his Resurrection (paragraphs 571–682)
     Excursus on the Jews and the death of Jesus   162
     John McDade SJ

The Holy Spirit (paragraphs 683–747)　　　　　166
  John O'Donnell SJ

The Church (paragraphs 748–975)　　　　　178
  J.M.R. Tillard OP, 1927–

Eschatology (paragraphs 988–1065)　　　　　205
  Brian E. Daley SJ

The sacramental economy (paragraphs 1066–1209)　　　　　225
  Regis A. Duffy OFM, 1934–

The sacraments of Christian initiation　　　　　242
  (paragraphs 1210–1321)
  Edward Yarnold SJ, 1926–

The doctrine on the Eucharist (paragraphs 1322–1419)　　　　　259
  Raymond Moloney SJ

Penance and reconciliation (paragraphs 1420–1498)　　　　　274
  Monika K. Hellwig, 1929–

The anointing of the sick (paragraphs 1499–1532)　　　　　288
  James L. Empereur SJ, 1933–

The sacrament of orders (paragraphs 1533–1600)　　　　　303
  Philip J. Rosato SJ

Marriage (paragraphs 1601–1666)　　　　　318
  Lisa Sowle Cahill, 1948–

Sacramentals and funerals (paragraphs 1667–1690)　　　　　330
  Kevin Donovan SJ, 1931–

Our human vocation (paragraphs 1691–2051)　　　　　336
  Gerard J. Hughes SJ

More than law and precept: commandments 1–3　　　　　357
  (paragraphs 2052–2195)
  Bernhard Häring CSsR, 1912–

You shall love your neighbour: commandments 4–10　　　　　367
  (paragraphs 2196–2557)
  Joseph A. Selling

The encounter known as prayer (paragraphs 2558–2758)　　　　　395
  Philip Endean SJ

The Lord's Prayer (paragraphs 2759–2865)　　　　　410
  Noel D. O'Donoghue ODC

Contributors　　　　　422

Scripture index　　　　　427

Index to the documents of Vatican II　　　　　431

Subject index　　　　　433

ACKNOWLEDGEMENTS

The Editor gratefully acknowledges the permission of Doubleday/Image Books, New York to reprint the poem by Anthony de Mello which appears on p. 48; of Oxford University Press for the quotations on pp. 52–3 from Richard Swinburne, *The Coherence of Theism*, on pp. 56–7 from James Barr, *Biblical Faith and Natural Theology*, and on p. 149 from *The Oxford Authors: Gerard Manley Hopkins*, edited by Catherine Phillips; of WCC Publications, Geneva, for the quotation on p. 92 from *Baptism, Eucharist and Ministry* (Faith and Order Papers 111); of HarperCollins (New York) for the quotation on p. 95 from Paul Ricoeur, *The Symbolism of Evil*; of Éditions du Seuil (Paris) for the quotation on p. 98 from Pierre Teilhard de Chardin, *Christianity and Evolution*; of SPCK for the quotation on p. 99 from *Readings in Christian Theology*, edited by P. Hodgson and R. King, and on pp. 149–50 from Hans Urs von Balthasar, *Elucidations*; of T. and T. Clark (Edinburgh) for the quotation on p. 153 from *The von Balthasar Reader*, edited by Medard Kehl and Werner Löser; of Burns and Oates for the quotation on p. 102 from volume V of *A Commentary on the Documents of Vatican II*, edited by H. Vorgrimler, and the quotation on p. 109 from the article by Giuseppe Alberigo in *The Reception of Vatican II*; of Michael Hamburger and Persea Books, New York, for the translation on p. 146 of the poem by Paul Celan; of The Lutterworth Press for the quotation on p. 152 from E. Hennecke's contribution to *New Testament Apocrypha*; of Liturgical Press/Michael Glazier of Collegeville, Minnesota for the quotation on pp. 298–9 from James L. Empereur *Prophetic Anointing*; of *Theology Digest* for the quotation on p. 329 of the précis of Norbert Greinacher, 'The problem of divorce and remarriage'; and of the Institute of Carmelite Studies, Washington DC for the quotation on p. 416 from St Teresa of Avila, *The Way of Perfection*.

Quotations of the *Catechism of the Catholic Church* are taken from the English translation for the United Kingdom, © 1994 Geoffrey Chapman–Libreria Editrice Vaticana, and are used by permission.

Citations of documents of Vatican II are taken from *Vatican Council II: Conciliar and Postconciliar Documents*, ed. Austin Flannery OP (Dublin: Dominican Publications and United States of America: Costello Publishing Company, 1975).

Excerpts from the English translation of the *Catechism of the Catholic Church* for the United States of America, © 1994, United States Catholic Conference, Inc. – Libreria Editrice Vaticana. Used with permission. Excerpts from the *Catechism of the Catholic Church*, © 1994, Concacan Inc. – Libreria Editrice Vaticana, for the English translation in Canada. All rights reserved. Used with permission.

ABBREVIATIONS

AAS	Acta Apostolicae Sedis
AG	*Ad Gentes*
CIC	Codex Iuris Canonici (1983)
CT	*Catechesi Tradendae*
DAS	*Divino Afflante Spiritu*
DS	Denzinger–Schönmetzer, *Enchiridion Symbolorum* (1965)
DV	*Dei Verbum*
FD	*Fidei Depositum*
EB	*Enchiridion Biblicum*
GS	*Gaudium et Spes*
JB	Jerusalem Bible
LG	*Lumen Gentium*
ND	Neuner–Dupuis, *The Christian Faith in the Doctrinal Documents of the Catholic Church*
NRSV	New Revised Standard Version
PG	Migne, *Patrologia Graeca*
PL	Migne, *Patrologia Latina*
PR	Prologue to the *Catechism of the Catholic Church*
RCIA	Rite of Christian Initiation of Adults
REB	Revised English Bible
RSV	Revised Standard Version
SC	*Sacrosanctum Concilium*
STh	*Summa Theologiae*
UR	*Unitatis Redintegratio*

INTRODUCTION
Apostolic Constitution *Fidei Depositum*
The Prologue
(Paragraphs 1–25)

Michael J. Walsh
Heythrop College, University of London

Important documents of the Roman Pontiff are traditionally known by the first two or three words of the Latin text. These words must therefore be chosen with care. The title of the Apostolic Constitution with which Pope John Paul II introduces the new *Catechism of the Catholic Church* is *Fidei Depositum* — 'the deposit of faith'. The deposit of faith is an expression in common use, at least within the Roman Catholic Church, and it is easy enough to describe what it means in general terms.[1] It is much more difficult, however, to be precise about it. It is not identical with the dogmas of the Church, nor with theological doctrines, though it necessarily underlies both of them. Nor is it identical with the Scriptures, though these sacred writings encapsulate the deposit of faith as they record the life and teachings of Christ.

As Pope John Paul says in the introductory section of *Fidei Depositum* (hereafter FD), the task assigned to the Second Vatican Council by John XXIII when he summoned it was to 'present better the precious deposit of Christian doctrine in order to make it more accessible to the Christian faithful and to all people of good will'. The deposit of faith, then, has to be articulated anew in and for every generation so they may understand it in their own terms. In saying this, the present Pope was re-echoing the words of Pope John in his opening address to the Council, *Gaudet Mater Ecclesia*, when he distinguished between the substance of faith and the language in which it was presented.[2]

In appealing to the experience of Vatican II, as Pope John Paul does in a moving tribute to the effect the Council had upon him personally, both the Apostolic Constitution and the Prologue to the *Catechism* avoid remarking that Vatican II had considered but had rejected the idea of a catechism to summarise the teaching. There was, of course, a distinguished precedent for such a book, as the Prologue (hereafter PR) notes in passing (cf. PR 9). The Fathers of the Council of Trent asked for a catechism to be produced to contain the teaching of the Council. The Latin edition was ready by 1556 — it had originally been written in Italian[3] — and was

1

published as the *Catechismus ex Decreto Concilii Tridentini ad parochos*, though it has always been more commonly known as the *Catechismus Romanus* or 'Roman Catechism'.[4]

Comparisons have been made between the catechism of Trent and this new volume claiming to represent the teaching of Vatican II[5] (whether it does so faithfully in particular areas is frequently discussed by the contributors to this *Commentary*), but the differences between the contexts in which they have been produced are considerable. Trent met at a time of extreme crisis in the Church, in an attempt to counter the Protestant Reformation. It formulated a large number of doctrinal decrees precisely in the form of decrees and condemnations, which lent themselves to relatively easy summary. Vatican II, under the guidance of Pope John, positively turned its back on such an approach. The documents it produced, though of varying quality, were in the nature of theological treatises which do not lend themselves to the traditional catechetical presentation. These documents were widely distributed in their entirety and in many languages, and have surely been read in the past quarter of a century by more people than ever read the Roman Catechism throughout all its numerous editions. Finally, the decrees of Trent were addressed to a much smaller world, and one of far less cultural diversity, than that which the Catholic Church has to address today.

This last is an important point, for one of the most serious objections launched against the *Catechism* by its critics, both contributors to this *Commentary* and many others besides, is that it is impossible to produce for so diverse a world a catechism which is equally intelligible to all, and equally applicable around the globe. In place of a fully-fledged catechism, in the aftermath of Vatican II there was produced a *General Catechetical Directory*, which proffered guidance for drawing up local catechisms suited to local needs. The best known of these (though it pre-dated the *Catechetical Directory*) was the Dutch Catechism, published in 1967.

Both *Fidei Depositum* and the Prologue to the new *Catechism* are clearly aware of the problem of cultural diversity. Both stress the need for adaptation 'required by the differences of culture, age, spiritual maturity, and social and ecclesial condition among all those to whom it is addressed' (PR 24; cf. FD, p. 6). Much therefore depends upon (1) the degree of authority to be attached to the text, and (2) the degree of independence local episcopal conferences will in practice have in undertaking adaptations for their own particular needs.

As far as (2) goes, the outlook is not encouraging, given the degree of control which the Vatican has exercised over the translation of the text into an English idiom suitable for today's Catholics in the British Isles and the United States. On (1), the degree of authority, Pope John Paul is surprisingly restrained. He says only that 'I declare it [i.e., the *Catechism*] to be a sure norm for teaching the faith and thus a valid and legitimate instrument for ecclesial communion' (FD, p. 5). The same might be said of, say, a report from the International Theological

Commission.

Nonetheless, there is a worrying degree of ambiguity in *Fidei Depositum*. It may be, and I suspect it is, unintentional, but there is an unfortunate parallel drawn between the recently completed renewal of the codes of canon law of both Eastern- and Western-rite churches, and the production of this *Catechism* (FD, p. 3). Law is, of its nature, imposed from above, no matter how willingly received: if this *Catechism* expresses as closely as possible the deposit of faith as articulated for the present generation, then it represents the faith of the Church as it is *already* accepted and believed by the People of God. The comparison with the Code of Canon Law suggests that the *Catechism* represents a norm which can be, like a law, imposed by authority. There is throughout the *Catechism*, as contributors frequently make mention, far too much emphasis on the authority of the magisterium (and see the excursus below, pp. 34–5, by Dr Robert Murray for an examination of the current misuse of that term), and far too little stress on the role of the Holy Spirit in the life of the Church.[6]

The second implication when the production of the *Catechism* is compared to the renewal of canon law is that the faith can be 'codified', reduced to a number of propositions which can be learned by rote. There was indeed something of this implied in the now traditional question-and-answer form of catechisms, but as the Prologue points out, quoting *Catechesi Tradendae* of 1979, the notion of catechesis is far broader (cf. PR 5), and it insists that the *Catechism* is to be treated as an organic whole, and read as such (PR 18). It is, however, not wholly consistent in this regard, for it says of the 'In Brief' sections scattered throughout the book that they are 'summaries [which] may suggest to local catechists brief summary formulae that could be memorized' (PR 22). But as, for example, Jean-Marie Tillard points out,[7] these 'In Brief' paragraphs may be sometimes inadequate, sometimes frankly inaccurate, summaries of the teaching contained in the body of the text.

The Prologue's mention of catechists raises the question of the intended readership for this book. Bishop David Konstant of Leeds, who was a member of the editorial committee and who is in his own right an expert on religious education, has commented: 'The text is for those who teach the faith. It is not intended for the direct use of children or young people. It will require discerning use.'[8] One could reasonably expect that the text of a document intended for teachers of the faith would represent the very best of modern scholarship in interpreting the deposit of faith for today's Church. But does it?

The Apostolic Constitution explains how the work of preparing the *Catechism* was undertaken. Although Vatican II had not called for one, an Extraordinary Synod of Bishops, assembled in January 1985 to celebrate the twentieth anniversary of the end of that Council, determined that a 'catechism or compendium of all Catholic doctrine regarding both faith and morals be composed' (FD, p. 3).[9] The following year a Commission of twelve cardinals and bishops, over which presided Cardinal Joseph Ratzinger, Prefect of the Congregation for the Doctrine of the Faith, was established. Under this Commission there was an editorial committee of seven diocesan bishops. The editorial committee had responsibility for drafting the text and incorporating the suggestions of the Commission, as well as those from theological consultors around the world.[10]

'As a whole', says *Fidei Depositum*, the plan 'received a broadly favourable acceptance on the part of the Episcopate' (FD, p. 4). It all depends what one means by 'broadly'. From many of those who were allowed to see the draft there came very vigorous criticism. In all, there were some 2,400 modifications proposed to the version circulated to bishops in 1989. Mgr William Shannon, for example, was asked to examine the first draft in March 1990: 'I was not impressed by what I read ... I had been asked to make suggestions to be sent to the commission writing the catechism, and I did so; but I honestly felt it was impossible to bandaid the text we had been given. It was "beyond redemption".' Three years later his views are significantly different: there had been a great deal of improvement to the document.[11] That was undoubtedly a view shared by many who have seen both versions. But how big an improvement?

There are undoubtedly many strengths to the *Catechism*: one, rightly emphasised by a couple of contributors to this volume, is the handling of Jewish–Christian relations, which is uniformly sensitive. To take another example, Father Brian Davies OP finds the doctrine of God in the *Catechism* very sympathetic, concluding that readers of this section 'have a solid and reliable guide in their quest for God' (p. 63) — though he also points out that other philosophers of religion would not necessarily share his view, and that the *Catechism* discussion of God is not as uncontroversial as the text appears to suppose.

Few of the contributors find nothing at all to welcome in the *Catechism*'s treatment of the topic they are discussing, some rather more so than others (Fr Gabriel Daly OSA, writing on original sin, is perhaps an exception), but the general view could be summed up in a remark made by Fr Philip Rosato SJ: 'The article on Orders is a text both conceptually inadequate and spiritually uninspiring' (p. 303). And the splendid discussion of the Jews simply serves to highlight the woefully inadequate treatment of world religions apart from Judaism and, indeed, of ecumenical relations with other Christian churches.

When I invited the authors to contribute to this *Commentary on the Catechism of the Catholic Church*, I suggested they entered into 'critical dialogue' with the text upon which they were commenting. They have, I believe, all done so excellently, and I am extremely grateful for the readiness with which they replied to my request and their promptness in submitting their articles. I would especially like to thank those two or three who, for one reason or another, had to undertake their task at extremely short notice, and in particular to thank Professor Joan Greatrex for so admirably translating the article by Jean-Marie Tillard.

Editions which have already appeared of the *Catechism* in languages other than English have had remarkably high sales. One cannot help wondering whether the volume will not be, like the Bible and Shakespeare, much bought but little read. This present volume was conceived as a commentary upon that text, but thanks to the diligence and the skill of the contributors it will in great part also serve as an up-to-date survey of the expert teaching of theologians on those topics in Catholic theology which are touched upon, often all too inadequately, by the new *Catechism of the Catholic Church*.

Notes

1   E.g., 'the definitive revelation of God given in Jesus Christ and entrusted to the church to be preserved and proclaimed with fidelity': Gerald O'Collins in Alan Richardson and John Bowden (eds), *A New Dictionary of Christian Theology* (London: SCM Press, 1983), p. 152.

2   Or did he say this? For the controversy, see Peter Hebblethwaite, *Pope Paul VI* (London: HarperCollins, 1993), p. 304 and footnote.

3   The working language of the group who composed the new *Catechism* was French, and it is from the French version, at least so far, that all authorised translations have been made. The French edition was also the first to be published.

4   The English translation, however, was titled *A catechism for curats* [*sic*].

5   Cf., for example, an article in the Madrid fortnightly *Vida Nueva* (2 January 1993), which has the title 'Dos catecismos, dos papas, dos epocas paralelas' (p. 20). Cardinal Joseph Ratzinger appears to subscribe to the 'parallelism', apparently seeing both Councils as occurring at periods which marked an abrupt break with what went before: see the interview he gave to Henri Tincq in *Le Monde* (November 1992).

6   Though see below Fr Jean-Marie Tillard's comments on the Holy Spirit, p. 183, in his discussion of the *Catechism*'s treatment of the Church.

7   Cf. below, pp. 181, 204.

8   'Understanding the Catechism', *Priests and People* (June 1993), p. 216.

9   Cardinal Ratzinger, in the *Le Monde* interview referred to above, says it took a generation after the reforms had been put into operation for a condensed form of the Christian faith to be possible.

10 Of course, someone had to write the texts which were submitted to the editorial committee. It is very obvious from the *Catechism* that many hands had been at work. The authors are not identified, or even acknowledged.

11 'The Catechism of the Catholic Church', *America* 168.19 (5 June 1993), pp. 6–10; the citation is from the first paragraph of the article. I have quoted Mgr Shannon simply because, at the time of writing this Introduction, his was the most recent *published* comment of that kind. Similar remarks have been made to me personally by very many others who had read the original draft, including contributors to this volume.

The Human Capacity for God, and God's Initiative

(Paragraphs 26–141)

Robert Murray SJ

Heythrop College, University of London

The first two chapters of the *Catechism* are closely connected by their complementary and reciprocally related subject-matter. Chapter One, however, calls for less detailed commentary, since its style is mainly more homiletic than dogmatic. Except for section III, it runs fairly easily, supported by quotations from Scripture, great Christian writers and the Vatican II Pastoral Constitution *Gaudium et Spes* (On the Church in the Modern World, hereafter GS). Section III, on the human capacity to know God, involves philosophical arguments developed by St Thomas Aquinas and others, and summarised in two Council texts, the Constitution on Catholic Faith of Vatican I and the Constitution *Dei Verbum* (On Divine Revelation, hereafter DV) of Vatican II. Since the latter is the main source of Chapter Two of the *Catechism*, here there is some overlap of material between its first two chapters; and since the framework of Chapter Two is more comprehensive and systematic, it seems best to keep the main discussions for that chapter.

It may be regretted that the variety of human expressions of desire for relationship with God, spread so widely in time and space, is alluded to so briefly in 28, when today it has become so necessary to understand peoples of different faiths. St Paul's words in Athens are of course the right text to quote, but some (at least summary) acknowledgement that there has been a 'preparation of the Gospel' in other religious cultures, and that the Holy Spirit has always been at work in the human race, would surely have been desirable. But we shall return to some themes of Chapter One below.

Introduction to Chapter Two

As was just observed, this chapter of the *Catechism*, dealing with revelation and its communication to us in Scripture and Tradition, fairly closely follows the Constitution DV of Vatican II, though with some

6

changes of order and emphasis, some abbreviation and some expansions. It is both right and inevitable that the *Catechism* here depends so much on DV, which is without doubt the most thorough piece of authoritative teaching on its themes in the history of the Church. Hence the best (indeed, essential) commentary on this chapter must be DV itself. Accordingly, it will be constantly referred to here. Further, though the *Catechism* is not structured in terms of theological debate, the controverted issues with which Vatican II had to deal will be outlined, in order to help the reader understand both DV and some aspects of the *Catechism*.

Of the four Council documents which bear the authoritative title of 'Constitution', only DV and *Lumen Gentium* (On the Church, LG) are called 'Dogmatic'. In terms of systematic theology, DV is the most fundamental document of Vatican II; rightly, therefore, its subject-matter is treated early on in the *Catechism*. However, DV is not an easy starting-point, for though it is comparatively short, it is also perhaps the document of Vatican II which makes the greatest demands on the reader. This is due both to the rather dense packing of ideas in many passages and also to the careful balance of many of its statements.

Indeed, for all its merits, DV requires fuller exposition, to explain some of its ideas and terms, to expand the rather limited scope of the chapters on the two Testaments, and to show how the Council was able to bring into balance a number of issues concerning biblical interpretation, Tradition and authority which had exercised theologians for some seventy years. The history of these issues has been well traced elsewhere,[1] but a brief sketch of some of them may be helpful at this point. They joined the unfinished agenda left behind by the interruption of Vatican I in 1870. That Council had produced a measured statement on Revelation, Faith and Reason; but on the nature of the Church, of which a full treatment was intended, papal jurisdiction and infallibility had been moved up the agenda and solemnly defined without being properly integrated with their wider context. When the Council was forced to adjourn, the public image of the Catholic Church was left looking much more like a centralised papal monarchy than it would have done if the Council had been allowed to complete its agenda.[2]

The following years saw the rise of a theological movement exploring a historical and developmental view of Catholic doctrine and biblical interpretation. This evoked a strong reaction on the part of theologians who saw the Church's doctrine and Tradition as enshrining divine truth immutably. For these, any suggestion that formulations of faith or doctrine could be affected by cultural factors or undergo development could only be due to poisonous influence by current evolutionist errors. Works by a varied range of theologians and historians were analysed and interpreted as forming one complex heresy which was given the name of 'Modernism'. This was condemned by Rome in 1907, and vigorous steps were taken to stamp out anything that looked like it in Catholic universities and seminaries; how this affected relationships within the whole work of teaching the faith is discussed later in this article.

7

Loyal Catholic biblical scholars and theologians knew that real problems of understanding Scripture and Tradition were being bypassed, and the work of interpretation hindered, in a way which must eventually harm faith rather than defend it. They lived through difficult years; but in 1943 Pope Pius XII, in his encyclical *Divino Afflante Spiritu* (DAS), discussed the methods of biblical study with understanding and encouragement for the scholars. This inaugurated a new spring in Catholic Bible study and teaching, and subsequent Roman documents became increasingly helpful to scholars and teachers. These developments prepared the way for Vatican II to produce a document which was to go further than ever before in bringing a number of disputes about biblical truth and interpretation to satisfactory conclusions.

The early drafts relating to DV,[3] presented to the Council in 1962, were prepared by theologians convinced above all of the need to root out and destroy what they still saw as dangerous traces of modernism. But the vast majority of the bishops knew that a different focus was called for, in the spirit of the vision with which Pope John XXIII had called the Council and invited it to review the Church's faith and life with joy and hope, always conscious that the Holy Spirit guides the whole Church; to communicate a vision and to encourage activity for the Gospel, rather than to identify new objects for condemnation or prohibition. Such vision and encouragement shine out in the last chapter of DV, and have already borne rich fruit in many parts of the Catholic world.

Since DV was promulgated in November 1965, much has been published, in many languages including English, to expound its contents for various kinds of readers, and to respond to the call in the last chapter of DV to develop use of the Bible in the Church's whole life and mission.[4] Surprisingly and regrettably, this chapter of the *Catechism* reflects little of that wealth of exposition and response; it keeps rather stolidly to its dogmatic sources, with a few expansions which, though they aim to fill real gaps in DV and are certainly traditional, are disappointing as guidance for effective preaching and teaching today.

In what follows, the *Catechism*'s first two chapters will be evaluated, not by commenting on every paragraph, but by concentrating on the presentation of certain crucial themes as they occur successively in the six chapters of DV: (1) the analysis of how divine revelation reaches its human addressees; (2) the balance, maintained by the Holy Spirit, between the total Church's response to revelation and the role of episcopal authority; (3) the relationship of Scripture, Tradition, magisterium and the Holy Spirit; (4) the various modes in which (as we believe) God speaks through Scripture, and how these are to be discerned and interpreted; (5) the value of the Old Testament in the Church, and how it can best be brought out; (6) the too limited scope of the sections on the New Testament and on how it uses the Old; (7) the importance of DV ch. 6, which is reduced to a few phrases in the *Catechism*.

1. How divine revelation reaches its addressees

1.1 Introductory

The *Catechism* approaches this subject in Chapter One by starting from the need and capacity for relationship to God on the part of the human race, and then the practical need for an initiative of revelation on the part of the Creator. These had been treated (together with the nature of faith) by Vatican I in the Dogmatic Constitution *Dei Filius*, though in terms of scholastic theories of knowledge, and models for thinking about nature and grace, which now appear less satisfactory (for reasons both philosophical and anthropological) to support a truly balanced theology. This change in theological perspective is due especially to those great theologians of this century whose work underlies much of the achievement of Vatican II, and in particular the Pastoral Constitution GS.[5]

On humanity's spiritual needs, longings and destiny, therefore, the *Catechism* does well to draw on GS, with some fine passages from St Augustine. On the powers and limitations of human reason and the consequent practical need for divine revelation, dealt with by Vatican I, the *Catechism* follows Vatican II in referring summarily to the former Council's treatment. In DV this is mentioned in 6, almost as an appendix to ch. 1; in the *Catechism* it is placed earlier in the argument (36 and 38). Here, however (as not in DV), the limitations of reason are underlined by quoting (37) a severe passage from the encyclical *Humani Generis* of 1950. This emphasises how easily we can be led astray by disorderly passions, but regrettably does not mention that the Holy Spirit, 'who fills the whole world' (GS 11), is also always at work, drawing minds towards the truth, wills towards the good and consciences towards moral conclusions, even before the gift of faith is accepted and assent given. This prevenient action of the Spirit is emphasised in several key passages of GS,[6] just as other texts of Vatican II acknowledge the working of divine grace outside the visible Catholic communion.[7] It is a pity that the Holy Spirit is not mentioned in Chapter One of the *Catechism*; one has the sense that the scales are somewhat weighted towards the darker side of the Augustinian legacy.[8]

It presupposes faith, of course, to speak of revelation by God to human beings: faith that God exists and is our Creator; that we, though mortal and finite, are yet made capable of conscious and intelligent contact with God; that humans have experienced such contact and have justifiably described the experience as 'revelation' (the 'unveiling' of divine truths hidden from our unaided powers of reasoning); finally, that humans can and do continue to enter into real contact with God through prayer, contemplation of the world as God's creation, and meditation on the acknowledged records of revelation, which we call 'Scripture'.

To unbelievers all this must seem an impossible mouthful, but it is only what is implied in being a believer in a personal God. Faith is needed at each stage, but what does the work is our human reason, illuminated by the grace of faith, yet still requiring to be satisfied at each stage that we are following the truth, for the human mind cannot assent to what it sees to be false.

Neither DV nor the *Catechism* analyses these stages, which belong partly to 'Natural Theology', partly to 'Fundamental Theology'. Vatican II surveyed more fields of theology and of Christian life than any previous ecumenical council, but the 'Fathers' deliberately chose a tone of proclamation of the Gospel rather than of theological controversy; this is immediately and strikingly expressed in the opening words of both LG and DV. The *Catechism* aims to serve the needs of teachers of the faith, but at senior school or adult level these will sooner or later need deeper treatments of many subjects than a single book can provide. The same is true of the present *Commentary*; what it can do is to indicate and evaluate the lines of exposition and argument which underlie the various chapters and sections.

1.2 The process of revelation in DV

DV's account, from God's initiative to the reception of revelation by humans, may be summarised in steps as follows:

(a) God has effectively revealed himself and, through Jesus Christ, made human beings able to share in his own nature.[9] God's way of revelation is by words and acts which illuminate each other (DV 2).

(b) God has made the world intelligible, and the human mind capable of reasoning validly from it to God as its Creator (DV 3, first sentence).

(c) From the beginning of the human race, God has communicated knowledge of himself as personal and concerned for our good. Such self-revelation was given particularly to Abraham and his descendants, especially through Moses and the prophets (rest of DV 3).

(d) Jesus, as God's Son in a true human nature, is the fullness of revelation: in his person, by his deeds and words, and supremely by his death, resurrection and gift of the Holy Spirit. Since his return to the Father, no further public revelation of God is to be expected till his final manifestation (DV 4).

(e) In response to God's revelation every human being is called to 'the obedience of faith', a total and free human act of self-commitment and at the same time a gift of God's grace, assisted and perfected by the Holy Spirit (DV 5).

It is in the context of this statement of the universal human need of faith in order to enter into relationship with God that DV briefly reaffirms the essentials of Vatican I's teaching on the basic capacity of the human mind for knowledge of God, which still leaves a practical need for revelation (DV 6).

(f) DV now returns to the point in the process summarised in (e) above, under the new chapter heading 'The transmission of divine revelation'. Jesus embodied and proclaimed the fullness of revelation and entrusted it, as the Gospel, to his chosen apostles. Guided by the Holy Spirit, they preached the 'Good News' and saw to it that the message was committed to writing (DV 7 §1).

(g) To preserve the Gospel in the Church which grew up in response to the apostles' preaching, these appointed bishops as their successors, 'handing on to them their own teaching function'.[10] Thanks to this link, the Church possesses the Gospel in its twofold form of apostolic Tradition and Scripture (DV 7 §2).

(h) This continuous succession enables the Church to maintain the Gospel, live by it and hand it on faithfully (DV 8 §1). Guided by the Holy Spirit, the apostolic Tradition 'progresses' in the Church,[11] as understanding on the part of its members deepens by contemplation, study and spiritual experience, and through the preaching of bishops, who receive 'the sure charism of truth' (DV 8 §2).[12] Apostolic Tradition is a living force in the Church; by its light the true canon of Scripture was discerned and the Bible more deeply understood. All these activities are guided by the Holy Spirit (DV 8 §3).

(i) Thus Scripture and apostolic Tradition are bound together in a close and reciprocal relationship, due to their common source and aim. Scripture has a fixed form; Tradition, under guidance of the Spirit, is guarded and interpreted by the bishops. 'The Church's certainty about all that is revealed is not drawn from Scripture alone' (DV 9). Scripture and Tradition form one 'deposit', to which the whole Church witnesses as one, united in a 'unique harmony' (DV 10 §1).[13]

(j) Finally, the task of authentically interpreting Scripture and Tradition 'was entrusted solely to the living teaching office (*magisterium*) of the Church, which exercises this authority in the name of Jesus Christ'.[14] But the *magisterium* is subordinate to the word of God, bound to listen to it and transmit it faithfully. This conclusion mirrors the opening sentence of DV 1.

1.3 Comment on the structure of the argument

The argument of these first two chapters (ten sections) of DV proceeds from God to the human recipients of revelation in two stages which balance each other. In the first, God reveals himself obscurely through creation and more clearly by communication to human minds, especially to the people of Israel, among whom Moses and the prophets stand out as mediators of revelation. Between this first stage and the second stands Jesus as the bridge, fulfiller, fullness and new source of revelation. With him begins the second stage, in which revelation is offered by Christ to the whole human race; now the primary focus is on his Church, in which the role of Moses and the prophets is now held by the apostles. These in turn entrusted their position as leaders and teachers to the bishops, who guard the tradition and interpret it with authority; but these are within the Church, not above it, just as they stand under the word of God, not in control of it. Far more is said about how the total Church responds to revelation and transmits it than about the special role of the bishops.

In an important respect this order of the argument of DV is significantly parallel to that of LG. In both cases the Council rejected earlier drafts structured on a descending hierarchical model: 'God — Christ — Peter and the apostles — the Pope and the bishops — the clergy — the laity'. In LG the Council was persuaded to insert a whole new ch. 2, 'On the people of God', before that on the Pope and the bishops; in this the messianic functions of prophet and priest are related to all members of

11

the Church, including the ordained, before the modes of the messianic functions proper to the bishops and the Pope are treated in ch. 3. The account of the prophetic functions and charisms in the Church as a whole in LG 12 is paralled by the account of how the whole Church maintains tradition in DV 8, which is thus implicitly shown to be likewise about the 'prophetic' function; and in the *Catechism* the two passages are combined (91–94).

1.4 The process of revelation in the *Catechism* (51–79)

If we now turn to the *Catechism* in the light of this examination of DV, how faithfully do we find it reflecting its main source? The quantity of quotations obviously suggests a positive answer; but how about the underlying structure of the argument, which determines how the *Catechism* makes DV understood?

The steps referred to above as (a) and (b) are represented adequately, in quotation or paraphrase, by 51–53 and 54.

Step (c) is much expanded in 55–64, but almost exclusively by reference to the Old Testament. The religious aspirations of all peoples have been mentioned in 28; here the availability of saving grace for all who seek the good is suggested under the heading 'The Covenant with Noah' (56–58), but the reality of some degree of revelation (traditionally referred to as 'seeds of the Word' and a 'preparation for the Gospel') in world religions other than those in the biblical tradition deserved a place here. Readiness to recognise this reality has been a fundamental principle of the greatest Catholic missionaries (in contrast with earlier Protestant theory), and is expressed, albeit cautiously, in the documents of Vatican II.[15] DV has at most a possible hint; the *Catechism* misses an opportunity to supplement it valuably. As it is, the biblical stories and persons mentioned in 56–58 (as not in DV 3) might be taken symbolically to indicate what could have been said more clearly in other terms; but the way in which these stories from Genesis 1 – 11 are here referred to, almost as if they were simply factual, with no discussion of the kind of truth which is to be ascribed to them, makes these paragraphs appear curiously naive, and certainly problematic as a basis for serious Christian teaching in a multi-faith world.[16] (However, the use of a phrase from Eucharistic Prayer IV in 55 was a happy thought.)

The other biblical examples, from Abraham to the Mother of Jesus (59–64), are likewise expanded from the last sentence of DV 3; but on the whole more satisfactorily, and with the sensitivity in referring to Judaism which the *Catechism* generally shows.[17]

Step (d), on Christ as the fullness of revelation (65), is, surprisingly, stated almost cursorily compared with DV 4, and then immediately overshadowed (65–67) by a long and repetitive comment on the last sentence of that paragraph (quoted in 66), which says that 'no new public revelation is to be expected before the glorious manifestation of our Lord Jesus Christ'. This is now sandwiched between a quotation from St John of the Cross and two additional paragraphs which, between them, significantly shift the emphasis from an explanatory negative statement about *public* revelation to an insistent warning that personal experiences which may seem revelatory in quality must be subjected to the Church's teaching authority. The drafters of DV were actually more interested in avoiding the ambiguous and unhelpful scholastic tag 'revelation was closed with the death of the last apostle'; they do not seem to have had private revelations in mind, and the *Catechism*'s focus on these is new.[18]

This may seem an over-insistent criticism of a point which certainly could have a legitimate place in a catechism. The New Testament contains warnings enough against claims to new revelations which can lead others astray; history contains disastrous examples, and the present century alone has presented not a few dubious cases. The apostolic charisms inherited by the bishops are indeed necessary for guidance. But what the *Catechism* does at this point in the argument of DV is actually to omit step (e) (DV 5), on how each individual responds to God's revelation by 'the obedience of faith' and the action of the Holy Spirit, and to replace it by this insistence on control of 'revelations' by ecclesiastical authority.[19] DV 5 is a most important section, which was particularly praised by the 'observers' Frères R. Schutz and M. Thurian of Taizé in their fine commentary on DV.[20]

DV next reaffirms the teaching of Vatican I on the capacity of the human mind to know God (DV 6); the *Catechism* places this as 36. Thus the carefully constructed argument of DV 4–6 is broken in the *Catechism*, and emphasis on every believer's growth in faith, through the Holy Spirit, is replaced by an extra stress on control by church authority.

What is really needed at this point is to introduce a distinction in the theological idea of revelation, showing how we affirm it (i) as God's *act* of self-communication, together with what believers recognise as the *record* of this (especially Scripture), and (ii) the *experience* whereby revelation is vitally apprehended by each believer. (This second sense is also common in ordinary speech, as when people say of an experience that gives them new insight, 'it was a revelation to me'.) G. O'Collins has helpfully called senses (i) and (ii) respectively 'foundational' and 'dependent' revelation.[21] It is supremely important in catechesis — the work of leading people to Christian maturity — not to neglect or undervalue the 'dependent' experience; indeed, it should be a main purpose of catechesis to collaborate with the Holy Spirit in fostering it. The *Catechism*, both by omissions and by its order, tends to underplay the importance of personal experience and the presence of the Holy Spirit to all members of the Church, and to put greater stress on obedience to external authority.

2. The balance between the total Church's response to revelation and the role of episcopal authority

We pass to the matter treated in DV ch. 2 and in the *Catechism*, Chapter Two, Article 2 (steps (f) and (g) in the analysis above): the transmission of the Gospel by Jesus to the apostles and by them to the bishops, by the twin modes of Tradition and the new Scriptures of the Gospel (DV 7–8).

First, however, since the term 'tradition' now begins to play an important part, it will be helpful to distinguish the various senses in which it is used, for these are several, rather as we saw above regarding 'revelation'.[22] 'Tradition' can denote (i) the *act* or *process* of handing on (say) a belief, a doctrine or a way of doing things, or (ii) the *thing* which is handed on (e.g., a belief or practice). This may be (a) something global, or (b) something particular. The sense of 'tradition' in DV 7–10 is generally 'global', referring to the whole complex of belief, practice and religious culture of the Church (as it can for any group). In Catholic and Orthodox theology 'tradition' in this sense is very often written (as in the *Catechism* and here), with a capital T; it is often used almost interchangeably with 'Gospel'. In the particular sense (ii.b) we speak of 'a tradition' or of 'traditions', without a capital, as in 83. This applies to practices in the Church which may be more closely related to the substantials of 'Tradition' (such as sacramental rites) or may be more variable (such as the use of beads as aids to prayer). With these distinctions of mind, it should not be difficult to decide in which senses 'tradition' or 'traditions' are being used when they occur in theological discussion.

Steps (f) and (g) are fairly fully represented in Article 2, 74–79; but step (h) (on how the apostolic tradition is received and treasured by the whole Church), which begins with the last sentence of DV 7 and runs right through DV 8, is all broken up in the *Catechism*, and its core (8 §2) is postponed till 94, after both step (i), on Scripture and Tradition, and step (j), on the *magisterium* of the Pope and the bishops. Though the eventual quotation of DV 8 §2 is enriched by being combined with a passage on the prophetic function in the Church (borrowed from LG 12), the dislocation of DV 8 still leaves the *Catechism* giving a more hierarchical picture of the Church's response to Tradition than is given in DV 8. What has been done calls for closer examination.

The fine last sentence of DV 7, which speaks of the Church as a whole contemplating God through the 'mirror' of Scripture and Tradition together on its journey through time, is removed;[23] the preceding and following sentences are so knitted together (77) that the only persons mentioned are the apostles and the bishops. 78–79 combine a sentence from DV 8 §1 with two from 8 §3, so as to allow ordinary believers just a mention; but the picture of the whole Church with all its members, both ordained and lay, maintaining and fostering Tradition, seems for two pages to have disappeared. It is, of course, brought in later: DV 10 §1 on the 'entire holy people, united with its pastors' is quoted in full in 84, but the diversified picture of the Church's activities in DV 8 §2 is held back until after the authority of episcopal *magisterium* and the binding force of dogmas have been firmly laid down (85–90).

When DV 8 §2 comes at last, the emphasis is on contemplation and obedient submission more than on the fruits of contemplation. The fairly extensive quotation from LG 12 in 91–93 is put under a cross-heading 'The supernatural sense of faith', which is indeed an important theme of the passage; but in its own context that section is expressly related to the prophetic function, as is recognised in the *Catechism's* section on the

Church (where also a brief summary of LG 12 is retained, 785). Whatever 'prophetic' means in the Church, it must be about more than contemplation; the word connotes utterance and communication, and the biblical models of prophecy by no means suggest restriction to official agents.[24] The quotation of DV 8 §2 which follows is under the cross-heading 'Growth in understanding the faith' (94); fair enough, but DV describes activities which bring it about that the gospel Tradition 'progresses' (*proficit*) in the Church',[25] even if actual verbal expression is mentioned only on the part of bishops 'who have received ... the sure charism of truth'.[26] But it is important that their activities are mentioned *among* the others; they have a special charism, but they are not said to be the only teachers. The 'study' on the part of others which is mentioned may reasonably be understood to imply also communicating the fruits of study.

Leaving to the next section the paragraph on the relationship of Scripture and Tradition ('step (i)'), let us look more closely at what is said in DV and in the *Catechism* about the teaching *function* and teaching *authority* in the Church ('step (j)'). The latter is the subject of one paragraph in DV, namely 10 §2. This is almost like a codicil to the account of the Church as bearer of Tradition. Codicils have, of course, the same authority as the documents to which they are added, but the proportions of a text are a clue to the comparative weight given to its parts.

The content of DV 10 §2 was summarised above. It is reproduced in 85–86. The sentence restricting 'the task of authentically interpreting the Word of God ... to the *magisterium* of the Church, which exercises this authority in the name of Jesus Christ' is taken from the encyclical *Humani Generis* of 1950,[27] but with an added clause identifying the holders of *magisterium* as 'the bishops in communion with the successor of Peter, the bishop of Rome'. This is common Catholic teaching, as in (for example) LG 25, and the 'Council Fathers', when considering the draft of DV 10, would not have located the Church's teaching authority anywhere else. Nevertheless, they did not say here that the *teaching function* itself (which is the basic and original meaning of *magisterium*) is restricted to the Pope and the bishops; neither in DV 9, which speaks of the bishops faithfully preserving, expounding and spreading the Word (quoted in 81), nor in DV 10. The final chapter of DV recognises that the teaching of Scripture in the Church depends on many (DV 23–25). It is the *authority* to supervise the Church's teaching, and on occasion to interpret God's word 'authentically', which is entrusted to the bishops as heirs of the apostles. But it is also important that, immediately after this statement, DV goes on to insist that the holders of *magisterium* are the servants of God's word and must listen to it humbly — words which the *Catechism* reproduces in full. The drafters' *relatio* on DV 10 explained that these words were intended to reassure the 'separated brethren' about the nature of the authority claimed for the *magisterium* in the Catholic Church.[28] The sentence was warmly welcomed by the 'observers' and is well discussed by Frères Schutz and Thurian.[29]

In Catholic usage till about the middle of the nineteenth century, the word *magisterium* regularly meant 'teachership', the *function* of teaching the faith, whoever exercises this in responsibility to our one *Magister*, Christ.[30] Of course all Catholics believe that the Pope and bishops are endowed with authority to teach and interpret apostolic Tradition; but it was only in the nineteenth century that *magisterium* began to be increasingly used in a sense which shifted the focus from the teaching *function* to the *authority* of Pope and bishops. This in turn rapidly led (especially in the anti-modernist documents of the early 1900s) to a personified use, with a capital M; it now regularly denotes 'the Authorities' who claim obedience in the name of Christ, especially the Holy See. As for the possibility of *magisterium* continuing to be used of members of the Church other than bishops, such pretensions were castigated in an encyclical of 1914.[31]

Fifty years later, in contrast, DV quietly left unsaid any exclusive restriction of *magisterium*.[32] Of course, in other documents the Council reaffirmed the teaching authority of bishops and Pope; but DV, the Church's most solemn document on Scripture and Tradition, does not qualify *magisterium* with that restriction which the *Catechism* adds in 85. Nor, of course, does DV use the word with reference to teachers other than bishops; but their importance in the Church is fully recognised in ch. 6. As the words of DV 10 stand, they are compatible with the traditional sense of *magisterium*, by which they could naturally refer to 'all who hold and teach the Catholic faith'.[33] After all, in DV 8–10 the action of the Holy Spirit is mentioned no less than seven times, and by no means with restriction to the successors of the apostles. 'Doctors of the Church' are honoured without restriction to ordained status, and the faith has had innumerable unsung 'doctors'.[34]

3. The relationship of Scripture, Tradition, magisterium and the Holy Spirit

The above discussion has concerned issues of balance in speaking of the Church and its teaching organs; in this the *Catechism*, while aiming to interpret DV, sometimes echoes earlier tones of warning and calling to submission which were muted or even absent in it. To complete these comments on the matter of DV ch. 2 other issues of balance remain to be discussed, and then how all these issues relate together.

The first concerns Scripture and Tradition ('step (i)', DV 9–10). DV had to deal here with a crucial point of debate between Protestants and Catholics since the sixteenth century, and, among Catholic theologians, a problem of definition and balance. *Scriptura sola* was the old Protestant slogan: revelation comes to us through Scripture alone. The Catholic reply was to insist on the apostolic antiquity and importance of many traditions,[35] which could be referred to collectively as 'Tradition'; but since the unique place of Scripture was not in question, the relationship of the two had to be worked out further than it had been at Trent. In the years before Vatican II such work had been developing with increasing ecumenical sensitiveness, especially in countries where Catholic and Protestant theologians, often brought together under persecution, had learned to listen to each other in real dialogue. In contrast, other Catholic theologians had hardly moved from the old confrontational apologetic. That was the tone which dominated the draft on Scripture and Tradition, insisting that they are two separate modes and repositories of revelation. Such separation was rejected by the majority at Vatican II, though its proponents went on urging it. It is indispensable to study the background of the problem in order to appreciate the final text of DV on this relationship.[36] Every phrase describing it was carefully weighed and subtly balanced, so as to respect as many as possible of the relevant considerations which were advanced in the discussions.

A key point is made already before the main paragraph in DV 8 §3. The conclusion as to which books were to be recognised as 'Scripture' could only have been made from outside Scripture, and reached (by whatever means) by the Church; the criterion must have been knowledge of the local churches' traditions on this question, which, we may suppose, revealed a consensus ascribable to the Holy Spirit. This is at least one firm point of distinction between the two modes in which the Church perceives revelation. DV 9 mainly expresses their closely intertwined relationship, but comes back before the end to assert again that the Church has some certainties which are drawn not from Scripture alone.[37]

The *Catechism* deals with this relationship in 80–83. These give the substance of DV 9, but with less clear coherence than the original, while the important point about the recognition of the canon of Scripture is moved so as to become a mere introduction to the list of canonical books in 120. Some explanations about 'Tradition' and 'traditions' are given in 83; but the importance of this whole subject for mutual understanding between Christians is not indicated.

The *Catechism* continues, under the cross-heading 'The interpretation of the heritage of faith', to reproduce DV 10 §§1–2, with an insertion, as analysed above (84–86). The next four paragraphs are not from DV. First (87) it is stated that 'the faithful willingly receive the teachings and directives their pastors give them, in different forms'. The other three are under the heading 'The Dogmas of the Faith'. 88 is on the defining of dogmas (truths contained in divine revelation or standing in a necessary connection with these) and their binding force for the faithful. 89 speaks of 'an organic connection' between dogmas and the spiritual life. 90 refers to the mutual coherence of dogmas, echoing a phrase from Vatican I, and follows this with a sentence from the Vatican II Decree on Ecumenism (*Unitatis Redintegratio*, UR) on the existence of a 'hierarchy of truths' in Catholic doctrine.

The effect of these supplementary paragraphs is to add enormous weight to that on the magisterium (85), though this is still framed (as in its source, DV 10) between a statement about the Church as a whole and another saying that the magisterium is the servant of divine revelation and is limited by its content. But here it is immediately followed by a statement (87) about the reception of authoritative teaching, which is asserted baldly, as if there were and could be no problem; as if 'reception' were not an important and debated theme in ecclesiology, not only in the Orthodox Church (which stresses it), but also in Catholicism, since the *sensus fidelium*, the mature understanding of the faith among the faithful, came back into prominence.[38] There is a stage missing here, a part of the process which is necessary for the 'unique harmony' of faithful and pastors to shine out. LG 25 spoke of reception of authoritative teaching as a duty on the part of the faithful; 87 speaks of it as a fact. Yet in truthfulness it must be acknowledged that reception of an act of the magisterium has not always been either joyful or immediate, especially if there has not been sufficient prior consultation, and such difficulty cannot automatically be put down to sin and ignorance.

The next paragraph (88), on the definition of dogmas, could be said to correspond to parts of LG 25, though the phrasing is more reminiscent of the anti-modernist documents. The assimilation of 'necessarily connected truths' to defined dogmas, so as to share their obligatory force, developed through interpretation of the definition of papal infallibility at Vatican I.[39] Here again is a bald statement on a topic of great ecumenical sensitiveness; the undefined scope of 'necessarily connected truths' is one of the areas of greatest unease for both Orthodox and Anglicans who attempt to enter into dialogue with Rome. Is it fitting for a universal catechism to touch so hastily on matter so delicate?

89 is less controversial; indeed the Creeds and the solemn definitions of the Church are signposts for growth in faith and love. It is strange, however, that only dogmas are mentioned here, since probably every Christian would ascribe this role first and foremost to Scripture. Further, many of the absolute fundamentals of Christian faith and living have never been made the subject of dogmatic definition. This is true even of so central a doctrine as the atonement.[40] Again, no ecumenical council in the history of the Church has ever promulgated teaching so extensive in doctrinal scope and so enriching for so many aspects of the Christian life as Vatican II; yet it deliberately abstained from claiming the status of irreformable dogmas for its documents.

Finally, 90 first develops a phrase from Vatican I (in the decree *De Fide*, DS 3016) and then quotes Vatican II (UR 11). The first sentence bears on the previous paragraph, duly qualifying what is said there about dogmas; now we are rightly reminded that they have their respective places and their mutual coherence within 'the whole revelation of the Christian mystery'. In that context, of course, no mature Christian need be troubled that some of the greatest truths of the faith have never been, and may never need to be, made the subjects of binding dogmas.

To pass to the second sentence, the principle that there is a 'hierarchy of truths' in Catholic teaching is one of the most luminously suggestive phrases formulated at Vatican II.[41] Here, however, it is inserted without any explanation as to how it is meant to relate to its new context. Its original context needs to be studied and digested; it concerns the sense of proportion which should guide Catholics in ecumenical dialogue with

Christians who share the fundamental (especially credal) doctrines, but to whom various emphases and developments in Catholic belief are strange. It is altogether excellent that this principle is brought into the *Catechism* here; it has the effect of notably qualifying and moderating the ecumenical insensitiveness of 88 and 89 — provided that the user of the *Catechism* realises this, for it is not made plain.

After this section on dogmas comes (as we saw above) that taken from LG on the Church's prophetic function (91–93), and then, at last, the gist of DV 8 §2 on the various activities of the Church as bearer of Tradition (94). This arrangement creates a considerable danger that the unwary reader will suppose that 91–94 are about the *laity*, at least until finally (and disjointedly) the phrase about the charism of bishops appears. (It is all too often noticeable, nearly thirty years after Vatican II, how many Catholics — even clergy — show that they mistakenly think that 'People of God' means the laity, when it means the entire Church.)

Finally, Article 2 closes (95) with the last paragraph of DV 10, on the interconnection of Tradition, Scripture and magisterium. In DV this is what sums up the finely balanced picture of the whole Church as bearer of Tradition. As for the *Catechism*, it is true that the greater part of the text of DV 7–10 appears in one place or another. But the above examination has shown that the primary focus on the total Church, its many activities being inspired and guided by the Holy Spirit, has been significantly weakened by both omission and displacement, so as to lay greater emphasis on the exclusive authority of the magisterium. Yet (as the Excursus to this article illustrates) the claim that 'authentic' interpretation is exercised solely by the magisterium in its modern sense is hard to verify from history. The present writer believes firmly that the Catholic bishops in communion with the Pope have inherited apostolic authority and exercise this in teaching and interpretation. But historically they have done this, both in conciliar acts and in 'ordinary' practice, with the help of theologians and relying on the whole structure of teaching in the Church. This is what *magisterium* has meant through most of the Church's history, a shared ministry; and the *singularis conspiratio*, the 'unique harmony' in the Church, has shone out best when this understanding of the relationship has flourished.

The closing paragraph expresses the ideal co-inherence and mutually dependent functioning of the two modes of revelation with the inter-pretative role of apostolic authority. But is it true that each *cannot* stand without the others? In fact the Latin is more correctly translated 'one *does not* stand without the others'.[42] This is not mere carping. The sentence describes how the three do in fact depend on each other, as understood in Catholic and Orthodox theology; but it does not venture to declare what God cannot do. Before anything was written and recognised as a true record of revelation, the experience of communication between God and humans was a reality and was forming a tradition, which had its principal bearers and interpreters. Likewise the Gospel tradition and its bearers were there before the new Scriptures were written. However, since Scripture (both the Old and New Testaments) took its fixed form, it

19

has a certain primacy in relation to Tradition and the magisterium. It does not depend on them for its power to feed faith and challenge consciences; its relationship to Tradition is of mutual support (as is well described in DV 9), but the Church's teaching function is their servant and answerable to God for interpreting them well.

It is also of great ecumenical importance to see and express the balance of this trio rightly. Many millions of Christians experience that their faith is instructed by Scripture alone; they have, of course, their own forms of tradition and authority, but they regard only Scripture as normative. The Decree on Ecumenism expressly recognises the reality of sanctifying grace among such Christians although they are separated from the Catholic communion (UR 21–23). It is not true that Scripture *'cannot stand'* without Tradition and authoritative interpretation. What DV 9–10 expresses is the Catholic belief that *Scriptura sola* does not exhaust the fullness of revelation; though the contents of Scripture alone can lead people to real holiness and union with God, God has in fact revealed more, which is preserved or made attainable by other channels which we include under the term 'Tradition'. Finally, it must be emphasised above all that this 'trinity' of Scripture, Tradition and the living interpretative function is maintained by the indwelling and action of the Holy Spirit in the whole Church, and Christ the Teacher speaks both through bishops and also wherever the word is truly understood and expounded; this does not always need guidance by external authority (cf. 1 Jn 2:26–27).

4. How God speaks through Scripture

The matter treated in the *Catechism*, Chapter Two, Article 3, 'Sacred Scripture' (101–120) is based on DV ch. 4 (11–13). The Council did not aim to do full justice to this whole subject, but rather to make clear statements on some basic points which had been much controverted, especially during the previous century. The *Catechism* attempts a little more on the principles of interpretation.

An introductory section is constructed from DV 13, a new paragraph, and two short quotations from DV ch. 6 (21, 24). This provides an attractive entry into fairly technical questions, by gathering some striking and illuminating analogies drawn by DV from Tradition to express the divine power which dwells, almost sacramentally, in Scripture. The first is based on two aspects of the incarnation: the wonderful 'condescension' of God in adopting human language, and the incarnate Christ's sharing in all human weakness except sin. The immediate source of DV 13 was the encylical *Divino Afflante Spiritu* (1943); this refers to St John Chrysostom, for whom this analogy was fundamental in his biblical teaching.[43] Balancing this insight from Antiochene exegesis is the analogy between Scripture and the eucharist (103, from DV 21), developed by St Augustine, though its roots are in the 'Bread of Life' discourse in John 6.[44] The last introductory analogy, or rather metaphor, sees Scripture as the medium of loving encounter and conversation between the Father and his human children (104, from DV 21). The one paragraph (102) which is not from DV focuses on the rich and multivalent term 'word', relating all the words of Scripture to Christ the 'single, unique Word, in whom everything is said' (referring back to 65), with a quotation from St Augustine. The cross-heading for this section, 'Christ — the unique Word of sacred Scripture', really refers only to 102. Certainly, its language reflects patristic expressions, but these often refer to more senses of *logos*, 'word', than merely those referring to Scripture and Christ, and the impression given here is misleading as regards the Old Testament. The latter subject is discussed further below.

The next section, under the cross-heading 'The inspiration and truth of sacred Scripture', reproduces the essentials of DV 11 in 105–107, with an additional paragraph 108. Like DV 11 itself, this section needs further explanation. Tradition uses the term 'inspiration' ('breathing-in') for the role of the Holy Spirit in the creation of the texts we call 'Scripture'. This is an early Christian metaphor,[45] using the same symbolism as God's 'breathing in' of life in Genesis 2:7 and Christ's gift of the Spirit (a higher level of life and power) in John 20:22. The metaphor indicates a mystery of communication between God and human minds, but leaves it a mystery. Also traditional is the application of the Latin term *auctor* to God. It is unfortunate that the version of DV which is used perpetuates the misleading word 'author' for this (105). *Auctor* means an originating cause, but not necessarily a writer;[46] it should be rendered 'originator' to avoid any suggestion that God dictated word for word. The actual relationship of God and the human writers is the subject of 106. This summarises the 'Neo-Thomist' account of inspiration,[47] which labours to avoid the faults of many earlier theories, but is both excessively complicated and psychologically hardly credible.

Simpler and in some ways more satisfying ways of interpreting the metaphor have been suggested: it might mean essentially (1) that aspect of ancient Israel's consciousness of their covenant with God in which the Holy Spirit creatively affected the minds of certain speakers and writers, and then analogously (2) that aspect of the founding of the Church in which the Holy Spirit likewise guided the minds of the apostles and apostolic writers.[48] Such a way of looking at the mystery has the advantage of not isolating the charism of the human authors, but locating it in the faith of the communities, first of Israel, then of the Church.

Another luminous analogy, close to those referred to in 101–104, is that which Newman briefly hinted at when he said that 'the Word of God . . . has the nature of a Sacrament, which is outward and inward, and a channel of supernatural grace'.[49] This still leaves the mystery intact, yet expresses another aspect of it: there is a power in Scripture which is released through reading (especially in the liturgy, when this is done with serious preparation and awareness that it is a most important ministry in the Church) and through well-prepared and selfless exposition; this power is analogous to that which we believe is there in the sacraments.

21

It is the recognition of such a divine power latent in the books of the Bible (without prejudice to what Christians may experience through reading other books, by saints or others) which must underlie the fixing of the 'canon' of Scripture (105 §2). This was brought about by a second activity of the Holy Spirit, the essential complement of 'inspiration', which led the two communities — first that of early Judaism, then of the Church — to recognise a divine quality in certain books. This recognition seems to have been reached by gradual consensus, eventually summed up by ecclesiastical authority in official lists.[50]

107 reproduces the sentence of DV on what used to be called the 'inerrancy' of Scripture. This had been perhaps the storm centre of official anxiety about biblical scholarship for about a century before Vatican II, and church authority had imposed extreme literalist interpretations on Catholic scholars and teachers, most of whom were far from undermining faith in the Bible as a medium of divine truth, but were aware that different kinds of literature have different ways of being true.[51] DV carefully moved away from a global assertion of inerrancy; it asserts firmly that God's truth is contained in the Bible, but defines it as 'the truth that God wanted to record ... for our salvation'. This proposes a qualitative criterion which calls for discernment, with the help of principles which are discussed in the next section.

Under the cross-heading 'The Holy Spirit, interpreter of Scripture' the *Catechism* in 109–114 summarises DV 12. That in turn largely depends on the encyclical *Divino Afflante Spiritu* of Pope Pius XII.[52]

The Bible exists for all to read, and people may assume, and look for, various kinds of truth. Too much time has been wasted interpreting Genesis 1 on mistaken assumptions, to show that science proves it false, or conversely that, since it must be true, it is compatible with scientific truth. DV teaches us to look only for that truth which God wishes to teach us, and also that God speaks through human agents and in human ways. In other words, we can know God's intended meanings in the Bible only through human accounts of them; there is no 'hot line' that could bypass the human writers.[53] But these human accounts use a whole range of images and metaphors for God and his purposes, including many based on violent human emotions and wild animals. Images and metaphors can often express truth more powerfully than cool factual statements, but they must be interpreted, and this would seem to involve determining what the writer intends to communicate.

Now we have a statement of St Luke's intentions at the beginning of his Gospel and of Acts, but for most biblical writers we have not, and the intentions of ancient authors prove almost as elusive as those of God.[54] All we have is *books*, separated from the personal experiences which gave rise to them by stages of tradition, interpretation and probably reinterpretation. It is these books which early Judaism and then the early Church recognised as vehicles of God's word. The only 'intentions' we can reach are those implicit in the natural sense of passages and books, in the light of what we know about the cultural context which each text reflects; the clues to this will be especially in the *style* of the writings

22

and the *literary genres* and *figures* which they exemplify. Study of these is the essential way to attune our 'ear' to what a biblical book is saying. Here 110 is thinner than DV 12 §2 and its source in DAS, and it should be studied in the light of them and with commentaries on them. As regards literary genres, these can be compared with examples in other cultures (even, to some extent, through translations). By such study it can become clear that not every prose narrative which begins 'and it came to pass' has to be read as claiming to be true as 'history', let alone as this is defined by modern criteria which were unknown in the ancient Near East.

The recognition of style is a subtler matter, but a reader can learn, even through the veils of translation, to become familiar with the characteristic style of 'schools' such as the 'Deuteronomic' or the 'Priestly'; this then can enable us to use other, related books of a 'school' to help to interpret passages with more confidence than would otherwise be justified.

In many cases it is a combination of recognising genres and developing a feel for style which enables us to see what a book really is and says. Take *parable*, for example. We do not read Jesus' parables as factual history, because the Gospels make it clear that he was using that literary genre to move his hearers to repentance or discipleship. But a narrative may not proclaim itself as a parable. Thus in 2 Samuel we have two episodes (ch. 12 and ch. 14) in which David was taken in by stories, told in order to move him to repentance and mercy; he mistook them for fact, and only then realised that they were parables directed at him. Now apply this to the book of Jonah, which was a focus of anxiety about 'inerrancy' in the time of Newman.[55] The story is attached to a historical name, but that does not prove that it is itself intended as factual history. There are strong literary grounds for taking it as a parable. That does not undermine its status as inspired: rather the opposite. Read it as a parable, brilliantly constructed with the arts of irony and satire in order to show up very defective ideas of God, and the power of the book springs from the page with new freshness.

The above examples are relevant also to the next paragraphs in DV (12 §3) and the *Catechism* (111–114). They first lay down, as a basic principle of interpretation following from belief in inspiration, that 'Scripture must be read in the light of the same Spirit by whom it was written' ('through whom' would be a better rendering). However, the *Catechism* handles its source so as to insist more explicitly on relating the whole Bible to Christ. DV says that for a right understanding of the texts we must bear in mind (1) the content and coherence of Scripture as a whole, (2) the living tradition of the Church and (3) the *analogia fidei*. While DV in its next chapter quotes traditional phrases relating the Old Testament to Christ, none of these three points requires the relationship to be made explicit all the time, as 112–113 tends to interpret them. The relationship may be a matter of cultural continuity, or of religious and moral teaching in the Old Testament which Jesus reaffirmed. The first point could be said to be illustrated by the examples above concerning the Deuteronomic and Priestly 'schools', though the connections noted there are only within the

Old Testament. The Church's traditions of exegesis form no monolith, and among the early Christian 'schools' it is the Syrian or 'Antiochene' (with their focus on the Old Testament in its own perspective and their sobriety in use of typology or symbolic exegesis) to whose method the balance held by DAS and DV perhaps comes closest.

The third point refers to the *analogia fidei*. Here some reflections are in place, not on the *Catechism* alone, but on the modern adoption of this phrase. It comes from Romans 12:6, where St Paul urges Christians to exercise spiritual gifts according to the grace given to each, and (as the best exegetes, patristic and modern, agree) 'in proportion to [the measure of each person's] faith'. The meaning given to the phrase in 114, following other modern Roman documents,[56] is very different from this, and uses 'analogy' in a way unfamiliar today. Exegetes are urged to attend to the *coherence* of the truths of the faith and the entire economy of revelation.

It is true that some exegetes have come into tension, in some cases unresolvable, with orthodoxy. But in all devotion to orthodoxy it must be said that the 'coherence' of the word of God in the Bible can be complex to the point of mysteriousness. In particular, the Old Testament contains elements which stand in a highly dialectical relation (not to say opposition) to each other. To take the most salient and profound example, the book of Job criticises and rejects a number of ways of speaking about God which are expressed elsewhere in the Old Testament. If the whole of Holy Scripture contains the inspired word of God, then God must also speak through its dialectical paradoxes, which challenge us to deeper thought. Is this not part of the duty of 'listening devotedly' to God's word (86; DV 10)?

The *Catechism* next inserts a further section on 'the senses of Scripture' (115–118) before returning to a last allusion to DV 12 in 119. It was a good idea to supplement the very concentrated teaching of DV at this point, but it is questionable whether the 'four senses' of medieval scholasticism should be recommended as an analysis of the ways to read a biblical text today. They call for explanation out of proportion to the scope of a catechism. The relevant sections of DAS are far more helpful.

The 'senses' raise problems both of terminology and of analysis. First, 'the literal sense' is a very misleading expression, but since it is there it has to be explained. The sentence in 116 is correct, but more is needed, because the traditional account of the 'literal' sense has tended to connect it mainly with 'historical' narrative (as in the old tag quoted in 118), and therefore to make people confuse it with 'literally' (that is, in common usage, 'factually') true. 'Literal' is no longer the suitable word to express what this aspect of meaning is really about: it is the *natural* sense of any human communication as it would be immediately comprehended by people understanding the speaker's language, cultural milieu and immediate context. It can even be immediately read off from metaphor when the latter is simple and transparent, as arises often in both Hebrew and English. In narrative the 'literal' sense is in the telling of the story; in the Psalms it is the praise of God or an outcry in distress; in Proverbs it gives advice, often using simple metaphors; in prophetic poetry it speaks of God's purposes, with rich yet still often quite transparent use of metaphor.

In 115 and 117 the other three senses are grouped together under the heading of the 'spiritual' sense, a term used by St Paul in 1 Corinthians 10:3–4. There it denotes a way of reading the Old Testament as containing a 'code' of symbols which can yield Christian meanings (this is dealt with in 128–130 and DV 16) but it can also refer to finding allegories in the Gospels, for example in Martha and Mary or the parable of the Good Samaritan. In the Fathers, a 'spiritual' interpretation is one which discovers a hidden 'mystery' or secret reference beneath the 'bodily' or outward sense. The clearest modern terms for this way of reading biblical texts are 'type' or 'symbol' for the patristic 'mystery', and 'symbolic' for 'spiritual'. The reader is aware of the 'literal' or natural sense (and may regard this as important in its own right), but, either by a flash of imaginative insight or following an established tradition, sees it as symbolising another level of meaning. The means, in varying degrees of complexity, can be metaphor, parable or allegory.

In the light of this explanation, it becomes clear that the other three senses, as traditionally defined, are not classified well in relation to the 'spiritual'. The 'allegorical sense' is really another name for the 'spiritual'; the 'anagogical' (or eschatological) has a particular kind of subject-matter, but may be either an allegorical way of reading a text ('Jerusalem' meaning heaven, etc.) or, despite much use of imagery, it may be the natural (and therefore the 'literal') sense of a passage, such as Jesus' parable of the Last Judgement.

As for the 'moral sense', this is surely the 'literal sense' (or part of it) of very many biblical passages: all those sermon-like episodes in the Old Testament 'historical books', the 'wisdom' books almost entirely, and much in both the Gospels and the epistles. Many Old Testament narratives are told with a bleak objectivity, yet an intention of evoking moral reactions of approval or abhorrence in the reader is often discernible between the lines. This is all quite different from the symbolic 'spiritual sense'. Is there a distinct 'moral sense' at all?

This discussion of the problems posed by commending the 'four senses' today without qualification may seem to leave the subject of scriptural exposition on a somewhat uncertain note. However, it can be said that, for preachers looking for a simple rule of thumb to find links between Old and New Testament readings in the Lectionary, the 'four senses' represent headings for a plan: 'What is the Old Testament passage primarily about? — Has it a lesson for us? — What relation has it to Jesus? — to the Christian hope?'

Finally, in 119 the *Catechism* returns to the last sentences of DV 12, on the work of scripture scholars in the service of the Church.

5. The value of the Old Testament in the Church

In the *Catechism* both Testaments come under one heading, 'The canon of Scripture', which begins (120) with a bare list of the Catholic canon as in

Trent. It is a pity that there is no mention of the 'Deuterocanonical' status of the books not in the Jewish canon. Catholic tradition, of course, is firm on their canonicity; but the distinction is still ecumenically sensitive, and it is not without importance for Catholics to know which books are involved and why there has been controversy about them. These and other, non-canonical writings of pre-Christian Judaism are coming to be more widely recognised as having great importance for understanding the immediate background of Christianity.

The chapter on the Old Testament in DV is its least meaty part, probably because here the Council was not faced with a hotly disputed issue. Many of the points made are traditional, going back to patristic commonplaces. DV 14–15 expands the Old Testament section 3, while 16 repeats traditional formulae on the relationship of the New Testament to the Old. The *Catechism* summarises all this even more briefly, but with a greater emphasis on the continuing value of the Old Testament. This is clearly stated in DV 14 and 15, and the *Catechism*, despite the brevity of this section (121–123), makes small but significant additions. In 121 there appears the striking phrase of John Paul II, 'the old covenant has never been revoked',[57] which adds further clarity to the passage of *Nostra Aetate* (4) in that sense. 123 adds (not in DV) that the Church has always opposed rejecting the Old Testament, ever since Marcion, in the second century, did so (and also pruned the New Testament of all that depended on the Old), This is important, and teachers using this *Catechism* need to be equipped to emphasise it. Marcionism is one of the most fundamental of Christian heresies, since it strikes at the very roots of New Testament revelation; and despite the Church's condemnation, fragments of its poisoned sting unfortunately remain in Catholic attitudes, both as practical under-valuing of the Old Testament and as tendencies to anti-Jewish prejudice. The relationship of the former covenant and its record in the 'Old Testament' to the Gospel, as carefully phrased in this section of DV and the *Catechism*, needs to be understood and taught as an extremely sensitive area. It must be emphasised that when the New Testament and Christians speak of the Old Testament as being in some ways 'incomplete' or as 'finding its full meaning in Christ', this is an expression of Christian conviction, not a judgement on those who in conscience cannot take this step. In general the *Catechism* handles these themes with care and delicacy.

The phrases in 122 (from the end of DV 15), listing a few of the reasons for treasuring the Old Testament, are too few and summary. Adequate Christian catechesis must have much more to say than this. Some reasons have already been touched on in the previous section of this essay, and more will come in the next.

6. The New Testament and how it uses the Old

DV ch. 5 (17–20) had one area to deal with, the historical value of the Gospels, which in the previous century had been at the centre of Rome's anxiety about the inerrancy of the Bible. The section on this (19) gave quiet approval to methods using analysis of form and tradition which had made their users the objects of vituperation by Italian conservatives.[58] For the rest, as in the chapter on the Old Testament, the Council was content to summarise traditional teaching in an almost homiletic tone. The remainder of the New Testament received the merest sketch (20).

The *Catechism* concentrates even more exclusively on the historicity of the Gospels (126), quoting the essentials of DV 19 accurately but without comment, even though teaching of great value has come from the Biblical Commission since the Council.[59] This section is framed by others (124–125 and 127) of the most general character, with two rather banal snippets out of the whole treasury of the saints. As for the rest of the New Testament, there is no section on it. Of course, there are occasional references elsewhere in the *Catechism*; but this failure even to mention the epistles, or the book of Revelation, misuse of which has caused such untold evil in the whole history of the Church, is simply inexplicable.

However, the *Catechism* inserts a section entitled 'The unity of the Old and New Testaments' (128–130, considerably expanding DV 16) which deals with an important aspect of the teaching in Acts and the Pauline and Petrine epistles. This is *typology*, one of the techniques of 'spiritual' or symbolic exegesis, which was discussed above. In patristic usage a *type* can refer to any entity (person, place, object or event, etc.) in the Old Testament, once it is perceived, with faith-filled imagination, as a prefiguring symbol of Christ, his cross, the resurrection, the Church or the sacraments, etc. The aspect of the New Testament which is thus seen as prefigured is strictly called the *antitype*.[60] The underlying principle for this whole procedure is faith that the same Holy Spirit guided the Old Testament writers who recorded the former events, and then guided the New Testament writers who saw them as prefigurations of Christ and expressed this. The imaginative process involved is the same as that of the poet who sees reality as potentially metaphoric and revelatory.

It is good that the *Catechism* gives attention to typology, because it is one of the principles on which Old and New Testament readings in the Lectionary are chosen to illuminate each other, and likewise it is the key to the fusion of themes which liturgical celebration enables worshippers to experience ever anew (e.g. the Passover lamb, the Suffering Servant 'led like a lamb to the slaughter', and Jesus the Lamb of God).

Typology is, however, only one of the three main uses of the Old Testament in the New and also in patristic writings. The others are (1) the construction of 'chains' of texts from the Old Testament, technically called *testimonies*; this method views the Old Testament as a whole tapestry of prophecy, all directed towards Christ, from which any selection could be used, without regard for context, to prove statements about him; (2) the construction of series of *examples* based on Old Testament persons (as in Heb 11) who illustrate virtues, vices, etc.; this method, of course, belongs to the 'moral sense' of Scripture. These other methods are no less widespread than typology in early Christian use of the Old Testament. (Incidentally, 'testimonies' and a kind of typology are also found in the pre-Christian Dead Sea Scrolls, serving sectarian Jewish purposes.)

7. Holy Scripture in the life of the Church

This all-important subject, which could be said to be about the divine purpose for which Christians have been given the Bible at all, occupies DV ch. 6 (21–26), or more than a quarter of the whole text. In the *Catechism* it is reduced to brief and general exhortations in 131–133, though material from DV 21 and 24 has been quoted in 103–104. Not only is there more valuable teaching in DV ch. 6, but the account of the various activities by which the Church uses and lives by Scripture is an inspiring expansion of the concentrated section on this in DV 8, the fate of which in the *Catechism* was traced at some length above. To read DV ch. 6 today is to realise what wonderful fruit it has borne since the Council, especially through ecumenical collaboration in the Bible Societies, and how much popular Bible study is flourishing, especially in Latin America. The work of biblical scholars is generously recognised and encouraged, and the importance of renewal of clerical formation for biblical preaching is emphasised. In the *Catechism* the latter receives a few words, but the other important aspects of the Church's developing use of Scripture are not thought worthy of mention, though in a catechism for the *Universal* Church many of them are of primary importance.

Looking back on this chapter of the *Catechism*, one must appreciate how extensively it reflects the greatest teaching document on revelation and Scripture in the Church's history. Yet detailed examination can cause anxiety. The activity of the Holy Spirit among all members of the Church is underplayed in comparison with DV, particlarly as regards scholars and teachers, whose role is only grudgingly mentioned; *magisterium* as centralised authority is emphasised far more than in DV. But most disappointingly of all, the handling of the Bible and biblical interpretation is less than impressive, and opportunities are missed.

Notes

1   See, e.g., Jean Levie SJ, *The Bible, Word of God in Words of Men* (1958; ET London: Geoffrey Chapman, 1961), chs 3–7.

2   Indications of the bishops' broader intentions are (1) the draft for a second Dogmatic Constitution on the Church, revised in the light of their comments, by J. Kleutgen SJ (July 1870), in *Mansi* LIII, cols 308–17, or in G. Alberigo and F. Magistretti (eds), *Constitutionis Dogmaticae 'Lumen Gentium' Synopsis Historica* (Bologna, 1975), Appendix 2; (2) the German Bishops' declaration (1875) countering Bismarck's allegation that the Catholic Church was now a centralised absolute monarchy, with Pius IX's solemn

approval of their teaching (DS 3112–3116 and 3117, and Alberigo, op. cit., Appendix 3).

3 The first draft document, 'On the sources of "Revelation"', insisted that Scripture and Tradition are two distinct sources, in a way insensitive to the whole ongoing theological debate, and then adumbrated some of the matter of DV chs 3–6. Another document, 'On preserving the deposit of faith in its purity', was prepared as a 'Dogmatic Constitution'; it dealt with some points which were to come up in DV chs 1–2, and others which had been raised in the encyclical *Humani Generis* (1950). Only the first of these drafts was discussed in the Council, and was rejected outright; the other was withdrawn. A new draft on revelation was then begun, and went through several revisions till it was accepted in 1965.

4 See, e.g., E. Bianchi, 'The centrality of the Word of God' in G. Alberigo *et al.* (eds), *The Reception of Vatican II* (ET London: Burns & Oates, 1987), pp. 115–36; R. Murray, *'Dei Verbum'* in A. Hastings (ed.), *Modern Catholicism* (London: SPCK, 1990), esp. pp. 79–80.

5 On nature and grace the writer has in mind especially H. de Lubac and K. Rahner; they are mentioned as influences on the theology of GS, not as its main architects.

6 Esp. GS 22 §5; 26, end; and cf. 57–58, which takes up the patristic recognition of a 'preparation for the Gospel' in human culture. See also Pope John Paul II, *Dominum et Vivificantem* (1986), 53–54.

7 E.g., LG 15–16, *Unitatis Redintegratio* (On Ecumenism; UR) and *Nostra Aetate* (On the Church and non-Christian religions).

8 This may be sensed again in the *Catechism*'s account of human conscience which, though not failing to mention the Holy Spirit, insists emphatically that the human conscience often needs an *external* authority to inform it soundly (1783, 1790).

9 The Latin makes it clear that this human access to God becomes a *reality* through Christ, not merely a matter of purpose. This nuance is correctly rendered in N. Tanner (ed.), *Decrees of the Ecumenical Councils*, vol. II (London: Sheed & Ward, 1991), p. 972; it is a pity that this more careful version was not chosen for the English edition of the *Catechism*.

10 The phrase is from St Irenaeus (*c.* AD 180), extant only in a Latin version: *suum ipsorum locum magisterii tradentes.* The Greek would have had *didaskalia*, which means 'teaching', either the function or what is taught.

11 *Proficit*: the paragraph is really about the development of doctrine, but many bishops were shy of the expression, which had been attacked in the first draft.

12 Again a phrase from Irenaeus in Latin, *charisma veritatis certum*. This is an important phrase which hints at what was to be called the Church's infallibility. It is more satisfactory, because it is couched positively, and thus avoids the endless difficulties which have been bred by the negative term.

13 *Singularis conspiratio.* 'Remarkable' is very weak. The phrase comes from the definition of the Immaculate Conception (1854), referring to the consensus which wide consultation had revealed in the Catholic Church; it implies an experience of shared belief, of a quality transcending other instances of agreement.

14 The phrase comes from the encyclical *Humani Generis* (1950). See further below. Though the Council no doubt meant the Pope and the bishops (as 85), the wording does not exclude or deny that they can share their magisterium with other competent teachers of the faith.

15   See LG 16; *Nostra Aetate* 2; *Ad Gentes* (on Missionary activity) 3 and 11, and
       the 'Apostolic Exhortation' *Evangelii Nuntiandi* ('Evangelisation in the
       Modern World') by Pope Paul VI (1975), 53. Most of these use the phrases
       quoted above and give references to their patristic authors.
16   Among matters for criticism, the Noachic covenant which, Gen 9 clearly
       states, is between God *and all creatures* (and is therefore the charter for
       Jewish and Christian ecological thinking) is declared in the main text (56) to
       refer only to interhuman relations; only in the later afterthought 'In Brief'
       (71) is the true sense of Gen 9 given, but without comment.
          The reference in 57 to belief in patron angels of the nations is interesting,
       but calls for more explanation than is likely to be available to most users of
       the *Catechism*. The trio from Ezek 14:14 mentioned in 58 also needs
       explanation; this 'Daniel' cannot be the hero of the biblical book.
17   However, note 17 on 59 is misleading: the last quotation renders Gal 3:8 but
       not the Hebrew or Greek of Gen 12:3.
          In 64, the role of women in the tradition of faith is justly emphasised, but
       Mary is oddly placed beside figures from whom she differs not only in purity
       but also in factuality.
18   *Acta Synodalia Concilii Vaticani II*, Vol. III.3, Relatio de n. 4 (F), p. 77, and
       vol. IV. 1, Relatio de n. 4, p. 345.
19   66 might aim to preserve a hint of DV 5, but the marginal reference is to 94,
       i.e., DV 8 §2.
20   R. Schutz and M. Thurian, *La parole vivante au concile* (Taizé, 1966); ET
       Revelation: A Protestant View (Westminster, MD: Newman Press, 1968),
       pp. 18–20.
21   G. O'Collins, *Fundamental Theology* (London: Darton, Longman & Todd,
       1981), pp. 99–102.
22   The *Catechism* offers a loose and partial explanation in 83. The 'classic' on
       this is Y. Congar OP, *Tradition and Traditions* (1960–63; ET London: Burns
       & Oates, 1966). Schutz and Thurian have a valuable discussion on pp. 28–33.
23   However, the key phrase is preserved, and turns up in the next 'In Brief'
       section (97). (These sections serve somewhat as did the twelve baskets after
       the feeding of the five thousand.)
24   'Would that all the Lord's people were prophets!' said Moses (Num 11:29),
       and Paul expresses the same wish at greater length in 1 Cor 14.
25   *Proficit* comes from the famous passage of St Vincent of Lérins (fifth century)
       on the development of doctrine, via Vatican I, *Dei Filius* 4 (DS 3020). The
       Catechism does not reproduce the statement that apostolic Tradition
       'progresses', but only says, weakly, that the Church's understanding 'is able
       to grow'. On this issue at the Council, see briefly J. Ratzinger in H. Vorgrimler
       (ed.), *Commentary on the Documents of Vatican II*, vol. III (ET London: Burns
       & Oates, 1969), pp. 186–9, and Schutz and Thurian, op. cit. (n. 20 above),
       pp. 33–40. In what sense Tradition (with a capital T) can be said to 'develop'
       remains at issue between theologians both within and beyond the Catholic
       communion. The *Catechism* offers no help to teachers here.
26   See n. 12 above.
27   DS 3886. Much more than DAS, this encyclical of seven years later renewed
       tones of warning to theologians, reminiscent of the anti-modernist
       documents. The exclusive ascription to 'the Magisterium' of the power to
       interpret Tradition 'authentically' would seem to imply that their charism of
       apostolic authority gives a guarantee that they will interpret a particular
       scriptural passage or point of Tradition correctly. It may be remarked that, at

least in the case of Scripture, this would seem to require, besides their episcopal charism, either personal mastery of the biblical languages or reliance on competent exegetes, so that to exclude the latter from any participation in magisterium would appear paradoxical.

28   *Acta . . . Vat. II* (n. 18 above), Vol. III. 2, Relatio de n. 10 (F), p. 87.

29   Schutz and Thurian, pp. 50–2.

30   This was amply researched by Y. Congar, 'Pour une histoire sémantique du terme "magisterium"', *Revue des sciences philosophiques et théologiques* 60 (1976), pp. 85–98. See also E. Hill OP, *Ministry and Authority in the Catholic Church* (London: Geoffrey Chapman, 1988), pp. 75–88.

31   By Benedict XV (DS 3625). For other effects of the new sense of *magisterium* during the early years of this century, see Excursus (pp. 34–5).

32   J. Ratzinger is excellent on this in Vorgrimler (see n. 25 above), vol. III, p. 196.

33   The Roman Canon (Eucharistic Prayer I).

34   At Vatican II the Maronite Patriarch, Paul Meouchi, urged that, in speaking of the whole Church as the bearer of Tradition, DV should mention the role of parents, other members of the laity, and theologians (*Acta . . . Vat. II*, vol. III.3, p. 854). In this he spoke for authentic Eastern Tradition, as the Eastern Catholic bishops so often did at Vatican II.

35   Trent, Session IV (1546), DS 1501.

36   Perhaps the clearest introduction is given by Schutz and Thurian, op. cit. (n. 20 above), pp. 40–9. For a fuller and more technical discussion, see J. Ratzinger in Vorgrimler (n. 25 above), pp. 184–96.

37   See J. Ratzinger, ibid., pp. 194–5; Schutz and Thurian as in n. 36.

38   See LG 12, which uses the term, and A. Grillmeier in H. Vorgrimler's Commentary (n. 25 above), vol. I, pp. 164–5. The *sensus fidelium* was often appealed to in the early Church (see Congar, *Tradition and Traditions* (ET 1966), pp. 314–32, and remains an important theme in the Orthodox Church: see, e.g., T. Ware, *The Orthodox Church* (Harmondsworth: Penguin Books, 1964), pp. 252–8. It must be emphasised that the Orthodox doctrine that even conciliar teaching must be 'received' by the whole Church does not say that such teaching requires confirmation by the laity before it has juridical authority. It is rather a matter of 'digestion', which may take some time.

39   For the kind of way this was treated in the scholastic manuals up to Vatican II, see, e.g., M. Nicolau and J. Salaverri SJ, *Sacrae Theologiae Summa*, vol. I: *Theologia Fundamentalis* (Madrid: BAC, 1955), pp. 729–47.

40   The term covers the range of possible answers to the question 'How is Jesus our Saviour?', corresponding to the range of emphases in the New Testament. Within that range, the atonement has never been a divisive issue between Churches. For many Evangelical Protestants a 'penal substitution' theory ('Jesus suffered the just penalty for my sin, in place of me') has virtually what Catholics would call 'dogmatic' status. The authors of the document on the 'Deposit of Faith', proposed for Vatican II (see n. 3 above), actually wanted the Council to dogmatise such a theory (ch. 10 in the draft); but the 'Fathers', in rejecting this with the rest of the document, maintained what seems a wise tradition in the Church, to respect the variety of ways in which the New Testament expresses Christ's saving work, and not to give dogmatic status to one. (See also below in the chapter on the death of Christ, pp. 144ff.)

41   See J. Feiner in H. Vorgrimler's commentary (n. 25 above), vol. II, pp. 118–21.

42   So the version in Tanner (n. 9 above), vol. II, p. 975.

43   The note on DAS 41 gives more references than that on DV 13. On this theme
      in Chrysostom see B. de Margerie SJ, *Introduction à l'histoire de l'exégèse,*
      vol. I: *Les Pères grecs et orientaux* (Paris: Cerf, 1979), who devotes the whole
      of ch. 8 (pp. 214–39) to his doctrine. The two previous chapters, on St Ephrem
      the Syrian and the exegetical tradition of Antioch, are also valuable.
      Ephrem, the greatest poet of the early Christian centuries, also expresses the
      incarnational analogy wonderfully.
44   Augustine interprets 'Give us this day our daily bread' of both Christ the
      Word and the eucharist in *Serm.* 56.10; 58.4 and especially 59.3. There are
      more texts in H. de Lubac SJ, *Exégèse médiévale,* vol. I (Paris: Aubier, 1959),
      p. 523. More familiar to many will be *The Imitation of Christ,* IV.11.4.
45   See R. M. Grant, *The Letter and the Spirit* (London: SPCK, 1957) for the
      history of this and analogous metaphors.
46   Thus in the Latin of Heb 2:10 and 12:2 Jesus is called the *auctor* respectively
      of our salvation and of our faith. Newman saw the true sense of the tradition
      of calling God *auctor* of Scripture; it was regularly followed by *utriusque
      testamenti,* 'of both Testaments', and was an anti-Marcionite formula, not
      intended to explain God's relationship to the human writers. See J. H.
      Newman, *On the Inspiration of Scripture,* ed. J. D. Holmes and R. Murray SJ
      (London: Geoffrey Chapman, 1967), pp. 129–31, and Introduction, pp. 53–9.
47   First propounded by M.-J. Lagrange OP, this theory was developed by P.
      Synave and P. Benoît (both OP) in *Prophecy and Inspiration* (Tournai etc.:
      Desclée, 1947; ET 1961). See also P. Benoît, 'Inspiration and Revelation',
      Concilium 10.1 (1965), pp. 5–14.
48   This kind of account was suggested for the New Testament by K. Rahner,
      Inspiration in the Bible (1961; ET in *Studies in Modern Theology,* London,
      1964), and developed for the Old Testament by J. L. McKenzie, 'The social
      character of inspiration' in *Myths and Realities* (London, 1963), pp. 59–69,
      though the actual formulations here are those of the present writer.
49   *On the Inspiration of Scripture* (n. 46 above), p. 114. Some personal notes by
      Newman on this theme were published by J. Seynaeve, *Cardinal Newman's
      Doctrine on Holy Scripture* (Louvain, 1953), pp. *127–8.
50   See R. Murray, 'How did the Church determine the canon of Scripture?', *The
      Heythrop Journal* 11 (1970), 113–26.
51   The problem preoccupied Newman: see his essays *On the Inspiration of
      Scripture* (n. 46 above), and the Introduction to that edition (pp. 48–96). See
      also briefly the Excursus (pp. 34–5).
52   Especially the sections quoted in DS 3826–3831. See J. Levie (n. 1 above), ch.
      VII, pp. 133–84.
53   This is said with precise reference to knowledge *through Scripture,* not to,
      e.g., certainties experienced in prayer.
54   Neither DAS nor DV 12 nor *Catechism* 109–110 shows awareness of this
      problem, so that many scholars reject the idea as naive, especially when (as
      has often been the case) figures such as Hosea and Jeremiah are pictured
      with not a little sentimental fantasy. Most modern hermeneutical theory
      would regard the quest for the author's intention as impossible;
      structuralists and their successors would add 'irrelevant'. Yet, if the inquiry
      is applied (as in the present discussion) to the biblical *texts,* whoever wrote
      them, the method remains valid and fruitful.
55   Even in the 1950s the writer heard a paper arguing that it cannot be proved
      impossible that a man might survive, at least for a reasonable time, in at
      least the mouth of some kind of whale.

56 Leo XIII, *Providentissimus Deus* (1893); DS 3283; allusions in Pius X, anti-modernist oath (1910), DS 3546, and Pius XII, DAS (1943), EB 551; *Humani Generis* (1950), DS 3887.
57 Allocution in Mainz, 17 November 1980.
58 See Holmes and Murray (n. 46 above), pp. 87–8, with further references there.
59 The documents of 1964 and 1985 are edited with full commentary by J. Fitzmyer SJ, respectively in *A Christological Catechism* (New York: Paulist Press, 1982) and *Scripture and Christology* (London: Geoffrey Chapman, 1986).
60 The mongrel word 'antetype' arose from a misunderstanding of 'anti-'; it causes confusion and should be helped to die.

Excursus

Further Reflections on magisterium and 'Magisterium'

If the actual task of interpreting Scripture 'authentically' is ascribed to 'the Magisterium' alone in the restricted modern sense, history raises problems. In the official Roman handbook of 'Ecclesiastical Documents Regarding Scripture'[1] (which typifies the modern use of 'Magisterium'), all the centuries up to 1893 occupy only one-seventh of the space, while the years 1893–1953 occupy six-sevenths. The long first period is that in which *magisterium* was applied to many members of the Church, some of whom became bishops and popes; the second period is that of the new sense of 'Magisterium'. In the 30 pages on the first period, many of the documents quoted are no more than brief recitals either of the Catholic canon of biblical books or of the traditional phrase calling God the *Auctor* of both Testaments. Authoritative interpretations of biblical texts hardly occur. During all those centuries the normative centres of Christian teaching were the catechetical schools, then some great monasteries, joined later by the universities. Conflicts might and did occur, but popes and bishops generally trusted theologians and exegetes. At Trent the bishops were regularly instructed by them.[2]

The short second period, which claims over 220 pages in the *Enchiridion Biblicum*, reflects how things had changed in the nineteenth century. The papacy had been forced on to the defensive. Its secular power could not survive, but its moral authority grew steadily, through a new development of encyclicals and, above all, the First Vatican Council. The keyword of this enhanced power was the new sense of 'Magisterium'. The half-century from 1893 to 1943 began and ended with major encyclicals encouraging study of the Bible in the Catholic Church,[3] and the Holy See founded a new Biblical Institute;[4] but this was also a period when Catholic scholars suffered much suspicion and harassment. The Pontifical Biblical Commission, founded in 1902 as part of the anti-modernist reaction, issued from 1905 to 1914 a series of *responsa* which Catholic scholars were obliged to regard as binding. These mainly imposed a literalist approach to biblical narratives which was unworthy

34

of the great tradition of Catholic exegesis and, in many cases, curiously comparable to positions taken by conservative Protestants who, in these same years, were rallying under the banner of 'fundamentalism'. The 'modernist crisis' had been about history and truth; but these *responsa* showed little awareness that there are different kinds of history, as of other forms of literature, and all have their own ways of being true. This series of interventions, unprecedented in the history of the Church, can only be read today with embarrassment, which 'the Magisterium' appears to share. The encyclical of 1943 was a major change of tack, and in 1954 two statements on behalf of the Commission quietly assured scholars that, on most of the questions dealt with, they have 'full freedom' to reach their own conclusions.[5] Since then, the few documents which have issued from the Biblical Commission have been increasingly helpful, and indeed represent an ideal collaboration in *magisterium* between teachers and church authority, fully in the spirit of Vatican II.[6]

The most recent of these, *The Interpretation of the Bible in the Church*,[7] largely corresponds in subject-matter to that of Chapter Two of the *Catechism*, though it differs in genre, structure and spirit, as well as in the depth of its treatment, since it includes description and evaluation of many methods of, and approaches to, biblical interpretation. There is hardly a point on which the *Catechism* has been criticised in the preceding pages which is not handled in a way which is above such criticism, and many points urged here are made even more clearly. This document will deserve the gratitude of every Catholic exegete and doubtless of others.

Notes

1 *Enchiridion Biblicum: Documenta Ecclesiastica S. Scripturam Spectantia*, 2nd edn (Naples–Rome, 1954). (Hereafter EB.)
2 See H. Jedin, *A History of the Council of Trent*, vol. II (London: Thomas Nelson, 1961), pp. 59–64.
3 *Providentissimus Deus* (Leo XIII, 1893) and *Divino Afflante Spiritu* (Pius XII, 1943). Between them, the anti-modernist documents of Pius X (1907) brought sore trials to loyal Catholic scholars, but encouragement began to sound again with *Spiritus Paraclitus* (Benedict XV, 1920).
4 Founded in Rome in 1909: EB 297ff. But it is ironic that the foundation in 1890 of the École Biblique in Jerusalem by the greatest Catholic exegete of modern times, M.–J. Lagrange OP, passes unnoticed in the EB, presumably because it earned no document of 'the Magisterium'.
5 For details see J. A. Fitzmyer SJ, *A Christological Catechism: New Testament Answers* (New York: Paulist Press, 1981), pp. 97–103.
6 See J. A. Fitzmyer SJ, *Scripture and Christology: A Statement of the Biblical Commission with a Commentary* (London: Geoffrey Chapman, 1986).
7 Libreria Editrice Vaticana, 1993. The document is prefaced by a fine address by Pope John Paul II and a short commendation by Cardinal Ratzinger.

The Doctrine of Faith

(Paragraphs 142–197)

Dermot A. Lane
Dublin

Anyone who is in touch with the catechical and theological life of the Church will be familiar with the challenges of communicating the truth of the Christian faith to the modern world. Part of the difficulty derives from the extraordinary cultural changes taking place in the world today: ecology, feminism and the new cosmologies. These changes, whether we like them or not, have a direct bearing on the teaching mission of the Church.

The decision to issue a universal catechism is one way of seeking to address the challenge of communicating the reality of the Catholic faith today. This decision has created great expectations, even among those who had misgivings about the wisdom of the decision. The *Catechism* offers a unique opportunity for the Church to present to the world the richness of the Catholic tradition, especially the spirit and substance of the Second Vatican Council. In a world that is at once anxious to know the truth, spiritually hungry, and increasingly in need of rediscovering its roots, there can be little doubt that the appropriate communication of the story of Christianity has much to offer.

My specific task is to comment on the doctrine of the faith as contained in Chapter Three of Part One of the *Catechism*. No doubt every section of the *Catechism* is important in itself. However, I would want to argue that the section on faith is foundational to the whole enterprise. Without a firm, convincing and credible account of faith the rest of the project could come crumbling down. Of course, it could be replied that the rest of the *Catechism* is itself a testimony of faith and is to that extent a source of faith. Nonetheless, it must be pointed out that the believer is faced in the end with the primacy of the personal act of faith. Further, it is hardly an exaggeration to claim that the fundamental issue facing the individual today is one of personal belief, especially in a world that is increasingly secular, self-sufficient, and pragmatic. We live in a situation of competing secular beliefs and faiths: the rise of cults, growing fundamentalism, the new age . . . To this extent the issue of faith, more specifically of religious

36

and Christian faith, is one of the most important challenges facing the Catholic Church at the close of the present millennium. The new *Catechism* understands itself as offering an opportunity 'to help deepen understanding of faith . . . towards the maturing of that faith, its putting down roots in personal life, and its shining forth in personal conduct' (23).

1. Part One, Section One, Chapter Three and Introduction to Section Two

Chapter Three of Part One, Section One, is made up of two articles entitled 'I believe' (21 paragraphs) and 'We believe' (129 paragraphs) respectively. The article on 'I believe' begins with a focus on the obedience of faith and holds up Abraham, Sarah and Mary as models of faith. This article then goes on to outline the trinitarian character of Christian faith centred on the revelation of God in Jesus (150–152). The *Catechism* also describes the various characteristics of faith (153–165): divine gift, a human act, the relationship between faith and reason, the freedom of faith, the necessity of faith, perseverance in faith, and faith as the beginning of everlasting life.

The article on 'We believe' discusses the relationship between personal belief and the belief of others (166–167), the faith of the Church (168–169), the language of faith (170–171), and the unity of faith (172–175). A short section summarises these many aspects of faith under 'In Brief' (176–184). This is followed by the formal texts of the Apostles' Creed and the Nicene Creed.

Finally, a part of Section Two of Part One, entitled 'The profession of the Christian faith: the creeds of the faith' (185–197) concludes the *Catechism*'s formal treatment of faith.

In general it must be said that the treatment of faith, like much of the *Catechism*, is highly condensed and as such calls out for commentary and clarification. The language is very traditional and will therefore be taxing to contemporary readers, with very few concessions to style or imagination. The text does not make easy reading and requires considerable concentration.

It is these two articles and the section following them that I propose to examine by way of commentary.

Article 1: 'I believe'
The overall context of the treatment of faith is the preceding chapter dealing with the revelation of God (Chapter Two). The opening sub-section is entitled 'The obedience of faith'.

The language of obedience, though biblical, is probably not the best way to introduce the complexity of faith. For many the use of obedience in a church document carries from a historical point of view negative and restrictive connotations. To be sure, there is a sense in which the act of faith does involve an important element of obedience, especially when the individual is faced with the impulses of conscience and the demands of truth. Responses to these impulses, however, are more often than not points of arrival in discussing faith rather than points of departure.

What is missing here and throughout the treatment of faith is an apologetic adequate to the demands of the modern world. No reference is made to the universality of faith as a basic ingredient of the human condition. No awareness is evident of the anthropological relationship that exists between human (primordial) faith, religious faith and Christian faith — not to mention what might be called Catholic Christian faith. In a world and a Church that recognises the importance of ecumenical and inter-faith dialogue, the *Catechism*'s treatment of faith is handicapped *ab initio* by ignoring these realities.

It is difficult to find a point of departure that will appeal to all women and men of goodwill, whether they belong to the Christian community or not. The nearest we get to this in the *Catechism* is to be found in Chapter One of Part One, which deals impressively with the human desire for God (27–30) and the human person's 'openness to truth and beauty, his sense of moral goodness, his freedom and the voice of his conscience, with his longings for the infinite and for happiness, man questions himself about God's existence' (33). But surely this desire for God and its many other unmentioned expressions such as the human experience of transcendence, limit-situations, and the pull of the future upon the present, constitute an important dimension of the stirrings of faith and should have been dealt with by the *Catechism* as *prologomena* to faith in Chapter Three.

Continuing with this section on 'The obedience of faith', the *Catechism* goes on to say that faith is 'to submit freely to the word that has been heard, because its truth is guaranteed by God, who is Truth itself' (144). This statement requires careful explanation, lest it be understood to beg the basic question of religious faith and involve the believer in something of a vicious circle. There is an important sense in which it must be pointed out that the justifying ground and truth of faith is available only within the experience of making the act of faith.

I have dwelt in some detail on the opening paragraph on faith, because one's point of departure is decisive for the rest of the treatment. In particular there is a need for a strong apologetic in relation to faith, especially an apologetic that takes account of the experiential and anthropological aspects of faith which seems to be missing in this section. A further reason for dwelling on this opening paragraph is that it sets the tone for what is to come.

In the next sub-section, on 'Abraham — "father of all who believe"', the figure of Abraham is put forward as one who embodies the basic characteristics of faith: obedience, setting out on a journey, assurance of things hoped for, the conviction of things not seen. This sub-section concludes with the Letter to the Hebrews, which describes Jesus as the pioneer and perfecter of faith. This important reference to Jesus is potentially one of the most promising statements in the *Catechism*'s discussion of faith. Unfortunately this reference is not developed, and there is no explanation of it given in the Christology section of the

Catechism that might show how Jesus enabled and facilitated faith in the past and continues to do so in the present. In fact, if anything the Christology of the *Catechism* would seem to be unsympathetic to the contemporary understanding of Jesus as the pioneer and perfecter of faith.[1]

In addition to Abraham, Mary is singled out as one who achieved the full obedience of faith. This suggestive reference to the faith of Mary is marred, however, by the historically unverifiable statement that Mary's faith never wavered and never doubted (149). Indeed this particular statement does not sit comfortably with the observation later on in the *Catechism* that when faith is tested we should turn to the witness of people like Mary, who in her pilgrimage walked into the 'night of faith' by sharing the darkness of her Son's suffering and death (165). In mentioning the faith of Mary, it would have been more helpful if the *Catechism* had linked the faith of Mary with the work of justice in the way that Paul VI does in *Marialis Cultus*.[2]

The next part, entitled '"I know whom I have believed", 2 Tim 1:12', outlines constructively the trinitarian character of Christian faith and focuses on Christ as the source of the Christian understanding of God. This section is doctrinally rich and describes faith as a personal commitment addressed to God. One particular remark, namely that 'Christian faith differs from our faith in any human person' (150), while true, is only half the truth. Surely there are some similarities, indeed important similarities from an apologetic point of view, between faith in a human person and faith in God.

The third part deals with 'the characteristics of faith'. This is the longest and most complicated section on faith in the *Catechism*. It begins by pointing out that 'Faith is a gift of God, a supernatural virtue infused by him', resulting from God's prevenient grace, and 'the interior helps of the holy Spirit' (153). No intimation is given, however, about how God's prevenient grace touches the human condition as put forward by, for example, the Second Vatican Council.[3] The *Catechism* then goes on helpfully to show how 'faith is a human act' (154–155) by drawing a parallel between trusting human beings and trusting God — in spite of seeming to deny this parallel earlier on in 150 as noted above.

Within this section the *Catechism* also deals with 'faith and understanding' (156–159). The text seeks to show that there is an underlying compatibility between faith and reason, suggesting that the assent of faith to divine revelation is supported by external signs. Among the external signs of credibility, the *Catechism* points to the 'miracles of Christ and the saints, prophecies, the Church's growth and holiness and its fruitfulness and stability' (156). This particular apologetic of Vatican I needs to be tempered by the acknowledgement at Vatican II of the Church 'as holy and at the same time in need of purification'.[4] In developing this relationship between faith and understanding, the *Catechism* highlights the creative dialectic that exists between faith and reason by quoting Augustine's perennially valid observation that 'I believe, in order to understand; and I understand, the better to believe'

(158). Consistent with this principle, the *Catechism* goes on to argue, with Vatican II, that the authentic search for knowledge and truth is supported by God who is the source of all knowledge and truth, whether secular or sacred (159) — a point that could have been developed a little more in the light of the new rapport that exists between religion and science. This part on faith and reason is logically followed by a useful treatment of 'the freedom of faith' (160). A short statement on 'the necessity of faith' for salvation leaves one with the impression that those who do not have faith will not obtain eternal life. Once again this quotation from Vatican I needs to be balanced by the more inclusive statement of Vatican II that '. . . we ought to believe that the holy Spirit, in a manner known only to God, offers to every human person the possibility of being associated with the Paschal Mystery'.[5]

From 'the necessity of faith' the *Catechism* moves on to discuss 'perseverance in faith' (162). Here the challenge of fighting the good fight and avoiding shipwreck is outlined. The need to grow in faith is signalled, and the importance of the relationship between faith, love and hope is indicated.

This part concludes with the sub-section on 'Faith — the beginning of eternal life' — a sub-section that is full of realism. While the goal of faith is eternal life, the journey of faith is often lived out in darkness and is frequently tested by evil and suffering, injustice and death. The *Catechism* acknowledges that faith can be shaken by these experiences. Many will regret, however, that the *Catechism* did not develop these significant openings, since they represent the experience of so many people today. This sub-section concludes with an appeal once again to the faith of Abraham and Mary, with particular reference to Jesus as the pioneer and perfecter of our faith (Heb 12:1–2).

Article 2: 'We believe'

In Article 2, 'We believe', like Article 1, 'I believe', there are three parts. These parts are introduced by a useful reminder that although faith is always a personal act, none the less it is never simply an isolated act. Instead, the personal act of faith is carried by the faith of others and is therefore linked to the great chain of believers. The *Catechism* points out that 'no one can believe alone, just as no one can live alone' (166). This significant point in the *Catechism* is worthy of further refinement, given the penchant of our age for individualism. This creative tension between individual faith and the faith of the community is seen to be paralleled in the relationship that exists between the Apostles' Creed said at baptism in terms of 'I believe', and the Niceno-Constantinopolitan Creed recited by the liturgical assembly in terms of 'We believe'.

Part I comments on the line from the liturgy, 'Lord, look upon the faith of your Church'. The faith of the Church precedes and grounds individual faith. At the same time the *Catechism* is careful to point out that while we receive faith from the Church, our faith as such is 'not in the Church as if she were the author of our salvation' (169).

Part II discusses 'The language of faith', quoting Aquinas's well-known and extremely important theological principle that the believer's act of faith does not stop at the expression, but at the reality expressed. This brings us to one of the principal issues that all catechisms must face — namely that the formulae of faith and doctrinal statements are not an end in themselves, but rather a means to opening up the incomprehensible mystery of God revealed in the person of Jesus. The Catholic Church has always taught this, and the new *Catechism* is particularly eloquent elsewhere in affirming this tradition. In Part One, Section One, the *Catechism* points out:

> God transcends all creatures. We must therefore continually purify our language of everything in it that is limited, image-bound or imperfect, if we are not to confuse our image of God — 'the inexpressible, the incomprehensible, the invisible, the ungraspable' — with our human representations. Our human words always fall short of the mystery of God. (42)

Given this theological principle, and the Thomistic distinction between the act of signification (*actus significandi*) and the reality signified (*res significata*), as well as the distinction between the act of faith (*fides qua*) and the content of faith (*fides quae*), a strong case clearly exists for variety and diversity in the language of faith and the approaches of faith to the one mystery of God. In effect, the greater the variety of doctrinal expression in our attempts to articulate the mystery of God, the deeper our experience and understanding of one and the same divine reality. This means recognising that the neo-scholastic language of faith does have a legitimate role in communicating the mysteries of faith. But equally, however, it implies that other tried and tested languages of faith, such as those of the existential, experiential, anthropological, shared praxis, narrative and story variety as developed by modern theology and catechesis also have a legitimate function in exploring the mystery of God and communicating the content of Christian faith. These other languages need not be seen as competing with or contradicting the neo-scholastic language — but rather as complementing and supplementing it.

There is of course the additional hermeneutical question: which interpretative language best communicates the object of personal faith? An answer to this question, over and above references to Scripture, Tradition and liturgy, is not given in the *Catechism*; yet such an answer is crucial to the future of faith and would surely have to include reference at least to human experience, contemporary culture, social justice, the praxis of liberation and the integrity of creation.

The new *Catechism* is less successful than it might have been because it has limited itself to one particular mind-set, namely the neo-scholastic one, in its treatment of faith. Within the confines of the neo-scholastic method the new *Catechism* could be said to succeed admirably. But, it will be asked, what about other conceptualities such as the turn to the subject and historical consciousness, the framework of modernity, process thought, and the emerging reconstructed post-modern ecological frameworks? This important section on the language of faith concludes with a brief observation on the role of the Church as guardian of the confession of faith received from the apostles (171).

Part III, entitled 'Only one faith', refers to the unity of faith down through the centuries found 'in so many languages, cultures, peoples and nations'. Recognition of 'one faith . . . in . . . many cultures' is one of the most significant paragraphs in the *Catechism*'s treatment of faith, and is re-echoed in Part Two in reference to liturgical diversity (1200). The *Catechism* quotes St Irenaeus of Lyons to the effect that the Church has always been conscious of her responsibility to preserve the unity of faith and tradition as something which comes to us from one house (173). At the same time the *Catechism* recognises that this faith 'is constantly being renewed' (175).

This chapter concludes with a block entitled 'In Brief' which summarises everything said up to now in ten propositions (176–184). These summaries are theologically rich, with the exception of one which says 'The Church is the mother of all believers. "No one can have God as Father who does not have the Church as Mother"' (181) — a statement which believers of non-Christian religions might well find objectionable because of the failure once again to distinguish between non-Christian religious believers and Christian believers.

Part One, Section Two, The profession of Christian faith: the Creeds

The purpose of this section is to help the reader understand the function and importance of the Creeds as confessions of faith, especially in view of the fact that a significant part of the *Catechism* is devoted to an extended commentary on the Apostles' and the Nicene Creeds.

Once again the *Catechism* returns to the close relationship that exists between 'I believe' and 'We believe'. From the beginning the Church expressed her faith in short formulae, and these in turn were gathered into organic summaries of faith (186). These became known as 'professions of faith', 'Creeds' (because of the use of the Latin word *credo* at the beginning of them), and 'symbols of faith' (187–188). Such statements of faith were expressed first at baptism in the name of the Father and of the Son and of the Holy Spirit. The basic structure of the Creeds is trinitarian, summarising the work of creation by the first divine person, the mystery of redemption by the second divine person, and the activity of sanctification by the third divine person (189–190).

The *Catechism* here alludes to a suggestion that according to an ancient tradition there are twelve articles in the Apostles' Creed, symbolising the entirety of the apostolic faith corresponding to the number of the apostles (191). It should be noted that this ancient tradition is probably based more on legend than on history, with very little hard evidence, either biblical or historical, to suggest that the twelve apostles were the authors in the literal sense of the Apostles' Creed — though of course most would agree that the Apostles' Creed is based on the apostolic teaching. Contemporary commentators on the Creed are agreed that a literalist interpretation of this ancient tradition ascribing the twelve articles of the Creed directly to the twelve apostles distorts its structure, which is primarily trinitarian.[6]

The *Catechism* notes that there have been many professions of faith articulated by councils and popes in response to the needs of different eras. None of these different creeds can be considered as superseded. Instead, they help to deepen faith. Among the different Creeds, the *Catechism* singles out the Apostles' Creed and the Niceno-Constantin-opolitan or Nicene Creed, which remain common to all the great Churches of both the East and the West. The *Catechism* follows the Apostles' Creed for its presentation of the faith because it 'constitutes, as it were, "the oldest Roman catechism"' (196). At the same time, this presentation of the faith is completed, it says, by constant reference to the Nicene Creed, which is often more explicit and detailed (196).

This section could have said something more explicit about the social, liturgical and doxological functions of these two Creeds. Creeds create communities of faith, shape liturgical celebrations, and express humanity's deepest need to worship.

What is perhaps most lacking in the treatment of faith in this *Catechism* is a clear statement of the classical distinction between the personal act of faith and the content of faith. The act of faith is expressed in code, creed and cult, which make up the major part of the *Catechism*. Yet the personal act of faith cannot be reduced simply to code, creed or cult. There is always something more to the personal act of faith. This more, this surplus, as it were, in the personal act of faith, creates a tension, a necessary and creative tension between the personal act of faith and the content of faith. Given the importance of the act of faith, much more attention should have been given to the foundations of personal faith. Likewise the awakening of personal faith is surely primary to the development of the details of faith. Instead the bulk of the *Catechism* in Part One, Chapter Three, and indeed throughout the *Catechism*, is given over to the elaboration of the content of faith. While this is understandable in one sense, it must be pointed out that the vitality and meaning of the content of faith ultimately rests on the personal act of faith. While the act of faith and the content of faith cannot be separated, they must be distinguished. Excessive preoccupation with the content of faith to the neglect of the personal act of faith runs the risk of 'handing on the faith without faith'!

2. Towards an evaluation of the *Catechism* on faith

In seeking to evaluate the *Catechism* in general, and in particular its treatment of faith, which is our primary task here, we must briefly refer to some of the terms of reference that the *Catechism* has set itself. In the Prologue it is stated: 'This catechism aims at presenting an organic synthesis of the essential and fundamental contents of Catholic doctrine, as regards both faith and morals, in the light of the Second Vatican Council and the whole of the Church's Tradition' (11). Further, it should be noted that the *Catechism* 'emphasizes the exposition of doctrine' and 'seeks to help deepen understanding of faith' (23). In addition, in various places the Prologue talks about the importance of apologetics or 'examination of the reasons for belief' (6). Lastly, the *Catechism* states that it 'does not set out to provide the adaptation of doctrinal presentations and catechetical methods' (24).

In the light of these aims and concerns, it must be said immediately that there are valuable openings for development in the *Catechism* concerning faith. These openings will be of considerable help to those charged with the responsibility of communicating the Christian faith. They include:

- the reference to Jesus as the pioneer and perfecter of our faith (149–165)

- the holding up of Sarah and Mary as models of faith (145, 148, 149, 165)

- the emphasis on the Trinitarian character of the Christian faith (152, 189, 190)

- the Christocentric focus of the Christian mystery (151, 158)

- the interplay between faith and understanding (156, 158)

- the unity of all knowledge and truth in God (159)

- the link between faith, hope and love (162)

- the recognition of 'one faith . . . in . . . many cultures' (172)

- the possibility of growth and renewal in faith (162, 175)

- the relationship between 'I believe' and 'We believe' (166)

- the coexistence of faith and darkness (164)

- the acknowledgement that the believer's act of faith does not stop at the expressions but at the reality expressed (170).

At the same time there are some striking omissions in the treatment of faith:

- the failure to differentiate between basic human faith, religious faith, Christian faith and Catholic faith

- a recognition of the intrinsic link between Christian faith, the work of justice and the integrity of creation

- references to the importance of ecumenical exchanges and inter-faith dialogue as sources of faith enrichment

- an acknowledgement of human experience as the matrix of faith

- a discussion of 'the stages of faith' that are now recognised by both psychology (J. Fowler) and theology (K. Rahner) as important for understanding the dynamics of faith

- the place of awe and wonder as well as affectivity and intuition in the genesis of faith

- an interaction of faith with doubt, unbelief and atheism.

These particular omissions, however, are related to a more serious issue, namely the extent to which the Second Vatican Council has influenced the *Catechism* on faith. One of the aims of the *Catechism* as noted above is to present the faith of the Church in the light of Vatican II. Now it would be quite unfair and factually inaccurate to suggest that the *Catechism* does not draw on Vatican II. After the Bible, the documents of Vatican II are among the most frequently quoted sources. In spite of this, however, one gets the impression from time to time that the spirit and substance of Vatican II is not always the driving force behind the *Catechism*'s treatment of faith. There are significant statements from Vatican II on faith that do not appear in the *Catechism*.

For example, the well-known opening statement on faith by John XXIII, designed to give direction to the Council and subsequently incorporated into the *Pastoral Constitution on the Church in the Modern World*, is omitted: 'For the deposit of faith or revealed truths are one thing; the manner in which they are formulated without violence to their meaning and significance is another.'[7] A second example comes from the Decree on Revelation: 'For there is growth in the understanding of the realities and words [of the apostolic faith] that have been handed down.'[8] A third example comes from the *Pastoral Constitution on the Church in the Modern World*: 'For faith throws a new light on everything, manifests God's design for man's total vocation, and thus directs the mind to solutions which are fully human.'[9] A fourth example must include the Decree on Ecumenism, which explicitly reminds us 'that in Catholic teaching there exists an order or "hierarchy" of truths, since they vary in their relationship to the foundation of the Christian faith'.[10] While it is clear that the *Catechism* abounds with quotations from Vatican II, it is not always clear that the actual spirit and substance of Vatican II permeates it in its treatment of faith.

No one doubts that something significant happened at the Second Vatican Council. One way of highlighting this is to contrast the style and language of the preparatory documents with the style and language of the finally approved documents of Vatican II. A dramatic shift occurred at the Council which is reflected in the approach, the spirit, and the language of the documents. In terms of approach, there is a move from a deductive, scholastic theology to an inductive, personalist theology.[11] In terms of the spirit, there is a new openness to the modern world and the signs of the times.[12] In terms of the language, there is a move from anathema to dialogue, from isolation to solidarity, from opposition to conversation.[13] A new way of doing theology came into being at Vatican II which embraced a turn to human experience,[14] the recognition of historical consciousness,[15] and an acknowledgement of pluralism.[16]

This new way of doing theology is summed up symbolically in the proposal of the Council that 'to carry forward the work of Christ' the

Church has 'the duty of scrutinizing the signs of the times and of interpreting them in the light of the Gospel'.[17] This particular proposal of the Second Vatican Council, which has biblical roots, has been used to great effect since the Council in the life of the Church: in international and local synods, pastoral letters, episcopal conferences, papal encyclicals and apostolic exhortations. It could have been used to greater effect in the new *Catechism*, especially in the treatment of faith. If it had been used more extensively in the *Catechism* on faith there would have been a more credible apologetic for faith and a greater engagement with contemporary culture.

There is an urgent need for a stronger apologetic concerning faith — not in terms of proving faith, but in terms of faith gaining a foothold in the crucible of human experience and of being in touch with the surrounding culture. A faith that is not rooted in human experience is a faith that is in danger of appearing abstract and becoming ideological. It is quite extraordinary that in the entire treatment of faith the *Catechism* makes only one reference to experience, and in this particular instance the reference concerns the obscurity between experience and the truths of revelation.

Likewise, Christian faith must express itself in the culture of the day if it is to have meaning in the lives of people. To be sure, some of the surrounding culture is reductionistic, but equally it must be acknowledged that parts of contemporary culture are sympathetic to the religious and Christian impulse: the univeral concern for human rights and gender equity, the search for a justice and peace that respects the integrity of creation, the continuous quest for human liberation and spiritual fulfilment, the direction of the new physics and post-modern cosmologies ... If the Church fails to incarnate her faith in association with the experience of people and contemporary cultural realities, there is the distinct possibility that the liberating message of the gospel will be discarded because of its association with abstractions and dated cultural forms.

Without this creative interaction with human experience and contemporary culture, there is the danger that we may end up passing on the dead faith of the living instead of the living faith of the dead. In this regard it is important to remember what John Paul II said about the process of inculturation: 'A faith which does not become culture is a faith which has not been fully received, nor thoroughly thought through, nor fully lived out.'[18] To suggest that the urgent task of apologetics and inculturation should take place at local level in and through the adaptation of the *Catechism* is to misunderstand the true nature of apologetics and inculturation.

When the Dutch Catechism came out after Vatican II, one of the most telling reviews of it was written by the then Professor Joseph Ratzinger. In his review Ratzinger pinpointed the problem facing the production of the Dutch Catechism, and by implication catechisms in general, in the following way: 'The form of our belief hitherto, built as it was on the old static geocentric view of the world and on an unassailable confidence in ontological thought is not fitted to cope with the questioning of the post metaphysical age.'[19] Ratzinger expands on this observation by suggesting that the challenge facing the Dutch Catechism, and presumably other catechisms, is one of 'translating doctrine from a medieval context into the modern world'.[20] The process of translation is, as he puts it, twofold. On the one hand the theology of the past must be translated into a theology of present-day realities. On the other hand this theology of present-day realities must 'be phrased in a language suitable for preaching and teaching the faith to modern man'.[21] Few would quibble with these criteria put forward by Ratzinger. The extent to which the new *Catechism* succeeds in realising the first task of translating the medieval theology of the past into present-day reality will become apparent to readers as they consult the commentaries that follow. Concerning the particular issue of faith in the *Catechism*, I have indicated above some of the successes and some of the neglects. As to the second task, of translating contemporary theology into a suitable language, it must be noted that according to the terms of reference within the *Catechism* this is the challenge that will follow the publication of the *Catechism*. This approach has the merit that the process of catechesis can overcome and make good what may be lacking in the first task of translating the old theology into a new theology as Ratzinger suggests. In this regard the guidelines given in the Prologue of the *Catechism* are worth noting. It is pointed out:

- that adaptation is indispensable

- that adaptation should take account of differences of culture, age spiritual life, and social and ecclesial conditions among the People of God

- that 'teachers must not imagine a single kind of soul as being entrusted to them', but rather recognise the great differences and needs that exist among their audiences

- that it is not necessary to follow one and the same method in all instances of teaching

- that account must be taken of the differences between newborn children, adolescents and adults

- that the presentation of the faith must be related to the maturity and understanding of the hearers.

On the other hand, it could be argued that there are also good pedagogical and pastoral reasons for keeping both theology and catechesis working together *in tandem*.

In conclusion, it is important to recognise that the *Catechism* is not an end in itself, but rather a catalyst to stimulate the lifelong process of getting to know in thought and action as well as experience and understanding the mystery of God made manifest in the reality of Christ Jesus — a living and liberating reality that cannot be confined to any

single book. The story of the mystic told by Tony de Mello SJ, is
instructive:

> The mystic was back from the desert.
> 'Tell us', they said, 'what is God like?'
> But how could he ever tell them
> What he had experienced in
> his heart?
>
> Can God be put into words?
> He finally gave them a formula —
> so inaccurate so inadequate —
> in the hope that some of them might be tempted
> to experience it for themselves.
>
> They seized upon the formula
> They made it a sacred text
> They imposed it on others as a holy belief
> They went to great pains to spread it
> in foreign lands
> Some even gave their lives for it.
>
> The mystic was sad
> It might have been better
> if he had said nothing.[22]

The mystic need not necessarily be sad — but that will depend in great
measure on the spirit in which the guidelines for implementing the
Catechism are followed.

Notes

1 See the helpful treatment of this subject in G. O'Collins and D. Kendall, 'The
   faith of Jesus', *Theological Studies* 3 (1992), pp. 403–23.
2 Paul VI, *Marialis Cultus* (1974), 37.
3 See LG 13; GS 18, 19 and 22.
4 LG 8.
5 GS 22.
6 See H. de Lubac, *Christian Faith: The Structure of the Apostles' Creed* (1970;
   ET London: Geoffrey Chapman, 1986), chs 1 and 2; B. L. Marthaler, *The
   Creed* (Mystic, CT: Twenty-Third Publications, 1987), pp. 1–5.
7 GS 62.
8 DV 3.
9 GS 11.
10 UR 11.
11 See DV 8 and 14.
12 GS 5.

13 See GS 1 and 3.
14 See DV 8 and 14; GS 33.
15 See GS 4 and 5.
16 See LG 23; DH 1 and 2.
17 GS 3 and 4.
18 Opening Address to the Council for Culture, available in *L'Osservatore Romano* (28 June 1982), pp. 1–8.
19 J. Ratzinger, 'The Dutch Catechism: a theological appreciation', *The Furrow* 22 (December 1971), p. 742.
20 Ibid., p. 751.
21 Ibid., p. 754.
22 A. de Mello, 'The Formula' in *The Song of the Bird* (New York: Image Books, 1982), p. 31.

The Doctrine on God

(Paragraphs 198–231)

Brian Davies OP
Blackfriars, Oxford

The great English philosopher Bertrand Russell (1872–1970) had views on the morality of war, and for these he spent time in prison. On one occasion a jailer asked him what his religion was. Russell said: 'Agnostic.' The jailer replied: 'Well, there may be many religions, but we all worship the same God.'

But do we? It is often said that all people who honestly profess belief in God certainly worship the same God (the one, true God). It is sometimes said that *bona fide* members of all the major world religions do so. Yet there are reasons for resisting this suggestion. The verb 'to worship' is an intentional one, like 'to support', as when we say that so and so supports a particular leader. And just as one can be mistaken about the object one *supports*, so one can be mistaken about what one takes oneself to *worship*.

Suppose I say that I support President Clinton and the Democratic Party. Suppose you question me about Clinton and the Democrats. Also suppose that discussion proves that I am confusing Clinton with Adolf Hitler, and Democrats with Fascists. In that case I do not support Clinton and the Democrats, for my beliefs about them are wildly off the mark. In saying that I support Clinton and the Democrats I might well be speaking in good faith. But I do not support what people who support Clinton and the Democrats support. By the same token, it could emerge that I do not worship the one, true God. If my beliefs about the one, true God are sufficiently off the mark, if I am sufficiently confused and in error about the one, true God, then the object of my allegiance will be something else. That is why idolatry is a serious possibility. One may worship as God that which is not God.[1]

If we are concerned with the one, true God, therefore, it matters that we are right in what we believe about divinity. And the chief business of 198–231 of the *Catechism* is to expound some basic truths about what it is to be God.[2] In particular, the paragraphs are concerned to insist on the uniqueness of God, and on the notion of God as Truth and Love.

50

But what the *Catechism* says about God is by no means as uncontroversial as might appear from this bald summary. All Christians may be expected to agree that God is unique. And all will be at ease with the formulae 'God is Truth' and 'God is Love'. But not all Christians will approve of the way in which the *Catechism* talks of God's uniqueness. And not all of them will be happy with what 'God is Truth' and 'God is Love' must mean in the light of the *Catechism*'s teaching on the uniqueness of God. For this reason, 198–231 is positively controversial.

From a reading of 200–201, this might not seem so at all. For here we are told that God is unique in the sense that there is only one God. Nothing controversial in that, you might say. All Christians are monotheists. None are polytheists. But having asserted that there is but one God, the *Catechism* promptly quotes from the Fourth Lateran Council (1215) to teach that the one, true God is 'eternal, infinite (*immensus*) and unchangeable, incomprehensible, almighty and ineffable, the Father and the Son and the Holy Spirit; three persons indeed, but one essence, substance or nature entirely simple'. And here the *Catechism* is being controversial on at least three counts.

'Eternal' and 'unchangeable'

To begin with, note the terms 'eternal' and 'unchangeable'. In 205 we read that God is 'beyond space and time', so in using the terms 'eternal' and 'unchangeable' the *Catechism* is evidently endorsing what is taught at length by theologians like St Anselm of Canterbury (1033–1109) and St Thomas Aquinas (*c.* 1225–74). According to these authors, to call God eternal is to say that he is wholly immutable and non-temporal.[3] Or, as the sixth-century thinker Boethius famously put it:

> Eternity, then, is the complete and perfect possession of unending life, all at once [*tota simul*]; this will be clear from a comparison with creatures that exist in time. Whatever lives in time exists in the present and progresses from the past to the future, and there is nothing set in time which can embrace all at once the whole extent of its life . . . Whatever, therefore, suffers the condition of being in time, even though it never had any beginning, never has any ending and its life extends into the infinity of time . . . is still not such that it may properly be called eternal.[4]

The idea here is that God differs from things in the world since his life is not one of limited duration. And to this idea is added the thought of him not having a life lived in time. The claim, therefore, is that God has nothing that we could recognise as a history or biography. As Anselm writes:

> You were not, therefore, yesterday, nor will You be tomorrow, but yesterday and today and tomorrow You *are*. Indeed You exist neither yesterday nor today nor tomorrow but are absolutely outside all times [*es extra omne tempus*]. For yesterday and today and

51

tomorrow are completely in time; however, You, though nothing can be without You, are nevertheless not in place or time but all things are in You. For nothing contains You, but You contain all things.[5]

Yet this way of talking is very much out of favour in many contemporary theological circles. According to a large number of authors, it is actually *incompatible* with belief in God. Hence, for example. J. R. Lucas bluntly declares: 'To say that God is outside time, as many theologians do, is to deny, in effect, that God is a person.'[6] According to Grace Jantzen, writing in a recently published *Dictionary of Christian Theology*:

> A living God cannot be static: life implies change and hence temporality. This means that the doctrine of immutability cannot be interpreted as absolute changelessness, which would preclude divine responsiveness and must rather be taken as steadfastness of character.[7]

We might also note that the notion that change is essential to God's being is fundamental to those twentieth-century theologians known as 'process theologians'. It is particularly prevalent in the work of the influential American author Charles Hartshorne. According to him, God is continually struggling against evil. God is also supremely sympathetic. He undergoes happiness as we flourish. And he grieves as we suffer. In the words of one of Hartshorne's more approving commentators: 'Hartshorne takes the statement that "God is love" to mean literally that God finds joy in our joys and sorrows in our sorrows. Love, as Hartshorne uses the word even in its application to God, means sympathetic dependence on others.'[8] For Hartshorne this means that God actually undergoes development, that quality and value get added to the divine life. He improves as time goes on.[9] Hartshorne also tells us God's knowledge grows with time and that people can be said to create themselves.[10]

And, so it is often said, to speak of God as changeless and non-temporal is to contradict what is said of God in the Bible. According, once again, to John Lucas (stating a frequently voiced opinion), 'the whole thrust of the biblical record' implies that God changes. The Bible

> is an account of God both caring and knowing about the world, even the five sparrows, which at one time had not yet been, and later had been, sold for two farthings, and intervening in the world, doing things, saying things, hearing prayers, and sometimes changing his mind.[11]

'The changelessness of God', says Lucas, 'is not to be naturally read out of the Bible, but rather was read into it in the light of certain philosophical assumptions about the nature of God.'[12] Here Lucas agrees with Professor Richard Swinburne, according to whom:

> The God of the Old Testament, in which Judaism, Islam and Christianity have their roots, is a God in continual interaction with

men, moved by men as they speak to him . . .If God did not change at all, he would not think now of this, now of that . . . The God of the Old Testament is not pictured as such a being . . . The doctrine of divine timelessness is very little in evidence before Augustine. The Old Testament certainly shows no sign of it . . . The same applies in general for New Testament writers.[13]

'Incomprehensible' and 'ineffable'

Now note the *Catechism*'s teaching that God is 'incomprehensible' and 'ineffable'. This teaching is a traditional one among writers in the Christian tradition (as well as among Jewish and Islamic authors). But many people now deny (either directly or by implication) that God is strictly incomprehensible and ineffable. They would agree that God is in some sense a mystery. But, so they would add, we can have a pretty good understanding of what he is, and we can capture him quite effectively in language.

Why so? The usual answer given is because God belongs to the same class as we do. I am a person. You are a person. And, so it is frequently said, God is a person. Hence, for example, Richard Swinburne maintains that theism (the belief that there is a God) is the belief that there is 'something like a "person" without a body (i.e., a spirit) who is eternal, free, able to do anything, knows everything, is perfectly good, is the proper object of human worship and obedience, the creator and sustainer of the universe'.[14] According to Swinburne, God is a conscious agent existing through time. He perceives. He learns. He changes. He even has beliefs. And words used in talking of people and of God bear the same sense.

Swinburne, I should stress, is by no means alone in speaking of God in this way. John Lucas, for instance, explains that 'The ultimate reality is a person . . . To be a person is to be conscious and to be an agent . . . We cannot understand the actions and feelings attributed to God in the Bible unless we can, at least to a limited extent, have some idea of God reaching a decision and caring about what happens.'[15] According to Professor Alvin Plantinga, one of America's currently best-known Christian philosophers: '*God* is the premier person, the first and chief exemplar of personhood . . . We men and women are image bearers of God, and the properties most important for an understanding of our personhood are properties we share with him.'[16] Swinburne, Lucas and Plantinga accept that God is in various respects different from human persons. But, like many other writers who could be cited, they are also convinced that God is very much like people and that people are very much like God. The *Catechism*, by contrast, is of a different mind. Hence it can insist that, though God is known by us, he is also 'infinitely above everything that we can understand or say'. In 230 it confirms this insistence by quoting St Augustine: 'Even when he reveals himself, God remains a mystery beyond words: "If you understood him, it would not be

God".' Such teaching points decidedly away from the direction in which authors like Swinburne, Lucas and Plantinga are headed.

'Simple'

That this is so can be further gleaned from the *Catechism*'s teaching that God is 'entirely simple'. For that teaching is quite incompatible with any idea of God literally being what an individual human person is. That is because to call God 'simple' is to deny that he is a member of any class at all. It is to assert a radical distinction between God and creatures.

The notion of divine simplicity is a very ancient one. It can be found, for example, in the writings of St Augustine. As he puts it:

> It is for this reason, then, that the nature of the Trinity is called simple, because it has not anything which it can lose, and because it is not one thing and its contents another, as a cup and the liquid . . . For none of these is what it has . . . those things which are essentially and truly divine are called simple, because in them quality and substance are identical.
>
> Now the reason why something is called a simple substance is this, because it does not possess anything that it can lose, or, to put it another way, because it is not different from what it has.[17]

The teaching that God is simple is also much emphasised by St Anselm and St Thomas Aquinas. As Anselm writes, in words addressed to God:

> You are therefore the very life by which You live, the wisdom by which You are wise, the very goodness by which You are good, to both good men and wicked . . . You are truth, You are goodness, You are blessedness, You are eternity, and You are every true good . . . There are no parts in You, Lord; neither are You many, but You are so much one and the same with Yourself that in nothing are You dissimilar with Yourself. Indeed You are unity itself not divisible by any mind. Life and wisdom and the other [attributes], then, are not parts of You, but all are one and each one of them is wholly what You are and what all the others are.[18]

In Aquinas's formulation:

> God is both simple, like the form, and subsistent, like the concrete thing, and so we sometimes refer to him by abstract nouns to indicate his simplicity and sometimes by concrete nouns to indicate his subsistence; though neither way of speaking measures up to his way of being, for in this life we do not know him as he is in himself.[19]

What is it that Augustine and Anselm and Aquinas are driving at here? They are basically saying that God cannot be thought of as a member of a world, as one of a kind. They are also arguing that we cannot think of God as something distinct from the nature he has. To put it another way, they are observing that God is not an individual in the familiar sense of 'individual', where to call something an individual is to think of it as a member of a class of which there could be more than one member, as something with a nature shared by others but different from that of things sharing natures of another kind, things with different ways of working, things with different characteristic activities and effects. In terms of the teaching that God is simple, God is the source of diversity and therefore the source of there being classes with different members, classes containing things with characteristic activities and effects. Or, as we may put it, *who* God is cannot be something different from *what* God is. Mary and John are both human beings. But Mary is not John and John is not Mary. They are individual people. And, though they are human, they do not, as individuals, constitute human nature. Along with many others, they exemplify it. Suppose we express this by saying that they are not, as individuals, the same as their common nature, that who they are and what they are can be distinguished. Then, so the teaching that God is simple holds, who God is and what God is are not distinguishable. We cannot get a purchase on the notion of a class of Gods or on the notion of God in a class.

As I say, this teaching is an ancient one. And it has been reaffirmed by councils of the Church.[20] But it is much resisted by many modern Christians (insofar as it is ever mentioned at all). As I have said, the notion that God undergoes change is now a very popular one. So anyone affirming change in God is implicitly denying that God is simple. But some authors explicitly deny that God is simple. Here, once again, we may cite the example of Plantinga. According to him, the notion that God is simple is in flat opposition to what Christians need to affirm. Why? Because, says Plantinga, it entails that God is a property, which cannot be true. In Plantinga's own words: 'No property could have created the world; no property could be omniscient, or indeed know anything at all. If God is a property, then he isn't a person but a mere abstract object; he has no knowledge, awareness, power, love or life.'[21] Plantinga seems to think that if God is simple, then God is identical with each of his properties, which entails that each of his properties are identical with each other, which entails that God is but a property.[22]

So, contrary to what readers might think on a first reading, 198–231 of the *Catechism* offers teaching which is heavily disputed. Its concept of God is at odds with that of many modern writers (*Christian* writers, not atheists or agnostics). And this, of course, raises an obvious question. Who is right? Is God truly as the *Catechism* says that he is? Or is he more like the picture given by those who dispute what it says?

That God defies our powers of understanding is a notion which the *Catechism* argues for chiefly on biblical grounds. It cites Lateran IV, of course, so its argument is not just biblical. But it does develop an argument based on Scripture. Unfortunately, however, the evidence which it cites is not enough to show that God is as Lateran IV taught, and it is not enough to justify the *Catechism*'s teaching that 'God is infinitely above everything that we can understand or say'. Nor does the biblical evidence cited by the *Catechism* justify the teaching that God is 'above space and time'. This is an important point, and it is worth pausing over for a while.

According to the *Catechism*, what we say about God can be derived from the teaching of Exodus 3, in which we are told how God revealed his name to Moses. With respect to Exodus 3, the *Catechism* makes the following points (among others):

1. The name revealed to Moses 'is mysterious just as God is mystery. It is at once a name revealed and something like the refusal of a name, and hence it better expresses God as what he is — infinitely above everything that we can understand or say' (206).

2. The proper understanding of God's name as revealed to Moses leads to the idea that God 'transcends the world and history' (212).

3. The name of God revealed to Moses indicates that 'God alone *is*', which means that 'God is the fullness of Being and of every perfection, without origin and without end. All creatures receive all that they are and have from him, but he alone *is* his very being, and he is of himself everything that he is' (213).

But is all of this so very evident? It is certainly true that the name given to Moses in Exodus 3 is a mystery. But that is largely because it is by no means clear how the name is to be interpreted. The name given is YHWH. But what is the significance of that? Readers of the *Catechism* alone will get no sense at all of the fact that this is one of the most unsolved and disputed questions in the area of biblical scholarship. Many learned essays have been written on the subject, but there is simply no single theory which commands universal assent on this matter. And even those with theories on the matter hold them with reservations. The *Catechism* translates the name as 'I am' or 'He is'. It also offers the rendering 'I Am He who Is', 'I Am who Am', and 'I Am who I Am'. In terms of available evidence, these renderings are possible. But they are debatable.[23] And it is therefore debatable whether the revelation of God's name to Moses evidently signifies that God is outside history (and therefore, presumably, outside time), or that he is his being (the notion that God is simple). Even if the *Catechism* is right to say that YHWH means 'I am', 'He is', 'I Am He who Is', etc., it does not follow that there is scriptural warrant for teaching about God as the *Catechism* does. The translations of YHWH offered by the *Catechism* do not clearly entail that God is wholly mysterious, outside time, simple, and so on. And, as many theologians have noted, there is plenty of scriptural warrant for thinking of God in terms quite opposed to that of the *Catechism* — in terms, for example, of authors such as Lucas, Swinburne or Plantinga. As James Barr puts it (with no particular axe to grind about what God is or is not):

The God of Israel is, in some ways, not so different from the Greek gods as has been supposed. By 'the Greek gods' I mean, of course, the gods of Homer, not the God of the Greek philosophers. The God of Israel is a clearly defined personality, as they are. He has a personal name, as they have. He speaks articulately in Hebrew, as they do in Greek. He has many anthropomorphic features, and they are highly anthropomorphic. He changes his mind, as they do, and allows himself to be persuaded to do so, as is the case with them. He intervenes in historical events, as they do. He favours certain individuals or social groups, as they do. He takes vengeance on those who have offended his will, as they sometimes do. He is interested in atonement for offences, as some at least of them are.[24]

Barr is not denying that one can quote from Scripture to defend a view of God which accords with that of the *Catechism*.[25] And neither am I. But it is a fact that if we are simply in the business of citing texts from Scripture, we shall be unable to decide as between the *Catechism* and those who embrace a different view of what it means to believe in God. We are in need of a standpoint from which to read Scripture.[26]

The *Catechism* clearly presupposes such a standpoint. And it comes near to admitting the fact explicitly in 213, where it says that YHWH means 'God alone *IS*', while adding that this is the understanding of the Septuagint (the Greek translation of the Old Testament) and 'following it the Church's Tradition', which holds that 'God is the fullness of Being . . . he alone *is* his very being'. Here the *Catechism* is passing beyond what biblical scholars may or may not come up with as an account of what is said of God in the Bible in this or that text (it is defending the notion of divine simplicity, which was not enunciated until well beyond New Testament times). Here, too, the *Catechism* is moving beyond the words of this or that biblical text. It is reading the Bible in the light of what is not explicitly present in the biblical text.

To be more precise, it is reading the Bible in the light of centuries of philosophical and theological reflection concerning divinity. And what it has to say would have been very welcome to many thinkers of earlier ages (to writers like Aquinas, for instance). With respect to God, the teaching of the *Catechism* is very traditional. But do we have any special reason to believe in its account of God (including its reading of what Scripture teaches about God)? After all, and as we have seen, many Christian writers would do no such thing.

Here we need to go back to basics. For how should we think of the one, true God? Indeed, should we suppose that there is a God at all?

Those who believe in God mostly started to do so because they believed those who told them that God exists. And what, we may ask, is wrong with that? The greater part of what we take for knowledge derives from what we have been taught in one way or other. The notion that I am only within my rights in believing what I have verified or confirmed for myself rests on a concept of knowledge and justified belief which is quite at odds with the way we actually learn.[27] It also fails to allow for the fact that, when we have done with reasoning and the production of evidence or grounds for beliefs, we are left with belief that is not based on reasons, evidence, or grounds.[28]

But this is not to say that our talk of God can be grounded in nothing but faith. And I do not wish to say that. On the contrary, I think that, whatever else may be said about it, belief that there is a God is a natural consequence of basic human curiosity. Or, to put things another way, it is what you end up with if you allow yourself to be sufficiently inquisitive or questioning. It is something that can derive from puzzlement, from wondering 'How come?'[29]

In asking 'How come?', of course, the objects of our concern will be fairly specifiable for the most part. We may, for example, wonder how it comes to be that some local phenomenon obtains. Why are there mountains to the east of Seattle? Why do I have brown hair?

Sometimes, however, the range of our inquiry may be wider. Someone might explain why there are mountains to the east of Seattle. But we might then wonder why there should be *any* mountains, whether east of Seattle or anywhere else. And we might wonder how there come to be people, whether brown-haired or otherwise. And if these questions are answered we might deepen the range of our inquiry. Mountains and people are there for reasons to be documented and explored by physicists, chemists, astronomers, and so on. These will tell us how it comes to be, not that this and that individual is there, but why things of certain kinds are there. And in telling us this they will be invoking levels of explanation which run deeper and deeper.

In doing so, however, they will always presume a background of things, a world or universe in the light of which explanation is possible. Mountains east of Seattle are explicable on geological grounds. And my brown hair is explicable in genetic terms. And if we ask why geology is possible and why genetics is possible, we shall again be looking for things of a kind behaving in certain ways.

But we might deepen the level of our inquiry. For we might ask, not 'What in the world accounts for this, that, or the other?', but 'Why any world at all?' How come the whole business of asking and answering 'How come?'

Now you may say that this is a question which should never be asked. You might, for example, side with Bertrand Russell in a famous debate which he had with Fr Frederick Copleston SJ. Copleston asked Russell if he would say that the universe is something 'gratuitous'. Russell replied 'I should say that the universe is just there, and that's all'.[30]

But this seems to me as unreasonable a position as it is possible to maintain. Confronted by cats, Russell would never have said 'Cats are just there'. Had Russell found a ton of mud in his office, he would never have said: 'The mud is there. This raises no questions.' He would have said that we can always ask why something is there unless it is intrinsically absurd to do so. And, so it seems to me, there is nothing intrinsically absurd in asking how it comes to be that there is a universe in which we can ask 'How come?'

Some questions *are* intrinsically absurd. An example occurs in a dialogue reported by Professor Peter Geach.[31] Two rabbis were debating Genesis 1:1 ('In the beginning God created the heavens and the earth'). The Hebrew for 'earth' is *eretz*, which does not contain the Hebrew letter 'gimmel', just as 'earth' does not contain a 'g'. The debate proceeds as follows:

> First Rabbi   'Why should there be a "gimmel" in *eretz*?'
> Second Rabbi 'But there isn't a "gimmel" in *eretz*!'
> First Rabbi   'Then, why isn't there a "gimmel" in *eretz*?'
> Second Rabbi 'Why should there be a "gimmel" in *eretz*?'
> First Rabbi   'That's what I just asked *you*!'

But 'Why should there be any universe?' is not intrinsically absurd. To ask the question is simply to carry on doing what we naturally do.

Or is it? In a sense it is, for asking 'How come?' is familiar enough. In particular, it is because people got into the habit of asking this question that science, as we understand it, ever got going in the first place. And, as we understand it, science advances as people continue to ask the question. But the 'How come?' question which I have now raised is clearly not a scientific one. For it is partly asking how come that science itself is possible. And its answer cannot be anything which a scientist could investigate or analyse. Scientific questions concern objects or events which are part of the universe. And their answers refer us to other things of the same kind, to more objects or events which are part of the universe. But the universe itself is not an object or event within itself. And whatever accounts for there being a universe cannot be this either. In asking how there comes to be any universe, we are effectively raising the topic of creation. And to say that something is created is not to locate it in historical terms or in terms of things having effects within the universe. It is to speak of it as derived, not because it has come from something equally derived, and not because it has come to be because something has been transformed, but because its existence as such is derived.[32] To view the universe as created is not to place it in a context of scientific causes. It is to see that there is a question to ask when science has done any work it can possibly do.

In the language of Aquinas, whom I cite because he is so unusually illuminating on the matter, there is a puzzle concerning the *esse* of things — the fact that they are there to be identified and spoken about and explained in terms of scientific or transforming causes. But Aquinas was not the only philosophical genius to see that there is a puzzle here, albeit one which is hard to articulate. The question that I am now talking about is sharply raised by Ludwig Wittgenstein in his *Tractatus Logico-Philosophicus*.[33] 'Not *how* the world is, is the mystical', says Wittgenstein, 'but *that* it is.'[34] For Wittgenstein, *how the world is* is a scientific matter with scientific answers. But, so he insists, even when the scientific answers are in, we are still left with the *thatness* of the world, the fact '*that* it is'.

As readers of Wittgenstein know well, that there is a world is not, for him, a factual matter. And that there is a world is not material for a question or answer that we can understand. As he puts it: 'We feel that even if *all possible* scientific questions be answered, the problems of life have still not been touched at all. Of course there is then no question left, and just this is the answer.'[35] But, as interpreters of Wittgenstein now generally admit, he does not mean that asking about the thatness of the world is unequivocal nonsense. He means that raising the question is to seek to go beyond familiar questions and answers in a way that leaves us at sea — at the limits of what can be said and understood.[36] And that is precisely what Aquinas thinks when he speaks of *esse* and creation. For him, the reason why there is any universe at all (the answer to 'How come any universe?') is radically incomprehensible to us. We can, he asserts, say *that* it is. But we cannot say *what* it is.[37]

For Aquinas, of course, God is the reason why there is any universe. His teaching, therefore, is that we cannot say what God is. And this teaching seems to me to be right. I do not mean, and neither does Aquinas, that we can make no true statements about God. I do not even mean that we cannot speak of God in positive terms, by saying that he can certainly be called such and such — good or powerful or loving, for instance. What I mean is that in speaking of God we must be careful not to attribute to him anything which is essentially creaturely, anything which cannot be true of whatever it is that accounts for there being any universe at all.

To put it another way, if our thoughts are to latch on to the one, true God, we need to become agnostics, though not in the usual, modern (Russellian) sense of 'agnostic'. The modern agnostic says 'We do not know, and the universe is a mysterious riddle'. Along with Aquinas, I want to say: 'We do not know what the answer is, but we do know that there is a mystery behind it all which we do not know. And if there were not, there would not even be a riddle. This Unknown we call *God*. And if there were no God, there would be no universe to be mysterious, and nobody to be mystified.'[38]

But what precisely might be meant by saying that in speaking of God we must be careful not to attribute to him anything which is essentially creaturely, anything which cannot be true of whatever it is that accounts for there being any universe at all? The question needs a lot of discussion. But one can still, I think, make a few points briefly.

We cannot, for example, suppose that God is part of the world of space and time. Nor can we suppose him subject to the limitations and changes which affect things spatial and temporal. So it will be nonsense to speak of God as literally being *here* as opposed to *there*, or as literally being *now* as opposed to *then*. And it will be nonsense to speak of God as literally being first *like this* and then *like that*. It will be nonsense to say that divinity is something passing through successive states. And it will be even more nonsense to think of God as changing because other things have an effect on him. So it will be wrong to say that creatures can do something to modify God somehow. It will be wrong to say that they can, for instance, cause him to know things or cause him to undergo emotions.

It will also, of course, be wrong to say that God has a character in any sense we can understand. Or, to put it another way, it will be wrong to assert that God is an individual — in the familiar sense of 'individual' where to call something an individual is to think of it as a member of a class of which there could be more than one member, as something with a nature shared by others but different from that of things sharing natures of another kind, things with different ways of working, things with different characteristic activities and effects. To conceive of God as the reason why there is any universe at all is to conceive of him as being the source of diversity and therefore as being the source of there being classes with different members, classes containing things with characteristic activities and effects. Or, as we may put it, *who* God is cannot be something different from *what* God is.

As the reader will doubtless gather, if what I have just said is right, then so is the *Catechism* in its fundamental teaching about divinity. And it is right for reasons which can be given without citing the Bible. With or without reference to Scripture, the *Catechism* is wholly sound in its basic concept of God. And its teaching represents a splendid alternative to other ways in which Christians have taught about God. But readers will clearly need to consider whether they can accept the sort of thing I am saying. And, if they do not, they will need to consider from where they might derive a true notion of God. You might say that we can learn how to think about God from the Bible. But, as I have indicated, the Bible does not interpret itself when it comes to a notion of divinity.

With all of that said, however, it would be wholly wrong to suppose that what is true of God is always something which can be worked out by means of ordinary, human reflection. Catholic theology has always insisted on there being a distinction between what can be known of God by reason and what must be believed in faith and without rational proof. And it is important to note that this tradition is very much alive in what the *Catechism* teaches in 198–231. Throughout these paragraphs the emphasis falls on what has been revealed, especially through Christ. At no point in them do we find anything which might be thought of as philosophical argument (there is no reason why we should). And it is with a matter of revelation that the paragraphs conclude their teaching concerning what God is. 221 links the teaching that God is Love with the doctrine of the Blessed Trinity (always, for Catholics, a matter of revelation, not human speculation). The link made here is an important one, and it is worth a bit of commentary.

Why should we ascribe love to God? People often reply that we should do so because God evidently loves us and other created things. But, though this answer makes sense, it is also deficient.[39] It is part of Christian orthodoxy that God's act of creation is free. God does not have to create, and there might have been nothing created. As Vatican I puts it:

The one true God, by his goodness and almighty power, not with the intention of increasing his happiness, nor indeed of obtaining happiness, but in order to manifest his perfection by the good things which he bestows on what he creates, by an absolutely free plan, together from the beginning of time brought into being from nothing the twofold created order, that is the spiritual and the bodily.[40]

But if God can only be said to love in the sense that he loves what is created, he would not be essentially love. If God could exist without creating, and if his love is only directed at creatures, then it is not God's nature to love. He could exist without loving.

But, so St John writes, 'God is love'. People often speak as though this were equivalent to 'God is loving', but one may, in fact, challenge the implied equivalence. Such, at any rate, seems to be the general verdict of the exegetes. Commenting on 1 John 4:8, Kenneth Grayston observes that we are dealing with 'a deceptively simple statement which it is difficult to analyse ... It is difficult to see how God's nature can be described by *love*; easier to see that his actions are being described as loving actions, as indeed they are in vv. 9–10.'[41] Grayston is presuming that 'God is love' does not mean the same as 'God is loving'. And his presumption is something of a scholarly commonplace. 'God is love', in 1 John 4:8, seems on a level with 'God is spirit' (Jn 4:24) and 'God is light' (1 Jn 1:5). Alluding to all three formulae, B. F. Westcott observes that they 'do not simply specify properties of God (as "God is loving"), but, so far as we can apprehend them, essential aspects of His Nature'.[42] C. H. Dodd notes that in 1 John God 'is presented as the personal Subject of the act of loving' but that 'the proposition, *God is love* is clearly intended to go further than the proposition "God loves us"'.[43] It means, says Dodd, that love belongs to God's very nature. The same note is struck by Raymond Brown. He draws attention to John 17:24, where 'Jesus makes it clear that he is speaking of a preincarnational love that existed before creation in the relationship between God and his Word'. The implication, says Brown, is that, in the 'God is' formulae of the Johannine corpus, 'while there is emphasis on God's activity, that activity is internally related to what God is before creation'.[44] Or, to put it another way, 'God is love' says that love belongs to God's essence, that it is not what exists between God and anything else, that its existence is given simply in the fact that God exists. We cannot therefore say, for example, that proof of God's love for us is proof that God is love, for God need never have made us (or anything). Assuming, as orthodox Christians generally have done, that God has no need of his creation, and that nothing compels God to create, it follows that there must be something in divinity itself which constitutes God as essentially loving.

On what basis, therefore, are we entitled to claim that God is essentially loving? It can only be that God is this if there is at least *one and another* in God. Or, in other words, if it is God's innermost nature to love, then that can only be because something like the doctrine of the

Trinity is true. And, since the doctrine of the Trinity is true, it is to that doctrine we may turn as we try to explain how God is love. It makes Christian sense to say that God is love because of what exists between Father, Son and Holy Spirit.

The *Catechism* brings this out sharply and well in 221. 'God's very being is love. By sending his only Son and the Spirit of Love in the fullness of time, God has revealed his innermost secret: God himself is an eternal exchange of love, Father, Son and Holy Spirit, and he has destined us to share in that exchange.' Most preachers dread the occasion of Trinity Sunday, for they wonder what to say about the doctrine of the Trinity. The *Catechism*, however, sees quite clearly that the doctrine of the Trinity is what finally allows us to say that God is essentially love.

All in all, then, 198–231 of the *Catechism* contains some provocative and arresting material. It stands firmly behind the view that there is truth about God to be taught, and what it teaches about him is by no means currently commonplace. It also indicates how revelation can help us to see what is unique to divinity, and how this connects with fundamental Christian teaching about God. And what it has to offer makes good sense, or so I have argued. This must be a plus for a text designed to teach and to draw people nearer to the truth. Readers of 198–231 have a solid and reliable guide in their quest for God.

Notes

1 For development and defence of this thesis, see P. T. Geach, 'On worshipping the right God' in P. T. Geach, *God and the Soul* (London and New York, 1969). Cf. also P. T. Geach, 'The meaning of God' in Martin Warner (ed.), *Religion and Philosophy* (Cambridge, 1992).
2 It is the chief business. But 222–227 is designed to indicate implications of holding true belief about God.
3 The same teaching is found in many patristic authors and in writers such as John Calvin (1509–64), René Descartes (1596–1650), and Friedrich Schleiermacher (1768–1834).
4 Boethius, *The Consolation of Philosophy*, V.6.
5 Anselm, *Proslogion*, IXX.
6 J. R. Lucas, *A Treatise on Space and Time* (London, 1973), p. 200.
7 Alan Richardson and John Bowden (eds), *A New Dictionary of Christian Theology* (London, 1983), p. 573.
8 Santiago Sia, 'On God, time and change', *The Clergy Review* LXIII (1978), p. 381.
9 Hartshorne's books are listed in Santiago Sia (ed.), *Charles Hartshorne's Concept of God* (Dordrecht/Boston/London, 1990). Hartshorne is criticised in this book by Norris Clarke SJ along lines I approve of. In this volume, too, he replies to Clarke.

10 Charles Hartshorne, 'The God of religion and the God of philosophy' in
    G. Vesey (ed.), *Talk of God* (London, 1969), p. 163; *Reality as Social Process*
    (New York, 1971), p. 206; *Omnipotence and Other Theological Mistakes* (New
    York, 1983), pp. 17ff.
11 J. R. Lucas, *The Future* (Oxford, 1989), p. 214.
12 Ibid., p. 215.
13 Richard Swinburne, *The Coherence of Theism* (Oxford, 1977), pp. 214ff.
14 Ibid., p. 1.
15 Lucas, *The Future*, pp. 212ff.
16 Alvin Plantinga, 'Advice to Christian philosophers', *Faith and Philosophy*
    1 (1984), p. 265. Throughout this essay Plantinga repeatedly uses the words
    'that there is such a person as God' to identify the issue at stake between
    those who believe in God and those who do not. Cf. pp. 261, 262, 264.
17 Augustine, *The City of God*, XI. X.
18 Anselm, *Proslogion*, XII and XVIII.
19 Thomas Aquinas, *Summa Theologiae*, I, 13, 1 ad 2.
20 The *Catechism* cites the Fourth Lateran Council. Most recently, the
    teaching that God is simple was reaffirmed by the First Vatican Council. See
    Vatican I's Dogmatic Constitution *Dei Filius* on the Catholic Faith, ch. 1:
    'Since [God] is one, singular, completely simple and unchangeable spiritual
    substance, he must be declared to be in reality and in essence distinct from
    the world . . .'
21 Alvin Plantinga, *Does God Have A Nature?* (Milwaukee, 1980), p. 47.
22 Plantinga's discussion of simplicity in God is directed against the teaching of
    Aquinas. Anyone who has read Aquinas seriously will know that Plantinga's
    points are wholly irrelevant to anything which Aquinas wants to affirm. See
    my *The Thought of Thomas Aquinas* (Oxford, 1992), ch. 4.
23 For a survey of the question, see G. H. Parke-Taylor, *Yahweh: The Divine
    Name in the Bible* (Waterloo, Ontario, 1975). For a biblical commentary
    documenting and discussing the problems of understanding YHWH in
    Exodus, see Brevard S. Childs, *The Book of Exodus* (Philadelphia, 1974),
    pp. 60ff.
24 James Barr, *Biblical Faith and Natural Theology* (Oxford, 1993), p. 139.
25 As well as drawing attention to biblical talk of God which points to the notion
    of God as a person with a clearly defined personality, Barr also notes biblical
    texts pulling in the opposite direction. Cf. ibid., p. 142.
26 As Barr (op. cit.) shows very well, even authors who take their stand on
    Scripture alone for an account of God use premises and principles of
    interpretation not explicitly derivable from Scripture.
27 Cf. G. E. M. Anscombe, 'What is it to believe someone?' in C. F. Delaney
    (ed.), *Rationality and Religious Belief* (Notre Dame and London, 1979).
28 Cf. Ludwig Wittgenstein, *On Certainty*, ed. G. E. M. Anscombe and G. H. von
    Wright, trans. Denis Paul and G. E. M. Anscombe (Oxford, 1974), paras
    160–167. See also Norman Malcolm, 'The groundlessness of belief' in Stuart
    C. Brown (ed.), *Reason and Religion* (London, 1977).
29 This idea is, of course, very much a feature of Catholic thinking. It lies, for
    example, behind Vatican I's teaching that 'God, the source and end of all
    things, can be known with certainty from the consideration of created things
    by the natural power of human reason: *ever since the creation of the world, his
    invisible nature has been clearly perceived in the things that have been made*'
    (*Dogmatic Constitution on the Catholic Faith*, ch. 2). Vatican I is here backing
    its claim with reference to Scripture. Many theologians, most famously Karl

Barth (1886–1968), have denied that what the Council teaches can be found in Scripture. For a solid refutation of this position, see James Barr, op. cit.

30 'A debate on the existence of God', reprinted in John Hick (ed.), *The Existence of God* (London and New York, 1964).

31 P. T. Geach, *Logic and Argument* (Oxford, 1976).

32 This is not to say that there is some property called 'existence' which needs to be explained, though some have thought that there is such a property. Cf. my 'Does God create existence?', *International Philosophical Quarterly* (June 1990). Also see C. J. F. Williams, *Being, Identity and Truth* (Oxford, 1992). For good accounts of Aquinas on *esse*, see Stephen Theron, 'Esse', *The New Scholasticism* LIII (1979) and Herbert McCabe, 'The logic of mysticism' in Warner (ed.), *Religion and Philosophy*.

33 Ludwig Wittgenstein, *Tractatus Logico-Philosophicus*, trans. C. K. Ogden (London, 1933); 'Wittgenstein's Lecture on Ethics', *The Philosophical Review* LXXIV (1965).

34 *Tractatus* 6.44.

35 Ibid., 6.52.

36 Cf. Cyril Barrett, *Wittgenstein on Ethics and Religious Belief* (Oxford, 1991); 'The logic of mysticism' in Warner (ed.), *Religion and Philosophy*.

37 Thomas Aquinas, *Summa Theologiae*, Introduction to I, 3.

38 Cf. Victor White, *God the Unknown* (London, 1956), pp. 18f.

39 It makes sense because we can think of love as a matter of willing the good for others, and because God wills any good which his creatures enjoy.

40 *Dogmatic Constitution on the Catholic Faith*, ch. 1.

41 Kenneth Grayston, *The Johannine Epistles* (London, 1984), p. 124.

42 B. F. Westcott, *The Epistles of St John* (Cambridge and London, 1892), p. 167.

43 C. H. Dodd, *The Johannine Epistles* (London, 1946), p. 107.

44 Raymond E. Brown, *The Epistles of John* (London, 1983), p. 195.

The Doctrine of the Trinity

(Paragraphs 232–267)

Catherine Mowry LaCugna
University of Notre Dame

The new Roman *Catechism* states that 'The mystery of the Most Holy Trinity is the central mystery of Christian faith and life' (234). Unfortunately this is a truth that has been forgotten in practice and in most doctrinal treatments. The *Catechism* promises that it is designed to state what is fundamental in the Christian message in a language more in keeping with the demands of today's world, in order to aid evangelisation. Thus we may ask whether the *Catechism*'s presentation adequately presents the doctrine of the Trinity, and whether it serves to restore this teaching to the centre of Christian faith. We look first at how the *Catechism* presents the doctrine of the Trinity; second, its placement in the whole of the *Catechism*; third, the history and development of trinitarian doctrine; and finally, its practical dimensions.

The *Catechism*'s presentation of the doctrine of the Trinity

The section on the Trinity is divided into four parts: an introduction, an explanation of how the Trinity was revealed, what the Church has taught regarding the Trinity, and the sending of Son and Spirit as the fulfilment of God's plan of salvation.

Introduction. This section begins with introductory statements that affirm the centrality of the doctrine of the Trinity to the whole of Christian faith. The liturgical starting-point is notable and effective. Baptism is the sacrament by which we are given access not to a generic God, but to the triune God (Mt 28:19). The triune name of God is *one* name, not three (233). The *Catechism* also reminds us that the original form of the baptismal confession was interrogatory; the one being baptised was asked three questions based on the structure of the Creed: Do you believe in God the Father Almighty? Do you believe in Christ

66

Jesus the Son? . . . Do you believe in the Holy Spirit, in the holy Church and the resurrection of the flesh? After each question the one being baptised would answer, *Credo* ('I believe').[1]

The *Catechism* affirms that the Trinity is 'the central mystery of Christian faith and life', *because* the Trinity is the 'mystery of God in himself' (234). While the positive intent of the statement is to be lauded, this phrasing is unfortunate because it reinforces the idea of an 'intra-trinitarian' life of God, when the equally important point of the doctrine of the Trinity is soteriological: God, Christ and the Spirit are equally essential to our salvation. Thus the mystery of God is also the mystery of God *for us*, not just the mystery of God *in se*.

The *Catechism* goes on to affirm that because of the centrality of the mystery of the Trinity, it is the source of all other mysteries of faith, the means by which to understand them, and 'the most fundamental and essential teaching in the "hierarchy of the truths of faith"'. There seems to be some confusion in this statement between the *doctrine* of the Trinity, and the divine *mystery* to which the doctrine refers.

This section includes an important statement about the nature of revelation: 'The whole history of salvation is identical with the history of the way and the means by which the one true God, Father, Son and Holy Spirit, reveals himself [to humanity] "and reconciles and unites with himself those who turn away from sin".' What is being affirmed is that God is none other in salvation-history than God is as such, and that the record of salvation-history is a reliable guide to the triune nature of God.

The introduction includes an excursus on the distinction between theology (*theologia*) and economy (*oikonomia*).[2] Theology is defined here as the mystery of God's intimate life *within the Trinity*, and the economy as God's works in creation and salvation-history. The economy is said to reveal theology, and theology to clarify the economy of redemption. The *Catechism* proposes the analogy that persons show who they are in their actions; the better we understand their actions, the more precise grasp we have of their personhood. I have argued at length elsewhere[3] why the definition of *theologia* as the mystery of God 'in Godself' prevents the practical implications of the doctrine of the Trinity from being realised. *Theologia* is indeed the mystery of God, however, that mystery is known to us only in the economy of salvation. We do not have direct knowledge of God's 'inner being', but only of God's self-revelation in the works of creation, in the person of Jesus Christ, and in the ongoing presence of the Spirit.

How the mystery of the Trinity was revealed. Without revelation we would have no knowledge of the Trinity; it is a mystery *stricte dictum*. Indeed, we knew nothing of God's triune being before the incarnation or sending of the Spirit.

In three paragraphs that are sure to be the least favourite among many theologians, the *Catechism* treats the name of God as Father (238–240). According to the *Catechism* God is Father in the generic sense as a deity, but Israel called God 'Father' as the Creator (Dt 32:6; Mal 2:10), because of the covenant and the gift of the law to Israel (Ex 4:22),[4] as king of Israel, and as Father of the poor, the orphaned and the widowed (2 Sam 7:14; Ps 68:5–6). While this Old Testament scriptural basis is hardly strong,[5] the *Catechism* interprets it to mean, first, that God is the origin and transcendent authority who is also good and kind toward his creatures (239). The *Catechism* admits that God's tenderness as a parent *can be* expressed by the scriptural image of motherhood (Is 66:13; Ps 131:2) which, according to the *Catechism*, brings out the intimacy between God and creature. No reason is given why fatherhood is linked with transcendence and motherhood with immanence. The *Catechism* goes on to say that despite the analogy between God and human parents, God transcends the distinction between female and male: God 'is neither man nor woman' [*sic*] (239). Perhaps this is the place to note that the non-inclusive language used throughout the *Catechism* (English translation) for both God and human beings is a blight upon the text and will be jarring and alienating to the majority of readers.

The New Testament evidence for God's Fatherhood is stronger. Jesus called God Father not just as the Creator, but in a highly personal sense: Father of the Son (Mt 11:27). Strangely, the *Catechism* does not mention the strong theme of Father and Son in John's Gospel. And this section contains no reference whatsoever to feminist scholarship or, more importantly, to the extensive discussion in the Church and in theology about the oppressiveness of the exclusive use of Father to address and conceptualise God. Further, the association of fatherhood with trans-cendence and motherhood with immanence reinforces what has been amply exposed elsewhere as a sexist and androcentric view of God and of human persons.

From this scriptural basis the *Catechism* moves quickly to the image of Jesus Christ as the 'Word' of God in the Johannine sense, and then to the Council of Nicaea (AD 325) which affirmed that the Son is *homoousios* (of the same nature) with God (242). The Council of Constantinople (AD 381) affirmed Nicaea's language with its assertion that Christ is the only-begotten Son of God, 'eternally begotten of the Father, light from light, true God from true God, begotten not made, consubstantial with the Father'.

The Holy Spirit, though active from the very beginning of creation, and active through the prophets, was sent in a special way by Christ. The *Catechism* leaps from this biblical datum to the dogmatic claim that the Spirit is revealed as 'another divine person' in relation to Christ and God (243). The eternal origin of the Spirit is revealed in the Spirit's 'mission' (sending) in the economy (244). The Council of Constantinople affirmed the divinity of the Spirit because the Spirit is worshipped and glorified as God, and affirmed also God the Father's role as the origin of Son and Spirit. The Eleventh Council of Toledo (AD 675) affirmed that the Spirit is from both Father *and* Son (*filioque*).

The *Catechism* gives a brief account of the *filioque* clause (the Spirit proceeds from both Father and Son), citing primarily the Council of Florence (AD 1438), which formulated Roman Catholic teaching on this topic. The *Catechism* acknowledges that the Council of Constantinople has no such phrase, and that its incorporation into liturgy and theology was quite gradual. The *filioque* first appeared in the liturgy in the eighth century.

The Eastern churches do not confess the *filioque*. As a matter of fact, the *filioque* is deeply troubling to the Orthodox, who feel that this phrase was unilaterally foisted upon them by the Western Church. The *Catechism* explains the Eastern belief that the Spirit comes from the Father *through* the Son, and suggests that there can be a 'legitimate complementarity' which, 'provided it does not become rigid, does not affect the identity of faith in the reality of the same mystery confessed' by East and West (248).

The formation of trinitarian dogma.[6] The *Catechism* asserts that the revealed truth of the Trinity was known from the very beginning of the Church's faith, mainly through baptism. For example, the Pauline salutation found at the beginning of the Eucharist reads: 'The grace of our Lord Jesus Christ and the love of God and the fellowship of the Holy Spirit be with you all' (2 Cor 13:14). It would help if the *Catechism* clarified that while the *truth* that would later be expressed by trinitarian doctrine is found at the origins of Christianity, there is no doctrine of the Trinity *per se* in Scripture. Certainly one can find the basic data that later (in the fourth century) emerge in the doctrine, but it would be anachronistic to look for the doctrine *per se* in the New Testament.

The first three centuries of Christianity were full of theological ferment, particularly in the areas of Christology and, eventually, trinitarian theology. Arius, though not mentioned, is clearly intended by the reference to 'errors that were deforming [the Church's faith]' (250). There is an excursus on some of the technical terms that theologians used, such as substance, *hypostasis* (person), and relation. 'Substance' means essence or nature, and designates the divine unity. '*Hypostasis*' refers to the distinctions among Father, Son and Spirit. 'Relation' refers to the 'fact that their distinction lies in the relationship of each to the others' (252). The *Catechism* points out that in using these terms the Church did not submit the faith to human wisdom, but redefined these terms 'which from then on would be used to signify an ineffable mystery' (251).

In the section on 'the Dogma of the Holy Trinity' the *Catechism* selects three basic affirmations that can be found in conciliar statements, particularly Toledo XI (AD 675), Lateran IV (AD 1215) and the Council of Florence (AD 1442).[7]

First, the Trinity is one. There are not three Gods, but only one God who subsists in three persons. Each of the divine persons *is* God wholly, that is, each divine person *is* the divine nature.[8]

Second, the divine persons are really distinct. These distinctions are real, which is to say, Father, Son and Spirit are not 'modes' of one divine being.[9] Interestingly, the *Catechism* uses the Greek rather than Latin view that the divine persons are distinct from one another by virtue of their 'relations of origin'.[10] That is, the distinctive character of each divine person stems 'from whence they come'. The Father is 'Unoriginate', coming from no one. The Son is 'Begotten', coming from the Father. The Spirit 'Proceeds', coming from the Father.[11]

Third, the divine persons are relative to each other. God's threefoldness does not 'divide' the divine nature.[12] Although the text does not use the words 'perichoresis' (Greek) or 'circumincession' (Latin), which mean interdependence, the text makes the point that while there are three persons who are really distinct, these three persons are really related to each other.[13] This interrelationship constitutes the divine unity. The text repeats the statement from the Council of Florence that 'everything [in God] is one where there is no opposition of relationship' (255).[14] Notice that in citing the Council of Florence the text reverts to the Latin, not Greek understanding of the distinction of persons according to 'relations of opposition'.

The sending of Son and Spirit into the economy. The final section deals with the divine missions, and the language is richly biblical and evocative. The text relies on the beautiful liturgical hymn in Ephesians 1:3–14 that describes the election by God before creation, the creation through Jesus Christ, and the providential plan of God in which we are to become adopted sons and daughters and conformed to the image of Christ, called to live for the praise of God's glory. This providential plan derives from God's love, is displayed in the work of creation, in salvation-history, and in the 'missions' of Son and Spirit which prolong the mission of the Church (257).

The economy is the work of three divine persons; since God's nature is one, the Trinity operates as a unity. At the same time, the distinctive identity of each of the persons must not be blurred by the unity. Thus creation is said to come from God *through* Jesus Christ *by the power of* the Holy Spirit. The sending of Son and Spirit and their presence in the economy of redemption must display what is unique to each of them (258–259).

Finally, the whole goal of the economy of redemption is to give the creature access to the life of the Trinity. The text ends with a prayer of Elizabeth of the Trinity in which she pleads for more perfect union with the triune God.

The placement of the doctrine of the Trinity in the whole text

Although the subject of the Trinity is mentioned elsewhere in the *Catechism* (notably with the sacraments), the main treatment falls under the first article of the Creed: 'I believe in God the Father.'

The placement of the doctrine of the Trinity is a notorious problem in dogmatic theology and in catechisms. In dogmatic theology it is an open and somewhat controverted question where exactly it belongs. In patristic theology the question did not arise, but in the medieval scholastic era, under the influence of Peter Lombard, Thomas Aquinas inaugurated the 'tract' approach to theology. One tract, *De Deo Uno*, treated the attributes of God, and *De Deo Trino* treated questions that properly belong to trinitarian doctrine. The merit of Thomas's approach was its consistency with the overall plan of the *Summa Theologiae*, namely, to consider all things 'from the perspective of God'. What is troubling for us today, however, is the implication, which Thomas Aquinas himself surely never intended and would not subscribe to, that the unity of God somehow precedes God's triunity, and that the trinitarian aspects of God's being are in a sense 'added on' to the divine unity. The preference today is clearly for a much more salvation-history orientated approach, according to which God is apprehended first in the incarnation of the Son and the sending and presence of the Holy Spirit. The question of God's unity arises only after the assertion is made that Father, Son and Spirit are 'equally' divine because of their role in our salvation.

Given the current emphasis on history as salvation-history, and the soteriological reorientation of the doctrine of the Trinity to mean the truth of God's being on the basis of God's self-revelation in Christ, the question of where the Trinity belongs has been reopened. It is entirely possible that a theologian would choose to begin a whole dogmatics with the doctrine of the Trinity,[15] but today it is unlikely that any theologian would adhere to the Thomistic separation of the two treatises on the unity and threefoldness of God.

It is also possible that the doctrine of the Trinity would be conceived as a soteriological doctrine, and thus be linked explicitly with Christology and with that most forgotten of doctrines, pneumatology. As a matter of fact, Trinity, Christology and pneumatology form a natural unity and reflect the pattern of salvation-history that is effected by God *through* Christ *by the power of* the Holy Spirit.

A further possibility is that the doctrine of the Trinity informs all areas of theology, especially sacramental theology, ecclesiology, theological anthropology, liturgical theology, and eschatology, along with Christology and pneumatology. In this option the doctrine of the Trinity would serve as an overall structuring principle, the inner rationale, as it were, of *all* Christian theology. In this way, theological reflection on *any* aspect of the Christian faith can legitimately be regarded as trinitarian.

At the same time, in order for any of these modern strategies to be effective, it is necessary to rethink completely the origins and evolution of trinitarian doctrine, and to restate it in a way that is intelligible to modern ways of thinking. On this score, the *Catechism* mostly fails because its main thrust seems to be the repetition of conciliar propositions, rather than a dynamic, vital restatement of what the doctrine of the Trinity really seeks to affirm, namely, that both God and human beings, and indeed all of creation, find their fulfilment in communion rather than solitariness. Even though the purpose of the *Catechism* is to teach, and to teach from out of the riches of the tradition, there are creative ways to teach the essential truths of doctrine without resorting to phrases and propositions that are, today, largely unintelligible not just to non-specialists but even to most theologians.

In any case, the *Catechism* has located the confession of faith in a triune God with the first article of the Creed: 'I believe in God the Father.' In itself this is not objectionable, but one wonders whether the better *catechetical* strategy would be to place it after the structure dictated by the Creed, that is, after the section on the Holy Spirit, to indicate the fact that trinitarian doctrine is the *summary* statement of Christian faith, not an *a priori* principle from which can be deduced all the truths of faith. The doctrine of the Trinity is *post facto* reflection on the whole truth of faith, understood according to the tripartite structure of the Creed itself. This alternative strategy would signal that the doctrine of the Trinity is just that: a *doctrine*, not divine revelation itself.

In the history of catechisms since the Council of Trent (AD 1559–65), we notice various options for the placement of the doctrine of the Trinity. The catechism issued by Trent is structured by the Creed. The doctrine of the Trinity is placed shortly after the article on God the Father, and there is a special section that deals with the view that creation is the work of the three divine persons.[16] The Baltimore Catechism of the 1940s treats 'the unity and trinity of God' as a separate topic, in the famous question-and-answer format, and in a way that reflects standard neo-scholastic theology.[17] The so-called Dutch Catechism issued in 1965 contains no separate section on the Trinity. Instead, the doctrine of the Trinity serves as an infrastructure, and the whole catechism is orientated to the history of salvation. The rationale given is as follows:

> The Bible does not use the word 'three' to speak of this mystery, any more than do the twelve articles of the Apostles' Creed, or the Nicene Creed. This does not mean that we must therefore avoid it. But it is a warning not to begin too readily with a brief formula in an attempt to proclaim the mystery which is so utterly comprehensive . . .
>
> But we are even shy about speaking of this mystery in biblical terms. After a whole volume in which everything spoke of the Father, the Son and the Holy Spirit, a 'treatment' in a few pages would be to set the mystery too much apart.[18]

The Dutch Catechism was criticised from many corners precisely because of the absence of any clear affirmation of trinitarian doctrine. Finally, the catechism issued in 1976, *The Teaching of Christ*,[19] is remarkable for the fact that its format is extremely close to that of the new Roman *Catechism*.

A blend of traditions: the history of doctrine

It is a temptation to see the *Catechism*'s treatment of the doctrine of the Trinity as simply a formal statement that has very little to do with the remainder of Christian faith. A student of the *Catechism* might legitimately wonder what the Trinity has to do with the believer or with the life of faith or the rest of the *Catechism*. It may be useful, therefore, briefly to reprise the historical development of the doctrine and its central truth claim in order to see how the doctrine of the Trinity might be related to spirituality, ethics, and ecclesiology.

It is well known that Eastern (Greek) and Western (Latin) traditions developed quite distinct and in some ways irreconcilable doctrines of the Trinity. The *filioque* is an obvious example. Still, both Eastern and Western doctrines of the Trinity developed in conversation with Arianism. Arius, a priest from Alexandria, held that while Jesus Christ was an important mediator in our salvation, he was 'less than' God. Jesus Christ, according to Arius, was the first-born and highest of all creatures, but a creature nonetheless. This position appeared to compromise the salvific role of Christ, who by that time was clearly acknowledged as divine.

The Council of Nicaea (AD 325) was called to refute the position of Arius; using non-biblical, metaphysical language, the Council affirmed that Jesus Christ was *homoousios* (of the same nature) with God. Still, the Council's affirmation did little to quiet the theological controversies over the exact status of Christ. Later in the fourth century Athanasius and the Cappadocians (Basil of Caesarea, Gregory of Nazianzus, and Gregory of Nyssa) launched a virulent attack upon the premises and position of Arius and his followers. In Athanasius' mind, since only God can save, and since salvation clearly comes through Jesus Christ, he must be on the side of God rather than on the side of the created order.

The Cappadocians, in the process of refuting Eunomius, a late fourth-century Arian, developed the first full doctrine of the Trinity. Eunomius had argued that the name of God's essence is 'Unbegottenness'. To be God is to be unbegotten, from no one. Since the Son is begotten, he cannot be 'of the same substance' as God. The Cappadocians were subtle and sophisticated thinkers, and through a genuine intellectual and theological revolution, they refuted Eunomius by arguing that the property of being unbegotten does not belong to the divine essence *per se*, but to only *one* of the divine persons, namely, God the Father. Thus the Father can be unbegotten, and the Son begotten, and still share the same substance, namely, divinity. The Cappadocian *tour de force* against Arianism and Eunomianism made it possible for the first time for there to be a genuinely trinitarian doctrine of God. Their emphasis on the distinctiveness of each divine *hypostasis* (person) was consistent with the pattern of the revelation of Christ and the Spirit in the economy of salvation. Further, by attributing unbegottenness to God the Father, they originated a new idea of God's Fatherhood: God is not just Father of creation, but the personal, eternal origin of the Son.

In the process of reaching this synthesis, a great sea change took place in Christian theology. Prior to Nicaea, affirmations about God, or about Christ's divinity, were exclusively biblical. After Nicaea, there arose the split between Christ's human and divine nature. For example, Athanasius argued that Jesus Christ suffered in his humanity, but not his divinity.

This split was reflected in the burgeoning doctrine of the Trinity which began to argue for the divinity of Christ and the Spirit not on the basis of their role in our salvation, but because they share the divine *ousia* (substance). This metaphysical argument to some extent displaced the usual soteriological argument about Christ and the Spirit with respect to our salvation. The tension between these two forms of argumentation is certainly present in the writings of the Cappadocians, but in general their focus remained on the economy of salvation. Metaphysical arguments were used in support of conclusions already reached on the basis of the scriptural testimony to Christ and the Spirit.

With Augustine in the West, a new kind of argumentation developed. Augustine, too, was concerned to refute the Arian heresy, yet his starting-point was not the distinctiveness of the divine persons in the economy of redemption, but the unity of the divine nature. According to Augustine, God's unity is primary; personhood is derived from the divine essence. The three divine persons are coequal because they share a common essence.

Augustine also believed that vestiges of the Trinity were present in the human soul, according to the text of Genesis that we are created in the image and likeness of God. The Christian life was a contemplation of that image within, by which we would ascend more nearly to God and be united with God. Augustine formulated a number of trinitarian analogies for the structure of the soul, for example, lover–beloved–love, and memory–intellect–will. The faculties of the soul are a mirror-image of God's own being: just as God knows and loves Godself, so we can know and love ourselves and thereby be united with God.

The effect of Augustine's approach was to locate the economy of redemption within the individual soul, instead of in history as such. Even though Augustine probably never intended such a thing, his interpreters in the subequent history of Christianity used his writings to promote the idea of a self-enclosed Trinity of persons who know and love themselves, and then reach out to the creature in one undifferentiated act. The doctrine of the Trinity soon acquired an unfortunate abstractness and distance from the concerns of everyday Christians.

Thomas Aquinas was very influenced by Augustine, and Thomas himself greatly shaped theology from the medieval period up until our own day. Many of the *Catechism*'s conciliar statements were developed in the period just following Thomas's own synthesis. Thomas attempted to combine the Eastern focus on the monarchy of the Father (the idea that the Father is the source and origin of Son and Spirit) with Augustine's idea of the soul as a mirror of the Trinity. Thomas also used the metaphysics of Aristotle, according to which God is the pure act of being. God alone is a self-sufficient act of being, whereas all creatures depend on God for their act of existing. As mentioned above, in the *Summa*, Thomas divided the section on God into two parts: *De Deo Uno* and *De Deo Trino*. The first treatise deals with the attributes of God, such as goodness and simplicity. The treatise on the Trinity begins with the idea that in God there are 'processions', that is, persons come from other persons. Then he

74

examines the concepts of relation and person, and then the unique characteristics of Son and Spirit. Thomas described divine relations as 'relations of opposition': the Father begets the Son, the Son is begotten by the Father, the Father and Son together spirate the Spirit, the Spirit is spirated by Father and Son. He defines a divine person as a 'subsistent relation', that is, a relation (such as begetting) that is constitutive of the person (the Begetter).

Thomas articulated a highly sophisticated metaphysics of intra-trinitarian relations. But in this account of the Trinity, the history of redemption does not play a prominent role. In the final question of the treatise on the Trinity, Thomas does raise the question of the divine missions, the sending of Son and Spirit into the economy of salvation. Still, the structure of the *Summa* shows that Thomas conceives of God first in terms of the divine unity, then in *intra*-trinitarian terms, and then he considers God's relationship to the creature. This unique approach, which he describes as 'seeing all things from the perspective of God', fits well with Aristotle's metaphysics. But, as I have argued elsewhere, the overall effect of Thomas's approach to the Trinity was to separate God-Trinity and creature by an ontological chasm that is difficult to overcome.[20]

In the Eastern tradition, a comparable development took place in the theology of Gregory Palamas (d. 1359), a monk from Mount Athos who is as important in the Orthodox tradition as Thomas Aquinas is in the Catholic tradition. Gregory wrote against the philosopher Barlaam, in defence of the practice of the Hesychasts (those who practise silent, contemplative prayer) who claimed that their union with God was unmediated. Barlaam insisted that God was too unknowable and inaccessible for such union to take place. Gregory's argument rested on the now-famous distinction between divine essence and divine energies. It is true, Gregory argued, that God's essence is, strictly speaking, unknowable and 'imparticipable'. But we are in union with the divine energies, which are the manifestations and expressions of God in the economy of redemption. These divine energies *are* the divine being, thus mystical union with the energies of God is union with God as such. The energies are 'enhypostatic', which means that they express the uniqueness of the divine persons.

Gregory's real concern was to preserve the Orthodox teaching on grace, understood as deification, 'becoming God'. Thus he wanted to maintain that our union with God is real, and that by this union we are deified, infused with divine life and grace. His position, however, tended to separate the divine persons from direct involvement in the economy of redemption, since the divine persons belong to the unknowable, imparticipable realm of God's being. Thus by the end of the medieval period, Gregory Palamas in the East, and Thomas Aquinas in the West, had succeeded in depicting the Trinity as a primarily intra-divine reality, self-sufficient, and somewhat unrelated to us. Thus divine life was located elsewhere than in the economy of salvation. The doctrine of the Trinity then became a matter of sorting out how many processions, relations, and persons there are, and how these function within God '*in se*'.

The *Catechism* is dominated by the type of trinitarian doctrine just described. Although the conciliar statements that are cited are modest, compared to the great number that could have been cited, the *Catechism* states that 'The mystery of the Most Holy Trinity is the central mystery of Christian faith and life. *It is the mystery of God in himself . . .*' (234). This shows that the *Catechism* does not see that the doctrine of the Trinity also articulates the mystery of *God for us*, which is the mystery and truth of our salvation.

Despite the general irrelevance of the *doctrine* of the Trinity, its central truth was preserved in mysticism, art, and especially in Christian liturgy. The movement in contemporary theology and catechesis is to retrieve the essential truths and insights of this doctrine, but to restate it in contemporary terms that are intelligible to modern persons, and thereby to make the practical and soteriological dimensions of the doctrine clear. In this respect the *Catechism* demonstrates no awareness of the important contributions of Karl Rahner and many others to the revitalisation and indeed rehabilitation of trinitarian doctrine.

The practical dimensions of trinitarian doctrine

The surest path towards seeing the practical implications of trinitarian doctrine is to recover the pre-Nicene emphasis on soteriology and the post-Nicene Cappadocian emphasis on the distinctiveness of the divine persons in God's saving acts in history. This tethers the doctrine of the Trinity to the actual economy of salvation, and curtails its tendency towards ungrounded speculation about God's 'inner life'.

The doctrine of the Trinity is 'practical' because its subject-matter is the shared life of God and creature.[21] Its practical dimension does not mean that it is a blueprint for resolving parish disputes or global issues of war and peace. Rather, the doctrine of the Trinity points to a wisdom, a means of discernment about what God is up to in the providential plan of salvation. Its primary direction is not metaphysical but soteriological; it intends the mystery of the God who saves us in Jesus Christ. The Christian life entails knowing, loving, and worshipping the God revealed in Christ, and acting in accord with this revelation. True Christian orthodoxy means 'right opinion' about the glory of God made manifest in creation and redemption, while Christian orthopraxis means right action in response to God's self-glorification in the economy.

Jesus Christ preached the coming reign of God and revealed the order of the new household of God, in which all persons, especially the outcasts, like the leper and the Samaritan woman, will live together in peace and harmony with those in privileged places. Indeed, this new order extends to the order of creation, for in that coming reign of God all creatures will find their fulfilment. In the vision of Isaiah, even the lion and the lamb will lie down together.

The *Catechism* acknowledges that 'the ultimate end of the whole divine economy is the entry of God's creatures into the perfect unity of the Blessed Trinity' (260). This is exactly right, but the language can give the impression that God's life is located somewhere other than 'with us'. We must keep in mind that entering into divine life requires also living fully, in right relationship, in God's economy. The next sentence of the *Catechism* is apropos: 'But even now we are called to be a dwelling for the Most Holy Trinity.' God's life is shared with us, and by God's grace we are caught up in that life. But living 'in God', or becoming a dwelling-place for God, does not result in an individualistic salvation. Indeed, the Christian vision is of the salvation of the community called the body of Christ. 'Entering into divine life therefore is impossible unless we also enter into a life of love and communion with others.'[22]

The rule (reign) of God preached by Jesus Christ gives specific guidelines about how to live. While Jesus certainly did not foresee every kind of ethical dilemma human beings face, there are certain principles that emerge from his teaching.[23] This teaching on God's reign is well expressed by the metaphor of the inclusive household (*oikos*) in which all those who repent of sin are welcomed and included, regardless of social, economic, political, or religious status.

Jesus' teaching on the new household and reign of God is reflected in the Cappadocian emphasis that all forms of monarchy (sole rule) are at odds with the Christian doctrine of God. Indeed, they argued that even God's *archē* (rule) belongs not just to one person, but is shared equally by three divine persons. Human socio-political arrangements are to mirror the divine arrangement. As we saw above, the whole point of refuting Arius was to eliminate all forms of hierarchy and subordination among (divine) persons. Applying this 'rule' to us means that no human being can be the *archē* of another, whether according to race, or sex, or some other classification. The inclusive household envisaged by Jesus Christ and the inclusive order of persons envisaged in the doctrine of the Trinity coincide. Hierarchical patterns of relationship among persons, whether sexual, economic, or ecclesiastical, are disallowed both by Jesus Christ and by the doctrine of the Trinity.

To make these considerations more concrete, and to illustrate the practical dimensions of trinitarian doctrine, we apply very briefly the insights of trinitarian doctrine to five areas: the nature of the Church, the sacraments, sexuality, ethics, and spirituality.[24]

The doctrine of the Trinity mandates that *the Church* is most effectively the image or icon of God when it embodies the eschatological hope of the inclusive household of God. The Church is to be a *visible* sign of the new order of relationships according to which all are one in Christ; in Christ there is no longer male nor female, free nor slave, Jew nor Gentile. The inclusiveness of Jesus' teaching on God's reign should be evident in the patterns of relationship within the Church. The trinitarian vision of the Church does not reduce its members to the lowest common denominator. Indeed, just as the doctrine of the Trinity affirms that Father, Son and Holy Spirit are equal though radically distinct in terms of personal identity, so too in the Church we can affirm the equality but sacred diversity of persons, gifts and charisms. Leadership is still a requirement in the Church, and it may be a charismatic, grace-filled endeavour, provided it is the leadership of service (*diakonia*) and not domination and control.

The *sacraments* give us entry into the household of God and engraft us into the life of God. Through baptism we 'put on Christ', making his identity our own. In the eucharist we celebrate the mystery of the communion of persons, both divine and human. The whole meaning of the eucharist can be summed up by the word 'communion', both that which we ingest and that new order of persons that the Holy Spirit creates. The sacramental life of the Church can be said to be 'catholic', that is, it embraces the whole of humanity, inviting all to share in the mystery of salvation through Christ. Whenever the eucharist is a sign of exclusion it contradicts what it stands for, namely, the new redemptive order preached by Jesus Christ.

Sexuality is an image of God, as Genesis attests. Sexuality is the drive towards personal communion with another, and in this way it is iconic of our fundamental desire for God. Sexuality is potentially holy, creative and fruitful, and at the same time capable of the gravest distortion through violence, selfishness, alienation and confusion. Even though one of the dynamisms of sexuality is towards exclusivity, the doctrine of the Trinity shows that sexuality must transcend itself and become inclusive and hospitable of the stranger, and in this sense 'catholic'.

Christian ethical life is impossible to pursue theoretically apart from the doctrine of the Trinity. One of the fundamental claims of the Christian doctrine of God is that we are created in the image of God, who dwells eternally in communion among persons. Given this, Christian ethics concerns those practices and acts that serve the communion among persons, that encourage human flourishing, that result in the praise of God, that recall Christ, that move away from sin towards conversion and authentic humanity. Christian ethical life consists in walking with God through service to others, love of the enemy, and the welcoming of the stranger into the household of God.

Finally, *Christian spiritual life* is the living out of what we believe and how we pray. The Holy Spirit makes us holy and gives us access to divine life. The terms used for this include grace, sanctification, and divinisation.[25] All these terms indicate that the Spirit of God conforms us to the person of Christ and in this way incorporates us into the communion of saints. The spiritual life is a means of 'discernment' of what God is doing in the economy of redemption. For this reason, spirituality is not an aspect of ourselves separate from every other dimension of our lives, but belongs to the very fabric of what it means to be human.[26]

Conclusion

The *Catechism* is right to stress the centrality of the doctrine of the

Trinity. Its presentation of this vital teaching begins in a promising way with the liturgical focus on baptism. But this concrete and accessible starting-point is not carried through the entire treatment, in the sense that no connection is shown between doctrinal affirmations and Christian life. The summary of church teaching on the Trinity is routine, and no reason is given why anyone should be interested in the doctrine of the Trinity, nor how and why it is central to our faith. This section also shows no awareness of current theological and pastoral literature in which a veritable renaissance of trinitarian doctrine is taking place. Finally, and the answer to this depends on other essays in this volume, does the whole *Catechism* reflect the claim made here, namely, that the Trinity is the source of all Christian mysteries?

The *Catechism* states that its primary audience is the episcopate, and that it is meant to encourage the writing of new, local catechisms. If such efforts are to be successful, they will have to compensate for the shortcomings of the Roman *Catechism*'s presentation by making the truths of trinitarian doctrine of vital interest to Catholic Christians.

Notes

1   This pattern is replicated in the modern Rite of Christian Initiation of Adults (RCIA). On the history of creeds, see J. N. D. Kelly, *Early Christian Creeds* (London: Longman, 1972) and Berard Marthaler, *The Creed* (Mystic, CT: Twenty-Third Publications, 1987). Note that the English translation of the *Catechism* renders 'Credo' as 'I do' rather than 'I believe'.

2   The text wisely avoids using the much more common distinction between the 'economic' and 'immanent' Trinity; these terms are open to much misunderstanding. For a full argument to this effect, cf. Catherine Mowry LaCugna, *God For Us: The Trinity and Christian Life* (San Francisco: HarperCollins, 1991), especially ch. 7.

3   Ibid.

4   The text reads: 'And you shall say to Pharaoh, "Thus says the Lord, Israel is my first-born Son".' No reference is made to God as Father.

5   The Old Testament contains other feminine images: God gives birth (Is 46:3–4; Dt 32:8); God is attached to her children as a mother is (Is 49:14–15); God has tender compassion (Jer 32:20; Is 66:12–13); see also Pss 131:1–2; 123:2; 22:9f. There are also numerous references to Wisdom as feminine; cf. Prov 9:1–6, 4:6–8; Wis 7:25 – 8:2; Sir 15:2.

6   The *Catechism* does not explain why the doctrine of the Trinity should be considered a 'dogma', nor what distinction there may be between doctrine and dogma.

7   These conciliar definitions can be found in any edition of H. Denzinger's *Enchiridion Symbolorum*, or in English in Roy J. Deferrari, *The Sources of Catholic Dogma*, translation of the 30th edition of H. Denzinger's *Enchiridion Symbolorum* (St Louis: B. Herder, 1957). References hereafter are to Deferrari (D).

8   Cf. Toledo XI (D 275–284, especially D 281); Lateran IV (D 428, 431–432).

9   Cf. Toledo XI (D 280–281).

10   In Latin scholastic theology the persons are distinct by 'relations of
     opposition'.

     Father → Son   (The Father begets the Son)
     Son → Father   (The Son is begotten by the Father)
     Father and Son → Spirit (The Father and Son spirate the Spirit)
     Spirit → Father and Son (The Spirit is spirated by Father and Son)

     Only three of these relations of opposition are 'person-constituting': the
     Father's begetting of the Son, the Son's being begotten, and the Spirit's being
     spirated. The spiration of the Spirit by Father and Son does not constitute the
     distinctive identity of Father and Son.
11   Cf. Lateran IV (D 428).
12   Cf. Toledo XI (D 278).
13   Cf. the Council of Florence (D 704).
14   (D 703).
15   This was Karl Barth's approach, in *Church Dogmatics*, vol. I/1, 2nd edn
     (Edinburgh: T. & T. Clark, 1975).
16   *Catechism of the Council of Trent for Parish Priests*, trans. by John A.
     McHugh and Charles J. Callan, 2nd rev. edn (New York: Joseph F. Wagner,
     1934).
17   *A Catechism of Christian Doctrine*, no. 2, rev. ed. (Confraternity of Christian
     Doctrine, 1941 and 1949). The questions are of the order 'Is there only one
     God?', 'How many Persons are there in God?', and so forth.
18   *A New Catechism* (New York: Herder & Herder, 1965), pp. 498–9.
19   Ronald Luber, Donald Wuerl and Thomas Lawler (eds), *The Teaching of
     Christ* (Huntington, IN: Our Sunday Visitor, 1976). At about the same time
     two other non-official catechisms were assembled: *An American Catholic
     Catechism*, ed. George Dyer (New York: Seabury, 1975) contains a very brief
     section, pp. 38–9; John Hardon's *The Catholic Catechism* (Garden City, NY:
     Doubleday, 1975) contains a fuller treatment of the Trinity, and tries to
     relate it to Christian life.
20   Cf. LaCugna, *God For Us*, pp. 143–80.
21   Ibid., p. 378.
22   Ibid., p. 382.
23   For fuller explication, cf. ibid., pp. 382–8.
24   For fuller explication, cf. ibid., pp. 400–11.
25   This is the preferred term used in the Orthodox Church. It means, literally,
     'being made God'. The Orthodox mean by this that as the Spirit gradually
     conforms us to the person of Jesus Christ, we are made 'Gods by grace', not by
     nature.
26   See Catherine Mowry LaCugna and Michael K. Downey, 'Trinitarian
     spirituality' in Michael K. Downey (ed.), *The New Dictionary of Catholic
     Spirituality* (Collegeville: Michael Glazier, 1993), pp. 968–82.

Creation and Original Sin

(Paragraphs 268–421)

Gabriel Daly OSA
Trinity College, Dublin

I

Creation

(Paragraphs 268–384)

The theme of creation has until recently remained relatively undeveloped in Christian theology, both Catholic and Protestant. The contemporary ecological crisis, however, has given it new relevance and potentially greater prominence on the doctrinal agenda. One happy consequence of its hitherto low profile in traditional theology is that it has not been a major battle zone of orthodoxy against heresy. The *Catechism* mentions Pantheism, Dualism, Manichaeism, Gnosticism, Deism, and Materialism (285), but we encounter no anathemas or warnings against views which are judged to be dangerous to faith.

What we do find, however, is a near total disregard for the difficulties and doubts which beset the average modern believer of goodwill and critical intelligence. The greater part of what appears in these pages could have been written hundreds of years ago. It is as if the modern world had not posed any significantly new questions for Christian faith. Faith is here taken to be as easy today as it was in the patristic or medieval periods. The effects of the Enlightenment, the scientific revolution, the turn to the subject, together with concern for human autonomy and suspicion of authority, are all in practice ignored. In the section which immediately precedes that on the Creator, the Roman Catechism is quoted to the effect that because nothing is impossible with God,

> Once our reason has grasped the idea of God's almighty power, it will *easily and without any hesitation* admit everything that [the Creed] will afterwards propose for us to believe — even if they be great and marvellous things, far above the ordinary laws of nature. (274; emphasis added)

Brave talk indeed; understandable perhaps in the sixteenth century, regrettable in the neo-scholastic period, but wildly out of touch with our age. Adult catechesis which does not reckon honestly with the genuine

82

problems and doubts which beset the modern faithful, intelligent, and questioning believer is failing in the first of its tasks.

This is the sort of approach of which Maurice Blondel, writing nearly a century ago, pleaded for reform. His arguments were aimed not so much at catechisms as at the apologetics of the time (which of course had far-reaching implications for certain types of catechism). He had become convinced that the Catholic Church was not giving an effective account of its faith, precisely because it was not speaking to modern men and women, whether within or outside its membership. The Catholic case, he felt, was going by default. It was derived from, and was being addressed to, another age and was therefore failing the first test of effective argument, namely, that it should speak to the actual condition of its hearers.[1] It is difficult to understand why this *Catechism* should so signally fail the very test that Blondel was talking about a century ago when mandatory neo-scholasticism was virtally unchallenged in the Church, and the Second Vatican Council was sixty years in the future.

Pope John Paul II sees the *Catechism* as a contribution to 'the renewal to which the Holy Spirit ceaselessly calls the Church of God, the Body of Christ, on her pilgrimage to the undiminished light of the Kingdom!'.[2] The pilgrimage of which the Pope speaks is marked by the struggle of faith to hear God's word in a world widely disposed to ignore or reject it. Church members need all the understanding and encouragement they can get from their pastors. The last thing they need is the sort of teaching which makes little or no effort to speak to an age beset by difficulties and hesitations, to say nothing of nihilism and cultural despair. It is a prime pastoral duty to recognise that there are people for whom the choice may be between an honest critically aware faith and no faith at all. The pretence that faith is easy constitutes a pastoral betrayal.

In the part of the *Catechism* dealing with creation there are three sections. The first is entitled 'The Creator'; the second, 'Heaven and earth'; and the third, 'Man'.

The Creator (279–324)

The section opens by quoting the first words of the Bible and the first words of the Creed and then goes on to note the place given to creation in the liturgy of the Easter Vigil (281). This neat linking of Scripture, Tradition and liturgy makes an impressive opening from a catechetical standpoint. It reminds us of the old dictum, *Lex orandi, lex credendi* (prayer is the measure of belief). A well-conducted Easter vigil, with its emphasis on the passage from darkness to light, can evoke with great effect the grandeur and elemental power of creation. A highly significant theological point is established in this context: creation is the foundation of all God's saving plans expressed in the mystery of salvation which culminates in Christ (280). We need this insight especially in view of a regrettable tendency in some circles today to separate the theme of creation from those of sin and redemption, on the grounds that traditional Western theology has sacrificed the celebration of the joys and glories of creation to a grim and joyless preoccupation with sin and redemption. If we wish to criticise the extremism of this type of creation spirituality, we would do well to take steps to avoid the sort of theology which treats creation as scarcely more than a backdrop to redemption. Creation is indeed the 'foundation of all God's saving plans' (280); but this should not be interpreted to mean that creation takes its theological significance only from human redemption.

The text then turns to the question of origins (protology) and ends (eschatology). It asks 'Where do we come from?' and 'Where are we going?' (282), and goes on to remark that the question of the origins of the world and of humans has been the subject of 'many scientific studies which have splendidly enriched our knowledge of the age and dimensions of the cosmos, the development of life-forms and the appearance of man' (283). These questions can be taken in either a scientific, philosophical, or theological sense; and it is important that they be distinguished from each other. The *Catechism* points out that questions about origins and ends go 'beyond the proper domain of the natural sciences' (284). Since this is one of the very few places in the *Catechism* in which science is mentioned in the context of creation, it deserves attention.

The text, in remarking that scientific studies have enriched our knowledge, is careful to avoid any suggestion of opposition between science and faith. This is important in an age when fundamentalism is all too ready to set up such an opposition. Insofar as the *Catechism* is intended to serve as a model for local catechisms, one can only regret that the question of science and religion receives such jejune treatment.

The Catholic Church has so far escaped the worst excesses of the creation/evolution conflict, but it cannot afford to be complacent in this regard. In an age of cultural insecurity and uncertainty, Catholics are by no means immune from the siren voices of a fundamentalism which offers confident and deceiving simplicities. Basic to these simplicities is a literal understanding of the Bible, especially of the book of Genesis. This literal understanding can easily produce a suspicion of, if not outright hostility towards, science and its findings. One might have hoped that the *Catechism* would recognise this danger and consequently would have demarcated the respective zones of science and religion more firmly, while at the same time recognising faith's proper interest in the findings of science.

The *Catechism* does give a valuable lead in a sentence which speaks about the power of these scientific findings to inspire in the believer admiration for, and gratitude to, the Creator 'for all his works and for the understanding and wisdom he gives to scholars and researchers' (283). This attitude is greatly to be welcomed (for all that it appears in small print and is left undeveloped). We cannot afford to forget our history here. Galileo and Darwin, two luminaries in the firmament of science, figure in church history in a role which does no credit to the Church. In these matters reform by amnesia is not enough. We need an admission of institutional guilt, an expression of institutional compunction, and some analysis of the reasons why former mistakes were made, if only to ensure that similar mistakes may be avoided in the future. If the Church warns scientists against exceeding their competence, it had better be sure that it is without guilt in this respect itself. The *Catechism* might here have aptly cited *Gaudium et Spes* 36:

> We cannot but deplore certain attitudes (not unknown among Christians) deriving from a shortsighted view of the rightful autonomy of science; they have occasioned conflict and controversy and have misled many into opposing faith and science.

For a variety of reasons, practical interdisciplinary bridgeheads between science and religion are not easy to set up. For most of the time the move towards dialogue will have to come from the religious side, since scientists who are not believers have no compelling reasons for taking the initiative, and a fair amount of prejudice to conquer even in responding to one. The problem is cultural as well as religious, as C. P. Snow suggested more than thirty years ago when he gave his lecture on 'The Two Cultures'.[3] If dialogue is difficult at a purely cultural level — a situation witnessed to in many universities today — theology, because of traditional suspicion on the part of scientists, can expect to find it doubly so.

Quite apart from bridgeheads between faith and science, there is the ecological crisis which is facing our planet, owing to our poisoning of lands, waters and atmosphere and our pursuit of unsustainable growth for which future generations will have to pay a heavy price. It is exceedingly important that religion play, and be seen to play, a significant part in the ecological movement and that catechisms, or equivalent educational programmes in the Church, should reflect the revitalising effect which ecological matters are having upon the contemporary theology of creation. The *Catechism*, in dealing with the creation of the visible world, notes that 'Each of the various creatures, willed in its own being, reflects in its own way a ray of God's infinite wisdom and goodness' (339). It goes on to exhort us to avoid the 'disordered use of things' which scorns the Creator and brings disastrous consequences on people and their environment. There are pointers here which, however understated and undeveloped, deserve to be carefully noted and followed up.

In the secular world the ecological crisis is properly regarded as a behavioural and prudential concern. This regard gives rise to an ethical programme of pressing importance: 'Think globally, act locally.' Christian theology and catechetics, however, can be properly expected to add a dimension to this programme. Theological reflection on the ecological crisis raises profound questions both about the intentions of the Creator concerning nature and about the role of human beings in promoting or obstructing those intentions.

The human component in creation can be either exaggerated or underestimated. The *Catechism* makes it very clear that it will certainly not err on the side of underestimation. One can therefore only regret that the text employs the strange phrase 'willed in its own being' instead, presumably, of 'willed for its own sake'. The point is important, because elsewhere the *Catechism* evinces a *very* strong anthropocentrism which needs balancing in favour of a recognition of the autonomous value of *all* creatures.

The Catholic Bishops of the United States, in their statement *Renewing the Earth: An Invitation to Reflection and Action on the Environment in Light of Catholic Social Teaching*, while recognising the special place of human beings in the scheme of creation, nevertheless write:

> The wonderful variety of the natural world is, therefore, part of the divine plan, and as such invites our respect. Accordingly, it is appropriate that we treat other creatures and the natural world not just as means to human fulfillment, but as God's creatures, possessing an independent value, worthy of our respect and care.[4]

When the *Catechism* speaks of each creature being 'willed in its own being', it can probably be taken to mean what the American Bishops mean by their phrase 'possessing an independent value'. Recognition of this independence leads to a new way of looking at nature and nature's relationship to its Creator. Not only does this recognition shape moral values and attitudes (such as avoidance of cruelty to animals), but it prompts the religious imagination to dwell on the reflection of divine beauty in all creation, especially as seen in the vast web of systemic relationships to be found in nature. Ecological respect and concern are more solid and secure for being rooted not only in prudential and even ethical considerations, but also in a sound theology of creation.

As things stand, the *Catechism* opts for a very strong anthropocentrism. In a passage which is primarily taken up with the ordered character of a good world, the goodness of which is a participation in God's own goodness, we are told that 'God willed creation as a gift addressed to man, an inheritance destined for and entrusted to him' (299). Later it says 'God created everything for man, but man in turn was created to serve and love God and to offer all creation back to him' (358). These statements appear to cut right across what ecologists are trying tirelessly to inculcate in their listeners and readers: the world of nature is *not* there simply for us. There is no valid reason why this ecological conviction should not receive strong theological endorsement. The *Catechism* goes near to, but finally falls short of, giving such a theological endorsement. More could have been made of the phrase 'entrusted to him' (299). It is true that not all ecologists are happy with the notion of human *stewardship* of creation, and some ecofeminists attack it for being patriarchal. Yet its value as a model comes from the circumstance that a steward shares in the creaturely condition and at the same time enjoys a measure of independence which allows for caring leadership.[5] 'There is', the *Catechism* remarks, 'a *solidarity among all creatures* arising from the fact that all have the same Creator and are all ordered to his glory' (344). St Francis of Assisi's *Canticle of the Creatures* is then invoked with pleasing effect, but the conclusion is never explicitly drawn that in view of the fact that all creatures are ordered to God's glory, they have a value in their own right and are not there simply for human use.

Anthropocentrism has been the almost inevitable product of regarding creation as little more than a backdrop to redemption. To be sure, certain biblical texts lend themselves to the sort of interpretation which appears to license domination if not exploitation of nature. The Priestly account of creation in Genesis gives both Adam and Eve supremacy over the rest of creation, more or less on the lines of Psalm 8: 'You make him master over all that you have made, putting everything in subjection under his feet' (v. 6 REB).

The biblical writers cannot be expected to share our anxiety and guilt about the way in which we have treated our world. The anthropocentric texts can and should be balanced by reference to texts like Psalm 104 which proclaim and celebrate nature in its own right. The first of the divine covenants recorded in the Bible depicts God saying to Noah and his sons: 'I am now establishing my covenant with you and with your descendants after you, and with every living creature that is with you, all birds and cattle, all the animals with you on earth, all that have come out of the ark' (Gen 9:8–10). It is especially appropriate that the natural phenomenon of the rainbow should be 'a sign of the covenant between myself and the earth' (v. 13), and that on seeing it God will 'remember the everlasting covenant between God and living creatures of every kind on earth' (v. 16). Any tendency to promote the human species at the expense of the rest of nature is effectively countered by God's splendidly ironic praise of creation in the book of Job: 'Where were you when I laid the earth's foundations? Tell me, if you know and understand. Who fixed its dimensions? Surely you know!' (Job 38:4–5)

The *Catechism* goes on to remark that God transcends creation yet is present to his creatures' inmost being (300). This is an important rejection of eighteenth-century Deism, which postulated a divine initiative to bring the world into existence but then dispensed with the need for any further divine presence or sustaining action. Here one might remember that the scientific use of the word 'creation' differs from the theological use. Scientists employ it to refer to the physical beginning of the cosmos. Sound theology uses it to refer to the totality of divine relationship with all that is not God. There is no warrant for taking the 'Big Bang' as the initial moment of creation in a theological sense. The fact that physicists recognise their inability to go beyond the 'singularity' of the Big Bang is no licence for religion to try to fill the gap. Revelation has nothing to say about the scientific details of how the cosmos began. Revelation deals with the matter in symbolic and mythological language from which a theological message can be extracted by a careful process of appropriate interpretation.

Creation in its theological sense is closely related to the providence of God, which the *Catechism* defines as the dispositions by which God guides his creation towards an ultimate perfection yet to be attained (302). The text notes that creation (i.e., the cosmos) 'did not spring forth complete from the hands of the Creator. The universe was created "in a state of journeying" (*in statu viae*) . . .' One may wonder whether the essentialist phrase *in statu viae* is appropriate in a context which clearly recognises process and development in creation; but by the same token one is grateful for any recognition, however inchoate, that we today see the world very differently from our biblical, patristic and medieval ancestors.

Scripture, says the *Catechism*, often attributes actions to God 'without mentioning any secondary causes'. 'This is not a "primitive mode of speech", but a profound way of recalling God's primacy and absolute Lordship over history and the world' (304). Why, one wonders, should it not be *both* a primitive mode of speech *and* a recognition of God's lordship? The mode of God's action in the world is a notoriously difficult theological problem. The fact is that we today know a great deal more about the scientific causes of, say, thunderstorms, volcanoes, eclipses, physical and mental diseases, and other natural phenomena than did the biblical writers or patristic and medieval commentators. It was possible for them to attribute such phenomena directly to divine action. Even the great Newton himself could appeal to the finger of God to account for planetary movements for which there was then no scientific explanation. Recourse to a 'God of the gaps' is, however, both bad science and bad theology. The Marquis Pierre de Laplace, the distinguished French mathematician and physicist, was right when, as the story goes, the Emperor Napoleon asked him why God was not mentioned in his recent book on astronomy. 'Sire', Laplace is reputed to have replied, 'I have no need of that hypothesis.' The remark may have been made by an atheist, but it contains a profound theological truth: God is not a hypothesis or a being existing alongside other beings. One would expect to find something along these lines in any modern catechism.

What one does find, however, is a remarkably strong association of divine providence with divine sovereignty. It would appear that neither process thought nor feminist critique has had the slightest moderating influence on these pages of the *Catechism*, in which God is the supreme controller, dominant, invulnerable, independent. Feminist theologians constantly point to the traditional projection upon God of these male preoccupations. They will find little in the *Catechism* to assure them that official attitudes are changing in this respect. The text, for example, notes that God, 'the sovereign master of his plan . . . makes use of his creatures' co-operation' for its fulfilment (306). 'This use is not a sign of weakness . . .' (One would need to be obsessed with power and control to think that it was.) Invitation to partnership with the Creator in the accomplishment of his plan, the text notes, contributes greatly to our dignity. This promising theological pointer is, however, not pursued, and the text returns to dwelling on the hierarchical theme of the grandeur of God and the insignificance of the creature.

Evil now makes its appearance with St Augustine's urgent question, 'Whence evil?' The *Catechism* asks why? rather than whence? (309), and remarks that there is no quick answer to this painful and mysterious question. Augustine is cited:

For almighty God . . ., because he is supremely good, would never allow any evil whatsoever to exist in his works if he were not so all-powerful and good as to cause good to emerge from evil itself. (311; citing *Enchiridion*, 3.11).

Augustine's invocation of divine omnipotence here is not honorific or hierarchical. In Augustine's view it is precisely because God is all-powerful that he can afford to allow evil to infiltrate his good creation. God's power is challenged but never defeated by evil. In fact one of the marks of omnipotence is that it can extract good from evil.

Here we must face a methodological difficulty. The one word 'evil' is used in reference to both moral evil and what the *Catechism* calls 'physical evil' (310). In an important address given to the American Academy of Religion in 1984 the French philosopher Paul Ricoeur drew attention to the serious ambiguity of the word 'evil':

The whole enigma of evil may be said to lie in the fact that, at least in the traditions of the West, we put under the same terms such different phenomena as sin, suffering, and death. However, evil as wrongdoing and evil as suffering belong to two heterogeneous categories, that of blame and that of lament.[6]

This simple but very important methodological observation alerts us to the existence of two distinct theological agendas, which can, indeed must, be interrelated, but each of which poses a different set of questions. Evil as blame has a much wider and more developed tradition, and in fact traditionally grounds the theology of sin and redemption; whereas evil as lament has often been treated as little more than an intellectual exercise in an area which, after Leibniz, is usually labelled theodicy. In the theology of Augustine it takes on what has been called an 'aesthetic' dimension.

In the sentence preceding that quoted in 311 by the *Catechism*, Augustine writes '. . . that which is called evil, well-regulated and confined to its own place, serves to give higher commendation to the good, making it, in comparison with the evil, more pleasing and worthy of praise';[7] and in the sentence following it he expresses his well-known claim that evil is merely the privation of good. The fact that the examples he chooses to illustrate his thesis are drawn from disease in animals (the privation of health) and 'evils in the soul' (privation of moral good), makes it clear that he amalgamates the categories of lament and blame. For him evil as blame is the cause of evil as lament, since suffering and death follow upon the first sin.

The word 'aesthetic' neatly describes Augustine's argument that evil (as both blame and lament) serves as a backdrop designed to highlight the good in creation.[8] The argument has a degree of metaphysical symmetry, but seems bloodless and insensitive when we think about innocent human and animal suffering. The scholastic tradition could be rather offhand about suffering, both human and animal. The convenient ambiguity of the word 'evil' allowed the category of blame to overshadow that of suffering, while a controlling supernaturalism offered the consoling reflection that all would be well in the next life. An analogous Protestant attitude could be found in the theology of Karl Barth, who refused to discuss the problem of evil, on the grounds that any attempt to justify God the Creator to his sinful creatures would be an impertinence and an affront to the divine sovereignty and majesty. God needs no defenders or champions, only obedient hearers of the word.

It was of course the Enlightenment which raised in new and more urgent form the problem of evil and which sought to treat it in a rationalist manner unbeholden to Christian revelation (yet curiously chiming in some respects with Augustine's 'aesthetic' argument).

The *Catechism* does not engage with the Enlightenment or with modernity. The fact that it sometimes appears to be in step with the anti-Enlightenment movement of today is purely adventitious. Post-modernity is a difficult phrase to interpret, but whatever else it is, it is not a return to pre-critical attitudes. The questions put to Christian faith by post-Enlightenment culture have not disappeared just because there is a dialectical swing away from scientism and rationalism. The contemporary catechist will find herself or himself faced with extremely serious and pastorally challenging questions on the meaning of suffering in a world proclaimed by revelation to be good. J. B. Metz, among others, has claimed that theology can never be the same again after Auschwitz. Neither the old pre-critical theology of the fall nor the Enlightenment-inspired theodicy of the best of all possible worlds will satisfy many thoughtful believers or potential believers today.

Theodicy which has not been chastened into intellectual modesty and existential sensitivity will be more likely to give offence than to justify the ways of God to people today. Augustine's question, 'Whence evil?', if taken in the sense of lament, has to be answered in the light of Ivan Karamazov's great cry of rebellion: '. . . if the sufferings of children go to make up the sum of sufferings which is necessary for the purchase of truth, then I say beforehand that the entire truth is not worth such a price.'

In the final analysis one has to deny Karamazov the right to place an *a priori* barring order on the very *possibility* of finding eschatological meaning in the 'tears with which the earth is saturated from its crust to its core'. The *Catechism* avoids the insensitivity of treating the whole matter as a bracing intellectual exercise, and is content to say that 'Only at the end, when our partial knowledge ceases, when we see God "face to face", will we fully know the ways by which . . . God has guided his creation to that definitive sabbath rest for which he created heaven and earth' (314).

Heaven and earth (325–354)

After treating of the weighty matter of evil, the *Catechism* turns to the credal phrase 'Creator of all that is, seen and unseen'. Readers should prepare themselves at this point for something of a cultural shock as they are conveyed abruptly to the thirteenth century, specifically to the profession of faith of the Fourth Lateran Council (1215) and its affirmation that God has created two orders of creatures, 'the spiritual and the corporeal, that is, the angelic and the earthly, and then (*deinde*) the human creature, who as it were shares in both orders, being composed of spirit and body' (327). The existence of angels is declared 'a truth of faith' (328), though the exact status of this truth is not specified. Angels are 'personal and immortal creatures, surpassing in perfection all visible creatures' (330). They belong to Christ, who 'is the centre of the angelic world' and who 'has made them messengers of his saving plan' (331). An accumulation of biblical references to angels follows. Finally St Basil is quoted: 'Beside each believer stands an angel as protector and shepherd leading him to life' (336).

What are late twentieth-century people to make of all this in a catechism which has so little to say about the relationship between faith and science, ecology, and other matters which many will think rather more pressing? Those who are used to symbolic thinking and to the interpretation of myth will have few problems with biblical references to angels as messengers of God. What *is* a problem, however, is the removal of mythological language from its natural literary context and its subsequent reduction to literalised dogmatic statement. Images which properly belong to poetic narrative cannot simply be reduced to prosaic, allegedly factual, descriptions which then become dogmatic statements. The authors of the *Catechism* show no sign of recognising that there are serious hermeneutical problems involved in dogmatising figurative (and especially apocalyptic) language, and that the revelatory intent of such passages has to be discerned *within* the poetic language before being reduced to flat dogmatic pronouncements.

Writing before the Second Vatican Council, Karl Rahner pointed out that angels are not the subject of express divine revelation. In divine revelation 'the angels are merely taken for granted and their existence experienced, as created, personal, structural principles within the harmony of the cosmic order'. 'Revelation is not interested in the details (the names, number, rank of the angels and so forth).'[9] Rahner in fact makes angelology 'an intrinsic element of Christology'. In short, Vatican II's concept of the hierarchy of truths needs to be recalled in any talk about angels.

Section 5 closes with a reflection on the sabbath, the seventh day when God rests from the labours of creation. 'Creation was fashioned with a view to the sabbath' (347). This remark deserves attention for two reasons. First, there is a link with worship, which is seen in the context of creation. In the industrialised world of today, the sabbath, given that it will survive in any form, is normally thought of as a rest from the labours of the week. It is an incidental break in the continuum of work. This is not how the Bible sees things, or how the *Catechism* puts it. The week is there for the sabbath, not the sabbath for the week. The sabbath is a foretaste of eternity — an idea which Peter Abelard expresses in his great hymn for Saturday vespers: 'There sabbath unto sabbath / Succeeds eternally, / The joy that has no ending / Of souls in holiday.'[10] This vision of the sabbath and of the worship associated with it is full of possibilities both for liturgy and for the theology of work. The fact that it cuts across the ethos and values of today's commercialised world is a reminder of the important counter-cultural element in Christianity.

A second reason why the connection between creation and the sabbath deserves attention is that it helps to offset any tendency towards undue anthropocentrism. Creation is there not for humankind, but for the sabbath. The *Catechism* neatly links creation with Christology and eschatology by referring to 'the eighth day', the day of Christ's resurrection. 'The seventh day completes the first creation. The eighth days begins the new creation. Thus, the work of creation culminates in the greater work of redemption' (349). This suggests a fruitful way of relating creation to redemption. The second creation is in full continuity with the first; indeed it *is* the first creation, only now it is transformed into what it was always destined to be.

A eucharistic connection might have been established here, with considerable theological, catechetical, and liturgical benefit to the text. Indeed there could even have been a valuable ecumenical input, if use had been made of the fine Lima document on the eucharist:

> The eucharist is the great sacrifice of praise by which the Church speaks on behalf of the whole creation. For the world which God has reconciled is present at every eucharist: in the bread and wine, in the persons of the faithful, and in the prayers they offer for themselves and for all people . . . The eucharist thus signifies what the world is to become: an offering and hymn of praise to the Creator, a universal communion in the body of Christ, a kingdom of justice, love and peace in the Holy Spirit.[11]

The human race (355–379)

We humans, says the *Catechism*, are created in the image of God, established in God's friendship, and given a unique place in creation. In our nature we unite the spiritual and material worlds (355). There is a great deal of compressed theological anthropology in these words, and the following several pages of the *Catechism* attempt to unpack it.

That the human race 'occupies a unique place in creation' is a claim that needs to be handled dialectically; that is, it must be related to context and 'corrected' to achieve a balance with its opposite. If, for example, the context is biological reductionism of the sort which sees human beings as nothing but one more among many living species, then we may properly feel justified in singling out for emphasis the special glory of being human. Human beings, as Goethe remarked, are the first conversation that nature holds with God.[12] Nor do we need to restrict the discussion to religious matters. Mozart, Shakespeare and Michelangelo are something more than the product of a more complex molecular arrangement within an evolutionary process each stage of which *adds* something to what has preceded it. Michael Polanyi, reflecting on the emergence of humankind from bacillus to noosphere, asks the question which reductionists seem impotent to answer, 'How can the emergent have arisen from particulars that cannot constitute it?'[13] In such a context it is proper to affirm that human beings occupy a unique place in creation.

If, on the other hand, the context is one of supernaturalism or creationism, where the processes of nature and the established findings of science about them are simply ignored or discounted, then it becomes necessary to reflect seriously on all that we humans have in common with our animal cousins — for example, a strikingly similar DNA structure. Perhaps we can give fresh currency and relevance to the teaching of the Fourth Lateran Council, cited by the *Catechism*, that in our human nature we unite the spiritual and material worlds. If the supernaturalists see only the spiritual and the reductionists see only the material, perhaps the task of the thoughtful believer is to reject the exclusivism of both and instead affirm the mysterious grandeur of the amalgamation of both spiritual and material in the human species.

The *Catechism* opts for a medieval anthropology enshrined in the teaching of the Council of Vienne (1312) that the soul is the form of the body (365). One needs to be well versed in the history of medieval philosophy and theology to appreciate what the Council is saying and why it is saying it. The *Catechism* points out that the language is Aristotelian — a helpful reminder that every doctrine has a historical context and that its meaning is to some extent limited by its context. The debate over whether the body has more than one 'form' was a lively one in the thirteenth-century schools. Vienne favoured the Thomistic (Aristotelian) contention that the human being is a unity brought about by the union of body and rational soul. Although, however, Aristotelian philosophy dominated other areas of church doctrine (on the sacraments, for example), it never displaced the Platonist doctrine of the soul as a separate substance preceding and succeeding its bodily existence. The *Catechism* simply juxtaposes the Aristotelian doctrine (365) with the Platonism of the following article which proclaims that 'every spiritual soul is created immediately by God . . ., does not perish . . . at death and . . . will be reunited with the body at the final Resurrection' (366).

The *Catechism* shows no sign of appreciating that body/soul language raises all sorts of problems today. It does not appear to recognise the difficulty of reconciling the Aristotelianism of its teaching on the unity of the human being with the Platonism of its teaching on the soul. Nor does it enter into the question of how such language is to be related to the Bible. It says nothing at all about what is rapidly becoming a very insistent question, namely, that of the relationship between the brain and the spiritual principle in human beings. We shall find it increasingly difficult to offer Christian comment on what is happening in neuro-physiological research, if we cannot get beyond the anthropological language of Greek philosophy or the matter/spirit dichotomy of René Descartes. This is a classic instance of the need to recognise the hermeneutical character of church doctrine, which cannot simply be read off the page of a catechism but needs to be historically and linguistically interpreted.

The *Catechism* pursues its anthropological theme with some reflections on the text 'male and female he created them'. The treatment here is brief and, one senses, wary. Genesis is freely quoted. Man and woman are equal and, each in their own way, 'reflect the Creator's wisdom and goodness' (369). Each is made for the other, and both, by transmitting life, co-operate in the Creator's work (372).

Six paragraphs (374–379) on 'Man in Paradise' provide a linking section between the doctrine of creation, which has preceded it, and the doctrine of original sin, which follows. At this point we enter a zone of serious theological problems which will in turn be reflected in equally serious catechetical problems. Nearly all of these problems stem from the difficulty of reconciling the pre-critical view of the Genesis stories with our contemporary knowledge of (a) the physical and biological origins of the human race; (b) the literary genre of the book of Genesis; and (c) the impossibility of conceiving of an actual *historical* 'original state of holiness and justice' (375) in which there was no pain or death.

The question which has arisen at several points in the teaching of the *Catechism* on creation now becomes insistent and unavoidable in the context of its teaching on original justice and the fall. The first three chapters of Genesis, we are told, 'occupy a unique place' and 'remain the principal source for catechesis on the mysteries of the "beginning": creation, fall, and promise of salvation' (289). This highly significant statement puts Genesis 1 – 3 in a remarkably exposed position, in that if there are serious critical objections to the traditional exegesis of these chapters, there will be a consequent effect upon the 'catechesis on the mysteries of the "beginning"'.

What hermeneutical principles, then, are the authors employing in their reading of the book of Genesis? They give the impression of trying to have the best of two very different worlds of discourse. First, they make cautious (and not obviously consistent) concessions to the symbolic character of the biblical text. Then they ignore these concessions when they turn to affirming the traditional dogma of original justice and the fall. This dogma, formally taught by the Council of Trent, is largely contingent upon a literal historical reading of Genesis. *Any* concession to the symbolic character of Genesis leaves the Tridentine doctrine of original justice and the fall without the biblical support which the Council itself invokes. Now the *Catechism* makes such concessions, and they are worth noting:

- 'Scripture presents the work of the Creator symbolically as a succession of six days of divine "work", concluded by the "rest" of the seventh day.' (337)

- 'The Church, interpreting the symbolism of biblical language in an authentic way, in the light of the New Testament and Tradition, teaches that our first parents, Adam and Eve, were constituted in an original "state of holiness and justice". This grace of original holiness was "to share in . . . divine life".' (375)

- 'The account of the fall in Genesis 3 uses figurative language, but affirms a primeval event, a deed that took place *at the beginning of the history of man*.' (390; original italics. The reference given in the text is to *Gaudium et Spes* 13. The conciliar text, however, does *not* affirm 'a primeval event'. It simply states that 'man abused his freedom from the very start of history'.)

- 'The "tree of the knowledge of good and evil" symbolically evokes the insurmountable limits that man, being a creature, must freely recognize and respect with trust.' (396)

These four passages acknowledge the existence of symbolic (or in one instance 'figurative') language in the biblical account of creation and the fall. Two concrete exemplifications are given: the six days of creation and the tree of the knowledge of good and evil.

Why are these singled out for explicit recognition as symbolic? Why does the *Catechism* not recognise that the *entire* creation/fall account is symbolic narrative? Instead of doing so, and in spite of its half-hearted concessions to symbolism, it affirms an idyllic state free from suffering, concupiscence, and death.

Unwillingness to abandon the literal historical interpretation of the first eleven chapters of Genesis is especially regrettable, first, because it places a totally unnecessary stumbling-block before critically minded believers of good will and ecclesial loyalty, and, second, because it deprives the reader of the riches which the Genesis narratives offer when they are interpreted symbolically. Paul Ricoeur said it all nearly thirty years ago:

> The harm that has been done to souls, during the centuries of Christianity, first by the literal interpretation of the story of Adam, and then by the confusion of this myth, treated as history, with later speculations, principally Augustinian, about original sin, will never be adequately told. In asking the faithful to confess belief in this mythico-speculative mass and to accept it as a self-sufficient explanation, the theologians have unduly required a *sacrificium intellectus* where what was needed was to awaken believers to a symbolic superintelligence of their actual condition.[14]

Pope John Paul II, in his Apostolic Constitution *Fidei Depositum,* remarks that the *Catechism* 'is offered to every individual who asks us to give an account of the hope that is in us and who wants to know what the Catholic Church believes'.[15] Was it not incumbent, then, on the authors to make it perfectly clear that the Catholic Church does not require of its members a literal, pre-critical, historicised understanding of the first eleven chapters of Genesis? Unhappily they have not done so. Instead, section 6 ends with the sombre, and apparently literally intended, assertion that the harmony of original justice 'will be lost by the sin of our first parents' (379). Section 7, on the fall, will compound all the problems of interpretation raised at several points throughout the previous three sections which deal with creation.

It is a sad note on which to end a section of the *Catechism* which could so easily have attuned itself to the needs and aspirations of contemporary Catholics without seriously offending the traditionalists. Instead, we are given verbal repetition of a doctrine which is desperately in need of reformulation in language which actually says something credible to contemporary men and women.

II

Original Sin

(Paragraphs 385–421)

If the doctrine of creation has been relatively free of conflict and condemnations, the doctrine of original sin has, on the contrary, been strongly marked by both. Part of the trouble stems from the phrase 'original sin', in which the word 'sin' functions ambiguously and the adjective 'original' focuses attention upon an anthropology which is seriously outdated. One result of this is that the Catholic Church has on its books, so to speak, a doctrine which *in its traditional formulation* simply invites disbelief and rejection. As a further and disturbing result a very important Christian doctrine is going by default because it has been tied to a mode of formulation which many thoughtful believers can no longer accept, namely, the committing by an original historical pair, Adam and Eve, of an offence against God which has been transmitted from generation to generation as a criminal record (to use Tertullian's phrase) affecting human nature itself.

The doctrine, in short, is so bound up with the literalisation and historicisation of the Adamic myth that any effort to demythologise the Genesis narrative has been routinely construed by the guardians of orthodoxy as an attack on the doctrine. As long as the doctrine continues to be expressed in the language of a discredited anthropology and a fundamentalist reading of sacred Scripture, a vitally important truth of Christian revelation will go by default in many pulpits and classrooms. This is a high price to have to pay for the verbal orthodoxy demanded by reactionaries in the Church.

Extremes tend to stimulate their mirror-opposites; and so there are today schools of 'creation-centred' theology and spirituality which are trying to contrive a radical dichotomy between creation and redemption, making each exclusive of the other and sponsoring the former over the latter. Much traditional presentation of sin and redemption has been moralistic, juridical and joyless, and as such gives impetus to the misguided programme of substituting creation-centred spirituality for fall/redemption spirituality. The most effective answer to this new and superficial trend is not a reissue of pre-critical and discredited formulations, but a sound theology of both creation and redemption which relates each to the other in a way which is positive and life-enhancing. A basis for such a theology is to be found in the Pastoral Constitution of Vatican II, *Gaudium et Spes*, on the Church in the World of Today.

The influence of Blaise Pascal on *Gaudium et Spes* is palpable (largely owing to the preponderance of French theologians who worked on the text). One of Pascal's deepest insights was his estimation of human beings as the glory and the scandal of the universe. He saw the problem as one of giving full weight to *both* light *and* darkness in any analysis of what it means to be human. It is a dialectical task calling for balance and subtlety of approach. Exaggeration of the light gives an unrealistic, superficially optimistic and ultimately disillusioning picture, because the reality will fail ludicrously to come up to expectation. Exaggeration of the darkness, on the other hand, kills hope, joy, and any practical initiatives designed to make the world a better place. If we wish to counter the false optimism of some 'creation-centred' spiritualities, we need to recognise that these are often mirror-images of gloom-laden spiritualities which are unhealthily obsessed with sin.

Teilhard de Chardin remarked that whenever he spoke on the evolutionary character of the universe, there would always be someone in the audience who would ask 'And original sin — what about that?'[16] Teilhard regarded this situation as 'unhealthy',

> An embarrassment or a stumbling-block to the well-meaning but undecided, and at the same time a refuge for the narrow-minded, the *story* of the Fall, as we can see for ourselves, is nullifying the attempt to introduce, as is so essential, a fully human and humanizing Christian *Weltanschauung*.[17]

Teilhard quite properly protested against the sort of sin-obsessed mentality which drains the spirit of spontaneous joy and celebration out of Christian consciousness. The doctrine of original sin has often been tactically invoked against any affirmation of goodness in the world and in support of the sort of *Schadenfreude* that actually rejoices in the discovery of human weakness and human failure, without going on to rejoice in the healing remedy brought about by the life, death and resurrection of Jesus Christ.

Yet nothing could be clearer than our need of a doctrine which realistically recognises the dark side of our human nature with its appalling history of violence, injustice, cruelty, oppression, and misuse of power, together with the proclivity to wrong-doing which any human being looking into himself or herself can so quickly discern. The core of the doctrine traditionally labelled 'original sin' is the assertion that to be human is to need redemption. The bare fact of being a member of the species *Homo sapiens* means that we need reconciling and healing by divine grace even before we have actually done anything sinful. Christians profess that the reconciling and healing is effected by a first-century Jew, Jesus of Nazareth, whose life, death and resurrection constitute a unique manifestation of God's salvific will and power. Christians call this manifestation the gospel, or good news, and they believe that they have been commissioned to proclaim it to a broken and sinful world. Many of them are anxious that unnecessary dogmatic obstacles shall not be placed in the path of thoughtful believers or would-be believers. An unreconstructed doctrine of original sin could easily be such an obstacle.

Some historical background is necessary if the teaching of the *Catechism* on original sin is to be placed in a context which might explain its concerns. The central point of reference for official church teaching is the Decree on Original Sin of the Council of Trent (1546) which set out to counter the teaching of the Reformers on the radical corruption of human nature by Adam's sin. Martin Luther had written:

> In accordance with Scripture, we should speak fully and bluntly of sin — or guilt, or inward evil — as a universal corruption of nature in all its parts . . . there is nothing profitable in those things which seem good as, for instance, arts, talents, prudence, courage, chastity, and whatever natural, moral, and impressive goods there are.[18]

In response to this comprehensive indictment of fallen humanity, the Council of Trent affirmed that Adam, the first man, by his sin lost the holiness and righteousness in which he had been constituted and brought death upon himself and his descendants. His sin, 'transmitted by generation and not by imitation', is proper to each one. Consequently infants must be baptised for the remission of sins, in order that regeneration may cleanse in them what they contracted by generation. Concupiscence (the disordered condition of human appetites), which is the source of evil, remains in the baptised not as sin, but *ad agonem*, as a test and a punishment.

The Council of Trent was concerned first and foremost with the teaching of the Reformers, who, so far from impugning the doctrine of original sin, had actually given it renewed emphasis. The Council had no quarrel with the Reformers over the main lines of the doctrine, namely, the sin of Adam and Eve, the loss of original justice, the incurring of divine wrath, the punishment of death, the transmission of the first sin to all the descendants of Adam and Eve. What it wished to do, in the Decree on Original Sin and in the Decree on Justification, was to affirm the ontological reality of what happens when justification takes place. Where Luther had taught the total corruption of human beings by sin, the identification of sin with concupiscence even in the justified, and the non-imputation by God of sin to the justified, the Council affirmed the essential goodness of human nature and the restoration of supernatural life in the justified by baptism. Like St Augustine, making his case against the Manichees, it recognised that such a strong statement in favour of the essential goodness of human nature left it open to the charge of Pelagianism, and so it reproduced the teaching of the Council of Carthage (418) and the Second Council of Orange (529) in its statement that the sin of Adam is passed on 'by propagation not by imitation'. The original context of this phrase is that of the late fourth and early fifth centuries. Pelagius and his followers were stern moralists who believed that the very idea of a sin of nature, transmitted by generation, simply played into the hands of the lazy and the morally uncommitted (of whom they believed, with some evidence, there were far too many in Roman society). Augustine's famous prayer in the *Confessions, Da quod jubes et jube quod vis* ('Give [the power to fulfil] what you command and command what you will'), seemed to the Pelagians to make a fatal concession to moral passivity.

The Pelagians saw the sin of Adam as bad example; it did not alter human nature. For them the roots of sin are to be found not in human nature itself, but in the external moral environment. Trent, in rehearsing the doctrine of fallen nature, was protecting the Catholic Church from any Protestant charge of Pelagianism; it was not actually engaging with Pelagianism as such. There were few, if any, theoretical Pelagians on either side of the confessional divide in the sixteenth century.

In the centuries which followed the Reformation, there was no significant development of the doctrine. The topic of original sin flickered briefly into life with the condemnation of Michel du Bay (1513–89) and Cornelius Janssens (1585–1638). In the light of what was to come, it might be argued that Jansenism's main contribution to modern Catholic theology was Blaise Pascal's *Pensées* — a book which was to have an important influence on the theologians who produced the text of *Gaudium et Spes* of Vatican II.

The century between the two Vatican Councils witnessed the reign of the neo-scholastic manual. Since manual theology structured the thought of those who drafted the first texts sent to the bishops of Vatican II, it may be helpful if we consider the main elements of the neo-scholastic theology of original sin as it was being presented on the eve of Vatican II.

A historical pair, Adam and Eve, were created by God and placed in idyllic surroundings. They fell from grace by disobedience and were banished from paradise. Their sin inculpated not only themselves but their descendants — the entire human race — and was transmitted 'by propagation' (or 'generation'), not by imitation, as the Pelagians had claimed. One of the last of the neo-scholastic manuals expressed this somewhat crudely as follows: 'As original sin is a *peccatum naturae* [sin of nature], it is transmitted in the same way as human nature, through the natural act of generation.'[19] The result of Adam's sin is a 'wounded', but not totally corrupted, nature, involving body as well as soul, in that not only is there an absence of sanctifying grace in the soul before it has been justified, but also a loss of 'preternatural' gifts such as health, immortality, 'integrity' (absence of the need for moral struggle), which are not restored by baptism. Concupiscence, which remains in the baptised, is not to be identified with sin, but is the 'tinder of sin' (*fomes peccati*).

The language here is static and heavily essentialist. It presents grace as a 'habit' inhering in the soul. It employs two contrasting, and in some ways conflicting models:[20] (a) generation and (b) nature; and it combines them in a manner which defies coherent linguistic analysis. It is, after all, people, not natures, who are generated. Far more serious than the philosophical deficiencies of the scholastic presentation of the doctrine of original sin were the implications for it, on the one hand, of critical biblical studies which showed the literary character of Genesis and, on the other, of the scientific anthropology which pointed to the evolutionary process that preceded the arrival of *Homo sapiens* on the scene.

The *nouvelle théologie* of the 1940s saw a turn, primarily in French theology, to biblical, patristic, historical and evolutionary perspectives. In this theology existentialism rather than Aristotelianism became the dialogue partner of Christian faith, with a consequent emphasis upon the human situation in the world. The implications of this for the theology of original sin were soon to become apparent.

In the meantime Pius XII's encyclical *Humani Generis* (1950) pursued a line of thought which had become a commonplace of papal teaching since the 1860s. Pius deplored the move from interpreting reality in terms of immutable essences to what he believed was a new and dangerous preoccupation with existence, historical situatedness, relativity of doctrinal enunciations, and, in general, to a reaction against the time-honoured certainties of scholastic thought. Lack of regard for scholastic theology, according to Pius XII, leads inevitably to lack of respect for the teaching authority of the Church. Pius IX and Pius X had said the same.

The encyclical concluded with a reflection on evolution. Souls do not evolve but are directly created by God. And bodies? 'Some [people] . . . act as if the origin of the human body from preexisting and living matter were already completely certain . . . as if there were nothing in the sources of divine revelation which demanded the greatest moderation and caution in this question.'[21] The encyclical also forbade Catholics to espouse the view that after Adam there were human beings who were not descended from him, or that Adam represents a certain number of first parents. The physicalism of these affirmations is remarkable in a document otherwise characterised by a notably abstract mode of thought.

Humani Generis was the swan-song of mandatory scholasticism. Ten years later, preparations had begun for the meeting of the Second Vatican Council, at which many of the theologians disapproved of by *Humani Generis* were to be guiding lights. Pope John XXIII, very different in temperament from both his predecessors and his successors, opened the Council on a startlingly upbeat note. He wanted no condemnations or anti-world sentiments. He reflected briefly and ironically on the 'prophets of gloom' to whom, he said, he often had to listen, and he asked that the Council would open itself to the world.[22] The Council responded to his wishes. It produced a document out of its own energies (the only document, in fact, to come totally from an impetus generated on the floor of the Council itself). The Pastoral Constitution, *Gaudium et Spes*, on the Church in the Modern World, was the most characteristic document of the Council in that it represented an opening to the world which was unique in the history of the Catholic Church in modern times.

It recognised that today humankind 'substitutes a dynamic and more evolutionary concept of nature for a static one, and the result is an immense series of new problems calling for a new endeavour of analysis and synthesis'. On original sin it speaks all too briefly, though its silences are eloquent. It appears to have registered Teilhard's weary reflections on the deadening effect of the doctrine of original sin in its traditional formulation. Article 13, on sin, affirms that man has abused his freedom from the start of history: '. . . [W]hen man looks into his own heart he finds that he is drawn towards what is wrong and sunk in many evils which cannot come from his good creator.' 'Man therefore is divided in himself.' The article closes with the Pascalian observation that 'Both the high calling and the deep misery which [people] experience find their final explanation in the light of . . . Revelation'.[23]

What is quite striking here is the absence of nature/supernature language, the avoidance of reference to Romans 5, the non-specification of the moment of the fall, and the use of 'man' rather than 'Adam'.[24] Commenting on this article in 1968, Joseph Ratzinger wrote:

> . . . in view of recent debates on questions connected with the original state of man and original sin, explicit treatment of this topic was avoided. Here, too, there was agreement that the essential content of Trent cannot be abandoned, but that *theology must be left free to inquire afresh precisely what that essential content really is.*[25]

Theologians were now displaying a fresh interest in a topic which had been freed by the Council from the constraints of exclusively neo-scholastic categories. It had become possible to think about sin in the light of evolutionary theory and existentialist insights. From the traditional issues of guilt, the fall, grace and nature, the transmission of sin, and the loss of preternatural qualities, attention shifted to the 'Sin of the World' and the human experience of division within the individual and society. 'Adam' and 'Eve' could now be thought of as symbols for the whole of humanity rather than as historical people. Creation could now be seen as a continuous process within which sin is interpreted as human resistance to God's purposes. '. . . [W]hat was at the start purely a not-yet-possessing, becomes a sinful absence, because the incompletedness, in conflict with God's will, is affirmed as a positive condition', wrote one of the post-conciliar biblical scholars.[26] This insight became a corner-stone of existential exegesis of Genesis. It responds to the widely accepted critical understanding of Genesis as an aetiological myth, i.e., a myth which is constructed to account for *present* human experience. It is offered as an answer to the question: How did we come to be the people we are, morally divided and predisposed to evil? The mythological answer it offers can make our present situation intelligible, if we interpret the symbolic narrative in the present continuous tense: we humans *are being* created, *are being* tempted to eat of the tree of the knowledge of good and evil, *are succumbing* to the temptation, *are paying* the price for our failure to be what we should be, and *are being offered*, in Christ, the means of healing our wounds and of being reconciled in Christ to God our Father. This interpretation of the myth is synchronic rather than diachronic: it reads the myth as representing the *present* situation rather than as merely a history of past events.

On the morrow of the Council a catechism was commissioned by the bishops of Holland and produced by the Higher Catechetical Institute at Nijmegen. In a foreword the Dutch bishops wrote of their 'hope to present anew to adults the message which Jesus of Nazareth brought into the world'.

Their aim was to 'render faithfully the renewal which found expression in the Second Vatican Council'.[27] In its section on original sin the *New Catechism* said of the story of the fall, 'This most moving text of Scripture can never be replaced as a summary of how man stands before God. But it can and must be replaced as a description of the beginning of mankind.'[28] This expresses the new interpretative technique in a nutshell. The early chapters of Genesis are a splendid representation in mythological form of *continuing* human existence before God. They say nothing at all about biological origins and the evolutionary emergence of *homo sapiens* from earlier and less complex living species. As Karl Rahner has put it:

> For Catholic theology, therefore, 'original sin' in no way means that the moral quality of the actions of the first person or persons is transmitted to us, whether this be through a juridical imputation by God or through some kind of biological heredity, however conceived.[29]

To historicise these chapters is not merely to fly in the face of scientific and critical thought; it is actually to miss the existential (synchronic) meaning of the biblical text. The 'Dutch Catechism', as it came to be popularly known, appeared to many people to make real sense of an otherwise obsolete doctrine. It therefore spoke powerfully to many of those who had been alienated from traditional catechisms. Its authors had shown that good catechesis was able to reckon with modern scientific findings and philosophical insights while remaining faithful to church teaching sanely understood. Conservative opinion, prominently represented in high places, chose to disagree with the new approach.

A Commission of Cardinals, set up by Pope Paul VI in 1967, declared that although the *New Catechism* was excellent in many respects, it did, however, contain certain opinions 'which have disturbed many of the Christian faithful'. With regard to original sin the Commission directed that the *New Catechism* should make clear that man, in rebelling against God from the beginning of history, lost for himself and his descendants the holiness and righteousness in which he had been placed. Adam transmitted to all 'a real state of sin through the propagation of human nature'. The *New Catechism* should avoid the sort of language which can be taken to mean that individual human beings contract original sin only because they are exposed from the start to the influence of human society where sin reigns.[30]

The Supplement to A New Catechism appeared in the following year.[31] Comparison of the amended with the original text is instructive. The amended text tried to adopt the style of the *New Catechism*, which was an exercise in open communication with thoughtful believers and would-be believers, but it failed to conceal an inquisitorial tone and a preoccupation with precisely those elements of the traditional doctrine which gratuitously invite incredulity today.

The Decaration of the Commission of Cardinals and the *Supplement to A New Catechism* indicate with remarkable accuracy the lines along which the *Catechism of the Catholic Church* would be composed. One notes with interest that original sin received a far greater proportion of attention than any other topic in the *Supplement*. It takes up nineteen pages. No other topic, including Christological and trinitarian doctrines, comes remotely near the extent of this coverage. One can only wonder why this should be. Evidently the teaching of the Council of Trent loomed large in the minds of all who were concerned in the production of the *Supplement*. Not for the first time a 'teaching of the magisterium' is seen as having to be defended at all costs and without hermeneutical nuance. Its defence witnesses to the tendency to reduce all doctrinal matters ultimately to the issue of ecclesiastical authority. It is less *what* the Council teaches than *that* it teaches it which matters. This is why Vatican II's concept of the hierarchy of truths is so important. It breaks with the integralism of the period between the two Vatican Councils. Integralism was (and apparently still is) a conception of theological orthodoxy which views the network of Catholic doctrines as an indivisible *whole*, and a divinely guaranteed whole at that. The true integralist sees no need to grade doctrines in terms of their importance to Christian revelation as a whole or to make any concessions to the process of interpretation.

The problem is a hermeneutical one: how are doctrines of the Church to be interpreted in a way which takes into account their historical and cultural limitations without rendering them obsolete in later ages? The doctrine of original sin is a particularly apt and uncomfortable illustration of the problem. The members of the Council of Trent followed their predecessors in historicising the early chapters of Genesis and in treating them as sources of factual information about creation and sin. The Tridentine doctrine of the fall together with the biological transmission of a damaged nature is inescapably tied to a literal and historical interpretation of Genesis. What therefore happens to that doctrine when such an interpretation of Genesis loses its credibility? Instead of facing up to this question, the authors of the *Catechism* (like the authors of the *Supplement* to the Dutch Catechism) fudge the biblical issues in order, as they see it, to defend the Tridentine formulation.

What had become apparent long before the *Catechism of the Catholic Church* was commissioned was the existence in the Church of two different, and at times conflicting, methodologies which formulate and attempt answers to different questions and different concerns, and do so in two different languages.

The *Catechism* on original sin represents a total victory for the pre-Vatican II mentality. Its authors make no effort even to *seem* to recognise that there are serious problems involved in the Tridentine and neo-scholastic formulation of the doctrine. One must, of course, be grateful that there are no condemnations. This new tactic, however, has probably more to do with image than with substance. The policy of the authors would seem to be to state the doctrine in its traditional formulation and simply ignore what has been going on in Catholic theology since Vatican II. In short, it is as if the reactionary minority at the Council had returned and had decided to write a text which makes no concessions to any viewpoint but their own.

The *Catechism* affirms the presence in human history of sin, which manifests itself 'as humanity's rejection of God and opposition to him' (386). The following paragraph points to our need of revelation in order to recognise sin as sin and not as merely 'a developmental flaw, a psychological weakness, a mistake, or the necessary consequence of an inadequate social structure, etc.'. That sin is *revealed* is an important truth expressed in Pauline teaching, reproduced here as a heading in the text: that where sin abounded, grace has abounded all the more. Revelation of the remedy takes precedence over revelation of the disease — an insight nicely reflected in the sentence 'We must know Christ as the source of grace in order to know Adam as the source of sin' (388).

All shades of theological opinion in the Church could respond positively to these opening passages; but this happy situation ends abruptly with 390. This is one of the paragraphs which make a vague concession to the use of figurative language in Genesis. Having made the concession, however, the paragraph goes on to claim that the fall in Genesis 3 was 'a primeval event, a deed that took place *at the beginning of the history of man*'. The French text of the *Catechism* reads '. . . un fait qui a eu lieu au commencement de l'histoire de l'homme'. The footnote reference here is to *Gaudium et Spes* 13. *Gaudium et Spes*, however, expressly avoids speaking of a primeval event taking place at the beginning of human history. The conciliar text says that man has abused his freedom *from the very beginning of history*. The Latin text reads . . . *inde ab exordio historiae, libertate sua abusus est* . . . The French, which was the original conciliar text, reads 'Etabli par Dieu dans un état de justice, l'homme, séduit par le Malin, dès le début de l'histoire, a abusé sa liberté . . .' Joseph Ratzinger's 1968 commentary on this article makes it plain that reference to a primeval event was expressly avoided; nor was Romans 5 in the Vulgate cited (*in quo omnes peccaverunt*). These silences are highly significant.

The *Catechism* now turns to the fall of the angels. The dismayed reader may begin to wonder what is happening here as we are once more plunged back into the realm of apocalyptic mythology reduced to flat statement. 'The Church teaches that Satan was at first a good angel, made by God' (391). The best the *Catechism* can do here is to produce a quotation from the Fourth Lateran Council (1215) in support of its contention. Only die-hard integralists will attempt to defend this literalised myth as pertaining to the core values of Catholic faith. The rest of us may draw some solace from Vatican II's doctrine of the hierarchy of truths. About the fallen angels we are told 'It is the *irrevocable* character of their choice, and not a defect in the infinite divine mercy, that makes the angels' sin unforgivable' (393). Announcing what God can and cannot do is presumptuous at the best of times, unless we are talking about logical contradictions; not even the most enthusiastic champion of eternal damnation, however, could claim that forgiveness of fallen angels entails a logical contradiction.

Putting this kind of thing in a modern catechism is simply incomprehensible; as is the remark that Satan's action in the world 'may cause grave injuries — of a spiritual nature and, indirectly, even of a physical nature' (395). Is this a reference to psychosomatic illness or to the kind of demonic activity often diagnosed by fundamentalists?

After this demonological interlude the *Catechism* returns to the Garden of Eden, where it finds something symbolic in the tree of the knowledge of good and evil, and having done so, rapidly reverts to a literal reading (396). Tempted by the devil, our first parents disobeyed God and lost the grace of original holiness (399). They also lost the harmony bestowed by original justice in which the soul had perfect control over the body. Relations between men and women were henceforth marked by 'lust and domination' (400).

As a result of the fall, '*death makes its entrance into human history*'. Writing in 1968, Joseph Ratzinger remarked, in reference to the view that human beings would have been immune from bodily death had they not sinned,

> This thesis in its classical dogmatic form is scarcely intelligible to present-day thought, but could be made so by means of an existential analysis of the constitutive features of human life which established a distinction between death as a natural phenomenon and death as seen in the personal categories proper to human life.[32]

The *Catechism* makes no such existential analysis, but leaves the bald statement, that in consequence of sin 'death makes its entrance into human history', to be taken literally as a natural phenomenon, and therefore in a form scarcely intelligible to present-day thought. *Gaudium et Spes* 13 is cited against the grain of its intended meaning. Romans 5 is cited twice, but Romans 7 (with its theme of inner division, so influential in *Gaudium et Spes*, especially GS 10) is not cited at all in this sub-section which reaffirms the transmission of original sin and states that this transmision 'is a mystery that we cannot fully understand' (404). Perhaps we could understand it a little better if we tried some of that existential analysis mentioned by Joseph Ratzinger.

By its commitment to interpreting the Genesis myth as history, and the transmission of Adam's sin as biological, the *Catechism* denies itself the opportunity of presenting a realistic estimate of the shadow side of human beings, of the societies they form, and of the history they both inherit and create.

It does refer to the Johannine 'sin of the world', which it sees as the product of original sin and of all the personal sins of humanity. 'This expression can also refer to the negative influence exerted on people by communal situations and social structures that are the fruit of men's sins' (408). This belated and laconic sentence is the nearest the *Catechism* comes to taking any notice of the vast amount of work done by Catholic theologians on original sin over the past three decades. (As we have seen, some of the earlier part of this work was reflected in the Dutch Catechism.)

G. Vandervelde, in his book *Original Sin: Two Major Trends in Contemporary Roman Catholic Reinterpretation*, asks why this 'explosion of literature on the doctrine of original sin' should have occurred as an almost exclusively Roman Catholic phenomenon.[33] He suggests, as one reason, that Protestant theology of sin is so radically bound up with its theological anthropology that the doctrine of *original* sin is 'less amenable to separate treatment', whereas the Catholic view of original sin is so tied in with its 'Adamic framework' that a major crisis is likely 'to be triggered by a changed view of human origins'.[34] The principal reason, however, is the climate created by the Second Vatican Council and by Pope John XXIII's celebrated distinction between the substance of a doctrine and the manner of its formulation. Pope John and his Council encouraged Catholic theology to break out of its medieval and Counter-Reformation enclosure and to measure itself with hope against the realities of the modern world. The result has been a crop of theories of original sin which Vandervelde classifies as 'personalist' and 'situationist'.

The personalist view reduces original sin to the *factual* universality of actual sins. Human beings are *de facto* sinners. This view thus dispenses with the quest for origins, either biological or anthropological, but seems to underestimate the depth dimension in human experience which evinces a predisposition towards sin.

The situationist view reflects the existentialist concerns of theologians such as Karl Rahner and Piet Schoonenberg who interpret men and women as historical beings who are related in freedom to their human environment. To be human, in this theological anthropology, is to be situated in a world which is sinful because it is the product of a sinful history. The strength of the situationist interpretation is that it de-privatises morality and takes socio-political sin with due seriousness. Its weakness is that it leaves itself open to the charge of Pelagian environmentalism, unless it takes especial care to make clear its recognition that the human tendency towards sin is antecedent to environmental exposure.

The move towards identification of original sin with the sin of the world has contributed greatly to a revitalisation of the doctrine of original sin, giving it badly needed contemporary credibility by breaking with the genetic and nature models (both of which are employed in the *Catechism*).

Environmental theories, however, are, in the last analysis, theories about *extrinsic* forces rather than about the *inherent* predisposition in human beings towards sin. The sin of the world and human environmental influences and pressures would be powerless if there was nothing intrinsic in human beings upon which they could act. This is the essential gravamen of the case against Pelagianism (though whether the fifth-century Pelagians themselves were guilty of it is quite another matter). We do not need to employ the genetic and nature models in order to safeguard the doctrinal truth that we are in need of redemption even *before* we are exposed to a sinful environment. Still less do we need to literalise and historicise the various myths which have been employed to express our human alienation from God and from our fellow human beings. Thus when the *Catechism* observes 'Ignorance of the fact that man has a wounded nature inclined to evil gives rise to serious errors in the areas of education, politics, social action and morals' (407), it is expressing in essentialist language a truth which can be expressed equally well otherwise without any loss to its doctrinal integrity.

What, then, are we to make of the assertion that 'the devil has acquired a certain domination over man' (407)? One is instantly put in mind of the 'devil's rights' or 'transaction' myth of atonement which flourished in patristic and early medieval times until it was dismissed by St Anselm. Is this what the text intends to suggest? If so, it does not tell us. The devil has been introduced to us as a fallen angel. How does he — 'he': one suspects that feminists will not be unduly disturbed to see him portrayed as a male! — exercise this 'certain domination'? Anselm, one feels, would have had a problem with the *Catechism*. It was Anselm who demythologised the devil's rights myth with the simple remark that he could not see what force it had.[35] The devil cannot have rights as a claim against God. However, the *Catechism* talks not about rights but about 'domination'. Does this amount to a significant difference?

To make the devil in any sense God's *vis-à-vis* is to advance down the road towards Gnostic dualism. The strange thing is that the *Catechism* does not appear to invoke Anselm's theory of satisfaction, which replaced the 'transaction' theory and went on to become the prevailing Catholic theory of redemption. It would seem that the *Catechism*'s preoccupation with the devil has served as a diversion away from the traditionally Catholic theory of satisfaction. This is an intriguing departure from the guidance given by the Commission of Cardinals in 1968: 'The elements of the doctrine of Christ's satisfaction which form part of the faith should be clearly given.'[36] The concept of satisfaction presents its own problems in respect of its implications for our image of God; but we are spared them by the fact that the authors of the *Catechism* have opted for a demonological interpretation of the contest between good and evil, thereby safeguarding the Tridentine formulation, which is quoted to the effect that original sin leads to 'captivity under the power of him who thenceforth had the power of death, that is, the devil' (407, with reference given to DS 1511). Since Trent, however, combines the myth of the devil's domination with the satisfaction theory, a desire by the authors of the *Catechism* to protect Tridentine teaching can hardly be the main reason for their demonological preoccupation. What, then, *is* the reason?

It would be naive to suppose that writing catechisms is an apolitical act. Perhaps the real key to understanding the strange preoccupation with devils is the 'restoration' programme now being mounted by ultra-conservative elements in the Church. According to this perspective on Church and world, there is a war to be fought. The enemy must be identified, named, and challenged. The forces of light must guard against any softness or any giving of comfort to the enemy, least of all to the effete 'liberals' within its own ranks. We are dealing here with what has been aptly named 'a green beret church', and it will find a congenial theology in these pages of the *Catechism*. Its members will not be at all disturbed by primitive demonology or historicised myths. This is their catechism. Others will have to pay the price for their fundamentalism and their wilful medievalism.

We have been told that this is the catechism of the Second Vatican Council, just as the Roman Catechism was the catechism of the Council of Trent. On the topic of original sin the *Catechism of the Catholic Church* is far removed not merely in spirit from, but even according to the letter of, Vatican II. The *Catechism* (409) cites from *Gaudium et Spes* 37. This conciliar article was much disputed on the council floor and recast several times. In its final form it reflected conservative *modi* (amendments). The *Catechism* quotes its most negative passage to the effect that 'The whole of man's history has been the story of dour combat with the powers of evil . . .' (409). There was a feeling at the time among some that the Council was taking too rosy a view of the world and was thus evincing too little awareness of the reality of sin. Those who drafted the text of *Gaudium et Spes* accepted the partial validity of some of these criticisms and made accommodating emendations to the conciliar text. They were, however, unwilling to allow conservative pessimism and negativity to divert them from Pope John XXIII's vision of a Church open to, and joyfully at work in, the contemporary world. *Gaudium et Spes* remains a powerful statement of joy and affirmation in spite of its eirenic concessions to the conservative minority — a courtesy not reciprocated by the authors of the *Catechism*. This mood, however, did not survive into the period which followed, when that minority had once again regained curial power. The distinguished church historian Giuseppe Alberigo reflects sombrely on the post-conciliar period:

> Recent years have seen a surprising revival of positions that were characteristic of more conservative circles of the Roman Curia and the episcopate in the 1960s. There has been, in other words, a clear return to attitudes that Vatican II unequivocally disavowed and overcame, attitudes that had found refuge in tiny groups of nostalgic individuals. A pessimistic vision of history, poisoned by Manichaeism, seems to be spreading abroad. There is a rejection of the Council's call to the churches to become once again pilgrims and missionaries, as though it implied the abandonment of tradition, and, finally, a revival of the 'closed' ecclesiology of the post-tridentine period in which the Church is a fortified castle, jealous of its own purity and bristling with condemnations.[37]

Alberigo's reference to Manichaeism is thought-provoking. The heavy emphasis placed by the *Catechism* on the devil and on the struggle between good and evil underwrites the programme of 'restoration' which has been mounted by the hard right in today's Catholic Church. We are back to the language of strife, to the notion of the Church 'as an island of grace in a world given over to sin'.[38] The section of the *Catechism* dealing with original sin seems to have been designed specifically to support the revanchist programme which is being imposed on the Church of today. According to this programme, 'The world is falling into misery, division, and violence. It is manifestly under the power of the Evil One.'[39]

While *Gaudium et Spes* may have taken too wide-eyed and optimistic a view of the contemporary world, one must remember that it was deliberately trying to offset a long history of entrenched gloom, by responding to the invitation of a joyful and hopeful Pope who actually loved the world which was being condemned by the conservative minority at the Council. The *Catechism* clearly does not see its task in the positive spirit of Vatican II, and it makes no concessions to the millions of Catholics who find themselves much nearer to the spirit of Vatican II than to the programme of 'restoration'.

In quoting passages from *Gaudium et Spes* which are least typical of its spirit, the authors of the *Catechism* pay that remarkable conciliar document an unintended compliment. Readers who follow up the references and put them into their context will discover a view of sin and salvation, Christ and culture, and Church and world alternative to that presented in the *Catechism*. It could prove to be a reassuring and liberating discovery; for by any ecclesial criterion, even the most conservative, a conciliar document takes precedence over a catechism.

Notes

1   Maurice Blondel, *The Letter on Apologetics and History and Dogma*, texts presented and trans. Alexander Dru and Illtyd Trethowan (London, 1964), pp. 129–31.
2   Apostolic Constitution *Fidei Depositum* (FD), p. xiv (= *Catechism*, p. 5).
3   C. P. Snow, *The Two Cultures: And a Second Look* (Cambridge, 1964). See also P. Medawar, *The Limits of Science* (Oxford, 1986), pp. 11–12.
4   *Origins* 21.27 (12 December 1991), p. 429.
5   See D. J. Hall, 'The integrity of creation: biblical and theological background of the term' in *Reintegrating God's Creation* (Geneva, 1987), p. 34.
6   P. Ricoeur, 'Evil, a challenge to philosophy and theology' in R. L. Hart (ed.), *Trajectories in the Study of Religion: Addresses at the Seventy-Fifth Anniversary of the American Academy of Religion* (Atlanta, GA, 1987), p. 68.
7   Augustine, *Enchiridion*, III, 11.
8   See J. Hick, *Evil and the God of Love* (London, 1985), pp. 82–9.
9   K. Rahner and H. Vorgrimler, *Concise Theological Dictionary* (London, 1965), p. 21.
10 As translated by Helen Waddell in *Medieval Latin Lyrics* (Harmondsworth: Penguin Books, 1952), p. 177.

11 *Baptism, Eucharist and Ministry*, Faith and Order Paper No. 111 (Geneva: WCC, 1982), p. 10.

12 F. Heer, *The Intellectual History of Europe* (London, 1966), p. 441.

13 M. Polanyi, *Personal Knowledge: Towards a Post-Critical Philosophy* (London, 1973), p. 393.

14 P. Ricoeur, *The Symbolism of Evil* (London, 1967), p. 239.

15 FD, p. xv.

16 P. Teilhard de Chardin, *Christianity and Evolution* (London, 1971), p. 188. 'Reflections on original sin' (pp. 187–98) was written in 1947 and 'offered for professional theological comment' (p. 187).

17 Ibid., p. 188.

18 Cited in P. Hodgson and R. King (eds), *Readings in Christian Theology* (London, 1985), p. 181.

19 L. Ott, *Fundamentals of Catholic Dogma* (Cork, 1962), p. 111. Consultation of this last of the neo-scholastic textbooks will provide revealing instances of where the *Catechism* has reverted to pre-conciliar modes of theological thinking.

20 A model is 'a sustained and systematic metaphor' (S. McFague, *Metaphorical Theology: Models of God in Religious Language* (London, 1983), p. 67). Models enable us to speak about God and God's dealings with human beings through analogies borrowed from human experience. Models are not literary embellishments; they are alternatives to silence.

21 *Some False Opinions Which Threaten to Undermine the Foundations of Catholic Doctrine* (Vatican, 1950), p. 14; Latin text DS 3896.

22 W. M. Abbott (ed.), *The Documents of Vatican II* (London, 1966), p. 712.

23 Austin Flannery (ed.), *Vatican Council II: The Conciliar and Past Conciliar Documents* (Dublin: Dominican Publications, 1975), p. 914.

24 'Man' causes problems today from the standpoint of sexist language, but in the context of the theology of creation and the fall its use in *Gaudium et Spes* is highly significant and marks a palpable advance.

25 H. Vorgrimler (ed.), *Commentary on the Documents of Vatican II*, vol. V (London, 1969), p. 125; emphasis added.

26 A. Hulsbosch, *God's Creation: Creation, Sin and Redemption in an Evolving World* (London, 1965), p. 50.

27 *A New Catechism: Catholic Faith for Adults* (London, 1967), p. v.

28 Ibid., pp. 262–3.

29 K. Rahner, *Foundations of Christian Faith: An Introduction to the Idea of Christianity* (London, 1978), p.111.

30 *Acta Apostolicae Sedis* 60 (1968), pp. 685–91.

31 E. Dhanis and J. Visser, *The Supplement to A New Catechism* (London, 1969).

32 Vorgrimler, *Commentary*, vol. V, p. 141.

33 G. Vandervelde, *Original Sin: Two Major Trends in Contemporary Roman Catholic Reinterpretation* (Amsterdam, 1975), p. 44.

34 Ibid., pp. 44–5.

35 Anselm, *Cur Deus Homo*, I.7.

36 AAS 60 (1968), p. 688; *Supplement*, p. 27.

37 G. Alberigo et al. (eds), *The Reception of Vatican II* (Tunbridge Wells, 1987), pp. 21–2.

38 A. Dulles, 'The reception of Vatican II at the Extraordinary Synod of 1985', ibid., p. 353.

39 Dulles, ibid., p. 353.

The Incarnation of the Son of God

(Paragraphs 422–511)

Jacques Dupuis SJ

Gregorian University, Rome

Christianity, it has been said, is not a 'religion of the book', but of a person. Hence, '"At the heart of catechesis we find, in essence, a Person, the Person of Jesus of Nazareth, the only Son from the Father . . . who suffered and died for us and who now, after rising, is living with us forever." To catechize is "to reveal in the Person of Christ the whole of God's eternal design reaching fulfilment in that Person. It is to seek to understand the meaning of Christ's actions and words and of the signs worked by him"' (426; cf. CT 5). This centrality of the mystery of Jesus Christ is clearly marked in the introduction to Part One, Section Two, Chapter Two of the *Catechism* (422–429). This centrality of Christ is indeed so true that 'everything else is taught with reference to him' (427; cf. CT 6). Earlier the *Catechism* has also said of the mystery of the Trinity of God that it is 'the central mystery of Christian faith and life' (234). Clearly, what is intended is that both mysteries are inseparable and constitute an indivisible whole. To show their intimate connection even better, it could have been explained that the mystery of God's inner life is manifested to us as God's self-revelation and self-gift in his incarnate Son. This is why 'Catechesis aims at putting "people . . . in communion . . . with Jesus Christ: only he can lead us to the love of the Father in the Spirit and make us share in the life of the Holy Trinity"' (426; cf. CT 6).

One question, however, arises from the outset: Does the centrality of the person of Jesus Christ stand out clearly from the *Catechism*'s general structure and development? One cannot fail to note a great difference between the space allotted to the triune God and the Christ-event on the one hand (199–267; 422–682) and to the Church and the sacraments on the other (748–975; 1210–1690). Admittedly, the importance of a doctrine is not necessarily gauged by the space given it; however, its place in the 'hierarchy of truths' that characterises Catholic doctrine, recalled by Vatican II (UR 11) and which the *Catechism* mentions explicitly (90), depends on a doctrine's relation to 'the foundation of the Christian faith' which in the Council's mind is the mystery of Christ.[1] Admittedly, the relationship of particular doctrines to the mystery of Christ is indicated everywhere in the *Catechism*. Yet would not the living centre of the faith have deserved a proportionately larger statement than it has been allotted?

It is true that the *Catechism* speaks of Jesus Christ explicitly in many places other than the section formally devoted to the Christological mystery. But this practice is not without adverse consequences where a complete presentation of the Christ-event is concerned. For this procedure results in a certain fragmentation. Many elements belonging to the mystery of the person of Jesus Christ have to be looked for in other sections. To give some examples: Jesus, fullness of divine revelation, is to be sought in the section on revelation (65–67); Jesus, revealer of the Father, is found in the doctrine of the Trinity (238–242; cf. 516); Jesus' humanity anointed with the Holy Spirit is reported in the section on the Spirit (727–730); Jesus, consecrated as the Christ by the Spirit in the mystery of the incarnation (with reference to Ps 2:6–7), is also mentioned in connection with the doctrine of the Spirit (745); Christ, unique Word of the Scriptures, is to be looked for under the section on sacred Scripture (101–104); the prayer of Jesus comes under Part Four on prayer (2599–2606).

We should add to these observations the fact that other aspects of the mystery of Christ's person, notably some belonging to Jesus' human psychology, are postponed till the *Catechism*'s later section on the 'mysteries' of his life, which lies beyond the scope of the present study. Examples are: Jesus and Israel's faith in the God of the Old Testament (587–591); his human freedom (609); his temptation (538–540); his suffering and agony (612); his sense of abandonment (603); his identification with the poor (544). Later, we will take note of some other Christological themes to which attention has not been paid explicitly. Such atomisation, while it makes for analytic clarity, is less apt to convey a synthetic picture of Jesus' person.

The avowed aim of the *Catechism* is to present 'an organic synthesis of the essential and fundamental contents of Catholic doctrine' (11). Where the incarnation of the Son of God is concerned, the impression is, however, created of a set of truths to be believed or held, rather than of an event to be proclaimed. One distinguishes with difficulty the essentials from the non-essentials. In sum, the content is more informative than inspirational. It may be regretted that, while the *Catechism* refers frequently to Vatican II, the great Christological texts of *Gaudium et Spes* (22 §2; 32 §§2–4; 45 §2) — all three, inspirational — though referred to piecemeal (for GS 22 §2 see 470, 521, 618; for GS 45 §2 see 450), have not been quoted at length. These texts express, more felicitously than do abstract formulations, Jesus' unity with humankind, his true identity and solidarity with us, as well as the central place and meaning of the Christ for human beings and their history.

The structure of the *Catechism*'s chapter on Jesus Christ is expounded in 429. Following Article 2 of the Apostles' Creed, it first explains the name of Jesus and the titles attributed to him in the NT (422–455). Then

113

follows Article 3, in which the mystery of the incarnation is first expounded (456–483), followed by his birth from the Virgin Mary (484–511) and the 'mysteries' of Jesus' hidden life (512–534) and public life (535–570). Articles 4 and 5 are devoted to the mysteries of Jesus' passover (571–658), and Articles 6 and 7 to those of his glorification (659–682). The present study is limited to Article 2 and the first two sections of Article 3 (422–511). It includes the titles of Jesus and the mystery of the incarnation as well as his birth from the Virgin Mary. Hence the two parts of the exposition: Christology and Mariology. Special attention will be paid here to the *Catechism*'s handling of the biblical data and of the genesis of the Christological faith in the NT and beyond.

I. Christology

The *Catechism* affirms that the resurrection of Jesus 'shows' that he was truly the Son of God (653), that 'only in the Paschal mystery can the believer give the title "Son of God" its full meaning' (444); and that in Pentecost the mystery of the Trinity has been fully revealed (732). It cites the admirable passage in which Gregory of Nazianzus shows the progressive revelation of the three divine persons, from the OT down to Pentecost (684). Yet the *Catechism* fails to give to the Easter experience of the disciples its full weight in the genesis of their Christological faith. It insists, for instance, on reading in Matthew 16:16 — without referring to the parallel texts of Mark 8:29 and Luke 9:2 — a profession of faith on the part of Peter in the 'transcendent character of the Messiah's divine sonship' (443; cf. 442–443, 424), even though Peter's recognition of Jesus' Messiahship suffices to explain Jesus' proclamation of his blessedness (Mt 16:17). Biblical scholarship today stresses with vigour the decisive influence of Jesus' resurrection on the making of the Christological faith of the disciples, an influence without which much of the gospel evidence would remain unexplained. Whatever they may have perceived earlier of his mystery fell short of the recognition of his divinity which they first truly perceived when faced with the risen Lord in whose glorified humanity the divine condition began to shine forth.[2]

The *Catechism*, on the contrary, tends to underestimate the path which the disciples had to travel in order to reach in their Easter experience a realisation in faith of Jesus' divine condition — a faith that passed through the crisis of total despondency brought about by the showdown of the cross. The disciples' slowness to believe and the long path through which their faith was finally born is of high pastoral relevance for the genesis of the faith of believers even today; therefore it should be of high value for catechesis.

The *Catechism*, however, undervalues this process of faith and, consequently, tends to level up the gospel texts concerning the person of Jesus to the high level of those in which his personal identity as the Son of God is clearly expressed, without due account for the different contexts and without distinguishing adequately different levels of comprehension.

114

Though the introduction to the *Catechism* mentions explicitly the three levels of composition of the Gospels recognised by Vatican II (DV 18) (125), the Gospels seem to be treated here as pure historical reporting. The method followed in reading them consists in searching for 'proof-texts' for the faith affirmation in the divinity of Jesus Christ. In the process the gospel and NT evidence about Jesus becomes a unitary historical account in which little attention is paid to the distinction to be made between pre-Easter or implicit Christology (Jesus' own self-awareness and revelation, and the disciples' understanding of their Master during his earthly life) and post-Easter or explicit Christology (the apostolic Church's Easter faith in Christ and its development through the NT writings).

No notice is taken of the redactional influence of the Easter faith on the gospel accounts, of the process of 'retrojection' that introduces the Easter faith into those accounts, nor of the real divergences that exist between the various accounts due to the authors' different intentions. The words attributed to Jesus are sometimes taken, without due caution, as the *ipsissima verba*. No account is given either of the plurality of NT Christologies. In particular, no attention is paid to the real development which took place from the Easter Christology 'from below', characteristic of the early apostolic kerygma, to the later, deeper perceptions 'from above' concerning the personal identity of Jesus as the Son of God incarnate, which may be said to culminate in the Gospel of John, notably in the Prologue. Here too a levelling up takes place which is more apologetic than historical, more dogmatic than biblical. The result is a uniform, incarnational, 'from above', model of Christology, directly in touch with the professions of faith and the Christological councils, but less so with the biblical evidence. These general observations, however, need to be substantiated in some detail.[3]

1. The titles of Jesus

The biblical Christology article opens with an account of the name 'Jesus' and of the main titles given him in the NT: Christ, 'the Only Son of God', Lord (430–455).[4] Necessary as it was to explain the meaning of the name and titles, the article turns out to build a 'title Christology' with a certain lack of sensitivity to the critical questions posed by them: did Jesus use them of himself, or were they used of him by others? If so, before or after Easter? With or without reference to OT prophecies; and in what sense and with which meaning? Distinctions are called for here.

Jesus. The meaning of the name is explained. It could, however, have been stated more plainly that: (1) the name expresses the function; (2) the name stands for the person. Had this been done, some intricate formulations would have been avoided. According to Matthew 1:21 it is Jesus, not God in him, who 'will save his [God's] people from their sins' (430). That in Jesus God 'recapitulates all of his history of salvation on behalf of men' is, of course, true. This leading thread and fundamental key of interpretation would have deserved ample development at an early stage (cf. 450). The *Catechism* does in fact develop a history of revelation, with its various stages, culminating in Jesus Christ who is the fullness of revelation (54–67); there the covenant with Noah offers an opportunity to say something about the religions of the nations (56–58), but nowhere is a coherent evaluation of those religions found in the *Catechism*. It should, in any case, not be supposed that the history of salvation begins with the liberation of Israel from Egypt (431); it embraces in fact the entire history of humankind. With reference to Philippians 2:9–10 it is said that 'it is the name of Jesus that fully manifests the supreme power of the "name which is above every name"' (434); what the text, however, says is that in exalting him God *conferred upon* Jesus 'the name which is above every name', that is the name *Kurios* (cf. Phil 2:11).

Christ. The origin and meaning of this term in the OT is explained. Why Jesus accepted it only with some reluctance when it was proposed by others (439) is also mentioned. What, however, is Jesus' *'eternal messianic consecration'* which is *revealed* during the time of his earthly life (438)? Acts 10:38, to which reference is made, speaks of Jesus' messianic anointing in his baptism (cf. also 453) — while, elsewhere, the *Catechism* pushes the anointing back to the incarnation itself (486; 745). Yet, according to the early kerygma, as represented by Peter's discourse on the day of Pentecost, 'God has *made* [Jesus] both Lord and *Christ*' in his resurrection (Acts 2:36). To say that he had been *revealed* as such in his resurrection (440) is to understate the real transformation of Jesus' humanity as he passes to the risen state, and the real conferring upon him by God of the fullness of his messianic power.

The Only Son of God. The *Catechism* recognises that in the OT 'Son of God' is often used with a metaphorical meaning which implies only an adoptive sonship — including the case of the Davidic king in whom the messianic expectation rests (441) — and that not all those in the Gospels who called Jesus 'Son of God' meant anything more by the title (441).[5] Yet, used of Jesus in NT Christology, the title is uniformly interpreted to convey the divine Sonship in the ontological meaning. The profession of faith by Peter in Matthew 16:16 has already been mentioned (cf. 442). It must also be recognised that in the early kerygma the title 'Son of God' is applied to the risen Jesus with a messianic meaning, as we see in the use made of the enthronement psalm, 2:7 (cf. Acts 13:32–33) (cf. 653): Jesus' resurrection at the hands of God is his enthronement as messianic king. Only progressively will the title take on its full ontological meaning. Even if 'from the beginning' the acknowledgement of Christ's divine Sonship was the 'centre of the apostolic faith' (cf. 442), it need not have been from the start expressed with the title 'Son of God'. Jesus had revealed himself as 'Son' related in a unique manner to the God he called 'Father'. The *Catechism* rightly refers to the 'hymn of jubilation' (Mt 11:27) — which would have been worth quoting in view of its special importance as evidence — to Matthew 24:36 and to the parable of the wicked tenants (Mt 21:34) (443).[6] Surprisingly no reference is made here

116

to Jesus' way of relating to God, his Father, as *Abba* (Mk 14:36), which later on the *Catechism* will understand as expressing the 'intimate and immediate knowledge' he had of his Father (473). This intimate knowledge flows from a personal relationship.

Less convincing is the mention made here of Jesus' baptism and transfiguration, where the reference in the theophany is to the Servant of God (Is 42:1), the anointed one in whom God 'is well pleased' (Mt 3:17; 17:5) (444; cf. also 422 on Jesus' baptism in Mk 1:11). That in John's Gospel Jesus' divine Sonship is understood as ontological is, of course, certain (Jn 3:16, 18; 1:11) as the term *monogenēs* makes clear (444). However, in Romans 1:3–4 the divine Sonship is to be found in v. 3 ('his Son'), while in v. 4 Jesus' designation as 'Son of God with power' refers once more to the fullness of messianic power conferred upon him through his resurrection from the dead, not as such to his divine origin in God: this is not a 'designation' of Sonship on the part of God (445; cf. 648), but a conferring of power on Christ's risen humanity.

Lord. The *Catechism* affirms that in the Greek OT the name YHWH is rendered by *Kurios* and that the NT uses the title Lord 'in this full sense' not only for the Father but for Jesus, who is 'thereby recognized as God Himself' (446). Distinctions need, however, to be made here. The title 'Lord' does not always have this strongest meaning wherever it is used of Jesus in the NT; nor can Jesus be seen too easily as identified with 'God', for this term is mostly used in the NT to designate the Father.

The *Catechism* rightly notes that the title 'Lord' addressed to Jesus is often on the part of his interlocutors a mere sign of respect (448). What it does not mention is that its use either by Jesus himself or by NT Christology at times expresses Messiahship rather than divinity. Such is the case in Jesus' controversy with the Pharisees (Mt 22:41–46), as is made clear by the quotation from a messianic psalm of enthronement (Ps 110:1) (447). The early kerygma of the apostolic Church will keep to the messianic meaning of the same Psalm 110 and apply it to Jesus' investiture with power in his resurrection (cf. Acts 2:34–35; cf. Heb 1:13). That Jesus' works of power showed his 'divine sovereignty' is true; but again it must be noted that the early kerygma assigned them in the first instance to God working through him (Acts 2:22). In the infancy narratives in the Gospel of Luke, Elizabeth's words about the 'mother of my Lord' (Lk 1:43) and the proclamation of Jesus as 'Christ the Lord' by the angels (Lk 2:11) could also be messianic. Or do they show a 'retrojection' of the divine title on the part of Luke (448)?

In any case, the divine title is much clearer in John 20:28 and 21:7 (448). It may be noted that Thomas's profession of faith — characteristically after the resurrection — is the first profession of faith about Jesus in which the term 'God' is added to that of 'Lord' (Jn 20:28) — witnessing to the use which is probably proper to John of the term *theos* applied to Jesus (cf. Jn 1:1, 18; 1 Jn 5:20). The same usage is unclear in the various passages of Paul sometimes cited in its favour, among which Romans 9:5 and Titus 2:13 are referred to here (449).[7] That in his pre-existence Jesus

Christ was in 'the form of God' is clearly affirmed by the Christological hymn used by Paul in Philippians 2:6. But again, according to the second part of the hymn it is not simply a question of the divine 'manifestation' of Jesus' sovereignty but of his being constituted *Kurios* in his humanity through his resurrection from the dead (Phil 2:9–11) — where the hymn links up with the Easter Christology of the early kerygma) (cf. Acts 2:36) (449).

In summing up the article on Jesus' titles, the *Catechism* aptly refers to John for the title 'Son of God' as conveying the 'unique and eternal relationship of Jesus Christ to God his Father' (454). It is less convincing when it cites Acts 8:37 to the effect that 'To be a Christian, one must believe that Jesus Christ is the Son of God' (454). This text, as is well known, is not authentic; it represents an ancient gloss preserved in the Western text, inspired by the baptismal liturgy.

2. The incarnation

As will have been noticed, the *Catechism*'s interpretation of the titles applied to Jesus in the NT not rarely tends to pull them unduly towards his divinity where a more sober reading would see in them his messianic investiture through resurrection. Justice is not done thereby to the Easter Christology 'from below' characteristic of the early kerygma. Instead, a 'from above' Christology tends to be read everywhere from the outset, as though it represented the only NT Christological model. The next section of the *Catechism* (456–463) will further develop the 'incarnation' model of NT Christology, from the pre-existence of the divine person to his human becoming. At work here is a process of harmonisation of differences between various NT Christological approaches which fails to convey the integral biblical picture of Jesus and to account for the full authenticity of his historical existence.

The section opens with the question: 'Why did the Word become flesh?' (456–460). The answer given is prompted by the Nicene Creed: 'For us men and for our salvation' (456). The *Catechism* develops that answer, with references taken from John (Jn 4:10, 14; 3:5; 1 Jn 4:9; Jn 3:16) (457–458): the incarnation of God's Son is willed by God for our salvation, thus manifesting God's love for us (cf. also 607). The truth of this statement cannot be questioned. However, in view of the centuries-old debate between Thomists and Scotists on the subject, the presentation made here will seem to endorse onesidedly the Thomistic view. Paul's more ample vision — which does not contradict John's — of Jesus Christ willed by God as the crown of creation under whom God 'would bring everything together as head [*anakephalaiōsasthai*]' (Eph 1:8–10; JB translation) is not taken into account. Lacking here is a cosmic Christology for which the New Testament provides foundation, especially in the Pauline literature (cf. Col 1:15–20; Eph 1:15–23; 2:10) and in John (Jn 1:1–18) (cf., however, 668). Instead, only the salvific purpose of the incarnation is brought out, with added references from Gregory of Nyssa (457); Irenaeus's idea of 'recapitulation' in Christ could have been felicitously used in a wider perspective.

118

The salvation of humankind through the Word's incarnation is rightly viewed, according to Irenaeus, as consisting in calling us to share in Christ's divine Sonship (460). That personal aspect is less apparent in the concept of our being made 'divine', expressed by Athanasius and St Thomas (460), and based on 2 Peter 1:4 (460). In any event, the Fathers' insistence on the deep insertion and immanence in our human reality of God's self-gift to us in his incarnate Son — and its implications for the Son's true identification with our human condition — could have been elaborated with profit. The Fathers saw in the event of the incarnation a 'marvellous exchange' between the divine and the human: the Son of God took to himself what is ours in order to share with us what is his (cf. 526).

The NT theology of the incarnation is finally developed with a threefold reference to John 1:14, Philippians 2:6–8, and Hebrews 10:5–7 (461–462). With differences, however; for while Philippians 2:6 clearly refers, as stated above, to the 'pre-existence' of Jesus Christ 'in the form of God' prior to his *kenōsis* in the 'form of a slave', John 1:14 expresses the Word's becoming human in terms of incarnation (cf. also the 'coming in the flesh' of 1 Jn 4:2 and the manifestation in the flesh of 1 Tim 3:16, quoted in 463). The meaning of 'flesh' (*sarx*) as referring to the weakness of human being could have been stressed; it corresponds to the *kenōsis* in the 'form of a slave' of the Pauline hymn. Both terms express the incarnate Son's deep identification with the concrete condition of humankind. John's Prologue (Jn 1:1–15, 14, 16–18) and the Pauline hymn (Phil 2:6–11) would have been worth quoting at length as eminent NT witnesses to the mystery of God's Son becoming human. As for Hebrews 10:5–7, 'when Christ came into the world' need not refer, as is understood here and explicitly stated elsewhere (606), to the punctual moment of the incarnation, but to Jesus' human condition and life; it does not necessarily imply an act of self-offering to God on the part of Jesus' humanity from the beginning of his human life.

3. The Christological dogma

The *Catechism* notes from the outset that the first-ever Christological heresy, Gnostic docetism, had to do with the denial of the truth of Jesus' humanity; John's letters already needed to uphold the reality of Jesus' humanhood against a docetic current (465). Elsewhere the *Catechism* will note how, against Apollinarius of Laodicaea's assertion that the Word took in Jesus the place of the human soul (spirit) with the result that his humanity was neither complete nor authentic, the Church affirmed that 'the eternal Son also assumed a rational, human soul' (471).[8]

For the rest, while stating clearly that Jesus Christ is as truly human as he is truly God — 'not . . . part God and part man' — the *Catechism* is overwhelmingly concerned with upholding the true divinity of Jesus Christ professed by the Church's dogma. The Council of Nicaea confessed the Son to be 'of one being' (*homoousios*) with the Father and condemned Arius who professed him to be 'from another substance' (465). Notice could have been taken of the fact that Arius denied the authenticity of

Jesus Christ's humanity as well: the created Word had assumed to himself not a complete humanity but human 'flesh' (body). The Nicene profession of faith, with its double affirmation 'He became flesh and was made man', meant to uphold the integrity of the Son incarnate's humanity.[9] His fullness of humanity was as important for the truth of our salvation through him as was his fullness of divinity.

Later, from the fullness of divinity and humanity the question shifted to the modality of the union of both. Against Nestorianism, the Council of Ephesus confessed that the Word, 'uniting to himself in his person the flesh animated by a rational soul, became man' (466). Against Mono-physitism, on the other hand, the Council of Chalcedon affirmed that the 'only-begotten Son is to be acknowledged *in* two natures without confusion, change, division or separation'; 'the same Son, Our Lord Jesus Christ: the same perfect in divinity and perfect in humanity, the same truly God and truly man, . . . consubstantial with the Father as to his divinity and consubstantial with us as to his humanity; "like us in all things but sin"' (467). The *Catechism* could have drawn attention to the fact that in the context of the Monophysite heresy Chalcedon's direct intention was to uphold the authenticity of the humanity of Jesus, which was in no way absorbed by the divinity in the process of being united with it.

The *Catechism* passes on to the second Council of Constantinople, which, against some who 'made Christ's human nature a kind of personal subject',[10] confessed him to be 'but one *hypostasis*, . . . one of the Trinity': 'He who was crucified in the flesh, our Lord Jesus Christ, is true God, Lord of glory, and one of the Holy Trinity' (468). The dogmatic value of the texts referred to is, however, problematic.[11] Texts whose authority is doubtful are here placed on an equal footing with those with the highest dogmatic value, without any distinction being made. Such indiscriminate levelling up is unfortunate, whatever the truth of the affirmations contained in the documents concerned.

Throughout this section the reader will be puzzled by the different meanings given in the various documents to the term *hypostasis*. In Nicaea it is identified with 'substance' (*ousia*) (465); in Ephesus it means the person (466); again in Chalcedon it refers to the person (467); in Constantinople II too it is equivalent to the person. Some explanation on the evolution in meaning which the term *hypostasis* has undergone, from 'nature' to 'person', would have been welcome.[12]

4. The true humanity of Jesus

The section starts by stating that, since 'human nature was assumed' by Christ's divine person, 'not aborbed' (GS 22 §2), the Church was led through the centuries to confess 'the full reality of Christ's human soul, with its operations of intellect and will, and of his human body' (470). All that is human in Jesus, however, belongs to the person of the Son of God who 'communicates to his humanity his own personal mode of existence in the Trinity', that is, his own divine personhood. From this it results that 'In his soul as in his body, Christ thus expresses humanly the divine ways of the Trinity' (470); which, expressed more clearly, means that in his humanity Jesus related in a human way to the Father and the Holy Spirit with whom in his divinity he belonged together in the mystery of God. The new section (470–478) studies Jesus' human psychology, his human soul and knowledge, his human will and body, respectively, and finally his human heart.

Because it is human, the human knowledge of Jesus was 'limited': Jesus could grow in wisdom and learn from experience. This limitation, it is explained, 'corresponded to the reality of his voluntary emptying of himself, taking "the form of a slave"' (472). The genuine identity of the Son of God with our concrete human condition — which goes beyond the assertion of the assumption of an integral human nature — could have been brought out more forcefully, with its concrete implications for the human psychology of Jesus. There is no hint in the *Catechism* that Jesus could grow in his human awareness of Messiahship and of his personal identity as the Son of God. On the contrary, it is said, quoting Maximus the Confessor, that 'the human nature of God's Son, not by itself but by its union with the Word, knew and showed forth in itself everything that pertains to God' (473). Taken literally, this quotation could tend to contradict Chalcedon's union of the two natures 'without confusion or change' (DS 302; ND 615).

It must be affirmed emphatically that in Jesus there is no communication of God's divine knowledge to his human intellect: his human knowledge is authentically and exclusively human in kind. Such is the case with the 'intimate and immediate knowledge' which Jesus had of the Father, as well as of his own human awareness of being Son (473). Such too was the case with Jesus' knowledge of the secret thoughts of the human heart. It was not a 'divine penetration' (473), but an infused human knowledge, comparable to that of the prophets, which Jesus received from God. That Jesus 'enjoyed in his human knowledge the fullness of understanding of the eternal plans he had come to reveal' (474) seems unwarranted by the evidence which is cited: the predictions of the passion (Mk 8:31; 9:31; 10:33–34) need to be handled with special care, inasmuch as they show a strong redactional influence in the light of the Easter event. What can and must be affirmed, in a more sober way, is that Jesus did know all that he needed to know for the exercise of his revealing and saving mission; no less and no more. This did not prevent on his part true, not feigned, ignorance (cf. Mk 13:32) (474). It did not exclude having to search for God's will in prayer, indeed, in the struggle of the agony in the garden; nor, even, in this case submitting to this will in 'blind faith' and obedience. But on the faith of Jesus the *Catechism* remains silent.

About Jesus' human will, the *Catechism* refers to the Third Council of Constantinople's affirmation of the existence in him of a human will and principle of operation (475). Since its integrity was preserved in the state of union, Christ's human will had to 'move itself', the Council explains, but it did so in perfect conformity with the divine will.[13] In such a way, 'two natural wills and actions concur together for the salvation of the

121

human race' (DS 637; ND 558). This 'concurring together' must not be construed to be an invasion of the divine will into the human, but the freely willed conformity of Jesus' human will in obedience to the divine will of the Father. But of Jesus' true human freedom even while he complies with the Father's will in his death, the *Catechism* will speak only later (609). The same is true where the temptations (538–540) and the mystery of the agony (612) are concerned. As for Jesus' cry on the cross, quoting Psalm 22:1 (Mk 15:34), the *Catechism* explains it — in a way which is both unfortunate and far-fetched — as said by him in our name (603). It would have been better to recognise that, faced with his violent death, Jesus could truly have had the sense of being abandoned by the Father, even while the Father remained close to him and 'sympathised' with him in his suffering.

Today it seems strange and somewhat preposterous to affirm that the human body of Jesus 'was finite' (*délimité*, in the French original).[14] It would have been more to the point to insist, here again, on Jesus' sameness with us in all things, including suffering, hunger, etc. But it seems even stranger to explain that it is possible to portray the human face of Jesus because it is 'finite' (477). Surely that could be taken for granted! It would have been better simply to base the legitimacy of the cult of holy images on the principle of the incarnation, as did the Second Council of Nicaea, to which reference is made (476–477): the body of Jesus is the body of the Son of God; the honour paid to it goes to the person. That 'the individual characteristics of Christ's body express the divine person of God's Son' (477), as the *Catechism* states, seems redundant. As for the heart of Jesus, the *Catechism*, following Pius XII, sees it as 'the chief sign and symbol' of Jesus' love for the Father and for humankind (478). It would have been helpful to base this doctrine on the biblical meaning of the 'heart' as symbolic of the 'person'. The cult of the Sacred Heart refers to that which is due to the person of Jesus himself.

The 'In Brief' of the section on Jesus' human psychology states that his 'human intellect and will [are] perfectly attuned and subject to his divine intellect and divine will, which he has in common with the Father and the Holy Spirit' (482). As has been noted earlier, this is said by Constantinople III with regard to the human will only. But in neither case must it be understood as an over-powering of the human by the divine which would destroy the authenticity of Jesus' humanhood. The *Catechism* speaks elsewhere of the human nature of Jesus as the 'sign and instrument of his divinity' (515; cf. 609). A Thomist tradition of the humanity as 'conjoined instrument' (*instrumentum coniunctum*) seems to underlie this concept. That tradition has its own validity, but care must be taken not to construe Jesus' humanhood as a blind instrument in God's hands, nor Jesus' intellect and will as invaded and over-powered by the divine. To see it thus would be to miss the authentic humanity of Jesus, his true identification with us and, even more, the historical reality of his human existence. This entire section of the *Catechism* is entitled: 'How is the Son of God man?' (470). It is not clear that it has shown us 'how human God's Son is'. This, however, is what concerns us more: he has not merely shared our nature, but our human condition with its limitations and imperfections, its struggles and problems; only then can he be said to be truly one of us in all things but sin (Heb 4:15).

II. Mariology

Our comments on the section devoted to Mary (484–519) will be considerably shorter. Following the Creed, the *Catechism* treats of Mary in relation to the mystery of the incarnation; the close connection between the Church's faith about Christ and about Mary is stressed (487). On the other hand, in keeping with LG, it also speaks of Mary in connection with the mystery of the Church (964–975). Elsewhere Mary is also seen in relation to the Spirit (721–726); thus the same fragmentation — perhaps unavoidable — is found here as has been observed earlier regarding the mystery of Christ. Other observations apply here as they did in the section on Christology: they concern the way biblical data are handled and the overall presentation of the Virgin Mary. While a full account is given of her God-given 'privileges' as truths to be believed, it is less clear that Mary stands out here as an inspiring model for our time.

The section deals first with Jesus' conception in Mary by the power of the Holy Spirit (484). The *Catechism* notes that 'the mission of the Holy Spirit is always conjoined and ordered to that of the Son' (485). This idea of a 'conjoined mission' of the Son and the Spirit — which requires some explanation — will be dealt with again later (690). Here it means that Jesus' humanity has been 'anointed by the Holy Spirit, from the beginning of his human existence (Mt 1:20)'. No hint is given at this point of the literary form according to which the infancy narratives in Luke and Matthew need to be interpreted (486; but cf. 498). The reference to Colossians 2:9 about the incarnation (484) seems unfortunate: in reality that text refers to the fullness of divine power in the risen humanity of Christ. As for using here Acts 10:38, it refers, as has been observed earlier, to Jesus' anointing with the Spirit at his baptism (486).

Now the *Catechism* turns to the Virgin Mary's free co-operation in her God-given vocation to become the mother of God's Son made man (488). Quoting LG, it shows Mary 'stand[ing] out' among many holy women of the OT who confidently awaited the fulfilment of God's promise of salvation (489). The immaculate conception of the Virgin Mary is based on Luke 1:28's *kekharitōmenē* (which, however, should be translated as 'favoured one', not by 'full of grace' (490; cf. 722)). The Church's tradition (including the Eastern tradition of the *Panagia*) has understood Luke 1:28 to refer to the privilege of the Immaculate Conception — proclaimed by Pius IX in 1854 (491) — 'by reason of the merits of her Son' (LG 53) (492). 'Mary remained free of every personal sin her whole life long' (493). In her free consent to her divine calling, Mary 'gave herself entirely to the person and to the work of her Son: she did so in order to serve the mystery of redemption with him and dependent on him by God's grace' (cf. LG 56) (494).

123

Since 'the One whom she conceived as man by the Holy Spirit, who truly became her Son according to the flesh, was none other than the Father's eternal Son, the second person of the Holy Trinity', Mary is truly the 'Mother of God' (*theotokos*), as the Church's faith confesses (495; cf. 466). Mary's virginity is treated at length, under three aspects. *Before birth*: the virginal conception is clearly meant in Matthew 1:20, 23; Luke 1:35 (496–497), although the argument, substantiated by a quotation from Ignatius of Antioch, that it is 'the sign that it truly was the Son of God who came in a humanity like our own' (496) is difficult to follow! *In birth* and *after birth*: her perpetual virginity is affirmed by tradition (499).[15] 'In fact', the *Catechism* adds with reference to Vatican II, 'Christ's birth "did not diminish his mother's virginal integrity but sanctified it" (LG 57). And so the liturgy of the Church celebrates Mary as *Aeiparthenos*, the "Ever Virgin" (cf. LG 52)' (499). The brothers and sisters of Jesus, referred to in the NT, are 'close relations', not blood brothers and sisters, according to an OT usage (500).

A final sub-section explains the meaning in God's plan of the virginity of Mary, the Mother of God's incarnate Son. The reasons 'touch both on the person of Christ and his redemptive mission, and on the welcome Mary gave that mission on behalf of all men' (502). Mary's virginity reveals God's absolute initiative in the incarnation (503); Jesus is conceived by the Holy Spirit because he is the New Adam, who ushers in the new creation (504); by his virginal conception, the New Adam ushers in the new birth of children adopted in the Holy Spirit through faith (505); Mary's virginity is the sign of her unhesitating faith and undivided gift of herself to God's will (506); at once virgin and mother, Mary is the most perfect symbol and realisation of the Church (507).

Whatever its merits, the Mariology of the *Catechism* strikes one as a privilege-centred Mariology. It does not adequately convey the picture of Mary as the woman who, from the beginning of her unique vocation, 'advanced in her pilgrimage of faith' (LG 58) and can inspire today the pilgrimage of believers, women in particular. The *Catechism* could have drawn on Mary's *Magnificat* in the first place (cf. 722), or even on Paul VI's apostolic exhortation *Marialis Cultus* (34–36; 57) for more vibrant accents in presenting Mary, the New Woman, model of womanhood and indeed of humankind in our own time. Here too, as in the case of Jesus Christ himself, the *Catechism* hands on truths of faith and doctrines more than it helps believers on their pilgrimage of faith. Such a doctrinal tradition is utterly essential, but we also need pastoral inspiration for our lives.

Notes

1 The *Catechism*, however, considers the mystery of the Trinity as the 'most fundamental and essential teaching in the "hierarchy of truths of the faith"' (234). Again, this is not to be understood as contradistinguishing the Trinity from the mystery of Christ.

2 See Rudolf Schnackenburg, 'Christologie des Neuen Testaments' in Johannes Feiner and Magnus Löhrer (eds), *Mysterium Salutis*, vol. III.1: *Das Christusereignis* (Einsiedeln: Benziger Verlag, 1970), p. 232.

3 The English edition has introduced the practice of gathering biblical references, spread over several notes in the French original, into a single note. The unhappy result of this practice is that the reader cannot make out to which exact words in the text each particular reference belongs. To find this out, one has to check the French original.

4 The titles 'Son of Man' and 'Servant of God' are treated only incidentally (cf. 440), without any discussion of their possible use by Jesus himself.

5 This applies not only to the centurion (Mt 27:54; Lk 23:47) (441), in whose exclamation (Mk 15:39), however, the Christian confession is said to be 'already heard' (444), but also to the question put to Jesus before the Sanhedrin (Lk 22:70; cf. Mt 26:64; Mk 14:61) (443): the question is about Jesus' claim to Messiahship.

6 See Jacques Guillet, *Jésus devant sa vie et sa mort* (Paris: Aubier, 1971), pp. 228–9.

7 Cf. Jacques Dupuis, *Who Do You Say I Am?: Introduction to Christology* (Maryknoll, NY: Orbis Books, 1994), p. 76, n. 13.

8 Reference is made to Pope Damasus I, DS 149. Another document of the same Pope is, however, more explicit (DS 148). Reference could, moreover, have been made to the profession of faith from the Council of Constantinople I, whose double affirmation 'He became flesh . . . and was made man', made in the same context, is intended to affirm the integrity of Christ's humanity (DS 150; ND (602), 12).

9 Cf. DS 125; ND (601), 7.

10 The authors incriminated here are named in the so-called 'three chapters'; they were, falsely perhaps, accused of Nestorianism. Cf. ND 620, introduction.

11 Reference is to the fourth and tenth anathemas attributed to the Council (DS 424; 432; ND 620/4, 620/10). However, the subsequent approval of the first ten canons by Pope Vigilius remains doubtful. The approval by the Pope seems to cover only canons 12–14 (DS 434–437; ND 620/12–14), directly concerned with the condemnation of the 'three chapters'. The significance of this council consists in a reiterated condemnation of the Nestorian heresy (cf. ND 620, introduction). One added reference is given, which the *Catechism* attributes to the Council of Ephesus: DS 255 (ND 606/4). However, the text comes from the fourth among the fourteen anathemas of St Cyril of Alexandria against Nestorius, appended to Cyril's 'third letter', which does not seem to have been officially approved by the Council. The dogmatic teaching of Ephesus is to be found in Cyril's 'second letter' to Nestorius, to which reference has been made above.

12 For clarification on the meaning of terms, eventually reached in the process of the development of the Christological dogma, cf. DS 421 (ND 620/1).

13 Cf. DS 556–558; ND 635–637.

14   The reference is to canon 4 of the Lateran Council of 649; *circumscriptum corpore* (DS 504); cf. ND 627/4; 'limited in the flesh'.

15   The documents to which reference is made for the virginal birth are: a letter of St Leo the Great (DS 291, 294); canon 6 of the Council of Constantinople II (DS 427), but see n. 11 above concerning the doubtful approval of this canon by Pope Vigilius; a letter of Pope Pelagius I (DS 442); canon 4 of the (local) Council of Lateran (DS 503); the (local) Council of Toledo XVI (DS 571); a Bull of Pius IV (DS 1880): *semper in virginitatis integritate, ante partum scilicet, in partu et perpetuo post partum.*

The Mysteries of Christ's Life

(Paragraphs 512–570)

Gerard O'Hanlon SJ
Milltown Institute, Dublin

Section I: Jesus' whole life is mystery (514–521)

This section is preceded by two paragraphs (512–513) which note that while the Creed says nothing about the mysteries of Christ's life, nonetheless it is legitimate for catechesis to make use of these mysteries as interpreted in the light of credal affirmations about Christmas and Easter. The *Catechism* proposes then to structure the discussion of Christ's life around the notion of mystery, with a first section on some elements common to all the mysteries of Christ's life, followed by sections on the mysteries of his hidden (II) and public (III) life. One notes the strategic importance of situating the discussion of Christ's life under the rubric of mystery — we will discuss the significance of this strategy below.

This first section makes three main points. First, what is said about the life of Christ in the Gospels is aimed to evoke faith in Jesus as the Son of God. Thus the evangelists are not interested in giving every detail of the life of Jesus as a biographical study. Rather, they are convinced that everything in his life is a 'sacrament', a 'sign and instrument of his divinity and of the salvation he brings' (515), and they make a selection of what to write down in confidence that the whole life of Jesus is mystery and so is suitable to express the invisible mystery of his divine Sonship. One notes that this approach is possible because the *Catechism* has already discussed the incarnation and the normative conciliar Christology of the early centuries and so can presume in faith the divine identity of Christ even as it presents the Jesus of history. This strategic option will bear fuller examination below.

Secondly, some characteristics which are common to all the mysteries of Christ's life are cited. These are the revelation to us of the Father, the redemptive nature of Christ's own life, and its ability to recapitulate the long history of the human family and all the stages of our lives. Regrettably one notes here, and indeed throughout the text, the

127

pervasive use of sexist language – the aim of Jesus is to restore 'fallen man', and Irenaeus is quoted to the effect that the recapitulation of Christ involves the 'long history of mankind' and gives 'communion with God to all men' (518). One notes too the weight of traditional, 'churchy' language such as redemption, atones (517), and recapitulation (518), which require some breaking down into a more contemporary idiom by the theologically informed catechist if they are to be fruitful mediations of the faith.

The third point notes that we are in communion with the mysteries of Jesus. This is so because Christ's whole life was 'for us . . . and for our salvation' (519), so that as 'the perfect man' he is a model that we are asked to imitate (520), and by uniting himself in some way with us all he gives us the enabling power actually to imitate him. What is noticeable here is the welcome inclusion of themes from soteriology and grace applied to the life of Christ. What needs further examination is the presumed universal applicability of the model of Christ as 'perfect man'. One notes finally what it is in Christ that is proposed to us for imitation – his self-emptying, his prayer, his poverty, deprivations and persecutions (520). It will be interesting to observe as we go along what sort of image of Christ is operative in the *Catechism*.

This section has presented us with a life of Christ which reveals God's saving love for us and which empowers us to accept and live out of this love. I propose now to move from this more general presentation to comment more specifically on three of the main issues which have arisen so far in our discussion.

1. The notion of mystery

The *Catechism* could have simply spoken of the life of Christ. Instead it chose to speak in terms of the mysteries of Christ's life. We need to examine in more detail the significance of the strategic option to structure the discussion in this way.

The notion of mystery has all kinds of resonances in the Christian tradition and has been developed in a very rich way in our own times.[1] Historically it is related to the deeply-felt patristic conviction of the incomprehensibility of God, signs of which, in a world-view influenced by neo-Platonism, are present in our created world and, in particular, in the events of salvation associated with Jesus Christ and his Church. Life, then, for the believer is sacramental, so that a revelation of the hidden God is present in nature and history, but particularly in the figure of Jesus Christ, and in the sacraments and liturgy of his Church.

A more precise explanation of what is meant by this may be sought in the context of the discussion of this whole area in Vatican I and subsequently. In defending the need for divine revelation against the post-Enlightenment movements of rationalism and semi-rationalism, the teaching of Vatican I (DS 3000–3045) maintained that human reason on its own cannot know certain things about God (mysteries, that which is properly supernatural). These truths are accessible only through God's free revelation, and when accepted in faith and investigated by human reason, a fruitful, if incomplete, understanding of these mysteries may ensue. Unfortunately, although Vatican I itself also declared that God is incomprehensible *in se*, the prevailing neo-scholasticism after the Council tended to understand mystery very much as due to human ignorance and to our status as pilgrims only. The suggestion was that in the Beatific Vision the mystery of God would finally be revealed.

Ultimately this position betrays a rationalist understanding of mystery from which modern theology has moved away. Karl Rahner and Hans Urs von Balthasar, for example, have argued for the intrinsic and enduring incomprehensibility of God who is *semper major*, always greater. They do so on the grounds that in the final analysis the mystery of God is one of interpersonal love, which depends on a freedom that goes beyond knowledge. In this respect Balthasar in particular notes the appropriateness of using metaphor and imagination in a theology which is conscious of having absolute love and beauty as its object.[2] He is however careful to note the need for conceptual control also, since God is absolute truth as well. In different ways too both authors note that God's self-revelation occurs in created figures which preserve their own relative autonomy in being signs of the divine. This is vital, since it is a temptation endemic to this kind of approach, as might be supposed given its influence from Platonism, to disallow the reality and otherness of the symbol in rushing to read off its meaning in what it signifies, the 'really real'. Instead, even in the qualitatively unique self-revelation of God in Jesus Christ, it is in the figure or symbol of Christ that the Father is revealed: there is no sense in which one could say that it is through Christ that we see the Father, if by 'through' one meant that Christ was in some sense dispensable. This means that the 'sign' value of Christ cannot mean that his humanity is downplayed, since it is precisely in his humanity that the truth about him and God is revealed. As we shall see, the *Catechism* has difficulty in using the term mystery in a way which gives full weight to the historical events of Christ's life.

There is available then a very rich theological notion of mystery, and this goes a long way to explaining the strategic option of the *Catechism* to structure its discussion of the life of Christ under this rubric. In an era of scientific and instrumental rationality, still very influenced by the Enlightenment and more latterly by the technological developments in its wake, there is need of a recall to a more holistic notion of the truth.[3]

2. A 'descending' Christology

As has already been indicated, this section on the life of Christ is situated firmly within a context which has established in faith that Jesus is the Son of God. This then is a 'Christology from above', a 'descending Christology' which builds on the given of the incarnation as developed in the Christological dogmas of the early councils. It is precisely this starting-point which allows the life of Christ to be discussed so readily under the rubric of mystery. I would argue that such a starting-point is not simply something neutral, without further consequences, and I would like to outline some of the implications that are involved.

The trouble with an excessively descending approach, as neo-scholasticism in particular discovered but as has been a recurrent tendency in post-Chalcedonian Christology, is that it is difficult to give full weight to the humanity of Christ.[4] If one is so conscious all the time that this is God, then there is a real difficulty about accepting Jesus as a man — which is the reverse of the situation of his own contemporaries, who fully accepted his humanity but were led through this to the surprising and problematic assertion of his divinity. Now of course in faith we accept that Jesus is divine, so there is no point in wishing to set that to one side and begin all over again. Nonetheless it is arguable that unless we have some kind of imaginative appreciation of the process that his own disciples went through we will too easily accept the divinity of Jesus in a way which masks the full humanity and ends up by being monophysite in effect. The pastoral implications can be legion — the process of becoming and history proper to humanity is downgraded, there is a tendency to content oneself with the 'spiritual' hidden assurance that all will be well in the next life while this life is seen as a testing-ground only without inner meaning of its own. In this context the model of authority is vertical, the *status quo* is supported, and preference is given to non-material aspects of reality in a dualist way. In the terms of John Courtney Murray,[5] there ensues an eschatological spirituality with strong focus on the 'not yet' of eschatology, with the humanity and especially the miracles of Jesus seen purely as apologetic instruments to show his divinity. Again in this context, priority is given to a sacramental, hierarchical model of the Church; the parish is the domain of believers with little outreach to the wider community; and prayer and spirituality are uneasy bed-fellows with business, politics, sex and pleasure.

It was because of these dangers that many theologians in the era after the anniversary of Chalcedon in 1951 chose quite deliberately to adopt a 'from below', 'ascending' approach to Christology. Their attempt has been to show in different ways that 'nearness to God and genuine human autonomy grow in direct and not inverse proportion' (Rahner),[6] that far from being an obstacle to full humanity, the divinity of Christ 'does not lie in what is not human in Jesus but precisely in his way of being human' (Segundo).[7] Now an exclusively ascending approach has its own risks, and Karl Barth and Hans Urs von Balthasar, among others, have shown that it is possible to adopt a perfectly orthodox descending approach. Indeed Segundo himself notes the need to take both starting-points in a complementary process, and Elizabeth Johnson analyses well how a keen appreciation of social justice may emerge from both a Christology from above (see Pope John Paul II's approach in *Redemptor Hominis*) and one from below (see the pastoral letters of the American Bishops on peace and on economic justice).[8] What is involved, then, is not so much an either/or dilemma, as an ability to strike a balance which obviates the dangers attendant on opting predominantly for one approach.

The *Catechism*, as we have seen, opts predominantly for the descending approach. It even speaks about the humanity of Christ as being 'the sign and instrument of his divinity' (515). There are good ways of under standing instrumental, sacramental causality — nonetheless we have adverted as well to the intrinsic tendency of such an approach to bypass the human, the symbol, and to focus too quickly on the 'really real' of what is signified. The *Catechism* is much too biblically based to fall into the more obvious pitfalls of neo-scholasticism in this respect. However, when one looks at the image of Christ which is presented for imitation above (p. 128), or at the end of this whole section on the life of Christ, one is struck by the rather one-dimensional figure that is portrayed. The 'In Brief' section at the end of each thematic exposition in the *Catechism* aims to provide a memorisable summary of what has immediately preceded (22). In the case of the life of Christ this 'In Brief' section (561–570) speaks of Jesus Christ in terms such as silence, miracles, prayer, love, weakness of a new-born child, obedience, humble work, holiness, servant, and so on. Perhaps a different approach might have taken into account the anger of Jesus, his strength and authority, his conflict with enemies, his sorrow and weariness, his sense of celebration. The catechist using this text would do well to supplement it with a wider cross-section of biblical material about the life of Jesus. But more importantly s/he would need to complement the approach 'from above' with a fuller indication of how an understanding of divinity flows from the richness of Christ's humanity and is not a preordained datum to which the humanity is somehow accommodated.

3. The model of 'the perfect man'
Jesus Christ, in a phrase taken from *The Church in the Modern World* (38) of the Second Vatican Council, is referred to as 'the perfect man', and as such is offered for our imitation (520). The presumed universal applicability of the man Christ as a model for both men and women needs to be examined. It is an issue raised by feminist theologians in questions such as: Can a male Saviour save women? The attempt to ghettoise the feminist issue as a rather elitist, middle-class concern, of interest to a small minority in the West, and particularly in North America, was rejected by Pope Paul VI back in the 1970s,[9] and more recently by the late Cardinal Tomas O'Fiaich at the Synod on the Laity. Christians must concern themselves with the sin of sexism as with any systematic erosion of human dignity and equality, and the present Pope John Paul II acknowledges this most readily in writings such as *Mulieris Dignitatem* (1988) and *Christifideles Laici* (1988). Obviously, when the humanity of Jesus is stressed it is relatively easy for both women and men to identify with him. And this is what is emphasised by the patristic maxim that 'what has not been assumed has not been saved', since the salvation of women is taken for granted as part of the mission of Jesus. The difficulty arises in acute form when even in official church teaching sympathetic to the feminist cause the maleness of Jesus is given a theological significance which results, for example, in the issue of the ordination of women being declared closed and not amenable to further discussion. In this context the *Catechism* does very well, in a section on God as Father, to note that God transcends the human distinction

between male and female (239).[10] However, it surely gives hostages to fortune in the section under discussion on the life of Christ by not even referring to Christ's unconventionally even-handed treatment of women in the course of his ministry, and by proposing without further ado a model of Christ as the perfect man.

There are a variety of theological approaches possible in this whole area.[11] In a broad sense one may speak of revolutionary and reformist approaches to feminist Christology — proponents of the former tend to reject the Church, the latter tend to work with liberationist models of Christology. Characteristic of the latter would be an awareness of the suffering of women, outrage at this, an attempt in groups by praxis and social analysis to change the situation, all inspired by a gospel vision of a new community of mutuality between men and women. There are three main steps to the theological inquiry stemming from this kind of approach — first, an analysis of the situation; secondly, a look at the Christian tradition for elements which have contributed to the oppression; and lastly an appeal to the liberating elements of the same tradition.

The appeal to the liberating elements of the tradition is to the ministry of Jesus, in particular to his preaching of the kingdom. Here the marginalised are first, the prostitutes gain entry before the religious leaders. God is now *Abba* in a way which subverts patterns of domination, including those of patriarchy. Jesus practises table-fellowship with all, has women disciples (unlike any of the other major groups within Judaism at the time), gives an apostolic role to the Samaritan woman. It is the women who stand by Jesus at the cross, they are first to hear of and bear witness to the resurrection. Both Acts and Paul speak of the prominent place of women in the early decades of the Church — as missionaries, teachers, preachers, leaders of house churches, and so on. In Christianity the cross is the opposite of power as usually understood, it is the *kenosis* of patriarchy, it is the radical challenging of all patterns of domination. Baptism, unlike circumcision, is gender-free, as witnessed by the great baptismal hymn in Galatians 3:28 (neither male nor female). There is even the naming of Jesus as Wisdom (1 Cor 1:24), a female personification of God, to balance out the more usual naming of Jesus as Logos with its associations of male rationality. However, besides any complementary use of female images in talking about God, there is need for more clarity on the analogical and metaphorical nature of all language as applied to God, need for a sensitivity to the 'is not' implicit in all non-univocal linguistic usage. And because of the long history of ascribing maleness to God through the use of male language in an operatively univocal way, there is need for respect for the difficulty many experience in addressing God by such traditional Christian symbols as Father and Son.

Jesus would have scandalised his contemporaries by the liberating way he related to women. This is the Jesus who can be a role model for women precisely because he empowers them. In this context it is the humanity of Jesus which is crucial for his solidarity with both men and women. We are at a point in human history and culture where we are no longer so sure about the anthropological and theological significance of gender as such. We need to be patient with one another as we explore this area further. However, we can at least be sure that it is wrong to understand this significance in terms of domination and subordination, that it is heretical to use the maleness of Jesus to treat women as lesser human beings. It is interesting to note that the issue concerning Jew and Gentile was resolved at least partly already within scriptural times; that the one concerning slavery took longer; and that it is only in our own era that we are coming to terms with the new relationship demanded in the kingdom between women and men (Gal 3:28). In this context it is surprising that the *Catechism* does not speak a little differently and a little more on this whole issue in its treatment of the life of Christ. And it is deeply disappointing that sexist language is used throughout the presentation.

Section II: The mysteries of Jesus' infancy and hidden life (522–534)

This is the second section of the *Catechism* on the mysteries of Christ's life. It deals with the time before the public life of Jesus. It notes first (522–523) that God prepared for the coming of Christ through the events of the first covenant in the Hebrew Scriptures and through the mission of John the Baptist in particular. One is reminded here of the relationship between prophecy and fulfilment, between what was once hidden and now is made clear (*latet/patet*), which was a characteristically patristic way of reading the Scriptures. This time of preparation is then related to the annual celebration of Advent by the Church (524). This is but one instance of the ability of the *Catechism* to relate faith to liturgy and spirituality, a very attractive feature of the text.

There follows a short treatment of the mystery of Christmas (525–526). It is noted that in the poverty of the stable is revealed the glory of heaven. This is a theme which receives a very rich theological treatment in the work of Hans Urs von Balthasar, who notes the shift in meaning from the glory of dazzling power, might and weight of the OT to that of the glory of vulnerable love in the birth, life and death of Jesus Christ.[12] The *Catechism* goes on to observe that we can only enter God's kingdom by being born again and in this sense becoming a child in relation to God. This fulfils the *admirabile commercium*, the admirable exchange by which God becomes human in order that we can share in divinity.

The *Catechism* goes on to deal with other mysteries of Jesus' infancy — his circumcision, a sign of his obedience to the law (527); the epiphany (528), the manifestation of Jesus as Messiah of Israel, Son of God and Saviour of all the world, including the pagans; the presentation (529), showing Jesus as the firstborn Son who belongs to the Lord and who encounters Israel; and the flight into Egypt and massacre of the innocents (530), revealing the opposition to Jesus. The treatment is instructive and spiritually nourishing. It is worth noting in particular the references to the opposition that Jesus will meet (529–530), and the only reference to Jesus as liberator (530) in the whole section on the life of Christ. It is affirmed that we participate in each of the different stages of Christ's life, a theme which is developed theologically in a very beautiful way by Balthasar.[13]

Finally in this section there is a treatment of the mysteries of Jesus' hidden life (531–534). It is noted that for much of his life 'Jesus shared the condition of the vast majority of human beings: a daily life spent without evident greatness, a life of manual labour' (531). One is reminded of the poet Patrick Kavanagh's observation that God is found 'in the bits and pieces of everyday'. It is noted that it is precisely through these ordinary ways of life that we can enter into fellowship with Jesus. This point is well taken, although once again one would have wished that in spelling out some of the detail of this ordinary life in the case of Jesus there might have been some attempt to admit to areas of conflict and misunderstanding which are surely most ordinary but which many of us as Christians tend spontaneously to think are not holy. So we are asked to learn from the silence of this period, from the holy love of family life, from the value of work (533). Might we not equally have been asked to meditate on the astonishment and lack of understanding of Joseph and Mary on the occasion of the finding in the Temple, their implied rebuke of Jesus, without too quickly hastening to conclude that though they 'did not understand these words ... they accepted them in faith' (534)? Attention is drawn to the significance of the obedience of Jesus to Mary and Joseph, anticipating his obedience to God on Holy Thursday, restoring what the disobedience of Adam had destroyed, and being the image in time and space of the Son's eternal obedience to his heavenly Father. However, it might also be opportune to note that in a post-Holocaust world it is not just women who spontaneously exercise a hermeneutic of suspicion when confronted with the notion of obedience as a value. This is another instance of time-honoured, traditional terminology requiring some theological mediation in order to make sense in a contemporary context. An Irish woman, Maura Lynch, offers such a mediation in a very simple theological reflection on how in her life as daughter, wife and mother, love had led to commitment, and commitment to all kinds of obedience in all kinds of ordinary ways.[14] So, for example, a mother is obedient out of love to the physical and emotional care of her baby. The obedience of Jesus, and the obedience which is asked of us, is rooted firmly in the give and take of love.

It is worth noting finally that whatever theological criticism one might make of individual parts of this text, one need not regret its devotional tone. This is achieved without sacrifice of solid, doctrinal content, and in this respect one is reminded of the approval expressed by Karl Rahner for Balthasar's dictum that theology should also be done 'on one's knees'.[15] Both these theologians were inspired in their academic theology by the Spiritual Exercises of St Ignatius, which gave a major role to the mysteries of Christ's life. For too long there has been a divorce between theology on the one hand, and spirituality on the other. The *Catechism* is to be applauded for its ability to express doctrine in a devotional way.

Section III: The mysteries of Christ's public life (535–560)

This is the final section of the *Catechism* on the life of Christ, and it deals with the mysteries of Christ's public life. First, there is a treatment of the baptism of Jesus (535–537). This historical event is presented very much from the viewpoint of faith as a trinitarian act in which Jesus anticipated out of love his future baptism of death for the forgiveness of sins. The *Catechism* does well to highlight the relationship between Jesus and his Father, but the significance of this relationship requires further development.

Next there is a treatment of the temptations of Jesus (538–540). These are seen in the context of the obedience of Jesus to his Father, in contrast to the disobedience of Adam and of Israel in the desert. It is noticeable here that the phrase 'obedience of . . . love' (539) is used, a helpful way of nuancing the notion of obedience in line with modern sensitivities. It is also pointed out that the temptations show the way in which the Son of God is Messiah, giving us courage to hope that we too need not be overcome by weakness or temptation. One is reminded here of the kind of pedagogy in the discernment of spirits which is central to the Spiritual Exercises of St Ignatius, and in particular to those exercises of the second week on the kingdom of Christ and the Two Standards.

There follows a long treatment of the kingdom of God (541–556). The good news is that this kingdom is near, a kingdom whose finality involves the gathering of humanity around the Son into communion with the triune God (541–542). Jesus proclaims this kingdom for all, but in particular he makes an active love towards the poor the condition for entry (544). Sinners too are invited to the kingdom. But entry for all involves conversion and radical choice, as the teaching of Jesus, most typically in parables, makes clear (545–546). The various miracles of Jesus are primarily signs of the presence of the kingdom in him (547–550). In this way they both evoke and presuppose faith — they are not designed to satisfy human curiosity or a desire for magic, and indeed those without faith reject the miracles as accomplished by the power of demons. In particular the faith-context of the miracles indicates that the goal of Jesus is to free people from sin and bring them to a right relationship with God — freedom from evils of other kinds (hunger, injustice, even death) is subordinate to this main goal.

The Church shares in the authority and mission of Jesus to proclaim the kingdom. There follows (551–553) a careful formulation of Roman Catholic teaching on ecclesial authority, based mainly on the well-known interpretation of the traditional texts in Matthew 16 and 18, Luke 22 and John 21. Thus, without specifying the exact nature of the relationship between Peter and the twelve, it is noted that the authority of Jesus is shared with the college of the twelve, among whom Peter occupies first place. In this context a specific authority is given to Peter, who alone explicitly receives the 'keys of the kingdom'. The power of the keys refers to authority to govern the Church, the associated power to 'bind and loose' refers to the authority to forgive sins, pronounce doctrinal judgements and make disciplinary decisions in the Church. The careful formulation of this section reflects well the current incomplete understanding of this issue as the Church continues to struggle with the integration of a more collegial notion of authority coming out of the Second Vatican Council with the hierarchical and centrist model of the First Vatican Council. There are, however, other issues surrounding this whole area of authority which the *Catechism* does not address, and to which we will return. The *Catechism* ends its treatment of the kingdom by considering how the transfiguration of Jesus is both a pledge of his resurrection and a foretaste of his glorious second coming and of the final actualisation of the kingdom (554–556). Once again, in an explicit link with the baptism of Jesus, it is noted that suffering and persecution are intrinsic to the love that brings about the kingdom. This means that the glory of the transfiguration is more that of vulnerable if ultimately triumphant love than that of dazzling power, as we noted already in commenting on the birth of Jesus above.

This whole section on the public life of Jesus ends with an account of his journey and entry into Jerusalem (557–560). It is stressed that Jesus decided to do this conscious of the possible, even probable, consequences for himself. The position of the *Catechism* on this matter is entirely compatible with the notion that Jesus would not have known in detail what awaited him, might even still have hoped against hope for some last-minute acceptance of his message, and was accordingly still living out of faith and the uncertainty which attends all human enterprises.[16] The whole treatment concludes with an 'In Brief' section (561–570) which presents a summary of the main teaching about the life of Christ.

It remains to comment in more detail on three main issues arising from the preceding discussion.

1. The relationship of Jesus to his Father

The *Catechism* has noted the importance of the relationship between Jesus and his Father in its treatment of the baptism of Jesus. In many other places too it is clear, as might be expected from a 'descending' Christological approach, that a trinitarian framework is central to the exposition. It will help to note some of the theological work done concerning the significance of this relationship and its foundation in the experience of the human Jesus.[17]

The main point to make here is that the unique intimacy which Jesus enjoyed with the one he called *Abba*, 'Daddy', was absolutely central and foundational for his whole mission. It is out of this experience of total acceptance by God that Jesus extends that unconditional acceptance to others, in particular the unacceptables of his day, which was so characteristic of his mission and of the kingdom which he proclaimed.[18] We may suppose that Jesus himself grew (Lk 2:52) in understanding and clarity about the nature of his experience of intimacy with the one he called *Abba*, and thus about his own identity as the Son of God. In this context it is not fanciful to suppose that there would have been key historical moments, perhaps in particular his baptism and transfiguration, in which earlier intuitions were confirmed and crystallised into a more adult grasp of self-identity. It is out of this sense of his unique relationship with his Father-God that Jesus offers to us participation in a relationship that is peculiarly his own.

Jesus, then, is captivated by his Father, this love is the centre of his life, it is what gives him energy, what frees him from undue fear, what allows him to struggle, get into conflict and even fail. It is in this overriding context of love that one speaks of the obedience of Jesus. And above all it is because of this foundational reality and experience that the kingdom of Jesus is shot through by the Holy Spirit of the unconditional love between Father and Son and not, *pace* human movements at the time and since, by an ethic of achievement.[19] This is what scandalised the scribes and Pharisees, the establishments of whatever hue, and what attracted the marginalised — Jesus was saying that this God of trinitarian relationship is love in the same way, as Simone Weil has put it so well, that an emerald is green.[20] This is the essence of God, and because there is no earning of love, then the hierarchies of value based on achievement so beloved of the powerful of this world simply become redundant. God is the Father in the parable of the prodigal, whereas we who have power identify so easily with the elder brother.

2. The kingdom or reign of God

It will help to link the presentation of the kingdom in the *Catechism* more closely to the *Abba* experience of Jesus, and also to bring out more clearly its profound historical, this-worldly implications, albeit within a finality which transcends history.

Jesus knew through being true to himself that God is love, that this love is generously self-emptying (kenotic), and that it expresses itself in solidarity with those who are easily forgotten in human calculations of lovableness. Reality, then, is intrinsically relational, and there is a lovely gratuity at the core of life, even when a warm word like relationality must be translated into a tougher word like solidarity to convey the fact that it will not do to pretend to love where relationships are founded on inequality and injustice. This basic core of loving acceptance, with its rejection of value based solely on achievement, was what attracted so many to the kingdom proclaimed by Jesus, in particular those whose potential for achievement was so limited by the system within which they lived. And if love is primary, and love is God, then one can well understand the need to teach that freedom from sin is at the heart of the mission of Jesus, which cannot be reduced to freedom from other evils like hunger and sickness, which do not of themselves separate a person from God.

However, is there no link between gratuity and achievement, between relationship with God and the socio-political context within which this relationship develops? Psychologists like Erikson, writing in the area of human development, note a positive correlation between good self-esteem and productivity. This approach can harmonise well with a notion of the kingdom which bases self-worth on being simply loved into existence by God, but then on that basis values human achievement, as the parable about the talents indicates. As Christians we need a more nuanced theology of the link between gratuity and efficacy than is usually available to us. We need to see that the two are not simply contradictory, and that Christianity does not involve a Manichaean dislike of success, even while it has its own unique insight into the value of failure. We need to develop an ethic which takes seriously the value of job- and wealth-creation, which encourages entrepreneurship, all within a context which calls for the sharing of wealth and which appreciates that the economism which measures all value by the economic yardstick of profit and loss has failed to strike the right balance in living out the link between love and achievement.[21] Aloysius Pieris notes in this respect that some of his Marxist friends discovered in Christians the ability to celebrate and give thanks, as well as to produce and achieve.[22] And Gustavo Gutiérrez[23] speaks about a spirituality of joy linking gratuity and efficacy. Coming at the same issue from a different perspective, Albert Nolan[24] notes that as church people we more easily espouse the sentiments behind the injunction to be as innocent or gentle as doves — we are less comfortable with the accompanying advice to be as cunning as serpents (Mt 10:16). The latter implies a strategic and engaged struggle in the many areas of human living in order to promote that culture of solidarity within which love may flourish. There is a proper sense in which riches are to be condemned and the rich called to conversion — but we do little service to the cause of the poor by expressing a chic option in their regard which masks a disdainful hostility to the world of business and an unchristian understanding of the link between gratuity and efficacy.

Allied to this latter misunderstanding can be operative a rather dualistic notion of the relationship between the this- and other-worldly aspects of the kingdom announced by Jesus. With all respect for that eschatological proviso or reserve which notes the ultimate trans-historical nature of the kingdom, one notes too the urgency with which Jesus preaches the 'already' of the kingdom, which leads to both his compassion towards victims and his anger towards victimisers. The founder of Christianity came to cast fire upon the earth, to bring the sword and not peace — why does consensus seem a more Christian word than conflict in a world riddled with division? Does this perhaps betray a bias towards a more middle-class culture of relative contentment?[25] There is no need always to suspect a socio-economic or political reduction of Christianity among those who look for signs of the kingdom to transform our culture — did not Jesus himself relativise the absolute primacy of God over humankind in the incarnation, in joining together the two great commandments, and in his identification with suffering humanity in the Last Judgement scene of Matthew 25?

On the basis of these kinds of observations modern theology has spoken of the option for the poor as being characteristic of the kingdom. It has drawn attention in phrases like social grace and social sin to the structural implications of the mission of Jesus, who need not himself have been aware of these implications in the differentiated way that is possible today. And it has recovered the sense that something decisive has happened with Jesus which has changed the course of human history in principle and can change it in fact as well. This latter happens to the extent that we learn to accept his kingdom as a gracious gift which eliminates neither human responsibility nor conflict, but which craves to be received with urgency and without putting limits to the anticipations of its final shape which are already possible within history. Most importantly, it should be noted in addition that many of these points are made repeatedly in the social encyclicals of John Paul II, and so have a claim to be considered as part of the faith of the Church and not just part of its theological resource. It is in the context of these observations that one regrets a somewhat spiritualised treatment of the kingdom in the *Catechism*. Perhaps this is another consequence of the option to focus on the life of Christ under the rubric of mystery and in the context of a descending Christology. Whatever the reason, one gets little sense that the rhetoric of kingdom values leads to a concentrated and serious focus on the bread-and-butter issues of daily life, particularly the life of those who are at the margins. One wonders if the Irish bishops who have recently brought out a very fine pastoral on unemployment called *Work is the Key*,[26] in which they encourage anger at the divided state of Irish society, would get much inspiration from this treatment of the life of Christ. My sense is that the *Catechism* has little bite when it comes to such human issues. To be fair, there does seem to be a greater awareness of the challenge Jesus posed to the religious and political establishment of his day in the discussion of the death of Jesus which follows immediately on the section about his life (see 574–594 in particular). But this begs the question why these issues are considered mainly in the context of the suffering and death of Christ — there can be an unhealthy mysticism of suffering which sees all human striving for a better world as vain and misguided, since this world is primarily a testing-place for entry into heaven.[27] One may very well hold on to the redemptive value of suffering and still hear in the call of Jesus an invitation to engage urgently now in the search for present, historical anticipations of the kingdom whose ultimate form lies beyond history. In this respect one would have welcomed a more robust portrait of Jesus in the *Catechism* — as one contemporary writer has put it, a God without teeth lacks credibility, particularly for those who are themselves victims.[28]

3. Church authority

The careful formulations of the *Catechism* concerning church authority are extremely eirenic in tone. Nonetheless it would have been both helpful and diplomatic, though perhaps it may not have seemed politic, for some mention to be made of the limits of authority, of its possible abuses, and of the notion of authority as service (Mt 19:24–28; Jn 13:1–20). I say this not out of any desire to downgrade the great value to the Church of the gift of office which is described in the sub-section on 'The keys of the kingdom' (551–553). What is at issue rather is a perception abroad that in its exercise of this office of authority, as evidenced in such matters as the appointment of bishops and the lack of tolerance for theological discussion and dissent, the Church can become oppressive in a way that needs challenging.[29] We have had a recent experience of the Church accepting it made a mistake in the case of Galileo: might it not in the end be both wiser and more politic to nuance the discussion of authority in the Church along the lines suggested? An interesting parallel from the secular world is the way in which the model of community development seeks to empower people to own their own gifts — if we as Church are convinced of the presence of the Holy Spirit in each Christian, then this might be a fruitful path to explore?[30]

Conclusion

There are many things to welcome in the *Catechism*'s treatment of the life of Christ. There is a good blend of spirituality and solid doctrinal content, giving evidence of attention to the findings of modern biblical scholarship. The tone is restrained, neither overemphatic nor aggressive.[31] There is much in it to nourish and sustain faith.

We have also noted that, perhaps because of its attempt to be universal, the *Catechism* in this section tends to be somewhat neutral and inoffensive in a way that belies the surprising and disturbing life of Jesus. One may respect the principle raised by Schweitzer in his critique of the unduly subjective nature of Liberal Protestantism's portrait of the historical Jesus without thereby domesticating this portrait to the point of harmlessness.[32] The *Catechism* runs this risk in presenting a rather one-sided, pious image of Jesus, not well rooted in the social context of his day, and without much inspiration to challenge the *status quo* of our day. There is an impoverished notion of spirituality underlying this tendency, very different from the judgement of Péguy that 'it is the mystic who nourishes politics'.[33] In this respect one remembers the critique of Segundo that Christology should focus on the historical project of Jesus and not simply on an imitation of his life and values in an atemporal way.[34] The argument for a more socially engaged image of Jesus can be based not simply on theological opinion but on the faith of the Church as outlined in papal and other magisterial documents.

Long before there existed a sociology of knowledge or the discipline of historical criticism in biblical studies, St Ignatius in his Spiritual Exercises included meditations on the Sermon on the Mount and on the cleansing of the Temple in his consideration of the mysteries of Christ's life. In the latter he noted that the poor sellers were treated more kindly by Jesus than the rich ones.[35] It is a lost opportunity that this instinct of faith is not given a more convincing modern interpretation in the *Catechism*. Such an interpretation would involve the complementing of the very sound Christology 'from above' in the *Catechism* by a Christology 'from below'. In this way the historical implications of the mysteries of Christ's life might be better appreciated, as might the contention that in the end there can be no such thing as a neutral presentation of this life.

Sadley the *Catechism* bears this out itself negatively in its systematic use of sexist language, a real blight on the entire presentation. This is a deep flaw in any contemporary text which wishes to be universal in a truly prophetic way, and its linguistic failure to address over half of its potential audience is deeply discrediting to its aims in most English-speaking countries. One can easily understand the response of women and men who feel insulted by this approach, and who will take a stand on it by refusing to buy a Catholic publication which deliberately chooses not to use inclusive language. One can only hope that this deeply offensive approach will in fact be a *felix culpa*, a happy fault, in that it will evoke the kind of constructive anger which Christ himself displayed at injustice, and will lead in the end to a real and more gracious acceptance of gender equality at all levels of Church life. Perhaps only through this conflictual process, and through a respect for the strong feelings on both sides of this argument, will there eventually result that goal of just reconciliation to which, as followers of Christ, we are all called.

Notes

1 For what follows, see K. Rahner, 'Mystery' in K. Rahner (ed.) *Encyclopedia of Theology* (London: Burns & Oates, 1975), pp. 1000–4; M. Kehl and W. Löser (eds), *The von Balthasar Reader* (Edinburgh: T. & T. Clark, 1982), pp. 113–46 (especially pp. 124–27).

2 See G. O'Hanlon, *The Immutability of God in the Theology of Hans Urs von Balthasar* (Cambridge: CUP, 1990), pp. 137–44.

3 See Patrick Kerans, *Sinful Social Structures* (New York: Paulist, 1974), chs 1–3.

4 See John P. Galvin. 'Jesus Christ' in F. Schüssler Fiorenza and J. Galvin (eds), *Systematic Theology* (Dublin: Gill & Macmillan, 1992), pp. 251–323; E. Johnson, *Consider Jesus* (London: Geoffrey Chapman, 1990), chs 1–2.

5 See J. Courtney Murray, 'Is it basket-weaving?' in *We Hold These Truths* (London: Sheed & Ward, 1960), pp. 175–96.

6 See Johnson, *Consider Jesus,* p. 29.

7 See J. Segundo, *The Christ of the Ignatian Exercises* (ET Maryknoll: Orbis, 1987), p. 35.

8 See Segundo, ibid., pp. 90–1; Johnson, *Consider Jesus*, ch. 5. See also D. Lane, *Christ at the Centre* (Dublin: Veritas, 1990), ch. 2.

9 See P. Hebblethwaite, 'Paul VI and the women', *The Tablet* (27 March 1993), pp. 398–9.

10 For a seminal theological treatment of this theme, see E. Johnson, 'The incomprehensibility of God and the image of God male and female', *Theological Studies* 45 (1984), pp. 441–80.

11 For what follows, see A. Carr, *Transforming Grace* (San Francisco: Harper & Row, 1988), especially ch. 8; Johnson, ch. 7; W. Thompson, *The Jesus Debate*

(New York: Paulist, 1985), ch. 13; D. Lane, ch. 2; E. Bredin, *Disturbing the Peace* (Mystic, CT: Twenty-Third Publications, 1985), ch. 7.

12 See H. U. von Balthasar, *The Glory of the Lord*, vol. VII: *The New Covenant* (Edinburgh/San Francisco: T. & T. Clark/Ignatius, 1989).

13 See H. U. von Balthasar, *Man in History* (ET London: Sheed & Ward, 1968), pp. 239–74; J. O'Donnell, *Hans Urs von Balthasar* (London: Geoffrey Chapman, 1992), pp. 50–1.

14 See M. Lynch, 'Married and religious obedience', *Religious Life Review*, 32 (1993), pp. 2–4.

15 See W. Dych, *Karl Rahner* (London: Geoffrey Chapman, 1992), pp. 28–9; H. U. von Balthasar, 'Theologie und Heiligkeit' in *Verbum Caro* (Einsiedeln: Johannes, 1960).

16 See H. U. von Balthasar, 'Fides Christi' in *Sponsa Verbi* (Einsiedeln: Johannes, 1960); A. Nolan, *Jesus before Christianity* (London: Darton, Longman & Todd, 1977), ch. 14.

17 For what follows, in addition to the Christological works already cited, see G. O'Collins, *Interpreting Jesus* (London: Geoffrey Chapman, 1983), ch. 2.

18 See B. McDermott, *What Are They Saying About the Grace of Christ?* (New York: Paulist, 1984), ch. 2.

19 See Bredin, *Disturbing the Peace*, ch. 5 and *passim*.

20 Johnson, *Consider Jesus*, p. 26.

21 See O. Maloney, 'Moral dilemmas in modern business', *The Furrow* 44 (1993), pp. 12–20; P. Vardy, 'Business morality: people and profit'. *The Way* 32 (1992), pp. 301–11; S. Murphy, 'The Church in socio-economic debate'. *Studies* 82 (1993), pp. 1–14.

22 Aloysius Pieris, 'Redefining religious life', talk given in Dublin, 1990.

23 G. Gutiérrez, *We Drink from Our Own Wells* (ET London: SCM, 1984), esp. chs 7 and 8.

24 A. Nolan, 'Transformation of the Church', text of a talk given to a Justice and Peace Conference in Johannesburg, November 1987.

25 See G. O'Hanlon, 'A middle-class Church for a working-class people', *The Furrow* 44 (1993), pp. 3–11.

26 The Irish Episcopal Conference, *Work Is the Key* (Dublin: Veritas, 1992).

27 See Segundo, *Christ of the Ignatian Exercises, passim;* J. Sobrino, *Christology at the Crossroads* (ET London: SCM, 1978), especially the Appendix on the Christ of the Ignatian Exercises; G. O'Hanlon, 'The Jesuits and modern theology—Rahner, von Balthasar and liberation theology', *Irish Theological Quarterly* 58 (1992), pp. 25–45.

28 See D. Nicholls, 'Trinity and conflict', *Theology* xcvi (1993), p. 23 (pp. 19–27).

29 See K. Kelly, 'Do we believe in a Church of sinners?', *The Way* 33 (1993), pp. 106–16. In this context Kelly quotes interestingly from Cardinal Ratzinger: 'Is it unconditionally a sign of better times that today's theologians no longer dare to speak prophetically? Is it not rather a sign of a feeble love which no longer makes the heart burn for God's cause (2 Cor 12:2)?'

30 See O'Hanlon, 'Jesuits and modern theology', pp. 9–10.

31 See also P. Valadier, *The Tablet* (21 November 1992).

32 See Galvin, 'Jesus Christ', p. 286

33 See S. Barrow, 'Mystique and politique: spirituality left or right', *The Way* 32 (1992), p. 43 (pp. 43–53).

34 Segundo, *Christ of the Ignatian Exercises*, ch. 7.

35 See L. Puhl (ed.), *The Spiritual Exercises of St Ignatius* (Chicago: Loyola University Press, 1951), nn. 277–8.

The Death of Christ, his Descent among the Dead, and his Resurrection

(Paragraphs 571–682)

John McDade SJ

Heythrop College, University of London

In its exposition of the death and resurrection of Jesus, the *Catechism* does not stray far from the statements of the New Testament, presumably for three reasons: (1) these foundational and normative statements are the privileged and inspired source of all subsequent soteriology; (2) there is a general reluctance on the part of the Church to treat soteriology with the precision which has characterised its treatment of Christology and Trinity; (3) the *Catechism* aims to offer teaching which will recall fundamentals, rather than propose a particular theological approach.

It is therefore difficult to specify the *Catechism*'s view of salvation, since it restates the common themes which have always stimulated the Church's prayerful reflection. The exposition it offers, for the most part, could have been compiled at any stage in Christian history. This has clear advantages, but weaknesses too: to judge from the *Catechism*, our contemporary context at the end of the second millennium makes no noticeable impact on how the Roman Catholic Church interprets the salvation brought by Christ.

The exception is a valuable and positive statement about the death of Jesus and the Jewish people: here one can see the benefit of the new approach to Judaism which has arisen since *Nostra Aetate*. It is no accident that this is the most coherently argued passage, since it is confident about what it needs to say, and says it well.

He suffered, was crucified and died

The Catechism of the Council of Trent, while recognising that 'it is on this Article, as on their foundation, that the Christian faith and religion rests', adds honestly: 'only with great difficulty can we grasp the fact that our salvation depends on the cross, and on Him who was nailed thereon.' The difficulty lies, for once, not in the obtuseness of the human mind, but in the foolish wisdom of God who decreed that humanity be brought to

143

glory through the crucifixion of Jesus and his exaltation (1 Cor 1:18ff.).

Christian theology has, classically, three answers to the question 'why are we saved in this way?', all of which belong together: the first and fundamental answer is simply that it is the will of God to make his love effective in this way. Jesus' teaching at Caesarea Philippi is still stark and shocking because it offers no help to the human mind: 'the Son of Man *must* undergo great suffering, and be rejected . . . and be killed, and after three days rise again' (Mk 8:31).

The second answer seeks to present this necessity as a fulfilment of anticipatory indications in the Jewish Scriptures which, because they seem to prefigure what happened, can be used to interpret features of the story. The risen Christ unlocked the key to the Scriptures and taught his disciples that 'everything written about me in the law of Moses, the prophets, and the psalms must be fulfilled . . . Thus it is written, that the Messiah is to suffer and to rise from the dead on the third day . . .' (Lk 24:44ff.). In this way, a coherence between the Jewish Scriptures and the life of Jesus is established, in which the language of the one casts light on the character of the other, and the words of the Scriptures are made to illuminate the Word made mortal flesh.

This way of reading the Jewish Scriptures is as old as the New Testament itself, which is suffused with the sense of the typological unity of literary anticipation and historical fulfilment in Jesus: *novum testamentum in vetere latet, vetus in novo patet*. The earliest Christian theology begins as exegesis of Jewish Scriptures in the light of Jesus and as the composition of Christian midrashim.[1]

Working from the first two, the third answer accepts Anselm's maxim that 'the will of God is never irrational' (*Cur Deus Homo,* VIII). Consequently we can seek the reasons — of 'fitting necessity' — which make the death of Jesus the means of our salvation. Anselm offers a strong version of this case: we could not have been saved in any way other than by the self-sacrifice of the incarnate Son on the cross. Less confident about what we can know, Aquinas, on the other hand, judges that we *could* have been saved in another way, but argues that since we have been saved in *this* way, we can discern features in the death of Jesus which make it a uniquely fitting means of salvation: 'It was better for us to have been delivered by Christ's passion than by God's will alone' (STh III, 46, 3). This third answer tries to discern, if not a necessity surrounding the death and resurrection of Jesus, then at least its supreme fittingness for God's purposes in relation to the creation.

The third approach, if handled with an agnostic reverence for God's mystery, seeks to amplify our understanding of the two factors whose confluence signals a terrible disorder, the resolution of which becomes the central focus of the salvation brought by Jesus: on one hand, God's freedom to make his love a tangible, vulnerable and effective reality among us and, on the other hand, our refusal to be the beloved sons and daughters of the Creator. Here God and humanity act, we might say, characteristically: God, by allowing his Son to be the healing victim of the sinful brutality which characterises human history, and human beings, by a combination of malice and blindness in the face of divine love. (Golgotha, not the Garden of Eden, is where the nature of sin comes to light.) It is this very act of violent rejection which brings the inexhaustible outpouring of the sanctifying Spirit, the gift both of the Father who hands his Son over to sinners, and of the Son who glorifies the Father in his death (614). The drama of salvation, with its double focus of God's self-gift and human resistance, becomes a dialogue of peace, culminating in the promise of the resurrection that it is God's mercy and not human sin which will have the last word on the destiny of the creation. In William Langland's words:

And all the wickedness in
this world   that man might work or think

Is no more to the mercy of God   than a live coal in the sea.

All three approaches have their place in the *Catechism*. The first locates in the 'mystery of God's plan' that Jesus 'was handed over according to the definite plan and foreknowledge of God' (Acts 2:23) (599). This scriptural testimony is interpreted with reference to God's eternal presence to all moments of time, and hence God's foreknowledge includes the knowledge of how human beings will act in their freedom (600). Although the issue is not pursued, Aquinas's view seems to underlie this brief incursion into philosophy.[2]

The second approach, bringing together Jewish Scriptures and Christian understanding, has always been a fertile source of imagery and typological thinking for a Church which values the theological unity of the two Testaments.[3] Although the theological tradition is rich, the *Catechism* does not offer a sumptuous biblical feast, and restricts its attention to the 'Suffering Servant' of Isaiah 52:13ff. (601; cf. 608; 615) and the Passover Lamb, 'the symbol of Israel's redemption at the first Passover' (608; cf. 613).[4]

The Suffering Servant of Isaiah 52:13ff. is the generative core of the earliest salvation formulae of the 'surrender' of Jesus (Rom 4:25; Gal 1:4; 2:20; Titus 2:14; 1 Tim 2:6; Mk 10:45; 1 Cor 11:25) and of his dying 'for many' or 'for us' or 'for our sins' (1 Cor 15:3; 1 Pet 2:21ff.; 3:18; Rom 5:6). The text acted as a catalyst which transformed the relationship of Jesus to the Scriptures: embedded within the Jewish Scriptures is a portrait of an innocent and righteous servant, whose election by God brings upon him rejection and affliction; though innocent, he is numbered among transgressors, and so his suffering is mysteriously related to the sins which he seems to bear 'for them'; his suffering brings healing to others and his affliction will make many righteous.

Pre-eminently, it provides a context for understanding the *event* of Jesus' suffering and death — it was foretold, and therefore falls within God's providence for the world — and of its *saving significance* — it takes place as an atoning intercession for sinners. Therefore other scriptural passages can be read in the same way: if Jesus' death marks the fulfilment of such a luminous prophecy, then it is right to search the

Scriptures for other texts which equally cast light on the death of Jesus. What I have called the third approach — the attempt to probe God's purpose in the death of Jesus — arises directly out of the reading of this text and others gathered by the early community in collections of *testimonia*. The programme behind the formula 'according to the Scriptures' (1 Cor 15:3 *et al.*) is the search for how to say that Jesus' death took place 'according to God's will', as indicated — where else? — in the sacred Scriptures.

The search has its origin, according to the *Catechism*, not in the early Christian community but in Jesus himself, who 'explained the meaning of his life and death in the light of God's suffering Servant (Mt 20:28)' and interpreted his mission in categories which flowed into the Church's understanding (Mk 10:45; 14:22ff.). It is notoriously difficult, exegetically, to isolate a core of teachings given originally by Jesus about his death from those developed by the early Christian community: it is more like the unmaking of an omelette — frustratingly impossible — than the unpeeling of an onion to reveal its core. However, the *Catechism* is rightly neither sceptical nor minimalist in its estimate of the scope of Jesus' own contribution to Christian soteriology.[5] Only a rigidly methodological scepticism would refuse to accord a centrality to his self-interpretation, shown especially in his actions at the Last Supper and in the traditions which issue in the passion predictions in the Synoptic Gospels.[6] Jesus is the first (exegetical) theologian of the salvation he brings.

The wealth of salvation in Christ cannot be exhausted by one particular formula, and so in 599–618 the *Catechism* recapitulates the range of fundamental interpretations of Jesus' death reached in the New Testament: it is 'a mystery of universal redemption' (601); an atonement to free us from the 'slavery of sin' (601); a reconciliation of sinners who had been separated from God by sin (603); a 'voluntary offering to the Father for the salvation of men' (610); 'the Paschal sacrifice that accomplishes the definitive redemption of men' (613); a 'reparation for our disobedience' (614); a 'redemptive sacrifice' (616); the sacrifice which completes Jesus' work of mediation (616). These great metaphors of salvation yoke together patterns of death and life; enmity and reconciliation; hatred and love; aggression and peace-making; sin and forgiveness. In the words of Paul Celan:

> A RUMBLING: truth
> itself has appeared
> among humankind
> in the very thick of their
> flurrying metaphors.[7]

All accounts of the significance of Golgotha depend upon flurrying metaphors, particularly the great 'root metaphors' of salvation, reconciliation and redemption. The phrases invite us to see the death of Jesus as, for example, the affliction of the Servant; an atoning sacrifice; an offering for sin; an act of liberation; a ransom for slaves; a High Priestly offering, a peace-making, etc. In Paul Ricoeur's phrase, 'the symbol gives rise to thought', and the resonances of these metaphors give rise to Christian soteriology. It is no accident that the language of salvation flows from a *complex* of images which, together, illuminate different aspects of what needs to be said: not everything can be said at once, so a cluster of images is required.

St Paul, for example, has to rely on *ten* different images to describe what Christ accomplished by his death: justification, salvation, reconciliation, expiation, redemption, freedom, sanctification, transformation, new creation and glorification. In addition, one might also mention themes of victory over death, the first-fruits of the general resurrection, the healing of the roots of human nature and the restoration of creation in Christ. Joseph Fitzmyer comments on Paul's multi-faceted approach:

> For each of these images expresses a distinctive aspect of the mystery of Christ and his work. If the Christ-event is conceived of as a decagon, a ten-sided solid figure, one can understand how Paul, gazing at one panel of it, would use one image to express an effect of it, whereas he would use another image when gazing at another panel.[8]

All metaphors hold together two realities, one of which is viewed as the other. In Owen Barfield's words, a metaphor is 'a deliberate yoking of unlikes',[9] held together in order that our account of one reality might acquire the transferred connotations of the other. 'Man is a wolf', 'spiritual decay is a cobweb on the soul', 'pleasure is a lighthouse flash across empty wastes' are new ways of thinking about man, spiritual decay and pleasure. When we make sense of metaphors like these, we engage in a type of 'stereoscopic vision' which brings together two points of view at the same time: the referents (man, spiritual decay, pleasure), without losing their own characteristics, are viewed in an entirely different way through being seen as 'wolf', 'cobweb', 'lighthouse flash'.

There is a particular appropriateness in the use of metaphors in this part of theology, because at the heart of Christian reflection is an analogous act of 'holding together' two disparate perspectives, one constituted by the facts of the event, and the other by the way these facts are seen in faith and in the light of the Jewish Scriptures. There is, on the one hand, the hard, factual reality that Jesus died as a blasphemer and a political criminal — this never loses its scandalous character — and, on the other hand, the assertion that this baseness is where God's love becomes an effective, healing reality in the world. The *fact* — 'Jesus is brutally executed' — and the *redescription* — 'God was reconciling the world to himself in this death' — are held together in a stereoscopic vision in which *one* is seen as the *other*.

Jesus' death is then the death of the Suffering Servant who bears our sins; it is the casting aside of the stone which then becomes the keystone (Ps 118:22; Mk 12:10); it is the death of the righteous one who has been subject to conspiracy, condemnation and a shameful death (Wis 2:12ff.), but who, through God's action, will be vindicated before his oppressors

(Wis 5:1ff.). Or using other images: his death can be seen as a ransom (Mk 10:45); the offering of 'a lamb without defect or blemish' (1 Pet 1:19); the sacrifice at the heart of the Covenant (Ex 24:8; Mk 14:24); the sacrifice of 'our paschal lamb' (1 Cor 5:7); the entry of the High Priest into the Holy of Holies to offer, not the blood of animals, but a complete offering of himself (Heb 9:12ff.). The metaphors of salvation, like starlings, love the company of others.

This 'stereoscopic vision' lies behind one of the most profound interpretations which opens the way to seeing Jesus' death in relation to the store of human sin: Paul, quoting from an earlier Christian tradition, sees the shedding of Jesus' blood as the sprinkling of blood on the golden lid of the ark of the covenant on the day of Atonement (Rom 3:25; Ex 25:17–22). The crucified Messiah is seen as the *hilastērion,* the 'mercy seat', the true locus of expiation, prefigured in the atoning rites of the Temple.[10] By extension, Golgotha, while remaining the place of the skull where criminals are executed, becomes the centre of the true Temple where there is the effective expiation of sins, since God 'condemned sin in the flesh' of Jesus (Rom 8:3). 'For our sake [God] made him to be sin who knew no sin, so that in him we might become the righteousness of God' (2 Cor 5:21).

Thus, in addition to seeing Jesus as the Servant who bears the iniquities of others (Is 53:11), the significance of his death is elaborated as an act of expiation for sin, willed by God for the purification and sanctification of humanity. The Temple imagery is further developed — metaphors are capable of indefinite expansion — in the Epistle to the Ephesians: in his flesh Jesus removes the wall which divides the court of the Gentiles from the inner court, eliminates the division between Jew and Gentile, and makes peace 'in order to create in himself one new humanity' (Eph 2:14ff.).

Although we may seem to have come a long way from Golgotha, this theological amplification never loses touch with the events of Jesus' death. Rather, it focuses a bright light on the cross as the drama between God's freedom to bestow mercy and to heal the effects of sin, and the freedom of creation which, in rejecting the Son, finds itself most intensely cherished and restored in peace. We are brought back again to the rightness of Aquinas's puzzling judgement: 'It was better for us to have been delivered by Christ's passion than by God's will alone.' Why? Because the cross is the effective moment of God's self-gift to the freely turbulent creation, and all the images we have used take us back to our first answer that this is simply God's loving will.

Can it be discussed further? Only by speaking in trinitarian terms, since if, as Rahner insists, the Trinity is a 'mystery of salvation', then salvation is grounded in the triune life of God. The *Catechism*'s summaries in 457–461 and 606 invite this perspective. Gerard Manley Hopkins, in his retreat notes of 1881, relates Jesus' death on the cross to the dynamic of love within the life of the triune God. The initiative begins in God, in the Son's desire to give glory to the Father:

Why did the Son of God go forth from the Father not only in the eternal and intrinsic procession of the Trinity but also by an extrinsic and less than eternal, let us say aeonian one?

— To give God glory and that by sacrifice, sacrifice offered in the barren wilderness outside of God, as the children of Israel were led into the wilderness to offer sacrifice. This sacrifice and this outward procession is a consequence and shadow of the procession of the Trinity, from which mystery sacrifice takes its rise . . . It is as if the blissful agony or stress of selving in God had forced out drops of sweat or blood, which drops were the world, or as if the lights lit at the festival of the 'peaceful Trinity' through some little cranny striking out lit up into being one 'cleave' out of the world of possible creatures.[11]

Six years later, Matthias Scheeben, with the same theological instinct, was to write that 'the idea of Christ's sacrifice thrusts its roots deep into the abyss of the Trinity' since it is both the expression of the trinitarian life and the means by which the creation is drawn into God's blessed life:

. . . Christ's sacrifice must be regarded as the perfect effusion and the most exalted outward representation of the eternal love which Christ bears for the Father as the Son of God . . . [We] can present Christ's sacrifice in the very form in which it was actually offered, namely, in the shedding of His blood to the last drop as *the highest expression of the Trinitarian relations and the most perfect vehicle of their extension to the outside world.*[12]

This approach invites us to say that the condescending movement towards the creation, focused in the incarnation and in the outpouring of the Spirit, and reaching its consummation in the death and resurrection of Jesus, is the expression of the love which is God.[13] In the paschal mystery, the Son identifies with a creation which has become lost in its experience of freedom, to seal such a strong bond of solidarity with those 'subject to the fear of death' (Heb 2:15), in taking their experience as his experience, that no part of creaturely life stands untouched by his presence (Rom 8:32). In Gabriel Daly's words, 'so pervasive of creation is innocent suffering that not even God's Son can escape it':[14] God takes seriously the disorder which the human will has inscribed on the whole of the world's experience, even to the point of taking it upon himself. God does not will to stand aside from the circumstances which free sin brings about, but enters it in all its lawlessness so that divine love and not human sin will determine the final destiny of the creation. If Jesus bears the sin of the world, he also bears the burden of being God's loving self-gift. Von Balthasar gives classic expression to this:

. . . the Son of God as man takes upon himself, out of the love of God, the sickness unto death of the creature who has strayed away from God and so goes to the place from which no man can rescue himself. . . . God causes God to go into abandonment by God, while accompanying him on the way with his Spirit. The Son can go into the estrangement from God of hell, because he understands his way as an expression of his love for the Father, and can give to his love the character of obedience, to such a degree that in it he experiences the complete godlessness of lost man.[15]

In that condition of estrangement, he renews the roots of free creaturely life, breaking the patterns of frustrated, cumulative sin (602), and draws human beings into an act of perfect prayer and praise in union with him (605; 618). Redemption is always eucharistic, since the death of the Son enables us to make valid prayer: we stand, no longer strangers (Eph 2:13ff.), but finally free children of God beside a brother whose death, with us and for us, has brought life.

The *Catechism*, in its treatment of the incarnation (457–461), recalls the Patristic tradition that the salvation brought by Christ is not restricted to the efficacy of his death: the 'taking of flesh' begins the work of healing and reconciliation. 'Christ's whole life is a mystery of redemption ... at work throughout Christ's entire life' (517). Maximus the Confessor said that Christ 're-established human nature in conformity with itself' (*Expositio in Orationis Dominicae*, PG 90, 877D): by the incarnation, the Son of God set the human will at peace with nature and with God. The Romanian Orthodox theologian Dumitru Staniloae, following Maximus, says that 'it is precisely through this harmonizing of the will that the reconciliation of man with God is achieved'.[16] It is a point which should not be ignored in our consideration of the saving work of Christ. The freedom of God to love, heal and bring about the good of the creation takes place in a way which respects and deepens the *freedom of the creation,* as reconstituted in the incarnate Son. He is — again a metaphor — the second root of the human race, according to Cyril of Alexandria, a source of holiness for all: 'In Adam, the root of the human race, like a mother, has died; but those who came forth from it — that is, we ourselves — have blossomed anew in Christ and we are saved if we have him as our life and our second root.'[17]

This tradition — of the healing of human nature in Christ — is worth recalling in the present context when some trinitarian theology, especially in the Lutheran tradition, focuses on the *death* of the Son of God as 'the death of God', God's struggle with 'the annihilating power of nothingness'.[18] Theologians like Jürgen Moltmann and Eberhard Jüngel treat death as the surd within the creation, the focus of destructiveness, which God resolves by absorbing it in the death of his Son. The *Catechism,* by contrast, makes sin, not death, the focus of God's action of salvation. We are redeemed not from death, but from sin, since the point of destructiveness within creation is not in the fact of death, but in the moral evil associated with human freedom: this is the point where the creation can be mortally self-destructive. We cannot envisage the creation without death — it is a fact of organic life — but in the person of Jesus we are asked to consider the creation *without sin,* because we are defined not by our resistance to God, but by our faithful responsiveness.[19]

At the level of our metaphors, however, death stands as the symbol of sinful destructiveness: this is how I would read the *Catechism's* statement 'Man's sins, following on original sin, are punishable by death' (602). As a bald statement it does not speak to the men and women of our time. We die, not because we are sinners, but because we are animals, and dying is what animals do. But nevertheless, there is a 'death' associated with sin which is a graver matter than physical dying: the closing of the human heart to God, particularly in the sinful killing of others. The witness of martyrdom — and Jesus is the great witness of faithfulness — is an assertion that there is, in all seriousness, a more destructive reality than death, namely, the option of rejecting God's love. It also affirms, as does the death of Jesus, that human identity is defined neither by its mortality nor by its inherited and wilful sinfulness, but by the exercise of its freedom in response to God. The Son of God takes the sphere of human freedom — the focus of disordered nature — and turns it into the place of love and obedience. In symbolic terms, the heart of Christ is the *locus* of salvation, the *hilastērion* within the Temple, where the sins of our nature are cleansed, and God is, finally, worshipped in spirit and truth (618).

In this perspective, the drama of the cross is not God's entry into death, but is the most intense focus of union between God and the creation when the incarnate Son in his testing (Heb 2:18) restores the non-divine order to a pitch of responsiveness and perfected identity. His physical death is the outward sign, the sacrament, of the union between our creaturely existence, which he assumes, and God. When Jesus entrusts his life to the Father in the midst of hatred and violence, his death, like the death of all of us, is disclosed to be not the entry into nothingness which the God-forsaken imagination fears, but the entry into the deepest dimension of creatureliness, namely God's love. His death, again like the death of all of us, marks a moment, not of emptiness, but of deeper union: not a hiatus, but a deeper blessedness. E. M. Forster's dictum 'Death destroys a man; the idea of death saves him' can be reversed with more truth than we might think.

From our consideration thus far, we can highlight a number of points: (1) dying does not destroy a person: instead, death is a deeper entry into God's love; (2) God's creative action does not cease, because, being a self-gift, it bestows on the world what we can only think of as a 'destiny' which marks the fulfilment of creatureliness; (3) we are loved for a purpose, and the death of Jesus is both a sign and a realisation (a 'cause', to use scholastic terminology) of the gift of God which marks the purposeful nature of God's self-gift to us. With these remarks, we are beginning, I think, to allow our understanding of death to go beyond the categories of pre-Christian thinking about death which still shape our thinking and feeling, and to uncover implications for our anthropology which might flow from the death of Jesus.

He descended to the dead

The early tradition found an important way of expressing a Christian understanding of death in the myth of the descent of Jesus 'to hell' ('Hades', or 'Sheol'), to 'the abode of the dead'. The *Catechism*, following the Creed, turns to this theme in 631–635. We should not be afraid to speak of this as a 'myth': it is a narrative in which death is portrayed as a journey to the underworld where the dead wait for God's salvation. Language of *descent* has a privileged place in the classic formulations of Christology. The Son of God *descends from heaven to earth*: the phrase is a mythical and imaginative equivalent of what is meant by saying, more technically, that the Son is 'of one substance with the Father', and becomes 'of one substance with us, though without sin'. It enables us to think of the 'descent' of the Son of God as a progressive movement or mission: first of all, to the womb of the Virgin where he assumes our condition; then into the waters of the Jordan at the Baptism where his Sonship assumes the role of the Servant of God; then, further, into the abasement of the cross; culminating in his burial in the tomb, when he shares the condition of all those who have died (632). Does his mission continue? The Christian imagination says that it does, and thinks of a mission of Jesus to the dead: he dwells in 'the abode of the dead', 'so that the dead will hear the voice of the Son of God and those who hear will live' (635; Jn 5:25).

The classic version of this story presents Satan and Hades (Death) holding prisoner all the saints of human history, who wait there until they can be freed. The gaolers look forward to finally being able to add Jesus to their number, but suddenly the gates of hell burst open and the 'King of glory' enters (Ps 24:9). He binds Satan, for 'no one can plunder the house of the strong man unless he bind him first' (Mk 3:27). Then Jesus takes the hand of Adam, and turns to those descended from him:

> 'Come with me, all you who have suffered death through the tree which this man touched. For behold, I raise you all up again through the tree of the cross.' With that, he put them all out. And our forefather Adam was seen to be full of joy . . . The Saviour blessed Adam with the sign of the cross on his forehead. And he did this to the patriarchs and prophets and martyrs and forefathers. And he took them and leapt up out of Hades. And as he went, the holy fathers sang praises following him and saying, 'Blessed is he who comes in the name of the Lord'.[20]

This story passes into Christian tradition in an abbreviated phrase in the Creed — 'he descended to hell' — but, more importantly, it becomes, through its representation in the icons of the Orthodox churches, the great symbol of the resurrection. In the icon, Jesus stands on top of the doors of hell which have fallen in the shape of the cross, takes the hands of Adam and Eve, the representatives of the creation which awaits salvation, and draws them out of death to heaven. Behind them always stand Moses and Elijah, David and Solomon and John the Baptist, the bridge between hope and fulfilment. The *Catechism* goes to the heart of what is offered by the myth and by the icon tradition:

> The descent into hell brings the Gospel message of salvation to complete fulfilment. This is the last phase of Jesus' messianic mission, a phase which is condensed in time but vast in its real significance: the spread of Christ's redemptive work to all men of all times and all places. for all who are saved have been made sharers in the redemption. (634)

Within recent Roman Catholic theology, this myth has been remarkably revived by Hans Urs von Balthasar: at a time when the call to 'demythologise' has been loud, he has shown that it is possible to revitalise the use of myth in Christian theology, and enable contemporary Christians to find their way to a 'second naiveté' (Ricoeur) in response to this ancient story. He finds a significance in Holy Saturday, the 'nontime' between Good Friday and Easter Sunday: on that day, there is the descent of the dead Jesus to the hell of sinners, expressing his solidarity 'with those who have lost their way from God'. He is dead 'together with them':

> And exactly in that way, he disturbs the absolute loneliness striven for by the sinner: the sinner, who wants to be damned apart from God, finds God again in his loneliness, but God in the absolute weakness of love who unfathomably in the period of nontime enters into solidarity with those damning themselves. The words of the Psalm, 'If I make my bed in the netherworld, thou art there' (Ps 139.8), thereby take on a new meaning . . . Only in absolute weakness does God will to mediate to the freedom created by him the gift of love that breaks from every prison and every constraint: in his solidarity from within with those who reject all solidarity.[21]

In his death, Jesus goes in search of the sheep that are lost, since his presence among both the living and the dead is a searching evangelisation among sinners who have existentially defined themselves against God. Balthasar's account, of course, goes beyond the boundaries of the early Christian myth, and suggests that we might *hope* — we can do no more! — that *all* will be saved. This perspective of universal salvation, which has haunted Christian theology since Origen, is raised by Balthasar's interpretation of Jesus' presence among the dead as a saving presence even to those who, in the exercise of their freedom, have shut themselves off from God's love. (It is worth remembering that the doctrine of hell is primarily not a doctrine about God, but a teaching about the scale of human freedom and choice: it tells us about what we recognise as the scope of human possibilities on a theoretical level. The doctrine of purgatory, on the other hand, is primarily a teaching about the immense scope of God's mercy in relation to human sin.)

Although the *Catechism* is clear that Christ's presence among the dead is not to be viewed as a deliverance of the damned from hell (633), we should remember that the Church has never said that anyone has actually reached that limit of self-damning choice: hell, we might hope, is an empty dark star. Balthasar's expansion of the myth of the descent need not conflict with the *Catechism*'s teaching on this point, but, instead, says to us that God's mercy, shown in the death of his Son who dies with sinners and for sinners, can have no limits placed on it by the human mind. An instructive insight into this is given in Dante's *Purgatorio:* the first soul Dante meets in the Ante-Purgatory is Manfred, the King of Sicily who died excommunicate and whose body was disinterred after his death and cast out of church lands by the Pope. In spite of these censures, he is not condemned by God, because as he tells Dante:

> My sins were horrible,
> but the infinite goodness has arms so wide
> that it receives whoever turns to it.

Words like this speak to us with a grace-filled intuition that divine mercy exceeds human constraints and may even embrace sinful freedom: God's words to Moses, 'I will be gracious to whom I will be gracious, and will show mercy on whom I will show mercy' (Ex 33:19), challenges any attempt to restrict the scope of divine forbearance. The theme of the descent of Jesus to the dead invites us to think that the bond of solidarity which the Son of God seals with us in our mortality is a saving presence whose scope extends to all those lost in the far country (Lk 15:13), since his death is an effective presence to sinners of every hue, and the hope it offers extends to the whole human family.

On the third day he was raised

Already, with this myth of the descent among the dead, we have begun to touch on the theme of resurrection. The two days of Good Friday and Holy Saturday — the days of Christ's suffering and solidarity with the dead — bear the lineaments of God's loving action towards the world, embracing the enigmas of sin, violence, suffering and death. Easter Sunday now brings the design in the threads into clear relief, since it is the day of revelation, the day of resolution, the day of completion, the day of transfiguration. On that day, Jesus enters the fullness of God's peace, and there takes place, in the words of Ignatius of Antioch, 'a clamorous mystery wrought in the stillness of God' (*Eph.* 19.1).

There is a loud proclamation — 'Jesus is risen' — but there is also the silence of what took place: the Church can only proclaim *that* Jesus is risen, without being able to say *what* took place, for the silence of God surrounds it. In the New Testament, unlike the Apocryphal Gospels, there is no attempt to describe the resurrection itself: the witnesses are only witnesses to what God leads them to believe, and what the risen Christ reveals to them (647). They carry no message about the nature of that event which remains uncharted: a 'theology of the resurrection' cannot transgress these limits and say what cannot be said. The resurrection of Jesus is the *sanctum* of inner silence within all Christian perception. The words of Coleridge are apposite here:

> I warn all Inquirers into this hard point to *wait* — not only not to plunge forward before the Word is *given* to them, but not even to paw the ground with impatience. For in a deep stillness only can this truth be apprehended.[22]

The resurrection is proclaimed; it is not understood. If it stands, as it must, as the union of the Son with the Father in the triune life (648), and, simultaneously, as the consummation of God's dealings with the creation, then our language fails on two accounts. First of all, we can describe the Trinity only in its saving action towards us, but we cannot deal with intra-trinitarian love except by images and analogies which have limited scope. The mystery of God is not removed by trinitarian theology. Secondly, we have no adequate language for the overarching relationship of God and the creation which here reaches its consummation.

On this latter point, the principles arrived at in the Church's Christology are important in discussing the resurrection: the Council of Chalcedon said of the union of the divine and human natures of Christ that they are 'without confusion, without change, without division, without separation'. The human nature of Jesus retains its characteristics in its hypostatic union with the divine Son of God. These Greek adverbs also regulate the two orders of God and the creation: whatever that relationship is, it is one in which God remains God, and the creation remains the creation. There is no fusion of the two orders, no mixing, no absorption of one in the other, but neither are the two orders of God and the creation separate, one from the other. In looser terminology, God remains 'transcendent' — not confused with the world — but is also 'immanent' — not detached from the creation which depends on God: God and the creation are neither *confused* nor *separate*. This is a way of identifying this primary relationship which excludes pantheism and deism, but it identifies the self-communication of God to the creation only *negatively*, since although we can say what it is not, we cannot positively specify its character. *A fortiori*, we cannot positively specify the character of the consummation which is the resurrection.

These controls on our theological language shape the way in which potentially misleading images such as the 'deification' or 'divinisation' of the creation ought to be understood. It is our destiny, not to be 'absorbed' into the divine, but to be brought to a fullness of creaturely identity under God's self-gift. Christian belief in the resurrection of Jesus affirms that whatever the completion of God's self-gift is, it has taken place in Jesus of Nazareth. 'For in [Christ] every one of God's promises is a "Yes"' (2 Cor 1:20). The related, and dependent, teaching about the Assumption of the Blessed Virgin says importantly that her role as 'the first of the redeemed', the archetype of the Church and saved humanity, is to be understood as including a realised participation in the completion God wills for Jesus. She is our redeemed and living sister.

We can relate this to our earlier discussion: if death marks an entry into a deeper blessedness, if it marks not a rupture in God's self-gift to the world, but a more profound entry into that love, then what is signalled in the resurrection of Jesus is the completion of the transforming self-gift of God. If the humanity that he took, 'like us in all things but sin', does not stand outside the transforming love of God, then the promise of the resurrection is that our death will be similarly blessed (655). It is a promise enunciated in Paul's sequential ordering of the consummation: '. . . All will be made alive in Christ. But each in his own order: Christ the first fruits, then at his coming those who belong to Christ. Then comes the end, when he hands over the kingdom to God the Father . . . The last enemy to be destroyed is death' (1 Cor 15:22ff.). The resurrection of Jesus is the opening of the coda, but he will not be raised without us.

The *Catechism* insists that the resurrection of Jesus is a 'real event' (639), 'essentially different' from the raising of those, like Lazarus, who returned to 'ordinary earthly life' (646). Its unique status, however, does not mean that it takes place 'outside the physical order'. The *Catechism* says that 'it is impossible not to acknowledge it as an historical fact' (643). Something *happened*, here and in our time. In a carefully fenced statement which affirms both its transcendent character and its character as 'event', the *Catechism* says:

> Although the Resurrection was an historical event that could be verified by the sign of the empty tomb and by the reality of the apostles' encounters with the risen Christ, still it remains at the very heart of the mystery of faith as something that transcends and surpasses history. (647)

The *Catechism*'s fundamental principle is that the resurrection was *real*. Negatively, it rejects the proposal that belief in the resurrection is a covert and coded way of saying that the mission of Jesus is still valid in spite of his death. Equally, it denies that belief in the resurrection is created by a prior faith or 'credulity' on the part of the apostles (644): instead, the antecedent action of God in the resurrection generates the Church's faith. Positively, it insists that the reality of the risen Jesus is not a datum in the mind of the witnesses, but is the result of the action of God which transforms the whole person of Jesus in the period between his burial and the discovery of the empty tomb. As Gerard J. Hughes puts it: 'To believe that the Lord is risen is to believe something about Jesus which is true of him independently of his effect on his disciples or on me.'[23]

In this respect, the *Catechism* repeats the realist claims consistently made by the Church in its proclamation, that this transcendent event of consummation has a bearing on the person of Jesus in an identifiable period between his burial and the discovery of the empty tomb, and therefore there is a 'moment in time' when it occurred. The historical dimension of the resurrection is central: it signals that 'God's saving activity is brought to completion *in the history that is actually ours* and not in some other dimension':[24] not elsewhere, but here, God's self-gift establishes a comprehensive harmony within the creation in which all discords are resolved and encompassed.

Using, inevitably, another image: God's self-gift to the creation can be seen as an *arch* which extends through all dimensions of the creation's life, from its beginnings, through its turbulent contradictions, to its completion. Within that arch, the moment we call 'salvation' — God's focused presence in the life, death and resurrection of the incarnate Son — is the modulation within God's action which arises in response to the emergence of created and human freedom. In that 'moment', our mortal flesh and human freedom become the expressive forms of the Son's glorification of the Father, so that human life might be delivered from patterns of destructiveness and be opened to receive the Father's love (654). The consummation which God wills to bestow is focused, initially, in the human form of the incarnate and dead Son: as with the incarnation, with which it is inseparably related, there is always a *focus* from which divine love radiates. The resurrection is the completion of the arch of God's self-bestowal to the creation: God has no more to give than what is conferred in the life of the risen Lord. Here the gift of perfected life is embedded within the very structures of the created and mortal world, and will not be frustrated (654).

That resolution, the completion of God's work of creation, cannot be contained, and bursts through the limits of its spatio-temporal location to extend its influence to all the living and all the dead (1 Th 4:13–18; Rom 8:18ff.) (645). The authority that Christ exercised in his descent to the abode of the dead touches the enigma of death: 'the dead will hear the voice of the Son of God, and those who hear will live. For just as the Father has life in himself, so he has granted the Son also to have life in himself' (Jn 5:25–26). The living, too, those still subject to incompletion, have been given the first-fruits of the fullness of the Spirit (Rom 8:23): 'If the Spirit of him who raised Jesus from the dead dwells in you, he who raised Christ from the dead will give life to your mortal bodies also through his Spirit that dwells in you' (Rom 8:11). The radiance of the resurrection shines in the hearts of all the living and all the dead who, 'with unveiled faces, seeing the glory of the Lord as though reflected in a mirror, are being transformed into the same image from one degree of glory to another' (2 Cor 3:18).

If we are to say more about the consummation which has begun in Jesus and will extend through the final destiny of the creation, it can only be, inevitably, through further images, especially those warranted by the Scriptures, since they invite us to think of a future when God's self-gift reaches its completion. First of all, there is a fruitfulness in God's self-gift which must reach an autumn to which all the seasons of the creation lead. In the resurrection, Jesus enters a fecundity of life no longer scarred by evil: his death bears fruit that will abide for the healing of the nations (Jn 12:24; 15:1ff.; Rev 22:2). Again, an early Christian ivory panel in Munich (*c.* AD 400) portrays, growing out of the empty tomb, a great tree, suggesting the Tree of Life as a symbol of life conquering death, but also the tree in the parable, grown from a mustard seed in which the birds of the air come and nest (Mt 13:31); the resurrection is the life of the kingdom to which God alone gives the growth, rising from the earth and sheltering the peoples of all nations. Or again, the Word of God coming forth from the mouth of the Most High (Sir 24:3; Jn 1:1) does not return to him empty: it establishes the human and non-human orders within creation so that God might finally dwell there (Sir 24:5–7). The tabernacle of divine presence (Jn 1:14) is the person of Jesus who is both the mercy seat of expiation (*hilastērion*) and the indissoluble union (*theopoēsis*) of God and the restored creation. The risen Jesus is the new *anthrōpos* where human hostilities are healed and both Jew and Gentile 'grow into a holy temple' in the Lord (Eph 2:15, 21).

The resurrection of Jesus is not his withdrawal from the world in the way in which the glory of God left the Temple in Ezekiel's vision (Ezek 10:1ff.): the idea of the risen but *absent* Christ is a betrayal of the central concerns of resurrection faith (647). Jesus has entered into a form of presence in relation to the world — the New Testament calls it a 'Lordship' or a 'rule' — in which he will continue to bestow peace (Jn 20:19), teach his disciples about the Scriptures (Lk 24:32, 45), ask women to witness to him in the Church (Jn 20:18), bring the sceptical to faith (Jn 20:26ff.), strengthen the confused and eat with them in the breaking of bread (Lk 24:13), commission his apostles in the ministry of reconciliation (Jn 12:24; 15:1ff.; Rev 22:2). Again, an early Christian ivory panel in Munich (*c.* AD 400) portrays, growing out of the empty tomb, a great tree, its transformation. Rilke's ninth Duino Elegy has the lines:

> *Here* is the time for the Tellable, *here* is its home.
> Speak and proclaim. More than ever
> things we can live with are falling away, for that
> which is oustingly taking their place is an imageless act.[25]

What can be told — the 'tellable' consummation of the creation — is prophetically enacted now on this earth, and the 'imageless act' of transformation takes place in the body of Jesus so that creation may not be finally marked by the violence of 'the things we live with'. The Son who bore the sins of the world now bears the sign of the world's fulfilment. This imageless act is the 'vision for the appointed time; it speaks of the end, and does not lie' (Hab 2:3). The resurrection is, *par excellence*, God's word of prophecy which both promises and brings about what God intends for the creation (655).

Jesus is so real in his expression of God's love that he can become, in his death, the victim of creation's rage against God; in his descent among the dead, he is the saving presence among those who have shut themselves off from God's love; in his resurrection, he becomes the radical blessedness of the creation's destiny. He is the first-born of many brothers and sisters who live and die and enter God's embrace. He still belongs within the world of stones cast aside only to become keystones in holy places; within the world of trees of life which build temples and arks, and trees of death which become gallows and racks; within a world of seeds which fall into the dark earth to give life. He is the pearl of great price that the world brings forth, first as an irritant on its surface, and then as the thing of beauty by which the creation, finally, praises God.

Notes

1   To take two examples among many: the Gospel of John, for example, presents Jesus as the fulfilment of themes associated with the Exodus: the Tabernacle (1:14); the paschal lamb (1:29); the bronze serpent (3:14); the manna from heaven (6:31ff.); the water from the rock (7:38–39; 19:34). The Epistle to the Hebrews audaciously relates Jesus' obedient Sonship to a priesthood deriving from the mysterious Melchizedek (5:5–6), and is able to present the unpriestly Jesus (7:14) as the unique High Priest in the heavenly sanctuary. Barnabas Lindars, *New Testament Apologetic* (SCM, 1973) remains a valuable study of early Christian scriptural *testimonia*.

2   Cf. Aquinas's judgement: 'It is impossible that God's foreknowledge should be erroneous and that his will or plan be frustrated. On the hypothesis, then, that Christ's passion was known and willed in advance by God, it was not at the same time possible for Christ not to suffer, or for man to be delivered in any way other than by his passion. This reasoning holds for everything that is foreknown and preordained by God . . .' (STh III 46, 2; Cf. I, 22, 4 and ad 1).

3   C. H. Dodd, *According to the Scriptures* (Fontana, 1963) is a simple and valuable study of the early Christian community's use of the Jewish Scriptures.

4   The 'passion psalms' (Pss 22, 31, 34, 41, 69, 109), for example, central to the Gospels' passion narratives, are passed over, save for an indirect reference in 603; the *Akedah* (Abraham's sacrifice of Isaac) is absent, even though generations of Christian writers have read it as a dark anticipation of the Father's deliverance of his Son to death. Missing, most notably, are the scriptural types of the cross favoured by patristic writers: the tree of life in paradise; the ark; the bronze serpent; the doors and lintels smeared with the blood of the lamb; Jacob's ladder, etc. It is remarkable that the richness of patristic exegesis of the Jewish Scriptures plays such a small part in this section of the *Catechism* 618.

5   The *Catechism* follows the International Theological Commission's 1979 statement on 'Select questions on Christology' in deriving the Church's soteriology from Jesus' own understanding: 'The origins and the core of the whole soteriology are to be found already in the early Church before Paul. This soteriology rests on the words and consciousness of Jesus himself. Jesus knows that he is to die for all, for our sins; in this perspective he lives out his entire life, he suffers, and he rises from the dead' (*International Theological Commission: Texts and Documents 1969–1985*, ed. M. Sharkey (Ignatius Press, 1989), p. 200). Cf. Hengel's judgement: 'There is nothing from a

159

historical or traditio-historical point of view which stands in the way of our deriving it [the theme of vicarious atoning death] from the earliest community and perhaps even from Jesus himself' (Martin Hengel, *The Atonement: The Origins of the Doctrine in the New Testament* (SCM, 1981), p. 64).

6 A penetrating discussion of the methodological issues involved in speaking of 'the historical Jesus' is found in Ben F. Meyer, *The Aims of Jesus* (SCM, 1979), pp. 76ff. His expansive and rich interpretation of Jesus' 'aims' is, I think, of exceptional and lasting value. 'Jesus understood his immediate messianic task to be the division of Israel between faith and unfaith; and he understood his messianic destiny (formally, enthronement and rule) to be scheduled for fulfilment only as the outcome and reversal of repudiation, suffering and death' (p. 216).

7 Paul Celan, *Selected Poems*, trans. Michael Hamburger (Penguin, 1988), p. 263.

8 Joseph A. Fitzmyer, *Paul and His Theology: A Brief Sketch* (Prentice-Hall, 1989), p. 59.

9 Owen Barfield, *Poetic Diction: A Study in Meaning* (McGraw-Hill, 1964), p. 81.

10 'In the perspective of this text, the forgiveness of sins had awaited the climactic, definitive, unrepeatable *yom kippur* of Golgotha': Ben F. Meyer, *The Early Christians: Their World Mission and Self-Discovery* (Michael Glazier, 1986), pp. 79–80.

11 G. M. Hopkins, 8 November 1881 (Long Retreat) in *The Oxford Authors: Gerard Manley Hopkins*, ed. Catherine Phillips (Oxford University Press, 1986), pp. 288–9.

12 M. Scheeben, *The Mysteries of Christianity* (1887; B. Herder, 1947), pp. 444–6 (emphases added).

13 Cf. J. McDade, 'The Trinity and the Paschal Mystery', *Heythrop Journal* 29 (1988), pp. 175–91.

14 Gabriel Daly, *Creation and Redemption* (Gill & Macmillan, 1988), p. 213.

15 H. U. von Balthasar, *Elucidations* (SPCK, 1975), p. 51.

16 Dumitru Staniloae, *Theology and the Church* (St Vladimir's Seminary Press, 1980), p. 190.

17 Cyril of Alexandria, *De Adoratione in Spiritu et Veritate* 10: PG 68, 704C.

18 E. Jüngel, *God as the Mystery of the World* (ET T. & T. Clark, 1983), p. 219. Both Jüngel and Moltmann speak of the death of Jesus as 'the breakdown of the relationship that constitutes the very life of the Trinity' (J. Moltmann, *The Trinity and the Kingdom of God* (SCM, 1981), p. 80). The *Catechism*, sensibly, will have nothing to do with such muddied gnosticism. For a sharp critique of these approaches, cf. 'Theology, christology, anthropology' in *International Theological Commission: Texts and Documents 1969–1985*, op. cit., pp. 219ff.

19 Cf. J. McDade, 'Creation and salvation: green faith and Christian themes', *The Month* (November 1990), pp. 433–41. I have drawn on this article for the present study.

20 The text is from 'The Gospel of Nicodemus/Acts of Pilate' in E. Hennecke, *New Testament Apocrypha*, ed. W. Schneemelcher (SCM, 1963), pp. 470ff.

21 Medard Kehl and Werner Löser (eds), *The von Balthasar Reader* (T. & T. Clark, 1980), p. 153.

22 Quoted, without further detail, in George Steiner, *Real Presences* (Faber & Faber, 1989), p. 224.

23 Gerard J. Hughes, 'Dead theories, live metaphors and the resurrection',
    Heythrop Journal 29 (1988), pp. 313–28; quotation from p. 323.
24 Pheme Perkins, *Resurrection: New Testament Witness and Contemporary
    Reflection* (Geoffrey Chapman, 1984), p. 409 (emphasis added).
25 Rainer Maria Rilke, 'Duino Elegy IX' in *Selected Works*, vol. II: *Poetry*, trans.
    J. B. Leishman (Hogarth Press, 1967), p. 245.

EXCURSUS

The Jews and the death of Jesus

In 574–591, the *Catechism* offers a valuable piece of teaching on Jesus and his Jewish context, particularly with regard to the circumstances of his death, in which the positive influence of the new approach to Judaism since Vatican II can be felt. In *Nostra Aetate* (1965), the Second Vatican Council took an irreversible step towards removing what Jules Isaac characterised as 'the Teaching of Contempt' towards Jews: in that tradition, Jews were pilloried as 'legalistic', 'carnal', 'usurious', 'spiritually blind', 'bloodthirsty' and, worst of all, guilty of 'deicide'. The insights of *Nostra Aetate* have been developed in two official documents: *Guidelines and Suggestions for Implementing the Conciliar Declaration* (1974) and *Notes on the Correct Way to Present the Jews and Judaism in Preaching and Catechesis in the Roman Catholic Church* (1985).[1] This section of the *Catechism* belongs to this new tradition which values the unique relations between Christianity and Judaism — traditions 'linked together at the very level of their identity' and 'founded on the design of the God of the Covenant' (Pope John Paul II).

In its discussion of the division and controversy which Jesus provoked among his Jewish contemporaries (587ff.), the *Catechism* follows the line taken by the 1985 Vatican Instruction (*Notes*) in two respects:

1. It highlights what Jesus had in common with the Pharisees: belief in the resurrection; expressions of piety (alms-giving, fasting and prayer); the liturgical practice of addressing God as Father; the centrality of the double commandment (575); the ideal of a spiritual observance of the Torah (579). 'An exclusively negative picture of the Pharisees is likely to be inaccurate and unjust ... if Jesus shows himself severe towards the Pharisees, it is because he is closer to them than to other religious groups' (*Notes* 19). In this section the *Catechism* makes no mention of Jesus' proclamation of the kingdom of God, in teachings and actions, which provoked controversy with the Pharisees and others.

2. It deliberately counters any attempt to blame the death of Jesus on the Jewish people. Although the *Catechism* does not raise the point, its

162

treatment is influenced by the acknowledgement in *Notes* that some New Testament writings particularly hostile to Jews — the Gospel of John, for example — have been influenced by an anti-Jewish polemic after the time of Jesus:

> It cannot be ruled out that some references [in the New Testament] hostile or less than favourable to the Jews have their historical context in conflicts between the nascent Church and the Jewish community. Certain controversies reflect Christian–Jewish relations long after the time of Jesus. (*Notes* 21)

The *Catechism* does not speak of 'the Jews' as collectively opposed to Jesus (595–597); his opponents are identified as 'certain Pharisees and partisans of Herod' (574) and 'certain teachers of the Law' (582); its favoured term for those opposed to Jesus is the 'religious authorities' (575; 587; 589; 591; 595; 596). In this way, the *Catechism* distances itself from the statements in the New Testament which suggest some form of collective responsibility on the part of 'the Jews' for the death of Jesus (cf. Mt 27:25; Jn 18:38ff.; 19:14ff.; Acts 7:51ff.). 597–598 follows *Nostra Aetate* and *Notes* in laying the blame for the death of Jesus not on the Jews, but on the sins of Christians. 'Christian sinners are more to blame for the death of Christ than those few Jews who brought it about — they indeed "knew not what they did"' (*Notes* 22). This is a welcome reassertion of the Tridentine tradition, and is free from the anti-Jewish polemic which has often coloured Christian preaching on the passion.

The *Catechism* sees a positive significance in the fact that when the Son of God enters human history, he is born under the Jewish law (Gal 4:4; 527; 532; 580), circumcised into the covenant God makes with Jews (Lk 2:21–22). and is trained in the observance of the Torah (577–582).[2] He celebrates the Jewish feasts, and exercises his ministry of teaching in both the synagogues and the Temple (583–584). He comes, as Paul says, as '*a servant of the circumcised* on behalf of the truth of God in order that he might confirm the promises given to the patriarchs, and in order that the Gentiles might glorify God for his mercy' (Rom 15:8).

Consequently nothing in his ministry and teaching annuls the validity of 'the adoption, the glory, the covenants, the giving of the Torah, the worship, and the promises' (Rom 9:4) which God wills to bestow on the Jewish people (577). These salvific gifts are not superseded by Jesus in his ministry; instead, he draws this framework of blessings, practices and guidance into his life and confirms them by offering himself to the Father as a faithful Jew whose identity is rooted in Israel's experience of faith.

It is in this sense that the *Catechism* interprets Jesus' fulfilment of the Torah (577ff.). Christians need to learn not to be negative about the Torah. Charlotte Klein points out that Torah means much more than law: 'it means instruction, path, God's word and call to Israel as part of his covenant; it is also Israel's grateful response to this covenant.'[3] W. D. Davies reinforces the point:

> It must be emphasized that the translation of the Hebrew word *Torah* by the English word *Law* has been doubly unfortunate.

> 'Torah' is a far wider term than the English 'Law': it stands for direction, teaching, instruction of a religious and moral kind. Indeed, it stands for what we call 'revelation' — the totality of God's will as revealed. It always retains a reference to law or commandment, but it is never exhausted in these terms.[4]

A liberalising theology which detaches Jesus from his Jewish context and sets the 'gospel of Jesus' in opposition to 'Jewish Torah' can be cast out only by prayer and fasting. The *Catechism*, by contrast, invites us to see the whole of Jesus' life and work as a faithful observance of the Torah — 'Torah', of course, being understood positively as an obedient and loving response to God's self-gift within Israel's life of faith. The statement in 580 that 'the perfect fulfilment of the Law could be the work of none but the divine legislator' comes from the sense that Jesus offers perfect praise and response to God — he is 'without sin' (Heb 4:15) — and therefore, as Pope John Paul said in the Rome Synagogue in 1986, 'Jesus took to its extreme consequences the love demanded by the Torah'. His commitment to the end is on behalf of those who are unable to maintain a right relationship with God (580).

The *Catechism* applies to Jesus the prophecy of Jeremiah, ' I will put my law within them, and I will write it on their hearts' (Jer 31:33): he is the one in whose heart the Torah becomes a life-giving principle of knowledge and worship of God, making him a paradigm of Torah-faithfulness. The God who gave the Torah and established eternal covenants through Abraham and Moses is the same God who sends his Son: these are 'inner moments' within revelation which belong within the divinely willed dispensation of divine love. All the features of God's revelation, however divergent and conflictual they may be in their refraction within human history, belong together as aspects of God's self-gift and must not be set in opposition to one another, since God's action is always unitary and is never at variance with itself (581).[5]

Yet this positive alignment of Jesus' faith and Torah-observance cannot ignore the ways, since the early Christian decades, in which the separation of Christian and Jewish communities has polarised these two 'moments'. The *Catechism* acknowledges that during his ministry Jesus was 'confronted by certain teachers of the Law who did not accept his interpretation of the Law' (582), and it understands how such an accusation could be made; yet it gives a high priority to Matthew's interpretation that Jesus' life and teaching perfects the practice of Torah-observance (Mt 5:17).

The range of approaches to Jesus and the Torah within the New Testamant — culminating in Paul's pained struggle to come to an adequate understanding in Romans and Galatians — is a paradigm of the difficulty which all subsequent Christian generations have experienced in relating the status of Jesus and the status of the Torah. The range of categories often used to describe Jesus' relationship to Jewish faith — 'fulfilment', 'transformation', 're-visioning', 'intensification', 'restoration', 'renewal' — shows that there is no exhaustive account of the relationship between them. John Barton's dialectical description — 'a reaffirmation that transforms what it reaffirms, a transformation that respects what is transformed'[6] — is as much a delineation of the difficulty as a resolution of the relationship between these central moments of God's action. The *Catechism* sensibly retains a preference for a positive relationship of 'fulfilment' between Jesus and the Torah. It thereby invites Christians to see their faith as inseparably bound to the patterns of Jewish faith which preceded Jesus, to the context of first-century Judaism in which his ministry was conducted, and to the continuation of that faith within the life of faithful Jews for whom the Torah, the feasts and the covenant mediate God's will and blessings.

Notes

1 The texts are available in Eugene J. Fisher and Leon Klenick (eds), *In Our Time: The Flowering of Jewish–Catholic Dialogue* (Paulist Press, 1990), which also contains a valuable thematic bibliography of recent writings on Christian–Jewish relations.
2 'Jesus was and always remained a Jew, his ministry was deliberately limited to "the lost sheep of the house of Israel" (Mt 15.24). Jesus is fully a man of his time, and of his environment — the Jewish Palestinian one of the first century, the anxieties and hopes of which he shared' (*Notes* 12).
3 C. Klein, *Anti-Judaism in Christian Theology* (SPCK, 1978), p. 39.
4 W. D. Davies, *Invitation to the New Testament* (New York, 1966), p. 29.
5 Cf. J. McDade, 'The continuing validity of the Jewish covenant: a Christian perspective', *SIDIC* (Service International de Documentation Judéo-Chrétienne), 23 (1990), pp. 20–5.
6 J. Barton, 'Preparation in history for Christ' in R. Morgan (ed.), *The Religion of the Incarnation: Anglican Essays in Commemoration of Lux Mundi* (Bristol Classical Press, 1989), p. 70.

The Holy Spirit

(Paragraphs 683–747)

John O'Donnell SJ

Gregorian University, Rome

1. Before entering into detail regarding particular points of the faith in the Holy Spirit as presented in the *Catechism*, we can note briefly at the outset a few general impressions. The first is that the *Catechism* adopts, at least in this chapter, a prevalently biblical approach, tracing the role of the Holy Spirit in the history of salvation. In a chapter of approximately fifteen pages there are roughly 125 quotations from the Bible. The few other references given are almost exclusively from the liturgy. Hence the *Catechism* follows the rule: *lex orandi est lex credendi* ('the law of prayer is the law of belief'). One notes as well that these references are taken from the liturgy of the Eastern Church. One has the impression that this section of the *Catechism* was developed by a theologian or theologians of the Eastern tradition.

Surprisingly, there is very little theology in this chapter, and I believe only one reference to a credal affirmation, namely to the Council of Constantinople in which the divinity of the Holy Spirit was defined. The *Catechism* remains content to state the definition without any explanation (see 685). Immediately following the definition, the *Catechism* declares that it will not deal with trinitarian theology, but only with the economy of salvation and hence the role of the Holy Spirit in the economy. This fact brings with it the interesting consequence that there is no reference whatsoever to the doctrine of the *filioque*, that is, to the clause inserted into the Nicene Creed, that the Spirit proceeds from the Father and the Son, an interpretation of the procession rejected by the Orthodox Churches.

A further point of general interest, and one which I would judge very positively, is that the *Catechism* is at pains to stress the joint working of the Son and the Spirit in the economy. This is mentioned at least three times in the body of the chapter on the Spirit and once in the summary. Reference is made to Irenaeus, who used the expression 'the two hands of God' to refer to the work of the Son and the Spirit. 704 thus states: "'God fashioned man with his own hands [that is, the Son and the Holy Spirit] and impressed his own form on the flesh he had fashioned, in such a way that even what was visible might bear the divine form."' This emphasis on the joint working of the Son and the Spirit is important in the light of the critique made against Western theology that it is Christomonic. An important contemporary author such as Yves Congar has adopted a similar approach to the economy, for example in his book *The Word and the Spirit.*[1]

A point which is underdeveloped is the universalist perspective which a theology of the Holy Spirit could give. The text almost immediately launches into the history of salvation and the role of the Holy Spirit in Israel, giving no attention to the work of the Holy Spirit outside the covenant community. Likewise the text concludes with the role of the Spirit in the Church. A broader perspective would be useful for the dialogue of Christians with those of other faiths and with non-believers. To this point we can return at the end of our commentary.

2. Early in the chapter (685) the *Catechism* offers its only dogmatic affirmation regarding the Holy Spirit. Faith in the Holy Spirit, it declares, involves belief that the Spirit is one of the persons of the Trinity, of one being with the Father and the Son, and then cites the Nicene Creed 'with the Father and the Son he is worshipped and glorified'. (More correctly this should be called the Niceno-Constantinopolitan Creed.)

Perhaps a few words of historical background to this definition might be useful. First, we note that this definition was given by the Council of Constantinople in 381. In the fourth century the Church was confronted by two vexing problems. One is known as modalism, a heresy which taught that in God there are no real distinctions, the divine essence being a bare monad. If this were the case, there could be no real distinction between the Father and the Son, the Son and the Spirit.

The work of the Cappadocian Fathers in the fourth century prepared the way to accept the full distinction of the persons of the Trinity by distinguishing the persons and the divine essence, in Greek the *ousia* and the *hypostases.* The *ousia* is one and indivisible; the three persons, however, really distinct among themselves.

The other problem was that of subordinationism. Arius taught that the Logos was an exalted creature, not of the same substance as the Father. This position was condemned by the Council of Nicaea in 325.

Later in the fourth century a group of heretical bishops known as the Tropici taught that the Spirit was ontologically inferior to the Son. Hence they saw a hierarchy in Being from the Father to the Son to the Holy Spirit. Athanasius waged a theological campaign against this doctrine, showing that the logic of Nicaea should lead to an affirmation of the full divinity of the Holy Spirit. Basil of Caesarea implicitly followed this line, including the Holy Spirit in the doxology with the formula 'Glory be to the Father and to the Son and to the Holy Spirit'. (Previously the liturgical tradition had been 'Glory be to the Father through the Son and in the Holy Spirit'.) Gregory of Nazianzus went further, specifically calling the Holy Spirit God and using the same term *homoousios* (one in being), which Nicaea had applied to the Son, for the Holy Spirit.

The Council of Constantinople did not explicitly say that the Holy Spirit was one in being with the Father and the Son, probably because it did not want to create new theological and political controversies. It did, however, say, as the *Catechism* quotes, that the Holy Spirit is worshipped and glorified with the Father and the Son. This affirmation effectively proclaims the divinity of the Spirit, for only God is worthy of adoration. Hence, in this brief phrase, the *Catechism* gives a summary of at least a hundred years of controversy in the patristic period in which the Church came to define the full equality and real distinction of the three persons of the Trinity.

3. Since the *Catechism* takes a historical-salvific approach to the mystery of the Holy Spirit, it is obvious that space is devoted to the period of preparation. The Spirit is at work in the Old Testament especially in the prophets, and the Spirit keeps alive in the people of Israel hope in the fulfilment of the promise. In the fullness of time God will send his Messiah, upon whom will rest the Spirit of the Lord (Is 11:2).

Interestingly, the *Catechism* notes that the first person of the Trinity to be known explicitly in the history of salvation is the Father, whereas the last to be recognised is the Holy Spirit (684). To this effect a text is cited from Gregory of Nazianzus (*Oratio Theol.* 5, 26).

But it is worth emphasising at the same time that from a soteriological perspective all three persons of the Trinity are always at work in history, though the pattern of their relationships differs in the three great epochs of the drama of salvation. In the period of the Old Testament the Father sends the Spirit to prepare humanity for the reception of the Son. In the fullness of time the centre of activity focuses on the Son. As Paul puts it, 'But when the time had fully come, God sent forth his Son, born of woman, born under the law, to redeem those who were under the law, so that we might receive adoption as sons' (Gal 4:4–5). Finally, in the period of the Church, the Spirit has the priority but the Spirit's work is to glorify the Son and through the Son lead the whole of creation back to the Father. Thus, in the present epoch, the Spirit is the power of the future. The goal, however, of all the activity of the Son and the Spirit is that the Father be glorified and that in this way 'God may be everything to every one' (1 Cor 15:28). Hence the story of salvation is an immense circle which proceeds from the Father and concludes in the Father.

4. In tracing the role of the Holy Spirit in the history of salvation, the *Catechism* notes how Jesus' earthly life begins with his conception by the Holy Spirit. 723 states: 'With and through the Holy Spirit, the Virgin conceives and gives birth to the Son of God.'

The work of the Holy Spirit in the incarnation is today the subject of much theological reflection. Hans Urs von Balthasar, for example, asks: Who is the subject of the act of the incarnation? In some texts of Scripture it looks as though the Logos itself is the subject. St Paul speaks, for example, of the self-emptying of the Son in the incarnation: 'though he was in the form of God, [he] did not count equality with God a thing to be grasped, but emptied himself, taking the form of a servant' (Phil 5:6–7). Likewise, in the Prologue of the Fourth Gospel, St John states 'the word became flesh' (Jn 1:14). Nonetheless, in the annunciation scene in Luke's Gospel, the angel declares 'The Holy Spirit will come upon you, and the power of the Most High will overshadow you; therefore the child to be born will be called holy, the Son of God' (Lk 1:35). Balthasar asks how we can put these various texts together.

He suggests what he calls a soteriological inversion. According to the long tradition of Western theology, in the divine Trinity, the Spirit proceeds as an act of love from the Father and the Son. Hence the role of the Spirit is passive-receptive. But it is equally true that the Son is always receptive towards the Father. His Sonship and his obedience always go together. Thus, in Balthasar's theology, the incarnation happens because the Son accepts the Father's plan of redemption. The Son, according to his receptive-obedience, lets himself be incarnated. But the active role in the incarnation is taken over by the Spirit.

What happens in the incarnation then becomes typical of the whole life of Jesus. Jesus lets himself be led by the inspirations of the Spirit. This receptivity lasts until the cross, when Jesus hands back the Spirit to the Father. At this point there is a new inversion: the Son becomes active again and pours out his Spirit upon the Church. From this point the activity of the Spirit is such as to conform men and women to Christ. The Spirit in this sense always has a Christological face.

5. The *Catechism* correctly associates Jesus' office as Messiah with his anointing by the Holy Spirit (711ff.). And interestingly the *Catechism* cites in this regard the significant text of Isaiah 61:

> The Spirit of the LORD GOD is upon me,
> because the LORD has anointed me
> to bring good tidings to the afflicted;
> he has sent me to bind up the broken hearted,
> to proclaim liberty to the captives,
> and the opening of the prison to those who are bound;
> to proclaim the year of the LORD's favour.

Many exegetes today believe that this text was applied by Jesus himself to his ministry. Not only does Luke place it at the beginning of his ministry as a programmatic summary of his mission, but a similar reference can be found in Matthew 11, where Jesus justifies his activity to the disciples of John the Baptist, citing Isaiah 61 and the prophet's prediction that the Messiah will preach the gospel to the poor.

The *Catechism* does not stress who are the poor. A contemporary theologian such as Jürgen Moltmann notes that Jesus and his disciples formed a movement of the literally poor. Moltmann observes that Matthew calls the people *ochlos*, that is, the poor in the sense of the oppressed, the destitute, the emarginated, the lost, the victims of violence. Jesus associates with these people and offers them hope for a new future in the reign of God. Moltmann stresses that Jesus gives them above all a new sense of their human dignity. What does Jesus give to the rich? Moltmann answers: the call to conversion. If they accept this call, they too can participate in fashioning the new creation. So Moltmann notes that Jesus' community is a contrast community. Jesus proclaims a new mode of existence, a new set of values, a form of living together not based on violence and exploitation, but on the value of the person and the law of forgiveness.

An interesting phrase in this text of Isaiah is the last one, where the prophet proclaims a year of the Lord's favour. To understand this we must first of all go back to the sabbath, the day of rest which recalls that the Lord is the Creator, a day which anticipates the new creation in which work will no longer have a place. In the Jewish faith there was also the tradition of the sabbath year every seven years in which the fields were not planted. This fact was understood as an act of trust that the Lord would provide. Then there was the tradition based on Leviticus 25:10 of a jubilee year every fifty years. During this year there was neither planting nor reaping. Slaves were freed and debts forgiven. When Jesus proclaims a year of grace, he is inserting himself in these traditions. In other words his ministry is the inauguration of the messianic times, his work is the beginning of the new creation, this is the fullness of time without end.

We should note that underlying the messianic hope of the Old Testament is the burning question of suffering. Why is Israel still in bondage? Why does the sinner prosper while the just are exploited? Why does evil still reign in what is God's creation? The coming of the Messiah is linked to the hope in God's future, a future in which God's goodness and justice triumph over sin and death. Unfortunately the *Catechism* does not underline the existential problem to which the coming of the Messiah is an answer.

6. Having looked at the role of the Holy Spirit in the life of Jesus, let us turn our attention briefly to the work of the Holy Spirit in the death of Jesus. In 730 the *Catechism* states succinctly: 'At last Jesus' hour arrives: he commends his spirit into the *Father's* hands at the very moment when by his death he conquers death.' Here the *Catechism* gives a reference to Luke 23:46 and John 19:30. Let us take a brief look at the Johannine text.

After handing over the beloved disciple to his mother, the evangelist continues: 'After this Jesus, knowing that all was now finished, said (to fulfil the scripture), "I thirst." A bowl full of vinegar stood there; so they put a sponge full of the vinegar on hyssop and held it to his mouth. When Jesus had received the vinegar, he said, "It is finished"; and he bowed his head and gave up his spirit.'

First we can note that already in John 7 Jesus had invited all those who thirst to come to him and drink, and he promised that out of his own heart living waters would flow. John comments that Jesus here spoke of the Holy Spirit, who had not yet been given (see Jn 7:37–39).

According to the Fourth Gospel the moment of the bestowal of the Spirit is the death of our Lord on the cross. In the text we are analysing Jesus thirsts, first in the sense of a physical thirst caused by his agony. But probably John intends more. John sees in this thirst the spiritual desire of Jesus to bring his disciples to the Father.

It is interesting that twice in this passage the evangelist says that all is completed. In 19:28 John comments that Jesus knew that all was now finished, that is, he looks back to his earthly mission and realises that he has accomplished all that the Father has given him to do. But then two verses later he proclaims 'It is finished'. Here the exegetes say that Jesus is looking forward, precisely to the salvation that he will bring to his disciples through his death and resurrection. And then we are told that he gives up his Spirit, that is, he surrenders the Spirit which was in him back to the Father, but at the same time this restitution of the Spirit is the setting free of the Spirit for the Church. The Spirit is given who will continue the work of Jesus after he ascends to the Father.

Another biblical text which speaks in a similar way is Hebrews 9:14. There the author states that Jesus offered himself without blemish to God through the eternal Spirit. Hence here too the New Testament affirms that Jesus' redemptive death on the cross took place through the Holy Spirit.

In a spiritual meditation upon this mystery, Pope John Paul II in his encyclical *Dominum et Vivificantem* reflects how the Holy Spirit as 'fire from heaven' works in the depth of the mystery of the cross. The Pope reflects how God has constantly sought the friendship of humankind, offering us the covenant of love; but the mystery of sin is that human beings have so often said no to this offer of friendship. This no to God, according to the Pope, has caused pain to the divine Trinity. The Spirit as the depth of the divine love leads the Son to the self-offering of the cross which will overturn the mystery of sin and lead human hearts back to God. The pain of sin thus leads to the suffering of God on the cross. As John Paul expresses it:

> Thus there is a paradoxical mystery of love: in Christ there suffers a God who has been rejected by his own creature: 'They do not believe in me!'; but at the same time, from the depth of this suffering — and indirectly from the depth of the very sin 'of not having believed' — the Spirit draws a new measure of the gift made to man and to creation from the beginning. In the depth of the mystery of the cross love is at work, that love which brings man back again to share in the life that is in God himself. (41)

7. Now that we have seen the role of the Holy Spirit in the life of Jesus, we can look briefly at his mission in the world today. At the Last Supper Jesus promised the gift of the Holy Spirit, whom he called the Paraclete. The *Catechism*, listing the titles of the Holy Spirit, affirms 'When he proclaims and promises the coming of the Holy Spirit, Jesus calls him the "Paraclete", literally, "he who is called to one's side", *ad-vocatus*.

"Paraclete" is commonly translated by "consoler", and Jesus is the first consoler' (692).

In calling the Holy Spirit another Paraclete, St John seems to be relying on an Old Testament tradition where a principal figure dies and leaves another to take his place, carry on his work, and interpret his message. One thinks, for example, of Moses and Joshua, Elijah and Elisha.

What is the significance of the word Paraclete? The background seems to be that of the law-courts. The Paraclete is a witness in the defence of Jesus and is a prosecuting attorney against the world which has rejected the ministry of Jesus and is responsible for his death. He proves the world wrong about sin, justice and judgement (Jn 16:8).

Raymond Brown in his commentary on the Fourth Gospel has pointed out that what is peculiar to John is the fact that the Paraclete is the personal presence of Jesus in the Christian while Jesus is with the Father. While Jesus is with the Father, the Paraclete guides the disciples to the truth and helps them to understand the revelation of Jesus which was obscure for them during his earthly ministry. Although Jesus is no longer with them in the flesh, his presence is assured because of the Paraclete who indwells the disciples.

In his encyclical *Dominum et Vivificantem* Pope John Paul II has reflected especially on the function of the Paraclete to judge the world. The Pope notes that convincing the world of sin refers to the fact that when the light came unto his own, his own refused him (Jn 1:11). The Holy Spirit also convinces of judgement. This means that the world is guilty in its rejection of Jesus. But, as the Pope points out, this judgement of guilt is not the last word. The Holy Spirit wishes to reveal the guilt of humankind so that men and women can repent and receive eternal life. For Jesus did not come to condemn the world, but to save it. And so the Holy Spirit also convinces of righteousness, that is, the definitive salvation which God wishes for all his creatures and which already belongs to Jesus through his glorification at the right hand of the Father.

Hence the Pope very much understands the situation of world history to be a drama between two opposing forces, the power of Satan, the father of lies, and the power of the Paraclete, the Spirit of truth. This drama is played out in every heart in the domain of conscience, where every man and woman is summoned to turn away from the lie of self-exaltation to the truth of self-gift. The Pope is fond of citing Augustine, who speaks of sin as the love of self to the point of contempt for God, whereas the mystery of the cross points to the love of God to the point of contempt of self (*De Civitate Dei*, XIV.28). Hence the cross points to the clash of two mysteries which the Pope calls the *mysterium iniquitatis* and the *mysterium pietatis* (48). It is the task of the Holy Spirit to lead us from the first to the second.

8. While the Paraclete acts as prosecuting attorney against the world, this is not the only mission of the Spirit. The Spirit is also the gift of God's love which comes to dwell in the believer. As the *Catechism* puts it, "'God is Love" and love is his first gift, containing all others. "God's love has been poured into our hearts through the Holy Spirit who has been given to us"' (733). This aspect is also stressed in the article on baptism. There we read 'Baptism not only purifies from all sins, but also makes the neophyte "a new creature" [2 Cor 5:17], an adopted son of God, who has become a "partaker of the divine nature", member of Christ and co-heir with him, and a temple of the Holy Spirit' (1265).

First of all, we could reflect for a moment on the word 'gift'. Since the time of St Augustine it has been common to refer to the Holy Spirit as the gift of God. In the life of the Blessed Trinity the Holy Spirit is already gift, for the Holy Spirit is the fruit of the love of the Father and the Son. The Father gives himself totally as gift to the Son. The Son returns the gift to the Father. And the Father and the Son do not retain this mutual gift for themselves, but they in turn breathe forth the Spirit who is pure gift, the fruit of their love. The mystery of the Holy Spirit is the mystery of love, a love which is open, open to the world and to history. God wishes to share the trinitarian love with creatures.

What is it that God gives? God gives nothing less than himself. Hence the giver and the gift are identical in the Holy Spirit. St Augustine saw a richness in the Latin word *donum*. The Spirit is the *donum* of the Father and the Son. But the Spirit is also what is given, *donatum*. Moreover, Augustine stressed how the mystery of the Trinity is the openness of divine self-communication. God is *donabile* in the Holy Spirit.

The culmination of God's salvific work is thus the indwelling of the Holy Spirit. With this indwelling God offers his friendship, and this friendship is accepted so that a union comes about between God and the creature.

Following the position of St Thomas, neo-scholastic theology tended to see this indwelling as merely appropriated to the Holy Spirit. The whole Trinity dwells in the creature insofar as the human being receives the gift of sanctifying grace which enables him or her to know and love God as he is. The scholastic tradition interpreted this grace as created grace, an effect of the Holy Spirit, since for these theologians an actual indwelling of the Holy Spirit was thought to compromise the divine transcendence.

More recently many theologians, including Karl Rahner and Walter Kasper, have argued for a personal indwelling of the Holy Spirit. As Rahner says, God so gives himself that he becomes a co-constitutive dimension of human subjectivity. Rahner too wishes to protect the divine transcendence, and so he applies the model of a semi-formal causality to shed light on the indwelling of the Holy Spirit. According to Aristotelian categories, the form and the matter are constitutive principles which together constitute a finite reality. Rahner argues that something analogous can be predicated of the relation between the Holy Spirit and the human subject. Without compromising the divine transcendence, God so offers himself as gift that he becomes, as it were, the form of the human subject. The goal of God's purposes for the world is thus realised. Through Christ and in his Spirit God becomes one with his creature. As Balthasar would say, the divine connubium is achieved.

9. Another important aspect of the work of the Spirit stressed by the *Catechism* is the restoration of the divine image. Already when speaking of the role of John the Baptist, the *Catechism* notes that the Holy Spirit began the restoration of the divine likeness, prefiguring what he would achieve with and in Christ (720). Then in 734 the *Catechism* states: 'The communion of the Holy Spirit in the Church restores to the baptized the divine likeness lost through sin.'

Here the *Catechism* echoes an important biblical theme, and one stressed by the Second Vatican Council, for example, in *Gaudium et Spes* 22. Recalling the text of Colossians 1:15, which speaks of Christ as 'the image of the invisible God', the Pastoral Constitution continues 'To the sons of Adam he restores the divine likeness which had been disfigured from the first sin onward'. Later in the same section the Council Fathers link this conformation to Christ with the first-fruits of the Spirit by which the Christian becomes capable of discharging the new law of love.

The Fathers of the Church, building on the affirmation of Genesis 1:26 that the human being is made in the image and likeness of God, taught that the image of God implanted in the human being with the creation was never destroyed, but the likeness was lost because of sin through which the creature used his freedom to seek a false autonomy and attempted an independence from God.

It is precisely the mission of the Holy Spirit to lead us back to true freedom. First, we can note that human freedom and divine freedom can never be in conflict with one another. When God creates, he truly lets the creature be. Hence when the human being accepts his creaturehood, he is free to be himself. Moreover, when the creature's freedom is marred by sin, the Holy Spirit leads the person back to the authentic sense of freedom. But what is the meaning of this freedom for a Christian?

First of all, freedom means the willingness to accept my life as a gift. As Gabriel Marcel says, the first gift of God to me is me to myself. Every dimension of my being reflects a dimension of giftedness. But secondly, in the light of sin and the history of the human refusal to accept the gift, there is the sense of wonder before the fact that God does not leave me in my misery, in a perverted freedom which leads to death. Rather, God sends his Son to rescue me from my situation of lostness and death. Hence the Christian has a new motive for thanksgiving. Not only does he thank God for his existence, but he is grateful for the gift of the Son as well. He cannot help recalling the words of the Easter *Exsultet:* to rescue a slave, you gave your Son. Hence the Christian meaning of freedom culminates in the eucharist, which expresses the fundamental attitude of the Christian towards God and his creation.

But as the Council stresses, this freedom is not only between the individual human being and God. Rather, the Christian is opened up to be free for his neighbour. He sees not only how much he has been loved, but also the fact that Christ has given his life for all men and women and so we are all brothers and sisters. Thus freedom becomes the willingness to serve. As Paul puts it so beautifully in the Letter to the Galatians, 'Through love be servants of one another' (5:13). Under the influence of the Spirit dwelling in his or her heart, the Christian is led to ever greater selflessness, to seeking the good of the neighbour, and in this way he or she is gradually restored to the likeness of Christ.

10. The chapter on the Holy Spirit concludes with the role of the Holy Spirit in the Church. 737 states: 'The mission of Christ and the Holy Spirit is brought to completion in the Church, which is the Body of Christ and the Temple of the Holy Spirit.' The idea of the Church as the temple of the Holy Spirit is also developed in the article on the Church. In 797 the *Catechism* quotes St Augustine, who wrote 'What the soul is to the human body, the Holy Spirit is to the Body of Christ, which is the Church' (see *Sermo* 267,4).

These ideas echo the teaching on the Holy Spirit in *Lumen Gentium* 7. There the Holy Spirit is called the soul of the Church, analogous to the life-giving principle of the soul in the human body. LG 7 also states that it is one and the same Holy Spirit who dwells in Christ and in his Church.

Reflecting on this affirmation, one modern theologian, Heribert Mühlen, has called the Holy Spirit one person in many persons. While Christ is a divine person with a human nature, the Church is constituted by the fact that the one divine person indwells all the human persons who make up the Christian community. Thus the Holy Spirit is the ontological bond of unity in the Church. The Holy Spirit unites each believer to Christ as well as the believers among themselves. In this sense Mühlen can define the Church as one mystical person.

Mühlen notes furthermore that one can see the mission of the Church as the prolongation of Christ's anointing with the Holy Spirit. We have already seen that the title of Messiah indicates that Christ was from the beginning of his life anointed with the Holy Spirit. But the fullness of the Spirit which was in him was meant to be shared with us. Each member of the community has some gift of the Spirit to carry on Christ's redemptive work of making God's kingdom present here and now in word and deed.

11. Perhaps in connection with the theology of the Church, it may be useful to say a brief word about baptism, for as the *Catechism* notes, 'Holy Baptism is the basis of the whole Christian life, the gateway to life in the Spirit (*vitae spiritualis ianua*), and the door which gives access to the other sacraments' (1213).

In the chapter on the Holy Spirit, when the *Catechism* comes to discuss the symbolism associated with the Spirit, the first reference is to that of water, which the *Catechism* links to the phenomenon of birth. Just as the foetus matures in the water of the womb, so the water of baptism signifies that our birth into the divine life is given in the Spirit (694).

Unfortunately, however, in this section the *Catechism* does not refer to the destructive power of water, water which is not only a sign of life but which can bring with it as well the threat of death. Here one thinks of the imagery of Psalm 69, 'Save me, O God! For the waters have come up to my neck. I sink in deep mire, where there is no foothold; I have come into deep waters, and the flood sweeps over me' (vv. 1–2).

This aspect is, however, brought out in the article on baptism in 1214, where it is stated that the word baptise means 'immerse' and it is explained that this immersion in baptism is a sign of the burial of the catechumen in the death of Christ, from which he rises with him as a new creature.

This symbolism is important, for its roots probably go back to Christ himself. Jesus, when speaking of his approaching death, exclaimed 'I have a baptism to be baptised with; and how I am constrained until it is accomplished!' (Lk 12:50). Here Jesus associated his death with baptism. Hence baptism is not a mere washing, but an entrance into the turbulent waters of Jesus' death and resurrection.

St Paul gave expression to this conviction in his theology of Christian baptism. For Paul, baptism has two dimensions: the Christological and the pneumatological. On the one hand, baptism means immersion into Christ's death and resurrection. On the other, it means new life in the Spirit. One comes out of the baptismal font a new man or woman. Because we have died with him and received the new life of his Spirit, we are enabled to walk in newness of life. We must consider ourselves as dead to sin and alive to God in Christ Jesus (see Rom 6:4, 11).

St John in his First Letter represents the same line of thought when he states 'No one born of God commits sin; for God's nature abides in him, and he cannot sin because he is born of God' (1 Jn 3:9). With this strong language St John is seeking to put into words the utterly new reality which has come into being through the power of the Holy Spirit in baptism. We are no longer sinners, we are new creatures. From this ontological reality there follows the Christian imperative: sin no more, love the brethren.

12. One of the limitations of the theology of the second millennium was its stress on the Church as institution and the sharp opposition which such a theology implied between Church and world. At the same time, one of the blessings of Vatican II was its openness to the presence of the Spirit in the laity, in members of other churches, and in the world at large.

As we have just seen, after tracing the role of the Holy Spirit in the history of salvation, the *Catechism* concludes its treatment of the third article of the Creed with the role of the Holy Spirit in the Church. Without doubt, this is very important. But at the same time one could wish for a more universalist perspective. As the biblical witness makes clear, the Holy Spirit is the power of the future, the power drawing the whole of God's creation back to the Father. This perspective is beautifully expressed by St Paul in his Letter to the Romans when he writes 'We know that the whole creation has been groaning in travail together until now; and not only the creation, but we ourselves, who have the first fruits of the Spirit, groan inwardly as we wait for adoption as sons, the redemption of our bodies. For in this hope we were saved' (Rom 8:22–24). Hence the work of the Holy Spirit is a work of hope, hope for all men and women, but hope especially for Christians, who have known the triumph of Christ in his cross and resurrection.

The Second Vatican Council in numerous places speaks of the Holy Spirit at work in the world. In *Gaudium et Spes* 22 we read 'Since Christ died for all, and since the ultimate vocation of humankind is in fact one, and divine, we must believe that the Holy Spirit, in a manner known only to God, offers to every person the possibility of being associated with this paschal mystery of Christ'. Later in the same document, the Council Fathers state 'Christ is now at work in the hearts of men and women through the energy of his Spirit. He not only arouses a desire for the age to come, but also vivifies, purifies, and strengthens those generous impulses by which the human family strives to render its life more human and to submit the whole earth to its goal' (38).

Although *Gaudium et Spes* 22 is cited in the *Catechism* in the article on baptism (see 1260), this universalist, future-orientated perspective is not found as such in the chapter on the Holy Spirit. Rather the discussion is strictly intra-ecclesial. While it is true that the *Catechism* is primarily for believers, and while we must recognise that it is not possible to say everything, a more universalist perspective on the Spirit would enrich the *Catechism* and add as well a particularly fruitful dimension of the theology of the Holy Spirit which was brought to light by the Second Vatican Council.

Note

1   Yves Congar, *The Word and the Spirit* (ET London: Geoffrey Chapman, 1986).

The Church

(Paragraphs 748–975)

J. M. R. Tillard OP

Dominican Faculty of Theology, Ottawa

According to the declaration of Pope John Paul II, the *Catechism of the Catholic Church* is intended for the use of both pastors and faithful in their local churches.[1]. We should be aware, however, that a catechism does not belong to the literary genre of an enchiridion in providing the essential documents on which our Christian tradition is based; nor is it a manual of Christian instruction. Moreover, the *Catechism* required by the episcopal synod was to be distinct from other catechisms produced at the national level. Its aim is to preserve what the Church has to keep faithfully in her 'memory' in order that the content of the faith may be lived and passed on in its plenitude and wholeness. The study which follows proceeds in this perspective.

We are concerned here only with the lengthy article on the Church, the perusal of which reveals the decision taken by the commission in charge of its preparation. The commission drew its principal support from the Dogmatic Constitution *Lumen Gentium* of Vatican II, supplemented and strengthened by some of the more robust assertions found in the decree *Unitatis Redintegratio* and other conciliar documents. Apart from a few quotations from the Code of Canon Law and from pontifical texts, the commission chose to be remarkably reserved, even reluctant, about referring to post-conciliar documents. This applies in particular to the conclusions of the Extraordinary Synod of 1985, despite its importance in ecclesiological terms. It applies equally to the extensive dossier to be found in *Mysterium Ecclesiae* and the *Tomos Agapēs* in which Paul VI made explicit use of several of the most profound intuitions of the Council on the nature of the Church, and in so doing 'received' them.

Throughout the entire article on the Church the imprint of a number of authors and the utilisation of a number of sources is easily discernable. The various titles given to Christ is but one of many examples: at times named simply as Jesus (which has an alien ring in the context),[2] at other times as Christ Jesus; and also, in the finest passages, he is addressed as Lord. Both authors and sources vary in quality, and it is to be regretted that some of the suggestions offered afterwards were accepted by the commission, for the result leaves the reader with a strange impression. At one point he is given an amalgam of notes with little semblance of unity; and at another he is offered the most profound statements in awkward association with texts which are quite different in style and based on a totally different perspective. As in a book of devotion, for example, we pass from Augustine through Gregory the Great and Thomas Aquinas to Joan of Arc.[3] Filial devotion on the part of the writer is an insufficient reason for presenting St Dominic as a model to illustrate the intercession of the saints when there is an abundance of traditional liturgical texts which would have been more apposite. One senses in certain paragraphs unmistakable signs of their origin in compromise, a disturbing attestation when it concerns a catechism. Finally, the résumés of paragraphs ('In Brief') are frequently inaccurate summaries of their contents, which is a dangerous procedure.

What is more worrying in the original French edition of the *Catechism* is the question raised by the translation of certain crucial texts from the Second Vatican Council,[4] in particular that of *Lumen Gentium* 8, of which two differing versions appear, both of them marred by a lack of clarity (816, 870). In one instance, especially, a declaration of fundamental importance which states that the one Church *subsistit in Ecclesia catholica* has been translated into French as 'it is in the catholic Church . . . that she [the one Church of Christ] exists' (870). The English version has accurately rendered it as 'the sole Church of Christ . . . *subsists in the Catholic Church*' (870). The first translation into French fails to give precise expression to the meaning that *Lumen Gentium* intended to convey[5] by interpreting *subsistit in* in a sense which no longer explicitly reflects what the Council Fathers 'recognised' as in conformity with the real nature of the Church of God. Here the English version is surely to be preferred. But why has the original text allowed an incorrect interpretation to stand in its résumé?

These preliminary remarks will serve to explain the approach taken in this commentary. The text of the *Catechism* is not presented in the form of an ecclesiological synthesis, that is, as an original piece of writing. It should rather be viewed as an 'official' recalling, in logical sequence,[6] of the principal statements on the Church which the magisterium holds to be essential. For this reason this commentary will not proceed from one number to the next except where required by the context. It will be more helpful to select from the compilation of citations from the Council the major ecclesiological themes which have been preserved by the living Tradition in its 'memory' and which, thanks to Vatican II, have been restored to their proper place in the life of the local churches in communion with the Church of Rome. For, as the text aptly expresses it, 'particular Churches are fully catholic *through their communion with one of them*, the Church of Rome "which presides in charity"' (834). It is the aim of this *Catechism* to be of service to this *communion of churches* in the 'catholic' faith.

I. The nature of the Church of God

1. The Church of God, communion

A careful and judicious reading of the *Catechism* leaves no doubt that it has endorsed the perception of the Church as *communion*. The meaning of this traditional perception has been well assimilated so as to become the dominant theme of the section which now concerns us, and it has been developed in several fine paragraphs belonging to another section of the *Catechism*, especially on the eucharist. Some of the expressions are both succinct and forceful.

The Church has been shown as intimately associated with the design of the Father which is 'to raise up men to share in his own divine life' (759; cf. 760). Moreover, we are reminded that in the Church this *communion* with God constitutes the end and governs all that exists; it is 'the purpose which governs everything in her that is a sacramental means, tied to this passing world' (773).

But this *communion* with God is inseparable from *communion* between men (775). God's desire is 'that the whole human race may become one People of God, form one Body of Christ, and be built up into one temple of the Holy Spirit' (776). God's 'ecclesial' design is identical with his love of humanity. Thus (751), he 'calls together', 'summons' (*ek-kalein*, from which *ek-klēsia* is derived), 'calls forth' from every corner of the earth a People whom he introduces into communion with his own life in order to wrest humanity from the consequences of sin which had brought about its downfall. This point is made in a striking passage summarising some of the patristic thought resumed by *Lumen Gentium*:

> The gathering together of the People of God began at the moment when sin destroyed the communion of men with God, and that of men among themselves. The gathering together of the Church is, as it were, God's reaction to the chaos provoked by sin. This reunification is achieved secretly in the heart of all peoples: 'In every nation anyone who fears him and does what is right is acceptable' to God. (761).

One would be hard pressed to express it more clearly. It is this 'calling together' or 'gathering together', at work in history until the second coming (the Parousia), that forms the Church; and only then will 'all the just from the time of Adam, "from Abel, the just one, to the last of the elect", be gathered together in the universal Church in the Father's presence' (769).

This *communion* takes *visible* form in 'the community of faith, hope and charity through which [Christ] communicates truth and grace to all men' (771). It finds expression in the *communion* in faith, the *communion* in sacraments, charisms and charity, and in the mutual sharing of possessions for 'the help of the needy and of [the] neighbours in want' (952).

Because all the members of the Church are sanctified by God — a point clearly stated in the Roman Catechism, which is taken up here — we are concerned with a '*communion* of saints' that includes the three stages in the life of its members: their earthly pilgrimage, the period of purification and the final contemplation of God in the full light of his presence (954, 955). This point is even more clearly affirmed in the *Catechism*'s commentary on the phrase of the Creed '*communion* of saints': in a way, this article is a further explanation of the preceding. What is the Church if not an assembly of the saints? The *communion* of saints is the Church (946).[7]

The Church is thus explicitly defined as *communion*, a *communion* which is at once already realised (946, 1325) and in a continuous process of actualisation in the ebb and flow of history. The emphasis here is on a mutual interdependence which permits us to state that through the *communion* of life with God and the unity of the People of God the Church is what it is (1325). The inadequate summary ('In Brief') of 'the mystery of the Church' is to be regretted because on this point it fails to do justice to the whole doctrine as presented in this document. Thus, it is not enough to say that 'the Church is . . . the sign and the instrument of the communion of God and men' (780),[8] for it *is* the *very communion* that it sacramentalises.[9] In the section itself this point is clearly demonstrated.

Communion with the Father and between men is 'in Christ'. Moreover, if the Church is the '*communion* of saints', this is because *the gifts of Christ* are communicated, through the sacraments and above all through the eucharist, to those who are open to receive them. The Church is holy through the holiness of Christ who is himself filled with the Spirit of holiness:

> The term 'communion of saints' therefore has two closely linked meanings: communion 'in holy things (*sancta*)' and 'among holy persons (*sancti*)'.
> *Sancta sanctis!* ('God's holy gifts for God's holy people') is proclaimed by the celebrant in most Eastern liturgies during the elevation of the holy Gifts before the distribution of communion. The faithful (*sancti*) are fed by Christ's holy body and blood (*sancta*) to grow in the communion of the Holy Spirit (*koinōnia*) and to communicate it to the world. (948)

'In Christ', therefore, the Church is *already* the gathering together of men and women of every nation, race, people and language, although the full realisation of this is still to come (775).

Nevertheless, the People of God is already in the process of being formed, and it is made one because the 'gifts' of Christ are passed on to all Christians, whatever their place of origin. These 'gifts' weld the faithful together in the *same* relationship of belonging to God, in the *same* birth through faith and baptism, the *same* liberty, law and mission, and in the *same* destiny (782). From this proceeds a participation in the priestly and prophetic functions of Christ and in his royalty (783, 786). However, this dignity, which has its origin in communion with Christ, carries with it a solemn responsibility in terms of mission and service (783). In contrast to 'all other religious, ethnic, political or cultural groups found in history' (782), this People (the Church) is at the same time visible in our midst and richly endowed with realities that are invisible, present in the world and yet alien, human and yet divine (771). The eyes of faith alone can see in its visible form the spiritual bearer of divine life (770). That part of the text of the *Catechism* which is concerned with the People of God is faithful to Vatican II. But there should have been more emphasis on the 'priesthood of the baptized' as a participation in the priesthood of the People *as such* (284). That is to say that the latter is the source of the priesthood of the baptised members and justifies it. On this point there remains a serious confusion which the text fails to clarify.

The People of God are the Body of Christ because he is their head who, 'by communicating his Spirit', gathers his members from all nations (787, 788). The unity of this Body is triumphant over all man-made ruptures: 'this unity triumphs over all human divisions' (791), to use the phrase in the text. Thus:

> The comparison of the Church with the body casts light on the intimate bond between Christ and his Church. Not only is she gathered *around him*; she is united *in him*, in his body. Three aspects of the Church as the Body of Christ are to be more specifically noted: the unity of all her members with each other as a result of their union with Christ; Christ as head of the Body; and the Church as bride of Christ. (789).

In this passage the *Catechism* provides a clear summary of the Church's teaching in accord with tradition.

Nevertheless, it is insufficient to make frequent reference to the eucharist (e.g., 766, 787, 790, 805, 832, 893, 901, 950, 960 . . .), to speak of the communion with Christ which unites his Body to the body of Christians through the sacrament of his flesh and blood (787), to give the eucharist the central place in the life of the local church (893), and even to say that 'it is primarily the Eucharist' that brings our communion with God and one another to completion (950), without dwelling in depth on the fundamental connection between Eucharist and Church. Instead of receiving due attention here, this important rediscovery of patristic ecclesiology is discussed later under sacraments (esp. 1396–1400), where the explanation is of a high theological quality. Unfortunately, however, it is unlikely that many of those who use the *Catechism* will think of turning to the Part on sacraments when they are concerned with the nature of the Church.[10]

At this point, for the article in question at least, we encounter one of the limitations of the *Catechism* which, by adhering too rigidly to the letter of the documents of Vatican II, has failed to take account of the fact that a quarter of a century of *reception* and of life, and the benefits gained from ecumenical dialogue, have prepared the ground for further elucidation. This is particularly true for the eucharistic dimension of the Church. One gains the impression that notes made from the principal conciliar texts have been strung together here without further reflection. This stands in sharp contrast to the unity and coherence of the catechism issued by Trent. Limitations such as these can only be regarded as unfortunate.

The section devoted to the Spirit is excellent. Probably inspired by the Roman Catechism, which in turn drew on the writings of Bonaventure, Albert the Great and Thomas Aquinas, it begins at once with the following declaration, based on article 9 of the Creed:

> The article concerning the Church also depends entirely on the article about the Holy Spirit, which immediately precedes it. 'Indeed, having shown that the Spirit is the source and giver of all holiness, we now confess that it is he who has endowed the Church with holiness.' The Church is, in a phrase used by the Fathers, the place 'where the Spirit flourishes'. (749)

This quotation is of central importance, but it does not stand alone. Further on in the text we are reminded that the pouring out of the Spirit reveals the Church (759, 778), that the Spirit guides and provides for the Church by means of the diversity of gifts both hierarchic and charismatic (768), that he distributes the grace of Christ through the seven sacraments (774), that he unites us in him in the new alliance (781), that we are born as members of the Church when we receive from him the new law of liberty (782) and the unction through which we are enabled to be in *communion* with Christ's consecration (783–786), that through him Christ constructs his Body (789), that the Church is his temple (797, 798) and is enriched by all his charisms (799, 800, 809). Of particular significance is the fact that the *Catechism* cites one of the key passages of the Decree on Ecumenism which affirms that the Church 'is one because of her "soul": "It is the Holy Spirit, dwelling in those who believe and pervading and ruling over the entire Church, who brings about that wonderful communion of the faithful and joins them together so intimately in Christ that he is the principle of the Church's unity"' (813).

Our attention is constantly directed to the Spirit throughout this section of the text (811, 819, 820, 823, 827, 828, 837, 849–856, 864, 867, 916 . . .), and one is aware of a conscious looking back to Tradition as the source of inspiration. The *Catechism* has achieved a balance here by successfully avoiding a frequent pitfall which consists in interspersing texts pertaining to an essentially Christomonist ecclesiology with allusions to the Spirit. There is cause for rejoicing that here the references to the Spirit have been judiciously chosen, and it is to be hoped that catechists will make good use of what has been placed at their disposal.

There can be no doubt as to the significance of the *Catechism*'s choice of a theme prominent in Augustine, that of Christ as bridegroom and the Church as bride (796).[11] Nevertheless, one may question whether the intended result has been achieved by the complex juxtaposition of biblical quotations taken from widely divergent contexts. Such a method is scarcely instructive as it is limited to a rapid skimming of the surface.

2. The Church, catholic and apostolic

(1) The *Catechism* is explicit in linking the catholicity of the Church to the action of the Spirit and to the dynamic of mission which sends the

Church out to all nations (767) to draw together 'in Christ' the whole of humanity (775). As in Vatican I (*Dei Filius*), it does not separate the unity and catholicity of the Church, but speaks of 'her catholic unity' (812).

Here is a precious designation which must be constantly borne in mind. This view of catholicity, presented by the *Catechism* with delicacy and discernment, is based on Tradition, but it has at times, in the West, been reduced to a mere geographical expression:

> The word 'catholic' means 'universal', in the sense of 'according to the totality' or 'in keeping with the whole'. The Church is catholic in a double sense:
>
> First, the Church is catholic because Christ is present in her . . . The Church was, in this fundamental sense, catholic on the day of Pentecost and will always be so until the day of the Parousia.
>
> Secondly, the Church is catholic because she has been sent out by Christ on a mission to the whole of the human race. (830–831)

868 summarises this well, but leaves out the reference to Christ:

> The Church is catholic: she proclaims the fullness of the faith. She bears in herself and administers the totality of the means of salvation. She is sent out to all peoples. She speaks to all men. She encompasses all times. She is 'missionary of her very nature'. (868)

Such a vision of catholicity permits the question of diversity to find its rightful place; this is a diversity in which both individuals and groups are concerned, as the *Catechism* makes clear:

> From the beginning, this one Church has been marked by a great *diversity* which comes from both the variety of God's gifts and the diversity of those who receive them. Within the unity of the People of God, a multiplicity of peoples and cultures is gathered together. Among the Church's members, there are different gifts, offices, conditions and ways of life. 'Holding a rightful place in the communion of the Church there are also particular Churches that retain their own traditions.' The great richness of such diversity is not opposed to the Church's unity. Yet sin and the burden of its consequences constantly threaten the gift of unity. And so the Apostle has to exhort Christians to 'maintain the unity of the Spirit in the bond of peace'. (814)

In this ordered diversity (887), the particular or local Churches are in *communion*, a *communion* such that in them 'though they may often be small and poor, or existing in the diaspora, Christ is present, through whose power and influence the One, Holy, Catholic and Apostolic Church is constituted (832). Thus, through the preaching of the gospel and the eucharist each one of the churches is the Church assembled, each one truly catholic because in each Christ is truly present (832). However, the churches experience the fullness of their catholicity only through their *communion* with one of their number, namely the Church of Rome 'which presides in charity' (834). The idea of *communion* is essential in this relationship, as the text of the *Catechism* makes clear in a passage inspired by *Lumen Gentium*:

> 'Let us be very careful not to conceive of the universal Church as the sum, or . . . the more or less anomalous federation of essentially different particular churches. In the mind of the Lord the Church is universal by vocation and mission, but when she puts down her roots in a variety of cultural, social and human terrains, she takes on different external expressions and appearances in each part of the world.' The rich variety of ecclesiastical disciplines, liturgical rites, and theological and spiritual heritages proper to the local Churches 'unified in a common effort, shows all the more resplendantly the catholicity of the undivided Church'. (835)

The source of this *communion* is in the eucharist. Our text affirms that *communion* with the Church which is located in Rome is its only basis and foundation. At this point the *Catechism* cites Maximus the Confessor (834), selected from among the Fathers as a privileged witness to Tradition, a choice which no doubt reflects a veneration shared by some of those who were chiefly responsible for the drafting of the text.

In so doing they made explicit their preference for a specific current within Tradition in an area in which the Fathers showed themselves far more skilled in formulating essential nuances. Augustine could (and should) have been cited also, and many other Fathers for whom 'the only basis and foundation' is, together with Christ, the faith as confessed by Peter in the sense that the Church makes its appearance only where his 'confession' as the *first among twelve* remains authentic and enduring. Furthermore, no one can be unaware that the most scholarly exegetes refuse to interpret the passage in Matthew which alludes to the gates of hell (Mt 16:18) as containing a reference to the Church of Rome in the sense that the quotation from Maximus implies, at least in the translation provided here. An affirmation such as this fails to give sufficient weight to historical evidence. It was equally strange to make use of this quotation in order to explain the meaning of the important declaration of Irenaeus on 'the more excellent origin' of the Church of Rome.[12] It is noteworthy that Paul's connection with Rome, which has its source in Tradition and was strongly reasserted by Paul VI, has not been stressed:

> Particular Churches are fully catholic through their communion with one of them, the Church of Rome 'which presides in charity'. 'For with this church, by reason of its pre-eminence, the whole Church, that is the faithful everywhere, must necessarily be in accord.' Indeed, 'from the incarnate Word's descent to us, all Christian churches everywhere have held and hold the great church that is here [at Rome] to be their only basis and foundation since, according to the Saviour's promise, the gates of hell have never prevailed against her'. (834)

Unfortunately the ambiguity of Maximus's phrase 'the great church' has been left unresolved: was he referring to 'the great Church' *as such* or only to the particular church at Rome?

For the above reasons it appears that, in an area of primary importance and that is fraught with consequences, the text of the *Catechism* is both good and disappointing. The sub-sections devoted to catholicity (830–856) are remarkable for the attention given to the local (here described as 'particular') church,[13] the respect for the ecumenical situation, the interpretation of 'no salvation outside the Church', the understanding of mission, all of which are presented with consideration and tact. But this success is somewhat marred by the way the importance and necessity of *communion* with Rome is expressed. The *Catechism* has confined itself to three quotations which are badly strung together and have been drawn from three entirely separate contexts; of these only one has been singled out in preference to other expressions of the many currents which flow from a tradition of great diversity and richness.

On the other hand it should be noted that the theme of catholicity and the several expressions of the Church's actual 'embodiment' are aptly shown to be convergent in the opening lines of the paragraph on the Church in the divine plan:

> In Christian usage, the word 'church' designates the liturgical assembly, but also the local community or the whole universal community of believers. These three meanings are inseparable. 'The Church' is the People that God gathers in the whole world. She exists in local communities and is made real as a liturgical, above all a Eucharistic, assembly. She draws her life from the word and the Body of Christ and so herself becomes Christ's Body. (752)

It is to be hoped that this short synthesis will not be passed over by the catechists.

(2) Having recognised the existence of a large variety of particular churches and their diversity (814), the *Catechism* is clearly concerned to stress the nature of the unity which stems from their *communion*. Here once again the text aptly incorporates some of the most felicitous and appropriate expressions from the Decree on Ecumenism (*Unitatis redintegratio*) and the decrees *Lumen Gentium* and *Gaudium et Spes*:

> *The Church is one because of her source:* 'the highest exemplar and source of this mystery is the unity, in the Trinity of Persons, of one God, the Father and the Son in the Holy Spirit.' The Church is one *because of her founder:* for 'the Word made flesh, the prince of peace, reconciled all men to God by the cross, . . . restoring the unity of all in one people and one body.' The Church is one *because of her 'soul':* 'It is the Holy Spirit, dwelling in those who believe and pervading and ruling over the entire Church, who brings about that wonderful communion of the faithful and joins them together so intimately in Christ that he is the principle of the Church's unity.' Unity is of the essence of the Church.

What an astonishing mystery! There is one Father of the universe, one *Logos* of the universe and also one Holy Spirit, everywhere one and the same; there is also one virgin become mother, and I should like to call her 'Church'. (813)

From the beginning, this one Church has been marked by a great *diversity* which comes from both the variety of God's gifts and the diversity of those who receive them. Within the unity of the People of God, a multiplicity of peoples and cultures is gathered together. Among the Church's members, there are different gifts, offices, conditions and ways of life. 'Holding a rightful place in the communion of the Church there are also particular Churches that retain their own traditions.' The great richness of such diversity is not opposed to the Church's unity. Yet sin and the burden of its consequences constantly threaten the gift of unity. And so the Apostle has to exhort Christians to 'maintain the unity of the Spirit in the bond of peace'. (814)

What are these bonds of unity? Above all charity 'binds everything together in perfect harmony'. But the unity of the pilgrim Church is also assured by visible bonds of communion:
— profession of one faith received from the apostles;
— common celebration of divine worship, especially of the sacraments;
— apostolic succession through the sacrament of Holy Orders, maintaining the fraternal concord of God's family. (815)

'The sole Church of Christ [is that] which our Saviour, after his Resurrection, entrusted to Peter's pastoral care, commissioning him and the other apostles to extend and rule it . . . This Church, constituted and organized as a society in this present world, subsists in (*subsistit in*) the Catholic Church, which is governed by the successor of Peter and by the bishops in communion with him.'

> The Second Vatican Council's Decree on Ecumenism explains: 'For it is through Christ's Catholic Church alone, which is the universal help towards salvation, that the fullness of the means of salvation can be obtained. It was to the apostolic college alone, of which Peter is the head, that we believe that our Lord entrusted all the blessings of the New Covenant, in order to establish on earth the one Body of Christ into which all those should be fully incorporated who belong in any way to the People of God.' (816)

Thus we understand that the unity of the Church is closely bound up with the unity of God himself in terms of his own trinitarian life and of the inauguration of his design through the economy of salvation. These bonds of unity, moreover, are spelled out according to their order of importance, thus fully respecting the thought expressed by Tradition, even if the absence of any explicit reference to the eucharist is regrettable. Most notable is the function assigned to the apostolic succession: that of maintaining the fraternal harmony of God's family as affirmed in *Unitatis Redintegratio* 2. I have already observed that the English version has happily corrected the imprecise French rendering of *subsistit in*.

To sum up, these important paragraphs are well balanced in their treatment of the (Roman) Catholic Church, and the presentation is free from any taint of triumphalism. The reference to Peter clearly portrays him in terms of complete dependence in relation to God, Christ and the Spirit, and is not isolated from the fundamental relation to the faith and the sacraments. The ill-judged citation of Maximus in 834 has thus been partially offset, even if its inclusion appears a mistake.

A similar tone of humble fidelity through which the Catholic Church must view itself and present itself to other religious groups, both Christian and non-Christian, pervades the next sub-sections: 'Who belongs to the Catholic Church?' (836–838), 'The Church and non-Christians' (839–845), and 'Outside the Church there is no salvation' (846–848). From these paragraphs the following extracts are worthy of note:

> 'The Church knows that she is joined in many ways to the baptized who are honoured by the name of Christian, but do not profess the Catholic faith in its entirety or have not preserved unity or communion under the successor of Peter.' Those 'who believe in Christ and have been properly baptized are put in a certain, although imperfect, communion with the Catholic Church'. With the Orthodox Churches, this communion is so profound 'that it lacks little to attain the fullness that would permit a common celebration of the Lord's Eucharist'. (838)

> To the Jews 'belong the sonship, the glory, the covenants, the giving of the law, the worship, and the promises; to them belong the patriarchs, and of their race, according to the flesh, is the Christ'; 'for the gifts and the call of God are irrevocable'. (839)

> The Catholic Church recognizes in other religions that search, among shadows and images, for the God who is unknown yet near since he gives life and breath and all things, and wants all men to be saved. Thus, the Church considers all goodness and truth found in these religions as 'a preparation for the Gospel, and given by him who enlightens all men that they may at length have life'. (843)

The nature of the Church could hardly be revealed more clearly than here. It is the divine plan for unity:

> To reunite all his children, scattered and led astray by sin, the Father willed to call the whole of humanity together into his Son's Church. The Church is the place where humanity must rediscover its unity and salvation. The Church is 'the world reconciled'. She is that bark which 'in the full sail of the Lord's cross, by the breath of the Holy Spirit, navigates safely in this world'. According to another image dear to the Church Fathers, she is prefigured by Noah's ark, which alone saves from the flood. (845)

These texts are laden with meaning. They are worthy to serve as inspiration for a catechesis which may, through their guidance, remain steadfast in its adherence to the faith as handed down by Tradition. At the same time they have been successful in restoring to visible unity its true signification. Thus

> The unity of the Mystical Body produces and stimulates charity among the faithful: 'From this it follows that if one member suffers anything, all the members suffer with him, and if one member is honoured, all the members together rejoice.' Finally, the unity of the Mystical Body triumphs over all human divisions: 'For as many of you as were baptized into Christ have put on Christ. There is neither Jew nor Greek, there is neither slave nor free, there is neither male nor female; for you are all one in Christ Jesus.' (791)

So strong is this *communion* into which we are incorporated through baptism, that it withstands the wounds inflicted by sin and cannot be completely destroyed.

> In fact, 'in this one and only Church of God from its very beginnings there arose certain rifts, which the Apostle strongly censures as damnable. But in subsequent centuries much more serious dissensions appeared and large communities became separated from full communion with the Catholic Church — for which, often enough, men of both sides were to blame.' The ruptures that wound the unity of Christ's Body — here we must distinguish heresy, apostasy and schism — do not occur without human sin:

>> Where there are sins, there are also divisions, schisms, heresies, and disputes. Where there is virtue, however, there also are harmony and unity, from which arise the one heart and one soul of all believers. (817)

> 'However, one cannot charge with the sin of the separation those who at present are born into these communities [that resulted from such separation] and in them are brought up in the faith of Christ, and the Catholic Church accepts them with respect and affection as brothers . . . All who have been justified by faith in Baptism are incorporated into Christ; they therefore have a right to be called Christians, and with good reason are accepted as brothers in the Lord by the children of the Catholic Church.' (818)

> 'Furthermore, many elements of sanctification and of truth' are found outside the visible confines of the Catholic Church: 'the written Word of God; the life of grace; faith, hope and charity, with the other interior gifts of the Holy Spirit, as well as visible elements.' Christ's Spirit uses these Churches and ecclesial communities as means of salvation, whose power derives from the fullness of grace and truth that Christ has entrusted to the Catholic Church. All these blessings come from Christ and lead to him, and are in themselves calls to 'Catholic unity'. (819)

The two kinds of unity have, admittedly, received ample treatment in these paragraphs: the unity God wills 'which subsists in the Catholic Church as something she can never lose' (820), and that which exists though impaired by rupture and schism, and is referred to as 'a certain, although imperfect, communion' (838). However, the appeal for ecumenical involvement which follows is far too weak. It is not enough to remark that 'the desire to recover the unity of all Christians is a gift of Christ and a call of the Holy Spirit' (820).

In the same way, the *Catechism* does not fail to note that unity is the concern of all the faithful, both clergy and laity (822), and it lists the obligations which this entails (821) through a selection of some of the recommendations in *Unitatis Redintegratio*. Nevertheless, the forceful conviction, so prominent in post-conciliar papal declarations — 'the Catholic Church's ecumenical engagement is irreversible' — is lacking. There is also some ambiguity here. For example it is not clear that, if we are expected 'to maintain, reinforce and perfect' unity (820), this is because it is regarded as an integral part of the Church's mission, or merely as a desirable activity in which participation is recommended, possibly in the context of works of supererogation (855). Finally, this appeal for the effective realisation of unity concludes (822) with a reminder of the difficulties to be faced, which is written in such a way that some may interpret it as providing ground for the belief that the task is impossible.[14] We are left unsatisfied.

(3) Mission is presented as a requirement of the Church's catholicity, the main source of inspiration here being the encyclical *Redemptoris Missio* of John Paul II rather than the decree *Ad Gentes* of Vatican II. The goal of mission is nothing less than *communion*:

> The Lord's missionary mandate is ultimately grounded in the eternal love of the Most Holy Trinity: 'The Church on earth is by her nature missionary since, according to the plan of the Father, she has as her origin the mission of the Son and the Holy Spirit.' The ultimate purpose of mission is none other than to make men share in the communion between the Father and the Son in their Spirit of love. (850)

Seen in this light, it is clear that *communion* can only be achieved through the power of the Holy Spirit (852) by following Christ in humility and poverty of spirit, and by having as companions *en route* the whole of humanity (854). This implies the founding of local churches in which the Gospel becomes incarnate within the culture of the region (inculturation) (854). It also requires patience in the face of adversity, accompanied by a whole-hearted commitment to the unity of all Christians. Only in this way will the message be supported by the example of a living witness (855).

There is neither triumphalism nor any hint of proselytism here, the text having been based on an arrangement of some of the profound observations of the decree *Ad Gentes* of Vatican II:

The missionary task implies a *respectful dialogue* with those who do not yet accept the Gospel. Believers can profit from this dialogue by learning to appreciate better 'those elements of truth and grace which are found among peoples, and which are, as it were, a secret presence of God'. They proclaim the Good News to those who do not know it, in order to consolidate, complete and raise up the truth and the goodness that God has distributed among men and nations, and to purify them from error and evil 'for the glory of God, the confusion of the demon, and the happiness of man'. (856)

With respect to social obligations towards societies, the authors may have been too reticent (854). But they wanted to stress the essential nature of mission.

The *Catechism* thus bears witness to a noble conception of evangelisation. Still, one cannot conceal great discomfort at the omission of any reference to the doxological dimension of mission, by which is meant the desire that God be 'recognised' for what he is in himself and glorified as such. *Communion*, which is well treated in the text, has its consummation in the eternal liturgy. God's glory is the end of mission, a perspective that was brilliantly expressed by Augustine but has subsequently vanished from consciousness within the Western Church as anthropocentrism has gradually usurped its place. Participation in a trinitarian *communion*, indeed (850), implies doxology. But the perspective conveyed here focuses on 'God's love for all men' (851). The result is that the opportunity to remind the Church in the West of an essential aspect of mission has been lost.

(4) It is a natural step to move from the 'mission of the Church' to the 'mission of the apostles' and the apostolicity of the Church. Thus, the section on the nature of the Church ends with the statement that 'the Church is apostolic'.

The impression obtained from a reading of 850–857 is that of a somewhat strange collection of statements from various sources. The last (857) consists of biblical citations woven together in order to explain the patristic understanding of apostolicity and to present the mission of the apostles as portrayed in the New Testament. This is the best part of a composite ensemble. It concludes as follows:

The Church is apostolic because she is founded on the apostles, in three ways:
— she was and remains built on 'the foundation of the apostles', the witnesses chosen and sent on mission by Christ himself;
— with the help of the Spirit dwelling in her, the Church keeps and hands on the teaching, the 'good deposit', the salutary words she has heard from the apostles;
— she continues to be taught, sanctified and guided by the apostles until Christ's return, through their successors in pastoral office: the college of bishops, 'assisted by priests, in union with the successor of Peter, the Church's supreme pastor':

> You are the eternal Shepherd
> who never leaves his flock untended.
> Through the apostles
> you watch over us and protect us always.
> You made them shepherds of the flock
> to share in the work of your Son . . . (857)

After recalling the distinction between the intransmissible and the permanent aspects of the apostolic commission (860), the *Catechism* inserts two quotations from *Lumen Gentium* on the continuity between the apostles and bishops, the latter 'taking over' the apostolic ministry and through their divine institution having a permanent pastoral office (861, 862). The passage from *Lumen Gentium* quoted in 862 without any explanation could give the reader the impression that the transmission of the apostles' pastoral office to the bishops is based on the same model as that of the primatial office to the bishop of Rome (862). This is an unfortunate blunder concerning a central issue. The editor must either have taken out the shortest quotation or have intended from the outset to uphold the Roman primacy. If the latter was the case, it was not the place for such an important stand, and the argument has a false ring. 863 and 869 also show signs of a similar approach.

The text then turns its attention to the classical conception of the apostolate as the 'communion of faith and life' with origins of the Church (863) that aims 'to spread the Kingdom of Christ over all the earth'. We are reminded, in a somewhat banal manner, that charity 'drawn from the eucharist above all' is 'the soul of the whole apostolate'. (864).

This section ends with a return to what appears to be a source more biblical and patristic in inspiration and closer to the intuitions issuing from Tradition.

> The Church is ultimately *one, holy, catholic and apostolic* in her deepest and ultimate identity, because it is in her that 'the Kingdom of heaven', the 'Reign of God', already exists, and will be fulfilled at the end of time. The kingdom has come in the person of Christ and grows mysteriously in the hearts of those incorporated into him, until its full eschatological manifestation. Then *all* those he has redeemed and made '*holy* and blameless before him in love' will be gathered together as the *one* People of God, the 'Bride of the Lamb', 'the holy city Jerusalem coming down out of heaven from God, having the glory of God'. For 'the wall of the city had twelve foundations, and on them the twelve names of the *twelve apostles of the Lamb*'. (865)

Once again, the 'In Brief' summary is misleading in its failure to explain the relationship between 'the Pope and the college of bishops', implying that the authority of both runs parallel (869). But the bishop of Rome is surely a member of the college, and as such is not one person added to that body. The college always includes Peter (*cum Petro*), and the primacy is that of one of the bishops inseparable from his brothers. In other words, the primacy is exercised *in* the college and has meaning only *in* the context of this belonging. Is this a simple matter of careless phrasing? *Lumen Gentium* 8 (cited in 870) speaks of Peter's successor and of *the bishops* in communion with him, not of Peter's successor and of the episcopal *college*. There is a subtle distinction here that is full of implications. Apostolicity, which is in question, concerns the episcopal college *as such*, and this college includes in it the bishop whose see is Rome. In this respect the *Catechism* falls prey to an interpretation which ignores the nuances of *Lumen Gentium* (especially LG 22).

II. The structure of ecclesial communion

The *Catechism* has chosen the title 'Christ's faithful, hierarchy, laity, consecrated life' for the section which describes the Church of God in its actual organisation as a visible society in the midst of other human societies. It relates this organisation to the Church's mission in which all persons participate according to their individual gifts and condition (871–873), everyone being of equal dignity before God. In an earlier paragraph (791) the point had been made that the unity of the mystical body 'triumphs over all human divisions', even those which have their origin in the diversity of functions of its members. This is because the Spirit ensures that the variety of conditions and of gifts is made to contribute to the well-being of *communion* and to the fruitfulness of mission. The hierarchical structure is thus regarded as participating in the profound reality of *communion*.

1. The hierarchical organisation of the Church

(1) Although an explicit statement is lacking, it is clear that the *Catechism* regards ministry, as it is realised in the episcopate, as the type or norm around which the other ministries are formed. It is in this light that the nature of ecclesial ministry *as such* is to be understood. The definition of ministry, which is conferred by means of a sacrament (875), describes it as 'at once a collegial and a personal service, exercised in the name of Christ' (879).

The *raison d'être* of such service is the well-being of the whole ecclesial body 'so that all who belong to the People of God ... may attain to salvation' (874). Its first aim is to announce the Gospel and to engage in activities related to this task. This calls for 'the mission and faculty ("the sacred power") to act *in persona Christi Capitis*' (875). This ministry is in itself sacrament, conferred by a sacramental rite.

Unfortunately, this paragraph tries to discuss too many important issues in a few brief sentences. Without any connecting link it jumps from the general proclamation of the Word to the whole action *in persona Christi capitis*. It seems also to move from the necessity to receive grace in order to be able to announce the Gospel to the necessity for every Christian to receive grace through ministers 'authorized and empowered by Christ'. Furthermore, one of the phrases is unclear: it is said that the minister does not speak as a member of the community, but speaks to it in the name of Christ. Indeed, the minister speaks and acts *in persona Christi*, but also *in persona Ecclesiae*, of which Christ is the head. Within the Church he is the member whom the Spirit, by means of sacrament, has invested with the power to act *in persona Christi capitis*, a Head who is inseparable from his Body. Certainly the minister presides, and in so doing he is for the community the *sacramentum* of Christ who is the source of grace, a grace that the community cannot give to itself but can receive only from Christ who offers and gives it. However, the minister also speaks and acts *in the community* as the servant *given* by Christ to that community to speak and act *within* it 'in his name'.

From this difficult paragraph let us keep in our minds the following perceptive formulation: Christ's envoys act, giving 'by God's grace what they cannot do and give by their own powers'.

All ministry performs its service (876) within the constraints set by the example of the Lord Jesus who came in the form of a slave. This service, however, always possesses a collegial character (877) which has its origin in the calling of the twelve. They were chosen *together*, sent out *together* and called to *fraternal unity* in the service of the fraternal *communion* of the faithful, in short a ministry which reflects and bears witness to the communion of the divine persons.

> from the beginning of his ministry, the Lord Jesus instituted the Twelve as 'the seeds of the new Israel and the beginning of the sacred hierarchy'. Chosen together, they were also sent out together, and their fraternal unity would be at the service of the fraternal communion of all the faithful; they would reflect and witness to the communion of the divine persons. (877)

Episcopal collegiality and solidarity within the diocesan *presbyterium* are grounded in both the origin and the finality of the state of all Christian ministry. Thus they are inherent in its very nature. We are here concerned with a ministry that is exercised in *communion* and occupied in supporting and strengthening the *communion* of the local churches and the faithful, through the grace of the *communion* of the divine persons which is the source and objective of all ecclesial life. These realities go far beyond the relatively simple question of administration.

The personal character of ministry is, indeed, preserved: every person receives a *personal* call and bears a *personal* witness and responsibility to Him who gives the commission to act in His name (*or person*) for others. Here the English translation is more illuminating than the French:

> Although Christ's ministers act in communion with one another, they also always act in a personal way. Each one is called personally: 'You, follow me', in order to be a personal witness within the common mission, to bear personal responsibility before him who gives the mission, acting 'in his person' and for other persons: 'I baptize you in the name of the Father and of the Son and of the Holy Spirit . . .'; 'I absolve you . . .' (878)

The minister is not an automaton.

Although this important section of the *Catechism* is faithful to conciliar teaching there is an omission which demands our attention. The theology of the period before Vatican II has found an echo in these particular pages by their emphasis on the aspect of ministerial service of the community to the neglect of another aspect, namely, that of the minister himself as a sign of Christ's presence in the midst of God's people. It is not merely a matter of speaking and acting *in persona Christi*, but also of being *in persona Christi* the *sacramentum* of the Lord who gathers together God's people. This implies holding them in his heart especially through prayer, striving to be 'the model for his flock' and guarding and guiding them by a spiritual conduct which is always open to the promptings of the Spirit. The plane of *being* must qualify and place its mark on the plane of *action*. Augustine made this point very clear while at the same time stressing that, despite the unworthiness of the minister, it is Christ himself who is at work. In a later passage (893) the *Catechism* does speak in this vein, although somewhat out of context, in its treatment of 'the sanctifying office':

> The bishop and priests sanctify the Church by their prayer and work, by their ministry of the word and of the sacraments. They sanctify her by their example, 'not as domineering over those in your charge but being examples to the flock'. Thus, 'together with the flock entrusted to them, they may attain to eternal life'. (893)

But this should have been mentioned in the discussion of the various aspects of ministry as well as in the context of ministerial responsibility and office. The minister, at all levels of the ministerial hierarchy, is by definition a particular kind of 'servant'. He is a 'servant' who is in *communion* with the other ministers in the episcopal college or the presbyterium, who is personally responsible *before God* for all that he does, who lays *before God*, above all in prayer, the portion of the People of God entrusted to his care with their problems, their sufferings, their joys, their search for truth. This all pertains to the sacramental nature of ecclesial ministry. But the *Catechism* remains silent on this point both here and in 1536–1600.

(2) Episcopal ministry is discussed by the *Catechism* in terms of the definition which is given for all ministry.

> Sacramental ministry in the Church . . . is at once a collegial and a personal service, exercised in the name of Christ. This is evidenced by the bonds between the episcopal college and its head, the successor of St Peter, and in the relationship between the bishop's pastoral responsibility for his particular church and the common solicitude of the episcopal college for the universal Church. (879)

It therefore presents 'the episcopal college and its head, the Pope' (880–887) together, regarding them as *inseparable*. This treatment is faithful to the relevant passages in *Lumen Gentium*, from which it quotes (esp. LG 22, 23), and is careful here (in contrast to 869) to consider the Pope and the bishops as a single whole (880, citing LG 22). The choice and compilation show scrupulous respect for the conciliar documents and draw attention to the nuances contained in them. On this occasion the French version is more accurate than the English in its rendering of *Lumen Gentium* 23. In French we read: the Pope who is 'principe perpétuel et visible et *fondement* de l'unité', which is much to be preferred to the Pope who 'is *the* perpetual and visible source and foundation of the unity both of the bishops and of the whole company of the faithful' (882). A felicitous phrase in 881 notes that the 'pastoral office of Peter and the other apostles belongs to the Church's very foundation and is continued by the bishops under the primacy of the Pope' (881). This passage bears quoting in full:

> The Lord made Simon alone, whom he named Peter, the 'rock' of his Church. He gave him the keys of his Church, and instituted him shepherd of the whole flock. 'The office of binding and loosing which was given to Peter was also assigned to the college of apostles united to its head.' This pastoral office of Peter and the other apostles belongs to the Church's very foundation and is continued by the bishops under the primacy of the Pope. (881)

An important pronouncement of Vatican II is repeated in 885:

> 'This college, in so far as it is composed of many members, is the expression of the variety and universality of the People of God; and of the unity of the flock of Christ, in so far as it is assembled under one head.' (885)

Clearly, then, the *Catechism* has conveyed the conciliar teaching on the 'supreme and full authority over the universal Church' which is possessed by the episcopal college in union with the Pope (883), and is also invested in the latter (882).

Despite its faithful adherence even to the letter of Vatican II, the *Catechism* has neglected to mention one of the post-conciliar fruits of the 'reception' of the Council. Certain texts of Paul VI and the encyclicals of John Paul II concerning Cyril and Methodius and the baptism of the Rus could have been used to show that the relationship between the bishops and the bishop of Rome gathered in the college is inseparable from the synodality of all the local churches. Episcopal collegiality becomes what it is only through the *communion* of local churches, a point referred to in 834. Moreover, it is this *communion* which is of primary importance. In the most ancient tradition the primacy of the bishop of the see of Rome (*sedes*) arose from the *principalitas* of the local church in Rome which was founded on the martyrdom of Peter and Paul.[15] It is to be noted that Irenaeus was not the only writer to hold this position which Paul VI reassumed in his dialogue with Athenagoras. Furthermore, it would have been wise to dispense with the title 'Roman Pontiff', which is omitted in the 'In Brief' résumé, but has been retained in several important passages in the text (882, 883). The *Catechism* appears to be uncomfortable with the traditional title 'bishop of Rome' (employed however in 882, 892,

936), preferring the more popular but more ambiguous 'Pope' or 'Vicar of Christ' (882, 936); these titles should have been explained.

886 is a good presentation of the place of the local bishop. The text consists of a complex weaving of conciliar texts, to which has been added a reference to the poor inspired by Paul's letter to the Galatians (Gal 2:10).

> 'The individual *bishops* are the visible source and foundation of unity in their own particular Churches.' As such, they 'exercise their pastoral office over the portion of the People of God assigned to them', assisted by priests and deacons. But, as a member of the episcopal college, each bishop shares in the concern for all the Churches. The bishops exercise this care first 'by ruling well their own Churches as portions of the universal Church', and so contributing 'to the welfare of the whole Mystical Body, which, from another point of view, is a corporate body of Churches'. They extend it especially to the poor, to those persecuted for the faith, as well as to missionaries who are working throughout the world. (886)

The episcopal office is then described, in accord with Vatican II, by means of the classical formulation of a threefold office; the office of teaching, of sanctifying and of governing. It is unfortunate that the sanctifying office is treated so briefly (in 893) and, as already noted, unsatisfactorily because it attributes to the *function* of sanctifying something far more comprehensive which is in fact a component part of the very *nature* of ministry.

The teaching office, on the other hand, has received good treatment. The infallibility of the bishop of Rome has been placed in its rightful setting, within the devotion of whole Church to the truth and in relation with the episcopal magisterium as such with its mission (889–890). The Pope is not isolated from the other bishops.

> In order to preserve the Church in the purity of the faith handed on by the apostles, Christ who is the Truth willed to confer on her a share in his own infallibility. By a 'supernatural sense of faith' the People of God, under the guidance of the Church's living Magisterium, 'unfailingly adheres to this faith'. (889)

> The mission of the Magisterium is linked to the definitive nature of the covenant established by God with his people in Christ. It is this Magisterium's task to preserve God's people from deviations and defections and to guarantee them the objective possibility of professing the true faith without error. Thus, the pastoral duty of the Magisterium is aimed at seeing to it that the People of God abides in the truth that liberates. To fulfil this service, Christ endowed the Church's shepherds with the charism of infallibility in matters of faith and morals. The exercise of this charism takes several forms. (890)

The treatment accorded to the ordinary magisterium is judicious, and *Lumen Gentium* has been interpreted in a broader sense than is the case in some post-conciliar documents (892), even if some tried to understand these lines in a still narrow way. The commentary on the assent of the faithful is noteworthy and bears repeating here:

> Divine assistance is also given to the successors of the apostles, teaching in communion with the successor of Peter, and, in a particular way, to the bishop of Rome, pastor of the whole Church, when, without arriving at an infallible definition and without pronouncing in a 'definitive manner', they propose in the exercise of the ordinary Magisterium a teaching that leads to better understanding of Revelation in matters of faith or morals. To this ordinary teaching the faithful 'are to adhere . . . with religious assent', which, though distinct from the assent of faith, is nonetheless an extension of it. (892)

This section of the *Catechism* is well written and clear. But is it entirely in tune with paragraph 88?

Finally, the governing office also receives fair treatment based on the essential points in *Lumen Gentium* 27. The authors have been mindful to affirm that, although it is necessary that episcopal authority be exercised in communion with the whole Church over which the Pope exercises his 'leadership', the bishops are not to be regarded as vicars of the Pope (895). On the contrary, it is the Pope's responsibility to confirm and defend the authority of the bishops.

> 'The power which they exercise personally in the name of Christ is proper, ordinary and immediate, although its exercise is ultimately governed by the supreme authority of the Church.' But the bishops should not be thought of as vicars of the Pope. His ordinary and immediate authority over the whole Church does not annul, but on the contrary confirms and defends that of the bishops. Their authority must be exercised in communion with the whole Church under the guidance of the Pope. (895)

This section concludes by recalling the relationship of ministers to Christ the Good Shepherd (896) as expressed in *Lumen Gentium* and by Ignatius of Antioch.

The only problem with this excellent section on the episcopal office is its undue brevity with respect to the sanctifying function (893). Also, the 'In Brief' summary (939) is unsatisfactory. The latter is especially regrettable. These summaries will presumably play a part in teaching and be used as a guide to the arrangement of the chapters. Hence the consequences of their failure to provide an accurate summary of the text.

This particular 'In Brief' is both incomplete and too condensed (938, 939). It does not indeed omit the essential affirmation that bishops are 'the visible source and foundation of unity in their own particular Churches' (938). But, it has neglected to include the equally essential statement of Vatican II (LG 27) that every bishop is the 'vicar and legate of Christ' (cited, however, in 894). This appellation, which is also used to describe the Pope (882, 936), enables us to understand how the bishop of

Rome and the other bishops stand in their communion with one another, and how in their relation to Christ they are, in sacramental terms, equals. The primacy is a service at the heart of this communion in which they are bound together in Christ.

This long section of the *Catechism* would have greater impact if more attention had been devoted to episcopal conferences (887), but here again post-conciliar developments have received little notice.

Moreover theologians no longer speak only of synods and of provincial councils, which are episcopal assemblies (887). Since the Council, diocesan synods, in which the laity participate, have recovered their importance (see 911). Once again, in the *Catechism*, although there are frequent discussions of the local (or particular) churches (814, 831, 834, 835), these are inadequate. This becomes evident when we check the list of 'In Brief' and discover that the 'particular Church' is mentioned once only (938), with reference to bishops. The text pays more attention to episcopal *collegiality* than to the synodality of the churches in *communion*, and lays more stress on the life of the 'universal Church' than on that of the local church. In this we have the mark of an unconscious tendency present in Western ecclesiology, although reactions in the opposite direction also exist. These could have been noticed, even if only from an ecumenical perspective.

2. The laity
In its opening paragraph concerning 'Christ's faithful' the *Catechism* has made it clear that all the faithful without exception participate in the priestly, prophetic and royal functions of Christ, each one in accordance with his or her own individual condition and circumstances (871). All contribute to the building up of the Body of Christ (872, 873). Having shown this to be true for the hierarchy, the *Catechism* now proceeds to do the same for the laity, a term for which the definition is taken from *Lumen Gentium*:

> 'The term "laity" is here understood to mean all the faithful except those in Holy Orders and those who belong to a religious state approved by the Church. That is, the faithful who by Baptism are incorporated into Christ and integrated into the People of God are made sharers in their particular way in the priestly, prophetic and kingly office of Christ, and have their own part to play in the mission of the whole Christian people in the Church and in the world.' (897)

It is obvious that the division of Christians into three groups is not without problems, because members of religious orders may be either clerical or lay and are not as a group part of the hierarchical structure.

For the *Catechism*, the vocation of the laity is closely bound up with the administration of worldly affairs, since it is they who 'seek the kingdom of God by engaging in temporal affairs and directing them according to God's will' (898). There is an emphatic insistence on the necessity of the lay apostolate, which, with its foundation in baptism and confirmation, is both a duty and a right (900). On several points the text is more precise than *Lumen Gentium*, and thus the presentation is more forceful. It declares unequivocally that the activity of the laity in ecclesial communities is so necessary that often 'the apostolate of the pastors cannot be fully effective without it' (900).

The participation of lay people in Christ's priestly office is amply covered (901–903), with the noteworthy inclusion of a quotation from Canon 230 (§3):

> Lay people who possess the required qualities can be admitted
> permanently to the ministries of lector and acolyte. 'When the
> necessity of the Church warrants it and when ministers are lacking,
> lay persons, even if they are not lectors or acolytes, can also supply
> for certain of their offices, namely, to exercise the ministry of the word,
> to preside over liturgical prayers, to confer Baptism, and to distribute
> Holy Communion in accord with the prescriptions of law.' (903)

But it would have been helpful to provide here further elucidation on several points concerning certain areas in which a state of confusion prevails. For example, some people are under the impression that, even in the presence of an ordained minister, baptism and other sacraments which pertain to the 'ordinary ministry' may be performed by a layman. Some even say that the nature of baptism calls for such a change in the practice.

On the prophetic role of the laity the relevant conciliar text is cited. This role is declared to be related to an understanding of the faith and grace to give voice to it (904), which goes beyond the mere witness of life (905). The examples given are catechesis, instruction in the sacred sciences and the various fields of social communication. 907 is particularly illuminating, with its authority stemming from the Code of Canon Law. But there seems to be a surprising silence about theological research, unless we are able to detect it in the use of the term 'competence' in this paragraph.

> 'In accord with the knowledge, competence and pre-eminence which
> they possess, [lay people] have the right and even at times a duty to
> manifest to the sacred pastors their opinion on matters which
> pertain to the good of the Church, and they have a right to make
> their opinion known to the other Christian faithful, with due regard
> to the integrity of faith and morals and reverence toward their
> pastors, and with consideration for the common good and the dignity
> of persons.' (907)

The 'participation in Christ's kingly office' (908) focuses on the gift of liberty. This gift is of importance first for the 'disciples' themselves but also for social institutions, which must be made just and well disposed towards the practice of virtuous living. Canon Law is again cited here in support of lay collaboration with pastors even in matters of government.

In the Church, 'lay members of the Christian faithful can co-operate in the exercise of this power [of governance] in accord with the norm of law'. And so the Church provides for their presence at particular councils, diocesan synods, pastoral councils; the exercise *in solidum* of the pastoral care of a parish, collaboration in finance committees, and participation in ecclesiastical tribunals, etc. (911)

In 910 the term 'ministries' is actually applied in this context. The sub-section concludes with a sentence from *Lumen Gentium* 33 which reflects the Council's high regard for the laity: 'Thus, every person, through these gifts given to him, is at once the witness and the living instrument of the mission of the Church herself "according to the measure of Christ's bestowal"' (913).

One cannot say of the above presentation that it reveals a clerical basis. Throughout this section obedience and submission to the hierarchy have been treated with discretion. It is to be noted also that the 'In Brief' summaries devoted to the laity are as many as four in number (940–943). Moreover the *Catechism* has succeeded in exposing to view the remark of Pius XII (repeated by John Paul II), which is quoted in 899, that the laity do not merely *belong* to the Church; they *are* the Church.

3. The consecrated life

After duly recognising that 'the state of life which is constituted by the profession of the evangelical counsels' is not part of the hierarchical organisation of the Church, the *Catechism* proceeds to discuss it at length (914–933). The text adopts classical terminology — though its theological application is awkward — and affirms that it is the *profession* of the counsels of poverty, chastity in a celibate life and obedience, in a life of stability recognised by the Church, that characterises the life consecrated to God (915). We are reminded that religious consecration is rooted in baptismal consecration (916); and we are called upon to recognise the eschatological aspect of such a vocation (916, 933).

The *Catechism* then describes the various forms of life grouped under the heading 'consecrated life': eremitic life, consecrated virginity, religious life, secular institutes and societies of the apostolic life (917–930). However, on account of the complex set of realities involved, it was risky to define so precisely the specific characteristics of each group. Although the editors have followed the distinctions found in the new Code of Canon Law, these are at times lacking in clarity. Monks, for example, are grouped with 'religious' (927), all, exempt or not, being associated as co-operators of the diocesan bishop in his pastoral office (927). No notice is paid to the recent appearance of groups that do not fit into any of the traditional categories. These new groups include married couples and are often half-way between a religious community in the strict sense and a secular institute, half monastic and half society committed to the apostolic life.

Finally, the section suffers from much repetition: 926 repeats 915, 931 repeats 916, 933 repeats 916. But, above all, there is a lack of unity and theological rigour throughout. For example, how can we accept that the Church is 'like the sacrament — the sign and *instrument* — of God's own life'? This is misleading. The English translation has shown wisdom in simplifying the original French of 933, which stated that Christ's coming is 'l'origine et l'Orient' of the religious life! This has an alien ring of 'enthusiasm'. Some readers may wonder what purpose is fulfilled by 931–933 that was not achieved by the succinct presentation in 915–919.

III. Mary's place in the Church

Paul VI's designation 'Mary Mother of Christ, Mother of the Church' has been chosen as the title of the lengthy final section in the article that deals with the catholic doctrine of the Church of God. Here, the nuances which were achieved after much painful formulation have been preserved, and a series of conciliar quotations, broken only by the interjection of a Byzantine troparion (i.e., a hymn) and a quotation from Paul VI, has been deemed sufficient. This is because the *Catechism* also contains references to Mary elsewhere.

The writers justify the use of the word 'maternity' to express Mary's relation to the Church by reference to her relation to Christ, the Head of the Church. Scripture itself provides constant witness, from the annunciation to the cross (964). Since she is mother of the Head, she is also mother of the members (963). Her relationship to the members is manifest in her presence in the midst of the nascent Church (965). Her maternal role in the order of grace, through her co-operation in the Saviour's work and her intercessory activity since her assumption, have been treated with discernment so as not to detract from the mediation which alone belongs to Christ.

> 'Mary's function as mother of men in no way obscures or diminishes this unique mediation of Christ, but rather shows its power. But the Blessed Virgin's salutary influence on men . . . flows forth from the superabundance of the merits of Christ, rests on his mediation, depends entirely on it and draws all its power from it.' 'No creature could ever be counted along with the Incarnate Word and Redeemer; but just as the priesthood of Christ is shared in various ways both by his ministers and the faithful, and as the one goodness of God is radiated in different ways among his creatures, so also the unique mediation of the Redeemer does not exclude but rather gives rise to a manifold co-operation which is but a sharing in this one source.' (970)

All this is well expressed. Nevertheless, as an aid to catechists there should have been an explicit warning of the danger inherent in certain forms of expression which emanate from persons as celebrated as Alphonsus de Liguori and which are making a reappearance in popular piety. These could distort the fine balance of what has here been reaffirmed.

In line with the Council, the text employs a variety of titles for Mary:

advocate, benefactress, helper and mediatrix (969). The appellation 'coredemptrix' has been avoided and in its place is the more exact title of 'mother in the order of grace' (968), closely akin to the title *Theotokos,* Mother of God, which is used in the liturgy (971). It is important to stress the place occupied by the *lex orandi* devotion in the expression of Marial doctrine in the Church.

But Mary's position in this part of the *Catechism,* which is concerned with the Church of God, may be explained by her function as an 'eschatological icon of the Church' (972). Indeed, tradition regards Mary's assumption as a singular participation in the glory of the resurrection of Christ, Head of the Church, and as an anticipation of the resurrection of other Christians (966). The following passage in the *Catechism* is to be seen in this light:

> After speaking of the Church, her origin, mission and destiny, we can find no better way to conclude than by looking to Mary. In her we contemplate what the Church already is in her mystery on her own 'pilgrimage of faith', and what she will be in the homeland at the end of her journey. There 'in the glory of the Most Holy and Undivided Trinity', 'in the communion of all the saints', the Church is awaited by the one she venerates as Mother of her Lord and as her own mother.
>
> In the meantime the Mother of Jesus, in the glory which she possesses in body and soul in heaven, is the image and beginning of the Church as it is to be perfected in the world to come. Likewise she shines forth on earth, until the day of the Lord shall come, a sign of certain hope and comfort to the pilgrim People of God. (972)

Conclusion

As the result of this analysis, based on a thorough examination of, and a critical commentary on, the text, the judgement on this article of the *Catechism* is generally favourable. At the same time one needs to point out certain imprecisions on important points; and express the concern that the 'In Brief' summaries lend support to a minimalist view which narrows the horizon. It is also to be regretted that the Bible itself has been cited only rarely; for reference to God's word, the source is almost invariably by way of a magisterial document or Tradition. On the whole, however, the section under scrutiny has shown itself generally faithful to the vision rediscovered by Vatican II of the Church-as-communion.

In spite of an overemphasis on the universal Church, to which attention has been drawn, there is no basis for the facile judgement expressed by some critics that the *Catechism* portrays the Church as 'heavily *sub Petro*'. Even though there are some awkward passages, the bishops have received adequate treatment and their role is clearly defined as *cum Petro et sub Petro*. Further, the Church does not appear as predominantly clerical, because the stature and the responsibilities of the laity are treated with respect. Nevertheless, it is unfortunate that the local church as such, though frequently mentioned in the text, is not given sufficient consideration. There are signs here of an ecclesiology which has a distinctly one-sided preference for the universal and is more concerned with the universal aspect of *communion* than with its counterpart on the local level. There also seems to have been an inability to find room for some serious discussion of ecumenism within the given theological framework.

May it be allowed to deplore the style in which the text is written and the heaping together of often disparate quotations. Both of these weigh down the reader. A little more attention to the art of writing well would have served a good cause.

Notes

1   As stated in the Apostolic Constitution *Fidei Depositum* of 11 October 1992: 'a reliable base for instruction in the faith'; 'an authentic and sound reference work for teaching Catholic doctrine and especially for the preparation of local catechisms'; 'an approved and invaluable aid in the service of ecclesial communion'.

2   For example in 787 and 788, which give the impression of a confused assemblage that does not hold together.

3   795. We are told that the quotation from Joan of Arc is a response to the desire 'to give witness to the feminine'. Is it not possible to find an example more universally recognised?

4   The original text of the *Catechism* is in French.

5   The translation of 816 is more exact but remains imprecise in the French version; see also 830, which declares that in the Church subsists the fullness of the Body of Christ . . .

6   The order followed is that of *Lumen Gentium*.

7   It is important to note that this is a quotation from Nicetas.

8   774 and 775 state that in the Church communion with God and among men has *already* begun!

9   The 'In Brief' summaries give a distorted vision of the ecclesiology of the *Catechism*.

10   For this reason it is all the more regrettable that the thematic index of the French edition fails to provide any substantial references to the article on the Eucharist under 'sacrement'.

11   This theme becomes even more pertinent as a result of the discussions in some Churches arising out of the ordination of women, the minister being the *sacramentum* of Christ the bridegroom.

12   On this, see E. Lanne, 'L'Eglise de Rome *a gloriosissimis duobus apostolis Petro et Paulo Romae fundatae et constitutae Ecclesiae*', *Irénikon* 49 (1976), pp. 275–322.

13   The more usual term 'local church' occurs in 854.

14   This attitude is well described in E. Lanne, 'Unité et diversité au sujet de quelques propositions récentes', *Irénikon* 60 (1987), pp. 16–46.

15   See J. M. R. Tillard, *The Bishop of Rome* (London, 1983), where I have discussed this point at length.

Eschatology

(Paragraphs 988–1065)

Brian E. Daley SJ
Weston School of Theology

In these two articles, the *Catechism* brings to an end the first Part of its presentation of the Church's faith, which is an exposition of the liturgical statement we know as the Old Roman or Apostles' Creed. Here, in developing what the Catholic community has classically understood by the phrases '[I believe in] the resurrection of the body, and the life everlasting. Amen', the *Catechism* takes up a range of doctrines known as Christian *eschatology*: reflection on the final meaning, beyond the limits of our changing human history, of the gift of salvation offered to us by God through Christ Jesus. By any estimate, eschatology represents some of the most challenging aspects of faith in God and in Christ: the conviction that death, though real and inevitable, will not be the end of our conscious life, and that even our bodies will somehow share in 'the life everlasting'; the expectation that death will bring us all to 'judgement' or confrontation with truth; the hope for complete fulfilment of all our desires in God; the recognition that we may need to undergo painful purification before that fulfilment is reached; the real possibility that any of us may freely reject God's invitation to happiness and condemn ourselves to eternal self-contradiction. Because the events and realities these expectations refer to all lie, for the believing and worshipping community, in the future, the concluding words of the Creed are really an expression of *hope*: the hope that is an indispensable element in all religious faith and that is central to every Christian's relationship to God (see Rom 4:16–18; 5:4–5; 8:24–25; Col 1:27; cf. 1817–1821). In the generally trinitarian structure of the ancient creeds the realisation of this hope is dealt with among the manifestations of the Holy Spirit: as God personally communicated to the believer and the believing community — as God 'given to us', 'love poured into our hearts' (Rom 5:5) — it is the Holy Spirit who brings to reality within us the transforming and indestructible life first realised in the risen Jesus (Rom 8:11).

Christian eschatology grows out of the conviction that Jesus' resurrection from the dead is real, and that it is 'good news' for all who believe in him. In calling the risen Jesus 'saviour' and 'redeemer' — in recognising him as the one who makes it possible for us to live free from the dangers that menace us most radically — the believer expresses the hope that the life given to Jesus by the Father in the Holy Spirit, after his experience of the full destructive force of human death, will also be shared with us after our own encounter with death. And the believer sees God's saving gift not simply as a promise to be fulfilled in a 'final' or eschatological state beyond this life and this human history, but also as a reality already tasted in the present life of the Church; so Christian writers often speak of the 'eschatological' dimension of the Church's sacraments and of the life of faith. God's presence, in Jesus and in the Spirit, is always the presence of a mystery of life beyond danger or decay, of ultimate truth, of unconditional and unwavering love. God himself is the *eschaton*, the goal and end of history, and his final salvation has already become concrete in human terms for us in the risen Christ.

This 'tension' between present and future reality gives a paradoxical but distinctive character to Christian expressions of eschatological hope. 'We hope for what we do not see' (Rom 8:25), for 'what no eye has seen, nor ear heard, nor the human heart conceived' (1 Cor 2:9): not simply because the fulfilment of our hope still lies in the future — because it has not yet happened to any of us who here profess it, has not yet become a *fact* for us — but also because its fulfilment involves a transformation of the present conditions of human life into something utterly beyond our experience. Yet our hope is nonetheless founded on experience: the experience of the changed quality of a life lived in hope, of the new freedom which the Christian shares, in the power of the Holy Spirit, because of faith in the risen Christ. So our convictions about the eschatological future are always based, as the theologian Karl Rahner pointed out, on our experience of the 'eschatological' character of the present life of grace, as that is revealed to us in the Good News about Christ, and on nothing more: 'The Christian knows of his future inasmuch as he knows of himself and his redemption in Christ through divine revelation.'[1] But because they are not simply statements about the realm of our ordinary experience, expressions of Christian hope must always be understood as *images* of what we hope for rather than as descriptions of what we know: metaphors for what is necessarily still unknown, extrapolated from a world of spiritual, internal experience that itself can only be alluded to by analogies.

For this reason, doubtless, the Catholic Church has always been noticeably reticent in its official teaching about the future details of salvation. Dogmatic statements representative of the Church's teaching office on eschatological subjects have been relatively few, and those that have been made usually avoid giving the impression of offering detailed information about the future. In fact, the Council of Trent's decree affirming the tradition of belief in purgatory expressly directs that Catholic teaching should avoid speculation on 'difficult and subtle questions' not related to the life of faith, and should omit whatever smacks of speculation or superstition.[2] In the same spirit, the Congregation for the Doctrine of the Faith, in a brief statement on eschatological questions issued in 1979, urged Catholic teachers against going beyond 'the images employed in the Scriptures' when dealing with Christian hope for life after death, and added, in conclusion:

> Neither Scripture nor theology provides sufficient light for a proper picture of life after death. Christians must firmly hold the two following essential points: on the one hand, they must believe in the fundamental continuity, thanks to the power of the Holy Spirit, between our present life in Christ and the future life . . . ; on the other hand, they must be clearly aware of the radical difference between the present life and the future one . . . We shall be with Christ and 'we shall see God' (cf. I John 3:2), and it is in these promises and marvellous mysteries that our hope essentially consists. Our imagination may be incapable of reaching these heights, but our heart does so instinctively and completely.[3]

The *Catechism*'s treatment of Christian eschatological hope, as it is expressed in the final two phrases of the Creed, reflects this same caution. Controversial theories without a well-established foundation in the Bible or the tradition of faith, such as that of a 'limbo' for unbaptised children innocent of personal sin, are avoided altogether. No attempt is made to present a single philosophical understanding of the human person — to define the 'soul', for instance (cf. 363), or to speculate about the qualities of the 'risen', eschatologically transformed human body. Spatial and temporal categories in the description of the process of purgation from sin after death, and speculation on the details of the joys of heaven or the pains of damnation, are also avoided; these 'states' are described either in simple biblical language or in terms of the relationship of the human person to the saving God. No conjecture is offered about when or how this world will come to an end, as if the biblical texts that refer to it were meant to convey information that could help us make exact predictions. Unlike many works on Christian hope composed in earlier times, the *Catechism* here seems deliberately to avoid presenting its readers with what might be taken as a treatise on human nature, a scenario for the final conflicts of human history, or a map of the 'world beyond'.

On the other hand, certain consistent traits can be noticed throughout the *Catechism*'s treatment of Christian eschatological hope.

(a) Whether it is dealing with the resurrection of the body, with human beatitude or with the final transformation of the material world, Christian fulfilment is presented here in explicitly *trinitarian* terms: as being involved with the risen Christ, through the presence and action of the Holy Spirit, in the eternal life that flows from the Father (see 988f., 1003, 1024, 1050).

(b) The details of final judgement and salvation are described primarily in terms of *relationship* rather than of events: the relationship of the believer to God through the risen Christ, who himself embodies the final fullness of grace (see 989, 994, 995, 999, 1001–1003, 1009–1010, 1021–

1022, 1025–1026, 1039). So, too, the suffering of the damned is presented as 'definitive self-exclusion from communion with God', on the basis of one's response to Jesus and his 'brethren' (1033).

(c) Final salvation or damnation are not presented primarily as the success or failure of individual lives, but as inclusion in — or exclusion from — a *community* of salvation, whose life is already anticipated in the sacramental life of the Church (1000, 1002, 1010, 1024–1027, 1029, 1033, 1045–1046). So the graced aspect of Christian death is seen in the context of the supporting prayers of the saints (1014), and the sharing of the dead in the eucharistic sacrifice of the Church is emphasised in several places throughout the *Catechism* (954–962, 1370–1372, 1684, 1689–1690). For this reason, the *Catechism*'s general practice of drawing on liturgical prayers and customs, and on the writings of the great saints of the past, as sources for communicating and interpreting the Church's faith, takes on particular importance in this context of Christian hope. To participate in a community of hope, one must pay particular attention to the voices of that community through the ages, as it worships God and expresses its awareness of his life-giving presence.

Article 11: 'I believe in the resurrection of the body' (988–1019)

I. Christ's resurrection and ours (992–1004)

The *Catechism* begins its explanation of these final two articles of the Creed by situating Christian hope for resurrection and life everlasting within the broad context of the Christian community's experience of God working in human history to save and give life — what we traditionally call the 'economy of salvation'. Hope that we will share God's gift of eternal life as complete, integral human beings — present to ourselves as conscious, self-determining spirit or souls, and rooted, as bodies, in a material world outside us — is really the hope that the *salvation* from enslavement to sin and mortal danger already experienced in Christ, already communicated to us by the Holy Spirit, will come to an eternal, indestructible fulfilment at the end of our history. So the *Catechism* rightly situates hope for eternal life as the culmination of faith in a God who creates, saves and makes holy (988); further, it rightly points out that hope for our own resurrection is based on our faith that Christ is already risen, and modelled on our present understanding of his risen life (989; see also 994–995, 999, 1002–1004), in which we recognise 'the work of the Most Holy Trinity' (989). It is the final stage of our incorporation, by the Spirit and according to the Father's will, in the mystery of Christ: of our adoption as children of God (see 1 Jn 3:1–2).

Hope in the resurrection of the dead is not simply a hope that we shall continue to exist, in some way, after our death, but also a hope for radical *transformation* of our humanity: so in professing faith in 'the resurrection of the body' or of the 'flesh', we express faith that even those aspects of ourselves in which we now most experience our weakness and mortality

(990) will share in a glorious life like that of the risen Jesus. 'We shall not all fall asleep', Paul wrote to the Corinthians, 'but we shall all be changed . . .' (1 Cor 15:51).

In fact, as the *Catechism* observes, faith in our own future resurrection, as well as in the present resurrection of Jesus, has been an essential part of Christian faith since apostolic times (991). The text quotes, in this connection, both 1 Corinthians 15, St Paul's most developed treatment of the implications of faith in the resurrection of Jesus, and the opening words of Tertullian's treatise *On the Resurrection of the Flesh*, written shortly after AD 200 — words which could also be translated '. . . believing this, we are what we are'. St Augustine, preaching two centuries later, insisted that hope for resurrection is 'the distinctive faith of Christians' (*Sermo* 241, 1), the distinguishing mark and focus of all Christian doctrine (*Sermo* 214, 12; 361, 2).

The *Catechism* develops its exposition of Christian faith in the resurrection in three steps: (1) its *foundation in Scripture*; (2) ways to a more exact understanding of its *content*; and (3) its *implications for our Christian life* now.

(1) Scripture. In saying that 'God revealed the resurrection of the dead to his people progressively', the *Catechism* is cautiously stating the recognised fact that the people of the Old Testament generally did not share faith in a coming resurrection, or indeed have any expectation of a genuinely human life beyond the grave, until the last two centuries before Christ. Like virtually all ancient peoples, Israel assumed — if only because of her occasional experience with mediums and ghosts (e.g., 1 Sam 28:6–25) — that the dead continue to exist in some shadowy way, in a dark pit or collective grave beneath the surface of the earth called *Sheol*. But life in Sheol was only a step short of complete oblivion: it was a 'land of silence' (Pss 94:17; 115:17), a 'land of forgetfulness' (Ps 88:12), where 'there is no work or thought or knowledge or wisdom' (Eccl 9:10) and where no one remembers or praises God (Ps 6:5; Is 38:18). The hope of individuals for some permanent validity, through virtually the whole Old Testament period, was conceived as a hope for descendants who would keep one's name and memory alive (e.g., Gen 12:2; Ps 22:29–30; Prov 10:7). A few passages in the Hebrew Bible (e.g. Ps 73:24) suggest traces of a hope that some people of outstanding faith might be 'taken up' into God's glory at the end of life, as Enoch (Gen 5:24) and Elijah (2 Kings 2:1–18) were, or even that the faithful dead of Israel might rise again (Is 26:19 — probably an addition from the fourth or third century BC). It was only at the very end of the Old Testament period, however, in passages like those the *Catechism* cites (992) from Daniel and the Books of Maccabees, that a clear hope for personal resurrection begins to be widely shared: sometimes simply as the ultimate reward of the faithful just (2 Macc 7:9–29; Eth En 91:10; 92:3f.; 100:5; Ps Sol 3:12), at other times as the preliminary to a universal judgement including sinners as well as saints (Dan 12:2; Eth En 51:1; 4 Ezra 7:32f.; 78–101). This became a standard feature of the apocalyptic literature of the 'intertestamental' period.

209

As the *Catechism* points out (993), Jesus and his more devout contemporaries, such as the Pharisees, clearly shared this lively late-Jewish expectation of a resurrection of the dead, and saw in it a prelude not only to God's judgement of all people, but to the transformation of the world and human existence (Mk 12:24–27; Jn 11:24; Acts 23:6). Jesus' identification of resurrection and eternal life with his own person, which the *Catechism* alludes to without comment (994), is, strictly speaking, part of the portrait of Jesus peculiar to the Fourth Gospel — a parallel, perhaps, to his insistence in the Synoptic Gospels that the coming of God's kingdom is revealed in his healing actions (e.g., Mt 11:4–5; 12:28, par.), and that entry into it will depend on our attitude to him and his followers (e.g., Mk 8:38; 10:23–27; Mt 25:40, 45).

The *Catechism* rightly notes (995) that the basis for the first apostles' witness to Jesus as Messiah and Lord was their experience of *fellowship* with him after his own resurrection — a resurrection that he is portrayed in the Synoptic Gospels as having predicted before his death (994). And just as this contact with the risen Jesus is the heart of the New Testament's witness to his role and person, so the continuing hope of Christians for a resurrection of their own is no longer simply the anguished longing for change that characterised apocalyptic Judaism, but is 'characterized' — 'completely marked', in the words of the French version of the *Catechism* — by the experience of Easter (995). The resurrection Christians hope for is not simply a miraculous resuscitation of the recently dead, similar to those performed by Jesus in the four Gospels, but an event 'of another order' (994), as his own resurrection was: permanent, totally transforming, and utterly mysterious. The life-giving force behind the future resurrection of the dead will itself be the risen Christ, in whose life — as the Adam of a new creation — all humanity will share (1 Cor 15:21–23, 45, 57; 997, 999–1000; cf. 1002–1004). When the Church, in the faith of Easter, professes hope in 'the resurrection of the body', it means 'we shall rise like Christ, with him, and through him' (995).

(2) Understanding the resurrection. The *Catechism* rightly points out that hope in a resurrection for all has been, since apostolic times, one of the great stumbling-blocks in the way of the acceptance of Christian faith (996). For the educated Greek world of the first Christian centuries, especially, where the hope was common that the immortal soul would be freed by death of all traces of materiality and corporeality, the notion of a restoration of the whole person from disintegration to unending life seemed both unintelligible and unseemly. Christian apologists of the second and third centuries like Athenagoras, Irenaeus and Tertullian argued with energy and passion that the God who has created the living human body is certainly capable of regenerating it in a new form, and that it is only in the hope for resurrection that the Christians' sense of the value of the body and the material world, and their daily struggle to integrate body and spirit, find meaning and support (e.g., Athenagoras, *On the Resurrection*, 12f.; Irenaeus, *Against Heresies*, 5, 1–15; Tertullian,

On the Resurrection of the Flesh, 15). But the credibility of hope for a resurrection clearly depends on the terms in which it is understood — on what Christians attempt to say about it with conviction and clarity, and what they are willing to leave enshrouded in mystery. This is what the *Catechism* attempts to outline, briefly and modestly, in the next five paragraphs (997–1001).

(a) The *Catechism* begins (997) by defining 'rising' as the reunion of the human soul, which has been separated from the body by death and which has been living in the presence of God, with its own body, once decayed and now incorrupt and glorified (cf. 1005, 1016). This language, which represents the most common way by which Christian theology has conceived of death and resurrection through the centuries, presupposes a conception of the human person many modern scientific and philosophical theories would not accept; the *Catechism*'s purpose here, presumably, is not to canonise any particular philosophical tradition, but to emphasise both the continuity between the present life and the life of glory — a continuity rooted in each person's free and conscious core — and the real break in our existence caused by death and physical disintegration. In the letter of the Congregation for the Faith of 1979 mentioned above (p. 207), the real point of using soul–body language is emphasised:

> The Church affirms that a spiritual element survives and subsists after death, an element endowed with consciousness and will, so that the 'human self' subsists, though deprived for the present of the complement of its body. To designate this element, the Church uses the word 'soul', the accepted term in the usage of Scripture and Tradition. Although not unaware that this term has various meanings in the Bible, the Church thinks that there is no valid reason for rejecting it; moreover she considers that the use of some word as a vehicle is absolutely indispensable in order to support the faith of Christians.[4]

Behind this emphasis on death as a separation of the person's conscious core from his or her bodily dimensions, both in the 1979 letter and here in the *Catechism*, may well lie a desire on the part of Vatican doctrinal authorities to distance themselves quietly from the tendency of several German theologians, in the 1970s and 1980s, to question the terms of traditional eschatology. The main target of this questioning has been the conception of a temporal interval or 'interim state' between the death of the individual and the resurrection, understood as his or her entry into final salvation or damnation as a whole, if transformed, person.[5] The final fulfilment of our personal existence, these authors argue, must occur for each of us at the end of this present life, when our ability to determine our acts and our character comes to an end; whatever 'resurrection of the body' is to take place, they suggest, must be part of our entry, as whole persons, into the presence of the God who is beyond time, and must be unaffected by the disintegration of the material molecules that have comprised our bodily existence within history. This interpretation of resurrection, however, which is sometimes called the theory of a 'resurrection in death', is regarded by its critics as overly spiritualised, and as implicitly minimising the importance of our rootedness as persons in the material world; it also seems to conceive salvation mainly in individual terms, distinct from the history of humanity that survives the individual's death. So both the letter of 1979 and this section of the *Catechism* take pains to emphasise that our entry as individuals into God's presence at death is a distinct but only a preliminary stage of eschatological fulfilment, and that the resurrection we hope for must be part of a re-creation and transformation of all humanity, and of the whole material universe in which our bodiliness is situated (997, 1021, 1038–1040; see also 671, 680–681), at the end of human history.

(b) The *Catechism* affirms clearly (997) that the resurrection of our bodies will be an act of God's almighty power, working through the risen Christ (cf. 1002). As St Thomas Aquinas insisted, it must be understood as a genuinely *miraculous* event, even though it will be the fulfilment of the innate needs and desires of our nature; 'in nature' by itself, after all, 'there is no active principle of the resurrection'.[6]

(c) The resurrection will include not simply the just or those who have hoped in God, but all who have ever lived (998). Thus it will be a *collective* event, involving and revealing the whole human community, and will set the stage for the judgement of all human works and their fitting retribution, accomplished by the manifest presence *(parousia)* of Christ at the heart of history (998, 1001; see below, pp. 220–1). As a result, it can only take place 'definitively' at the end of all history (1001), even though it may be anticipated in a variety of partial ways in the individual's death and even in the quality of his or her earthly life (see 1002).

(d) What the resurrection will mean concretely, and how it will take place, simply exceeds our powers of imagination (999–1000). The *Catechism* quotes 1 Corinthians 15 to remind us that despite the familiar images used in preaching and theological speculation, resurrection will be a transformation of our human existence, in both its spiritual and material dimensions, to a state wholly unlike the present one. To acknowledge frankly the limits of our understanding in this aspect of our faith is not obscurantism or deliberate vagueness, but a recognition that our future transformation in Christ is a central implication of the mystery that challenges us, by its very nature, to trust in the unknown.

(3) Relevance of the resurrection for Christian life. The *Catechism* reminds us that hope for the resurrection of our bodies, although shrouded for us in God's future, also exercises a profound influence on our present life of faith. Alluding to Colossians 3:1–3, the text reminds us that the baptised Christian already has passed with Jesus, in liturgical mystery, through death to life; the present life of the Christian is not simply one isolated human existence, borne by its own limited powers, but shares, through the gift of the Holy Spirit, in the life of the risen Christ which for now is 'hidden' within the mystery of God (1002–1003). The *Catechism* quotes the teaching of St Irenaeus, however, that our present sharing in the

Eucharist is a preparation for the full, bodily realisation of that life given us in Christ, a pledge in simple, physical terms of the transformation of our humanity that will be revealed at the end of time (1000, 1003). Christian salvation includes the body as well as the mind and heart; Christian worship involves the body and bodily things as well as words and ideas. The implication is that our bodies share in our dignity as people who belong to Christ, and demand from us respect, care and love (1004). As the second-century apologists insisted, the serious Christian lives even in this life as one who expects to rise again.[7]

II. To die in Christ Jesus (1005–1014)

In the second part of its treatment of Christian hope in the resurrection, the *Catechism* turns to the Christian's understanding of *death* within the perspective of faith. As Paul insisted to the Corinthians, resurrection always presupposes that death has been experienced in its full reality (1 Cor 15:20–24, 26, 30–31, 42–50); so what gives Christian hope both its challenge and its power is the fact that it is a hope for indestructible life in the face of genuine, unavoidable human death. Resurrection to eternal life cannot mean, for the Christian, an escape from the certainty of death or an avoidance of its violence and terrors, but rather a life given to us gratuitously by God, in and beyond death. And if our hope for resurrection is derived from our faith in the risen Jesus, and will be brought to realisation by the Holy Spirit through Jesus' power and presence, then our death, too, must also be reinterpreted and transformed in some way by our relationship to him: 'to rise with Christ, we must die with Christ' (1005).

So the *Catechism* briefly considers here what the Christian understands death to be, in the context of the mystery of salvation in Christ; it then goes on to reflect on the transformed attitudes Christians might be expected to have towards the prospect of death. Since it is the end of human activity in the world and of interpersonal communication as we know it, death is now a closed reality to us: at worst, it appears simply as the negation of all we are; at best, it is darkness and mystery. The *Catechism* quotes the beginning of Vatican II's brief reflection on death, reminding us that 'it is in regard to death that man's condition is most shrouded in doubt' (GS 18), and then goes on to make three further assertions about what our faith *is* able to say on the subject.

(a) In one sense, the *Catechism* reminds us, death is utterly *natural*, the obvious termination of an existence bound by time and characterised by change (1006–1007). Quoting the book of Ecclesiastes (Qoheleth) in the Old Testament, it observes that the inevitability of death, and the limits it places on our ability to shape our lives, gives drama and seriousness to each of our moral choices. As St Athanasius and St Gregory of Nyssa recognised in the fourth century, death and corporeal disintegration is simply a natural consequence of our being animals, the outcome of our organic participation in a world of growth and decay.[8]

(b) Yet biblical faith, as the *Catechism* also reminds us, sees death as the result of *sin*, and thus as something *not* simply natural, not intended

213

by God for his human creation but brought about by human infidelity to God (1006, 1008). This teaching can be understood in at least two senses: first, that death as it presently confronts us, as it darkens our lives with fear, is not simply the natural termination of our organic processes, but finitude seen through through the lens of sinful self-interest and self-affirmation; and second, that God's plan for humanity, since its origins, has been to offer it a share in his own transcendent life in a way that would lift it beyond the capabilities of its own nature — a plan that humanity has resisted by seeking instead to become master of the universe independent of God.[9] This second view, which sees the prospect of our undergoing a simply 'natural' death precisely as the result of our forfeiture of God's 'supernatural' gift of life, seems to form the background of the assertions of the Council of Trent cited here (1008; see ND 508–509), and it paves the way for a third line of reflection: on the transformation of death by the grace of Christ.

(c) The *Catechism* points out the central *role of Christ* in changing the meaning of death for the Christian believer: 'For those who die in Christ's grace it is a participation in the death of the Lord, so that they can also share his Resurrection' (1006). In living out a fully human life, God the Son suffered the death that is both life's natural conclusion and coloured by our collective history of sin; but by accepting this death freely and obediently, by making it into an expression of his faith and trust in the God he calls Father, Christ has 'transformed the curse of death into a blessing' (1009). For those who can enter into death in solidarity with Jesus and in his spirit of obedience and trust, death itself becomes a door to life with God, a moment of transforming grace.

In the light of this new understanding of death, the Christian can approach death, as the *Catechism* suggests (1010–1014), with a new range of attitudes.

(a) Death remains the complete and authentic termination of life as we know it; Christian hope is not a hope for reincarnation, or for a simple continuity that would reduce the seriousness of the choices we must make to determine the shape of the life we now lead (1013). The *finality* of death — and thus the uniqueness of this present life — is not an illusion.

(b) Yet because of the freedom and hope revealed in Jesus' death, and the promise of transformed life for us all revealed in his resurrection, the Christian can see death, with Paul, as a 'gain' and a *way to God* (Phil 1:21–23). Although we remain morally responsible to care for our lives, and have no right to take steps to hasten our own deaths (see 2280–2283), we may certainly *desire* death as the path to union with the risen Christ and to deeper immersion in the mystery of God (1010–1011). The *Catechism* cites St Paul and St Ignatius of Antioch as writers who express this Christian longing for death in an authentically Christian way.

(c) Through *baptism*, the Christian already enters into this transformed reality of death during the present life. Baptism, in Paul's view, is a sacramental way of entering into the death of Christ (1010); physical death accepted in faith, for the baptised person, is thus simply a way of living out to its human fullness the identification with Jesus in his death and resurrection which baptism has begun. So the Catholic funeral liturgy can say, with startling simplicity, that for God's 'faithful people life is changed, not ended' in death (1012); the eternal life into which we enter at baptism continues in a new, unimaginable way when this physical life reaches its end.

(d) The Christian understanding of death contributes an added *urgency* to our everyday actions; so spiritual writers have traditionally urged their readers to see life as a preparation for death, and to live each day as if it were their last (1014).

(e) The *Catechism* also suggests that the Christian view his or her own death in the context of the whole *Church*: so we traditionally ask the saints to intercede for us at the moment of our death (1014), recognising that they, too, as dead persons of faith, form an essential part of the living community that is the Body of Christ.[10] Christian death, like Christian salvation, is not simply an individual experience; it is an individual's full realisation of the paschal mystery at the heart of the Church.

Article 12: 'I believe in life everlasting' (1020–1060)

The eleventh article of the Creed, which we have just discussed, presents us with the core of Christian hope for the final fulfilment of the salvation we already share: the resurrection and almost unimaginable reintegration of our whole person, beyond death and beyond the completion of all human history. The twelfth article is closely paired with it, pointing to the new state of humanity and the world for which the event of resurrection is the necessary prelude: eternal, indestructible life in the condition of joyful beatitude with Christ, or anguished, self-destructive resistance to him, in a transformed cosmos that will truly be 'a new heaven and a new earth'.

The Christian tradition has generally assumed that there will be *continuity* between the present life of faith or unbelief, expressed in the choices we make here, and that final fulfilment: a state of anticipation or a process of preparatory purification experienced by the conscious core of each person, despite the disintegration of the material body, which, as we have said, theologians often refer to as the 'interim state', since it occupies the interval between the individual's death and the end of human history. After quoting a dramatic passage from the Western Church's Prayer of Commendation of a dying person, in which death is conceived as an embarking on our homeward journey into God (1020), the *Catechism* here develops the main features of the Church's understanding of this passage into eternal life, both in its interim and final forms, under six headings: the 'particular' judgement of each person's life, which occurs at his or her death; heaven, or beatitude; purgatory, or purification after death; hell, or permanent separation from God; the final judgement of the whole human race as a single community; and the renewal and transformation of the universe we now live in. Its presentation of all of these facets of Christian eschatological hope is modest in its affirmations, and interprets them more in terms of personal relationships — with God, with the human community — than of concrete images and events. Nevertheless, all of them belong to the content of Christian hope, and to a fully rounded Christian understanding of God and ourselves.

I. The particular judgement (1021–1022)

Although the term 'judgement' suggests a forensic process of investigation, verdict and sentencing, the *Catechism* rightly points out that in biblical terms it 'primarily' means a 'final encounter with Christ': the entry of an individual or of the whole mass of humanity, in that form of our being which our own freedom has finally determined, before the illuminating truth of God, as it has been revealed in the human figure of Jesus (see Jn 3:19–21; 5:22–24; 12:31–32).

Because Christian faith calls us to take death seriously, to see it as the end of the life we now live, theology has generally insisted that death ends our ability to make the choices that determine our fundamental relationship to God, to accept or reject God's grace (1021); so, for instance, Pope Leo X condemned, among other theses of Martin Luther, the notion that the souls in purgatory continue to be capable of sin, and remain unsure of their salvation (DS 1488–1489).[11] At death, we are what God's grace and our own free response have made us; further, several passages in the New Testament suggest that the person of faith should expect to be 'with the Lord' immediately after death (Phil 1:23; Lk 23:43), and so to discover then the full meaning of his or her own life in Christ's presence. Therefore, although the New Testament's depiction of God's judgement through Christ is conceived as a judgement of all humanity at history's end, theologians since the early Church have understood that this judgement is anticipated for each individual when she or he encounters Christ at death.[12] So Pope Benedict XII, in 1336, as well as a number of medieval synods of the Western Church — all cited here by the *Catechism* (footnotes to 1021–1022) — taught that both the beatitude of the just and the punishment of the damned must be thought of as beginning 'immediately' at the death of each individual. As we have mentioned already (above, p. 211), some contemporary theologians have raised questions about the necessity or plausibility of such an 'interim' state;[13] without discussing the issue directly, the *Catechism* follows the Congregation for the Faith's letter of 1979 (see above, pp. 211–12) — and cites, in passing, a line from a poem of St John of the Cross (1022) — in affirming the more traditional conception of a judgement and recompense realised for each individual at death, as something distinct from the bodily resurrection and judgement of all humanity at the end of history.

II. Heaven (1023–1029)

The *Catechism* next treats of the real object of eschatological hope: 'the ultimate end and fulfilment of the deepest human longings, the state of supreme, definitive happiness' (1024), which we usually speak of as 'heaven'. Although it alludes briefly to some of the images used in the

Bible for this final and blessed fulfilment (1027), the text emphasises that the reality of heaven is enshrouded in the mystery of God, and so 'is beyond all understanding and description' (1027). What can be said about it is that it is the fulfilment of all the relationships that define our personal being and bring it to perfection: our relationship with God, our Creator and Saviour, and our relationship with those other human beings who share God's life with us. So the *Catechism* here defines heaven as a 'communion of life and love with the Trinity, with the Virgin Mary, the angels and all the blessed' (1024), as 'blessed communion with God and all who are in Christ' (1027). It is, in fact, the full realisation of the communion with God and with other men and women which is now the heart of the Church, and which reveals to us, in our experience of the Church's life, what God is: a mystery of love and communication who involves us in his own inner rhythm of life, drawing us, in the power of the Spirit within us, on the way of Jesus, our brother, towards the source of all being whom he and we call Father. As such, heaven is the final form of the present community of disciples, 'the blessed community of all who are perfectly incorporated into Christ' (1026).

The *Catechism* also reminds us of three other aspects of the Church's traditional hope for heaven. First, it speaks of final fulfilment as 'the beatific vision' (1028), a relationship of complete mutual openness with God that is best imagined in terms not simply of knowledge but of contemplation or sight. After quoting at some length Pope Benedict XII's definition of 1336, in which he speaks — in Thomistic terms — of beatitude as seeing 'the divine essence with an intuitive vision, and even face to face, without the mediation of any creature' (1023),[14] the *Catechism* emphasises that such an interior 'vision' always exceeds the mind's natural powers, and is possible only by God's transforming gift (1028). Second, it makes the point that this final union with God, through Christ, will not simply absorb us into the primal ocean of being in a way that destroys our personal identity; 'the elect live "in Christ"', as in an all-sustaining environment, 'but they retain, or rather find, their true identity, their own name' (1025). Participation in the life of God is precisely what perfects our distinctive existence as persons. Third, the *Catechism* suggests that the communion among created and redeemed persons in heaven also continues to involve them in the life of the Church on earth, where the mystery of shared life in Christ has already begun: 'in the glory of heaven the blessed continue joyfully to fulfil God's will in relation to other men and to all creation' (1029). This same idea of the 'communion of saints', as a vital network of transformed human relationships, is touched on in several other places in the *Catechism*: in the section on the Creed's affirmation of the 'communion of saints' (954–962); in the discussion of the practice of prayer for the dead, particularly at the Eucharist (1370–1372); and in the treatment of the Christian celebration of funerals (1684, 1689–1690). In all of these sections, expression is given to the ancient Christian conviction that the living and dead remain in communion with one another in the one Body of Christ.[15]

III. Final purification or purgatory (1030–1032)

The *Catechism* next treats of the Catholic belief in a process of personal purgation after death for those whose lives are essentially directed towards God, yet lacking in the integrity and simplicity of commitment, the purity of heart, that would seem to be requisite for contemplative union with God. A number of important early Christian writers (e.g., Lactantius, Augustine, Paulinus of Nola, Maximus the Confessor), drawing on Jewish apocalyptic tradition, imagine the final judgement of Christ as involving a fire through which all the dead must pass, a fire that will consume the wicked and purify the remains of sin in the just. Some later Latin Fathers (Caesarius of Arles, Gregory the Great) also speak of fiery purgation for individuals immediately after death, while others (Clement of Alexandria, Origen, Ambrose, Gregory of Nyssa) imagine a gentler and less picturesque process of healing and instruction, prior to full sharing in the presence of God. In the medieval Western Church, this *process* of purgation after death came to be understood as a *state* or even as a *place* of purgation, a 'purgatory', to which souls are confined for a time in the interim before resurrection, until they are fully ready to be engaged in the beatific vision of God — a conception which both Orthodox and Protestant Christians have frequently called into question, as lacking in scriptural evidence and leading to an over-material, even superstitious understanding of life beyond the grave.

The *Catechism* here cites the Councils of Florence and Trent, in their replies to these objections, as well as Pope Benedict XII: all simply assert that a process of purgation for the dead *is* possible, and that our prayers and liturgical commemorations of the dead are therefore especially appropriate (1031). Indeed, the *Catechism* rightly stresses the importance of such liturgical practices (1032) since they offer perhaps clearer evidence of the Church's conviction that healing and growth may take place after death than the scriptural passages traditionally referred to (1 Cor 3:15; 1 Pet 1:7) in support of a doctrine of purgation (1031).[16] In fact, all that official Catholic teaching holds is that 'there is a purgative process (*purgatorium esse*)' and that those dead who are undergoing it are helped by the prayers of the eucharistic community on earth.[17] Behind this, doubtless, is the assumption that final union with God presupposes a total conversion of the human heart from the selfish pursuit of our own interests in this world, and that such a conversion may involve a more elaborate process of growth and detachment than everyone's life on earth affords. How, if at all, one may conceive such a process after death in temporal or spatial terms, and whether it need even be separated from the potentially painful experience of death itself, must be left to theological speculation. The *Catechism* prudently avoids further development of the subject.

IV. Hell (1033–1037)

Next the *Catechism* turns to consider the possibility of eternal life in a negative sense: an existence permanently alienated from God, and so definitively contradicting its own welfare and meaning. This condition is what Christian faith calls *hell*, which the *Catechism* here defines as a 'state of definitive self-exclusion from communion with God and the blessed' (1033; cf. 1035).

The roots of the Christian conception of hell lie also in the preaching of Jesus and in the images of apocalyptic Judaism on which he drew: for Jesus and early Christianity, those who refuse to heed the gospel of God's kingdom and who fail to 'bear fruit' in deeds of reverence and love will be cast, at the final judgement, into the 'unquenchable fire' of Gehenna (e.g., Mk 9:43–48; Mt 3:10–12; 5:22; 13:40, 42; 25:41). Once again, these images must be interpreted cautiously and modestly. The *Catechism* presents the doctrine of hell, like that of heaven, in essentially relational terms, and explains both its possibility and its importance as an outgrowth of human freedom. To affirm the existence of hell, in fact, is nothing more than to affirm the possibility that we are made by God capable of frustrating both God's purpose in creating us and our own ultimate well-being, by choosing not to acknowledge our dependence on him with gratitude and self-transcending love. Put another way, the Church's doctrine of 'the existence of hell and its eternity', which is presented here (1035), is really the doctrine that it is possible for God's primary plan of salvation to fail in the case of some individuals, because they are created free; it is the recognition that even God's grace can be rejected, and that creaturely freedom is powerful enough to become the means of conscious and permanent self-contradiction, by denying God's role as Creator and Lord.

So while the *Catechism* alludes to the traditional image of hell, as a fiery place of torment beneath the earth (1034–1035), its emphasis here is not on the psychological or physical pains that we imagine to be the result of human separation from God, so much as on the utterly destructive character of that separation, and on the fact that we freely impose it on ourselves (1033). Consequently, with a reference to Vatican II's *Lumen Gentium*, it emphasises also the importance of the doctrine of hell as a summons to 'the responsibility incumbent upon man to make use of his freedom in view of his eternal destiny' (1036). It is only if we see hell as a real possibility for us all that the full seriousness of our freedom, in responding to God's gifts, can be recognised.

The *Catechism* is also careful to point out that the Catholic Church does *not* believe God actually *predestines* anyone to hell, or that God has created anyone with any other purpose than to share in his life (1037). Both the liturgy and the official teaching of church councils have suggested, rather, that the reality of damnation, like the reality of evil itself, consists in the paradoxical choice of creatures to turn away from their intended destiny — a choice that God may allow, out of respect for his own creation, but that God certainly does not desire. The very torments of final damnation, however we picture them, can best be understood as the discovery by the creature of all the personal implications of his or her choice to deny the full reality of creaturely existence.

The *Catechism* does not deal here with the question of whether or not anyone, in fact, *has* been or *will* be damned; it simply presents the

Church's teaching that permanent damnation is, from our perspective, a real possibility. Since the early Church, theologians have grappled with the question of whether God, in his mysterious power and love, would ever in fact allow any of his creatures to remain unconverted and unhealed until the end. So Origen, in the early third century, followed by Gregory of Nyssa, Ambrose and other Church Fathers, developed the theory of universal salvation or *apokatastasis*,[18] according to which it is assumed that God's grace will triumph finally in all intelligent creatures, even the evil spirits, by moving them to return freely to him in creaturely obedience and love. This theory was condemned, along with other positions attributed to Origen and his followers, by a local synod at Constantinople in 543, a condemnation ratified by the Fifth Ecumenical Council held in that city ten years later.[19] Catholic theology has generally understood that decision to mean that the Church may not teach with dogmatic certainty that all *will* be saved; nevertheless, the Church has also never affirmed the certainty that any individual is damned, and has always recognised that the workings of grace in each human heart are simply beyond our grasp. Although the question of the reality of damnation remains hotly debated in our own time, Christian theologians and mystical writers through the centuries have often presented the possibility that all will be saved as something the Christian may and should hope for.[20] The *Catechism*, too, points out elsewhere (1058) that the Church prays for the salvation of everyone, understanding this as something which is both possible and consonant with God's own plans, and it insists that each of us should hope to persevere, by God's grace, in our desire for God and so come to the joy of heaven (1821).

V. The Last Judgement (1038–1041)

Next the *Catechism* presents the Christian hope in the 'Last Judgement': a final disclosure to all humanity, in the moment of resurrection at history's end, of the meaning of that history as a whole and of the part each of us has played within it. Earlier, the *Catechism* discussed the expectation of the Christian faithful that the risen Christ, in whom God's kingdom has now been achieved, 'will come again in glory to judge the living and the dead', and the reign of God in the world will then move from the struggles of its present hidden reality to luminous realisation (668–682).

Here the focus is on the implications of this 'second coming' of Christ for our present hope. The *Catechism* presents the Last Judgement less in the image of a courtroom event than in terms of *revelation*: it will be history's final 'moment of truth', brought about by the then-obvious presence (*parousia*) of the glorified Christ in the midst of the world as Truth itself (1039). In coming to *see* Christ, in his integrated humanity and divinity, as the personal embodiment of what creation was meant to be, 'we shall know the ultimate meaning of the whole work of creation and of the entire economy of salvation, and understand the marvellous ways by which God's providence led everything towards its final end'

(1040). In hoping for such a final judgement, the Christian is really hoping that the true value of human actions and suffering within history will someday become apparent to all, and that Christ will be the heart of that vision, as he is now the heart of our hope.

The *Catechism* also points out the importance of this hope for Christian moral responsibility, especially for our engagement to work now for the realisation of justice in the world, in conformity with the gospel. Our faith that God is just, our conviction that God's demands are serious, requires us to hope that the justice or injustice of all human actions will, in the end, be revealed in the radiant presence of Christ. So the *Catechism* remarks that the expectation of final judgement 'calls men to conversion' in our present circumstances, 'inspires a holy fear of God', who has serious expectations of us all, and 'commits' us to the justice of his kingdom (1041). Only if Christ is to be judge of all can his role as saviour of all be seen as demanding a real transformation of the human heart.

VI. The hope of the new heaven and the new earth (1042–1050)

In this final section of its discussion of our hope for 'the life everlasting', the *Catechism* turns to the vision of universal transformation — the transformation of both human society and its material setting — which Christian faith in final salvation implies. This transformation will be the fulfilment of the reign of God, which has already begun in the person of the risen Christ, and will include both the full realisation of the Church's own identity and the renewal of all creation (1042). The *Catechism* describes this fulfilment — which, again, can only be conceived in metaphor — primarily in terms of *unification*: 'it will be the definitive realization of God's plan to bring under a single head all things in Christ' (1043), 'the final realization of the unity of the human race . . . of which the pilgrim Church has been "in the nature of sacrament"' (1045). And it will include a new integration of our material environment with the needs and desires of the human community, so that the cosmos itself will share both the glory and the harmony of a unified humanity (1046–1047).

The means of this ultimate transformation, the *Catechism* suggests, will simply be, once again, the obvious presence of Christ as the focal point of perfected human communion, and the vision of God which will consequently be made available to all, through Christ, as 'the ever-flowing well-spring of happiness, peace, and mutual communion' (1045). This sense of the transforming role of Christ's presence at the end of history, movingly presented here and reinforced by passages cited from Vatican II, recalls the expectation of the great twentieth-century Jesuit scientist and theological visionary Pierre Teilhard de Chardin:

> One day, the Gospel tells us, the tension gradually accumulating between humanity and God will touch the limits prescribed by the possibilities of the world. And then will come the end. Then the presence of Christ, which has been silently accruing in things, will suddenly be revealed — like a flash of light from pole to pole. Breaking through all the barriers within which the veil of matter

and the water-tightness of souls have seemingly kept it confined, it will invade the face of the earth.[21]

As before, the *Catechism* emphasises (1048) that this hoped-for transformation is, for our present minds, mysterious, only dimly imaginable; yet the importance of this hope for our present action in the world is considerable. Quoting the Second Vatican Council's Constitution on the Church in the Modern World (*Gaudium et Spes*), it reminds us that this hope should encourage our commitment to cultivate and care for the earth, to work for the order and progress of human society, and to try to achieve through our efforts a unity of the human and material worlds that will always be less than the kingdom of God, but nevertheless 'of vital concern' as an image and herald of that kingdom (1049-1050).

The *Catechism* ends this section with a quotation from one of the *Baptismal Catecheses* of the fourth-century bishop Cyril of Jerusalem, which reminds us that 'life everlasting', though including all these aspects of revelation and transformation for which the Church hopes, is in fact something inestimably more mysterious; a share in the life of God, who is Father, Son and Holy Spirit, and who communicates also to us, his creatures, the love that is, in the end, the core of his own reality.

The End of the Creed: 'Amen'

The *Catechism* concludes this first book, its summary of Christian doctrine about God and his plan of salvation based on the 'Apostles' Creed', with a brief reflection on 'Amen', the word that brings the creed — like most of our prayers and like the New Testament itself — to a conclusion (1061). As the text here observes (1062), 'Amen' is a Hebrew adverb meaning 'truly', related to a verb expressing the idea 'confirm', 'support' or 'assure'. To add 'amen' to an assertion is to affirm one's belief that it is thoroughly credible, assuredly so. Thus, as the *Catechism* here observes (1064), the 'Amen' with which the Creed ends is the counterpart of the 'I believe' with which it begins; at both ends of this profession of faith, the believer expresses the trust and personal commitment on which that faith rests. The Christian's commitment to the Church's proclamation of a mysterious, loving God who acts in history to save and transform what he has created — the Christian's ability to say 'Amen' to the Creed, and to live it out in the concrete, active fidelity of daily life — is only possible because he or she recognises the infinite fidelity of God, revealed to us in the Bible and especially in the resurrection of Jesus from the dead. The God of Israel, in a biblical phrase (Is 65:16) cited here, is the 'God of the Amen' (1063); and Jesus, whose fidelity unto death was transformed into glory by the Father's continuing fidelity to him, became in his whole person 'the definitive Amen' (1065), God's 'Yes' to us, who expresses for us and in us our final 'Amen' to God (Rev 3:14; 2 Cor 1:18–21). In the very act of proclaiming our faith in the God of our history, in Father, Son and Holy Spirit, we have already begun to share by grace in his own fidelity, in the love and obedience which is both a response to and a rejoicing in the Truth (1064).

St Augustine, whom the *Catechism* cites here (1064), spoke several times in sermons of the blessedness of heaven as the endless chanting of 'Amen' and 'Alleluia'[22] — as echoing, with the angels and all the company of saints, the joyful affirmation of all that God is, and all that he has done for us. The Creed, and the faith the *Catechism* here attempts to summarise, is simply the narrative of those deeds, the enumeration of those gifts. To say 'Amen' and 'Alleluia' is to rejoice that these things are so.

Notes

1 K. Rahner, 'The hermeneutics of eschatological assertions' in *Theological Investigations*, vol. 4 (London, 1966), pp. 332, 335.

2 Decree on Purgatory, Twenty-fifth Session of the Council of Trent (1563): ND 2310 (p. 687).

3 Letter of the Sacred Congregation for the Doctrine of the Faith on Certain Questions concerning Eschatology (17 May 1979): ND 2317 (pp. 692f.).

4 Ibid. The phrase, 'though deprived for the present of the complement of its body', which clarifies the 'disembodied' or separate character of the human person's life between death and resurrection, does not appear in this letter as first published in *Osservatore Romano* (23 July 1979), and seems to have been added for its official publication in *Acta Apostolicae Sedis* 71 (1979), p. 939: see ND 2317, preliminary note (p. 691).

5 See, for instance, K. Rahner, 'The intermediate state' in *Theological Investigations*, vol. 17 (London, 1981), pp. 114–24; W. Breuning (ed.), *Seele, Problembegriff christlicher Eschatologie* (Quaestiones Disputatae 106; Freiburg, 1984); G.Greshake, *Auferstehung der Toten* (Essen, 1969); G. Greshake and G. Lohfink, *Naherwartung — Auferstehung — Unsterblichkeit* (Freiburg, 1975); G. Greshake and J. Kremer, *Resurrectio Mortuorum. Zum theologischen Verständnis der leiblichen Auferstehung* (Darmstadt, 1986). In his book *Eternal Life?* (New York, 1984), Hans Küng discards the soul–body distinction as obsolete and irrelevant (p. 110), and presents both eternal life and resurrection as a process of 'entering into the infinite' and taking on, in God, a 'transpersonal' reality (pp. 111f.); this implies an even greater distancing from the traditional conception of personal immortality, the 'interim state', and future resurrection than the authors mentioned above suggest.

6 Thomas Aquinas, STh, Supplement, 75, 3.

7 See, e.g., Justin, *Apology I*, 19, 57; Athenagoras, *Plea for the Christians*, 36.

8 Athanasius, *On the Incarnation*, 4–5; Gregory of Nyssa, *Great Catechetical Oration*, 8; *On the Soul and the Resurrection* (PG 45, 15A-C).

9 For an exposition of this view of death as the loss of God's 'second gift' of incorruptible life, and as the return to the 'simply natural' state of animal life, see especially Athanasius, *On the Incarnation*, 3–5.

10 See St Augustine, *City of God*, 20, 9: 'For the souls of the pious dead are not separated from the Church, which is even now the kingdom of Christ; otherwise there would be no remembrance made of them at the altar of God

in the partaking of the body of Christ, nor would it do any good in danger to run to his baptism, that we might not pass from this life without it . . . For why are these things practised, if not because the faithful, even though dead, are his members?'

11 See also Augustine, *Enchiridion*, 29, 110.

12 See, for example, Tertullian, *De anima*, 55–58; Augustine, *De natura et origine animae*, 2, 4, 8; Gregory the Great, *Hom. in Evang.* 2, 39, 8.

13 See Rahner, 'The intermediate state' (above, n. 5).

14 See Thomas Aquinas, STh, Supplement, 92, 1.

15 See above, n.10.

16 See the 1979 Letter of the Congregation of the Faith, sec. 4: 'The Church excludes every way of thinking or speaking that would render meaningless or unintelligible her prayers, her funeral rites and religious acts offered for the dead. All these are, in their substance, *loci theologici*' (ND 2317).

17 Council of Trent, Session 25, Decree on Purgatory: DS 1820; ND 2310.

18 This Greek word really means 'restoration to an original state', and suggests, in patristic theology, that the ultimate salvation of all creatures will be a return to the state of loving harmony with God in which God originally conceived and created them.

19 See DS 411; ND 2301.

20 For a discussion of the history of this question, and a passionate affirmation that such a hope is not only possible but incumbent on every Christian in charity, see Hans Urs von Balthasar, *Dare We Hope 'That All Men Be Saved?'* and *A Short Discourse on Hell* (San Francisco, 1988). Balthasar's treatment may well have influenced this section of the *Catechism*, as well as others. See also J.R. Sachs, 'Current eschatology: universal salvation and the problem of hell', *Theological Studies* 52 (1991), pp. 227–54.

21 P. Teilhard de Chardin, *Le milieu divin* (London, 1960), p. 151.

22 See especially *Sermo* 362, 28, 29 (PL 39, 1632f.) : 'When we see face to face what we now see "darkly, in a mirror" (1 Cor 13.12), then we shall say, in a way different beyond words, "It is true"; and when we say this, surely we shall be saying "Amen", but with a satisfaction that knows no satiety . . . And because we shall see the Truth without any trace of boredom, but in unending delight, because we shall gaze on it with incontrovertible certainty and shall be inflamed by love of that Truth, and cling to it with a sweet, chaste, incorporeal embrace, we shall also praise him in that same breath, and say "Alleluia". Encouraging each other with burning charity to join in this praise, all the citizens of that City shall say to God "Alleluia", because they shall say "Amen"!' See also *Sermo* 243, 9; *Enarr. in Ps.* 85, 11.

The Sacramental Economy

(Paragraphs 1066–1209)

Regis A. Duffy OFM
University of Notre Dame

'The celebration of the Christian mystery', the heading for the second Part of the *Catechism*, is developed in two Sections: the sacramental economy and the seven sacraments of the Church. My task is to comment on some of the issues raised in the first of these headings, the sacramental economy which is described as 'the communication (or "dispensation") of the fruits of Christ's Paschal mystery in the celebration of the Church's "sacramental" liturgy' (1076). This description includes the two topics to be discussed: the paschal mystery in the time of the Church (Chapter One) and the sacramental celebration of the paschal mystery (Chapter Two). The titles of these chapters promise a theology of the liturgy rather than an approach that is usually described as 'the sacraments in general'.

The overall tone of the section is conciliar, more theological than pastoral, and uncontroversial. As indicated in the text (1075), since the *Catechism* must serve a variety of rites and cultures, only what is basic and common to all local churches is discussed. This approach presumably puts considerable responsibility on local churches to adapt the discussion of liturgy to the particular historical and cultural situations in which they minister. In English-speaking countries, the catechetical and liturgical ministries have usually produced a substantial number of studies of their own situations.[1]

These studies represent, to some degree, the actual praxis of the local church. The question, then, is whether to proceed from the theory of the universal *Catechism* to its local application in the national catechism or to examine first the liturgical praxis of a local church and the questions it suggests about the received teaching of the universal Church. Much of what today is considered classical liturgical teaching began as the liturgical experience of local churches. This certainly is one of the meanings of the axiom, 'the law of worship establishes the law of belief'. Therefore, the received teaching of the Church on liturgy should not simply be dismissed as theological theories that bear little relation to

225

pastoral experience and praxis. On the other hand, the contemporary liturgical experience of a local church should also be examined with due respect, for God does not cease to teach the Church in its worship.

Therefore, the universal *Catechism* should not be expected to do that which only a local church with its particular knowledge of the cultural and historical obstacles and advantages can hope to do: set up a creative and tensive dialogue between praxis and theory. Little consolation, then, can be taken from the conciliar tone of the *Catechism* if it is not matched by a critical assessment of the ongoing evangelisation and conversion in the local situation. Nor can the universal *Catechism* reflect all the important post-conciliar work of theologians. Where the insightful contributions of a Karl Rahner, for example, on liturgy and sacrament have achieved a certain classical theological status, the local church would be remiss in not employing such insights in its adaptation of the *Catechism*.

These suggestions have guided the way in which I have commented on the text assigned to me. The text, as it stands, is fairly clear and obvious. A rephrasing of this text would not be theologically helpful, nor would it serve any practical purpose for those who must work with it. On the other hand, there is a certain logic to the arrangement of topics, and my discussion will follow this order. Therefore, after giving a précis of the section under consideration, I have chosen to point out the theological and pastoral implications as well as some of the cultural corollaries of the text. Other readings of the text are obviously possible. My purpose is to promote a positive and pastorally useful discussion.

How to describe the liturgy

The text begins by apparently answering the classic questions about the why, what and how of the liturgy (1066–1075). In treating the purpose of the liturgy, the *Catechism* makes several important points. First, it links worship to the Trinity in terms of how God saves us. Second, it challenges us to look at the Church out of our liturgical experience. Third, it stresses the importance of catechesis for any fruitful appropriation of liturgy. I will comment briefly on each of these points.

First, the Trinity is liturgically presented in terms of our salvation. This is a welcome approach. Ever since the seminal article of Lothar Lies calling for such connections and the working out of a trinitarian model in liturgical theology by Edward Kilmartin, theologians have made an effort to rethink this pivotal doctrine within the law of worship, *lex orandi*.[2] Catherine LaCugna has cogently argued that in the early tradition of the Church, the economy and the theology of salvation were intimately connected. (In fact, this is another way of stating *lex orandi lex credendi*.) With the Arian controversies, the price of trinitarian orthodoxy was a split between economy and theology. Ontological explanations of the Trinity which found little insight in the liturgy became the rule:

The doxologies that arose naturally out of the Christian experience of being saved by God through Jesus Christ, such as 'Glory to the Father through the Son in the Holy Spirit', were replaced by *homoousios*-structured doxologies, for example, 'Glory to the Father and the Son and the Holy Spirit'.[3]

This salvation approach to the Holy Trinity is a fine example of how liturgical experience provides a pastorally accessible understanding of this mystery while inviting us to value more deeply this mystery in its celebration. Since God has never encountered us in a neutral or abstract fashion, but always in terms of our redemptive need, we are challenged to speak and think of God in the practical categories of our living which is where God saves us. The combining of the sign of the cross with the naming of the persons of the Trinity is the beautiful liturgical expression of this perspective.

A second challenge of the introductory section is to provide a liturgical focus for looking at the Church. Citing Vatican II's Constitution on the Liturgy, the *Catechism* insists on the liturgy as the privileged means of discovering the 'real nature of the true Church' (1068). Once again, we are not being offered a theoretical definition of the Church, but rather, a reminder of the practical way in which we best encounter the meaning of the Church. Because Christ's self-sacrificing work is at the centre of all worship, then both the wider meaning of liturgy as service to God and others and the liturgical role of the Church as servant are encountered in all worship. In other words, the dramatic ritual of the presider of the Holy Thursday liturgy, whether he be Pope, bishop, or priest, washing the feet of other Christians (therefore, not only those of men), reminds the gathered Church of its everyday role of servant.

The theory behind this theological observation is absolutely correct. But the actual praxis of a local church may contradict this theory and also point to a credibility gap in the experience of parishioners. Liturgies of affluent churches, for example, in the midst of ignored poverty or discrimination, do not disprove, but they do contradict, what the liturgy teaches about the servant conduct of a discipled church. Arrogant posturing on the part of the ordained (or unordained) ministries cannot be defended unless the liturgical model of the Church as servant is conveniently set aside. While these observations are certainly not new, the catechism of a local church must take into account how seldom some Catholics have seen the servant aspect of Church in their own experience. There is, in other words, an implicit warning here not to offer idealised images of the Church which will only frustrate our hearers. Liturgy always offers beliefs and images that are both true and 'doable' because the liturgy enables Christians to be what they see, to paraphrase Augustine.

Finally, the liturgy is the practical pastoral situation in which most catechesis is actually done and where it is best done (1074). In the pre-Vatican II Church, Catholics came together for devotions and parish missions as well as for the liturgy. As recent studies have shown, it is

227

very difficult to get people (at least in the United States) to come out during the week for any pastoral gathering because of the decreasing amount of personal time available in our culture and also because of the fear of urban crime. The Sunday homily should be a pastorally cherished opportunity for such catechesis, but again, the studies of Andrew Greeley and others are not encouraging here. The generally poor quality of the Sunday homily is linked not only to lack of preparation in some cases, but also to the inability of many homilists to address the religious experience of their communities in the real world.[4]

The *Catechism* recalls the classical mystagogical process of forming Christians as going 'from the visible to the invisible, from the sign to the thing signified, from the sacraments to the mysteries they represent' (1075). Liturgy is an excellent teacher, not because it contains any sort of audio-visual library, but because it addresses the religious experience of participants in an unequalled way. Both preachers and teachers should be encouraged, in the national catechisms, to imitate the liturgy in their preaching and teaching by valuing the religious experience of their hearers and helping them to find in that experience the footprints of God.

The sacramental economy

The term 'economy' in its theological Greek meaning refers to God's plan for our salvation. 'Sacramental economy' includes the ways in which liturgical and sacramental life help us to enter into God's plan. The role of the Church provides an important context for the treatment of the sacramental economy. In the early and crucial periods of the development of Western sacramental theology, the practical liturgical issues that occupied the attention of Cyprian (on rebaptism) and, later, Augustine (on ministerial holiness) are inevitably linked to the larger questions of the ecclesial community that celebrates the paschal mystery. In other words, in what kind of church community should sacraments be celebrated and received?

One might suggest an axiom that the real ecclesiology of a particular Church and period may best be found in its sacramental and liturgical practice. We will shortly have opportunities to return to this axiom and its applications. A significant line of the introductory paragraph, then, sets a certain tone: 'In this age of the Church Christ now lives and acts in and with his Church, in a new way appropriate to this new age' (1076). It remains to be seen what this 'new way and age' might be. With these general remarks in mind, I turn to the first chapter of the 'sacramental economy' which is entitled 'The Paschal mystery in the age of the Church'.

'Paschal mystery', of course, is one of those expressions that teachers use regularly until they find out that their students still cannot describe what it means. The *Catechism* intriguingly adopts the biblical approach to paschal mystery: it begins by blessing and thanking God for the mystery of our salvation, appropriately citing the *berakah* of Ephesians 1:3–6 (1077).

If there is one area of liturgical scholarship that has reaped a rich harvest of pastoral and theological insight, it is that of *berakah*, the ancient and originally improvised prayer whose spirit, if not its form, so influenced early liturgical worship in such sources as the *Didache*, and the eucharistic prayers of Addai and Mari and that of the *Apostolic Tradition* of Hippolytus.[5] The importance of this form of prayer, too often missed, is the profound *experience* of salvation that it presupposes. Even our inability to translate literally the complexity of the Hebrew term *berakah* that includes notions of thanksgiving, praise, and acknowledgement only underlines the complexity of our contact with the mystery of salvation. If there is one form of prayer that is adaptable to the contemporary situation in liturgical and non-liturgical situations, it is this understanding of blessing. The *Catechism* succinctly points out the complementary dimensions of blessing: a 'divine and life-giving action' of the Father and our own 'adoration and surrender to [our] Creator in thanksgiving' (1078).

In doing this, the *Catechism* has signalled an important pedagogical approach. Rather than speak of the redemptive work of the Holy Trinity in abstract terms, it broaches the subject in the way the liturgy does, with an exclamation of praise and acknowledgement. In a similar way, in citing the Ephesian *berakah*, the *Catechism* points to the Trinity in the historical way in which humankind has experienced it, i.e., in its work of saving us. Again, the national adaptations of this teaching should employ the successful methods already used in national catechetical texts in the past two decades, where the religious experience of the student is an essential dynamic in opening them up to a new appreciation of God's mystery in their lives. In response to some criticism that this approach is responsible for contemporary young Catholics not knowing the 'essentials' of their faith, I would respond that this biblical method links knowledge and ongoing conversion, when it is successfully carried out.

Another biblical retrieval in this section of the *Catechism* is the notion of *zakar*. In three paragraphs (1079–81) the *Catechism* highlights turning-points in the history of salvation (e.g., Noah, Abraham, Isaac, etc.) as grounded in this understanding of blessing. Summing up this overview, the *Catechism* then says: 'The Law, the Prophets and the Psalms, interwoven in the liturgy of the Chosen People, *recall* these divine blessings and at the same time respond to them with blessings of praise and thanksgiving' (1081). The term 'recall' underlies the technical idea of *anamnesis* (the recalling of salvation events in liturgical prayer) and the Jewish notion of *zakar*. Unfortunately, the word 'recall' as normally understood in English reflects neither notion. In Western languages, to 'recall' is to return to a past event in a historical, not a salvific, way, much as if one were watching a newsreel of a past event.

More recent biblical scholarship has emphasised the complex use of *zakar* in the Scriptures. While the word may refer to the recollection of a past event, it often indicates the *actualisation* of a past salvific event in the present, especially when employed in liturgical sections of the Scriptures. In other words, *zakar* may also mean 'to be present'. Brevard

Childs captures this special meaning: 'Memory has a critical function of properly relating the present with the past . . . When Israel observes the Sabbath in order to remember the events of her redemption, she is participating again in the Exodus event. *Memory functions as an actualization of the decisive event in her tradition.'*[6]

The importance of this notion for the celebration and theology of liturgy will be obvious. In contrast to commemorations, liturgical 'remembering' brings participants into contact with saving events and allows them to welcome the salvation they bring. 'Remembrance equals participation. The present rupture in the relationship of Yahweh with his people stems from Israel's failure to understand the saving acts.'[7] Since God is the source of all liturgical 'remembering', then every liturgical event makes available this empowering presence to participants. A practical corollary of this discussion is that terms such as 'presence' or 'actualisation' are to be preferred to 'recall' or 'memory' because current English usage does not correspond with the biblical meaning or liturgical usage.

Throughout this article (1077–1109), the connections between liturgy and the Holy Trinity are noted. One particularly classic retrieval of these connections is pithily expressed in 1108: 'Communion with the Holy Trinity and fraternal communion are inseparably the fruit of the Spirit in the liturgy.' As discussed earlier, the liturgical references to the Trinity usually praise God for 'economic reasons', i.e., our salvation. Each divine person is then described in terms of blessing: the Father as the source, the Son as the epitome of blessing, and the Spirit as the active expression of all blessing, 'the Gift that contains all gifts' (1082). From this starting-point the double link between the praying Church and the Trinity flows: ecclesial thanksgiving and praise to the Father is always made in the company of Christ and the Holy Spirit. As a response the Church offers to the Father his own gifts while asking for the sending of the Spirit over them and over the assembled community (1083). What the *Catechism* is doing, in effect, is to make the economic or experienced event of salvation within the Church a structural component of liturgical understanding.

A faithful transposition of this approach to the particular concerns of a national catechism would require a close scrutiny of how the host culture assists (or perhaps, dilutes) the actualisation of a saving past into the present. Cultures, after all, provide significant contexts for our most prized religious texts and experiences as well as suggesting potent images and symbols for them. An audio-visual culture that increasingly dominates most English-speaking countries is, I would argue, a form of cultural actualisation for younger generations. It regularly universalises and images certain notions, for example, of 'salvation' and 'redeemer' that may bear little or no connection with the Christian understanding of those terms. In the past, however, Christian evangelisation at its creative best has known how to take powerful cultural elements of a pagan or dechristianised tradition and transform them into telling announcements of what the triune God is doing in their midst. (We will return to this point in a later section.)

Liturgy's Christ and Holy Spirit

The ensuing sections deal with the work of Christ and the Holy Spirit in the liturgy (1084–1109). The reader is immediately struck by a comparatively short Christological treatment of the sacraments, but a closer reading reveals how the following section on the Spirit continues and amplifies the first section. This section begins with a Christological description of the sacraments as Christ's actions which communicate his grace (1084). In an amplification of the classic definition of sacrament, these signs in words and actions 'make present efficaciously the grace that they signify' by Christ's action and the Spirit's power. (The pneumatological reference is an important addition which will be further developed in the following section.) The institution of the sacraments is spoken of in a general way without making the older distinctions between major and minor sacraments or between direct and indirect institution.

At this point, the liturgy is presented as the teacher of the paschal mystery (1085). In corroboration of our discussion of *zakar*, the *Catechism* notes that this mystery cannot be fixed in time since Christ now transcends all such boundaries. The experience of Christ's death and resurrection is to be found in the liturgical celebrations of the Christian community. Citing Vatican II (SC 7), the text reminds us that the presence of Christ is found not only in the liturgy of the sacraments but also in the reading of the Scriptures and in the prayer and song of the Church (1088). Since the *Catechism* does not comment on the conciliar description of 'presence', it is all the more important that commentators, teachers, and authors of religious education texts do. In contrast to the static pre-conciliar descriptions of 'presence' (usually limited to the discussion of real presence in the eucharist), the Council acknowledged the celebratory and experienced dimensions of the liturgical presence of Christ. Furthermore, this conception of presence with its ecclesial context is a classic one that permeates, for example, the writings of Augustine.[8]

At this point, the *Catechism* quotes the conciliar description of the present liturgy as affording Christians an initial experience of and participation in the heavenly liturgy (SC 8; cf. LG 50) with its strong eschatological longing (1090). This is the only reference, to the best of my knowledge, to the eschatological dimension of liturgy in Section One, and yet it is one of the most crucial qualities of authentic liturgical participation. At the centre of Jesus' preaching was the announcement of the coming reign of God. In contemporary language, Jesus spoke of God's future as profoundly affecting the way in which his followers would live in the present. Since the characteristics of God's future include unity, peace, justice and true worship of God, these same interlinking qualities must begin to shape the conduct and attitudes of Christians in the present. The practical corollary is that the easy toleration of injustice and disunity seriously calls into question the honesty of our worship.

Once again, the cultural corollaries of time are intimately linked to the appropriation of any eschatology. In other words, we have been formed in the cultural ways of conceiving and dealing with time. We start from our acculturated sense of time in thinking about a 'non-time' or God's future. In the American culture, for example, the proverb 'Time is money' is probably more true now than when it was coined. The ironic corollary is that the higher one ascends in the corporate and educational world, the less time one usually has. We will postpone further discussion of this important point until later. Secondly, the very qualities of justice and peace that the *Catechism* quite correctly links to a Christian notion of eschatology are always attached to, and sometimes qualified by, lived time. The sense of time among the deprived and homeless is culturally and psychologically different from those more fortunate. The local church has the important responsibility of translating the eschatology of the universal *Catechism* into the language and praxis of its members.

The work of the Spirit

Having dealt with the work of the Father and the Son in the liturgy, the *Catechism* now turns to the crucial work of the Holy Spirit. It has been a commonplace in discussions of the history and theology of liturgy and sacrament to note the apparent absence of liturgical reference (*epiclesis*) to the Spirit. During the sessions of the Council of Florence (1439), the Greeks seem to have taken scandal at the lack of an actual *epiclesis* (a calling down of the Holy Spirit over the gifts and people) in the celebration of the Eucharist, as well as any theological reflection on the role of that Spirit. Profiting from both the conciliar and post-conciliar importance given to the pneumatological dimension of all liturgy, the *Catechism* offers a rich if succinct theology (1091–1109) in five short sub-sections.

In the initial two paragraphs (1091–1092), the *Catechism* answers the implicit question of all liturgy: How can a flawed Christian community hope to offer God honest worship? The answer is a précis of liturgical pneumatology: 'In the liturgy the Holy Spirit is teacher of the faith of the People of God and artisan of "God's masterpieces", the sacraments of the New Covenant' (1091). The Spirit is constantly enabling the Church to encounter the risen Lord and to welcome his mission which is inseparable from such an encounter.

A later paragraph (1098) expands on this notion of sacramental encounter by noting that it is the action of the Spirit that prompts us to a deepening faith, conversion of heart and commitment to God's will. When the Spirit recalls God's saving events in the liturgical anamnesis, it enables the community to thank and praise God more profoundly (1103). This teaching is a partial response to the pastoral question: Why is there so much sacrament and so little apparent commitment?[9] The Spirit's initiative is always present in liturgical and sacramental events to enable individual participants as well as the ecclesial community to enter more deeply into God's meaning and purpose and its practical corollaries for their lives.

In a statement that is ecumenically important, the document then notes that the Spirit makes Christ present by its transforming power (1092, 1107). This is a retrieval of constant patristic teaching that reassures the Eastern Church about our sacramental praxis and also affects the ecumenical question of the validity of sacraments in other Christian churches.[10] Long before the theory of matter and form gained classical status in the Western Church as a description of how to determine a valid sacrament, the calling down of the Holy Spirit in the sacramental event was seen as essential. In the liturgical practice of the Western Church, however, the actual epicletic prayer had disappeared, for example, in the Roman Canon of the eucharist.[11]

Equally important is the *Catechism*'s refreshing emphasis on the role of the Holy Spirit in enabling Christians, individually and communally, to become a 'living sacrifice' (1105, 1109) by a spiritual transformation. Other characteristics of this ongoing conversion are a concern for the Church's unity and an active commitment to the mission of the Church (1109). In the same way, it is the Spirit's abiding and indefectible presence, intimately renewed in the liturgy, that enables the Church to be 'the great sacrament of divine communion' (1108).

In an interesting and unexpected approach, the intimate connection between the Hebrew and Christian Scriptures is discussed in the light of the work of the Spirit which makes known the mystery of Christ already announced in the figures of Noah's ark and the crossing of the Red Sea. In a fairly long paragraph (1096), the *Catechism* succinctly sketches some of the important connections between Jewish and Christian liturgy. Once more, there is an obvious ecumenical effort to acknowledge the unique role of the Jewish people in God's plan. (The occasional reference to the 'Old Testament' might be better phrased, as it regularly is in ecumenical and academic dialogue, as the 'Hebrew Scriptures' or similar phrases that avoid any pejorative connotation.)

This attentive understanding of the Scriptures as they are proclaimed in the liturgical year enables participants to relive 'the great events of salvation history in the "today" of [the] liturgy' (1095). It is the Spirit, 'the Church's living memory' (1099) who 'recalls the meaning of the salvation event to the liturgical assembly' so that it may be lived out by the community (1100). Moreover, in every liturgical action the Church encounters Christ as it is gathered and enabled by the Spirit to celebrate fruitfully and to welcome the salvation it proclaims (1097–1098). Finally, the ecumenically and pastorally important question of whether the liturgy repeats or actualises the mystery of salvation is clearly answered: 'in each celebration there is an outpouring of the Holy Spirit that makes the unique mystery present' (1104).

But it is important to add that the action of the Spirit does not occur in a vacuum, but rather in the specific personal and cultural context of a participant's life. Thus, the Spirit ensures a fruitful listening to and understanding of God's word so that it might then be lived out by the hearers of that word (1100–1101) in a historical and cultural situation. (The catechetical unfolding of this highly condensed presentation might take the very concrete discussion of Paul VI in *On Evangelisation* as a way of examining the cultural and pastoral implications of this teaching.) In the summary statement (1112), there is an excellent and concise recapitulation of the *Catechism*'s pneumatology: 'The mission of the Holy Spirit in the liturgy of the Church is to prepare the assembly to encounter Christ; to recall and manifest Christ to the faith of the assembly; to make the saving work of Christ present and active by his transforming power; and to make the gift of communion bear fruit in the Church.'

The paschal mystery in the Church's sacraments

This second article of Chapter One (1113–1134), as indicated in the heading, deals with the sacraments from several foci generated by the paschal mystery. The discussion is narrowed even further to the doctrinal dimension of sacraments, while the discussion of their celebration is delayed until the next chapter. This article continues the generally positive liturgical tone, with some disappointing exceptions.

The question of sacramental institution by Christ is treated first (1114–1116). None of the scholastic distinctions on the question (direct/ indirect, major/minor) are employed. In their place, the *Catechism* offers Leo the Great's classic axiom, 'what was visible in our Saviour has now passed over into his mysteries' (1115). Thus, institution is grounded in an incarnational theology which values the whole life of Christ, since it 'anticipated the power of his Paschal mystery' (1115).

Even more interesting is the description of sacraments as powers rooted in the body of Christ, as actions of the Spirit in the Church and as 'masterworks of God' (1116). The text is using the term 'powers' in its biblical meaning of *dunamis*, the God-crafted strength that resides in Jesus.[12] This biblical approach not only avoids the problems of matter/ form definitions, but also offers a much richer context for appreciating the theological and historical development of sacraments and its corollary, the question of the authority for such developments. The *Catechism* notes parallel cases in the gradual recognition of the canon of sacred Scripture and the doctrine of the faith (1117). The general argument, then, would seem to be that in the eventual development and recognition of seven sacraments the prophetic and healing ministries of Christ are continued, and the sacraments are empowered in a similar way to Christ's ministry.

The insistence that the recognition and celebration of the sacraments occur within the body of Christ is further explained by the phrases 'by her' and 'for her' (1118). Since the sacraments are ministered by the Church, the ministry of a sacrament is anchored in an acceptance of the Church herself as 'the sacrament of Christ's action'. The celebration and reception of sacraments are also for the Church, since they have as their purpose a sharing in the life of God which renews the Church. The baptismal priesthood of all the faithful flows from this larger discussion.

Despite the assertion that the ordained priesthood is at the service of this more fundamental priesthood of the faithful (1120), the description of ministerial priesthood reverts to a 'link in the chain' explanation of apostolic succession and continuity. Thus, this priesthood is a 'sacramental bond' that connects liturgy to the apostles, and thus to Christ. The allusion to sacramental character as indelible rounds out this approach to priesthood (1121).

While it would be naive to expect the complete reversal of this traditional theology, the careful biblical research of the last decades on the origins of ministries in the Church (which, to the best of my knowledge, has not been questioned by Rome) could certainly enrich this discussion.[13] Continuity with Christ and the first generation of apostolic ministries has always been considered a *sine qua non* for any theological examination of ministerial priesthood. Locating the baptismal and ordained priesthood firmly within the larger mission of the Church as the body of Christ has also been a constant theological concern. The same might be said for the question of character. While the *Catechism* attempts to avoid an ontological description of character, the original Augustinian explanation of character as an external mark that would be to the Christian's everlasting glory or shame was connected to the larger discussion of how sacrament and Church are related.[14] This would seem to be a more fruitful and classical way to develop the question of why certain sacraments are not repeated.[15]

What God does so that we can do

The final three short sections of Article 2 (1122–1130) are best commented on together, since they are connected by the themes of faith and salvation. There is, first of all, an important principle that sacramental participation nourishes faith and instructs the believing Church, for the Church believes as she prays (*lex orandi, lex credendi*) (1123–1124). As noted above, this axiom is an important guideline in understanding the gradual articulation of theological doctrines such as the Trinity. But equally important is an indication that what is crucial to the salvation of the liturgical participant is found in praying liturgically. In Romans 8, where the context is liturgical prayer, it is the Spirit who both formulates and reveals the profound redemptive need of the praying assembly.[16] Given the importance of this teaching, it deserves more discussion in the national catechisms.

One of the important theological retrievals for the Roman Catholic community in this century has been a clear articulation of the connections between faith and sacrament. (Karl Rahner is especially remembered with gratitude in this regard.[17]) The tone of the discussion is best captured in the *Catechism*'s phrase 'the sacrament is prepared for by the word of God and by the faith which is assent to this word' (1122).

But succinct and accurate theological statements do not necessarily deal with pastoral reality. For most people, the reformed Sunday liturgy of the word with its three readings, responsorial psalm and homily has been a mixed blessing. Even in the best of situations, where the readings receive an intelligent and accessible exegesis in the homily, this does not, of itself, result in a more profound faith. Faith is, after all, an assent of the will as well as of the mind.

Therefore, the connection between the word and the ongoing conversion of the listener is crucial. The national catechism is in a better pastoral and cultural position to know the specific ways in which the believer might be helped to participate more fully in the liturgy of the word and is thus able to develop these connections in the universal *Catechism*. The perennial Christian wisdom has consistently made a link between the word of God (and its appropriation in faith) and the lived experience of the listener. The need for redemption as well as the marks of God's presence are eloquently attested to in the pages of our own religious autobiographies. The word specifically addresses not only the narratives of our experience but also the implicit meanings we attach to them.[18] It would seem important, then, that the national catechism lead the neophyte to understand and value their religious experience in the light of God's word.

Pedagogically speaking, the logic of the text then leads to an explanation of the objective dimension of sacrament (the medieval term *ex opere operato* is relegated to a footnote). The faith of the believing community or individual does not give the sacrament its efficacy. In the patristic formulation, it is Christ who baptises and presides in all sacramental action (1127). In an even more complete explanation, the Father accedes to the prayer of the Son's Church which is expressed in the *epiclesis*. This insight rules out any misunderstanding about the dispositions of the sacramental minister or recipient as effecting a sacrament and thus detracting from the gratuitous action of God (1128). On the other hand, once the sacramental action is celebrated, the fruitful participation in it reflects the dispositions of the recipient. A forceful statement of the forward movement of all liturgy towards the final reign of God rounds out this second article (1130).

What is strikingly absent from the above discussion is the larger corollary of liturgy: the mission of Christ's Church to proclaim and work for the reign of God. Liturgy is not a pious corollary to the actual work of the Church. Rather, it is one of the principal ways in which she accomplishes that work, for all liturgy effectively symbolises in an incipient way the reign of God. Much of the Reformation and Counter-Reformation debate on the *ex opere operato* and justification dimensions of liturgy and sacrament lost sight of this larger issue. In contrast, more recent biblical discussion of justification has pointed to the ecclesial dimensions of that doctrine.[19] The implication is that the Church is not saved for its private purposes, but exists to do the work of Christ. In a similar way, can the 'fruitful dispositions' of the liturgical participant be reduced to certain moral attitudes divorced from all discussion of participating in the work of saving others? These are important aspects of a contemporary understanding of liturgy and sacrament that might attend to some of the causes of the Reformation disputes.

The sacramental celebration of the paschal mystery

Under this heading, Article 1 deals with what is common to all liturgical celebration (1136–1199) while Article 2 treats liturgical diversity and the unity of the mystery (1200–1209). In Article 1, 'Celebrating the Church's liturgy', the who, how, when, and where of celebration is studied (1135).

In answering the question of who celebrates, the text returns constantly to the book of Revelation for its inspiration. The purpose of this approach is to connect contemporary liturgical participants with the liturgy that has begun in the reign of God 'where celebration is wholly a communion and feast' (1136). The Spirit and the Church make this possible (1139). This short section is pedagogically important because it then serves as a foundation for discussing particular liturgical ministries.

The *Catechism* repeats the teaching of Vatican II on the communal nature of all liturgy and the baptismal priesthood of all the faithful (1140–1141). The subsequent discussion of the ordained ministries also follows the conciliar treatment: the Holy Spirit empowers such ministers to act 'in the person of Christ the head for the service of all the members of the Church' (1142). The non-ordained liturgical ministries (servers, readers, choir, etc.) are also recognised.

This *in persona Christi* theology can be misunderstood, so that the ordained person might think of his calling as a personal possession rather than as an ecclesial task. (In this view, the concealed intention, e.g., of the presiding priest could invalidate a sacramental rite which is a public rite of the gathered Church.) The ordained minister has a unique role in the liturgy, 'the action of the whole Christ' (1136).[20] What is crucial is how that uniqueness is described. The *Catechism* does this by saying: 'The ordained minister is, as it were, an *icon* of Christ the priest' (1142). This manner of speaking recalls the statement of the Anglican–Orthodox Doctrinal Commission: 'The celebrant in his liturgical action has a twofold ministry: as *icon* of Christ, acting in the name of Christ for the community, and also as representative of the community, expressing the priesthood of the faithful.'[21]

Edward Kilmartin has cogently argued that the priest as liturgical presider is 'a public person who places a public act in the context of a community of faith'.[22] He thus acts as a representative of Christ who is the Head of the Church, and his ritual action expresses the faith of that Church. But this action of the Church is possible only because of the power of the Spirit of Christ who unites Christ and the Church. From this perspective, 'the priest acts as minister of Christ by acting as minister of the Church'.[23] Thus, the priest can be said to act *in persona ecclesiae*, which explains his action as *in persona Christi*.

The importance of symbols

In response to its own question, 'How do we celebrate?', the *Catechism* offers a fairly lengthy argument for the origin of signs and symbols in

God's creation and redemption (1145–1149), and their liturgical expression in words, actions, music and images (1153–1162). This section, as it stands, is quite good in its discussion of some of the dimensions of liturgical signs. In particular, in 1158 the *Catechism* notes the enriching effect of specific cultural heritages when used in liturgical words, actions, music and images.

While recognising the value of this emphasis on inculturated symbols, I believe that the national catechisms must then spell out the specific heritage of their audiences' cultures and the obstacles to cultural participation. After all, the language and gestures from which cele-brations are created are themselves the products of a particular culture. The notion of liturgical time (1163–1165) also depends on the cultural sense of time that is available. The *Catechism* notes this: 'The liturgy of the Church presupposes, integrates and sanctifies elements from creation and human culture, conferring on them the dignity of signs of grace, of the new creation in Jesus Christ' (1149).

There are three aspects of this cultural dimension that I would cite as examples of areas the national catechisms should treat. The first is the specific modes of communication that are favoured in a particular culture. In the United States we have a whole generation of young people who have received many of their images, vocabulary, and perhaps values from the audio-visual world. Cultural critics of these communication forms point to the over-simplification of complex problems, the levelling of diverse topics into a homogeneous product for easy consumption, and a shift from intrinsic values to external evaluations.[24] To the extent that these criticisms are valid, the process of continuing evangelisation becomes much more specific and demanding while some of the assumptions of liturgical participation are directly challenged (e.g., the ease with which we attend to a liturgical action or word). A national catechism, then, must sharpen the focus of the universal *Catechism* by pin-pointing the cultural strengths (e.g., response to movement more than to word) and weaknesses (e.g., a tendency to level complex symbols to one-dimensional signs).[25]

A second cultural concern is the sense of time. Liturgical celebration presumes a gradual unfolding of word and action that requires time. But time has become a cultural victim of our American life (I suspect this would be true of other English-speaking countries to various degrees). Personal time and leisure time seem to have been progressively shortened in the past decades, for the upwardly mobile population as well as for the economically less privileged. In quite different ways, the elderly, the homeless, and families where both parents work are preoccupied with the scarcity of time.[26] The ways in which the poor and the affluent experience the lack of time may be markedly different.[27]

Christianity normally requires some leisure time to reflect religiously and to participate symbolically. In a culture where commuting time to and from work can easily average two to four hours, such time for reflection, liturgical prayer, and some participation in the mission of the Church may be difficult indeed. The significance of the liturgical year and of the Lord's Day may remain a theological ideal rather than an experience to which more than minimal time can be given. The *Catechism* eloquently states that 'the economy of salvation is at work within the framework of time, but since its fulfilment in the Passover of Jesus and the outpouring of the Holy Spirit, the culmination of history is anticipated "as a foretaste", and the kingdom of God enters into our time' (1168). But the daily demands of a culture may effectively eradicate the needed leisure time and space in which to respond. The American bishops, for example, admitted that if the Christian sense of time is to be retrieved, then 'the use of leisure may demand being countercultural'.[28]

Does inculturation have a future?

Article 2 has an interesting heading, 'Liturgical diversity and the unity of the mystery', but is given only seven paragraphs (1200–1206). As already indicated earlier in this discussion, the question of how the liturgy and a host culture interact is crucial for an accessible and meaningful celebration of the mystery of salvation. Frankly, this section is somewhat disappointing, not for what it says, but for what it omits.

The selective use of sources is indicative of the problem. Paul VI's classic letter on evangelisation, for example, is cited once (to note the complementarity of particular churches' liturgical traditions, 1201) but some of the Pontiff's trenchant statements on the need for inculturation, linked to a missioned Church proclaiming radical conversion, rather than simply adaptation, are passed over.[29] The teaching of Vatican II praising the liturgical life of the local church is acknowledged (1202), but this seems to be understood as a historical reference, since liturgical adaptation seems confined to 'cultures of peoples recently evangelised' (1205). The Council's openness to wider adaptations, not limited to mission countries, is not mentioned.[30] This generally conservative tone is reinforced in the final paragraph (1206), which is a citation from a letter of John Paul II warning about the dangers of liturgical diversity. Actually, John Paul II has followed, with some reservations, the direction of Paul VI in some fairly forceful statements.[31] Although it is true that certain national conferences have had great difficulties with Rome on the question of even minor adaptations, there are other encouraging examples from Zaïre in Africa and from the Church in India.

The practical corollary to this discussion is that the national catechisms once again have a golden opportunity to reassess the ways in which the liturgical reforms have been received within the culture (or cultures) of the country. Such a vantage point provides a fine teaching moment to make certain important connections between creation and redemption, and between ongoing conversation in a culture and social justice, as celebrated in the liturgy within a missioned Church.

Some concluding remarks

At the beginning of this piece I noted my generally positive impressions of the liturgical sections of the *Catechism*. I also admitted that a universal *Catechism* cannot be expected to deal with particular questions better left to the competence of those who will write the national catechisms. My critical observations have centred on the connections between liturgy and its cultural expression because this is where the pastoral currency of rather general liturgical principles is tested. Good liturgical theology has historically emerged from the liturgical praxis of churches as different as that of Rome and North Africa or Gaul and Ireland. The current efforts to construct authentic liturgical theologies cannot be done apart from the liturgical praxis of contemporary churches as they struggle with and benefit from their particular cultural heritages. The authors of the liturgical sections of the universal *Catechism* have done a reasonably commendable job, and it remains for the catechetical writers to develop these insights for the benefit of their particular churches.

Notes

1   In the case of the United States, for example, The Notre Dame Study of American Parish Life, the extensive studies and analyses of Andrew Greeley, etc., are examples of such work.
2   L. Lies, 'Trinitätsvergessenheit gegenwärtiger Sakramententheologie', *Zeitschrift für katholische Theologie* 105 (1983), pp. 415–29; E. Kilmartin, *Christian Liturgy*, vol.1: *Theology* (Kansas City: Sheed & Ward, 1988), pp. 100–79.
3   C. LaCugna, *God for Us: The Trinity and Christian Life* (San Francisco: Harper, 1991), p. 134.
4   Cf., e.g., A. Greeley, *The Catholic Myth: The Behavior and Beliefs of American Catholics* (New York: C. Scribner's, 1990) pp. 148–53.
5   For the state of the question and a balanced position on this subject, see P. Bradshaw, *The Search for the Origins of Christian Worship* (New York: Oxford University Press, 1992), pp. 25-30, 158 (consult subject index for other references). For a strong critique of using *todah* as a paradigm, see H.-J. Klauck, *Herrenmahl und hellenistischer Kult* (Münster: Aschendorff, 1982).
6   B. Childs, *Memory and Tradition in Israel* (London: SCM Press, 1962), p. 53; my emphasis.
7   Ibid., p. 56.
8   Cf. W. Gessel, *Eucharistische Gemeinschaft bei Augustinus* (Würzburg: Augustinus-Verlag, 1966), esp. pp. 147–53.
9   This question is the principal theme of my book *Real Presence: Worship, Sacraments, and Commitment* (San Francisco: Harper & Row, 1982).
10 In the document *Baptism, Eucharist and Ministry* (Geneva: World Council of Churches, 1982), this epicletic principle is fruitfully employed; cf. section C on the Eucharist (p. 13) and section B on Ministry (p. 22).

11   See A. Nichols, *Rome and the Eastern Churches* (Collegeville, MN: Liturgical Press, 1992), pp. 269–72, for a useful summary of the problem.

12   This is evident from the Lucan sources cited: 5:17; 6:19; 8:46.

13   Cf., e.g., A. Lemaire, *Les Ministères aux origines de l'Eglise* (Paris: Cerf, 1971) and J. Delorme (ed.), *Le Ministère et les ministères selon le Nouveau Testament* (Paris: Seuil, 1974).

14   See N.H. Haring, 'St Augustine's use of the word character', *Medieval Studies* 14 (1952), pp. 79–97.

15   Cf. R. Duffy, 'Baptism and confirmation' in F. Fiorenza and J. Galvin (eds), *Systematic Theology*, vol. 2 (Minneapolis: Fortress, 1991), pp. 222–4.

16   Ernst Käsemann is particularly eloquent on this point in 'Cry for liberty in the Church's worship' in *Perspectives on Paul* (Philadelphia: Fortress, 1971), pp. 122–37.

17   Cf., e.g., Rahner's 'The word and the eucharist' in *Theological Investigations*, vol. 4 (Baltimore: Helicon, 1966), pp. 253–86, and 'What is a sacrament?' in *Theological Investigations*, vol. 14 (New York: Seabury, 1975), pp. 11–20.

18   Cf. Duffy, *Real Presence*, pp. 58-107.

19   Cf., e.g., C. Müller, *Gottes Gerechtigkeit und Gottes Volk: Eine Untersuchung zu Römer 9–11* (Göttingen: Vandenhoeck & Ruprecht, 1964).

20   H. Vorgrimler points out that Vatican II in using this and similar classic phrases wished to indicate the 'special and direct relationship of the priest to Jesus Christ'. Cf. his *Sacramental Theology* (Collegeville, MN: Liturgical Press, 1992), p. 264.

21   As cited in E. Kilmartin, 'The active role of Christ and the Holy Spirit in the sanctification of the eucharistic elements', *Theological Studies* 45 (1984), pp. 225–53, here p.237; my emphasis. As Kilmartin points out, other Orthodox theologians (e.g., P. Evdokimov and C. Kern) would have problems with an *in persona Christi* theology and would substitute *in nomine Christi* (the priest as icon places the sign but acts *in persona ecclesiae*: ibid., 236).

22   Ibid., 240.

23   Ibid., 241.

24   Cf. R. M. Merelman, *Making Something of Ourselves* (Berkeley: University of California, 1984), pp. 70–115; N. Postman, *Amusing Ourselves to Death* (New York: Penguin, 1985), pp. 99-113.

25   Cf. P. H. McNamara, *Conscience First, Tradition Second: A Study of Young American Catholics* (Albany: State University of New York, 1992).

26   Cf. J. Nowotny, 'From the future to the extended present' in G. Kirsch et al. (eds), *The Formulation of Time Preferences in a Multidisciplinary Perspective* (Aldershot: Gower, 1988), pp. 17–31.

27   Cf., e.g., J. P. Robinson, *How Americans Use Time* (New York: Praeger, 1977), pp. 27–31; M. Jahoda, 'Time: a social-psychological perspective' in M. Young and T. Schuller (eds), *The Rhythms of Society* (London: Routledge, 1988), pp. 154–72.

28   *Economic Justice for All: Catholic Social Teaching and the U.S. Economy* (Washington, DC: National Conference of Catholic Bishops, 1986), #338.

29   Cf. *On Evangelisation*, par. 15.3, and his allocution to the African Bishops in *Notitiae* 5 (1969), p.346.

30   *Constitution on the Sacred Liturgy*, 40 and 44.

31   Cf. his annual address (1984), e.g. to the College of Cardinals in 'One Church, many cultures' in J. Gremillion (ed.), *The Church and Culture Since Vatican II* (Notre Dame: University of Notre Dame Press, 1985), p. 215, and similar texts, pp. 162–222.

The Sacraments of Christian Initiation

(Paragraphs 1210–1321)

Edward Yarnold, SJ

Campion Hall, Oxford

1212. It was not until Vatican II that it became normal for baptism, confirmation and first communion to be linked together as 'sacraments of Christian initiation'. The Decree on the Liturgy called for a revision of the rite of confirmation so that 'the very close connection of this sacrament with the whole process of Christian initiation may become more clearly visible' (SC 71).

The word 'initiation' is to be understood in more than one sense. First, by these sacraments we enter into the Church. If the sacraments are celebrated in the order in which they are described in the documents, we enter the Church at baptism, our membership is confirmed and we receive new responsibilities at confirmation, and the process is completed at our first holy communion, when through receiving the body of Christ we become fully members of his body which is the Church: according to St Paul, to receive holy communion is not only to share in Christ's (eucharistic) body, but also to become one body with fellow communicants (1 Cor 10:16–17). The same truth is sometimes expressed in terms of the new covenant. Baptism has replaced circumcision as the rite of entry into the covenant-people — 'In him also you were circumcised with a spiritual circumcision . . . when you were buried with him in baptism' (Col 2:11–12) — while in the eucharist the new Christian may receive the 'blood of the New Covenant' (cf. Mt 26:28).

Secondly, the rites are initiatory for the Christian life of the individual, laying the 'foundations of every Christian life'. This is the emphasis expressed in the *Catechism*'s quotation from Paul VI's Apostolic Constitution *Divinae Consortium* which inaugurated the new rite of confirmation: through the rebirth of baptism, the strengthening of confirmation and the food of the eucharist, Christians 'receive in increasing measure the treasures of the divine life and advance toward the perfection of charity'. The three sacraments thus form a progressive initiation into the mystery of Jesus Christ.

Baptism

1213. Baptism, as the first of the sacraments of initiation, is appropriately described as the 'basis', the 'gateway' and the 'door'. This is true even when the three sacraments are celebrated together, and is even more evident when there is an interval between baptism and the other two. Already by baptism we are freed from sin, incorporated into the Church which is Christ's body, reborn in Christ and given a share in the Church's mission.

1214–1216. Baptism has been given various names. (a) The name 'baptism' itself, a word which originally meant 'dipping' and could refer to such actions as bathing and plunging hot iron into water, reminds us that in baptism we symbolically go down with Christ into his tomb in order to rise with him to new life. Among the several Pauline passages which the *Catechism* quotes, the best known is Romans 6:4: 'Therefore we have been buried with him by baptism into death, so that, just as Christ was raised from the dead by the glory of the Father, so we too might walk in newness of life.' (b) The name 'washing' expresses not only the removal of the stain of sin but also the new life of Christ which is well symbolised by water, the source of refreshment and life. The link between water and rebirth is made not only by Jesus' words to Nicodemus about being born again[1] by water and the Spirit, but also in the reference in the Epistle to Titus to 'the water of rebirth and renewal by the Holy Spirit' (Jn 3:5–8; Titus 3:5). (c) The name 'enlightenment' (derived from Heb 6:4) suggests the Christian's union at baptism with Jesus Christ, the Light of the World (Jn 8:12; cf. 1:9), a union which is symbolised by the lighted candle given at the baptismal ceremony. This enlightenment includes the catechesis which the adult candidate will have received, but involves a reality which is deeper than instruction, namely union with Jesus Christ — the Word who makes the Father known (Jn 1:1, 18), 'the Way, the Truth and the Life' (Jn 14:6) — and the indwelling of the Holy Spirit, who leads the Church into all the truth (cf. Jn 16:13).

1217–1222. The *Catechism* quotes a form of words used at the blessing of the font at the Easter Vigil which refers to water as a 'rich symbol' of baptismal grace. This is true in the first place of the natural value of water as an indispensable source of life and as a means of cleansing. The blessing goes on to trace the role of water in the history of salvation, namely in the account of God's creation of the world from the primal waters (Gen 1), the waters of the flood (Gen 7 – 8) which made 'an end of sin and a new beginning of goodness', and the waters of the Red Sea which the Israelites crossed on their journey from captivity in Egypt to the Promised Land (Ex 14). In the third passage the drowning of Pharaoh's army shows another side of the symbolism, namely water's capacity to be a means of death. The *Catechism* also recalls the water of Jordan which the Israelites crossed when Joshua led them into the Promised Land (Josh 3). One could add the use of water as a symbol for moral purification, the best-known example of which occurs in Psalm

243

51(50):7: 'O purify me, then I shall be clean; O wash me, I shall be whiter than snow' (Grail translation).

1223–1225. John the Baptist was not the first to use a rite of baptism. Josephus records that the Jewish Essene sect practised ritual washings once or perhaps twice a day (*Jewish War*, 2, 8, 5), and that after a year's novitiate the members were admitted to the 'purer kind of holy water' (ibid., 2, 8, 7). The community at Qumran, where the Dead Sea Scrolls were found, similarly admitted candidates to 'purifying water' after a period of probation.[2] A form of baptism also featured in mainstream Jewish practice, together with circumcision, as part of the rite by which Gentiles entered the Jewish community, but it is not certain that this practice already existed when John began his baptising.[3] John's baptism, however, seems to have contained at least two novel elements. First, whereas in earlier baptisms the candidates seem to have immersed themselves, John was the 'baptiser' (Mk 1:4); secondly, John's baptism did not involve entry into the Jewish community, but rather moral preparation for the coming of the messianic kingdom.

Jesus' own baptism seems to have been a turning-point in his life. Though himself sinless, he submitted to this penitential rite to 'fulfil all righteousness' (Mt 3:15) — either to show his solidarity with sinners, or else because it was right for the Messiah to transform the community of those awaiting the Messiah into an actual messianic community. The words of the Father, 'You are my Son, the Beloved; with you I am well pleased' (Mk 1:11), and the descent of the Holy Spirit, revealed him as the prophesied Servant of the Lord who would be anointed and filled with the Holy Spirit to bring relief to the weak and suffering (Is 42:1–4; 61:1–3). St Luke shows Jesus led by the Holy Spirit into the desert to face his temptations, returning full of the power of the Spirit, and applying the first of these Isaian passages to himself in his sermon in the synagogue at Nazareth (Lk 4:1, 14, 16–19); he records a speech by St Peter (Acts 10:37–38) in which Jesus' baptism is regarded as the moment when he received the office of the Messiah or Christ (the two titles derive respectively from the Hebrew and Greek words meaning 'the Anointed One'). It was perhaps these passages from Isaiah which led Jesus himself to regard his baptism as the beginning of a task which would lead him to his death: 'I have a baptism with which to be baptised, and what stress I am under until it is completed!' (Lk 12:50); 'Are you able to drink the cup that I drink, or be baptised with the baptism that I am baptised with?' (Mk 10:38). It is also possible that the Father's words, 'You are my Son, the Beloved', are an echo of God's words to Abraham, 'Take your son, your only son Isaac, whom you love, and go to the land of Moriah, and offer him there as a burnt offering' (Gen 22:2); the Father in his love for the world is giving his beloved Son to a mission that will end in the cross (cf. Jn 3:16).

Early church writers commonly taught that the Christian in accepting baptism was being united with Jesus' own baptism. By entering the water Jesus was believed to have sanctified all baptismal water; the font was accordingly sometimes called the 'Jordan'. The *Catechism* sees the cross to be the link between Christ's baptism and ours — a truth symbolised in the Johannine writings by the water which flowed from his pierced side (Jn 19:34) and the water which, together with the blood and the Spirit, testify to Christ (1 Jn 5:7).

1226–1228. St Luke in his account of the beginnings of the Church in the Acts of the Apostles gives many descriptions of the baptism of converts. A key moment came when the decision was taken to baptise the Gentile Cornelius and his family without requiring them first to become Jews (Acts 10:47–48). The statements in Ephesians 5:26 and 1 Peter 1:23 which link baptism with God's word refer to the faith which in the case of adults was a necessary condition for the reception of baptism. This subsection concludes with a brief account of the effects of the sacrament, which will be discussed at greater length below.

1229–1233. The second chapter of Acts depicts a kind of compressed catechumenate which the first converts went through on the day of Pentecost. They heard instruction from St Peter; they believed what they heard; they repented of their sins; they were baptised; they received the Holy Spirit; they celebrated the eucharist (the 'breaking of the bread'). In subsequent centuries the process became much longer: in the third century, three years were laid down as the norm (Hippolytus, *Apostolic Tradition* [Dix], xvii.1). Various rites, such as scrutinies and exorcisms, formed part of the process, the last part of which was a period of more intense preparation, generally coinciding with Lent and culminating in baptism, confirmation and first communion at the Easter Vigil.

The prebaptismal catechumenate, which had gradually died out as adult baptisms became less common, was restored by the Second Vatican Council. This new Rite of Christian Initiation of Adults (RCIA), which was published in 1972, reintroduces many of the practices of the early Church. The rite is divided into four periods linked by three steps. The first period of evangelisation and precatechumenate, during which the candidate makes a first exploration of the Church and reaches an initial conversion, is terminated by the step of entry into the catechumenate, which forms the second period. This catechumenate, which will commonly last six months or even much longer, is a time not only for instruction but also for an introduction into the life of the parish. It ends normally at the beginning of Lent with the second step of enrolment or election, when the candidates are admitted to the final preparation for baptism. This third period of purification and enlightenment has as its most intense moments the three scrutinies (which are rites at which in the presence of the community the candidates in deep silence examine their readiness to accept the obligations of a Christian life) and the presentations at which they are formally taught the Creed and the Lord's Prayer. The third step is the celebration of baptism, confirmation and first communion at the Easter Vigil. Finally, in the fourth period of post-baptismal catechesis or mystagogy, the new Christians familiarise themselves with the sacramental life of the Church.

When babies are baptised, however, arrangements must obviously be different. The catechumenate which is impossible before baptism must be given later, as the child grows up. In the Catholic Church as we know it in Britain (still called the 'Latin' rite even though the liturgy is usually celebrated in English), the three sacraments of initiation are separated; in most dioceses first communion will be made about the age of seven, and confirmation received several years later. In the Eastern Catholic rite, however, as in the Orthodox Church, even babies receive the three sacraments at the same time, in the spirit of Jesus' words, 'Let the little children come to me' (Mk 10:14; cf. 1244, below).

1234–1245. In the early Church the rites of initiation were so powerfully expressive that it was thought more effective to delay the explanation of them until after they had been celebrated. This subsequent explanation was given the name 'mystagogy'. The *Catechism* borrows it for the title of this sub-section which gives an account of the rites. Somewhat strangely, the account corresponds more to the rite of infant baptism than to that of adults, in which the ceremonies are spread out throughout the process leading up to baptism.

The *sign of the cross* is traced on the child's forehead by the priest, parents and godparents to show that the child now belongs to Christ. When babies are to be baptised, the *proclamation of the word* is evidently not for their immediate benefit, but for that of the parents, godparents and the congregation; indeed the rite suggests that the babies may be taken away during the liturgy of the word, presumably to prevent them from distracting the listeners. The *exorcisms* were originally addressed to the devil, commanding him to depart from the candidates, or to God, asking him to expel the devil from them; the latter type can still be used, though alternative versions are in the form of prayers that the candidate may be cleansed from original sin. In the RCIA, exorcisms may be celebrated at the reception into the catechumenate; further exorcisms are celebrated during the catechumenate and as an essential element in the scrutinies which take place during the period of enlightenment. Closely linked with the exorcisms is the *anointing with the oil of catechumens* (plain olive oil), as a sign of spiritual strength; in the RCIA this may (at the discretion of the bishops' conference) be celebrated earlier on Holy Saturday or omitted altogether. There follows the candidate's *renunciation of Satan* and the *profession of faith in Christ*; when babies are baptised the parents and godparents make these undertakings as an acknowledgement of the faith of the Christian family and of the congregation which is assuming responsibility for the child's education in the faith.

We now come to the central act, baptism itself. The *epiclesis*, which forms part of the *blessing of the water*, is a prayer that God the Father will make the baptismal water a source of rebirth through the power of the Holy Spirit. Throughout Eastertide the water blessed at the Easter Vigil is used. *Baptism* itself is celebrated in its most expressive form when the candidate is totally immersed three times; the immersion and subsequent emersion were sometimes taken as a symbolic burial and resurrection in union with Christ. It is not uncommon nowadays for fonts to be built which allow for this practice. Often, however, a simpler form is used in which water is poured three times over the candidate's head. The two forms of words used respectively in the Latin and Eastern Churches refer to the name of the Trinity; the triple immersion is intended to have the same reference. It is this immersion in water or pouring of water in the name of the Trinity which constitutes the essential rite of baptism ('In Brief', 1278). Both the Church's commission to baptise and the use of the trinitarian name derive from the words of the risen Lord in St Matthew's Gospel: 'Go therefore and make disciples of all nations, baptising them in the name of the Father and of the Son and of the Holy Spirit' (Mt 28:19).

Immediately after baptism the neophyte (the newly baptised) receives the *anointing with chrism*, which is scented oil. Since the name Christ comes from the Greek word 'chrism' — the name Messiah comes from the Hebrew and Aramaic translation of the same word — this anointing symbolises the candidates' union with Jesus Christ the anointed priest, prophet and king; though Jesus was not literally anointed, his baptism in the Jordan was regarded as a figurative anointing (cf. Acts 10:37–38). As Isaiah prophesied that the anointed bringer of liberation would receive the Spirit (Is 61:1), chrism also serves as a sign of the gift of the Holy Spirit which the neophytes have already received in baptism and which will be given a new significance when they are confirmed. However, if confirmation is celebrated immediately after baptism (as is the case with the baptism of adults), this 'messianic' anointing is omitted; sadly the accompanying prayer (Rite for the Baptism of Children, 62), which contains the only reference to Christ as priest, prophet and king, is also omitted. The neophytes are then clothed in a *white garment* as a sign of their new life of innocence in Christ, and given a *lighted candle* to indicate their share in Christ, the Light of the world. In baptism, which is the new birth in water of which Jesus spoke to Nicodemus (Jn 3:5–6), the Holy Spirit, the 'spirit of adoption', makes us sons and daughters of our heavenly Father; this new relationship is expressed in the *Our Father* which is said after baptism (when the sacrament is celebrated during Mass, the regular recitation of the Lord's Prayer fulfils this purpose).

When adults receive the sacrament, their baptism is followed not only by confirmation but also by *First Communion*, which is the final sacrament of initiation: 'we who are many are one body, for we all partake of the one bread' (1 Cor 10:17). The *Catechism* compares the white-robed neophytes to wedding-guests at 'the marriage supper of the Lamb' (Rev 19:9). When little children who are too young to make their first communion are baptised, they are brought to the altar in anticipation of what lies in store. The baptism of babies concludes with a special *blessing* for the mother and father, and then for all the congregation.

1246. Baptism cannot be repeated. Consequently baptised members of other churches who become Catholics may not be rebaptised. However, if there is doubt whether the non-Catholic was baptised in the proper way, they are baptised 'conditionally'; i.e., this new ceremony will be a true sacrament only if the first was for some reason invalid.

1247–1249. When adults are baptised, the RCIA introduced after Vatican II is used. In preparation for their baptism they take part in a lengthy catechumenate, which is discussed above (1229–1233), with a triple purpose. (1) The periods of catechumenate and enlightenment, with their accompanying rites, and above all the scrutinies, are designed to help the candidate to undergo a progressive *conversion*. (2) The instructions on Scripture, doctrine and morals, again together with the rites, are intended to promote the candidates' growth in *faith*. (3) Through the liturgy and by other means they are gradually introduced into the worship and mission of the local *community*. The participation of representatives of the parish in the instructions and the liturgy helps to reinforce this message.

The entry into the catechumenate is a serious step. According to Vatican II, catechumens are 'already united with the Church' and 'already belong to the household of Christ' (Decree on Missions, AG 48). They are admitted to Christian marriage and, if they die before baptism, to Christian burial.

1250–1252. When the Church began regularly to baptise babies is disputed among scholars. J. Jeremias[4] argues that the practice existed from New Testament times, taking as evidence for this view Jesus' command to let the little children come to him (Mk 10:14), and various references to whole 'households' receiving baptism. The practice is clearly attested by Tertullian and Hippolytus early in the third century, but seems to have become less common for a while towards the end of the fourth.

It has been argued that since the establishment of the RCIA the baptism of adults is the *'norm'*, though that is not to say that it is the *usual* way of celebrating the sacrament.[5] Just as the norm for the Eucharist is the celebration by the bishop with all the clergy and the local church, even though such formality will be a rarity, so too, it is argued, the baptism, confirmation and first communion on a single occasion of those who are old enough to participate with faith is the form of celebration which is 'normal' in the sense of showing most fully the nature of Christian initiation; the baptism of babies will then be a 'benign abnormality' [6] dictated by pastoral reasons in perhaps the large majority of cases. However, the Congregation for the Doctrine of the Faith in 1980 published a statement on infant baptism entitled *Pastoralis Actio*, which seems to be intended as a rebuttal of this argument:[7] the Church 'knows no other way apart from baptism for ensuring children's entry into eternal happiness' (13). Moreover, the fact that they are brought to baptism without any choice of their own is a sign that the sacrament is a completely undeserved gift from God (26).

1253–1255. In the long ending of Mark (Mk 16:16) faith and baptism are linked together as conditions for salvation. Baptism is therefore appropriately called the 'sacrament of faith'.[8] For the adult, the catechumenate is a process which enables the candidates' faith to grow to the point when they are ready to receive the sacrament. However, the gift of faith is also one of its effects of the sacrament: when the candidates for entry into the catechumenate are asked what they are seeking, the usual reply is 'Faith'. The renewal of the baptismal profession of faith at confirmation and on other occasions such as succeeding Easter Vigils is a reminder that even the habitual faith of the baptised needs to be reaffirmed and to grow.

The baptism of babies is also a sacrament of faith, for it sets them on the way of receiving the grace of faith in the Church; but in their case the faith that is required as a precondition is not their own, but that of those who welcome them into the Church and accept the responsibility of bringing them up to the point where they are able to choose the faith freely for themselves. This is the meaning of the profession of faith which the parents, godparents and the congregation make. Canon law allows the baptism of babies only if there is 'well founded hope' that they will be brought up as Catholics (Canon 868.2).

1256. Apart from bishops, priests and deacons, who are the ordinary ministers of the sacrament, in an emergency baptism can be conferred by anyone, even by people who have not themselves been baptised or do not themselves share Christian faith. Such cases can easily occur in a maternity hospital, when it may fall to a non-Christian nurse to confer the sacrament on a dying baby. All that is necessary is that water be poured while the trinitarian baptismal formula is recited. The minister does not need to *believe* in the effect of the sacrament; what is required is simply the *intention* of 'doing what the Church does', i.e. of performing the Christian rite.

1257–1261. Jesus' saying, 'No one can enter the kingdom of God without being born of water and Spirit' (Jn 3:5), is the ground for the Church's teaching that baptism is necessary for salvation (see 'In Brief', 1277). *Pastoralis Actio* reaffirms the Church's teaching on the 'necessity' of infant baptism (34). The *Catechism*, however, does not endorse the tradition (which was never a defined dogma) that babies who die without the rebirth of baptism go not to a heaven, but to a state of purely natural happiness called limbo. On the contrary, it is stated that *'God has bound salvation to the sacrament of Baptism, but he himself is not bound by his sacraments'* (1257). God's desire that all should be saved (1 Tim 2:4) and Jesus' appeal that little children should be allowed to come to him (Mk 10:14) are cited as grounds for the hope that 'there is a way of salvation for children who have died without Baptism' (1261). The Vatican II Decree on the Church in the World suggests that they share in Christ's death and resurrection 'in a manner known only to God'.[9] The Requiem Mass for a deceased child in the new Order of Christian Funerals contains prayers for a child who has died without baptism.

The Church has long specified some of the ways in which the unbaptised can be saved. (1) Unbaptised martyrs who die for and with Christ are said to receive 'baptism of blood'. (2) Those, such as catechumens, who have repented and wish to be baptised, but who die before their wish can be realised, are said to receive 'baptism of desire'. (3) From God's will to save all mankind, we can conclude that those who seek the truth and do God's will as they see it will be saved, even if they know nothing of Christ. We can attribute to them a form of baptism of desire because if they had understood the need for baptism they would have desired it. (4) Although the *Catechism* does not consider the salvation of the good atheist or agnostic, many theologians would hold that their openness to truth and their fidelity to their conscience constitute an unrecognised faith in 'the Way and the Truth and the Life' (Jn 14:6). Karl Rahner described such people as 'anonymous Christians'. **1262–1274.** The *Catechism* lists five effects of baptism.

(1) The forgiveness of sins. After the outpouring of the Holy Spirit at Pentecost, St Peter told the cosmopolitan group of listeners to 'Repent, and be baptised . . . so that your sins may be forgiven' (Acts 2:38). This effect of baptism is often referred to as justification: 'you were washed, you were sanctified, you were justified in the name of the Lord Jesus Christ and in the Spirit of our God' (1 Cor 6:11). The *Catechism*'s explanation of baptismal forgiveness is based on the definition made by the Council of Florence. Baptism, when received with faith and contrition, removes *original sin*, i.e., the separation from God and the lack of grace with which the neophyte entered the world as a member of a sinful human race. It also removes all *actual sins*, i.e., the personal sins which the neophyte has committed. Furthermore, it annuls the *'temporal punishment'* consequent upon sin, so that a person who died immediately upon baptism would have not need of purgatory. Baptism cannot however heal all the consequences of the fall: there still remain various human frailties, such as mortality and weakness of will, which because of the fall we experience as afflictions. This purifying effect of baptism is symbolised by the cleansing properties of water: before 'sanctifying' his bride the Church, the Bridegroom 'cleansed her by the washing of water with the word' (Eph 5:26 RSV). For St Paul, immersion in the water symbolised death, an end of the old sinful life, as well as a mystical sharing in the death of Christ (Rom 6:2–3). Baptism involves the removal of sin even for babies, because, although they have not been guilty of any actual sins of their own, the original sin with which they enter the world needs to be put right.

(2) New Creation. Baptism is not only a death, it is a new beginning; having died with Christ we rise again with him to a new life (Rom 6:4). Water is a source of life as well as a means of cleansing. Jesus' words to Nicodemus link baptism with new birth (Jn 3:3–6). In explaining the meaning of this new birth the *Catechism* refers to various passages in the epistles of Paul and Peter which do not however make explicit mention of baptism: God makes of us a 'new creature' (2 Cor 5:17) and 'partakers of the divine nature' (2 Pet 1:4); the Holy Spirit comes to dwell within the baptised as in a temple (1 Cor 6:19), but also as the life-giving Spirit (Rom 8:11) who makes us sons and daughters of our heavenly Father like Jesus Christ our Brother, and sharers of his inheritance (Rom 8:15–17).

In the words from 1 Corinthians 6 quoted above under (1), justification is not simply the negation of our sins, but is linked with sanctification. Accordingly the new life which the Holy Spirit imparts is called sanctifying grace, and is a share in Christ's own life. We become the branches who draw life from the True Vine (Jn 15:5), a life which is based on faith, hope and charity — the three virtues which are called 'theological' because they are related immediately to God. This life of grace is not a hidden reality, but issues in new lives of Christian morality (Rom 6:4).

(3) Incorporation into the Church, the body of Christ. Baptism is initiation into a society, which is on one level the visible community of the Roman Catholic Church, but at the same time the body of Christ: 'in the one Spirit we were all baptised into one body' (1 Cor 12:13). The first Epistle of Peter, which many scholars take to be a treatise on baptism, enlarges on the nature of the community of the baptised, applying to it the description in Exodus of the people of the old covenant: 'if you obey my voice and keep my covenant, you shall be my treasured possession out of all the peoples ... you shall be for me a priestly kingdom and a holy nation' (1 Pet 2:5; Ex 19:5–6). This membership implies a share in the mission of Jesus, who was, as we have seen, the anointed king, priest and prophet. The baptised fulfil their priesthood by witnessing to God's 'mighty acts' (1 Pet 2:9), by presenting to God lives of holiness and generous service as 'a living sacrifice' (Rom 12:1), and by taking a full part in the liturgy, especially the sacrifice of the Mass. The duty of the baptised to 'obey and submit to the Church's leaders' which the *Catechism* recalls must be placed in the context of the *sensus fidelium*, the instinct for truth which is called metaphorically the 'anointing' of the Holy Spirit: 'the anointing that you received from him abides in you, and so you do not need anyone to teach you' (1 Jn 2:27).

(4) The sacramental bond of Christian unity. The Catholic Church recognises the validity of baptism administered in other Churches when duly performed with the pouring of, or immersion in, water in the name of the Trinity. The Vatican II Decree on Ecumenism speaks of the 'imperfect communion' that exists among all Christians who have received this 'sacramental bond of unity' (3).

(5) Indelible spiritual mark. Baptism cannot be repeated: 'It is impossible to restore again to repentance those who have once been enlightened [= baptised]' (Heb 6:4). Even though by mortal sin we can extinguish the sanctifying grace which is produced by the presence of the Holy Spirit, and can cease to be members of the Church, there remains an ineradicable effect of baptism. Such a permanent sacramental effect or *character* is conferred by three sacraments, baptism, confirmation and holy orders: we cannot cease to be baptised or confirmed or ordained, or need to have these sacraments repeated after any kind of lapse, however grave.

St Augustine seems to have been the first to use the word 'character' in this sacramental sense; it means literally an impression made by a seal, and the word 'seal' is sometimes used as a synonym. Although the *Catechism* describes it as a 'sign on the soul' (1280), such language is evidently metaphorical. St Thomas regarded the character as a sign that one was destined for heaven, and as a share in the priesthood of Christ (STh III, 63, 3). Thus the *Catechism* sees the character as a commission ('commits') and a source of power ('enables'), so that the baptised may participate in the Church's liturgy and give witness to Christ by the holiness of their lives.

Confirmation

1285. Confirmation is the second of the three sacraments of initiation — second not only because it is normally listed between baptism and Eucharist, but more importantly because logically confirmation comes before first communion, which is the completion of the process by which we become members of Christ's body in his Church. This is the understanding of Vatican II, which describes how through the preaching of priests 'the faithful, already sealed by the holy sign of ownership in baptism and confirmation, are fully absorbed into the body of Christ by the reception of the eucharist', to which the other sacraments are 'attached' and 'lead' (Decree on Priests, PO 5). Similarly the General Introduction to the RCIA, after explaining summarily the effects of baptism and confirmation, continues: 'Finally, coming to the table of the eucharist, we eat the flesh and drink the blood of the Son of Man . . . (2).

Pastoral reasons, however, often lead the order of the sacraments to be changed, so that confirmation is postponed until several years after first communion. In explaining to people who do not see the point of confirmation that initiation into the Church is incomplete without the sacrament, it is appropriate to indicate the 'special strength' and 'stricter obligation' which confirmation conveys. We shall discuss below how these differ from the strength and obligation already conveyed by baptism.

1286–1292. This section of the *Catechism* is in effect a history of confirmation. It begins with the Old Testament prophecies that the Holy Spirit would rest on the Messiah to strengthen him for his mission of mercy (Is 11:2; 61:1), and also on the whole people (Ezek 36:25–27; Joel 2:28–29 [=in some editions 3:1–2]). The first prophecy was fulfilled when the Holy Spirit descended on Jesus at his baptism, as Jesus' own address in the synagogue at Nazareth testified, when he declared he was the one who according to Isaiah was to receive the Spirit (Lk 4:18–21). The second was fulfilled when the Holy Spirit came down first on the apostles at Pentecost, and then on those whom they baptised: 'Repent, and be baptised . . .; and you will receive the gift of the Holy Spirit' (Acts 2:38).

The Acts of the Apostles contains several accounts of baptisms, some of which describe a rite of the laying on of hands. It is not certain that this rite was in every case attached to baptism, nor what its significance was. Paul VI's Apostolic Constitution *Divinae Consortium*, which established the revised rite of confirmation in 1971, suggests that the laying on of hands regularly followed immediately after baptism as a rite for the giving of the Holy Spirit. The Pope observes that the Epistle to the

Hebrews includes the hand-laying among a number of items connected with initiation (Heb 6:2), and concludes that this apostolic practice was 'the origin of the sacrament of Confirmation, which in a certain way perpetuates the grace of Pentecost in the Church'.

Although two passages in the New Testament, 2 Corinthians 1:21 and 1 John 2:20–27, speak of an anointing in connection with the gift of the Holy Spirit, it is possible that the language is metaphorical, as it is when Jesus' own baptism is described as an anointing (Acts 10:38), in the light perhaps of the anointing received by kings, priests and prophets. By the third century, however, it is clear that an anointing was regularly added to the imposition of hands;[10] by the fourth we can be sure that perfumed oil, called 'chrism' or 'myron', is used. Thus by being anointed with chrism we become Christians, other Christs, anointed like him with his messianic Spirit and so strengthened for the fulfilment of our Christian calling.

At first the development of this rite in the Western Church was quite different from that in the East.[11] In the West in the third century the main emphasis was on the laying on of hands for the giving of the Holy Spirit. In the East, especially the Syriac-speaking areas, more importance was attached to the anointing with chrism, originally celebrated immediately *before* baptism, with the gift of the Spirit often being associated with the whole rite of chrismation plus baptism, or even with the water rather than the chrism; eventually, however, chrismation became located after baptism, and was explicitly linked with the gift of the Spirit. The name 'confirmation', which was adopted in the West in the fifth century, at first denoted the *completion* of baptism by the gift of the Spirit; it was only later that it was taken to express the *strengthening* of the recipient (see p. 255, below).[12]

As early as the third century there are signs that in the West baptism and hand-laying were on the way to being regarded not just as two moments in a single rite, but as two distinct sacraments.[13] This view prevailed when the widespread practice of infant baptism, together with the principle held in the West that only bishops could confirm (see p. 256, below), led to the postponement of hand-laying/chrismation until a bishop could be present. In addition, an extra rite of chrismation was added, to be celebrated by the *priest* or a *deacon* immediately after baptism; it was not, however, directly associated with the gift of the Spirit (see p. 247, above). In the East, however, the acceptance of the baptising priest as the normal minister of chrismation has allowed the two rites to be celebrated together, even though here too they are regarded as two distinct sacraments. As the *Catechism* observes, while the Eastern practice better emphasises the unity of initiation, the Western more clearly expresses unity with the bishop.

1293–1296. The symbolism of anointing is very expressive. St John Chrysostom in the fifth century explains that the oil symbolises athletic strength, the perfume a bride.[14] St Paul calls Christians 'the aroma of Christ to God' (2 Cor 2:15). Psalm 45:7 speaks of the 'oil of *gladness*'. In the parable of the Good Samaritan, oil is a means of healing (Lk 10:34).

The act of anointing is accordingly a suitable sign for the healing of the effect of sin (the anointing of catechumens), physical healing (the sacrament of the sick), the share in Christ's messianic mission (confirmation), and the consecration of the priest's hands for his sacred work (ordination).

As we shall see, confirmation is 'the *seal* of the gift of the Holy Spirit'. The word 'seal' recalls not only the mark which authenticates a document, but the brand which was stamped on cattle, and the mark, perhaps a tattoo, which was put on slaves and soldiers to identify their owner or leader. At one place in the Gospels Jesus states he has been sealed by the Father (Jn 6:27). In a verse which collects several terms later used in connection with confirmation, St Paul states that Christians are anointed (or commissioned), sealed and given the Holy Spirit (2 Cor 1:22).

1297–1301. The chrism which is used at confirmation will have been blessed by the bishop one day near Maundy Thursday at the Chrism Mass at which as many priests of the diocese as possible concelebrate with the bishop and renew their priestly commitment. In the course of this ceremony the bishop pronounces the *epiclesis*, the prayer in which God the Father is asked to send his Spirit on the chrism so as to make it a means of grace.

If confirmation is celebrated some time after baptism, the candidates renew their baptismal promises as a sign of the unity between the two sacraments. This connection is emphasised if one of the godparents also serves as sponsor at confirmation (1311). The connection with the Eucharist, the third sacrament of initiation, is expressed if confirmation is celebrated at Mass (1321). In the Latin rite the bishop, extending his hands over the candidates, in a prayer which recalls that they have been freed from sin by baptism, first asks the Father to send on them the Holy Spirit with his seven gifts of wisdom, understanding, right judgement, courage, knowledge, reverence and awe in God's presence. The list of these gifts is derived from Isaiah 11:2–3.

There follows the essential part of the sacrament, the anointing with chrism, with the laying on of the hand. This hand-laying is not the extending of the bishop's hands described in the last paragraph, but the touch of his hand in the very act of anointing. In the Latin Church it is only the forehead which is anointed, in the Eastern Churches also the organs of sensation and other parts of the body. As Pope Paul VI explains in *Divinae Consortium*, the revised rite of confirmation published in 1971 adopted the form of words used in the Eastern Churches: 'Be sealed with the gift of the Holy Spirit.' The different translations which the *Catechism* gives for the Latin and Eastern rites obscure the fact that the forms are identical.

1302–1311. If the history of confirmation is a complicated subject, the definition of the effects of the sacrament is even more so. As long as the two rites of baptism and hand-laying/chrismation were celebrated *together* there was no great difficulty, because there was no need to distinguish between their effects. Paul VI indeed acknowledges that it took time for the Church to recognise confirmation as a separate sacrament.[15] However, when, as explained above, pastoral reasons led to their separation, it was inevitable that it should be asked what confirmation added to baptism. The *Catechism* (1285) repeats the answer given in the Vatican II Dogmatic Constitution on the Church (LG 11) and quoted by Paul VI in *Divinae Consortium*: 'by the sacrament of Confirmation, [the baptized] are more perfectly bound to the Church and are enriched with a special strength of the Holy Spirit. Hence they are, as true witnesses of Christ, more strictly obliged to spread and defend the faith by word and deed.' The *Catechism* adds three other ways in which confirmation increases and deepens the grace of baptism: confirmation deepens our adoption as sons and daughters of God, unites us more firmly to Christ (1303), and gives a character which 'perfects the common priesthood of the faithful' (1304–1305; cf. 1273).

Thus it seems that there is no grace given by confirmation — whether membership of the Church, the commission to bear witness to Christ and the strength needed for that task, adoption by God, or union with Christ — which has not already been given by baptism. All that can be said is that through confirmation the effect of baptism is perfected and realised *more* intimately, *more* strictly, *more* deeply, *more* firmly, with *special* strength.

The earliest attempt to explain the distinctive significance of confirmation is contained in a sermon generally attributed to Faustus of Riez (*c.* 408–*c.* 490):[16] 'In baptism we are born again to life, after baptism we are confirmed for battle. In baptism we are washed, after baptism we are strengthened.' [17] This view was accepted by the old 'Penny Catechism', according to which confirmation made us 'strong and perfect Christians and soldiers of Jesus Christ'. Another view was that confirmation was an opportunity for Christians to make the public profession of faith and commitment to Christ which they had been unable to make for themselves if they were baptised as babies. The revised rite of confirmation promulgated in 1971 supports neither of these explanations. The intention of the rite is expressed in the Introduction to the rite: 'This giving of the Holy Spirit conforms believers more fully to Christ and strengthens them so that they may bear witness to Christ for the building up of his Body in faith and love. They are so marked with the character or seal of the Lord that the sacrament of confirmation cannot be repeated' (2).

This reference to the character or seal contains the clue to the answer we are seeking. Any sacrament not only is a means of grace but also establishes the recipient in a new or deeper relationship with the Church; in baptism, confirmation and holy orders, however, this new relationship, being irrevocable, is given the name of a 'character'. The character, which St Thomas, as we have seen (p. 252, above), envisages as a share in Christ's priesthood, entails new responsibilities within the Church. The new responsibility given at confirmation is that of being a witness to Christ. Although from baptism *all* Christians have a call to witness, this task becomes the *distinctive* responsibility of the confirmed. Accordingly the Holy Spirit, who from baptism has been given as the source of the Christian's new life in Christ, is now invoked as the source of power and strength for the new responsibilities.[18]

1306–1311. Whereas in the Eastern Churches confirmation is given immediately after baptism, the canon law of the Latin Church lays it down that the sacrament should be conferred 'about the age of discretion' (CIC 891), which is equivalent to the attainment of the 'use of reason' required for first communion (CIC 914). Nevertheless, the first of these two canons gives bishops' conferences the power to determine a different age for confirmation. There is, however, no uniform practice at present.

In determining the age for confirmation false reasons should not be allowed to be decisive. The *Catechism* warns that the fact that confirmation is sometimes called the sacrament of Christian maturity is not a valid reason for postponing reception of the sacrament until adulthood has been reached (1308). A choice has to be made between two aims which are not totally consistent. If priority is given to the understanding of confirmation as the sacrament of Christian apostolate, a somewhat later date than the age of discretion seems indicated, though even seven-year-olds can be challenged to be faithful to Christian values in the face of hostile pressure from their companions. If, however, it is considered more important to preserve the order of baptism–confirmation–first communion which we have seen is implied by the documents of Vatican II, the sacrament will be given shortly before first communion at the age of about seven. Whichever decision is taken, careful preparation appropriate to the age of the candidate should be given, and in danger of death even younger children may be confirmed. On the age and conditions for the reception of confirmation see 'In Brief' 1318–1319.

1312-1314. The tradition that confirmation originates with the bishop is very old. The incident in Acts quoted in 'In Brief' 1315 was cited in support of this tradition: it was argued that although the deacon Philip was competent to baptise the people of Samaria, only apostles, and subsequently their successors the bishops, could give the Holy Spirit in the sacrament of confirmation.[19] Although modern scholars offer different explanations of this passage, the principle remains that the bishop's involvement more fully expresses the unity of the diocese and of the whole Church.

In the Eastern Catholic and Orthodox Churches, although chrismation is normally performed by the priest, the chrism must be blessed by the bishop or patriarch. In the Latin Church the bishop is the 'ordinary minister', but he may delegate power to confirm to priests, though again the chrism must have been blessed by the bishop. Moreover, since 'adults are not to be baptised without receiving confirmation immediately afterward' (RCIA 208, Eng. edn), normally it will be the baptising priest who confirms them.

Similarly when baptised members of other Churches are received into the Catholic Church, the priest who receives them will normally confirm them at once. Priests may also confirm a Christian who is in danger of death.

Notes

1 The Greek can also mean 'born from on high'.
2 *Manual of Discipline* (or *Community Rule*), chs iii and v.
3 See G.R. Beasley-Murray, *Baptism in the New Testament* (1962; repr. Grand Rapids, MI, 1988), pp. 18–31.
4 J. Jeremias, *Infant Baptism in the First Four Centuries* (London, 1960).
5 See, e.g., A. Kavanagh, *The Shape of Baptism: The Rite of Christian Initiation* (New York, 1978), ch. 4.
6 Ibid., p.110.
7 'Some people propose that the order "preaching, faith, sacrament" should become the rule' (*Pastoralis Actio* 17; cf. 31). The document is contained in A. Flannery (ed.), *Vatican Council II*, vol. 2: *More Postconciliar Documents* (Leominster, 1982), pp. 103–17.
8 St Augustine, *Epistle* 98.9.
9 GS 22.
10 Hippolytus, *Apostolic Tradition* (Dix), xxii, 2; Tertullian, *De Baptismo*, 7.
11 For the early history of the sacrament, see C. Jones, G. Wainwright, E. J. Yarnold and P. Bradshaw (eds), *The Study of Liturgy*, 2nd edn (London, 1992), pp. 112–52.
12 See ibid., pp. 149–50.
13 St Cyprian indeed applied the words 'each sacrament' (*sacramento utroque*) to the two rites (*Ep.* 72, 1; 73, 21); but it must be remembered that in his time 'sacrament' had a much less precise meaning than it had acquired by the time Trent defined the number of sacraments as seven.
14 Chrysostom, *Baptismal Instructions* (Papadopoulos–Kerameus), 3.27 (trans. Harkins, *Ancient Christian Writers*, vol. 31, 11.27).
15 'In many Eastern rites it seems that from early times a rite of chrismation, *not yet clearly distinguished from baptism*, prevailed for the conferring of the Holy Spirit . . . In the West there are very ancient witnesses concerning the part of Christian initiation that was *later* distinctly recognised to be the sacrament of confirmation' (*Divinae Consortium* in *The Rites of the Catholic Church*, vol. 1A: *Initiation* (New York, 1988), p.475) (italics mine).
16 The attribution is questioned by G. Winkler, 'Confirmation or chrismation? A study in comparative liturgy', *Worship* 58 (1984), p. 13.
17 The sermon is quoted extensively in A. P. Milner, *The Theology of Confirmation* (Cork, 1972), pp. 44–7.
18 Since the Middle Ages theologians have set out the effects of a sacrament on three levels. First there is the sacramental sign itself (e.g., in confirmation the anointing and laying on of hands), known in Latin as the *sacramentum*. The second and third levels concern the effect (*res*) of the sacrament: the second is a new relationship with the Church (in confirmation, the status of witness), which in its turn is the sign of the third, which is the grace conferred individually on the recipient (in confirmation, the grace to be a witness). As both effect and sign, the new relationship was called *res et sacramentum*, whereas the individual effect is only the *res*. For an exposition of this understanding of the sacraments, see, e.g., E. Schillebeeckx, *Christ the Sacrament of the Encounter with God* (London, 1963), ch. 5.
19 Pope Innocent I argued in this way early in the fifth century (*Epistle XXV ad Senarium*, 6; PL 59, 403). Moreover, in the third-century *Apostolic*

Tradition (at least in the form in which it has come down to us), though priests could baptise and perform the first post-baptismal anointing, it is the bishop who lays on his hand and anoints in connection with the gift of the Spirit.

The Doctrine on the Eucharist

(Paragraphs 1322–1419)

Raymond Moloney SJ
Milltown Park, Dublin

After baptism and confirmation, the *Catechism* turns to the Eucharist as the completion of the process of Christian initiation. This third of the three sacraments of initiation celebrates and deepens the day-to-day life of the initiated believer within the Christian community. As the *Catechism* itself points out (1324), all the other sacraments are directed to this one, and so it is not surprising that the *Catechism* devotes such a generous portion of its text to this 'source and summit of the Church's life' (SC 47).

The treatment of this sacrament is divided into seven sections, the headings of which are some guide to the content. A person using the *Catechism* as a basis for instruction should notice the selection of topics which the authors have considered significant and the order in which they are presented. In general they correspond to the standard topics of a theological treatise on the subject. Indeed most of them may be found in Aquinas's articles in the third part of the *Summa Theologiae* (III, 73–79). The main topics in each section may be listed as follows, designating them according to headings more usual in doctrinal theology:

I   The importance of the Eucharist (1324–1327).
II   The names of the sacrament (1328–1332).
III   The matter of the sacrament (1333–1336).
       The institution of the sacrament (1337–1344).
IV   The liturgical structure of the Mass (1345-1355).
V   Eucharistic sacrifice: Thanksgiving and memorial (1356–1372).
       Eucharistic presence (1373–1377).
       Tabernacle devotion (1378–1381).
VI   The meaning of holy communion (1382–1388).
       Communion in both kinds (1390).
       The effects of the sacrament (1391–1397).
       Intercommunion (1398–1401).
VII The eschatological aspect (1402–1405).

From this plan it appears that the approach is a gradual one, beginning with the more experiential aspects of the sacrament and then moving on towards the inner meaning of the rite, which is presented mainly in the fifth section. On first reading, one will need some patience with the earlier parts, since the main questions in the minds of most people are dealt with only in the fifth section. However, the overview of the plan presented above shows the logic of the method and its usefulness for purposes of teaching and study. This commentary will now follow the same plan, going through the article, section by section.

I. The Eucharist — source and summit of the Church's life

The *Catechism* leads off in this section with a strong affirmation of the central role of the Eucharist in the whole life of the Church. The content of the section is well summed up in the phrase in the heading, an expression taken from Vatican II (*Lumen Gentium* 11), but the thought behind it comes from Aquinas, who sees the Eucharist as the consummation and goal of all the sacraments (STh III, 73, 3).

II. What the sacrament is called

The name we apply to the Eucharist has a certain importance. It tells us something about how we understand the sacrament, and often it helps to locate our understanding in particular historical circumstances. In this section the *Catechism* lists no fewer than sixteen different names for the rite, but of these the most important is that constantly used by the *Catechism* itself, 'the Eucharist'. According to the dictionary, this is the Greek word for thanksgiving, but the role of thanksgiving in the Mass is scarcely sufficient to explain how this word came to be the name of the Christian act of worship. Since understanding this aspect throws considerable light not only on the name of the sacrament but also on the kind of ritual it is, and since it also prepares for the next section on the institution of the sacrament, the point deserves to be explained in more detail.

Jewish origin of the Eucharist
When our Lord came to give his community a form of worship, he did not start from zero. He adapted a form of prayer which was familiar to every Jew, the rite of grace before and after meals. From earliest times Jews have loved the prayer of blessing, praise and thanksgiving. 'Blessing' here means primarily that believers praise God for his goodness in himself and thank him for his benefits to the world. While this prayer could be carried out at any time of the day, it was associated in a special way with the family meal. There the father of the house led his family in prayer. Grace before meals was a ritual of blessing God over bread and

then sharing the bread among those present. Grace after meals was a similar ritual, but with wine.

Today many scholars consider that, in instituting the Eucharist at the Last Supper, our Lord did so by celebrating these table rituals in a new way, relating his act of worship at the supper to his act of worship on the cross, and so giving the familiar rituals a totally new meaning. It is quite likely that at first the Eucharist was celebrated before and after a community meal. At this stage the whole complex would have been referred to as 'the breaking of bread', naming the whole from the introductory rite (cf. the texts in 1342). Then as the Church became more conscious of the unique meaning of the Lord's new rituals, the meal began to drop out and the two rituals over bread and cup were fused into one and offered to God in one great prayer of blessing and thanksgiving modelled on the one previously said over the cup. This is the origin of our great prayer of offering, the Eucharistic Prayer (cf. 1352–1354), and the whole ritual was named *eucharistia*. At first it was a name for the whole ritual action, but then, quite early on, it was extended to the sacramental gifts themselves (see the quotation in 1355). Both of these usages are preserved down to our own day. *Eucharistia* therefore does not refer simply to the prayers of thanksgiving in the Mass. It is really a Christian transposition of the ancient ritual of *blessing* as this was carried out in the table liturgy of the Jews.

III. The Eucharist in the economy of salvation

In this third section the *Catechism* deals with the institution of the Eucharist on the occasion of the Last Supper, but it begins with the significance of the bread and wine which are the focal point of every Eucharist. Here one has to keep before one's mind the account of the origin of the sacrament which was given in the previous section of this commentary. In instituting the sacrament our Lord did not start by taking two objects to change them into something else, as though he were simply some kind of wonder-worker, or even magician. He began as a man of prayer. He took an action of prayer, the Jewish ritual of grace before and after meals, of which bread and wine were part. In taking this ritual he transformed it, giving it a new and sublime meaning, and by that very fact he transformed the bread and wine. Bread and wine actually have certain associations from salvation-history, which the *Catechism* explains, but these associations are secondary to the funda-mental reason just described as to how bread and wine came to be the matter of the Christian sacrament.

In locating the institution of the Eucharist at the Last Supper, the *Catechism* adopts the viewpoint of the Synoptics that this supper was a celebration of the Passover. This assumption is attractive, since it facilitates the presentation of the Eucharist as a kind of Christian Passover, but unfortunately the historical assumption on which it is based is far from certain. In the Fourth Gospel the Passover occurs on the evening of our Lord's death, not on the day assigned in the Synoptics. This problem has exercised the minds of scholars down through history, some following the Synoptics, some following John. Even if one opts for the latter position, one can always say, with Raymond Brown, that the supper on the Thursday evening would inevitably have Passover characteristics, since that whole week in Jerusalem was filled with the atmosphere of the feast.

On the other hand, one cannot press too literally the notion of the Eucharist as a Christian Passover. There is a certain analogy between the two celebrations, since, as we will see below, both are forms of a Jewish ritual memorial, but it is clear that the Eucharist was not instituted on the elements proper to the Passover. For instance, unleavened bread was never used in the early centuries, and from the beginning it has not been simply an annual celebration. Even if the Last Supper were a Passover, the Eucharist was established on elements common to any Jewish festive meal, whether Passover or not.

The key truth in this whole section is the fact of divine institution itself. The Eucharist was instituted by the Son of God as God's chosen way for offering worship pleasing to him. This truth is fundamental not only to the divine efficacy of the sacrament, but also to the obligation which Christians have always felt to celebrate it, an obligation familiar to us in the custom of Sunday worship.

IV. The liturgical celebration of the Eucharist

One reason why Christians go to Mass on Sundays is to follow Christ in doing things which he did. As the *Catechism* notes in 1346, the Mass comprises two main actions, the liturgy of the word and the liturgy of the Eucharist. Each of these actions has a separate origin in customs with which our Lord was familiar. The liturgy of the word comes out of the synagogue service in which our Lord participated every sabbath (Lk 4:16). The liturgy of the Eucharist, as has been explained above, comes out of the table rituals with which every Jew was familiar from childhood on.

The basic structure of the liturgy of the word is in three parts: readings, preaching, prayers. These were found in the synagogue of our Lord's time, as they are to this day. The liturgy of the Eucharist is more complicated. At the Last Supper there were seven main gestures of our Lord to be noted: (1) he took bread; (2) he blessed his Father over it; (3) he broke the bread; (4) he gave it to the disciples. After the meal, (5) he took the cup, (6) again he prayed a prayer of blessing to his Father; (7) he then shared the cup with them. Some time in the first decades of Christianity, the meal, which had separated the ritual over the bread from that over the cup, dropped out. At that stage the seven original gestures of the Lord fused into the four basic actions of our ritual: he took bread and wine (*the Preparation of the Gifts*); he blessed his Father (*the Eucharistic Prayer*); he broke the bread (*the Breaking of Bread*); he distributed host and cup (*Holy Communion*).

Such is the origin of what the *Catechism* calls 'the fundamental structure' of our worship. At some point in the first century of the Church, the Christian versions of these rituals of word and Eucharist were brought together and fused into that one single act of worship which we call the Mass. The earliest witness to this development is the striking text of St Justin given in 1345. If the Eucharist celebrates especially the Lord's paschal mystery, and the liturgy of the word brings before us the other events of his life on earth, then the entire Mass can be seen to encapsulate for us the whole sweep of our Lord's mystery, in his life, death and resurrection, as one great Christ-event, which is the source of salvation for the world.

V. The sacramental sacrifice

In this fifth section of the article, the *Catechism* reaches the most important and controversial part of its task. In describing the liturgy of the eucharist in the preceding section, the focus was on *how* we celebrate it. Now that we come to explain the nature of the Eucharist, the focus is on *what* we celebrate. Two topics in particular are covered, the meaning of Eucharistic sacrifice and the meaning of Eucharistic presence. The first of these is treated in two sub-sections (1359–1361; 1362–1372), beginning with the Eucharist as thanksgiving.

Sacrifice of praise and thanksgiving (1359–1361)

The *Catechism* opens its account with a reflection on the Eucharist as sacrifice of praise and thanksgiving. Following the principle of basing one's explanation on the texts of the Mass itself, this is one of the aspects of the Eucharist which it is easiest to point to in the Mass and to explain. There are not only prayers like the Gloria and the Alleluia in the liturgy of the word, but there is above all the way the great prayer of offering, the Eucharistic Prayer, opens with this theme in the preface and closes with it in the doxology. The preface is that part of the Mass which expresses most clearly the identity between the offering of the Church on earth and the worship of God carried out by the angels and saints in heaven.

That praise and thanksgiving should be the dominant theme of the prayer of the saints in heaven was something that was realised already by the Jews. The Talmud declares that the day will come when all prayer will be silent on human lips, save the prayer of thanksgiving and of praise. But it is not at all obvious that this theme should give its name (cf. 1328) to the worship of those still faced with the struggles of this life. That it should do so is not due to some flight from reality, but it is a tribute to the transformation of life and to the anticipation of heaven which the paschal mystery makes possible.

If we read the whole of Psalm 21(22), we will see how Christ's prayer of desolation on the cross was transformed into one of thanksgiving. If through the Eucharist we are to share in the praise and thanksgiving of Christ's victory, it is only by first entering into his self-oblation. The thanksgiving that defines the Eucharist is the fruit of union with his sacrifice in both his death and resurrection. This twofold mystery has its counterpart in our worship when our praise rises out of our oblation. The Eucharist is thanksgiving, not just because of particular prayers on this theme in its liturgy, but because it is the climax of a sacrificial offering in the proper sense of the term.

The sacrificial memorial (1362–1372)

In 1362 the *Catechism* takes up a more theological presentation of the Eucharistic sacrifice. This question has been the subject of much reflection in the past, where scholars have developed many ingenious theories to attempt to throw some light on the mystery. The *Catechism's* approach is predominantly that of avoiding such theories and of taking its cue from the Second Vatican Council. Here one should notice in particular the quotation given without comment at the outset of the whole article in 1323. This paragraph is the principal statement on Eucharistic sacrifice in the contemporary magisterium, and so this passage, rather than that from the Council of Trent cited in 1366, deserves to be taken as basic in any catechesis on the Eucharist today.

Of this paragraph, and of the whole approach to the Eucharist in Vatican II, Edward Schillebeeckx wrote as follows: "The Council relinquished the old sacrificial concept common to various religions and reached out directly to the biblical and ecclesial sacrificial concept with the paschal mystery at its centre.'[1] The old concept, to which Schillebeeckx refers, was primarily a cultic one. It emphasised the mediatorial role of the priest carrying out some sacrificial protocol, often focused on sacrificial immolation. Such a notion stands in the background of many of the older theological theories, bringing their attention to bear with particular emphasis on the death of Christ.

The newer concept is primarily historical rather than cultic. It is what the ancient writers meant by the expression 'spiritual sacrifice' and the scholastics by the term 'sacramental sacrifice'. As we shall see below, this notion stresses the role of the whole assembly in the offering of our worship. The meaning lies in our union through ritual with the historical events of the paschal mystery, and so it clearly embraces not only the death but also the resurrection of Christ. This perspective culminates in the heavenly sacrifice of Christ, which is the view of the Eucharist which predominates in the *Catechism's* presentation from the first mention of it in 1326 to the quotation in 1372.

This is the notion of sacrifice to which the *Catechism* is turning when in 1362 it takes up the question of the meaning of memorial in the context of the Eucharist. At the time of the Reformation the divisions among Christians over the Eucharist could be summed up in the way they understood the little word 'memory' in the phrase 'Do this in memory of me'. Both sides took the word in what today we would call a purely subjective sense: 'memory' meant simply calling to mind an event of the past; it was something that simply happened in the mind. Against the Catholic doctrine of the Eucharistic sacrifice, the Protestants commonly described the Eucharist as simply a memorial of Christ's 'once for all' sacrifice on the cross. The Catholics insisted that, as well as being a 'memorial' of the cross, the Eucharist was a 'sacrifice'. In this way the two terms, memory and sacrifice, came to be set in a certain opposition.

One of the features of Scripture scholarship in this century has been the study of the Jewish background of the New Testament. It was this line of approach that led to the discovery that memory in the context of worship had a very special meaning for a Jew. A specific characteristic of biblical faith is the belief that God is the Lord of history. Not only does he intervene in history, but when he does so, all of history is equally present to him. As a result we find statements in the Old Testament which indicate that the great redemptive events are carried out not just for the people of a particular time, but for all the succeeding generations as well. When the contemporaries of Moses were liberated from Egypt in the Exodus, this event contained within it a grace of liberation for every Jew. This grace of liberation is then believed to become present to believers when they pray, for instance in the Psalms, but especially when these events are commemorated in the liturgy.

One very clear example is the annual festival of the Passover. In the Passover the Jew commemorates the Exodus under Moses, but, as many of the Passover texts show, when the people today commemorate these events of so long ago, they are not simply calling them to mind. By the power of the Lord of history, those events are in a sense made present in the liturgy, so that the worshippers are living them again in their own lives. A Jewish ritual memorial, therefore, is no mere thinking of the past; it is a memorial filled with the reality of that which it commemorates.

This, then, is the context for understanding the word 'memory' when our Lord says 'Do this in memory of me'. Just as Moses focused the minds of Jews on the events of the Exodus by the institution of the Passover (Ex 12), so does Christ by his Eucharist focus our minds on the salvific events of the new law, namely on his own death and resurrection. It is worth noting that in one place in the New Testament (Lk 9:31 in the Greek) these two events are actually referred to as Christ's 'exodus'. Consequently the phrase 'Do this in memory of me' points to the fact that, just as the Jewish Passover contained the events of the Exodus under Moses, so Christ's eucharist contains his 'exodus', namely his death and resurrection.

The ecumenical importance of this discovery is obviously far-reaching. We know from elsewhere in the New Testament (e.g., the Letter to the Hebrews) that Christ's death and resurrection constitute the great sacrifice of our redemption. As a result, this notion of Jewish ritual memorial has opened up for us a whole new avenue of approach to the vexed question of Eucharistic sacrifice — and that grounded in the very phrase of the New Testament which was once interpreted to exclude it. All this has the added advantage that the exegetical exploration of this discovery was shared by Catholic and Protestant scholars alike. These scholars do not necessarily agree in all details concerning the implications of their findings, but the notion of Jewish ritual memorial has certainly placed the whole discussion of the Eucharist on a new plane, and divisions which once seemed unbridgeable are beginning to fall away. By this one stroke we have at once established that in some sense the Eucharist is a sacrifice and that it is so by being one with the sacrifice of the cross. As the *Catechism* puts it (1365), the Eucharist is a sacrifice *because* it is the memorial of Christ's Passover.

Having established the principle of Eucharistic memorial as the basis of a new notion of sacrifice, the *Catechism* goes on to develop its approach by showing how comprehensive a notion it is. It encompasses in one sweep all subsequent celebrations of the Eucharist, which in turn bring into one great act of worship the Head, the members, the living, the clergy, the saints, the dead. The unity between the Eucharist and the cross is the basic reason for seeing the Mass as the sacrifice of Christ the Head. From this the *Catechism* goes on to reflect on how the Mass is also the sacrifice of the members of Christ in his Church. This represents the view of the Eucharist which is reflected significantly in the main Eucharistic Prayers of the Church, not least the Roman Canon. Commemorating the various members of the Church is a way of exercising our communion with them, so that we can regard this commemorating as another way of celebrating the Eucharist as communion.

A further key aspect of this truth is mentioned in 1368, but maybe not clearly enough. The Mass is not only something offered for the Church, but something offered *by* the Church. It is not only offered by the priest, but by all the faithful as well. This teaching, which was already clarified for our times by Pius XII in *Mediator Dei*, was repeated unambiguously in the Vatican Council: the faithful 'offer the divine Victim to God, and themselves along with It' (*Lumen Gentium* 11). The point is a central one for the role of the laity in the modern liturgy. It is also a key one for the theology of the Eucharist, since it specifies *who* is the celebrant of the Eucharist. It is the whole body of Christ, Head and members, which offers the body of Christ, Head and members, to the Father, but the different people act in different ways, with the priest alone acting in the person of Christ the Head, and he alone consecrating the gifts.

Returning to the question of the Eucharist as communion and to the commemoration of various people within the body of Christ, three categories of members can be picked out for special mention. Firstly, there are the ministers of Christ on earth, with the Pope at their head. Every Eucharist is an act of ecclesial communion. This is why the naming of the Pope and the bishop in the Eucharistic Prayer is more than just a prayer for them. It is an expression of our being members of the one body with them in the community of faith.

Secondly, we commemorate the saints. Sometimes we mention the names of particular patrons. Sometimes, as with some of the saints in the Roman Canon, we scarcely know who they are. But it does not matter. The important thing is our communion with all those, named and unnamed, who are now gathered before the throne of God in heaven. As the preface of the Eucharistic Prayer clearly brings out, in every

Eucharist we form one assembly with them in heaven, not only sharing in their worship, but drawing help from their intercession in the one communion of saints.

Thirdly, we commemorate the living and the dead, for whom we pray at Mass and for whom we offer the divine Victim to God. The offering of the Mass for the living and the dead was one of the main points of contention at the time of Trent and was what they principally had in mind when they described the Mass as a propitiatory sacrifice. The issue was connected with the question of Mass stipends, which is often a problem for people, then as now. The Reformers particularly objected to the notion that the Eucharist should benefit people who are not present at the celebration. The Council went some way to meet their difficulties when it taught that only those already disposed by faith and repentance can benefit from the Mass (DS 1743). The Mass is not magic! At the same time, the Council rightly saw that the nub of the question was in fact that the Eucharist is a true sacrifice. Petition is one of the ends of sacrifice, and just as prayer can be offered for the living and the dead, so can the sacrifice of Christ and his Church.

The *Catechism* concludes its treatment of the Eucharistic sacrifice with a quotation from St Augustine (1372). This quotation makes an excellent summary of the view of the Eucharist presented by the *Catechism*. It clearly relates the Eucharist to the heavenly sacrifice. It underlines who offers the Eucharist and who is offered in it. The one who offers is the one who is offered, namely the body of Christ, Head and members, now united in one great communion of worship. As a theological explanation of the nature of the Eucharist, the notion of the heavenly sacrifice only carries us a limited distance, but it has the great advantage of immediacy and of according well with the texts which the people hear being celebrated in the liturgy itself. Furthermore, it is a sufficient basis for conveying something of the majesty and seriousness of the rite, so that the Mass may be seen as considerably more than just a local assembly at prayer.

The mystery of presence (1373–1381)

When it comes to the question of Eucharistic presence, the *Catechism* takes as its starting-point the teaching of Vatican II on the plurality of ways in which Christ is really present in his Church. This approach is a significant one, which should be seen as setting an example for teachers and catechists generally. It is presented by the *Catechism* in a summary way in 1373, but it will be found more fully in the liturgy constitution (SC 7), and even more fully in Paul VI's *Mysterium Fidei* 35–38. There are two points in particular which need to be stressed about this teaching.

First of all, this approach places the mystery of the Eucharistic gifts within the context of liturgical presence generally and of the diversity of modes of Christ's presence in the Mass. In the past people tended to think in terms of only one mode of 'real presence'. The very expression, as the *Catechism* notes, citing Paul VI, seemed to imply that the other modes of presence were not real. The change of bread and wine into Christ's body and blood was understood to occur within a context of 'real absence'. The signal of his approach was the bell at the consecration.

Nowadays, the doctrine of the many modes of Christ's presence marks a return to an earlier perspective on the mystery of presence. The Church itself is the fundamental mystery through which the problem of distance between Christ and ourselves is overcome (cf. Mt 28:20). Christ's presence to his Church is the presupposition of any liturgical celebration, so that any particular mode of his presence within that context comes about not in order simply to establish a presence, but in order to deepen our response to a presence already there. Consequently, the change that takes place in the Eucharistic gifts does not come about as though the problem to be overcome were still one of spatial distance. The real problem is one of what we might call moral distance, namely one of our lack of response. He comes close to us under the species of bread and wine primarily in order to deepen our response to this and to the other modes of his presence by drawing us into an altogether special union with himself through holy communion. He then continues his presence among us in the tabernacle in order to keep that union alive in our hearts from Mass to Mass and from communion to communion.

There is a second important point about the real presence implicit in this teaching of Pope and Council, though one left by them to the theologians to develop. If there are several ways in which Christ is really present to his people, the teacher has to be able to give a reason for this plurality. Would not one mode of presence be enough? The answer lies in the fact that the presence we are concerned with is not just spatial but personal. The diversity of modes of presence is necessary if God is to become present to us in the varying facets of our personal lives. Indeed, in its higher forms, presence is something mutual as well, where the response of one person to another is part of the very reality of the presence.

This helps us to understand why there is no rivalry between the various modes of presence. Each of them is different in kind, and each complements the other. At the centre of them all there is Christ's presence in host and cup which, as the sacrament of presence *par excellence*, helps to maintain all the others and keeps us sensitive to them. In particular there is no rivalry between Christ's presence in the tabernacle and his presence in our neighbour, for in each case the appropriate response is different. We respond to his presence in others by serving them. We respond to his presence in the tabernacle by prayer and adoration. The former gives our prayer greater realism. The latter gives our service greater depth. This treatment of presence has seemed necessary in this commentary since the *Catechism* itself does not face up to the problems created by the teaching of the contemporary magisterium with which it opens its own account. Even more clearly than in the case of Eucharistic sacrifice, the *Catechism* moves from Vatican II to the Council of Trent, and most of what it then says is focused on the central concerns of the earlier Council with its insistence on the reality of Christ's presence in the consecrated species (1374–1377). This teaching is of course a necessary part of any catechesis, even today, but it is regrettable that the *Catechism* did not address itself in addition to the concerns which surround the documents of Vatican II.

In particular one will notice the absence in the *Catechism* of any reference to the controversies concerning real presence which, though not discussed in the documents of Vatican II, were much spoken of at that time and were the occasion of Paul VI's encyclical *Mysterium Fidei*. These controversies centred on certain new approaches to this truth which received such names as transignification and transfinalisation. The absence of any reference to these approaches in the *Catechism* fits in with its tendency to avoid theological theories, but since these approaches have been widely discussed and can be the source of questions in people's minds, some mention of them seems necessary today.

This is not the place to go into these theories in detail. Suffice it to say that they arise in the context of a more personalist philosophy than that which was basic to Catholic theology in the past. In general they try to describe the mystery of change in the Eucharist in terms of a change of meaning in the bread and wine. It is important to realise that these new approaches are more a style of approach than one monolithic account. Theologians differ in the way they explain the matter, some clearly taking note of the points to which the Church is committed, some being not so careful. It was because of the confusion in this area that Pope Paul VI wrote his encyclical. In it he draws attention to the key points which remain binding for Catholic teaching on the subject. However, it is essential to realise that the Pope did not close the door on the new approaches. Indeed he himself in the encyclical uses some of the language of a 'change of meaning' in explaining the Eucharistic mystery. Consequently the whole question has been left to Catholic theologians to work out with loyalty and creativeness. It will be for the Church of the future to pass judgement on their conclusions.

In 1378–1381 the *Catechism* concentrates on devotion to the reserved sacrament. The context for this insistence is a certain change with regard to this devotion since the Vatican Council. Even if the tabernacle does not have the central place it once enjoyed, it is still important to appreciate that this devotion continues to be recommended to the faithful by the highest authorities in the Church. For this the *Catechism* cites Paul VI and John Paul II. It could also have cited the Vatican Council itself, *Presbyterorum Ordinis* 5 and 18, as well as several documents of the Holy See dealing with the new liturgy. In this light, and recalling what was said above, we can see that the change in attitude to the tabernacle is not so much a decline as a change of emphasis, as this devotion is set in the wider context of presence envisaged by Vatican II. Shortly before his death Karl Rahner could write with confidence of the place of this devotion in the spirituality of the future: 'This ancient custom contains a blessing for the future, a blessing we should not miss.'[2]

VI. The paschal banquet

In this section the *Catechism* takes up the question of holy communion. It dwells on the dispositions with which the sacrament should be approached, the manner of its celebration and the effects of grace it bestows on the participants. In the opening paragraph (1382) it lays down the important principle that sacrifice and banquet belong together. Since taking part in the Mass without going to holy communion is such a familiar feature of Catholic life, the impression could easily be created that holy communion is simply an 'optional extra' for the worshipper. The *Catechism* make the point that the whole meaning of Mass culminates in the Eucharistic banquet, and so it is the desirable climax of anyone's participation in the rite. Conversely, it can be said that holy communion is essentially a sacrificial act. It is not just a visit to 'my Jesus'. It is a way of entering more deeply into the whole movement of that sacrifice of Head and members spoken of by Augustine in 1372.

In 1384 the *Catechism* expresses the invitation to communion in the words of John 6:53. In the fifteenth and sixteenth centuries this verse was a controversial one. It was a favourite text of those who opposed the Catholic custom of communion in one kind only. By reaction, some began to doubt whether John 6 referred to the Eucharist at all. Today a Eucharistic interpretation of John 6:51–58 is widely admitted among exegetes, and the invitation to the use of the cup is in fact taken up by the *Catechism* in 1390.

Next the *Catechism* turns to our preparation for communion. While the best preparation for communion lies in offering the Mass with attentiveness to the liturgy and commitment to God and neighbour, the *Catechism* concentrates on the aspect of examining one's conscience, drawing on the words of Paul in 1 Corinthians 11:22–29. This way of presenting the matter could easily be taken in a purely individualistic way, which is not only contrary to the sense of communion as a banquet, but also scarcely in keeping with the actual text of Paul. When the apostle wrote the quoted words from 1 Corinthians, he was concerned with cliques and divisiveness in the local congregation. Indeed some exegetes have proposed that 'discerning the body' refers to the ecclesial body directly. However, the view implied by the *Catechism*, that 'body' here refers to the body of the Lord in host and cup, is well supported by exegetes; but even in this approach the ecclesial sense should not be seen as absent. Holy communion summons us not only before our responsibilities directly to God, but also before those owed to our fellow human beings in justice and love. All these aspects should have a place in our examination of conscience before communion.

The following paragraph (1388) brings two points to our attention. Firstly, it underlines, as already mentioned at the beginning of this section above, that reception of holy communion is integral to the Mass. The liturgical movement has encouraged the faithful in the many ways of active participation in the liturgy, singing, reading, offertory processions, and so on; but we must always remember that our active participation in the Mass is seriously incomplete if we do not go to communion as well. The *Catechism* then reminds us of a point stressed by the magisterium ever since Pius XII, but still too often neglected, that the Eucharistic gifts offered to us in holy communion should be consecrated at the same Mass. Though still a recommendation rather than a requirement, this simple arrangement is a very direct way of bringing out how our communion is integral to the Mass, for it is the divine confirmation and deepening of the offering we have just made.

The reception of communion under both kinds is raised by 1390. The custom of communion under one kind, which was usual for the communion of the sick in the early Church, became general in the Western Church only during the Middle Ages. It has never been the norm in the Eastern rites, and since the Second Vatican Council there has been a movement in the Western Church to return as far as practical to the more common Christian usage. The Western Church has always had to defend the legitimacy of communion under one kind. This was done most notably at the Council of Trent, where it taught that those who receive communion under one species alone are not thereby deprived 'of any grace necessary for salvation' (DS 1729).

This way of putting it may be contrasted with that used in the *Catechism* where it speaks of 'all the fruit of Eucharistic grace'. This latter phrase is misleading. It refers to the fact that under *either* species Christ is present, whole and entire, body, blood, soul and divinity. It could, however, give the impression that reception under both kinds is a purely ceremonial matter and does not affect the grace of the sacrament. Trent's mode of expression is more precise. It leaves room for the possibility that communion under both kinds can in fact be more fruitful of grace for the recipient. Symbols speak to the heart and dispose us to be more open to the ways of God. The dispositions of the worshipper condition the fruitfulness of all the sacraments. The cup of Christ's blood is such an intimate sign of his love that it is not impossible that it should open us up to depths of response which the host alone would not evoke.

The effects of holy communion (1391–1401)

The last topic to be taken up in this section deals with the effects of the sacrament in our lives. In doing so the authors have in mind in particular the effects of holy communion, but, if we are to be faithful to the *Catechism*'s own principle of the basic unity of sacrifice and banquet (1382), then something of these effects must be said to flow into those who simply participate in the Mass without going to holy communion. They are not only effects of holy communion, but of the Eucharist as such — though, of course, they are found most clearly and most deeply in those who come with faith and love to the Eucharistic table.

The *Catechism* presents us with three main effects of the sacrament: (a) union with Christ; (b) forgiveness of sins; (c) union with others: the Church, the poor.

Union with the life of Christ is the most obvious effect of the eating and drinking of Christ's body and blood. The *Catechism* describes this as the principal effect, citing in its support some verses from the Eucharistic passage in John 6. As 1392 points out, this is the effect suggested by the very symbolism of the sacramental signs. Just as bread and wine nourish our natural lives, so do Christ's body and blood nourish the life we have from baptism.

Underlying this principle is the great mystery of that life of which John's Gospel speaks. Christ has come that we may have life and have it more abundantly (Jn 10:10), but this is not simply the life we have already, the human life of natural creation, though it does include it. It has to be above all a new life, a 'born again' life, a new creation, and this is nothing less than the divine life, the life of God himself shared with us. Indeed, if we expand the notion of life spoken of in John 6 with the teaching about divine life in John 13 – 17, then the life which the Eucharist is to nourish is the life of the three persons, Father, Son and Holy Spirit, shared with us already here below in the mystery of divine grace.

The second effect of the sacrament, according to the *Catechism*, is the remission of sins. This doctrine still comes as a surprise to many people, since we associate the forgiveness of sins rather with the sacrament of penance. However, as the texts cited by the *Catechism* in 1393 show, it is clear from the beginning that there is some link between the Eucharist and forgiveness. If the Eucharist helps to increase our love, by that very fact it withdraws us from that darkness of selfishness which is sin. Consequently, the Eucharist has some effect both with regard to venial sin and to mortal sin, as 1394 and 1395 indicate respectively. In the former case, we can speak of forgiveness; in the latter, of a strengthening against future falls. We could sum up this teaching in a paraphrase of St Ambrose: the Eucharist is our daily bread for our daily sins.

Inevitably, a Catholic will wonder where this doctrine leaves the sacrament of penance. First of all, it is far from implying that the latter sacrament is unnecessary. Not only is there the question of mortal sin, for which the sacrament of penance is the normal remedy, but there are all the grey areas in life, for which we will always need not only healing, but counselling. To deal with the darker aspects within us can never be the principal function of the Eucharist. Every so often, then, whether we like it or not, we will have to face up to these negative aspects of our lives, and for that the normal sacramental way will always be to go to confession. At the same time the above teaching on this effect of the Eucharist does make a difference with regard to the sacrament of penance. It implies that perhaps we go less often than before, and that when we do go, we do so more personally and profoundly.

The third effect of the Eucharist is our ever-deeper incorporation into the mystery of Christ's body, the Church. This aspect of the Eucharist is very profoundly and beautifully developed in the writing of the Fathers of the Church. Henri de Lubac summed them up when he wrote, in a phrase that has become famous, 'The Eucharist makes the Church'. Indeed, we can say that the body of Christ makes the body of Christ: the sacramental body makes the ecclesial body.

With this teaching we are faced with some of the ambiguities which always attend the notion of 'community'. We could take it on two levels. There is the general level of the universal Church. Certainly the Eucharist helps the Church to grow on this level. Some people would see the development of the Church in the twentieth century, its theological growth at Vatican II, its expansion in the Third World, as fruits of the increased recourse to holy communion inaugurated by St Pius X at the beginning of the century.

But there is also the local level. One of the dominant concerns of Vatican II with regard to the Eucharist was to heighten awareness among the faithful as to the social implications of the sacrament. Often we hear people lament the passing of aspects of the pre-conciliar liturgy, and in particular its sense of mystery. Though there must always be some sense of mystery in the liturgy, it is true that the conciliar reforms reduced it. This will always be seen as regrettable if we do not appreciate the increased sense of social commitment which more than compensates for the former. Christianity has to be about love of neighbour, and clearly this must come to expression at the common table of the Eucharist. This gives us one norm for measuring our liturgies: the more they succeed in involving the community, in expressing community, and so in celebrating and deepening the sense of community, the more Christian they will be and the more in keeping with the meaning of the sacrament.

VII. The pledge of future glory

This final section of the article deals with the eschatological aspect of the sacrament. In many manuals of theology this aspect has been presented as an additional effect of the sacrament. The presentation in the *Catechism* has the advantage of underlining that this aspect is really a dimension of all the effects of the Eucharist. Each of the three effects already listed will be found in this section in some form, for the truth of the matter is that the anticipation of the banquet of heaven is another way of describing the whole mystery of divine grace. The life mirrored in the image of the banquet is the life of God himself, Father, Son and Holy Spirit, shared with us. Eternal life will be our communion with them forever, but this communion is already a reality for us in the communion which we celebrate in every Mass.

Notes

1   Edward Schillebeeckx, *Vatican II: The Real Achievement* (London, 1967), p. 28.
2   Karl Rahner, *Theological Investigations*, vol. 23 (London, 1992), p. 115.

Penance and Reconciliation

(Paragraphs 1420–1498)

Monika K. Hellwig

Georgetown University, Washington DC

1. The historical context

The sacramental celebration of reconciliation has a long and complex history in the Church, one which does not appear in the *Catechism*. Although we find the text, 'Receive the Holy Spirit. For those whose sins you forgive, they are forgiven . . .' in Scripture (Jn 20:22–23), we know from patristic sources that formal rituals of reconciliation and forgiveness emerged only gradually and experimentally. The major occasions of repentance and reconciliation for the earliest Christians were baptism and after that the eucharist. But we also find references to the reconciling significance of the thrice daily recitation of the Lord's Prayer;[1] and even when public penance and the order of penitents appear, the assumption is that most Christians will never have cause to participate in this discipline which appears to be reserved for seriously scandalous occasions.[2] Indeed, it was debated whether such a solemn reconciliation could occur more than once for the same individual.

The medieval history of penance and reconciliation in the Western Church seems to have developed from two sources, a gradual refusal of the Christian people to participate in the increasingly onerous public penance system, and the emergence of alternative traditions. Little known but significant among the latter is the Spanish Good Friday ceremony of the Indulgentia, with its general absolution given to the pilgrim crowds who took part.[3]

More widespread and more enduring in the tradition was the private penance tradition which came from the British Church, having been adopted and adapted from Celtic monastic traditions, possibly to be traced to the desert hermits of Egypt.[4] It is noteworthy that this tradition, which involved specific confession of personal sins, was not in the first place a jurisdictional matter, but a matter of spirituality in the quest for continuing conversion. Nor was it in the earlier phases linked to the ministry of the ordained priesthood. People simply sought guidance in conversion of life from a wise and holy person.

274

What happened at the Fourth Lateran Council of 1215 is that the two traditions of Roman or public penance and of British or private penance, which had been the subject of fierce debate and rivalry, were blended into a hybrid form, later re-endorsed by the Council of Trent. This form combined the individual and specific confession of personal sin from the northern tradition with the element of official jurisdiction exercised on behalf of hierarchical church authority, and represented as a kind of tribunal. It is essentially still this hybrid form which is celebrated in the first and second rites in use since 1973,[5] and the understanding of the rite as a tribunal where a judgement is pronounced is still found in canon law (CIC 978).

Whatever may be the questions raised by the earlier history about this understanding, it is in the context of this development and present situation that the universal *Catechism* presents the sacrament of penance and reconciliation.

2. The theological context

As the title of this chapter of the *Catechism*, 'The sacraments of healing', implies, the essential issue in the understanding of the sacrament of penance is that of the redemption. Jesus preached the coming reign of God, that is the conversion of all human life, behaviour, social structures, values, relationships and expectations to the will of God in creation and grace. Under the influence of Scripture, liturgical and patristic studies, and with the strong impulse to return to the sources of our tradition, the Second Vatican Council focused clearly on the social and communal dimensions of the redemption. Both in *Lumen Gentium* and in *Gaudium et Spes*, the role of the Church as the People of God in human affairs is stressed in such a way that attention is focused on public and communal responsibilities and hopes.

To think about the redemption not as the cumulative saving of isolated souls out of the world, leaving the world of human affairs essentially untouched, but rather as the saving of the world in all its dimensions, turns the focus away from preoccupation with itemising specific actions as sinful and towards the discernment of attitudes, values, expectations and fundamental orientations from which such actions spring. There is an important shift here, which is not well represented in the universal *Catechism*. It is a shift away from scrutinising one's behaviour and impact by measuring them against the accepted norm within one's society, and towards critically evaluating to what extent that norm really conforms to the demands of the reign of God. Many questions of social justice would never emerge by the former scrutiny, but are seen as urgent by the latter.

This has immediate relevance to the formation of conscience and therefore to catechesis of the sacrament of penance, as well as to its practice. It suggests some mode of return to the sense of sin in the early Church which took shape in the consciousness of the believers from the

275

experience of adult baptism and the sharp contrast experienced between the way of light and the way of darkness,[6] that is the contrast between life in the community enlightened and empowered by the risen Christ and that other, confused society outside. In other words, the shift that is so noticeable in the Council documents directs our attention to original sin and its implications of distortion of values and vision. Particular actions are symptomatic of a larger more pervasive distortion, and it is this larger distortion which is the principal matter for the redemption.

It is clear that in our own time no sharp contrast is experienced between life in the Church and life outside it. Therefore a critical function of sacramental celebrations of conversion must be the fostering of discernment and evaluation of the values and attitudes and expectations with which we are surrounded and which we have absorbed from our infancy. For that vast majority of Catholic Christians who were baptised in infancy, post-baptismal catechesis and church experience must play that role, and the catechesis relating to the sacrament of penance is crucial in setting a direction for progressive discernment. It may well be that the suitable celebration of the communal rites achieves this best.

3. The pastoral context

It is no closely guarded secret that in many parts of the world, including the English-speaking countries, the practice of individual sacramental confession among adult believers has dwindled rapidly. Official and unofficial surveys to determine why this has happened have usually come up with a very wide range of answers; people find that the eucharist, with its initial penitential rite and its following of the Lord's Prayer with the passing of the peace, seem to fulfil the role of sacramental reconciliation; or they ask forgiveness of God and enlightenment and conversion in their prayer privately; or they talk to someone whom they trust but who is not an ordained priest; or they do not really think they are in need of repentance, possibly thinking preoccupation with failure morbid; or they find that they are no longer so clear about what is sin, and simply do not know what they should say in a confession; or they confessed formerly because of social pressure, and the pressure is no longer there.

All of these reasons are very important to consider in shaping a catechesis for our time. But one answer is definitely not helpful: to try to compensate for the absence of the adults and their inability to see sacramental confession as meaningful, by putting stronger social pressure on younger children. This is not only theologically problematic in itself, but certain to be counter-productive, conveying the message that when no longer immature and defenceless one escapes from the social pressure and no longer participates.

Behind the question of how Catholics think about the sacrament of penance is the larger question of how they understand their calling and responsibilities as Christians. This understanding is no longer shaped by a unified Christian culture. Most Christians today have had daily encounters with people of other traditions, and have had occasion to reflect on alternative visions of what makes a good life. They have also been subjected to the influences of increasingly secularised laws and customs at local, national and international level, leading them to question many aspects of public and private morality. Clearly, we need strong Christian formation to counter this, but such formation can only be effective if it takes into account the realities of contemporary society and culture, and if it does not claim authority arbitrarily.

One dimension of contemporary consciousness well based in observation and study is the realisation that human freedom is not absolute, but extensively conditioned by genetic factors, upbringing, economic circumstances, conditioning and other forces operating on each individual to shape perception, judgement, attitudes and expectations, and therefore behaviour in society. For this reason, contemporary Catholics do not easily accept the clear-cut definitions of what is sinful, and particularly what is gravely sinful. Nor do they respond readily to any claim to judge degrees of guilt when so much has clearly demonstrated that this is a claim that cannot be justified. Yet they will admit that there are attitudes and actions that are destructive, unjust, dishonest, and must be changed.

These attitudes and expectations are not necessarily in conflict with the gospel. The emphasis in the teaching of Jesus was not on determination of guilt, much less degrees of guilt, but on invitation and empowerment to conversion and the life of the reign of God. In all the gospel scenes in which Jesus is shown in conversation with sinners, the point of the narrative is precisely that he does not want to dwell on the past, because guilt is paralysing, but directs attention to the future and its possibilities for change. This appears in the story of the prodigal son (Lk 15:11–32) and in the two parables that precede it. But it also appears in the encounters with Zacchaeus the publican, the Samaritan woman at the well, and so forth.

A return to sources suggests that not everything in contemporary culture and understanding is a deterioration of earlier ways of living and thinking. The contemporary pastoral context certainly offers some new and special challenges, but it also offers new opportunities. Not least of these is this sense that it is not useful to look back and assign blame, but better to look forward and ask what may be done.

In a similar way, it may be noted that while on the one hand there is a tendency in modern industrialised society towards individualism, materialism and hedonism, on the other hand the experience of democracy, of mass communication media, and of a certain popular assimilation of insights from psychology and the social sciences, has brought ordinary people to a level of awareness of the suffering and needs of others which is new.

4. The structure and content of Article 4

The structure of this article is rather difficult to follow because it is not at all clear to whom it is addressed. In part it seems to be an exhortation to confessors, in other sections information to the uninformed, with a long excursus on the theology of indulgences according to the Council of Trent and the Apostolic Constitution on the topic by Paul VI. It is clearly not a text to be used directly in the preparation of children for the sacrament of penance, and might be quite confusing if followed too closely in an adult initiation programme. In fact, this article seems to follow, though not in the same sequence, the headings of Book IV, Title IV, of the Code of Canon Law. After an introductory discussion of terms and of the need for continuing conversion, the article deals with the role of the penitent, the role of the minister of the sacrament, indulgences, and the liturgical patterns of celebration.

Almost the whole of this article describes and discusses the rite for the reconciliation of a single penitent, and in spite of four references to *Lumen Gentium* and one to *Sacrosanctum Concilium*, the teaching given is really that of the Council of Trent and its interpretation of the earlier tradition. This leaves a great deal that must be supplied from elsewhere to take full note of the teaching of Vatican II and the directives from post-conciliar instructions.

5. The purpose of the sacrament (sections I, II and III)

1422 is a direct quotation from LG 11. It focuses on the twofold function of forgiveness from God and reconciliation with the Church. This might usefully have been expanded at this point to show why a ritual celebration is helpful in the process of redemption: it shows that sin is not only alienation from God, but the rupturing of the fabric of human society; it indicates, therefore, that the redemption likewise has to do with relations among people and the building of true human community in which the community of the faithful should be a 'seed of unity and hope and healing for the whole human race' (LG 9).

The logic of the first paragraph of this section 'What is this sacrament called?' is not immediately evident, but is theologically important. The first half states that conversion begins with a divine initiative expressed in the call of Jesus and modelled on the parable of the prodigal son. The first sentence of 1423, with the designation of the sacrament as one of conversion, says that what is happening here is precisely that the sacrament constitutes the divine initiative in the call of Jesus. This is an important point: the very existence of a sacrament of repentance and conversion is a pledge and an invitation — a pledge that conversion is possible by God's grace, and an invitation to make the turn.

Having made this point, this section goes on to consider the other ways the sacrament has been named: 'penance', not particularly well explained; 'confession', given an explanation which requires further comment;

'forgiveness', likewise requiring more comment; and 'reconciliation', which is related both to God and to fellow human beings.

The explanation given for calling the sacrament 'confession' is that 'the disclosure or confession of sins to a priest is an essential element of this sacrament'. This is certainly a correct rendering of the Tridentine position and the Roman Catechism, but it may be misleading as a statement of the Tradition from its beginnings (given the Celtic-British tradition that was not connected with ordained ministry), and it may be misleading as to the present situation after the decree on the three forms of the rite given in 1973. The term 'disclosure or confession' can of course be understood to include the generic confession of sinfulness by the congregation in the third rite. But it is necessary to make that point because there is much in this article of the *Catechism* that seems to ignore the existence of the communal forms.

Nevertheless, almost as an afterthought, there is reference to the older patristic focus in which confession is primarily the praise or declaration and witnessing of God's merciful goodness. This is linked with the comment that we are dealing with a sacrament of 'forgiveness' because it is 'by the priest's sacramental absolution God grants the penitent "pardon and peace"'. Claiming to be based on the formula of absolution, this statement seems to go further in a way that is theologically problematic. The formula of absolution contains the *prayer* 'through the ministry of the church, *may* God give you pardon and peace'. The change of the verb into the indicative in the *Catechism* makes the larger claim with no qualification, that pardon and peace are brought about by the priest's absolution. However, we know from Scripture and from our theological tradition that repentance and forgiveness are two aspects of the same moment, and that peace in any experiential sense of the term may or may not result for a particular individual. Therefore, while the formula of absolution respects the distinctions to be made, the formulation in the *Catechism* does not, and this problem arises again in 1440–1442. The Church, after all, no matter how solemn its declarations or how elaborate its canon law, cannot legislate what God may or may not do, nor require God to act only through official church channels, and therefore we are not entitled in our catechesis to give the impression that God's forgiveness and grace are contingent upon the judgement or action of any church functionary. What we can say is what is in the formula for absolution, namely that we act in sacraments, expressing the divine invitation and initiative, hoping to facilitate encounter with the divine and conversion, and praying that God's pardon and peace may effectively happen for particular individuals.

1425–1429 contrasts the conversion of baptism with the continuing conversion called for in the Christian life. Weaving together texts from Scripture, 1425 and 1426 make the point that the welcoming into the grace of Christ in the community of believers does not eliminate human frailty or the heritage of distortions that we know as original sin. This sets the stage for the next three paragraphs, which exhort to a continuing struggle against evil but without conveying much sense that what is required is not only the avoidance of obviously immoral acts, but growth in discernment tending towards a completely counter-cultural, redemptive style of life. Because such reflections on Christian spirituality are conspicuously missing from what is said about conversion throughout the article, it does not support a catechesis arousing vision, enthusiasm and commitment, but rather leaves a heavy sense of institutional control demanding passive conformity. Anyone referring to the *Catechism* as a resource for catechesis will have to draw inspiration and enthusiasm from elsewhere in order to evoke a truly personal response from those being instructed.

What is particularly disappointing in this discussion of continuing conversion in a guide for the shaping of catechesis is that no attention is given to the contemporary catechist's chief problem. In almost all cases our basic and intensive catechesis is directed to children who have been baptised in infancy. Therefore, it is unrealistic to move from the assumption that a wonderful, truly radical conversion has happened at baptism. Instruction relating to confirmation, eucharist and penance is therefore almost always evangelisation of a primary kind. Under those circumstances, serious thought must be given to the role that instruction about the sacrament of conversion, as well as its practice, must play in the initial turn to Christian faith and life, if it is not to become an experience of something quite inauthentic. There is a recurring problem in this article, that it assumes that if people are properly tidied into the official rules and observances, an authentic personal Christian life will follow. In the training of catechists and the shaping of catechetical programmes, this is even less likely to be successful in our days of independent critical thinking and experiences of a plurality of traditions than it has been in the past.

6. Repentance and works of penance (sections IV and V)

1430–1439 forms a section distinguishing and relating to each other the inner impetus of repentance and outer works of repentance. Beginning with the invitation of Jesus, the text in 1431 states explicitly that inner repentance involves a radical reorientation of one's whole life. But it then seems to equate this with 'an end of sin, a turning away from evil, with repugnance toward the evil actions we have committed ... accompanied by a salutary pain and sadness ... (affliction of spirit) ... (repentance of heart)', and the realisation of the need of God's grace for conversion. There are two problems here. First, this is not an adequate statement of what is involved in a Christian conversion. Secondly, people living as observant Catholics (who are the only ones likely to hear this message) are very unlikely to recognise this as a description of their own existential situation.

A call for Christian conversion is not simply a call to turn away from obvious specific sinful actions, regret them, and stop doing them, but rather a call to open one's eyes to the illumination that Christ offers and accept the empowerment he holds out, so as to attain a radically new vision in which we recognise the hidden distortions of values, relationships, expectations, identities, and so forth which are the heritage of original sin. Because this is subtle and gradual it involves a lifelong continuous conversion of what we see and understand and how we then respond in our lives, relationships and decisions.

1434–1439 expands the traditional categories of fasting, prayer and almsgiving along lines drawn from Scripture and from the Church Fathers: reconciliation with others, concern for the poor and for justice, amendment of one's life, acceptance of life's difficulties, examination of conscience, spiritual direction, and so forth. The list is unexceptionable and comes from the highest sources, but one might have hoped for a closer link with the subject-matter of the redemption. We are invited to do these things not only because they are a kind of private balancing of a spiritual account, good works to compensate for bad ones, but because they are supposed to be making a difference in the community's welcoming of the reign of God into the world to replace the reign of sin and selfishness. Beyond this, Scripture, Eucharist and the liturgical year are mentioned as instrumental in continuing conversion. This might have been expanded to show how and why. Finally, in this section, the parable of the prodigal son is explicitly invoked as prototypical model of conversion.

7. History of the sacrament and role of the penitent (sections VI and VII)

1440–1449 offers what is basically a historical justification of the sacrament of penance, which seems still to argue against Protestant positions. Beginning with the thesis that God alone can forgive sins (1441), that Jesus being divine exercises this divine prerogative, and that he shares it with other human beings in the Church, the exposition goes on to the very important point (1442) that the Church as a whole is intended to be instrumental in forgiveness and reconciliation in all its members and activities. This is a point which might be emphasised and given more space, because it concerns the active vocation of all Christians.

The next point made in the same paragraph is awkward. It claims, on the authority of 2 Corinthians 5:18, that Jesus 'entrusted the exercise of the power of absolution to the apostles'. The text from Corinthians speaks of the task of reconciliation left by Jesus to those who have themselves been reconciled. This seems to be concerned with that general mission of the community of believers to be reconcilers, but 'absolution' is such a specific and technical term used for something that emerged in the course of time, that the referral of the Corinthian passage to a gift or mandate of Jesus to the narrower circle of the apostles to exercise 'power of absolution' seems misplaced and unhelpful. The next three paragraphs (1443–1445) seem to use the New Testament references more appropriately in emphasising the importance of reconciliation with the community. However, the simple equation in 1445 of ecclesial excommunication with loss of communion with God, asserting impossibility of reconciliation with God without institutional sacramental reconciliation, is theologically indefensible.

1446 speaks of the reason for the existence of the sacrament as the need to offer a second chance to those who sin gravely after baptism so as to lose grace. Though this bypasses the question as to why we practise devotional confession, it certainly accords with what we know of the historical emergence of the sacrament (which is noted briefly in 1447). It is, however, unfortunate that the text here still uses the expression 'Christ instituted the sacrament of penance'. Institution refers to a specific juridical, organisational act, such as diligent Scripture study cannot find in the New Testament; therefore the continued use of this term may well turn sincere seekers away because they see it as untruthful. More significantly, 1448 makes the very important point that in all the historical changes (of which only the transition from ancient public penance to subsequent private penance is mentioned), what remains stable is the interaction of the individual penitent, already moved by grace (the Holy Spirit), and the divine power outwardly manifested and mediated by the Church. In 1449 the formula of absolution now in use in the Latin Church is proposed as a summary of the theology of the sacrament. This is a very important point, and might well be elaborated when the *Catechism* is used as a resource.

1450–1459 are paragraphs devoted to the acts of the penitent, among which contrition is given pride of place. The traditional distinction is maintained between perfect contrition stemming from love of God and imperfect contrition stemming from fear. It is a distinction that cannot be made in practice to discern someone's state of mind with any hope of certainty or accuracy, and indeed it is possible that there is often some mixture of both. Yet it may be quite helpful to point out the qualitative difference that can be there. What is problematic again is the assertion (based on Trent, DS 1677) that perfect contrition obtains forgiveness of mortal sins '*if* it includes the firm resolution to confess sacramentally as soon as possible' (1451). It is not theologically possible to restate the claim by saying that people may have *perfect* contrition for sin but God will not forgive them because the thought of sacramental confession as soon as possible was not part of their conversion by perfect contrition (because, for instance, they are not Catholics, or the practice of individual confession has more or less disappeared as far as their experience of the local church is concerned, or because they were never very well instructed, or for any other such reason). It is simply contrary to the meaning of the terms to say that someone could repent with perfect contrition and yet not be forgiven by God, because God is not less faithful than human creatures. Whatever the reasons, therefore, for the proposing of this formulation in the heat and confusion of the Protestant Reformation, it is unhelpful to repeat it now, with all the misconceptions to which it can lead. What can be said without fear of confusing the issue is that the discipline of the Catholic Church requires the integral confession of serious sins, even if they have been previously repented, as a condition of reconciliation with the Church.

1454 gives the briefest of comments on examination of conscience in preparation for confession, pointing out that it is most helpful to do this in the light of Scripture, particularly the teachings of the New Testament. This leads into several paragraphs discussing the reasons for explicit confession of sins, namely that it is liberating (1455), that it is intrinsic to the sacrament (1456–1457), that it helps in the formation of conscience (1458) and that it encourages one to be more merciful to others (1458). These are certainly goals to be striven for, but 1457 also reiterates the rulings of canons 989, 916 and 914, that all Christians from the age of discretion should confess serious sins at least once a year, that those who have committed serious sin should not receive communion, even if the sin has been fully repented, until they have confessed this sin, and that children 'must go to the sacrament of penance' before first reception of communion.

This last has been debated extensively on pastoral and psychological grounds. If adults are required to confess only when in a state of grave sin, why are children to confess without further qualification before first receiving communion? It may be quite problematic to combine the instruction of Pius X about early access of children to the eucharist with the requirement of canon law that they make a sacramental confession first, without risking the introduction of inauthenticity in the practice of confession that could be very damaging not only in childhood but later. Small children are easily bullied, especially when marched through as a class, but what is the result of this, especially at a time when it is clear that few of the adults avail themselves of individual confession? Is this really what Jesus would have wanted? Because this has been written into the Code, it will remain a pastoral problem and may become the major scandal that drives many Catholics away from the Church in adolescence or early adulthood because the practice of the faith has been experienced as inauthentic.

The final two paragraphs of this section deal with the third 'act' of the penitent, satisfaction. The issue is clearly that regret does not undo the damage done, so that true repentance must include the effort to restore what has been destroyed, and 1460 seems to be an encouragement to confessors to impose appropriate penances, while reiterating that these receive their value by incorporation in the redemptive action of Jesus.

8. The minister and effects of the sacrament (sections VIII and IX)

The discussion of the minister of the sacrament begins with the reiteration (1461) that Christ entrusted the ministry of reconciliation to his apostles (this time citing Jn 20:23 as well as 2 Cor 5:18 cited before), and states that bishops and presbyters continue the ministry because the sacrament of orders gives them the 'power to forgive all sins' in the name of the triune God. As mentioned before, this glides over some questions of biblical interpretation, of continuity of orders as understood in different times of earlier church history, and the nuances of what is meant by saying that the ordained have the 'power to forgive sins'. These questions are certainly not ones that can become part of catechesis, but it may be necessary to state the practice and teaching of the Church without making claims of historical fact that can be called in question by the more educated on solid scholarly grounds.

1462–1467 are paragraphs largely describing with relatively little explanation the current practice and canonical regulations concerning confessors. Significant points are: the emphasis (1462) on the function of reconciliation with the Church as well as with God, and the consequent function of the bishop in regulating penitential discipline; what is meant by excommunication and how it can be lifted; the need for priests to be available and compassionate and to exercise good judgement (1464 and 1465), as well as having good understanding of human behaviour and loyalty to church teaching (1466); and finally the explanation of the sacramental seal of secrecy (1467). It is not clear why these paragraphs were included, as they are less a matter of knowledge required for those who plan catechesis than a matter of exhortation to confessors.

Following the above is the short section of three paragraphs on the effects of the sacrament. 1468 names as the first effect the restoration of grace and the dignity of 'children of God' enjoying God's friendship. This obviously concerns confession and absolution of grave sins, and does not speak directly to the practice of devotional confession. Here and elsewhere in the article this is confusing; one assumes the emphasis on maintaining the practice of individual confession and of bringing small children to it before first communion are not based on the supposition that practising Catholics are habitually in a state of serious sin. 1469, concerning reconciliation with the Church as the second effect of the sacrament, also focuses on restoration to ecclesial communion, assuming that this has been lost. In using this text as a resource for catechetical planning, it will be very important to expand this explanation of the effects of the sacrament to include the intended outcomes of the practice of repeated (even frequent) devotional confessions, namely continuing conversion through developing more sensitive discernment and more consistent commitment. 1470 adds an interesting thought drawn from several New Testament texts: a third effect of the sacrament is that final judgement has been anticipated.

9. Indulgences (section X)

A whole rather long section, 1471–1479, is given to a defence of the practice and theology of indulgences. The definition and much of the explanation are taken from the teaching of Paul VI in the Apostolic constitution *Indulgentiarum Doctrina* of 1967, which was almost entirely a compilation and restatement of various much earlier texts. The definition of indulgence speaks of it as 'remission before God of the temporal punishment due' for sins that have been forgiven, the remission being due to the merits of Christ and the saints, and mediated by the Church. The underlying idea is certainly that we are in a history of grace and redemption in which the consequences of our actions are always rather better than could be expected on a principle of simple proportionality. There is some risk that this definition by itself might suggest a kind of legalistic balancing of pain against wrongdoing, in spite of the fact that the pain can, so to speak, be commuted by qualifying for indulgence. 1472, however, warns against this by insisting that there is nothing arbitrary about the idea of sin once forgiven leaving a residue of 'punishment'; it is simply a way of saying that destructive deeds have consequences which must be undone. 1473 describes the ordinary way that such damage is undone in people's lives: suffering adversity and death patiently, and engaging in good and charitable works. But by the Christian understanding of redemption and Church, people are not left to struggle in isolation but are drawn into the communion of saints (1474), sharing so intimately in the life of Christ and of one another that the undoing of evil and the fashioning of a holy people becomes a single project among the participants (1475–1477).

This much is clear, and can be explained rather easily to people of modern mentality. Considerably less intelligible to the modern mind is the further statement (1478) that the hierarchy of the institutional Church was given by Christ, under the designation of binding and loosing, control over the flow of redemptive grace and new life among the members of that communion. This may well seem almost like a contradiction in terms to many thoughtful and faithful contemporary people. One might be tempted to wish that this issue of indulgences had been left to rest quietly, so that what is of God in it would survive and flourish and what is not would fade away quietly. As it is, this may revive tensions and difficulties that had long been dead.

10. The liturgical celebration (section XI)

1480–1484 is concerned with the ritual aspects of the sacrament. The first paragraph (1480) describes the current Rite for Reconciliation of Individual Penitents. It is presented simply as the norm, the other two rites being mentioned almost as an afterthought and in smaller print (1482, 1483). Indeed the third rite is mentioned as available only in case of urgent need, and with the caution that the absolution is valid only for those who intend to confess any grave sins explicitly 'in the time required' (according to CIC, Canon 962, no. 1, before again receiving general absolution). This follows exactly Canons 961–963, and therefore simply informs as to what the law is. But this will not prevent observant inquirers from noting that it seems to contradict the underlying spirit of the post-conciliar opening up of the three rites.

1481, however, offers an absolution formula of the Byzantine liturgy as commentary on the meaning of the sacrament. Noteworthy in that formula is the accumulation of biblical examples of God's forgiveness, culminating not in a declaration that the priest absolves (using a judicial power), but in a prayer that God will forgive through the priest, also a sinner, and will not in the final judgement condemn. It is worth giving much reflection to the rather different perspective offered by this prayer of absolution.

The final paragraph (1484) repeats, needlessly in the light of what has gone before, that individual complete confession and absolution are the only ordinary means of reconciliation with God and the Church for any member of the Church conscious of mortal sin. Noteworthy here is the re-introduction of the term 'mortal' rather than 'serious', which refers back to the need to determine whether conditions for mortal sin are met. This in itself has proved very elusive in the light of what we know today about human psychology. By the fact that this is the last paragraph (except for the brief outline résumé of the entire article), what is conveyed is a certain defensiveness, and this will unfortunately be less than helpful in a matter in which much help is needed if the sacrament is not to slide quietly into desuetude.

Concluding reflections

By constantly addressing the issue of serious sin and loss of grace, the text achieves a burdensome and depressing effect which cannot be helpful to catechesis. What one might have hoped to find is some foundation for genuine enthusiasm and the expansion of vision of what Christian life in the world might be. In order to encourage the regular, and therefore devotional, participation in the sacrament of conversion, one would need to invoke not only canon law and moral theology, but much more dominantly and prominently spiritual theology. To reduce the continuous living of Christian life to an ever-repeating cycle of turning away from obvious, not to say serious, sinful actions and mourning them may prove to be not only discouraging but disabling by its sheer negativity and lack of newness. What we really need in catechesis certainly includes knowledge about the dark side of history and the possibility of rescue even from the worst moral and spiritual disasters, but the focus of attention cannot be on this if we hope to maintain a faithful community which is a 'seed of unity and hope and healing' for the whole human race.

If this last is what we are seeking, and if we are looking to the sacrament of reconciliation and conversion to further the quest, we need a theology of the sacrament that understands Christian conversion in a radical, biblical, communal, progressive and challenging way. We need to show that there is always something further to see and to which to respond, that there is a wonderful possibility of increasing integration in entering further into the mind of Christ, and that there is nothing else in the world so well worth doing. We need to see the repeated celebration of reconciliation and conversion as the progressive righting of distorted perceptions, and as a constant widening of horizons within which we are empowered to make a difference.

Notes

1 Hippolytus, *Apostolic Tradition*.
2 Cf. Bernard Poschmann, *Penance and the Anointing of the Sick* (New York: Herder & Herder, 1964).
3 See Oscar D. Watkins, *A History of Penance*, vol. 2 (London: Longmans Green, 1920), pp. 585–7.
4 Cf. Poschmann, op. cit.
5 See *The Rite of Penance*, English translation by the International Commission on English in the Liturgy (New York: Catholic Book Publishing Company, 1975).
6 Cf. *Didache*, first part.

The Anointing of the Sick

(Paragraphs 1499–1532)

James L. Empereur SJ

Santa Clara, California

Article 5 deals with the sacrament of the anointing of the sick. As would be expected, the content does not go beyond the references which are restricted to Scripture and some documents of the Church, especially from the Council of Trent and the Second Vatican Council. The reader of whatever ideological bent who is acquainted with the theology and practice of this sacrament will find nothing new or surprising here. This article is but a reaffirmation of what is already found in the introduction of *The Pastoral Care of the Sick*. This may be a relief for people on both ends of the theological continuum. The question remains, however: Of what use is this Article 5? It is too general to be a source of theological reflection. It is too minimal to be of any pastoral assistance. The nature of this commentary, then, will be to fill out the text to enhance it as a resource for preaching and sacramental celebration.[1]

The article begins with a quotation from *Lumen Gentium* 11 which sets the foundation on which this sacrament is based, namely that it is through anointing and prayer that the Church commends the sick person to Christ, praying for their relief and salvation, with the exhortation that they join themselves with the passion and death of Christ for the good of the people of God.

There are five major sections to Article 5: (1) Foundations of anointing in the plan of salvation; (2) Who receives and administers this sacrament; (3) How is this sacrament celebrated? (4) The effects of the celebration of this sacrament; (5) Viaticum, the Christian's last sacrament.

The movement in the first section on the place of anointing in the plan of salvation is from a theology of illness to Christ the Healer to the sacrament itself. Illness in human life is viewed primarily in negative terms, 'among the gravest problems confronted in human life'. Here we experience our powerlessness, often in the face of death. The side-effects of illness are also negative: 'anguish, self-absorption, sometimes even despair and revolt against God'. There is the suggestion that some good can come from such affliction. There is no question that illness places one

288

in an ambiguous situation of liminality. Here we experience the loss of personal unity and bodily harmony. For many the loss of control at this time is more debilitating than the disease itself. Not only is there the physical separation from home and friends, but also the inner isolation of loneliness and inability to make meaningful human contact. Fragmentation follows upon such radical changes in relationships. One is now in a different role *vis-à-vis* society. One becomes marginal, one of the 'sick'. One becomes an object. Our technological world has only accelerated this dehumanisation process. Life-support systems when all hope of a human life has vanished are the ultimate in the objectification of the person who is ill. It is no wonder that such alienation from the human community brings the threat of loss of contact with God. Self-doubt and anger projected on to God and the inability to pray are all signs of crisis at this time.

But sickness as a human phenomenon is not solely negative. The *Catechism* does not bring out well what is positive about sickness in itself. It seems to suggest that this can only be discerned in the light of faith and is only available to Christians. But while it is true that this Christian sacrament of anointing removes the ambiguity of the experience of being ill, yet there is a sense in which illness is salvational on what might be called the human level only. For all people are challenged to deal with the mystery of life and death in terms of this limit experience. Others besides Christians see death as an entrance into another kind of existence, and even for those who do not, there is the call to live in a more fully human way.

Sickness becomes that mobilising experience where we can recognise (and feel) the coming together of our physical, emotional, mental and transcendent dimensions, because their very unity is under threat. The power of witness that the sick person possesses (as the text of the *Catechism* states: 'to the good of the People of God') is not the monopoly of the Christian. This is dramatically demonstrated every time a non-believer confronts sickness and death with equilibrium and peace, with gentleness to self and with a resignation that is a positive encouragement to friends, family, and care-givers. At times this stands in embarrassing contrast to the Christian who undergoes illness or who passes into new life in a mean-spirited way, more in protestation than in evangelical proclamation.

The next paragraph of this section, 'The sick person before God', is but a transition to the consideration of Christ as the Physician. It is a very brief summary of the meaning of sickness in the Hebrew Scriptures. Illness was the occasion of lament and prayer to God which sought for forgiveness. Sickness and sin were connected, although there was no systematic development of that notion. Sickness was not only a physical reality, because the prophet saw that personal suffering 'could also have a redemptive meaning for the sin of others'. The messanic time was seen as the time when there would be no illness.

The notion that sickness is a form of punishment is now generally rejected. It does not accord with the image of a loving God, and most theologies of the human person see the cause of disease in other categories than moral. This is not to deny the place of personal responsibility, both physical and psychological, in the matter of sickness. We know that a positive self-regard and feeling of acceptance by God has healing qualities. Today, we are much more aware of the societal effects, which are often referred to as sinful structures, on our physical and psychological well-being.

Closely associated with this more negative view would be the consideration that illness is a kind of discipline. This is the 'if it hurts, it must be good' syndrome. This is a basically dualistic form of spirituality which sees the material and spiritual dimensions of the person at odds with each other, at war in some sense. Sickness becomes the opportunity to conquer the physical, the triumph of the spiritual. Ironically, where sinfulness and sickness are still connected is in the way secular society defines the sick person. For often the social condition of the sick person is one which is isolating, having been pushed to the margins of ordinary life. So-called healthy society tries to conceal the sick and elderly. Even those without contagious diseases are treated as though they had such. Perhaps our moving away from an excessively individualistic view of sin permits us to connect sin and sickness in a different way. Now much disease and sickness may be manifestations of the sin of society.

The connection between sin and sickness resonates in the picture of Christ the Physician, who is the one who not only heals, but forgives sins. But here the point is that the connection is a way of signifying the whole person. Christ's identification with those afflicted with illness demonstrates a preferential option for these particular marginal ones. The kingdom of God is revealed in Christ's compassion towards the sick.

In Christ sickness and healing are tied to both faith and the physical (spittle, laying on of hands, washing). This ministry of Christ is placed in the context of the sacramental principle: that salvation is made available in an incarnate way, which is both spiritual and material and where the invisible is symbolised in the visible.

Jesus was not a miracle-worker, nor was he primarily interested in manifesting his power or in gathering followers. Healings were signs of the kingdom. They were kinds of proclamations, forms of the good news, the victory over sin and death through his dying and rising. He made it possible to search the depths of suffering and to find there the opportunity to create our lives so that they become more like his.

What is missing from the *Catechism*'s treatment is the connection between Jesus' ministry of healing and the justice dimension of the kingdom of God. Healing is eschatological, but is not only a future reality. The kingdom has already been inaugurated. This ministry reveals that God is just, for God sent Jesus into our world, and so God was faithful to the promises made. Jesus' ministry manifests this divine uprightness. For when people have faith in Jesus, the justice of God is a possibility for them. The sick can participate in the righteousness of God, not because of personal merit, but because of a total commitment to God in faith. This righteousness of God becomes the norm of their lives. Jesus' healing ministry shows that God is faithful, and so they can depend on

God in their own faithfulness.

The ministry of healing is Christ's gift to the Church, first given to the disciples and now as our way of participating in his compassion and healing. The recovery of those touched and anointed through this ministry is a sign of the risen Lord and his mission. But such healing is not a mere service of wonder. The present sufferings we undergo are to make full the body of Christ.

In 1509, the *Catechism* hints at the larger healing ministry, one which is beyond prayer, charismatic or otherwise. This is the ministry of pastoral care. But it is a mere hint, because the *Catechism* locates the healing presence of Christ in the sacraments, especially the eucharist, and refers to St Paul, who connects the eucharist to bodily health. And then, it states that there is the Church's own rite for the sick, the apostolic sacrament of anointing.

Here the *Catechism* asserts the sacramentality of anointing as witnessed by the councils throughout history. This is unexceptional. But it also claims that it is attested to by St James, and quotes the traditional text (Jas 5:14–15). It is not that a reference to James is inappropriate here, for it has had a singular place in the tradition. But there is also an implication here regarding the institution of the sacrament. Present biblical and theological understanding would be more nuanced, lest the impression be given of the origin of this sacrament in apostolic times as a certainty. There is no indication in the *Catechism* that this sacrament and its recognition as a sacrament emerged over a relatively long period of time, which is not to deny that it can be seen as in continuity with Christ's healing ministry and as a sacramentalisation of an ongoing experience in the Church.

The *Catechism* simply repeats the brief teaching from the Council of Trent. It does not deal with the ambiguity of Trent. On the one hand, Trent says that anointing is definitively presented for the dying, but on the other, that it should be administered while the person is still conscious. The *Catechism* notes the change in discipline ushered in by the Second Vatican Council, but this is primarily a change in name and time of administration. What is more significant about the Second Vatican Council is that anointing was affected by the placing of all the sacraments in a larger ecclesial dimension. And most importantly, enlarging the sacramental experience of anointing to the larger context of the pastoral ministry to the sick and elderly has more radical ramifications than whatever might be implied in the demise of the term 'extreme unction'.

The phenomenon of the communal anointing service, which is a product of the Vatican II reforms, indicates a paradigm shift from anointing on death-beds, at the time of traffic accidents, and in emergency rooms to a full liturgical setting which involves the friends, families and care-givers of the sick and elderly so honoured.

The second section of Article 5 deals with what has traditionally been known as the subject and minister of the sacrament. It clearly reiterates that the sacrament is not limited to those in the last hours of their lives, but it still sees 'danger of death' as a necessary condition for anointing, although this does not mean 'at the point of death'. It is possible to be quite generous in judging who may be anointed if one sees the danger of death as a remote possibility. This would cover most of the cases where anointing would be desired. But today we tend to shy away from using the phrase 'in danger of death', unless death is realistically probable. As a result, the text, which says 'as soon as anyone of the faithful begins to be in danger of death from sickness or old age', is not a helpful pastoral guideline. Apparently, the original wording to the introduction of the rite had suggested 'seriously ill', but this was not accepted by the Vatican. It is in fact the actual working pastoral rule of thumb.

While this section speaks of the repetition of anointing when the sick person recovers and falls ill again, or if the condition becomes more serious, and permits anointing before surgery or when an elderly person is notably weakened, nothing is said about anointing young children or the mentally ill. This writer would include 'persons suffering from alcoholism and drug abuse, noticeable depression, and other psychological problems such as discouragement and scrupulosity'.[2] Today, pastoral sensitivity requires that we consider offering the sacrament to those who are handicapped if they so desire.[3]

What the text says about repeated anointing may be good as far as it goes, but it offers no help for a contemporary problem, that of indiscriminate anointing. Although the older practice of extreme unction was pastorally and theologically unsound, it was simple to judge the time of administration. 'Seriously ill' or 'danger of death' introduces a necessary vagueness. This is usually problematic on the occasion of communal anointing when all people who feel they are in need of anointing are invited to come forward. Such a practice can only reinforce a magical approach to the sacrament, which is probably the last thing intended by those who hold these services. But when hundreds step forward for anointing, it is doubtful that the experience is in a larger context of pastoral care. And without such a context, the rite of anointing itself becomes deprived of that which gives it its meaning and purpose, and which would rescue it from any merely formal instrumentalism.

The following sub-section of this second section is devoted to the minister of the sacrament. It briefly restates the present discipline that only bishops and priests can anoint. It quite rightly calls upon all pastors to contribute to a meaningful celebration of the rite and to instruct the faithful on this sacrament. It encourages the sick to call a priest and to prepare themselves to receive this sacrament in community.

This is, of course, nothing but a restatement of the present legislation. The ordinary ministers are the bishop, the pastor of the sick and elderly persons, religious superiors, and priests who work in hospitals. While this rule makes sense in terms of to whom the responsibility is entrusted, it is increasingly unrealistic in application because of a scarcity of ordained ministers. As is true of so much in regard to the sacrament of anointing, one can only wonder what may be the value of restating this position. Although one would hardly expect the *Catechism* to call for the extension of the ministry of this sacrament to others such as deacons, sisters, brothers, and many lay people involved with the sick and elderly, still it would have been appropriate to refer to those people who help create the larger sacramental context of anointing, since they too are ministers of this sacrament in a real sense. At the present time they are not permitted to do the actual anointing. But they most probably are doing most of the ministry connected with the sick and elderly. It is a distortion to reduce sacramental ministry here to the one who applies the oil, especially when, as is so often the case, the priest comes into this whole process for only a few minutes, having had little or no contact earlier, and possibly having no further contact. If the sacrament is to be seen in terms of the larger context, then some recognition of those who counsel and comfort the sick and elderly should be acknowledged. In the history of the Church the administration of this sacrament was not always confined to presbyters, and hopefully the official Church will see its way to further change, or, even better, will recapture a more authentic tradition of extending the full ministry of anointing to those who are not ordained presbyters. The *Catechism* gives the impression that such is not even a possibility. The catchesis should speak of ministry here in broader terms. If one of the purposes of the *Catechism* is to serve as a basis for the teaching in the Church, then some mention of the broader ministry would be appropriate.

While the *Catechism* says that 'only priests (bishops and presbyters) are ministers of the Anointing of the Sick', Trent said that the priest alone is the *proper* minister of this sacrament.[4] Trent's wording is actually preferable, because it leaves open the possibility that, while the priest is the ordinary minister of the sacrament, there can be extraordinary ministers of anointing.

The movement away from the practice of self-anointing as well as lay anointing which existed in the Church until the eighth and ninth centuries was connected with the view that tied the sacrament to the forgiveness of sins. Now that we have loosened that relationship and no longer view anointing as the last sacrament, a more inclusive view (at least in theory at the present time) seems called for in a document which is to serve the teaching ministry of the Church.

In section III of Article 5 we find three paragraphs which deal with how this sacrament is to be celebrated. It clearly states that anointing is liturgy and therefore communal. It may take place in the family home, in a hospital or in church, and is most appropriately situated within the eucharist. It may be preceded by penance and followed by the eucharist, as the eucharist is the last sacrament of our lives, our viaticum.

Although this section is relatively brief, it is the one most in need of catechesis, because it also refers to the pastoral practice regarding this sacrament. As is the case with all sacraments and liturgy, if they are to achieve their purpose in Christian life, the catechesis will need to be effective. There is a particular need here because it is impossible to catechise effectively those already sick or debilitated by old age. Adequate teaching will be to the community still well and in some vigour of life.

Such catechesis may well begin with the rites themselves, but rites which are placed in a larger framework. This context has many dimensions. The most significant aspect is a changed attitude on the part of Christians regarding sickness, that being 'ill in the Church' has a salvational character to it. Sickness can be neither treated as a meaningless and unfortunate event in one's life nor as something which can be fully explained in medical categories. Therefore, the sick will be seen as contributing to the healing ministry of the Church. When the local community indicates its interest in the sick and elderly, praying for their recovery, then those anointed will have a more authentic experience of what is claimed in their prayers. Especially in regard to this sacrament, catechesis will often take the form of pastoral visitations, public celebrations in church, and home liturgies with families and care-givers.

It is not even implied in the *Catechism* that the renewed rite of anointing has changed the image of the priest and the meaning of his presence in this situation. He is no longer to be seen as the harbinger of death, as death personified. He is the presence of the community to the person anointed, so that all may grasp more profoundly the meaning of sickness, old age and death. Because he is a symbol of the ministering community, there is more to the celebration than the act of anointing with oil. More than touching them momentarily with oil, the priest must touch the individual with his whole being so that he may serve as a connecting point between the sick or elderly person and the other members of the community, both well and marginal.

What is implied in the *Catechism*'s brief statement regarding the celebration of anointing is the importance of when the priest needs to become involved. What takes place in the last moments of death or when the person is already unconscious or in the inevitable emergency-room situations can hardly be described as liturgy. More than anything, the regular practice of communal anointing will help alleviate this problem. But congregations need to be reminded about the appropriateness of anointing by a priest when a person is confined to a home because of serious illness, is elderly or weak, or is immobile because of something like arthritis. Another situation would be where a person is dying, probably from old age or an extended illness, and may have already been anointed. The repetition of anointing is appropriate. And when anointing is not called for, as in the case of someone recovering from disease or surgery, or when someone has died, the visit by the priest or parish staff is still very much in order. Other ministrations are possible. It is a serious shortcoming that the *Catechism* does not deal with the fullness of the sacrament, but continues to see it confined to the ritual of anointing itself.

Perhaps the greatest implication of the acknowledgement that anointing is liturgy is that it places it firmly in a faith context. There is no more justification to treat it as something magical. It is prayer. It is an act of thanksgiving for what God is proclaiming to the Christian community through this person. It is an appeal for healing on many different levels in the human person. Faith contextualises the healing. Faith does not produce it. And faith is not in competition with the medical profession. Perhaps the greatest task regarding the implementation of this sacrament is the conversion of attitudes on the part of so many concerning what they think this sacrament is about.

The rite of the sacrament itself is not contained in Article 5, even in brief. The *Catechism* notes only that there is a service of word and sacrament with a rite of reconciliation at the beginning. It mentions what it would consider the significant elements of the rite: the priests lay hands on the sick in silence, they pray over them with the proper invocation, they anoint with oil. The section ends with the quizzical statement: 'These liturgical actions indicate what grace this sacrament confers.' Is this one grace? Many graces? Do the texts of individual parts of the rite indicate a specifically different grace? As the statement stands, it is doubtful that it can do more than leave the reader bewildered.

As is characteristic of post-Vatican II liturgical revisions, the rite is to be celebrated in different settings. This only emphasises that it is the pastoral care of the sick and elderly which indicates the meaning and purpose of this sacrament, and not the actual anointing itself. It may be that individual anointings are more frequent in most pastoral situations, but the norm remains the communal celebration. Thus, any implementation of the rite should envision that others are present at the ceremony. It is still true that for the sacrament to be effective, the celebration must be well done. If truncated celebrations are unavoidable because of circumstances, it is all the more necessary to have others which make full use of the symbols so that the liturgy remains an action expressive of the Church. Services of healing and other liturgies which make a connection with anointing can be helpful in moving this sacrament out of the hospital emergency room into the larger context of the ministry to the sick and elderly in the Church. The symbols of anointing should speak like artistic symbols through which people can touch more deeply their feelings, joys, doubts, and fears. Although it may be too restrictive to see anointing only as a sacrament of healing, it is at least that, and its symbols should be allowed to function in a healing way.

Anointing takes place outside of Mass or during Mass. When there is no eucharistic celebration, the introductory rites contain a sprinkling with holy water and a penitential rite. After the liturgy of the word, the rite of anointing itself moves through several elements: litany, laying on of hands, prayer over the oil, anointing prayer after anointing, and Lord's Prayer. There is usually a liturgy of holy communion and then the concluding rites.

In the rite during Mass, the reception of the sick replaces the sprinkling with holy water, and the Lord's Prayer is in its usual place. 1518 says that 'word and sacrament form an indivisible whole'. This means that whatever the circumstances, some proclamation of the word is in order, even if it must be minimal. There may not be a formal homily, but personal expressions and comments in the liturgy should convey what is the theology of anointing and the biblical understanding of this ministry.

What may be helpful is for the priest to have a good acquaintance with the James 5:13–16 text so that he can choose a sentence or phrase to emphasise. It would not be appropriate to exegete the entire text. For instance, one could take verse 15a: 'And the prayer of faith will save the sick person.' Here the connection between the prayer of faith and healing could be brought to light using instances from Scripture. The minister could bring out that this is more than the prayer of the faithful person. It is one uttered *in the name of the Lord*. The prayer arises not only from the trusting believer, but from the whole Christian community. The prayer is offered by the priest (and those present) in the name of the Church. The efficacy of the prayer, as in all prayer, is due to Christ, but in this instance the believing community is also exercising its ministry of worship based upon its baptismal status.

What is meant by 'will save' in this text? It implies all the biblical notions of salvation such as grace, justice, freedom from sin, and peace. It surely means the breaking of the power of sin and its historical manifestations such as are found in disease and death. It is embodied salvation, not purely spiritual or corporeal, not simply invisible grace or a charismatic physical healing. It means a disposition of the spirit which is open to the word of God. But especially as depicted in James, salvation in the larger flow of Jesus' healing ministry means that the healing is actually conditioned by the faith of those who are healed. The woman with a haemorrhage (Mt 9:22; Mk 5:34; Lk 8:48), the blind man (Mk 10:52), and the ten lepers (Lk 17:19) are all instances of healings based on faith. Whatever healing of the body takes place is a sign of Christ's power over the kingdom of darkness. The effect of the prayer is the same as that of the act of anointing: victory over sin and its accompanying effects such as old age. But victory is not the same as physical cure or personal immortality.

The rite begins with the laying on of hands, the basic sacramental gesture. It demonstrates love for the person; it is a sacramental caress; it is a symbol of the community's care for the person. It is regrettable that the Vatican cannot see its way to permit all those present to engage in this action. With the accompanying silence such an action helps to render this a time of compassion for the sick whereby the faith of the person anointed and of the community becomes visible.

The oil used in the rite may have been previously blessed at the chrism Mass. Times will arise when it may be more pastorally helpful to bless the oil in the liturgy of anointing. It will be a matter of judgement whether a particular need or situation supersedes the usual value of maintaining the connection with the bishop. In any event, the symbol of oil should have its full value. This requires enough oil to anoint liberally, an appropriate container, and an aesthetically pleasing setting. Oil should be seen, felt, and smelled. The anointing itself should not be limited to a sign of the cross. For those who are to receive the eucharist, anointing on the back of the hands rather than the palms is the more logical thing to do. Other parts of the body besides the forehead and hands can be anointed. It is worth noting that the formula used to accompany the anointing does not have the strong penitential character of the previous rite. The ritual offers numerous prayers to correspond to the particular situation of the person anointed, such as before surgery or for a young person.

In many ways this is one of the more successful ritual reforms of Vatican II, because it is relatively simple and flexible, open to the adaptations which will be required. The minister would be untrue to the rite if he treated it out of a mentality of a new kind of rubricism. Above all else, this is liturgy; it is prayer. It should be as fully human as possible. Hopefully, the ministers of this sacrament will be comfortable with silence and non-verbal symbols which work best with the sick and elderly. The use of oil will be meaningless if the minister has not communicated the meaning of life and Christian hope in the midst of suffering. It is an empty rite unless the person anointed can minister to the larger Church in some way.

In the fourth section of Article 5 four effects of the celebration of the sacrament are elaborated. The first is a gift of the Holy Spirit of 'strengthening, peace and courage to overcome the difficulties . . . of serious illness or the frailty of old age'. The Holy Spirit is the help in these times of temptation to discouragement and despair as one faces death or its possibility. 1520 affirms the traditional teaching that this sacrament forgives sin. A second effect is union with the passion of Christ. Through this configuration to Christ's passion, suffering achieves a new meaning, a more transcendent one. The third effect is ecclesial grace. This is what the sick and elderly give to the rest of the Church. Basically, what is affirmed here is that the Church prays for those anointed, and they in turn pray for the Church (or perhaps, in accord with the *Catechism*'s mentality, merit grace for the Church). The final effect refers to those situations where the sacrament is given to those who are dying, or as the *Catechism* in referring to the Council of Trent puts it: 'The sacrament of those departing'. What baptism began, anointing concludes. There is an anointing in both sacramental rites. In baptism we are sealed to new life, in confirmation we are strengthened for life's struggles, and in anointing itself we are fortified at the end of life 'like a solid rampart for the final struggles before entering the Father's house'.

The original ambiguity of Trent and Vatican II is still present here. It is as if there are two sacraments, one for the dying and one for the sick and elderly, and they have been conflated. Fortunately, the *Catechism* does not overstate the removal of sin as an effect. And since it shies away from any reference to physical well-being or cure, it avoids the dichotomy between the spiritual and the physical. It seems to have cast its lot with the position which opts for primarily spiritual effects of the sacrament.

This kind of theological isolationism is, however, not very helpful, for a recovered sense of the incarnate nature of the human person keeps together these various dimensions and calls for a more synthetic experience of this sacrament. In that sense, one cannot opt for two kinds of effects, physical and spiritual, or for one or the other. There is only one effect of anointing, because a whole undivided person is anointed. It is not that the sacrament affects the soul in one way and the body in another.

The traditional theological approach did try to frame a more holistic view. Sickness consumes the whole person and becomes an obstacle to a person's spiritual growth. There are the ever-present fears of the unknown and loss of meaning. To raise the question of the significance of life is to produce anxiety. Anointing is to assist the person in their growth towards God. What this means is that grace permeates the body, mind and imagination so that the person has the strength and peace to move to greater freedom.

While the *Catechism* in the spirit of Trent and Vatican II does not claim physical healing to be a primary effect of this sacrament, one can ask whether physical healing can be an effect of this sacrament in any sense. For many people the healing of anointing is confused with charismatic healings. But the sacrament is more about the pastoral care of the sick and the elderly. It is not aimed at individual therapeutic results. From the beginning of the Church, the power of physical healing has been seen as a gift, a charism not attached to office or sacramental rite.

A way of seeing the effects of anointing as unified or as holistic would be to understand it as that special liturgy of the Church which is directed specifically to those who are *sick in the Church*. They constitute an identifiable group. Just as life in the Church is of a particular kind, so is being sick and elderly in the Church. Sickness and old age are part of the mystery of human evil, and this sacrament brings the power of Christ to such situations. It is an instance of the Church focusing the power of Christ on a limit situation, a Christian in need. With or without a physical healing, what the Christian who is anointed and the Church as a whole pray for is a spiritual authority over sickness and old age.

Almost always the effects of anointing have been seen in terms of the individual Christian who is anointed. But since sacraments of the Church are the way the Christian community maintains its identity, the effects should be applied to the community also. That is, this sacrament is effective when the community hears the proclamation that there is more here than disease or death, that the passage through sickness, old age and death can be made without fear, that we are not alone in these situations, and that salvation is found in personal self-integration and reconciliation with others and with ourselves.

Although one would not expect the *Catechism* to engage in theological speculation, if it is to be pastorally useful it should offer some directions that affect pastoral practice and preaching. An approach which would look at this sacrament from a different perspective, and which broadens the notion of the effects of anointing, is one developed by this author some years ago:

> Anointing can also be that sacrament which recognizes that there is a special vocation in the Church of the sick and the aged.
> Anointing is the ritualization of that vocation. This sacrament is a celebration of the fact that because of Christianity the sick and old person who is fragmented can be brought back together again. It is

an articulation of the truth that by dying to oneself, by being the kind of marginal human being a sick and old person is, one opens oneself to a far greater wholeness. In turn, the sick and old person who is anointed, as well as the rite itself, speaks to the Church, reminding it that there is a deeper meaning to sickness and old age than what can be explained by the medical and psychological professions. Thus, those anointed minister to the rest of the Church who are well and in the fullness of life. They are called to proclaim that sickness and old age need not be a threat to their fellow Christians whose lives need not be characterized by fragmentation. The sacrament of anointing removes the ambiguity from those endless situations in daily living which bring salvation. The salvational aspect of sickness and old age may be obscure, but it is the liturgy of anointing which can show them for what they are: real events of personal triumph over the past and present, and representations of growth toward new life.[5]

In this perspective anointing is joined with baptism, orders, and marriage as a vocational sacrament and a rite of passage. This theological approach takes the emphasis away from the preparation for death, and sees sickness and old age as liminal experiences of growth. The anointed are those who are in the cracks of the social structure. Our ordinary status roles cannot countenance these marginal people. Anointing is a liminal liturgy because sickness and old age are liminal. As a rite of passage the sacrament of anointing ritualises first a separation, usually from ordinary life patterns, secondly, an ambiguous situation which is their present disease or weakness, and thirdly, a reintegration. This third may include a more intense community integration, a renewed understanding of one's life, or deeper union with God. Anointing both removes the ambiguity regarding sickness and old age and proclaims the ministry of the sick and elderly to the whole Church.

The final section devotes two paragraphs to 'Viaticum, the last sacrament of the Christian'. To receive the eucharist (and it mentions both body and blood) at the time of death has its own special significance. It is the sacrament of the passover of Christ from death to life, and so also for the Christian it is the 'seed of eternal life and the power of resurrection'. This article closes appropriately with the observation that just as we begin our Christian lives with baptism, confirmation, and eucharist, so we close them with penance, anointing, and the eucharist. These latter bring to a close our earthly journey.

As is the case with anointing, there are two main forms for viaticum, during Mass and outside of Mass. In most pastoral situations the administration of viaticum during a eucharistic celebration would be considered an ideal but not the normal occurrence. It is, however, clearly the norm. There will be times when such is possible even in a hospital-room setting. Probably the rite outside of Mass will be the more common experience. This is structured in a way similar to the ordinary rite of communion of the sick. There are introductory rites (sprinkling with holy water, instruction, penitential rite., etc.), a liturgy of the word with the baptismal profession of faith and a litany, the liturgy of viaticum, and the concluding rites which close with the sign of peace.

In practice viaticum has been restored to its position as the final sacrament. It is now more clearly seen as a final rite of passage. Again (as is the case even more so for anointing) families should not delay in calling a minister to bring viaticum. Neither sacrament can be well celebrated when the person is preoccupied with all the instruments of intensive-care units or is unconscious. There are three elements of the viaticum liturgy which emphasise that this is a sacrament of the dying: (1) a renewal of baptismal promises, (2) the plenary indulgence formula which states 'May almighty God free you from all punishments in this life and in the life to come', and (3) the possibility of reception of the eucharist under both kinds, the fullness of the symbol.

Francis J. Buckley SJ, in a review of the *Catechism of the Catholic Church*, makes a number of observations which have relevance for this commentary on Article 5.[6] Many of his comments on the *Catechism* in general are verified in this writer's critique of the article on the sacrament of anointing. For instance, he remarks 'It is not designed to be used directly with children or adults ... It makes no pretence of adaptation to age or culture.' In the case of Article 5, this means that such a bare-bones presentation of doctrine with references to the Bible and church documents is not helpful on the level of ordinary catechesis, liturgical theology, or pastoral practice. One can only ask: For whom is the article on anointing written? It has all been stated elsewhere, and in more appropriate contexts.

'Its use of scripture is not kerygmatic: the Bible is not the source of the teaching but is confirmation of some doctrines already decided upon.' As is the case with the whole *Catechism*, the scriptural texts relevant to anointing are not given in full, and they are treated as footnotes to be checked if someone needs further confirmation. There is no indication that a solid hermeneutic underlies the selection of texts except that they are the 'usual' ones.

There is no distinction of what is central to this sacrament, what is peripheral, although it may well be that Article 5 offends in this area less than in other parts of the *Catechism*. In fact Buckley remarks: 'Its treatment of anointing of the sick is quite pastoral.' Given the reservations regarding the pastoral applicability of Article 5, one can only wonder what the pastoral orientation of the rest of the document is like.

'The *Catechism* is reluctant to admit diversity or doubt in anything.' There is not the slightest hint that the celebration of anointing would be different in different cultural settings or that the ministry of this sacrament might be more fully extended. When Buckley says that the *Catechism* could have been written before the Second Vatican Council, with references to the Council added later, one can apply that to Article 5, although there is the obvious updating of the name from *extreme unction* to the *anointing of the sick*. However, although Article 5 may well be one of the least problematic parts of the *Catechism*, it still presents that pre-Vatican II mentality of unchangeableness in matters sacramental. The feel of Article 5 is that it need not depend on ordinary human experience to authenticate what it claims. As Buckley puts it: 'Its approach is too dry, too rational, too cold.' When Buckley states that the *Catechism* 'is not another step forward but a retreat to the classic approach', one must agree that although the article on anointing would escape many of the criticisms of the *Catechism* in general, it is still vulnerable to this one.

Two examples of this distressing situation are the absences of the relationship of anointing to social justice and the significance of a theology of anointing for understanding the human body. These are not optional aspects of the Christian message, and deserve a place in a document which claims to be a compendium of that message.

Since in anointing we ritualise the Christian's passage to Christ, it must include that life which made it possible for humankind to be free of injustice and oppression. An aspect of Christ's healing ministry is that he is a vindicator of the poor and that through our sacramental life there is released in our world the new energy of humanising love and mutual concern. Anointing is but another way in which the community of Christ comes to visible expression, this time in terms of overcoming the destructive forces and situations which stand in the way of a more human life.

The sacrament of anointing is the Church as counter-cultural, calling into question the presuppositions of our society not only about sickness and old age but also about the meaning of personal fulfilment and the good life.

The laying on of hands and the anointing with oil embody another counter-cultural aspect of the sacrament. Such embodied gestures claim the anointed from their situation of isolation and fragmentation. But more, they symbolise human presence and community bonding. They state clearly that the body beautiful is not the one of magazine covers and inserts, or of TV deodorant commercials, but the one that has been touched humanly and can touch humanly in return. That what is supposed to be the *Catechism of the Catholic Church* finds no place for social justice, the body, the mission of the Church, or the way Christ is incarnate today can only leave the reader bewildered and sad. The real catechism of the Roman Catholic Church is still to be done, for as Lawrence S. Cunningham observes:

> It desperately needs a prophetic edge to its prose and a narrative
> style that would relieve its unremitting plodding assertiveness. It
> is, alas, the work of intelligent clerical theologians (did any lay
> persons have a hand in its formulation?) written for the higher
> clergy with an eye on Rome and not on the faithful of the world.[7]

Notes

1   Works which deal with anointing at some depth, both theoretically and
     pastorally, would include: James L. Empereur SJ, *Prophetic Anointing*
     (Collegeville, MN: The Liturgical Press, Michael Glazier, 1982); Peter Fink SJ
     (ed.), *Alternative Futures for Worship*, vol 7: *Anointing of the Sick*
     (Collegeville: The Liturgical Press, 1987); and Charles Gusmer, *You Visited
     Me: Sacramental Ministry to the Sick and Dying* (Collegeville: The Liturgical
     Press, 1984).
2   Empereur, *Prophetic Anointing*, p. 106.
3   For a full treatment on the relationship of the sacrament of anointing and the
     handicapped see James L. Empereur, 'Anointing and the handicapped', *The
     Way* 25.2 (April 1985).
4   DS 1719.
5   Empereur, *Prophetic Anointing*, pp. 141–2.
6   Francis J. Buckley SJ, *National Jesuit News* (March 1993), pp. 6, 9. Father
     Buckley is a professor of theology at the University of San Francisco who has
     written extensively on catechesis.
7   Lawrence S. Cunningham, *Commonweal* (12 March 1993), p. 11.

The Sacrament of Orders

(Paragraphs 1533–1600)

Philip J. Rosato SJ

Gregorian University, Rome

Before offering detailed observations on Part Two, Section Two, Chapter Three, in which Orders is presented as a sacrament in service of ecclesial communion, this commentary opens with some general remarks, both critical and constructive in kind. This procedure is deemed necessary since the treatment of Orders, despite the alleged intention of its editors to centre on one of the prominent themes of Vatican II, rests on certain unstated theological and historical premises which grievously impede it from showing that this sacrament indeed serves genuine unity in the Church. Moreover, since it appears that the editors purposely disregard other equally important conciliar motifs such as collegiality *ad intra* and evangelisation *ad extra*, the article on Orders is a text both conceptually inadequate and spiritually uninspiring. This critical observation is made for no other reason than to safeguard the dynamic nature of the theology of Orders in the Catholic tradition itself, which has repeatedly proven to be adaptable in the face of the changing religious self-consciousness and pastoral needs of the faithful throughout the centuries.

These general remarks are also meant to be constructive, since they aim at correcting the subtle impression, created by the questionable premises underlying the text, that all loyal Catholic theologians should advocate that the structure of sacred ministry be restricted in every respect to its present contours. However, no truly Catholic presentation of Orders should be based on opposition to its further efficacious development as a prophetic stimulus not only of communion, but also of collegiality and of evangelisation. Thus, the constructive criticism of this commentary entails indicating at the very start the restrictive presuppositions of the editors, and complementing them with more suitable ones. Once having been made aware of other premises which counterbalance the narrow scope and negative tone of the text, contemporary readers might better appreciate its positive affirmations. These will deservedly be highlighted in the course of the detailed remarks to follow.

The questionable premises of this article of the *Catechism* can be

303

illustrated by means of pairs of contrasting approaches, the first of which are adopted in the actual text on Orders, and the second of which are suggested here as complementary ones which would render it more precise regarding theological content, and more acute regarding pastoral insight. These premises concern:

1. Methodology: a deductive manner of reasoning prevails throughout, rather than one which begins with induction deriving from the universal phenomenon of religious leadership, and only then exposes the inherent credibility of the data of Scripture and Tradition concerning ecclesial ministry. The result of the method employed in the *Catechism* is that no effort whatsoever is made by the editors to allude to the anthropological and sociological bases of statements found in the Christian sources with regard to the necessity and function of Orders as a service both of the internal unity and of the external mission of the Church.

2. Trinitarian theology: a Christological viewpoint, modified by few pneumatological and doxological considerations, constrains the editors to ground Orders only in the second article of the Creed, and thus to obviate the essential trinitarian dimension of this sacrament. No reference is made to the Father–Creator who first sends the Son–Redeemer on the temporally circumscribed mission of becoming the definitive prophet, priest and pastor of humanity. Nor is it then explained how the Father through the Son initiates the temporally continuous mission of the Spirit–Sanctifier who grants charisms to all members of the priestly people, and to the ordained who are chosen from its midst, in order to animate its evangelical, sanctifying and pastoral task in the world.

3. Ecclesiology: a juridical concept of the Church and of the sacrament of Orders dominates the text, rather than a missiological and eschatological one which, while respecting the advisability of some uniform legislation, does not repress the fundamental connection between this sacrament and the prophetic nature of the Church. In the actual text, some major themes of the theology of Orders advocated by Vatican II remain unmentioned, such as the role of the ordained in urging the faithful to discern more effective forms of lay ministry by which to inaugurate in history a foretaste of the Kingdom. Instead, an excessive concern is manifested for the role of the ministerial priesthood in assuring internal discipline and obedience on the part of the faithful. Thus the recent prophetic declarations and actions of bishops, presbyters and deacons in diverse cultures, which have led to persecution and even to martyrdom, are passed over in silence.

4. Development of dogma: a biased rather than objective stance is taken in the text with regard to the various culturally and pastorally conditioned forms which Orders has assumed in the past, and may assume in the future. These forms have hitherto been determined, as the magisterium, guided by the Spirit of Christ, was challenged to acknowledge and empower new ministries in a given place which corresponded to the problems of inculturating the gospel there. Similarly, as the Church becomes an ever more universal phenomenon, reliance on the principle of the organic development of dogma could

enable innovative forms of ordained ministry to be approved which would facilitate dialogue and collaboration with the diverse religious leaders of the globe.

Considered altogether, the questionable premises underlying the presentation of Orders in the *Catechism* reveal the constricted theological and historical understanding of its editors who claim to articulate a contemporary view of this sacrament without reference to the similarities between the epochal conceptual and spiritual shift occurring in ordained ministry since Vatican II, and other such shifts which took place in previous periods of ecclesiastical history. Instead, the editors seem to reject the thesis that the present transition in ordained ministry will be complete only when every ecclesial community has ordained members sufficient in number, and truly representative of its diversity of gender, culture and charism, so as credibly to carry out its prophetic mission in society. The presentation of Orders in the *Catechism* refers neither to the present lack of ordained persons in the Church, nor to the existence of many communities which as a result do not have regular contact with sacramentally authorised preachers, liturgical leaders and pastors. Surely, the impression of being indifferent to the psychological and spiritual sufferings of many Catholics who are affected by the current shift in ordained ministry was not intentional on the part of the editors.

Nonetheless, this impression can legitimately be perceived as the by-product of their prevailing concern both to placate those who lament the demise of the so-called traditional model of ministry, and to restrain those who press for imminent resolution of the pastoral harm caused by the shortage of ordained ministers. Even if it is granted that a middle course between the extreme theological positions of classicists and revisionists had to be taken by the editors of the *Catechism*, it can be said that the manner in which they did so is deprived of anthropological reflection, pneumatological and doxological content, missiological and eschatological orientation, and historical objectivity.

Since the detailed remarks which follow intertwine positive and critical observations, it should be stated here that the standards used in formulating them are not arbitrary. Not only the pronouncements of Vatican II with regard to Orders but also the post-conciliar theological literature on its various dimensions and prospects provide sound criteria by which to judge whether a faithful yet progressive comprehension of ecclesial ministry is achieved by the *Catechism*. In order to summarise what has been indicated in these general remarks, it can be observed that the *Catechism* underscores chiefly the ontological affirmations on Orders as found in the documents of the Council, to a lesser degree treats those that are existential, and for the most part omits those that are practico-social and eschatological.

Furthermore, biblical and historical research has resulted in an understanding of Orders as both a constant and a flexible reality in the life and mission of the Church. Constant, because its principal purpose of fostering the faith, the holiness and the apostolate of the common priesthood has remained unchanged for two millennia. Flexible because, before and after being determined by the triad bishop—presbyter—deacon, it has repeatedly assumed, and then often abandoned, different forms of actualising itself. This combined constancy and flexibility guarantees that its unique and eschatological dimensions can effectively adjust to the religious needs of the faithful on the one hand, and to their cultural situations on the other.

Detailed remarks

1533–1535. Here Orders is defined, along with marriage, as a sacrament in service of ecclesial communion. The essentially diaconal understanding of the existence and the function of the ordained in the Church is rightly accentuated at the start, and the sanctifying grace received by them is not detached from their service of building up the People of God. Thus, the personal salvation of the ordained is said to be achieved through their mission on behalf of the communion of the faithful, that is, of the baptised and confirmed. The stress placed by the editors on the intra-ecclesial aspect of ministry is announced in the *Catechism* when, in 1535, a phrase from *Lumen Gentium* regarding Orders is cited, so as to explain this sacrament as a form of consecration in Christ's name 'to feed the Church by the word and the grace of God' (LG 11).

Yet, as laudable as this accent on intra-ecclesial service is, it limits the social impact of Orders by not emphasising that the ordained receive a prophetic calling which contributes, along with the similar calling of the baptised and confirmed, to the evangelisation of the world. It would be quite misleading to maintain that the ordained serve the inner communion of the Church while the faithful alone render it the universal sign of salvation for the world. Left unmentioned in the *Catechism*, therefore, is the missiological and public function of the ordained which is pointedly expressed in the section of *Presbyterorum Ordinis* dedicated to pastoral service. The prophetic and cultic actions of presbyters, so as to be sincere and thorough, 'must lead to various works of charity and mutual help, as well as to missionary activity and to the different forms of Christian witness' (PO 6). Furthermore, a public mission among the socially marginalised is explicitly assigned to the ordained: 'Although they have obligations toward all people, the presbyters have the poor and the lowly entrusted to them in a special way. The Lord himself showed that he was united to them, and the fact that the Gospel was preached to them is mentioned as a sign of messianic activity' (PO 6). Only at the very end of the presentation on Orders is it asserted that the ordained should manifest 'gratuitous love for all and a preferential love for the poor, the sick and the needy' (1586).

1536-1538. In these paragraphs the predominantly Christocentric and juridical approach to the presentation of Orders in the *Catechism* becomes quite noticeable. Here the incomparable achievement of Christ in instituting the Church as an eschatological reality seems far to surpass the continuous work of the Holy Spirit in directing it to its fullness in the Kingdom. This remark does not mean in any way to deny the fundamental truth of the opening statement of 1536: 'Holy Orders is the sacrament through which the mission entrusted by Christ to his apostles continues to be exercised in the Church until the end of time.' Yet in this text Christ alone is said to have been active in initiating the mission of the twelve and in establishing the Church, as if the Holy Spirit who guided his ministry and who was bestowed on his apostles at Pentecost were not equally active in inspiring them to take up their mandate and thus to determine and animate the life of the Church.

In fact, the Holy Spirit is referred to only in a secondary manner in this section when, in 1538, Orders is described as conferring 'a gift of the Holy Spirit'. This gift is then immediately interpreted in Christocentric and juridical terms, since it 'permits the exercise of a "sacred power" (*sacra potestas*) which can come only from Christ himself through his Church'. Therefore, the 'sacred power' received through Orders is not primarily understood by the editors in pneumatological and liturgical terms, that is, as a self-bestowal of the Holy Spirit on the ordained through the sacramental laying on of hands by the bishop. The absence of these insights explains why ministry is not presented in the *Catechism* as an enduring eschatological empowerment for the charismatic service both of the unity of the Church and of the transformation of the world according to the values of Christ. Even though the editors refer to the gift of the Holy Spirit, 'sacred power' is conceived by them as an authorisation of the ordained by Christ that is granted not through the liturgical rite of Orders, but through the juridical act of the college of bishops as represented by the local ordinary. The result of the ambiguity of 1538 is that Orders is *de facto* treated in the *Catechism* as a canonical empowerment for intra-ecclesial governance.

The reason for the dominance of the Christocentric and juridical viewpoint in these paragraphs becomes clear when the text forcefully asserts that ordination 'goes beyond a simple *election, designation, delegation* or *institution* by the community' (1538). The editors want to ensure that the baptised and confirmed, guided by the Holy Spirit, do not overestimate their part in approving who can or cannot be ordained. However, such a theological stance is not justified, since it contradicts the pneumatocentric and ecclesiocentric understanding of Orders which prevailed in the first millennium of the Church. For example, the editors make no mention of the fifth-century affirmation of Leo the Great: 'the one who is to preside over all ought to be chosen by all . . . no one should be consecrated bishop against the desire of Christians and without having been explicitly elected by them' (*Ad Anast.*, PL 54, 634). The lack of historical objectivity in these paragraphs of the *Catechism*, and the resulting emphasis on the Christocentric and juridical theology of the second millennium, causes the editors to omit the patristic tenet that the mature opinion of the baptised regarding the dignity of those to be ordained is considered a determining factor of Orders, since only recognised charismatic leaders are to be able to foster rather than disrupt ecclesial unity.

Because of its sparse references to the Holy Spirit, which are made chiefly in quotations of other documents, as in 1556, 1558, 1563 and 1587, the editors of the *Catechism* propose the view that the sacrament of Orders is effective solely because it was instituted by the incarnate Word for the sake of the unity of his followers. Yet the Gospels unambiguously state that Jesus the Christ was anointed, illumined and guided by the Pneuma of God, so as to carry out a unique messianic mission. Moreover, Jesus encouraged his disciples to trust fully in the pneumatic empowerment they would receive, so as to extend his unique mission to many people. In the Scriptures, therefore, the activity of the Holy Spirit inserts the ministries of Jesus and of the disciples within the history of salvation, and lends them a missiological and eschatological efficacy.

Invariably the text of the *Catechism* adheres, however, to the Christocentric and canonical scheme which can be designated by the sequence: Christ → Church → sacrament of Orders. This concept of sacred ministry validly underscores that each sacrament is salvific only in that it is an action of Christ and of the Church. Yet, in order to be interpreted in a biblical rather than juridical manner, this understanding should be completed by pneumatocentric and missiological elements, as is the case in the sequence: Christ → Spirit → sacrament of Orders → Church → world. Here the actions of Christ and the Spirit are viewed as enabling the liturgical celebration of the sacrament of Orders repeatedly to constitute and mission the Church as the universal sign of salvation for the world. If the text on Orders had included such intuitions, it would have been enhanced by the more balanced and dynamic trinitarian perspective. According to the latter, the concerted missions of the Logos and of the Pneuma call forth and consecrate prophetic leaders for the service of the unity and the apostolate of the baptised in order to signify how God the Creator, through the agents chosen by the Son and the Spirit, brings humanity to the fullness of salvation.

In this context it can be noted that the order of deaconesses is conspicuously absent from the list of former ecclesial ministries provided in 1537. At first this omission is particularly striking, because many contemporary theologians are advocating the restoration of this feminine ministry, which is described in a most favourable light in the New Testament, and which endured in the West until the eleventh century. Once again it seems that certain historical facts are not alluded to by the editors, lest they inadvertently support insistent calls for reform of the sacrament of Orders, and thus render the *Catechism* controversial rather than acceptable to those who do not desire any such development. Then, however, the failure to allude to the deaconesses becomes more intelligible when the text goes on to affirm that 'integration into one of these bodies in the Church was accomplished by a rite called *ordinatio*, a religious and liturgical act which was a consecration, a blessing or a sacrament' (1538).

The advocates of the restoration of the deaconesses can be most gratified by this statement, since they are often countered with the observation that the scarce historical evidence at hand does not warrant

308

the supposition that the deaconesses underwent a liturgical ordination, or consecration, which entailed the laying on of hands. In 1538, were the editors attempting, in an indirect way, to leave open the possibility of a future liturgical ritual or ordination for deaconesses, even though they had excluded them from the foregoing list of once extant orders? What is intended here is not exactly patent: a restricted historical stance appears to be juxtaposed to an unrestricted one. The attentive reader is therefore constrained to conclude that obfuscation of the essentially flexible structure of the sacrament of Orders accounts for the contradictory stances adopted by the editors.

1539–1545. Here the sacrament of Orders in the plan of salvation is treated under two headings: the priesthood of the old covenant, and the one priesthood of Christ. The editors strive to attain a balance between recognising the inherently sanctifying role of the priesthood of Aaron, the service of the Levites and the functions of the seventy elders, and admitting that these sacred ministries were prefigurements, 'powerless to bring about salvation' (1540), of the sacrifice of Jesus Christ and of the ordained ministry of the new covenant. This presentation is praiseworthy in the light of the Christian obligation to respect the revelation and call to holiness given by God to the chosen people of Israel, while at the same time affirming the uniqueness of Jesus Christ, the Saviour, as the fulfilment of this revelation and holiness. It is not initially clear, however, why the *Catechism* emphasises only the cultic functions of Hebrew religious leaders, and not their prophetic and pastoral ones as well, which are equally efficacious in bringing about salvation.

This decision of the editors to concentrate only on the cultic or sacrificial character of the Hebrew priesthood becomes evident only when their attention is then directed to Jesus and to the ministers of the new covenant: 'The redemptive sacrifice of Christ is unique, accomplished once for all; yet it is made present in the Eucharistic sacrifice of the Church. The same is true of the one priesthood of Christ; it is made present through the ministerial priesthood without diminishing the uniqueness of Christ's priesthood: "Only Christ is the true priest, the others being only his ministers"' (1545). Even if it is rightly pointed out this text that the cultic function of the ordained does not diminish the definitive nature of the sacrifice of Jesus Christ, but simply makes it present, the ministry of presiding at the Eucharist seems to overshadow that of preaching of the word which is its necessary precondition, and that of exercising pastoral love which is its indispensable criterion of sincerity. More than thirty years after a major council, which accentuated the triple functions of the ministry of Jesus Christ and of his followers — prophetic preaching, cultic gestures and pastoral care (PO 4–6) — it is legitimate for the contemporary reader to ask why the editors chose to describe Orders chiefly in terms only of one function.

Besides the predominance attributed to the sacrificial function of Hebrew and Christian priesthoods, the paragraphs under consideration are marked by another form of unilateral thinking. They do not state, even in a cursory manner, that the divine plan of salvation includes all the positive aspects of prophetic, cultic and pastoral leadership as practised for centuries, and in many cases still being carried on, by adherents to faith systems other than that of Israel. A brief treatment of this theme would not have required any speculative invention on the part of the editors, since the documents of Vatican II clearly indicate the salvific nature of other religions, and thus interpret the credal statement that the Holy Spirit 'has spoken through the prophets' in an inclusive rather than exclusive manner.

In *Lumen Gentium*, it is asserted that 'those also can attain to everlasting salvation who through no fault of their own do not know the gospel of Christ or his Church, yet sincerely seek God and, moved by grace, strive by their deeds to do his will as it is known to them through the dictates of conscience' (LG 16). An even more clear reference to the sacred duties performed by leaders of other religions is made in *Nostra Aetate*: 'The Catholic Church looks with sincere respect upon those ways of conduct and of life, those rules and teachings which, though differing in many particulars from what it holds and sets forth, nevertheless often reflect a ray of that Truth which enlightens all people' (NA 2). These texts might have helped the editors to have been more aware of the sensitivities of Christians whose forebears were led to divine truth and salvation by the grace bestowed on them through the mediation of the leaders of their indigenous religions.

In contrast to the decision of the editors not to include some inductive reasoning in the presentation of Orders, the Gospels attest how throughout his ministry Jesus appreciated the authenticity of the faith, hope and love exhibited by apparently godless Samaritans, Phoenicians and Romans who had nevertheless heeded the voices of their respective religious leaders. Thus, at the end of the century in which the magisterium is urging the faithful to undertake a new evangelisation among people everywhere who doubt the inherent truth and social relevance of Christianity, it is difficult to understand why the editors were content to make no reference to the continuity and discontinuity between Orders and other types of prophetic leadership. Despite its potential or proven ambiguity, such universal prophetic activity has the capacity to promote social cohesion and moral unity in various cultures, and to encourage greater dialogue with adherents of Christianity and of other religious traditions.

The option not to include such fundamental theological insights in the text on Orders renders its deductive thought-pattern inconsistent both with the tolerance advocated by Jesus and with the experience of contemporary Christians, many of whose relatives are not baptised. Of course, it might be objected that the editors could not have started with fundamental theology in each chapter of the *Catechism*, lest one theme after another would have had to be rooted in human experience, as if the logical connection with previously well-grounded statements were not evident. Yet the presentation of Orders under discussion is not useful to Christians engaged in dialogue with a religion other than that of Israel. This is the case, since the text of the *Catechism* does not furnish at least some initial and recurring reflections on the relationship of this sacrament to the universal phenomenon of religious prophecy. The latter is considered by many Catholic theologians as a constituent aspect of the human transcendentality which is facilitated and perfected by the Holy Spirit.

1546–1547. This section is among the most felicitous in the presentation of Orders, since it describes the relationship between it and the sacraments of baptism and confirmation by synthesising quite well what is one of the significant developments of dogma proposed by Vatican II, namely the interrelation of the two means of participating, common and ministerial, in the one priesthood of Christ. In 1546 the unilateral emphasis on the cultic mission of Christ the priest which was noted in 1544–1545 is corrected by the addition of references to his prophetic and regal or pastoral missions: 'The whole community of believers is, as such, priestly. The faithful exercise their baptismal priesthood through their participation, each according to his own vocation, in Christ's mission as priest, prophet and king.'

Particularly Spirit-centred and fraternal is the manner in which the distinction, as well as the correlation, between the common and the ministerial forms of partaking in the one priesthood of Christ is formulated in 1547:

> While the common priesthood of the faithful is exercised by the unfolding of baptismal grace — a life of faith, hope and charity, a life according to the Spirit, the ministerial priesthood is at the service of the common priesthood. It is directed at the unfolding of the baptismal grace of all Christians. The ministerial priesthood is a *means* by which Christ unceasingly builds up and leads his Church. For this reason it is transmitted by its own sacrament, the sacrament of Holy Orders.

In these phrases the balance between the Christocentric aspect (the Word grants the Church its form) and the pneumatocentric aspect (the Spirit grants the Church its vitality) of baptism, confirmation and Orders is properly maintained by the editors. Furthermore, this sub-section unambiguously affirms both the existential view of Orders as a self-giving service of the universal priesthood, and the dynamic role of baptism, confirmation and Orders in constituting the Church ever anew as the universal sacrament of salvation.

1548–1553. In these paragraphs the ordained are described as acting on behalf both of Christ the Head, and of the Church, his body. The mere fact is to be acclaimed that the editors attempt here to emphasise the two inextricable forms of representation which the ordained embody, and which the current debate on sacred ministry views as the paramount issue: the trans-historical form, since they symbolise the transcendent Head of the Church and thus act *in persona Christi*, and the historical form, since they symbolise the time-bound body of the Church and thus act *in persona Ecclesiae*. Yet, whereas the shortage of canonically acceptable candidates for Orders has caused the current debate to focus

311

on the urgent need to stress the ecclesial form of representation along with the Christological one, the editors seem intentionally to subordinate the former to the latter. They simply assert that the transcendent form is the prerequisite of the historical one: 'It is because the ministerial priesthood represents Christ that it can represent the Church' (1553). The result of this statement is that, under the appearance of being theologically correct, it in fact obscures the inherent interconnection between the two forms of representation. In other words, the editors do not raise the truly relevant question: If the corporate group of the ordained do not represent the Church as it actually exists, how can it be said authentically to symbolise its Head?

Once this major flaw is pointed out, it should be remarked that this sub-section contains one of the two truly candid references in the *Catechism* to the crisis or shift in ordained ministry presently facing the Church. Since the ordained are consecrated so as to make Christ 'visible in the community of believers' (LG 21) and to exercise his sacred power through them, the editors ask how it is to be explained that they are not 'preserved from all human weaknesses, the spirit of domination, error, even sin' (1550). In response, a pneumatological insight is offered: the power of the Holy Spirit does not guarantee all acts of ministers in the same way as it does their specifically sacramental ones, and thus their infidelity to the gospel can harm the apostolic efficacy of the Church.

In the course of accounting for the sinfulness of the ordained, reference is made to the frequent discrepancy between the objective, *ex opere operato*, dimension of their sacramental acts, and the complementary ethical, *ex opere operantis*, dimension. While such a distinction is valid, it should not be confined solely to the cultic functions of the ordained, but applied as well to their prophetic and pastoral ones. In any case, 1550, as well as 1584, do allude to the public disedification occasioned by those members of the clergy who do not attain the ideal integration of the objective and the ethical aspects of their ministry. Yet the text does not admit that during the present phase of the post-conciliar period many of the ordained must labour under extreme psychological and pastoral tension precisely because the sacrament of Orders is still not being received by a greater number of the faithful. The most that the editors seem to concede here when confronted with the crisis of ordained ministry is that they describe the 'sacred power' of Christ, in which the ordained share, in a far less juridical fashion than they did in 1538. The power of the ordained is not one of domination, but of love: 'the exercise of this authority must therefore be measured against the model of Christ, who by love made himself the least and the servant of all' (1551).

As indicated above, the treatment of the historical or ecclesial form of the representation which is inherent to the sacrament of Orders is so cautiously formulated that its theological impact for contemporary Catholics is greatly muted. After having briefly stated that the ordained act 'in the name of the whole Church' (1552), and after having decidedly restricted this representation to the eucharistic sacrifice, the editors do not elucidate this important theme in a more positive manner. Instead, they proceed in the next paragraph to explain what such representational action in the name of the whole Church does not imply. Here the inability of the editors to manifest a sound understanding of the development of dogma once again comes to the fore. Notwithstanding the fact that prominent Fathers of the Church advocated the right of the faithful to elect their sacred ministers, the following is boldly affirmed: "'In the name of the *whole* Church" does not mean that priests are the delegates of the community' (1553).

It is certainly true that, once the ordained are consecrated to preach the word of God, to preside at the liturgy and to promote the unity of the Church, they are bound to challenge their fellow believers with the truth of the gospel, whether it pleases them or not. However, to claim in the late twentieth century that those who act in the name of the faithful are in no way their delegates denies the anthropological principle underlying the concept of ministry prevalent in the first millennium: the Christian people will find obedience to sacred ministers repugnant if the latter are not perceived by them as their accepted delegates, even if their office necessitates that they often enunciate Christian teachings which place in question many of the cultural values and practices of their parishioners. This is not a twentieth-century opinion, based on an erroneous view of the Church as a democracy, but a perennial one, founded on the very criteria proposed for ecclesial leaders in the Scriptures and in Tradition.

1554-1574. In these paragraphs the treatment of the three grades of the sacrament of Orders — bishop, presbyter, deacon — can be said to mirror perfectly the ontological aspects of the doctrine of Vatican II, to mention in passing its existential aspects, but to overlook for the most part its practico-social and eschatological ones. In order to underscore that the conciliar statements rest on the ontically real distinctions between the three grades of the hierarchy, the editors cite those texts from *Lumen Gentium* which employ the term 'subordination'. The text concerning priests, which is quoted in 1564, states: 'Notwithstanding the fact that they depend on the bishops in the exercise of their own proper power, the priests are for all that associated with them by reason of their sacerdotal dignity' (LG 28); that concerning deacons, which is cited in 1569, reads: 'At a lower level of the hierarchy are to be found deacons, who receive the imposition of hands "not unto the priesthood, but unto the ministry"' (LG 29). The pronounced emphasis on this ontic concept of subordination is somewhat mitigated in the *Catechism*, as is far more the case in the documents of Vatican II, by references to the existential bond which unites the members of the hierarchy; this motif is accentuated in the following phrase: 'The bishop considers [the presbyters] his co-workers, his sons, his brothers and his friends' (1567).

It has already been pointed out previously in this commentary that the practico-social dimension of Orders, which Vatican II regards as Christ-like service of the most poor and weak in society, receives negligible attention in the *Catechism*. Thus, here it suffices to add that the intra-ecclesial understanding of the editors with regard to this sacrament

313

appears to exonerate the ordained from the task, to be achieved through word and action, of promulgating the social teaching of the Church. That the eschatological dimension of Orders, as found in the documents of Vatican II, is also scarcely treated in the *Catechism* is less comprehensible, since the conciliar texts in which it is articulated clearly refer to the unitative role of the ordained, and thus should have been perceived by the editors as in keeping with their central theme. A forceful example of the link between the service-centred and the future-orientated dimensions of pastoral ministry is the following: 'Exercising within the limits of their authority the function of Christ as Shepherd and Head, the presbyters gather together God's family as a brotherhood all of one mind, and lead them in the Spirit, through Christ to God the Father' (LG 28).

What is most noteworthy in the discussion of the three grades of Orders is the fact that the variegated history, and the still open future, of this sacrament are not adequately alluded to. This prudent silence contrasts with the innovative decision of Jesus to urge his male and female followers to assume humble forms of authoritative ministry which would alleviate the material and spiritual sufferings of people around them. This decision of Jesus was the basis for the subsequent practice of church leaders to share their authoritative service with others as need arose. The text on Orders does indeed provide some historical references to the gradual comprehension, on the part of the first Christians, of the difference between the Hebrew and the Christian concepts of priesthood (1544), to the many previously extant orders such as those of cate-chumens, virgins, spouses and widows (1537), and to the recent restoration of the permanent diaconate to which even married men might be admitted (1571). Yet these few selective references appear to ignore the sociological and pastoral problems underlying the current meta-morphosis of ministry in the Catholic Church, and that surely yet to occur. It is thus all too evident that the editors assume a cautious rather than courageous attitude to the essentially open question about how the sacrament of Orders may be structured in the future, as local bishops are empowered to discern which new ministries should share to some degree in the fullness of their priesthood.

1575–1580. This sub-section treats matters such as female ordination and priestly celibacy, which most members of the theological magisterium would not consider dogmatic issues, but canonical ones open to further revision as social conditions and pastoral needs change. Yet the editors, following the official magisterium, do not make such a clear distinction between matters of faith and matters of law, with the result that the question of female ordination seems linked inextricably to Christology, and that of priestly celibacy to eschatology. With regard to the first of these questions, it has already been pointed out that the deaconesses are not mentioned at all in the *Catechism*, although they constituted an order in the Church throughout the first millennium. Thus, the question of female ordination enters only towards the end of this treatment of Orders by means of the following sentences: 'The Lord Jesus chose men (*viri*) to form the college of the twelve apostles, and the apostles did the same when they chose collaborators to succeed them in their ministry . . . The Church recognizes herself to be bound by this choice made by the Lord himself. For this reason the ordination of women is not possible' (1577). The final phrase of this statement is ambiguous, since it seems to imply that females may not enter any of the three grades of Orders, whereas in fact they had already done so as deaconesses.

What is at issue here is whether or not the college of bishops is free to choose to share the fullness of its priesthood with women, in the same way it does with men. If in the present century the question of the gender of sacred ministers is being discussed as it has not been since the beginning of the second millennium, this fact alone does not justify defensive stances based on Christological tenets. That for more than a thousand years deaconesses carried out prophetic, cultic and pastoral functions, such as instructing and baptising female catechumens, is proof enough that formerly bishops deemed women worthy of sharing in their apostolic task of fostering ecclesial communion and service. That reflections similar to these are not provided by the *Catechism* at a time when many competent Catholic theologians are advocating the restoration of the order of deaconesses is a grave oversight.

Furthermore, in so categorically stating the argument that baptised women are excluded from episcopal, presbyteral and diaconal ordination because Jesus of Nazareth chose men alone as his disciples, the editors reveal that they were not permitted to engage in serious theological reflection, but were constrained to limit themselves to the pronouncements of the official magisterium which, although not infallible, does enjoy a certain authority. Thus the *Catechism* proposes theses which claim to be rooted in sound Christology without considering at all the serious discussion which has been taking place since Vatican II regarding the historical conditions by which the incarnation of the Word was bound. This dogma is not properly understood, unless it is viewed as implying that the Son of God assumed all the inherently imperfect dimensions of existing in history, including those caused by the psychological and sociological prejudices of a particular place and time.

Just as the question of the ordination of women is placed within a Christological framework in the *Catechism*, that of priestly celibacy is placed within an eschatological one:

> All the ordained ministers of the Latin Church, with the exception of permanent deacons, are normally chosen from among men of faith who live a celibate life and who intend to remain *celibate* 'for the sake of the kingdom of heaven' . . . Celibacy is a sign of this new life to the service of which the Church's minister is consecrated; accepted with a joyful heart, celibacy radiantly proclaims the Reign of God. (1579)

Although it is indeed valid to base a general theology of celibacy on the eschatological teachings of Jesus, the impression should not be given that the canonical requirement that the ordained remain single is the only way in which the end-time power of God is made manifest in pastoral ministry.

Since the ordained preach the definitive word of God, celebrate the unique prognostic gestures of Jesus, and provide pastoral care so as to lead the baptised towards the Kingdom, sacred ministry is eschatological because of its essential relation to the first and last comings of the Lord. That the Kingdom of God is not mentioned at all throughout the presentation of Orders in the *Catechism* prior to the discussion of celibacy appears to mean that the editors were not able to integrate the eschatological dimension of this sacrament into their fundamental outline. They thus relate the Kingdom only to the canonical question of celibacy, and not to the dogmatic question concerning the triple ministry of the ordained which shares in the being and mission of Christ who has come, is in glory, and will come again. The impoverishment of the dogmatic treatise on Orders for the sake of the elevation of its canonical stipulations appears to be the principal theme which unifies the statements concerning both the ordination of women and the celibacy of sacred ministers in the *Catechism*.

1581–1589. The closing paragraphs of the presentation of Orders concern its effects, namely, the grace of holiness, the authority of office and the conferral of character. Although this sub-section is composed of many citations drawn from ecclesial Tradition, the editors do unite them by viewing all the effects of Orders as means by which the ordained receive a permanent configuration to Christ the head of the Church, so that they can act in his name with holiness and authority. Moreover, because of the Eastern Christian sources cited here, this final part of the treatment of Orders is also marked by a balance between its Christocentric and pneumatocentric aspects. The grace, the authority and the character granted to the ordained are attributed to the Holy Spirit who alone can render them ministers of Christ.

Yet it should be pointed out that some confusion exists in the text between the grace of holiness and the special or indelible character, even if both effects do configure the ordained to Christ. Grace should be presented as the personal aspect of this configuration — a self-communication of the Holy Spirit is bestowed to guarantee the fundamental holiness of the ordained. In turn, character is the ecclesial aspect of this configuration — a share in the transcendent Head of the Church enables the ordained permanently to teach, sanctify and guide his social body. As it is, little difference can be noted between the contents of 1581 on the spiritual character, and of 1585 on the grace of holiness.

The striking citations with which the section of the *Catechism* on Orders ends serve, in a slightly ironic manner, as counterpoints to the predominantly ontic and juridical tone adopted for the most part by the editors themselves. One of these citations, inserted into 1589, is taken from a prayer of Gregory of Nazianzus: 'Who then is the priest? He is the defender of truth, who stands with angels, gives glory with archangels, causes sacrifices to rise to the altar on high, shares Christ's priesthood, refashions creation, restores it in God's image, recreates it for the world on high and, even greater, *is divinized and divinizes*.'

316

In contrast to the intra-ecclesial and canonical emphasis of the text itself, this citation views Orders as ultimately orientated to glorifying the Creator and to renewing creation. In order words, the work of Christ and of the Spirit in and through ecclesial ministry has a doxological goal, in that the ordained are empowered to praise the Father by divinising their fellow Christians, and by being divinised in the process. Furthermore, this doxological goal of Orders includes preparing the whole world for its entrance into the Kingdom, a truth which is enforced by the use of the three verbs 'refashioned', 'restored' and 'recreated'. Perhaps the editors themselves sensed that the vast scope granted to Orders in this patristic text would best relativise their own dilemma in not being able to transcend the narrow confines of some post-conciliar reflection on ecclesial ministry.

Marriage

(Paragraphs 1601–1666)

Lisa Sowle Cahill
Boston College

Introduction

Marriage and sexuality are perhaps the most controverted issues in contemporary Catholic theology. One must evaluate the *Catechism*'s treatment of them in the light of its purpose — and within the realm of the possible. It would unrealistic to expect a 'catechism' to be the site of theological innovation. In the Roman Catholic tradition, this is particularly true of moral teaching, since it is morality (especially sexual) that in the popular, and in large degree the pastoral, mindset most defines Catholicity. It is hardly surprising that the *Catechism of the Catholic Church* does not exceed the parameters established by recent magisterial teaching about sexuality and marriage. The more interesting question is how this teaching is presented.

Two items are of particular note. First, the teaching itself represents the introduction of modern Western values into traditional understandings of sexuality and of the marital relationship. Secondly, as these new approaches to married couples are opened up, the pastoral responsibilities of the Church towards marriage are emphasised.

Key to the presentation of marriage in the *Catechism* is one quite traditional affirmation: the unity and indissolubility of marriage as signifying the relation of Christ to Church. On the basis of these properties, divorce and polygamy are excluded. Yet the *Catechism* also and more positively envisages marriage as an intimate and loving partnership of spouses, expressed sexually, and does not give procreation an overriding emphasis. However, procreation is still seen as a natural and morally compelling aspect of the marital relationship, which should be 'open' to it. This implies that artificial birth control is excluded, as are homosexual relationships or temporary heterosexual liaisons, but these topics are not treated in the section on the sacrament of marriage itself. Insofar as marriage is presented within the treatment of sacraments, the requirements and limits of marital behaviour are defined according to canon law.

318

As indicated above, a critical appreciation of the *Catechism* requires examination of the ways it may reflect values newly prized by the cultures and audiences addressed. Restatements of 'traditional' values may actually represent changes in relation to past magisterial teaching or canon law, changes which are responsive to contemporary cultural sensitivities about sex, gender, and family. Three examples of clear recent shifts in the Church's teaching about marriage, as represented by the *Catechism*, concern the nature of the marital relation as an interpersonal and not primarily a procreative union, the equality of women, and the presumption of a moral obligation to control fertility (only in this century a reliable practical possibility). It should also be noted that, in addition to some predictable defensive concerns about sexual morality and the permanency of marriage, the *Catechism* includes a platform for positive pastoral outreach to Catholics in mixed marriages, to the divorced and remarried, to single persons, and to infertile couples. One serious gap is receptiveness to non-Western experiences of Christianity and of marriage customs; diversity is minimised, rather than viewed as a source of insight (1603).

Because the *Catechism* incorporates twentieth-century personalist values in marriage, several tensions remain with older approaches. They result in fundamental questions about how to interpret the perspective on marriage which the *Catechism* advances. How does the new personalist view of the marital relation, with its emphasis on love, relate to an older social, economic, and kinship model of marriage, with its focus on procreation? If the love relation of spouses presupposes their equality, how does that square with the Church's asymmetrical valuation of the parenthood of women, and the exclusion of the most secure means to control births, so as to facilitate women's public participation? How would the *Catechism*'s abstract definitions of the properties of marriage stand up to a deeper exploration of the evolution of the understanding of marriage in the Catholic tradition, as implied in the first place by the fact that the *Catechism* takes as its point of departure a 1983 Code recently revised from the 1917 version? How are scriptural, natural law, and canonical resources for the definition of marriage reconciled — do they at any point yield different implications? Does or can the ideal of marriage proposed engage effectively enough with the concrete and often difficult circumstances in which people live their lives?

One also cannot fail to note the effects on equal partnership of the non-inclusive language in this translation. Often the text uses the inclusive 'spouses'. But, especially in its opening sections, it uses 'man' for both sexes. Sometimes this seems to make women marginal to the human ideal (as in 'God who created man out of love also calls him to love', and 'man is created in the image and likeness of God' (1604)); sometimes it seems to denigrate men ('Every man experiences evil . . . within himself' (1606)), and sometimes it is jarring, as when 'pain in childbearing' is the first example of a punishment for 'sinful man' (1609).

The teaching: history and context

Marriage in the New Testament and early Christianity was not totally transformed from a secular into a sacramental reality, but, along with other spheres of life, was understood to take on a special quality in view of discipleship. For instance, Paul (1 Cor 7:3–5) rejected the extreme asceticism of celibacy in marriage, but did adopt a more moderate preference for virginity as a way of life (1 Cor 7:7, 8). Christians also linked marriage with religious symbols as a graced or transformed relationship (Eph 5:25; 1 Cor 7:13–14). However, there is no explicit or full-blown doctrine of marriage as a sacrament to be found in Scripture. Paul's analogy of husband and wife to Christ and Church stands in the text (Eph 5) simply as an exhoration to Christians regarding specific and practical marital behaviour. It can hardly be taken as an abstract principle, much less turned around as a statement of fact about all marriages. As Theodore Mackin rightly observes, 'An analogy consisting of Christ's metaphoric marriage with a metaphor of the Church cannot produce an ontological effect in an actual marriage'.[1] One can conclude at most that 'the ideal model of Christian marriage has been assumed into the love relationship of Christ and the Church'.[2] Although the New Testament portrays marriage as a graced reality, the doctrine of marriage as a sacrament developed only gradually.

The understanding of marriage as 'sacramentally' signifying God's presence eventually became detached from the immediacy of eschatological community, and was advanced instead by means of canonical regulation and moral restrictions on sexual behaviour. Since the Middle Ages, the Church has understood marriage to be created by consent to a contract. The contract also grounds marriage's sacramental significance, though marriage was not formally defined as a sacrament until the Council of Trent (1563). In subsequent centuries, the sacramentality of marriage was virtually reduced to the permanency of the contract, easier to supervise canonically than the presence of divine love through a relationship.

Historically, discussion about the formation and properties of marriage reflected different perspectives on what is most essential to it as a reality: sexual intercourse or social and domestic partnership. The medieval theologians tended to see the consent which establishes marriages as directed to a mutual personal and social relationship (thus protecting the marriage of Mary and Joseph), but canonists sided with the more practical criterion of sexual intercourse. In the early Middle Ages, the Church had legal jurisdiction over marriage, and problematic cases were brought to it for resolution. Partly because the process of resolving such cases required a practically applicable test, the indissolubility of the bond became linked to consummation. Such a criterion also would have permitted the later dissolution of childhood marriages undertaken to consolidate family alliances. In the twelfth century, Gratian's decretals and Pope Alexander III established what continues to be Roman Catholic practice: marriage is valid and sacramental by virtue of the partners' consent. Yet a valid unconsummated marriage can be dissolved on the condition of a legal declaration within the Church that it is 'null and void'. What is indissoluble in principle (a marriage established by valid consent) differs from what is indissoluble in fact (a valid marriage which has not yet been consummated).[3]

The Church also stipulates that any marriage of two baptised persons is by definition sacramental (and thus indissoluble). In other words, the contract cannot be separated from the sacrament, even in cases in which the baptised do not practise the faith, and do not intend the sacrament when they marry. This position is the historical result of a struggle for juridical control over marriage between the ecclesiastical and civil authorities in eighteenth- and nineteenth-century Europe. Pius IX condemned the idea that the contract could come under state power (which would leave only the sacrament to church jurisdiction), and insisted that as two inseparable realities, both contract and sacrament must be governed by canon law. A resulting theological and practical problem for today is the situation of so-called 'baptised nonbelievers', whom the Church must regard either as administering to one another a sacrament they do not accept, or as having no right at all to marriage, otherwise regarded as a natural human prerogative.[4]

The 1917 Code secures and controls marriage as a social institution by defining it as permanent and monogamous, and brought into being by consent. That to which consent is given determines the real nature of the relationship. In the act of matrimonial consent, a man and a woman exchange the mutual and exclusive right to one another's bodies in regard to those acts which are ordered by their nature to procreation (Canon 1081.2 of the 1917 Code). Community of life is secondary to sexual intercourse and procreation, and tends to be envisioned primarily in terms of providing the social institution necessary for the upbringing and education of offspring.

In the documents of Vatican II and in the 1983 Code the picture changes. Under the influence of the 'personalist' philosophies of the 1930s, the Church comes to recognise the foundational nature of the interpersonal relationship in marriage. The intimate relationship of spouses as a community of life and love begins to make inroads into the procreative, institutional and contractual understanding of marriage favoured by canon law up to 1917. A new language of marital union begins to emerge, and is incorporated into the 1983 Code without completely transforming it.

Personalist authors, such as Herbert Doms and Dietrich von Hildebrand, found the meaning of both sex and marriage in the love relationship of the couple (heterosexual spouses). According to von Hildebrand, it is love which gives marriage its primary meaning, as a complete and exclusive self-offering or self-surrender of each spouse to the other.[5] Although the suggestion that love in marriage is not essentially subordinate to procreation was condemned by the Holy Office in 1944, magisterial teaching was itself to become heavily though incompletely influenced by the modern emphases on the dignity of the person, the importance of the personal relationship in marriage, and the emerging equality of women. This was already evident in *Casti Connubii* (1930), which gave new attention to marital love, even as it reasserted the primacy of procreation. Since the 1960s, the magisterium has treated love and procreation as equal ends of marriage. *Gaudium et Spes* (1965) does not rank these ends, though it sees conjugal love as 'ordained' to procreation (GS 48, 50). It uses covenant *(foedus)* rather than contract language to indicate the relation to which spouses give consent, and speaks of an 'intimate union' of persons who 'render mutual help and service to each other' (48). Conjugal love is a form of 'mutual self-giving', expressed in 'the marital act', but involving 'the good of the whole person' (49); it is a 'communion of life' (50).

In *Humanae Vitae* (1968), Paul VI specifically recognises changes in the status of women and in the evaluation of love in marriage and in sexual acts (2). The love of wife and husband is a 'reciprocal personal gift of self', a 'communion of their beings in view of mutual personal perfection', 'free', 'total', and 'a very special form of personal friendship' (8–9). For the baptised, it 'represents the union of Christ and Church' (8). The unitive and procreative meanings of sex are stated to be inseparable (12), but a duty of 'responsible parenthood' is also affirmed (10), to be exercised of course through natural means. John Paul II continues this line of reinterpretation. *Familiaris Consortio* idealises Christian marriage, sacramental and indissoluble, as a 'covenant of conjugal love freely and consciously chosen, whereby man and woman accept the intimate community of life and love willed by God himself . . . ' (11). 'Fecundity' is the sign of this love and of 'full reciprocal self-giving' (28), and again may be controlled only by natural means.

The personalist conception of marriage also informs the 1983 Code, as is especially evident in its use, following *Gaudium et Spes*, of the term 'covenant', and in the fact that 'a partnership of the whole of life' takes precedence over contractual rights to sexual intercourse:

> The matrimonial covenant *(foedus)*, by which a man and a woman
> establish between themselves a partnership *(consortium)* of the
> whole of life, is by its nature ordered toward the good of spouses and
> the procreation and education of offspring; this covenant between
> baptized persons has been raised by Christ the Lord to the dignity of
> a sacrament. (Canon 1055.1)

The ambiguity of the fact that the covenantal definition of marriage cited above is immediately followed by a reference to marriage as a contract ('a matrimonial contract cannot validly exist unless it is also a sacrament by the fact', Canon 1055.2) has been noted often.

One important consequence of the revised definition arises in regard to declarations of nullity for those marriages to which consent has not been properly given. Whereas formerly the parties only had to be able to give and fulfil consent to intercourse, it is now seen that those intending to marry must be willing and able to establish 'a partnership of the whole of life'. An original incapacity of one or both spouses to enter into such a partnership, and hence to form a genuine marriage, may only be revealed in the course of a relationship. An annulment may be granted on the basis of a general investigation of the quality of the relation established, as revealing its original conditions, even in the absence of evidence that lack of knowledge or external pressures influenced marital consent as a specific act performed during the wedding ceremony.[6]

More radically and more significantly, both the 1983 Code and *Humanae Vitae* present a vision in which a covenantal partnership of love and life, characterised by mutual intimacy and generosity, defines marriage. (The 1983 Code refrains, however, from using the word which would indicate the highest form of interpersonal union, *communio*, which certainly *de facto* does not typically characterise marriage in many cultures of the world today.) Some still-debated questions necessarily follow, both about whether it is still appropriate to specify marital sexual morality in terms of the procreative potential of distinct sex acts, and about whether 'indissolubility' can in any meaningful way be said to characterise a relationship in which virtually all the ideal personal characteristics of the marital bond have ceased to exist.

Though the 1983 Code assimilates Vatican II's personalist theology of marriage, it leaves essentially intact the juridical criteria and procedures by which marriage is controlled. Personalist understandings of marriage fit uneasily into the canonical framework because personal relationships are not easily scrutinised by objective and universalisable criteria, and because personalist characterisations of the marital relationship are more persuasive as ideals rather than as descriptive characterisations of what it is that real marriages always have in common. The same might be true of 'sacramentality'. Peter Huizing says 'marriage is a mandate to accomplish' the 'evangelical principle' of 'lifelong fidelity'. However, as are other human efforts to live the gospel, marriage is still 'exposed to irreversible failure'.[7] Bernard Cooke also invokes absolute fidelity as an eschatological ideal for marriage, rather than a juridicial norm: 'A Christian marriage is indissoluble, but short of the eschaton it is incompletely indissoluble.'[8]

What does the *Catechism* say?

The new *Catechism* picks up where *Familiaris Consortio* and the 1983 Code left off, but without elucidating the historical development behind the current magisterial teaching on the natural reality, the sacramental meaning, and the juridical status of marriage. Furthermore, it defends most of the traditional positions about the behaviour marriage requires, despite the fairly radical shifts in the presentation of the meaning of marriage which recent theological developments have produced.

The programmatic statement on marriage is:

> The matrimonial covenant, by which a man and a woman establish between themselves a partnership of the whole of life, is by its nature ordered toward the good of the spouses and the procreation

and education of offspring; this covenant between baptized persons has been raised by Christ the Lord to the dignity of a sacrament. (1601)

The statement cites and incorporates the definitions of *Gaudium et Spes* and of Canon 1055 (1983 Code). The language of covenant and of a partnership of life govern, and procreation and spousal welfare are presented on equal terms, as emerging from human nature, not just from Christian faith. Christian identity (baptism) provides the sacramental meaning of the marital covenant.

Both the natural and the sacramental aspects of marriage are defended biblically. The section begins with an appeal to the creation of 'man' in God's image and as called to love. 'Man and woman undertake steward-ship of creation as a common work', and are 'fruitful' as parents (1604). The woman is the 'equal' of the man, and their union is to be intimate and permanent (1605). The distortion of marriage by sin in recognised, and discord and domination, seemingly universal, are attributed to original sin. The document incorporates the thesis of many feminist critics that the portrayal of the results of the fall in Genesis 3, in the past offered to justify the rule of men over women, really depicts a disturbance of the order of creation, which should and can be healed by grace (1607–1609).[9] The text also mentions the law of Moses as 'protecting the wife from arbitrary domination by the husband', even if inadequately so in light of the later teaching of Jesus (1610).

The *Catechism* portrays a movement away from polygamy in the Old Testament (1611), a movement consummated in the teaching of Jesus and his reference back to the will of God in the creation (1613–1614). It asserts not only that the biblical story of Jesus' presence at the wedding feast at Cana is adequate to ground the sacramentality of marriage (1613), but also concludes to Jesus' 'unequivocal insistence on the indissolubility of the marriage bond' (1615), and cites in support Ephesians 5 (1616). Although these texts may indeed display the early Christian vision of all relationships as transformed by membership in the body of Christ, it is overstating the case to assert that they provide a clear and adequate ground for Roman Catholicism's sacramental theology of marriage. This theology emerged as a historical reflection on marriage, and is not contained in the Bible in full-blown form. It is especially important, for instance, that the New Testament authors themselves qualified Jesus' teaching on divorce, when they had to apply it to particular situations in their own communities (Matt 5:32; 19:9; 1 Cor 7:10–12, 15). St Paul specifically distinguishes his own teaching (as not 'binding' a Christian spouse to a marriage which the pagan partner has abandoned) from that of Jesus (no divorce at all). A criticism made by David Power of the first draft of the *Catechism* still applies, at least in the case of marriage. He says that the sacraments are treated as though 'development' is merely 'the unfolding of a treasure' which 'existed from the first days of the church'. But 'failure to see things in their historical context both misrepresents history and makes it difficult to address current issues'.[10]

A section on virginity (1618–1620) extolls it as a sign of the kingdom, without denigrating marriage. The two ways of life are said to 'reinforce each other' (though a quoted text from John Chrysostom contains the view that virginity is more excellent).

The sections on the celebration of the sacrament of marriage stress its Christian meaning and its public and ecclesial reality, mention differences in the Latin and Eastern rites without developing their significance, and restates that consent is the 'indispensable element' in constituting marriage (1626), though consent 'finds its fulfilment in the two becoming one flesh' (1627). Proper preparation for marriage is given considerable attention, as are the special pastoral care and ecumenical sensitivity required by mixed marriages and 'disparity of cult' (1632–1637).

Finally, the bond established by marriage is said to be permanent and exclusive *by nature* (1638); moreover, for any baptised persons, this bond is a sacrament and 'can never be dissolved' (1640). The indissolubility of the sacramental marriage is 'guaranteed by God's fidelity'. 'The Church does not have the power to contravene this disposition of divine wisdom' (1640). The rationale for asserting so categorically that it is God's will that all baptised persons must undertake sacramental and indissoluble marriages if they are to marry at all is not explicated further at this point. However, we are assured that God through Christ will provide all sacramentally married couples with the grace to attain love and unity in their lives together (1641–1642).

A section on 'the goods and requirements of conjugal love' touches on the standard questions of sexual morality in marriage. The answers proceed from an appeal to the nature of marriage as a 'deeply personal unity'. This unity 'leads to forming one heart and soul; it demands *indissolubility* and *faithfulness* in definitive mutual giving; and it is open to *fertility*' (1643). Both polygamy (1645) and divorce (1646–1647) are excluded.

Although permanent monogamy 'can seem difficult, even impossible', the actual accessibility of this ideal is established with reference to the 'definitive and irrevocable love' with which God loves humanity, and in which 'married couples share'. Hence, even in 'very difficult conditions' absolute fidelity is possible and demanded (1648). The question here would be why it is that married couples are required to live up to an absolute standard of participation in God's faithful love, whereas the possibility of failure is admitted and forgiven for single lay persons and for clergy, and in spheres of life outside the sexual (e.g. economic sharing, nonviolence, etc.). Certainly all Christians are called to be witnesses to the kingdom on earth. But Jesus himself does not single out the married state as the area *par excellence* where the kingdom shall be realised.

Despite its high expectations, and fundamentally exclusionary attitude towards those whose marriages fail, the *Catechism* is not without pastoral concern for the divorced and remarried. First of all, it admits that separation may sometimes be permitted, though it adds that 'the best solution would be, if possible, reconciliation' (1649). Civil remarriage, however, is denied ecclesiastical recognition because Jesus is said to have condemned it as adultery (citing Mk 10:11–12). No mention is made of the fact that Matthew, Mark and Luke all render Jesus' teaching against divorce somewhat differently; that Matthew and Paul both seem to contemplate exceptions of some sort; or that Paul specifically distinguishes his own teaching from that of Jesus, evidently on the assumption that later interpretation is not precluded by the original teaching.

Despite the condemnation of remarriage after divorce, both the clergy and 'the whole community must manifest an attentive solicitude' for people in such situations, 'so that they do not consider themselves separated from the Church, in whose life they can and must participate as baptized persons'. Reception of the sacraments is excluded as a mode of such participation, while raising one's children in the Catholic faith is commended (1650–1651).

Marriage is 'ordered to' parenthood as its 'crowning glory'. A positive approach to children as marriage's 'supreme gift' is outlined (no specific mention is made here of the ban on artificial birth control) (1652). Through parenthood, spouses participate in God's own creativity, and enjoy a family life which enhances their own well-being, as well as that of their offspring. The emphasis on children as a fulfilment of marriage is affirmed 'without diminishment of the other ends of marriage' (1652), and marriages to which 'God has not granted children' can still be 'full of meaning' as they 'radiate a fruitfulness of charity, of hospitality and of sacrifice' (1654).

The final section of the treatment of marriage follows *Gaudium et Spes* and *Familiaris Consortio* in referring to the family as a 'domestic church' (1655–1657). The potential of this metaphor for affirming and supporting family life as 'the first school of Christian life and "a school for human enrichment"' is diminished somewhat by the imagery of antagonism between family and world, and even of Christian retreat from a world depicted as 'alien', 'hostile', and 'unbelieving'. A concluding approach to single persons as also belonging to the inclusive family of the Church likewise loses something in the presentation, which makes it obvious that this population arrives in the picture quite as an afterthought to the marital paradigm ('We must also remember the great number of single persons') (1658).

The *Catechism* offers its own eight-point summary of the highlights of the marriage teaching, and makes it apparent which perceived threats in the contemporary setting this catechetical endeavour has in view. The points include the sacramental and indissoluble character of marriage as instituted by Christ himself; 'the consent of the contracting parties' as constituting marriage (reinforcing the Western, juridical framework); the necessity of a public ceremony; the unacceptability of polygamy, divorce, and 'the refusal of fertility'; and the ban on eucharistic communion for the divorced and remarried.

The significance of the *Catechism's* teaching

What are the strong points of the *Catechism*'s presentation of marriage? Incorporation of modern values in relation to marriage will make its teaching more encouraging and attractive to couples today, especially in the West. Of particular importance is the window opened on to equality of women and men in marriage, and the expectation that their co-operation in home and society will be premised on a mutually respectful as well as intimate relationship. Counterbalancing uses of 'man', stewardship of the creation is called a 'common work', and parenthood is not portrayed as a specifically female task (1604). Catechists can and should capitalise on the assertion that the woman is the man's 'equal' (1605). Also important is the abandonment of other hierarchies which have often characterised Catholic views of marriage, namely the ranking of virginity over marriage, and the primacy of procreation over union. By no longer dwelling on the contrast of marriage with celibacy, the *Catechism* communicates that holiness can be accomplished through the body and through everyday life, not only through asceticism. Control of fertility in service of other ends is a legitimate goal and value.

The *Catechism* provides Christian spouses with the opportunity to view marriage as an important Christian vocation in its own right, and to ground its contribution primarily in the love union which they establish, a union which founds both their social contribution and their shared parenthood. This construal will be useful and prophetic in situations and cultures in which women are disadvantaged, dominated or even abused. The image of the 'domestic church' can be supportive of families in their struggles to live out the Christian calling, if it is not applied as a 'blueprint' from above. Rather, the image can communicate to families of all racial, ethnic, cultural, and class identities that they are included in the mission of the Church, whatever their concrete problems and even failures.

Also helpful is the encouragement to pastoral ministry to persons who fall somewhat outside the parameters of the norms the *Catechism* upholds. It is notable, however, that the exceptional situation is envisaged more in the context of problems which have been highlighted in Western culture (the divorced and remarried, the infertile, the permanently single person, and the evangelisation of young couples approaching the Church for marriage preparation), whereas less adaptation is contemplated in regard to problems which have arisen in non-Western cultures (such as arranged marriages, progressive marriages and polygamy). The emphasis on marriage preparation does help place marriage commitment within a process, rather than placing the whole burden on a moment of consent, and calls attention to the fact that pastoral care for the couple is at least as important as ensuring that their entry into the married state is accomplished in conformity with certain juridical norms. It will be up to dioceses, parishes and pastors to employ the process of preparation as a means of attracting the laity to the positive values the Church associates with marriage, rather than primarily as a means to restrict access to the sacrament.

The presentation also has deficiencies. First of all, the emphasis on the sacramentality of marriage, as requiring unity and indissolubility, is cast in categorical terms which seem more juridical than inspirational. As has already been noted, the introduction of personalist values into the Roman Catholic understanding of marriage may have weakened fatally any effort to comprehend it in a primarily legal framework, for instance, as excluding any exceptions to the requirement of indissolubility. The *Catechism*'s insistence that the teaching on the sacramentality of all marriages between baptised persons has been a part of Christian belief from the New Testament onward, and that even creation as presented in Genesis clearly requires monogamy and indissolubility, is fallacious. Moreover, historically, the specifically Roman Catholic tradition on marriage and sex comes more from canon law and natural law than from the Bible. Hence the *Catechism* obscures rather than builds upon the parameters and strengths of the tradition on related points. Simplistic appeals to the Bible to ground teaching which has developed gradually are not only unconvincing to theologians, but are likely to alienate lay persons who, upon consulting Scripture, discover that the texts used to warrant exceptionless positions seem rather far afield or only loosely related to them.

An alternative and more Thomistic approach would be to look at human marital experience itself, with its intrinsic characteristics, purposes, and values, as a starting-point for Church teaching on the nature of the marital relationship. This approach is contained within the *Catechism*, but not given as high a profile as the argument from biblical authority. A possible reason for this neglect is that the magisterium's readings of what marital experience requires in the concrete (especially on indissolubility and artificial birth control) have been widely challenged. A crying need is an honest investigation of the human reality of marriage, incorporating testimony from married persons themselves, across cultures. The capacity of a human relation to function as a sign of a divine reality must necessarily build on the nature of the human signifier itself. To say in effect that the infinite faithfulness of God to the Church needs a created representation, and that, since Christian marriage has been chosen as the sign, it must in every case manifest properties which quite exceed the human reality as widely experienced, is surely to put the cart before the horse. (The bond between mother/parent and child almost seems a better natural sign of the unity and indissolubility of God's love for God's people, especially as it implies an appropriate hierarchy, rather than the submission of women to men as Christ's image, a conclusion too frequently drawn from Ephesians 5.)

A concluding word should draw attention to a fundamental besetting problem of Catholic teaching about marriage: a conflation of the ideal and the real. A picture of marriage as 'total' self-gift which could attract and inspire were it held out in the same evangelical mode as Jesus' commands to 'love your enemies' or 'leave all and follow me', becomes oppressive and alienating when it skewers married persons on standards which are not only impossible, but also inequitable in relation to church expectations in other realms of life. Describing Jesus' prohibition of divorce as a 'revolutionary, radical demand', Norbert Greinacher develops this point:

> Jesus applied this same prophetic radicality in the Sermon on the Mount where with similar decisiveness he condemned anger against one's neighbor, swearing, oaths, indeed, any kind of force. The concern here revolves around a prophetic call, radical norms, passionate ethical instructions. But it was a far-reaching and fatal misunderstanding in Christian history to make a church law out of this prophetic call.[11]

The same is true of church teaching on the 'total' character of marital intimacy, of the couple's 'openness' to procreation, or for that matter, of sexual communion. Sexual intimacy, like the interpersonal relation of which it is a part, is realised along the length of the marriage only if it is nurtured. Pastors and catechists in the Catholic Church are challenged to use *The Catechism of the Catholic Church* in order to nourish marital commitment and parenthood, as well as personal and sexual intimacy in marriage, the equal participation of men and women in family and in public roles, and attitudes of inclusion and reconciliation towards those whose situation in life falls beyond the traditional (and canonically legitimated) marital model.

Notes

1 Theodore Mackin, *The Marital Sacrament* (Mahwah, NJ: Paulist Press, 1982), p. 673.
2 Ibid., p. 634.
3 On the history of marriage in canon law, see Ladislas Örsy, *Marriage in Canon Law* (Wilmington, DE: Michael Glazier, 1986), pp. 13–37.
4 See Peter J. Huizing SJ, 'Canonical implications of the conception of marriage in the Conciliar Constitution *Gaudium et Spes*' in William P. Roberts (ed.), *Commitment to Partnership: Explorations of the Theology of Marriage* (Mahwah, NJ: Paulist Press, 1987), pp. 26–7.
5 Dietrich von Hildebrand, *Marriage* (New York: Longmans, 1932), pp. 5, 9, 16, 49. Originally published as *Die Ehe* (Munich: Kösel-Pustet, 1929).
6 Huizing, 'Canonical implications', p. 116.
7 Ibid., p. 126.
8 Bernard Cooke, 'Indissolubility: guiding ideal or existential reality?' in Roberts (ed.), *Commitment to Partnership*, p. 71.
9 1609 uses the word 'punishments' of 'pain in childbearing' and the toil of work, which could seem to support the controverted conclusion that these realities, possibly along with the domination of women by men, are God's *present* will for humanity. On the whole, however, the *Catechism* leans towards including all the disasters of Genesis 3 among sin's effects, to be overcome by grace in the present order.
10 David N. Power, OMI, 'The sacraments in the Catechism' in Thomas J. Reese SJ (ed.), *The Universal Catechism Reader* (New York: HarperCollins, 1990), pp. 16–17.
11 Norbert Greinacher, 'The problem of divorce and remarriage'='Zur Problem von Scheidunge und Wiederverheiratung', *Theologische Quartalschrift* 167.2 (1987), pp. 106–15, as summarised in *Theology Digest* 35 (1988), p. 222.

Sacramentals and Funerals

(Paragraphs 1667–1690)

Kevin Donovan SJ
Heythrop College, University of London

Sacramentals

This first article of the final chapter in Part Two rounds off the lengthy treatment of the Church's official worship and sacraments with a brief consideration of what might at first sight seem rather fringe liturgies — sacramentals, blessings, exorcisms and various expressions of popular piety. Their importance is not to be underestimated. Popular devotions such as pilgrimages, rosaries, medals, statues and even religious dance are for many people their main contact with Christianity, and such practices penetrate ordinary life in a way that the seven sacraments often fail to do. Drawing on the documents of Puebla, the *Catechism* offers a quite profound and sympathetic analysis of popular devotions and the Christian world-view they enshrine — an account which should be borne in mind by all who might be inclined to dismiss such manifestations as syncretistic or superstitious. The *Catechism* commends, but has difficulty in accounting for, a popular religious sentiment which is independent of hierarchical control. The treatment would perhaps have been strengthened if it had integrated a more consistent theology of the Holy Spirit, such as is found in *Lumen Gentium*, with that of its main sources, which are *Sacrosanctum Concilium* and the Code of Canon Law.

Another weakness is the failure to give a satisfactory basis for the sharp distinction it draws between sacraments and sacramentals. This distinction, only finally established at the Council of Lyons in 1274, was orginally based on the view, no longer widely held by Catholic exegetes, that Jesus personally instituted the seven sacraments. It followed that these would give grace in a way that church-based sacramentals could not. Today, it is recognised that

> Institution by Christ means that those actions we call sacraments
> are specifications and applications of a power that during his
> ministry and after his resurrection Jesus Christ gave to his church
> in and through the apostles — a power containing what was
> necessary to make God's rule or kingdom triumph over evil by
> sanctifying the lives of people from birth to death.[1]

331

The Church makes sacraments as much as it does sacramentals, and Karl Rahner's warning should perhaps be heeded: 'The difference is not at all as radical as a rather mediocre theology would suppose.'[2]

Perhaps more could have been said to clarify why it is that the Church officially recognises that certain signs, because they accompany key moments in life, are privileged occasions for encountering the grace of personal union with God. An indication might have been given that in the individual situation, there is no guarantee that the offer of grace will be more certainly accepted in the case of official sacraments than of sacramentals. As it is, although its original basis is weakened, the traditional distinction is strongly maintained, and the *Catechism* goes even further than *Sacrosanctum Concilium* and the Code of Canon Law when it asserts that 'Sacramentals do not confer the grace of the Holy Spirit in the way that the sacraments do' (1670). This is the only reference to the Holy Spirit in this article, and it seems a trifle adventitious, since it usually adopts the more Christocentric theology of *Sacrosanctum Concilium* and speaks of 'the divine grace which flows from the Paschal mystery of the Passion, Death and Resurrection of Christ. From this source all sacraments and sacramentals draw their power' (1670). Significantly, the Code only manages a single reference to the Spirit in the 419 canons which comprise its Fourth Book on the Sanctifying Office of the Church. Grace remains an impersonal power entrusted to the official Church to be administered in its ritual system. The perspective of *Lumen Gentium* is missing, with its 90 references to the Spirit, as against a meagre four in *Sacrosanctum Concilium*. This is not just a question of statistics, but of a rediscovery of the role of the Holy Spirit in the sanctification of all men and women — and not just Christians. Such a theology would arguably have afforded a better basis for understanding both sacramentals and popular piety.

Extensive quotation is impossible, but we give just two instances, as well as an example of the important post-conciliar developments in the theology of grace to which they have given rise. 'Christ Jesus vivifies them [the laity] in His Spirit, thus as worshippers whose every deed is holy, the laity consecrate the world itself to God' (LG 34). 'We ought to believe that the Holy Spirit in a manner known only to God offers to all people the possibility of being associated with this paschal mystery' (GS 22). In other words, 'God's Spirit is a constant and intrinsically present element of daily life, and the response to grace is mediated by human situations and people that make the ordinary events of life'.[3] On such a view, the Church's liturgy would serve to focus God's call and our response with an explicit reference to Christ and his message for key areas of life. The rest of life, however, is not profane in the sense of being ungraced, for 'the Father sent the Holy Spirit upon all men that he might inspire them from within to love God with their whole heart and soul . . . and one another as Christ loved them' (LG 40).

The *Catechism* in general prefers an older theological emphasis, with greater stress on the official Church's activity (twenty references in all). Any suspicion of magical efficacy is guarded against by several references to the prayer and intercession of the Church, and the dominance of the institution is further mitigated by the very positive attitude shown towards the non-ordained ministry of the baptised. 'Sacramentals derive from the baptismal priesthood: every baptized person is called to be a "blessing" and to bless' (1669). In the face of this magnificent statement, one might be forgiven for thinking that more than one hand has been at work in compiling this section.

Among the prayers and blessings which are distinct from, but related to, the official sacraments, the *Catechism* gives special attention to exorcisms, both the simple forms found in baptism and the solemn forms requiring episcopal authorisation, in which the Church strives for 'the expulsion of demons'. There appears to be an assumption that the world-view of the contemporaries of Jesus, or of the Middle Ages, should be shared by everyone today.

Catechists might wish to consult some up-to-date exegetical help on this question. This might enable them to add to the distinction already made by the *Catechism* between demonic possession and psychic illness, and make further useful distinctions between the medical presuppositions of an earlier age and our current medical knowledge of conditions such as epilepsy. While accepting that there can be (rare?) cases of demonic possession, should there not be some reference also to the supra-personal social manifestations of evil which we are surely also called upon to renounce in baptism?

Christian Funerals

The opening paragraphs of this article condense the introduction to the Order of Christian Funerals. The goal of sacramental initiation and life is our ultimate sharing in the paschal mystery of Christ, the passover from death to life, and this hope is proclaimed in the funeral liturgy. The treatment is quite biblical, but makes rather heavy weather of stressing that the funeral and its various blessings are not a sacrament. It is in the eucharistic sacrifice that the offering of the child of grace by Mother Church into the Father's hands is fully celebrated — a somewhat obscure if lyrical passage.

The final page is clearer and offers a summary of the funeral liturgy which could form the basis for a good catechesis on the Christian understanding of death. It could have been widened by introducing the perspectives outlined in the discussion of the eschatological nature of the Church from *Lumen Gentium*. However, the authors may have felt that to treat of the way in which 'the human race as well as the entire world ... will be perfectly re-established in Christ' would have been beyond the immediate scope of a funeral. If so, this would be in keeping with the general approach of this chapter, which has concentrated on the Church's sanctifying role towards its own members, rather than on its mission to be both sacrament to the world and instrument for achieving union with God and the unity of all humankind.

Notes

1   Raymond E. Brown, *Responses to 101 Questions on the Bible* (New York: Paulist Press/London: Geoffrey Chapman, 1990), p. 107.
      Using the traditional format of a catechism, a distinguished scripture scholar distils a vast amount of information in a style which is more accessible than more technical works. Excellent for catechists.
2   Karl Rahner, *The Church and the Sacraments* (ET London: Search Press, 1963), p. 28.
3   Roger Haight in L. Madden (ed.), *The Awaking Church* (Collegeville, MN: Liturgical Press, 1992). Haight's article on the 'Community consciousness of grace' develops Rahner's ideas in a way that throws great light on sacramentals. 'The immediate purpose of liturgy is to bring grace to conscious expression, and this occurs in a great variety of ways . . . the immediate purpose of liturgy is not to cause or confer grace where it does not exist' (p. 33). For a more technical presentation, see his *An Alternative Vision* (New York: Paulist Press, 1985), esp. ch. 10; and for a full exposition of Rahner's views, Michael Skelley, *The Liturgy of the World: Karl Rahner's Theology of Worship* (Collegeville, MN: Liturgical Press, 1991).

Our Human Vocation

(Paragraphs 1691–2051)

Gerard J. Hughes SJ

Heythrop College, University of London

In Part Three of the *Catechism*, 'Life in Christ', the first Section is intended to provide the general theological and philosophical background against which Christian deliberation about morality ought to take place. The more directly theological issues (the biblical tradition, and the theology of grace and salvation) come right at the begining and also at the end. I shall take these two sections together. Sandwiched between them is a fairly long and largely philosophical section on general ethical theory and on social ethics.[1] Both in subject-matter and in style, then, the text is not at all homogeneous, and it is not always easy to see it as a whole. I hope that my subdivision of the main topics will be a help to this end, even if, as a result, I do not proceed by commenting on all the passages strictly in order.

1. Christian ethics in the Bible

Christian moral living is presented as the way in which we can realise our vocation to the blessedness to which we are called in Christ. Created in the image of God, redeemed and ennobled in Christ, we are enabled by the gift of the Spirit to live as members of Christ's body. A proper catechesis therefore begins with a catechesis of the Spirit (1697), and has the person of Jesus as its 'first and last point of reference' (1698). In practice, the emphasis turns out to be less on the imitation of Jesus, and much more on living by the teachings of Christ, as summing up and perfecting the teachings of the Jewish tradition.

The *Catechism* contains very many allusions to the biblical writings, from both the Christian and the Jewish Scriptures. Many of these references are extremely brief—an illustrative example, or sometimes simply an occasional word or phrase. But the key texts on which the *Catechism* relies are the Beatitudes in their Matthaean version (1716ff.), and the Ten Commandments as reiterated by Jesus in his conversation

336

with the rich young man (Mt 19:16–19; 2052ff.). Other moral texts are mentioned, such as Romans 12 – 15, 1 Corinthians 12 – 13, Colossians 3 – 4, and Ephesians 4 – 5, and are said to be fittingly added to the Sermon on the Mount (1971). The New Commandment in John 15 is given a passing mention (1970). In the opening section of 'Life in the Spirit', the entire presentation is centred on the Beatitudes; the other shorter texts come much later, in the chapter on 'Law and grace'; and the Ten Commandments have an entire section devoted to them alone, in Section Two of this Part.

It is indeed refreshing that the reader is first presented with the Beatitudes as the sharpest and most attractive expression of the Christian vocation and hope. But although the *Catechism* states that 'the Beatitudes are at the heart of Jesus' preaching' (1716) and 'depict the countenance of Jesus Christ and describe his charity' (1717), and that 'the beatitude of heaven sets the standards for discernment in the use of earthly goods in keeping with the law of God' (1729), this approach is not developed in any detail. Although the approach to Christian ethics through moral philosophy is treated at some length, and an entire part is devoted to the Ten Commandments, the *Catechism* does little to elaborate its initial statement that the heart of the Christian vision of the moral life is to be found in the Beatitudes and the person of Jesus which they portray. One cannot help feeling that a valuable opportunity has been missed to present a fresh and more positive picture of the moral demands with which the gospel confronts us, by developing the Beatitudes at much greater length.

The way in which the *Catechism* uses the Scriptures, and especially the Christian Scriptures, pays little attention to the way in which the biblical texts came to be written. One would hope that catechisms based upon this document would do much more to encourage their readers to appreciate the *diversity* of views and approaches to morality in the Christian Testament. The Beatitudes themselves are notably different in Matthew and in Luke, for example, and the attitudes to the Mosaic law exhibited in Matthew, Luke, Paul, and in the Johannine writings, are far from identical, for the very good reason that the authors were trying to apply their understanding of Jesus in different circumstances and for the benefit of different audiences. It is surely important to point out that these writers might themselves have been *using* rather than simply repeating what Jesus himself might have said. So one might have expected an explanation of why the Fourth Gospel should so stress that Jesus gave a *new* commandment; while, on the other hand, it is an important fact that some New Testament writers seem to have used existing secular sources in order to provide an outline of the virtues which Christians should practise.[2] Above all, it is essential to explain the process whereby some parts of the Sermon on the Mount (for instance the total prohibition of oaths) came to be downplayed by later tradition, whereas other parts have been taken to express demands to which no exception is possible.

Instead of this, the reader is presented with a picture of a totally homogeneous tradition, in which the biblical writers merely repeated what they had heard, and never had to *work out* what they should say about the Christian life in order to respond to the needs of their audiences. The *Catechism* at times gives the impression of using texts with little concern for their real character,[3] and of offering superficial harmonisations where a much richer and more instructive approach, taking into account the vast amount of work done since *Divino Afflante Spiritu*, could have been offered instead. In so doing, it runs the risk of perpetuating a false picture of how the inspired writers thought about morality, and why they thought about it as they did. As a result, it offers little or no encouragement to the development of a style of catechesis whose aim is to enhance an understanding of the biblical texts in their own terms, as an essential prelude to using them in thinking about contemporary moral problems.

II. Method in Christian ethics

So how *should* one go about thinking about morality as a Christian?[4] Not surprisingly, the *Catechism* makes no attempt to approach such a theoretical question directly. To do so would be quite out of place in a work of this kind. But it does contain some intriguing remarks which have some bearing on the thorny and much disputed questions of the proper method for Christian moral reasoning.

There are three somewhat different issues which are involved:
A. The relationship between grace and our natural abilities.
B. The role in Christian ethics of reasoned moral reflection independent of biblical revelation.
C. The role in Christian ethics of revelation, and especially revelation in Christ.

A. Grace and nature
The long-running disputes about the relationships between divine grace and human nature have their roots in the controversy with the Pelagians. In part, the Church was concerned to insist that the initiative in our salvation rests wholly with God; even the first efforts we might make towards belief in Christ, or repentance for our sins, are prompted by God's action, not by our own unaided efforts. The gift of the Holy Spirit is just that, gift, and the blessedness of heaven to which we are called is not something which we can achieve by ourselves. Protestant theologians, much influenced by Augustine's anti-Pelagian writings, have tended to take the view that any attempts to come to a true knowledge of God and of his will for us by using our human powers of intellectual or moral reasoning are doomed to failure, and almost idolatrous in their implications. The Catholic tradition, less pessimistic in its estimate of fallen human nature, on the whole saw the action of God's grace as prompting and supplementing the human powers of reason and will which, despite the fall, remain substantially intact. Positions on these

issues have inevitable implications for the view to be taken on B and C above. The more 'Protestant' view has tended to emphasise the importance of revelation in ethics rather than moral reasoning operating independently of revelation; the Catholic tradition has been on the whole more sympathetic to what human beings can discover without appeal to specifically Christian revelation. Nevertheless, there are *two* issues here, not one; for it might be held that human beings, with the grace of God, can think adequately about morality without the benefit of explicitly Christian revelation. Whether they can do so without grace is a separate question.

The medieval theologians typically saw grace as building upon and extending the powers of unaided human nature. More recently, writers like Henri de Lubac and Karl Rahner, emphasising the fact that all human beings are created *in Christ*, have argued that, though there is a theoretical distinction to be made between our 'natural' abilities and our abilities stemming from God's grace in Christ, this does not mean that there are in fact human beings existing in a 'purely natural' order. So there is in practice no question of anyone trying to think about ethics by using their purely natural abilities. On the medieval view, the grace/nature relationship has a direct hearing on method in Christian ethics, since it was commonly held that some human beings might think about ethics without being aided by grace. Could this be done at all, let alone successfully? On the more recent view, the possibility of people doing moral reflection outside the order of grace is not taken to describe the situation in which human beings in fact find themselves, and so poses no actual problems about method in Christian ethics.

The chapter of the *Catechism* on 'Law and grace' relies heavily on the formulae of the Council of Trent, stressing that God's gift of grace makes an intrinsic difference to those who receive it, and enables us genuinely to co-operate with the promptings of the Holy Spirit (1987–2011).[5] By and large, therefore, the *Catechism* is content to repeat the medieval view of these matters, and does not comment on the more modern developments at all, favourably or unfavourably.

Thus, the happiness to which we are called in the Beatitudes 'surpasses the understanding and powers of man. It comes from an entirely free gift of God: whence it is called supernatural, as is the grace that disposes man to enter into the divine joy' (1722). 'Since it belongs to the supernatural order, grace escapes our experience and cannot be known except by faith' (2005). I take it that the *Catechism* is here simply repeating the teaching of Trent.[6] One might go on to say that, while it is indeed true that the whole economy of salvation can indeed be known only by faith, and that without faith we would have no reason to identify anything in our experience as stemming from the gift of God's Spirit to us, it does not follow that 'grace escapes our experience'. After all, the whole tradition of Christian discernment presupposes that our experience *can* be recognised as being coloured by the promptings of God's Spirit. The *Catechism* presumably does not intend to deny this.

Something of the methodological difficulties created by the two-stage medieval interpretation of the relationship between nature and grace emerges at various points in the *Catechism*.

> The precepts of natural law are not perceived by everyone clearly and immediately. In the present situation sinful man needs grace and revelation so moral and religious truths may be known 'by everyone with facility, with firm certainty and with no admixture of error.' The natural law provides revealed law and grace with a foundation prepared by God and in accordance with the work of the Spirit. (1960)

One might perhaps wish that the need for grace and the need for revelation had been kept rather more separate than they are here, and I shall discuss the questions concerning revelation below. For the moment, it is worth noting that the passage tends to assume that it is possible to exercise 'natural' reason outside the order of grace, and asserts that this natural activity at least in principle can provide a good basis on which grace can then build.[7] More recent views might suggest that, since we are all created in Christ and so are *already* in the order of grace, we never in fact exercise purely natural, unaided, reason, though we can obviously reason, as many people do, without reference to Christian revelation.

It is quite important to ask whether knowledge of the nature of God, and knowledge of how to live morally are *equally* difficult for us to attain. The passage quoted here by the *Catechism* comes directly from Pius XII's encyclical *Humani Generis*. Pius XII in one important respect goes beyond what was said by Vatican I, which he is here citing. Vatican I in *Dei Filius* had said that although *in rebus divinis* ('where the nature of God is concerned') human reason is not powerless, nevertheless God's revelation is offered to confirm and correct what we might ourselves have discovered; Pius XII applies exactly the same argument *in rebus religionis et morum* ('in what concerns matters of religion *and morals*'). Is revelation *equally* needed to correct or to confirm our thinking about God and about ethics? And does revelation in fact contain answers to questions *about ethics* which would otherwise be unavailable? The answer to that question has obvious implications for how Christian moral reasoning ought to be conducted. One might perhaps have more confidence in graced human reason when thinking about ethics than when trying to fathom the mystery of God. It seems to me that, overall, the *Catechism* takes this general line, and so devotes a good deal of space to the philosophical basis of ethics, as well as to revelation.

B. The role of reason in Christian ethics

In the Catholic tradition, the *Catechism* lays great stress on the 'natural law', so called because it is formulated by reason, and reason is proper to human nature (1955). 'The natural law expresses the original moral sense which enables man to discern by reason the good and the evil, the truth and the lie' (1954). Cicero is adduced in support of the view that right reason can provide a true law (1956) precisely in order to make the point that reasoned thinking about ethics is the privilege of all human beings. The Decalogue, which we know has close parallels elsewhere in the ancient world, is said by the *Catechism* to present the chief commandments of the natural law, which are 'authenticated within the covenant of salvation' (1955, 1961). 'The natural law, the Creator's very good work, provides the solid foundation on which man can build the structure of moral rules to guide his choices' (1959). The *Catechism* is carefully nuanced: the principles of natural law are indelible in every human heart, and underlie the 'flux of ideas and customs'. Yet although it is in this sense unchanging, 'application of the natural law varies greatly; it can demand reflection that takes account of various conditions of life according to places, times, and circumstances' (1956–1958). Here, and elsewhere as we shall see, the *Catechism* relies a great deal on the treatment of natural law in Aquinas's *Summa Theologiae*.

The remark that the Decalogue is 'authenticated within the covenant of salvation' is a recognition of the fact, demonstrable also from the Christian Scriptures, that the inspired writers were on occasion quite willing simply to incorporate moral insights from the non-Christian world into their writings. This is no more than one might expect, given that men and women of good will have devoted such effort to thinking about ethics. The same no doubt holds good in our own day. Christians have no monopoly on moral truth, and should be ready and willing to learn from the reflection of others, as well as being willing to apply their own tradition to the altered circumstances of our age, or to the different needs of different peoples and cultures. One might remark that the decisions arrived at in the context of civil and criminal legal deliberation might be expected to provide much that is best about human moral thinking, stemming as they at least often do from a deliberate effort to be impartial, respectful of conflicting interests, and mindful of the complexities of our modern world. Despite the caricatures often presented of the science of casuistry as practised by moral theologians, it might be said that it has always flourished and been respected in the ordinary business of the law.[8] Perhaps similar lessons are to be learned from non-Christian moral philosophers too. At any rate, the stress on the importance of moral reflection independently of Christian revelation is a valuable asset to Christians living and working with people who do not share their faith. This is all the more important since Christians, and perhaps Catholics above all, are so often seen as not willing to enter honestly into serious discussion of controversial issues, or to learn from such a shared reflection. Such an impression is all too often a counter-witness to the faith we profess.

C. The role of revelation in Christian ethics.
It is clear from the *Catechism* that the revelation of God in Christ puts the entire enterprise of moral living in a new light. It is not simply a life of respect for the dignity of one's fellow human beings; it is part of a growth towards the fullness of all things in Christ, part of a development into the light of God's kingdom (1691–1709). Such a vision is both enriching and motivating. It is not theologically controversial that

revelation makes this kind of difference to Christian ethics.

What is much more controversial is whether, and how, the revelation of God in Jesus gives any *content* to Christian ethics which could not be obtained by moral thinking independent of revelation. Here, both explicitly and by implication, the *Catechism* is perhaps less clear. The new law of the gospel '"fulfils", refines, surpasses and leads the Old Law to its perfection' (1967). From this and the following paragraph it appears that the fulfilment consists in showing, for instance in the Beatitudes, the connection between the Christian's moral life and the blessedness of heaven. The old law is 'surpassed', not by the addition of new external precepts, but by reforming our acts at their root. The allusion is to the stress in the Sermon on the Mount on the internal moral attitudes that a person has. Fundamentally, however, the new law just is the gift of the Holy Spirit, who writes a new law upon our hearts.[9] In general, then, the *Catechism* lays comparatively little stress on any difference of *content* between Christian ethics and the ethics which is in principle available through moral reflection independently of the revelation of God in Jesus.[10]

It is therefore not too clear what the *Catechism* means by saying that beatitude 'sets the *standards* for discernment in the proper use of earthly goods in keeping with God's law' (1729), especially since, as I have already remarked, there is no attempt made to provide a worked-out version of how such standards might operate, in contrast to the detailed exegesis given to the Decalogue, which derives from natural law.[11]

If this is a correct reading of the *Catechism*'s overall estimate of the role which specifically Christian revelation plays in Christian moral reflection, and of the kinds of differences which knowledge of that revelation might be expected to make, then there are some consequences which are worth pointing out.

Firstly, in Aquinas's view the role of philosophical reflection about ethics, or about the existence and nature of God, is not simply that of establishing a preliminary framework, which revelation can then fill in with what is really interesting. Such a picture is not even an adequate picture of Aquinas's view of how theology deals with the mysteries of God and God's dealings with us in Christ. It is still less adequate as an account of his view of the relationship between natural law and revelation.[12] In Aquinas's view, philosophical reflection establishes not merely (among other things) that revelation is possible, and that it is reasonable to believe that God has in fact revealed himself; crucially, it must be used to determine the limits of acceptable interpretation of that revelation. So he points out that once one has, by philosophical reflection, established at least some basic truths about what God is like, it follows at once that many biblical passages must be interpreted metaphorically and not literally.[13] More relevantly to our present purposes, even when (at times on the basis of the inadequate exegetical assumptions with which he was working) he took it to be revealed truth that God commanded conduct which was apparently demonstrably immoral on philosophical grounds, he endeavours to show that these examples do not in fact violate natural law after all.[14]

In short, the proper interpretation of the content of revelation can never conflict with what can be established by the proper use of human reflection which is independent of revelation. If such a conflict apparently exists, then either revelation has been misunderstood, or the philosophical argument is defective. *Both* must therefore be re-examined. So it follows that when the *Catechism* says[15] that 'sinful man needs grace and revelation so religious and moral truths may be known by "everyone with facility, with firm certainty and with no admixture of error"' (1960), things may not always be quite as straightforward as that remark might suggest. For it may not be obvious whether it is our ordinary (graced) powers of moral reflection which are in error, or our interpretation of revelation. Merely to assert that some truth is contained in revelation does not resolve the problem unless there are solid exegetical grounds for saying so, and unless it can also be shown that the proposed solution can be satisfactorily reconciled with an improved moral reflection. It hardly needs saying that to decide this question will not always be a simple matter.[16]

III. Basic moral concepts and principles

The *Catechism*, having stated that human beings are made in the image of God,[17] that the special dignity of human beings lies in their possession of reason and free will (1701–1715), and that they are called to happiness as outlined in the Beatitudes (1716–1729), then goes on to talk further about freedom, and to discuss the morality of human actions which are the products of reason and free will. This is the setting for the largely philosophical section of the treatment of the Christian moral life (1730–1802), after which the *Catechism* goes on to consider the virtues, sin, grace and law. Perhaps the fact that this philosophical section is placed at the beginning of the discussion of the basic concepts of ethics reinforces my earlier suggestion that the *Catechism* opts for a natural law approach to Christian morality, to which revelation provides in the main a Christian motivation and context.

Be that as it may, the philosophical discussion is quite detailed and is far from easy reading. It relies very much on Aquinas's treatment of many of these issues, especially in *Summa Theologiae* I-II, 18–21 and 90–94.

A. Freedom
The discussion of freedom (1730–1742) uses the word 'freedom' in two or even three very different ways, unfortunately without much warning. In one sense of 'free', a person acts freely if at the moment of choice, different choices (including not acting at all) are still open; in the other, more Augustinian, sense, 'freedom' refers to freedom from the bondage of sin. In the first sense, freedom excludes being predetermined. Since an event either is causally predetermined or it is not, freedom in the first sense does not admit of degrees. In the second sense, freedom does admit of

degrees, since one can be more or less given over to a sinful way of life. At least on the traditional view, the blessed in heaven are no longer *able* to reject the goodness of God; so they are, on that view, no longer free in the first sense, although they are now supremely free in the second sense.[18]

Both senses can be seen in 1731:

> Freedom is the power, rooted in reason and will, to act or not to act, to do this or that, . . ., on one's own responsibility [*first sense*] . . . [Freedom] attains its perfection when directed toward God, our beatitude [*second sense*].

Hence the *Catechism* can say that freedom (in the first sense) is the basis of praise and blame, reward or punishment (1732); and that freedom makes us *responsible* for our acts to the extent that they are 'voluntary'. It can also point to various causes which can diminish or remove responsibility (1735). This is perfectly intelligible if it is taken to refer to freedom in the first sense; sometimes it is indeed hard to say that a person's choices could have been made differently. But the *Catechism* can also say that 'The more one does what is good, the freer one becomes. There is no true freedom except in the service of what is good and just. The choice to disobey and do evil is an abuse of freedom and leads to the slavery of sin' (1733). These remarks, if they are to be consistent, must take 'free' in the *second* sense. The intention, I think, is not to suggest that we enjoy a higher degree of free will, and hence of responsibility, the more good we do, or that the bondage of sin destroys moral responsibility which depends upon freedom of choice.

The *Catechism* notes that responsibility can be diminished or even suppressed not merely by those factors which have long been recognised such as fear, ignorance, violence and immoderate affections, but also by 'other psychological *or social* factors' (my italics). I take it that here the intention is to refer to mental illness, and also to the defects in a person's upbringing and social conditioning which might bring it about that some choices, which perhaps theoretically they might have made, simply did not even occur to them as possibilities to be considered, or could not, given their cultural background, even appear to be in any way good. This is a most welcome and pastorally useful statement.

On the other hand, exactly *how* these various factors diminish responsibility, and whether they do so by removing free will (as, for instance, ignorance and threat do not, but the kinds of illness which result in compulsive behaviour presumably do) is a complex philosophical question. The *Catechism* (1735), rather unhelpfully to my mind, introduces technical terminology without really solving the problems.[19] It might have been better to rest content with the general statement of principle.

The *Catechism* goes on to deal with the exercise of freedom, pointing out firstly that there is not an unlimited right to do anything we choose. Secondly, and more interestingly, it stresses that for an individual to be able to act as they have every right to act, it is not sufficient for that person to have free will; the person needs a just economic, cultural and political setting in which to be able to make the choices which they have every right to make (1740).

The transition to the following paragraph is extremely abrupt. The reader might well ask what the proper exercise of freedom and the conditions which should be provided for it have to do with salvation and the freedom which Christ has won for us all, which is the burden of 1741. I surmise, from the title of this paragraph ('Liberation and salvation') that the link might be found in the controversies which have arisen in connection with liberation theology. If that is correct, then 1741 might be seen as an attempt to balance, or perhaps to correct, the previous one in which the emphasis was on the ways in which unjust social structures can be a violation of the rights of people to the just exercise of their freedom. It has sometimes been alleged that 'liberation theologians' have focused on social and political liberation to the exclusion of any other sense in which human beings might stand in need of liberation. Of course social and political liberation is not identical with the freedom with which Christ liberates us from the power of sin. (It may indeed be doubted whether any responsible theologian in fact identifies them.) So perhaps the point of 1741 is to say just that. Still, it remains important to say that the struggle for social and political liberation is nevertheless a requirement on those who claim to have been liberated from sin by the freedom Christ has won for us, in order to counteract a *wholly* 'other-worldly' interpretation of what Christ has done. I hope that this is a correct interpretation of the logic behind the two paragraphs, but the *Catechism* makes no comment on how its authors intended them to be connected.

B. The morality of human acts

Here again the *Catechism* generally follows Aquinas. The morality of an action depends on its object, on the agent's intention, and on the circumstances. For an action to be morally good, all of these elements have to be good.[20] The general picture is clear enough: for an action to be right, it must be the *kind* of action which is at least permissible; if it is done to achieve some further specific end,[21] that end must also be a good end; and the incidental circumstances in which it is done must not be such as to alter its moral quality.

The decision to base the treatment on Aquinas means that the *Catechism* is heir to some of the problems and obscurities which commentators have long noticed in Aquinas's own text. A full discussion of these would need to be very long, and I can here give only some indications of the points which have presented difficulty.

The *Catechism* states that 'the object chosen is a good towards which the will deliberately directs itself' (1751). But in the following paragraph, it states that 'In contrast to the object, the intention resides in the acting subject ... The end is the first goal of the intention and indicates the purpose pursued in the action' (1752). So what, then, is the precise relationship between the object and the intention of an action? There are various possible answers to this question. One could take it to mean that, morally speaking, the object of the action is simply the action-as-the-agent-sees-it, since it is that towards which the will deliberately directs itself. On this reading, object and intention tend to coincide.[22] Thus a government might in all honesty see a curtailment of normal human rights in an emergency as essential for the common good. In such a case, one could argue that both the object, and the intention, are 'to pass an Emergency Powers Act for the common good'. This would square with the *Catechism*'s account of intention, and of the object of the action as 'a good towards which the will is deliberately directed'. Of course, that still leaves open the question whether the measure was justified or not. For the same measure might be regarded by others as an immoral denial of individual rights, and hence as wrong no matter for what purpose it was done.

Another reading of 'object' is suggested by the *Catechism*'s immediately following remark that '*objective* norms of morality express the rational order of good and evil, attested to by conscience' (1751; my italics). So perhaps the object of an action is how that action would *ideally* be regarded, as distinct from how the agent *thinks or intends* that it should be regarded? In that case, whether the measure curtailing human rights was wrong or not depends on the 'objective' facts of the matter, and not on how the government, or the opposition, sincerely believes things to be.

On yet a third reading, the 'object' is simply the curtailment of human rights, and the 'intention' (in this case equivalent to 'end') is the improved national security which the measure is designed to promote. The object has to be evaluated *separately* from the end which is aimed at. But neither this, nor the previous interpretation in terms of the 'objective' facts, is easy to square with the *Catechism*'s initial definitions of 'object' and 'intention'. The average reader is certainly not going to be able to sort all this out, and it seems a pity that the authors have chosen to adopt a terminology which raises so many technical problems which the *Catechism* of its very nature cannot be expected to solve. In practice, the reader should remember that there are various aspects of an action, which all need to be considered in order to give a well-rounded judgement, both of the agent and of what the agent did.

In one significant way, the *Catechism* departs from Aquinas's treatment, whether in an attempt to be simple or by way of deliberate correction it is hard to say.

> It is therefore an error to judge the morality of human acts by considering only the intention that inspires them or the circumstances (environment, social pressure, duress or emergency, etc.) which supply their context. There are acts which, in and of themselves, independently of circumstances and intentions, are always gravely illicit by reason of their object; such as blasphemy and perjury, murder and adultery. One may not do evil so that good may result from it. (1756)

Firstly, this paragraph is hard to reconcile with the account of object and intention which was asserted in 1751. Moreover, it runs together two

346

very different questions: How would the agent describe what they were doing?, and Does a good end ever justify a means which is wrong in itself? That these questions *are* different can be seen by contrasting a government which sees the curtailment of some human rights as a reasonable sacrifice to require for the common good with one which sees it as wrong, but seeks to justify the injustice by the intended outcome. In the first case, the government does *not* intend to do evil that good may result; in the second case it does. 1756 seems to assert that whether the measure is illicit or not is to be settled by looking at the object *as distinct from* the intention of the government, contrary to 1751–1752. But in that case, the *Catechism* offers no clear test for determining what the object of the action itself is.

Secondly, while the *Catechism* repeats Aquinas's view that circumstances can change the *degree* of rightness or wrongness of an action and are in that sense 'secondary elements of a moral act' (1754), it nowhere repeats Aquinas's further view that in some cases circumstances are more properly to be considered *part* of the object of the action itself.[23] 1756 would have been acceptable to Aquinas only if it were to stipulate that those circumstances which make a difference to the species of an action itself, whether to make it good or to make it bad, have *already* been taken into account in saying what the object of the action is. This is no mere quibble. It underlines the difficulty already mentioned that these apparently technical paragraphs in fact fail to provide any general criterion for deciding what the action in itself is, and hence for deciding which actions in themselves are illicit no matter what good results they might have or in what circumstances they are performed.

If one turns to the treatment of such issues in later sections, we find cases where circumstances have indeed been considered part of the action itself, as traditional moral theology would lead us to expect; thus, for instance, 'lying' is defined as 'to speak or act against the truth in order to lead into error someone *who has the right to know the truth*' (2483). Given that definition, of course, one need never admit that one might sometimes have to lie to preserve a professional (or confessional) secret; which would be a case of the end justifying an illicit means; for in such cases, telling an untruth simply does not count as lying at all, according to the definition. Similarly, the prohibition against oaths is defined in such a way as not to exclude oaths taken for a good reason (2154), and the duty to take part in the eucharist on Sundays is also defined in such a way as to provide for legitimate reasons for not doing so (2181). To omit going to Mass in order to tend a seriously ill parent, for example, does not count as 'the end justifying an illicit means'. But this desirable result is achieved only by redefining the terms 'lie', 'oath', and 'Sabbath obligation' so as to include circumstances in the definition, contrary to the explicit statements of 1756.

The frequency with which the prohibition against appealing to a good end to justify an illicit means is mentioned (1753, 1754, 1755, 1756, 1759, 1761, 1789) is in itself simply a reiteration of the traditional view that certain types of action are wrong no matter what the circumstances. The

347

difficulty with it is that it is radically question-begging, unless *independent* arguments are brought to show which are the cases in which circumstances or ends alter the very nature of what is being done. An assessment of the principle here must therefore depend on the strength of the arguments used elsewhere in connection with specific issues, such as those mentioned in the previous paragraph. To say that the end does not justify the means is not therefore an argument which can be effectively used to settle controversial issues, and it would be unfortunate were the principle to be presented as if it were. The tradition of the Church has always recognised a difference between, say, omitting to go to Mass on a Sunday in order to care for a sick relative, and framing an innocent man in order to be seen to crack down on drug dealers. *In the light of* these assessments, the second is therefore described as an instance in which the good end does not justify a wrong means; and the first is not so described. 1756 should be read as making this point, but not as foreclosing debate on issues which are still properly open to discussion. Similar remarks might also apply to parallel passages in *Veritatis Splendor* about exceptionless negative moral norms.

C. Conscience

The section on conscience begins by combining the beautiful passage from *Gaudium et Spes* 16 with the more technical definition of Alphonsus Liguori (1776, 1778). This is a helpful starting-point, combining as it does the intensely personal tones of *Gaudium et Spes*, and the cool reminder, still catechetically necessary, that conscience is not some kind of feeling, but rather a *judgement* which therefore stands accountable to reason. As is not uncommon with Vatican documents, the article on conscience sometimes states as facts what are, alas, no more than ideals. It may well be that in one's conscience one is 'alone with God whose voice echoes in his depths'; but the voice one hears might often enough be no more that the voice of one's own prejudices. It may be that 'by the judgement of his conscience . . . man perceives and recognizes the prescriptions of the divine law', but it may also be that we only *think* we do.

Of course the *Catechism* recognises this, and contains a whole sub-section on erroneous conscience, on which more presently. But the tendency to idealise sometimes leads to statements such as 'In all he says and does, man is obliged to follow faithfully what he *knows* to be just and right' (1778; my italics). That is true, but it is also true that we are obliged to follow what we sincerely *believe* to be right, even if we are mistaken. There is perhaps a similar difficulty with 1790, where it is said that 'A human being must always obey the *certain* judgement of his conscience' (again, my italics). If 'certain' here means 'of which we are completely convinced', then the statement is true, but might give the erroneous impression that we should not, or may not, follow judgements of conscience which seem to us on balance to be true, but not to be certain. If 'certain' means 'true', then again the unfortunate impression is given that these are the only judgements of conscience that we should follow. And although 1793 does say that if we follow an inculpably erroneous conscience, we cannot be blamed, it is less clear than Aquinas's assertion that we are positively *obliged* to follow our conscience in such a case.[24] The very proper concern to avoid encouraging laxity thus unfortunately leads to statements which are less clear than they might be. On these points the *Catechism* is to be interpreted in the light of the traditional teaching on the duty to follow one's best judgement even when it is mistaken.

The *Catechism* stresses the importance of moral education and the proper formation of conscience (1783–1789). While much in this article is straightforward and unexceptionable, there are two passages which, as it seems to me, could be very seriously misleading, and possibly in the technical sense scandalous. They read as follows:

> The education of conscience is indispensable for human beings who are subjected to negative influences and tempted by sin to prefer their own judgement and to reject authoritative teachings. (1783)

> Ignorance of Christ and his Gospel, bad example given by others, enslavement to one's passions, assertion of a mistaken notion of autonomy of conscience, rejection of the Church's authority and her teaching, lack of conversion and of charity; these can be at the source of errors of judgement in moral conduct. (1792)

The first passage certainly does not *say* that to prefer one's own judgement to that of some authority is to be tempted by sin, but it might easily give that impression. Were 1783 to be read that way in all its breadth,[25] it would rule out any dissent from one's parents, or from the laws of a state which is in general a just one, or from non-infallible teachings of the Church. That would be an absurd position. The view that it is sinful to 'prefer one's own judgement' seriously misleads, if only because one has to judge upon the credentials of any given authority on a given point. One should *never* abandon one's own best judgement, least of all when judging that the statements of an authority should be accepted. The antithesis set up in 1783 is a false one, unless it is much more carefully nuanced and explained. This misleading impression could easily be reinforced by 1792, even though this passage, too, can be interpreted in a reasonable sense. It is indeed possible that all the items mentioned *could* be the 'at the source of errors'; but not all of them inevitably are. Not, for instance, ignorance of Christ and his gospel. For while it may be that the revealed gospel is a help to moral discernment, as the *Catechism* has earlier remarked, the general position taken by the *Catechism* is that this help is certainly not *essential*, as the lives of many saintly non-Christians might testify. But it is at least unfortunate that the *Catechism* does not recognise, either in 1792 or in 1783, that people might dissent from some non-infallible authoritative teaching *and be correct*, having been led to dissent by a love of truth itself. Examples abound. The authoritarian tone of these two passages runs the serious risk of undermining what is said elsewhere in this article. Far from encouraging a love and respect for the authority of the Church, such views can easily serve to diminish it. The important and valuable point surely is that people should be taught to be discerning about their own motives, and encouraged to be sufficiently honest to recognise when they are being tempted to ignore the Church by motives which are dishonest or sinful in some other way.

In 2038–2039 the *Catechism* states that the Church has need both of the 'knowledge of theologians and the contribution of all Christians and men of good will'. 'Thus the Holy Spirit can use the humblest to enlighten the learned and those in the highest positions.' It then goes on to say that 'Personal conscience and reason should not be set in opposition to the moral law or the Magisterium of the Church'. This last sentence will have to be read in the light of the preceding ones, and as stating an ideal which may not always be realised in practice. Surely the Church should formulate its authoritative teachings in such a way that their grounding in revelation, reason, and the experience of the faithful is manifest. It must therefore be clear to the catechumen that those teachings and 'those in the highest places' have in fact been enlightened by the faithful, as well as the other way round. As the *Catechism* itself points out, 'Faith and the practice of the Gospel provide each person with an experience of life in Christ, who enlightens him and makes him able to evaluate the divine and human realities according to the Spirit of God'. The crucial point, surely, is that the catechumen, more than anyone, has to make a judgement, a judgement which will be made on what can be seen of the interaction between the Spirit-enlightened experience of Catholics and the authoritative teachings of the Church as a whole. The holiness of the Church as a whole is supposed to provide one of the motives which might lead a catechumen to accept the gift of faith.[26] The Church must therefore commend itself to the person seeking faith, among other things by an obvious willingness to listen to the views and experience of its members. Such a willingness is not displayed by describing all dissent as inadmissible.

D. The virtues
The article on the virtues requires little by way of commentary. But one minor point is perhaps worth making. In 1804 virtues are defined as habitual dispositions of the intellect and will. I would have thought that the better tradition distinguished between intellectual virtues (especially, in this context, the intellectual virtue of 'prudence') and the moral virtues, which, to put the matter in modern terms, have more to do with the balance of our emotional and instinctual responses.[27] On this view, the perfectly virtuous person, who has the emotional balance called 'temperance', does not *need* self-control, as is indeed suggested by 1810, but not suggested by 1809. Self-control is required when one's emotional and instinctual responses are *not* in harmony with what one judges ought to be done. That lack of harmony is what was traditionally meant by lack of the moral virtues. Temperance is a moral virtue, consisting in the proper balance of one's appetites for pleasure (in contrast to fortitude,

which is to have a balanced degree of aggression). Temperance is therefore *not* best translated 'self-control'. The *Catechism* has not really made up its mind whether to define moral virtue in terms of habitual choices (which are a matter of intellect and will) or in terms of habitual emotional dispositions.

E. Sin

In 1849 Aquinas I-II, 76, 1 is cited for the definition of sin. He there makes it clear that when it is said that sin is 'an utterance, a deed or a desire contrary to the eternal law', it is voluntary desires which are in question, not simply spontaneous ones. Unless 1849 is read against its original context, it could give the impression that the mere occurrence of a desire might constitute a sin.

In distinguishing between mortal sin and venial sin, the *Catechism* repeats Aquinas's doctrine that the Ten Commandments deal with matter which is in itself serious (1858). This too is to be taken in the context of his immediately following remarks. The *Catechism* is not saying that all sins against the Ten Commandments involve grave matter, but merely that they involve the kind of areas which are potentially grave matter. Thus, killing, adultery, lying are by their very nature serious issues. But not every failure to observe the commandments is necessarily equally serious. Once again, the original context in Aquinas must be understood, or the brief remark in the *Catechism* could mislead.

The *Catechism* does not discuss the theory that it would be rare to find an individual action which so fully expressed the rejection of God as to deserve exclusion from Christ's kingdom. 1861 does indeed point out that mortal sin, like love itself, 'is a radical possibility of human freedom', a remark which could be one element in such a theory; and the comparison between mortal sin and love perhaps suggests that mortal sin is unlikely to be an *isolated* action. In any event, the *Catechism* is content to say only that we should exercise caution in making any definitive ascriptions of blameworthiness. A more elaborate, and controversial, discussion of these issues is given in *Veritatis Splendor*.

IV. The human community

The *Catechism* deals with Christian social ethics by giving an admirable summary of the main lines of thought developed in the recent documents of Vatican II and the social encyclicals of recent popes. These are well known and are so clearly expressed as not to require much in the way of detailed comment here.

It might be worth remarking that in general the social and political theory of the Church is much more Aristotelian in spirit than more recent contractarian theories. That is to say, it starts off with a view of human beings as by nature social beings, rather than with the more typical Enlightenment view that they are individuals who have to construct a society by mutual agreement (1879). It has long been regarded as a difficulty with contractarian theories that they find it very difficult to derive anything like an adequate theory of social justice from their individualistic starting-points. On the other hand, one might say that the more Aristotelian theories are at their strongest when societal groups are sufficiently small to make mutual interdependence a real part of people's everyday experience. (See some remarks to this effect in 1882.) Perhaps in this context, the stress on the Principle of Subsidiarity is all the more important (1883–1885). Interdependence is more of a practical and psychological possibility when the group with which one is involved is smaller rather than larger.

In 1888, the *Catechism* tries to balance the view that it is unrealistic to expect individuals to convert to a more just way of living while unjust structures remain in place, against the view that unless individuals are converted, unjust structures never will be removed. It does so, I think, by refusing to say which of these must precede the other *in time*; perhaps the view is that both must proceed hand in hand. The difficulties of our own day, where new states are endeavouring to replace previously unjust structures almost overnight, provides a ready example of the practical problems which underlie this paragraph.

The remainder of this chapter reiterates already well-known principles: that the flourishing of individuals is the primary aim of communities; that the common good requires solidarity of all classes, and a just reward for labour; that the authority of the state and its laws depends on their being so organised as to serve the common good. It is especially noteworthy that the *Catechism* stresses the plight of refugees (1911), the corrosive effect of fraud and corruption in public life (1916), and the scandal of unjust inequalities (1938). While it mentions the wrongness of discrimination on grounds of race, sex, creed, class, language or religion where such discrimination infringes on the basic rights of persons (1935), there is no elaboration upon the evils of racism, or upon the rights of women or the specific forms of discrimination to which women are subjected. Given the detailed elaboration of other moral issues, it seems quite disproportionate that these major contemporary problems receive such cursory treatment.

The whole chapter on social justice is remarkable for its humane tone, and for the very general level at which it is formulated. It proposes ideals which have to be borne in mind, but on the whole does not descend to the details of particular issues. In this, it is in sharp contrast with the way the *Catechism* treats other moral issues. It is not easy to say which approach is the more helpful. Some might wish for more detailed remarks on exactly which kinds of discrimination infringe on basic personal rights; others might have wished for less efforts to give detailed opinions in other areas of morality. As Aquinas pointed out, the more detailed one tries to be, the less likely it is that one will be correct about every case.[28] Either way, though, there is in the end no substitute for practical wisdom, and for the gift of Wisdom that is the Holy Spirit.

V. Conclusions

This Part of the *Catechism* is in many respects a very traditional document, in that its overall approach repeats in outline, and often in detail, the treatment of these topics in Aquinas. It is therefore illuminating to see the points at which the concerns of the authors have led them to depart significantly from a tradition to which they are in general very sympathetic.

There are, I think, three such concerns. The first is the most positive of the three, to place the entire topic of Christian ethics in the context of the Beatitudes. This would be a most welcome development, had it been more systematically carried through. In fact, though, the rest of the Part is influenced hardly at all by its starting-point, despite the emphasis there given to what is said to be the heart of the gospel. The second concern is with the absoluteness of certain moral values, which leads to the repeated emphasis on the thesis that a good end cannot justify a means which is in itself wrong. The target here is evidently the views of those who would be more flexible in the way that acknowledged values have to be pursued, and hence less absolutist in their approach to the more controversial moral issues of the day. I have already remarked that the *Catechism* itself, like the Catholic tradition generally, is by no means consistently absolutist in its own treatment of such issues. The principle that the end does not justify illicit means holds good as a shorthand way of expressing a conclusion which has already been reached. It is less effective as an argument in favour of some conclusion, which is how it appears to be presented in the text. The third concern is to increase the scope and the power of authority in moral matters, which has as a result that the details of its remarks on the relations between conscience, revelation, authority, and moral judgements are almost incoherent in places. Whatever one might think of the extent to which authority needs strengthening in scope and in power, the *Catechism* seems at times to try to achieve this by means of statements which might well have just the opposite effect. On all these points, it seems to me that the *Catechism* should be read and interpreted in the light of the tradition, rather than the other way round.

The *Catechism* mentions the need for the Church to learn from the work of theologians and the experience of the faithful. Unfortunately, it seems to have made little use of any contemporary biblical scholarship in its approach to the biblical texts, and little use of the work of contemporary moral philosophers or theologians elsewhere. While there are no doubt advantages in resting so much on the text of Aquinas, doing so with little effort to express his views in more modern terminology makes the text in many places somewhat inaccessible. The section on the philosophical basis for ethics, in which the terminology is very largely medieval and highly technical, contrasts markedly with the wholly contemporary 'feel' of the sections on social ethics. Why is the one so nervous and defensive in tone, while the other is so challenging and idealistic? One cannot escape the impression that it is because the faithful have largely accepted the contemporary social teaching of the Church with gratitude, whereas they may have many more reservations in other areas. If that is the explanation, an opportunity has surely been missed to put the *Catechism*'s own teachings more obviously into practice.

Notes

1   1691–2051. The chapter headings in this Section are 'The dignity of the human person', 'The human community', and 'God's salvation: law and grace'. Especially the first of these gives only the slightest indication of the contents.

2   See the so-called Household Codes, Col 3:18 – 4:1, Eph 5:21 – 6:9.

3   A particularly glaring example of this is the citation of Jer 1:5 and Ps 139:15 in the context of abortion (2270).

4   One constructive suggestion might be that one should try to learn how the biblical writers, the doctors of the Church, and the great moral theologians, in their different ways, thought, reasoned and argued. Garth Hallett's *Christian Moral Reasoning* (University of Notre Dame Press, 1983) is a good example of how such a suggestion might be developed.

5   For a comparatively recent discussion of the controversies to which the Council of Trent was responding, the reader might wish to consult Hans Küng, *Justification* (London: Burns & Oates, 1981).

6   The point which Trent was addressing had to do with whether a human being could know with certainty that they would be saved, or were in a state of sanctifying grace. See DS 1533.

7   Aquinas in similar vein writes 'Faith presupposes natural knowledge, just as grace presupposes nature': *Summa Theologiae* I, 2, 2 ad 1.

8   This is not, of course, to deny that there can be individual laws which are unjust, nor indeed that entire legal systems might be corrupt in theory and in practice. I suggest merely that, where this is not the case, Christians should be as willing to learn from the deliberations of the law now as the Israelites were from the legal enactments of their own non-Israelite contemporaries.

9   It will help to notice that the use of the phrase 'the new law' in the *Catechism* is complex. On the one hand, the new law is identified with the grace of the Holy Spirit (1966); but it is also said to contain the Beatitudes, the Sermon on the Mount, and other biblical texts (1971), as well as precepts and counsels (1973). This twofold use of the phrase goes back to Aquinas, who says that in its primary sense the new law just is the gift of the Spirit; but secondarily, the phrase can also be applied to the words and writings which are used to dispose people to respond to the gift of the Spirit (STh I-II, 106, 1).

10 Where clear mention is made of additional content, the result is not very happy. The claim (which is also to be found in Aquinas) about the newness of Jesus' teaching on the importance of internal attitudes as well as external behaviour is much exaggerated. Jesus here aligns himself with strands in the Jewish tradition which were already well established. (See, e.g., Mk 7:6–8, and Eusebius's comments in *Hist. Eccl.* I, 15–16.) The mention of the evangelical counsels as manifesting the fullness of charity, and as offering a readier means of developing charity than is involved in keeping the commandments (1973–1974) is indeed, as the *Catechism* says, a traditional

doctrine; but one which surely ought to have been re-thought.

11   It is surely an overstatement to suggest, in connection with the Beatitudes, that they reveal to us that 'true happiness is not to be found in any creature, but only in God' (1723). Creatures, in so far as they reflect the goodness of God, can and should be rejoiced in, and should be a source of true happiness. One ought not to *oppose* the love of creatures and the love of God, even when one says that our *ultimate* happiness is in God.

12   The rather simple model offered by Vatican I, especially if it is extended beyond questions about the mystery of God to include ethics which is not in that sense a mystery at all (see above, p. 338), is very incomplete in contrast with the treatment of these issues offered by Aquinas.

13   A complete list of examples would be very long: but a good idea of the general approach can be found in the replies to the objections in the various articles in STh I, 3; see also 10, 1 ad 4.

14   STh I, 100, 8. Among the examples, the command to sacrifice Isaac, Hosea's relationship with a woman who was not his wife.

15   As Aquinas also says: STh I-II, 99, 2 ad 3.

16   I have not here dealt with the more technical questions concerning what precisely is meant by 'revelation', and how exactly one is to relate the truth that Jesus is the primordial revelation with the common usage which identifies revelation with a set of *statements*. These issues are more properly considered elsewhere.

17   In passing, one might note the remark in 1703 that human beings are the only creatures on earth which God willed for their own sake, quoted from *Gaudium et Spes* 24 §3. A different view might be that since all creatures in their way reflect a perfection of God, they are all to that extent 'willed for their own sakes', even if one wishes to say that they are also willed for the sake of human beings. One might perhaps not wish to foreclose debates about morality and ecology quite so brusquely. 2416–2418 presents a very different picture, however.

18   The whole subject is a minefield of possible equivocations and unclarities. Aquinas's views, on which the *Catechism* draws, are to be found in STh I-II, 10, 1–2, and 113, 3. But the issue is made more complex by the fact that Aquinas can speak not only of *liberum arbitrium*, but also of *voluntarium*, cf. STh I-II, 6. There is no one unambiguous translation of *voluntarium* in English. The *Catechism* uses 'voluntary' in its technical sense, which it does not fully explain. Aquinas's general position is that human beings by natural necessity will their happiness; and when, as in the unique case of the beatific vision, they know this happiness in its fullness, they are determined by natural necessity also to will it. This act of will would *not* be an instance of *liberum arbitrium*, free will; but it would in the highest degree be *voluntarium*, since the willing is in the fullest accord with the desire of a person for good. But the detailed application of these notions, in Aquinas as in Aristotle, is still a matter of scholarly debate.

19   See the previous note.

20   STh I-II, 18.

21   There is a problem about the best translation of *finis* here in Aquinas. The *Catechism* opts for 'intention', which is unsatisfactory, since the object of the action is also intended. The simplest example in Aquinas is a military manoeuvre for the sake of a victory (STh I-II, 18, 7), but he also considers stealing in order either to give alms, or to commit adultery. 'Aim' might have been better; and at least 'end' would have been non-committal.

22   At least one widely held interpretation of 'intention' is that the agent's
     intention consists in the way that the agent would describe the action. On
     this reading, it might include both Aquinas's *objectum* and his *finis*. Thus, a
     general might intend to manoeuvre to gain a victory.

23   STh I-II, 18, 10, and the replies to the objections. One might, for instance,
     wonder whether someone who has been living in an invalid second marriage
     for ten years can properly be said to be committing adultery in anything like
     the same sense as someone who is unfaithful to an otherwise valid and
     successful marriage commits adultery.

24   STh I-II, 19, 5.

25   Perhaps 'authoritative teachings' here is intended to refer only to the
     authoritative teachings of the Church; but the text does not say so.

26   Vatican I, *Dei Filius*, ch. 3, DS 301.

27   See, for instance, Aquinas, STh I-II, 58. One might also remark that
     'practical wisdom' or even 'moral discernment' might be a much better
     contemporary translation of the Latin *prudentia* and the Greek *phronēsis*
     than the now misleading 'prudence'.

28   STh I-II, 94, 4.

More than Law and Precept: Commandments 1 to 3

(Paragraphs 2052–2195)

Bernhard Häring CSsR

Gars-am-Inn

The third Part of the new *Catechism* deals with the perspectives, dimensions and tasks of moral theology. After a careful reading, it has to be said that it is a most earnest and encouraging effort to understand the moral teaching of the Catholic Church in the light of the Second Vatican Council, which asked for an especial effort to be made to renew moral theology in the light of salvation-history and the mystery of Christ.[1] For this reason I suggest that no one should read the Section dealing with the 'Ten Commandments' before having carefully studied the first Section on 'Man's vocation: life in the Spirit'.

The renewal of moral theology is also evident in the decision to treat sacramental life (the second Part of the *Catechism*) before the treatise on moral theology. I would remind the reader that most of the manuals of moral theology after the Council of Trent treated the sacraments after the commandments as a means to, and providing strength for, heeding all the commandments and laws of the Church. In the new *Catechism* there appears the joy of faith and of celebration of the Christian mystery. Only by beginning there can we understand Christian morality as 'Life in Christ' (the third Part of the *Catechism*). These are without doubt major changes in the right direction, and they help to consolidate the renewal of Christian ethics within the Catholic Church.

It is clear that one of the main perspectives of the Bible, that of bearing fruit in love, justice and peace for the life of the world, characterises the thrust of the new *Catechism*.

As I have been asked to write a commentary on Section Two, 'The Ten Commandments', and particularly on the first three commandments, I will confine my reflections to this part, though always, of course, in the light of the whole work.

1. A free choice

There was no obligation to choose the Decalogue as the outline. The authors know that it has only been 'since St Augustine [that] the Ten Commandments have occupied a predominant place in the catechesis' (2065). More characteristic is a catechesis on the Christian life cast in the light of the Sermon on the Mount. The new *Catechism* proves, however, that an outline based on the Decalogue can integrate well the main vision and dynamic of the Beatitudes.

One advantage of doing so is the convincing presentation that is made of the continuity between the old and the new covenant. What is said about the relationship between 'Covenant and Law' (2052 and elsewhere) is indeed helpful. Christian moral life, even more so than in the Old Testament, is a *covenant morality*. The Israelites venerated 'the tables of the Testimony . . . in the ark' (2058). Observing the law has its depth and strength in gratitude for the gift of the covenant. For us Christians, Christ himself is the covenant: not law by itself, but covenant is the key word of the Old Testament. Christ, the non-violent servant, is foretold as 'the covenant of the people'. 'I am the Lord, I have chosen you in righteousness . . . I have given you as the covenant to the people, the light of the nations' (Is 42:6; author's translation throughout). In his dialogue with Trypho, a Jew, Justin insists that for us Christians Christ 'is the law and the Covenant'.[2] This is reason for joy, and a call to solidarity: 'We share in a common life, that life which we share with the Father and his Son, Jesus Christ. And we write this in order that the joy of us all may be complete' (1 Jn 1:3–4). The new *Catechism* makes an effort to keep this perspective alive. This is a strong motive and call to overcome individualism (2060–2063, 2069 and elsewhere).

2. In the light of the twofold gift and law of love

The first table of the Decalogue tells us what contradicts the covenantal relationship with God the Creator and Liberator. The *Catechism*, however, centres on a positive approach: the infinite love of God for his people and for every human being, the gift of his love in Jesus Christ and through the Holy Spirit, and then the kind of response, love in return, which God rightly expects from us. The model is the Lord's Prayer: the first three petitions deal with the love of God, of his holy name, the longing for the coming of his reign, the fulfilment of his loving plan of salvation (his holy will).

The *Catechism* insists on God's initiative, his self-revelation, his gift of love. Love is infinitely more than law, precept, commandment. It is the supreme gift, the loving presence of God's grace enabling us to abide in his love, and to respond lovingly in faith, hope, love, in prayer and in all of life.

The second table of the Decalogue is presented just like the second part of the 'Our Father', as the several dimensions of love of neighbour. Here, too, the covenant dimension is ever present with its distinctively Christian aspect — love of neighbour 'as Christ has loved us', and as abiding in the love of Jesus who shares his love with all of us.

3. The paracletic dimension

The new *Catechism* gives due attention to the paracletic quality of a distinctively Christian moral theology. This comes to the fore not only throughout the whole Section on 'Life in the Spirit', but also in the explanation of the Decalogue in the light of the Old and New Testaments. The prologue to the Decalogue reminds the Israelites of the great deeds of God the Liberator; it reminds Christians of the even greater deeds of God in Christ the Liberator, the Saviour. From this remembrance comes not a dry imperative but a well-grounded expectation that gratitude will inspire us to respond gratefully, faithful to the covenant morality.

The enormous importance of a grateful memory, shaped and strength-ened through the celebration of the covenant, cannot be overlooked. It is there already in the epilogue to the Decalogue: 'Hear, O Israel, the Lord is our God, one Lord, and you are expected to love the Lord your God with all your heart, and soul and strength. These commands which I give you this day are to be kept in your memory. You shall repeat them to your sons' (Dt 6:4–7). The whole of Christian life receives its strength and joy through the memory of him, through a grateful memory of all the signs and deeds of his love (cf. 2074, 2083–2085 and *passim*).

To the extent that we fully understand the paracletic dynamism and learn to communicate it, bad moralism will be overcome. Then will Christian life bear fruit in joy, peace, love and justice.

4. Emphasis on the newness of Christian life

The decision to follow the outline and structure of the Decalogue demonstrates a desire to show the continuity from Old to New Testament, though without neglecting to show equally the newness of authentic Christian life. 'Love your neighbour as yourself' is the abiding natural law written on the hearts of all and explained and deepened by the Old Testament. But the Christian knows the love of the Father in a new way, for Christ shows us the Father: 'Anyone who has seen me has seen the Father' (Jn 14:9). We Christians have in Jesus the unique *eikōn*, the image of the Father, the unsurpassable embodiment of the love of God in Jesus Christ. To know him with heart and mind teaches us what true, redeemed and redeeming love demands.

Similarly, due attention is given to the solemn words, 'You have learned ... but what I tell you is this ...' (Mt 5:17–46), leading to the supreme, all-embracing commandment, 'There must be no limit to your goodness, as your heavenly Father's goodness knows no bounds' (Mt 5:48; cf. the parallel in Lk 6:36, 'Be compassionate as your Father is compassionate').

The new *Catechism* firmly excludes a mere borderline moralism. The Decalogue speaks to us in the light of the morality of the Beatitudes, of each of which Christ himself is the complete embodiment (cf. 2055, 2074, 2012–2016).

All this clearly shines through the section on the Christian life and also in the section on the Decalogue. But it is most beautifully and convincingly present in the final sections of the *Catechism*, where prayer is presented as the integration of faith, adoration and life. The faith, hope and love which we express in our prayer (especially in the 'Our Father') become for our thoughts, desires, deeds and our human relationships the rule by which we live, and the air with which we breathe.

5. Outline of a faith-ethic

One of the guidelines for the entire Part on Christian morality is that of faith bearing fruit throughout the whole of our lives. The completeness of our conversion to the gospel embodied in Christ, the faith-conversion, is the condition for, and fruitful soil of, a life rich in the harvest of the Spirit.

Although the magisterium's role in both faith and morals is strongly emphasised, the *Catechism*'s understanding of faith-ethics is far deeper and very attractive. It is faith gratefully lived, shared in the faith-community, nourished by the liturgy and by a profound life of prayer; faith as joyful, grateful acceptance of God's self-revelation in Jesus Christ; and faith as a response coming from the heart and mind, and shaping all our life. It is all this that is meant by faith-ethics and its moral fruitfulness, its radiance and its testimony. It should not be overlooked that the new *Catechism* repeatedly places due emphasis on God's own initiative. The emphasis is correctly and coherently placed on joyous, grateful faith making us ready for genuine obedience and responsibility, and making all our life fruitful in love, peace and justice.

Yet whenever moral norms, which are in no way part of revelation, are insisted upon by church authorities in the name of God, and as a requirement for the spirit of faith, there is, and especially in our critical age, a considerable danger of serious misunderstanding, and a rejection of faith-ethics within the Church.

The main thrust of the new *Catechism* is surely not an external obedience, but a profound vision of the 'obedience of faith' in its mystical dimension. The 'fruit of holiness' is explained as a life made fruitful by union with Christ. When we believe in Jesus Christ, participate in his mysteries and keep his commandments, the 'Saviour himself comes to love, in us, his Father and his brethren, our Father and our brethren. His person becomes, through the Spirit, the living and interior rule of our activity' (2074). In such a vision there is no place for authoritarian moralism.

6. The liberating power of religion

The liberating power of Christianity has become a chief concern of our times. It is also a central sign for discernment within the Church.

The liberating power of the Decalogue, considered of course in its dynamic fulfilment in the new covenant, is mentioned with reference to the observance of the sabbath, for Christians Sunday, the day of resurrection.

A growing awareness of this dimension can already be found with the history of the formulation of the Decalogue. In the text of Exodus 20 there is mentioned only — but forcefully — the liberation of the people from servitude in Egypt, while Deuteronomy 5 introduces a partial liberation of slaves and servants, making a practical expression of justice towards the weaker members of society.

A similar progress can be discerned in the case of women. In Exodus 20:17, coveting one's neighbour's wife comes within the same list as 'slave, ox, ass' — anything, in other words, which belongs to one's neighbour. In Deuteronomy 5:21, however, the prohibition against coveting one's neighbour's wife is given a specific category, transcending that of property. The *Catechism* does not deal with this question of development. It would have been an appropriate place to discuss the long, and sometimes humiliating, history of the role of women in society and in the Church. Pope John XXIII recognised this issue as one of the signs of our times. It is one of the most contentious issues in the life of the Church of today — and will be in the Church of tomorrow.

The new *Catechism* deals only indirectly with the liberating power of the eucharist, and of Sunday. The otherwise beautiful treatment of the eucharist in Part Two (1322–1419) pays no special attention to the dimension of liberation. Was this an explicit rejection of liberation theology, or simply a lack of awareness of this most burning issue? Does the memorial of the paschal mystery awaken in the Christian community, and in the heart and mind of each Christian, a strong commitment not only to liberation from the servitude of power and money, but also to liberation of the oppressed and exploited, a healing liberation for oppressors and for all who profit from the present unjust and sinful structures of wealth and power?

When dealing with the complex problem of atheism (2124) a 'form of contemporary atheism' is mentioned, one which 'holds that religion, of its very nature, thwarts such emancipation by raising man's hopes in a future life, thus both deceiving him and discouraging him from working for a better form of life on earth' (cf. GS 20 §2). At this point the *Catechism* seems rather to remain at the level of apologetics. Liberation theology, on the other hand, argues quite differently: while Marxism teaches that this is an iron 'law' of dialectical history, liberation theology calls for a serious examination of conscience on the part of all, even of those in the highest authority. Any abuse of religion, or any toleration of such abuse, is not at all inevitable. It is a crime that cries to heaven. It must be unmasked.

Only indirectly, under the heading 'Blasphemy', is there mentioned sin against the liberating power of God's law and covenant: 'It is also blasphemous to make use of God's name to cover up criminal practices, to reduce peoples to servitude, to torture persons or put them to death' (2148). The word 'also' already demonstrates the weakness of the qualification. One might have expected the text to have the courage to say that such a temptation has invaded even the Church itself, and at all levels.

Atheism is today's number one problem. It is said, as in the Second Vatican Council, that

> 'Believers can have more than a little to do with the rise of atheism. To the extent that they are careless about their instruction in the faith, or present its teaching falsely, or even fail in their religious, moral, or social life, they must be said to conceal rather than to reveal the true nature of God and of religion.' (2125; GS 19 §3)

Who is to be included under 'believers'? In the world of today, and in the light of the crisis within the Church, one might have expected a suggestion that difficulties and temptations also arise from church structures, and from improper ways of using power — for example, from the rift between official church teaching on the basic principle of subsidiarity, and the ever-increasing centralism of power and control. And do troubles arise only from false explanations of doctrine, or do they arise more particularly from false teaching, and from the unwillingness to admit to mistakes? How will people feel within the Church — and, even more, how will those God-seekers outside the Church feel — when they are told, with the First Vatican Council, that 'The Church herself, with her marvellous propagation, eminent holiness and inexhaustible fruitfulness in everything good, her catholic unity and invincible stability, is a great and perpetual motive of credibility and an irrefutable witness of her divine mission' (812)? Is not the Church, in this critical age, still too apologetic? Should it not rather accept humbly the challenge of those who tell it, whether in love or in anger, that it should look more redeemed, more humble, if it is to turn our eyes to the Redeemer and Liberator whom it proclaims?

By the declaration on religious liberty the Catholic Church has removed one of the greatest obstacles to credibility (2104–2109). It appears as a confidence-inspiring sign that the Church feels strongly that it can gain credibility only through absolute honesty and sober humility about its past and its present. A Church which confesses its sins and shortcomings before God and the human race is more attractive than a triumphalistic Church. A firm 'yes' to the religious liberty of all, combined with the fulfilment of its liberating mission, will ever more appeal to the upright consciences of sincere seekers of liberating and saving truth.

7. Between the paradigm of obedience and that of responsibility

The first significant catechism based on the Decalogue (St Augustine's *De catechizandis rudibus*) was intended for people who had little education. The long tradition of catechisms, of which the *Catechismus Romanus* was the highlight, served more or less the same purpose. The 1994 *Catechism of the Catholic Church* is written for a wholly different audience. But will it appeal to modern adults with a high level of education? There are living today probably more theologically educated people than lived in all of the first nineteen centuries of Christianity put together. Our generation has lived through the criminal use of 'obedience' by Stalin and Hitler in particular, but by others as well. Those Catholics who, during Hitler's war, refused military service, did not find support among their bishops. Within the Christian community it was common teaching that it fell to the state to decide whether or not a war was just. All moral theologians worth their salt have therefore worked strenuously for a radical change of the paradigm — from (almost) blind obedience towards responsibility. Readers of this new *Catechism* will see how far, if at all, this paradigmatic shift is reflected within its pages.

There is much in this *Catechism* to educate believers in discernment, and the acceptance of responsibility in the secular world. But this intention will be effected chiefly to the extent that the paradigm of 'responsibility' prevails over that of one-sided obedience within the Church itself. Responsible obedience is characterised by mutuality.

The moral life is understood as a response to God's initiative, and as responsible co-operation with the plan God pursues in history (cf. 2062). In the same way, it is explained that the Decalogue teaches us 'true humanity' (2070), and, with a reference to Irenaeus, it is remarked that this is also the purpose of the 'natural law' (2071). When the *Catechism* affirms that the Ten Commandments are 'fundamentally immutable' (2072), it is presumed that people have learned to discern what that 'basic content' may be.

There are, however, some formulations which seem one-sidedly to place the fault on the side of those under authority, without any suggestion of responsibility on the part of those in authority. For example: 'Doubt voluntarily entertained about faith is disregard for or refusal to hold as true what God has revealed and the Catholic Church proposes' (2088). It is not only true of this *Catechism*, but it is also a widespread practice of ecclesiastical authority, to fail clearly to distinguish what is revealed by God from what is church doctrine not based on a clearly-revealed truth. It cannot be overlooked that ecclesiastical authority has sometimes placed more emphasis on doctrines and precepts which do not arise from revelation and which sometimes, after a long period, have been discarded either as not true or as not important. In my view it is one of the new *Catechism*'s greatest weaknesses that alongside basic truths, revealed and shining forth in the holy Scriptures, there are many doctrines and norms which can hardly be shown to belong to the deposit of faith. Yet there is no indication of such a distinction which, in our tradition, has been a constant hallmark of good theology. One of the most striking examples is the way in which, throughout the whole work, original sin is presented without mentioning the present position of most biblical scholars and theologians on its *genus literarium*, and ignoring our current knowledge of historical anthropology.

Another example is the way in which schism is treated as 'the refusal of submission to the Roman Pontiff or of communion with the members of the Church subject to him' (2089). This formulation using the words 'submission' and 'subject' shows little sensitivity for ecumenism. There is, furthermore, no mention of the historical responsibility of the papacy. The view of ethics as obedience (submission) here prevails over a broader vision of our shared responsibility.

Probably the most striking example of a one-sided ethic of obedience is 2181. It is of considerable moment for our Church today. It says 'The Sunday Eucharist is the foundation and confirmation of all Christian practice'. This is beautifully said, and of the greatest relevance for our faith and life. But it then goes on: 'For this reason the faithful are obliged to participate in the Eucharist on days of obligation, unless excused for a serious reason (for example, illness, the care of infants) ... Those who deliberately fail in this obligation commit a grave sin.' My first question is what image of God is implied if a believer, simply for deliberately missing one Sunday Mass, should be guilty of mortal sin and worthy of eternal damnation? But there is another problem which more directly touches our present concern. From those *under* authority obedience is required, with the severe sanction of 'grave sin'. There is not even a hint about the responsibility of those *in* authority. What, for example, if by clinging to a merely human tradition they hinder, Sunday by Sunday, a large, perhaps even the larger, part of Catholics from attending the regular celebration of the Eucharist? I am, of course, referring to the insistence on celibacy as an absolute condition for ordination to the priesthood in the Latin Church. I am firmly convinced of the value of celibacy freely chosen for the sake of the kingdom of God, but Christ chose Peter and other married men, and only afterwards the celibate Paul. I detest the argument frequently heard from churchmen that, were celibacy not required by law as a condition for the priesthood, there would soon be only a small number of celibate clergy. This argument seems to ignore the essential character of charism — not under law but under grace. Fewer celibate priests living the charism joyfully alongside holy, married priests would give an even better witness to celibacy than a larger number upon whom it has been imposed by law. But more important still is this, that no human tradition may contradict the beautiful statement of this *Catechism*, that the eucharist regularly celebrated is 'the foundation and confirmation of all Christian practice'.

The criticism of there being a lack of consistency as far as the paradigm of responsibility is concerned is also valid for my own earlier work *The Law of Christ* (1954).[3] While I argued strongly for a turning towards the ethics of responsibility, I failed to apply it to the duty of the church authorities not to block the basic right of all Christians regularly to celebrate the eucharist: I stopped after having insisted on the duty of the faithful regularly to participate. I, too, considered only the duty of those under authority. To turn from an age-old paradigm to one of shared responsibility is difficult for the individual theologian, and much more so for those responsible for 'law and order'.

In this regard, however, the situation of the Church has changed profoundly since 1954. In Germany at that time, and in Europe more generally, there was no notable shortage of priests. Like most of my colleagues, I was still a prisoner of a Eurocentric vision, unmindful even in so basic an issue of the situation in Latin America, Africa and Asia. Since that time we have learned how to think in a more global manner. This was also the consequence of the Second Vatican Council, which was, more than all other councils of the Church, ecumenical in the sense that all continents were represented by indigenous bishops.

More important still is the renewed self-understanding of the Church since the Council. It sees itself as a 'People of God': all the faithful share a strong co-responsibility for the Church. They are, and constantly become more, aware of their basic rights and duties. I do not think it requires a spirit of prophecy to foresee that in this and similar questions change is already on the way, thanks to strong convictions and world-wide public opinion. The new *Catechism* will not curb this development. On the contrary, it will strengthen the process of discernment so necessary for the future of the Church, and for its mission in the world.

8. Jesus the *eikōn* of the Father

The *Catechism* also discusses the 'veneration of images' (cf. 2129–2132, 2141). The text rightly states that 'By becoming incarnate, God's Son introduced a new economy of images' (2131). In this I miss an aspect very dear to the Orthodox Churches: Christ himself is the *eikōn*, the unique image, of the Father. 'Anyone who has seen me has seen the Father' (Jn 14:9). As Christians, in all things we look to Jesus: to know him, and through him the Father, 'this is eternal life' (Jn 17:3).

The new *Catechism* gives due attention to the main task of all of us to know and love Jesus in order to know and love the Father, and to know our lofty vocation 'in Jesus'. But attention is never drawn to a critical point: do we test all our doctrines, and especially our moral teaching, in this perspective? What image of God spells out this or that doctrine, this or that norm, this or that threat of 'mortal sin'? Before the Second Vatican Council all too many Catholics saw God above all as a 'judge', even though Jesus told us that he did not come to judge but to heal and to save. Overall, however, the *Catechism* is on the right lines.

9. 'The Lord's Holy Name'

What is said so beautifully in the section on God's Holy Name (2142–2159) is treated with even greater beauty and depth in the section on the petition 'Hallowed be thy name' (2807–2815) in the last Book of the *Catechism*.

In 2143 the *Catechism* says: 'Among all the words of Revelation, there is one which is unique: the revealed name of God.' In the Old Testament there was a great change, from names of God which above all inspired fear to a trust-inspiring name, 'I-am-here'. But I miss in this section any mention of the even greater event: Jesus revealing by the whole of his life, by his proclamation of the good news, and even by his death on the cross, the dearest name of God: 'Abba'. In the prayer of his great hour (Jn 17), six times Jesus begins with 'Abba!', and he rejoices 'I have made thy name known to those whom thou didst give me out of the world' (Jn 17:6). It is our highest privilege to exclaim, in union with Jesus and in the power of the Holy Spirit, 'Our Father!'

Next the Catechism treats blasphemy, magical use of the divine name and 'false oaths' (2149–2155). 'An oath or swearing is to take God as witness to what one affirms . . . An oath engages the Lord's name' (2150). 'An oath . . . cannot be taken unless in truth, in judgement and in justice' (2154). Not one self-critical word is said about the use of oaths within the Church. What is said is, rather, apologetic. It is extraordinary that the saying of Jesus on divorce which occurs in the same passage (Mt 5:31–32) is interpreted rigidly in the Western Church, allowing of no exceptions, while today's Church is turning to new and frequent requirements for the taking of oaths of loyalty and similar things. I am not suggesting that the Church should forbid any kind of oaths, but the words of Jesus, 'Plain "Yes" or "No" is all you need to say; anything beyond that comes from the devil' (Mt 5:37), are to be taken most seriously as an instruction from Christ, a goal towards which the Church itself should strive with great earnestness. This would lead to healthier relationships within the Church, and to greater credibility before the world.

Notes

1   Cf. *Optatam Totius* 16.
2   Justin, *Dialogue with Trypho*, chs 11, 24: PG 6, 497, 528.
3   Original German edition 1954, English translation 1963.

You Shall Love Your Neighbour: Commandments 4–10

(Paragraphs 2196–2557)

Joseph A. Selling[1]
Catholic University, Louvain

In the press statements that surrounded the first publication of the new, universal *Catechism* for the Catholic Church, and in the official statements of the hierarchy in the same regard, we were told that the text of this *Catechism* is not intended for direct, local consumption by the faithful, but rather that this text should serve the purpose of providing bishops' conferences with a 'reference text ... for preparing local catechisms'.[2] This being understood, it still remains to ask who the intended audience for this text might be. Is it the bishops themselves? Is it catechetical commissions or drafting commissions working on local texts? Should this audience include the staff of local seminaries, theologically trained professors whose instincts will lead them back 'to the source' as it were, evaluating or perhaps even writing local texts on the basis of the Vatican's example? How one is to understand the *Catechism* will have a good deal to do with a fair conception of its intended audience.

Some of this questioning may be superfluous for much of the *Catechism*'s text. However, it appears to be crucial to the development of those sections pertinent to the area of moral theology, especially when we take into account the words of John Paul II, who writes that the *Catechism* 'is meant to encourage and assist in the writing of new local catechisms, which must take into account various situations and cultures, while carefully preserving the unity of faith and fidelity to Catholic doctrine'.[3] Certainly the elaboration of norms is closely tied to 'various situations and cultures'. At the same time, this begs the question of the content, specificity and relevance of various aspects of the 'faith' and 'Catholic doctrine' with respect to the task of formulating norms or guidelines for moral decision-making.

At the heart of these considerations, it is equally appropriate to consider questions of style, form and method, as well as those of content, when it comes to Part Three of the work, on 'Life in Christ'. It is simply observed by the official commentators that this Book will be based upon the Ten Commandments, as if it is a foregone conclusion that the similar structure of the Roman Catechism (the Catechism of the Council of Trent) is normative or even desirable. One could ask whether this is a sufficient excuse to adapt a system that ultimately became one of the pitfalls of Counter-Reformation theology, giving rise to the debates about probabilism, making itself vulnerable to rationalism, and fostering a legalistic ethics devoid of scriptural, theological or Christological insights. Overcoming these biases turned out to be a tremendous task that culminated in the achievement of Vatican II. Is it therefore necessary to repeat the experience all over again?

Before getting to the commandments themselves, the *Catechism* itself indulges in an introductory work of 'fundamental moral theology' which has already been commented upon by others. While this work starts out on what I would consider to be the right foot, taking the dignity of the human person created in the image of God as its starting-point, it quickly turns into a more traditional textbook form of moral theology that is reminiscent of pre-Vatican II thinking. Slowly but surely, most of the traditional categories of thinking are introduced into the text: the subtleties of directness and voluntariness with regard to 'effects' are introduced at 1736–1737,[4] the *tres fontes moralitatis* are addressed at 1750, and intrinsically evil acts make their appearance at 1756. Even the notion of *sunderēsis* pops up in paragraph 1780.[5] In the midst of this traditional structure we find the exposition of conscience which, although it begins with the famous description of *Gaudium et Spes* 16 as a faculty of moral discernment (1776), quickly deteriorates into describing a mechanism of rational judgement that must be rightly 'formed' in order to function properly in carrying out the dictates of the moral law. It is on the basis of this 'fundamental' outlook that one discovers the central place of rules, norms, regulations, or, in the Judaeo-Christian tradition, commandments. For even though the text follows its discourse on conscience with a treatise on virtue, it is clear that the author(s) of the *Catechism* maintain the central place of commandments in the exposition of morality, even moral theology.

The fourth commandment

Traditionally, if I may use that term, the fourth commandment has provided an occasion for discussing all forms of authority, thus not simply that of the family. One's expectations will not be disappointed in the 50 paragraphs that the *Catechism* devotes to this commandment, although one might be surprised at how little attention is actually paid to the 'broader perspective', as it were. Since Chapter Two of the preceding Section of the *Catechism* already touched upon the question of authority and social living (1897–1917), the author(s) may have considered this repetitious.

The very first paragraph (2197) draws attention to the idea that all authority is ultimately derived from God, who distributes it for the purpose of our well-being. This is followed by the somewhat novel idea that the fourth commandment, putting forth the concept of general authority, somehow introduces the 'particular' aspects of human living that will be covered by the subsequent commandments (2198). It is presumably this call to heed authority that is said to be 'one of the foundations of the social doctrine of the Church'. Then, in an effort to extend the scope of what will follow, 2199 proposes that the fourth commandment applies not only within families but also 'to the duties of pupils to teachers, employees to employers, subordinates to leaders, citizens to their country and to those who administer or govern it'. One may wonder about the invocation of the authority–obedience schema in reference to the employer–employee relationship. Fortunately, this article never returns to this area, except for a brief mention of 'right relations between employers and employees' in 2213. I believe that such an approach would have been a mistake, if not merely confusing for those who have read *Laborem Exercens* (1981), for it could then be open to the accusation of introducing paternalism into the work-place.

On the other hand, there are a number of very positive ideas in this article. The text emphasises the equal dignity of all human persons, including every member of the family (2203), that is based upon creation in the image of God, being children of God, so that every relationship with the neighbour is really 'personal in character' (2212). Further, it is proposed that the way in which children 'learn moral values' (2207) is not simply by imposition but by good example, even by parents 'knowing how to acknowledge their own failings' (2222–2223; cf. 2232). This puts forth a high standard or pedagogical model that contrasts with the older but still present models of rigid authoritarian structure in the family that elicit obedience as response (2216–2217). As a parent, I must admit that the text left me somewhat cold. The kind of obedience that I expect from my children is not the kind of simple, absolutistic, unquestioning and uncritical obedience that I see described here (2216–2217). Perhaps I was reading into the text, but the unattributed quotation found in 2217 appears to substantiate such a notion when it speaks to the 'emancipation' of children at the age of majority when 'obedience towards parents ceases'. In other words, I find unequal and inconsistent images of the parent–child relationship described here that do not necessarily help me understand my responsibilities either as a child or as a parent.

The greater part of this article deals with the family, relations between family and society, and relations within the family itself. The bases for the article are set upon such notions as the common good, the well-being of all persons, and the principle of subsidiarity. For once there is more material on the duties of parents than those of children. However, there appears to be a rather simple presumption that if the family gets it right, everything else will fall into place. For the vast majority of the people of the world, this is simply not the case. Calling the family the 'original cell of social life' (2207) does not make it so. A number of bishops represented at the 1980 Synod on the Family apparently felt the same thing when they accused the preparatory documents for that meeting of 'family-ism', the notion that the family is virtually the exclusive agent of social justice.[6] Quite the contrary was the experience of many that the family is more the victim of poverty, structural injustice, and political and economic dictatorship. One does not recognise the family as victim of social injustice in the text of the *Catechism*, leaving one to lament the fact that little or nothing is said about this very real situation.

The fifth and last section of the article, on 'Authorities in civil society', is much more thought-provoking. What we find here is by and large classical moral theology, enhanced with the substantiating but unsubstantiated arguments from the 'fundamental rights of persons' (2237, 2242, 2246).[7] Such references to rights, in particular 'political rights' (2237), beg the question of how the document arrives at its notion of human rights. The absence of any argumentation makes the subsequent (and predictable) invocation of 'the duties of citizens' (2238–2243) appear apodictic. Still, what is written here has already made many people sit up and take notice when parts of the *Catechism* were leaked to the press some months ago. Stating that it is 'morally obligatory to pay taxes, to exercise the right to vote, and to defend one's country' (2240) will be applauded by many, not the least of whom will be political leaders. When the applause dies, however, we are still left with the real ethical questions about how to solve conflict situations: when taxes imposed are exorbitant (or unjustly levied), when voting does nothing more than exchange one corrupt politician for another, or when defending one's country is tantamount to defending communist or capitalist dictatorship. Further, the same paragraph appears to undermine its own argument with a quotation from an anonymous ancient work that refers to Christians as 'resident aliens' whose 'way of life surpasses the laws'. Centuries of argument about whether Christians should participate in military activity have apparently been forgotten, or at least suspended, by the author(s) of this text.

At the same time, it is good to see that 'a spirit of criticism'[8] as the 'right and at times the duty' of 'loyal collaboration' in society has been institutionalised in this text (2238). Abandoning the traditionalist prejudice that civil authority is *ipso facto* legitimate unless proved otherwise beyond a shadow of a doubt — a position that was taught up until the time of the world wars in this century — the *Catechism* understands that our relation with political and civil power is much more complex. Traditionally, the thinking on this subject was based upon the idea that no one is obliged to follow the directives of (even a legitimate) authority when this violates conscience or the moral order (2242; cf. 2217 on the relations between children and parents). The thinking progressed when it was finally admitted that the abuse of authority can destroy any claim to legitimacy, so that existing power structures themselves may have to be removed or even destroyed. The first movement of the magisterium towards adopting this position was put forth by Paul VI in *Populorum Progressio* (1967) and is now being officially repeated. However, when it comes to the question of armed insurrection, the presumption would appear to be on the side of authority, even oppressive political power. When we read that 'Armed *resistance* to oppression by political authority is not legitimate, unless all the following conditions are met' (2243), we are reminded of something akin to the theory of the just war. We will evaluate the five conditions given here when we touch upon that theory below (2309).

Finally, yet more provocation will be found in the *Catechism's* statement that 'The more prosperous nations are obliged, to the extent that they are able, to welcome the *foreigner* in search of the security and the means of livelihood which he cannot find in his country of origin' (2241). Despite the fact that the smaller print in this paragraph suggests that the 'exercise of the right to immigrate' may be subjected to 'various juridical conditions', one could not help but think of the issue of so-called 'economic refugees' currently being turned away from the borders of the prosperous nations. Here, I would suggest, is a debate that has not taken place and probably never will do so because the majority members of society are made to feel threatened by the issues. Poverty is a relative thing, and it needs to be spoken of in context, even if one could venture that something like 'absolute poverty' could be used to refer to the deprivation of the basic necessities of life. The experience of poverty on a relative scale means that families that are struggling to survive in the prosperous countries, even though they are themselves prosperous in comparison to families in the poorest countries, are made to feel threatened by the onslaught of yet millions more people trying to share shrinking resources. The issue of 'economic refugees' will remain a political hot potato until our most basic instincts lead us to conclude that we do indeed have it all wrong, that the protection of our wealth is an inappropriate argument to ban those less well off from crossing our borders. When we reach that point, the gurus of the economic *status quo* will probably suggest that it would be more appropriate to (re)build the infrastructure of 'those' countries so that indigenous persons can remain where they are and hence protect their social, cultural and familial values and traditions. Would it not have been preferable if the *Catechism* had hastened this debate by dropping its bombshell on the 'economic refugees' question right here and now? I sincerely hope that this is one passage that does not get watered down through interpretation.

The fifth commandment

One of the shortest of all commandments is not necessarily one of the simplest. When the *Catechism* translates Exodus 20:13 as 'You shall not kill', it completely avoids a controverted exegetical question that has important implications for the rest of theology. This 'ordinary' version of this commandment that most of us grew up with left generations of persons wondering how self-defence, war, and capital punishment could be justified, even by churchmen, while killing is clearly condemned in the Bible. One can add to this the question whether the prohibition found in the commandment extends to animals. The *Catechism* chose to deal with relations with animals under the seventh commandment on 'Respect for the integrity of creation' (2415–2418).

The text of Exodus itself uses the relatively rare Hebrew word *rasah*, which is better translated as 'murder' rather than 'kill'. My colleagues who study the Old Testament in a great deal of detail and depth inform me that this word is translatable as 'to slay', thus suggesting that the killing taking place is less than morally neutral. At the same time, one 'slays' the enemy in a justifiable manner in battle, but 'slays' one's brother unjustifiably when there is no cause. In other words, most of the words that one might choose to translate this commandment will be ambiguous.

There is an issue here that goes far beyond a choice of words, an issue that is both linguistic and moral. As for the first, the alternative passage quoted at the beginning of this article (Mt 5:21–22)[9] includes a reference to anger that shares a similar problem of precise meaning. Contemporary human sciences and Christian ethics have confirmed what most of us already knew as 'common sense': there is a difference between anger which is simply an emotion and thus not morally qualifiable, and 'unjustified, unbridled, blind, destructive anger' that is better referred to as hostility, belligerence, vengeance, or perhaps even (disproportionate) aggressiveness. Anger in this second sense is not an emotion but an attitude, a disposition, a way of relating to others. This is the concept of anger as a capital sin (cf. 1866) which, unfortunately, the *Catechism* fails to clarify. It is not until 2302, on 'Peace', that the text of the *Catechism* decides to define anger as 'a desire for revenge'. This rather gratuitous definition, which can hardly be substantiated on the basis of earlier teaching, does not solve the problem of the multiple meanings of the word in common usage. By the same token, the word 'kill' admits of an entire range of meanings, from ritual sacrifice to murder, from self-defence to genocide. Glossing over this problem does little to aid our understanding.

The second aspect of this problem is indicated by the linguistic issue, but is more specifically ethical. If killing is not a good thing, and the text of the *Catechism* goes on at quite some length to demonstrate this, it becomes clear that there are occasions when (morally relevant) circumstances may have to allow for killing to take place. These circumstances do not make the killing 'good', even though the human act performed, understood in its entirety (and thus including the physical act of killing), may be said to be a 'correct' or 'right' one. The recognition of these circumstances neither turns killing into a good thing nor compromises the moral order or the integrity of the moral person. It simply admits that we must sometimes deal with aspects of life that are not *simply* good or evil.

The *Catechism* is very traditionalistic in its approach to this subject-matter in that it invokes a list of classical distinctions to get around the difficulty. We find reference to the qualification of killing 'the innocent and the righteous' (2261), to the role of one's attitude and intention, namely 'anger, hatred and vengeance' (2262), to the specification of murder as 'intentional killing' (2263), and to the distinction between that which is 'direct and intentional killing' (2268) and that which is 'indirectly bringing about a person's death' (2269).[10] All of these distinctions have been used at one time or another to avoid the difficulty of having to deal with the perpetration of something that is 'evil' (taking human life can hardly be called a 'good' thing) either along the way to or as the result of achieving some other good. Textbook theologians prefer to admit only the second category, pretending that each and every perpetration of an evil can somehow be called a consequence or 'effect' of an otherwise 'good' human activity. Such a position ignores the complexity of modern warfare, the clearly chronological series of events in the use of capital punishment, and any host of other examples that do not necessarily have to do with the loss of life. By setting up the problem in this way, the textbooks shunted off every perplexing issue on to the sidetrack of 'double effect'.

Nor is it immediately clear that the magisterium itself has come to terms with the issue. If we look at the text on 'Respect for the person and scientific research' a little further on, we see that in the case of organ transplants, 'physical and psychological dangers and risks may be incurred by the donor [that] are proportionate to the good sought for the recipient' (2296). Then we are told that 'it is morally inadmissable directly to bring about the disabling mutilation or death of a human being, even in order to delay the death of other persons'. However, this appears to be directed to some intervention taken towards a third party, presumably without their consent, and hardly does justice to the just admitted 'proportionate dangers and risks' incurred by a voluntary donor. Nor does the issue become clear in the following paragraph on bodily integrity that states 'Except when performed for strictly therapeutic medical reasons, directly intended *amputations*, *mutilations* and *sterilizations* performed on innocent persons are against the moral law' (2297). We are left with the simple fact that any donor for whatever organ is going to undergo some form of 'mutilation', however slight or heroic, however justified by good intentions and love of neighbour. What is at issue here is not whether organ transplantation is moral or immoral. What is at issue is whether we are willing to admit that mutilation constitutes an evil that we are willing to tolerate so that a good can come about through the use of this means.

A final criticism of the methodology employed in this article concerns the argument for self-defence. Thomas Aquinas used the idea that 'one is bound to take more care of one's own life than of another's' (2264, quoting STh II-II, 64, 7). Many people believe that we have gone beyond this form of argumentation and should be able to deal with self-defence without suggesting that self-love is somehow the primary moral consideration. Perhaps the methodology of the *Catechism* dictates its own approach (so that the death of the aggressor becomes merely an 'effect' of exercising self-love). In any case, the chosen methodology of this article, and indeed this text as a whole, makes the remainder of the issues that are dealt with predictable.[11] Abortion, euthanasia and suicide are dealt with in this manner, resurrecting old arguments ('the natural inclination of the human being to preserve and perpetuate his life', 2281) or quoting heavily from existing documents. The abortion issue is argued almost exclusively from the text of *Donum Vitae*,[12] while the *Catechism* makes no mention of the 'Declaration on Procured Abortion' by the same Congregation for the Doctrine of the Faith.[13] The text on euthanasia quotes from the Vatican's own Declaration[14] on the subject, but without providing specific reference, which is regrettable, since many moral theologians consider this Declaration to be one of the Vatican's best examples of contemporary moral methodology.

The second section of the article on the fifth commandment turns to other things that the *Catechism* considers to be harmful to persons, beginning with scandal as harmful to eternal life. The text gives a rather simple definition of scandal as 'an attitude or behaviour which leads another to do evil' (2284), apparently leaving aside any nuanced consideration of freedom (intention), foreknowledge (circumstances) or detailed description of what is happening (object). Dismissing this criticism with the idea that 'we all know what is meant here' only underscores the weakness of the text, the only saving feature of which is its particular emphasis upon the misuse of authority to perpetrate evil and lead others to the same.

It is in this section of the *Catechism* that we find a number of things mentioned that earlier press reports referred to as 'new' sins. While the only thing 'new' here might be that these actions are specifically named, it is perhaps good to note that the concrete norms enumerated include over-indulgence in food, alcohol, tobacco or medicine; drunkenness or immoderate speed 'on the road, at sea or in the air' (2290); production of, trafficking in or the use of drugs (2291); kidnapping, taking hostages, terrorism, and torture (2297). I expect that the Christian community did not need to be told that such activities constitute wrong behaviour and have to be judged as immoral when performed with foreknowledge and freedom.

The final section on the fifth commandment deals with peace and war. As for peace, the *Catechism* supports the positive, constructive and developmental notion of peace as 'more than the absence of war'. Personally, I consider it a shortcoming of the text that not a single reference is given here to Paul VI and his many writings and speeches. With respect to war, the text is based largely upon that of *Gaudium et Spes* and includes at least one reference to *Populorum Progressio* (2315, note 110) condemning the arms race. To its credit, the *Catechism* draws attention to the issue of manufacturing and trafficking in arms (2316). It is also very explicit about war crimes and the inadequacy of 'obedience' as an excuse. However, the centrepiece of this short text is the classical 'just war theory'.

I mentioned above that in dealing with the 'armed *resistance* to oppression by political authority' (2243) five conditions were enunciated that closely resembled the conditions of the just war theory presented here (2309). At this point it may be helpful to list the arguments side by side (the order is that given in the text).

Resistance	Just War
(1) there is certain, grave and prolonged violation of fundamental rights;	— the damage inflicted by the aggressor on the nation or community of nations must be lasting, grave and certain;
(2) all other means of redress have been exhausted;	— all other means of putting an end to it must have been shown to be impractical or ineffective;
(3) it will not provoke worse disorders;	
(4) a well-founded hope of success;	— there must be serious prospects of success;
(5) it is impossible reasonably to foresee any better solutions.	— the use of arms must not produce evils and disorders graver than the evil to be eliminated.

It is clear that the *Catechism* is using the same criteria to deal with cases of both armed resistance and just defence. There is little surprise in this, though it would have been interesting indeed if the author(s) admitted this from the beginning and attempted to demonstrate how and why these common elements could be invoked for two seemingly separate questions. The astute reader will recognise the similarity immediately. We can only speculate why the author(s) here did not do the same and become explicit about their methodology. Had they done so, and had they remained just a bit more true to the tradition itself, perhaps they would not have avoided the use of the word 'proportionate' in both expositions.

The word 'proportionate' does appear several times in the text of the *Catechism*. However, every use of the term is carefully chosen to coincide with the possible application of the principle of double effect. Nowhere in this article do we find an admission that 'fifth commandment issues' are not simply matters of right or wrong, moral or immoral.[15] Many, if not most, moral issues related to the fifth commandment are borderline cases that call for prudential judgement. The *Catechism*, however, prefers to leave its readers with the impression that morality can be decided in a manner that is 'objective', non-circumstantial, a-historical, uninvolved with detail or motivation, and still a matter of virtually universal consensus. Who is going to say that torture is good or that murder is sometimes acceptable? Obviously no one. Being forced to 'agree' with the treatment of fifth commandment issues as 'objective', we may not realise that we have been set up for what follows. The sixth commandment will approach human sexuality in the same (objective) spirit as the life-and-death issues of the fifth commandment.

The sixth commandment

I feel compelled to begin this section of my commentary with a personal note. As a Roman Catholic I find myself called by a spirit of loyalty to the hierarchical magisterium of the Church, just as I feel called to loyalty to the remainder of the institutional structure, including and especially when that structure exercises its function of teacher. As a moral theologian, I find myself called to critically assess every form of scriptural, historical, 'traditional', philosophical and theological argumentation used to establish, substantiate, or attempt to convince others of a particular position that is taken on a moral question by those of us who claim to share a common faith in Jesus Christ and the gospel. As a lay person, spouse and father, and as a sexual human being, I find myself called to be attentive to the experience of my own sexuality, the testimony concerning sexuality communicated to me by those around me, those with whom I share my life and those whom I have come to know personally and professionally. Unfortunately, my problem at this point is that I find myself being called in three different directions. It is a problem because, depending upon which call I heed, I might have to say something different about a number of the issues that are raised by the *Catechism* in its exposition of the sixth commandment.

An additional problem that one may experience in commenting on the *Catechism*'s text is that we all know what the outcome of this treatment is going to be: a condemnation of masturbation, any form of non-marital sexual behaviour, and homosexual acts (*Persona Humana*), and contraception (*Humanae Vitae*); and the proposition that conjugal sexual intercourse carries two *inseparable* 'meanings', one unitive and one procreative, that for some reason which will not be explained must always *both* be present (even during periods of infertility) lest the 'moral law' be somehow offended. One could expect that a number of 'sexual sins' will also be mentioned, while the reader's attention should not neglect possible omissions in that list of sins as well.

The text begins with a general introduction that uses a number of scriptural quotations and references. In the midst of this somewhat random collection we find a rather positive observation, reminiscent of *Gaudium et Spes* and echoed even in *Persona Humana*, that '*sexuality* affects all aspects of the human person' (2332). This open, all-encompassing view appears to be carried into the following paragraph, where 'gender' is used to designate the hypothesis of the 'physical, moral and spiritual difference and complementarity' concept that has been becoming more prevalent in the contemporary teaching.[16] Whatever the text intends with sexuality, gender, or 'difference and complementarity' is then said to be 'oriented toward the *goods of marriage* and the flourishing of family life' (2233, emphasis added; cf. 2351, 2353, 2363 and 2366). Thus we find one of the key concepts, that of the 'goods of sexuality and/or marriage', being subtly introduced into the progression of ideas.

In the second section it is interesting to note that the article chooses to take on the entire area of human sexuality under the auspices of 'The vocation to chastity' (2337–2359).[17] The virtue of chastity is said to combine 'The integrity of the person' (2338–2345) and 'The integrity of the gift of self' (2346–2347), and is manifest in three forms: chastity for the virgin or celibate, for the married (conjugal chastity), and for the not (yet) married (2348–2350). While the *Catechism* distinguishes the first from the other two, which are said to be 'prescribed by the moral law', the functional difference actually lies between 'conjugal chastity' and the other two, which demand nothing less than total continence.

The reflections upon the 'integrity of the person' open with an obscure paragraph which we quote in full: 'The chaste person maintains the integrity of the powers of life and love placed in him. This integrity ensures the unity of the person; it is opposed to any behaviour that would impair it. It tolerates neither a double life nor duplicity in speech' (2338).

I showed this text to several people to read, hardly any of whom could make any useful sense of it. Then I suggested that the paragraph may contain a certain amount of jargon. For instance, the 'powers of life and love' may refer to the 'inseparable connection between the unitive and procreative meanings' of sexual intercourse. The behaviour which would 'tolerate a double life', then, becomes contraceptive behaviour, which the defenders of natural family planning claim is tantamount to 'a falsification of the inner truth of conjugal love' (2370; cf. FC 32). At the same time, the 'duplicity in speech' and the 'behaviour that impairs' could refer to those who engage in sexual behaviour without reference to the 'unitive meaning', i.e., outside the bonds of matrimony. With an explanation of the 'code words', the paragraph began to make more sense. The equally obscure footnote reference to Matthew 5:37 also began to come clear. 'Let what you say be simply "Yes" or "No"; anything more than this comes from evil' is a text about taking oaths (cf. 2153 and 2466). If one applies this saying to the 'innate language that expresses the total reciprocal self-giving of husband and wife' that contraception 'objectively contradicts' with a 'language of not giving oneself totally to the other' (2370; cf. FC 32), the connection becomes more obvious. Speaking *one* 'language', engaging in *one* 'doubly meaning' behaviour, is equivalent to the 'simply "Yes" or "No"'. 'Anything more than this . . .' becomes the sexual language that has one 'meaning' without the other, so that contraception is equivalent to taking an oath in the name of the Lord when one's word would have been sufficient. Of course, this interpretation must forget the exceptions, nuances, and multiple meanings of real *languages*, not to mention the need for a sense of proportionality, such as when it is necessary to deal with questions such as the 'just war' that had been mentioned at the end of the previous article. It would be difficult to imagine how Christians could speak about self-defence or just war with a language of 'simply "Yes" or "No"'.

The remainder of the text on the 'Integrity of the person' places its entire emphasis upon self-control and asceticism as the source of living out the cardinal virtue of *'temperance*, which seeks to permeate the passions and appetites of the senses with reason' (2341). The *Catechism* recognises that the project of building self-control is a long-term process

(2342), governed by the 'laws of growth' (2343), that it is cultural, and demands the 'right to receive information and an education that respects the moral and spiritual dimensions of human life' (2344). Turning to the 'Integrity of the gift of self' (2346–2347), we are reminded that, like all virtues, chastity is animated by love. Thus, practising chastity moves one towards friendship that, after the model of Christ's love for his friends, is everlasting and thus a 'promise of immortality'.

This said, the *Catechism* then lists the 'Offences against chastity'. They are: lust (2351, cf. 2517),[18] masturbation (2352), fornication (2353), pornography (2354), prostitution (2355), and rape (2356). Most of this is self-explanatory. I would, however, mention the continuous references to 'procreative and unitive' (2351) and 'sexuality which is naturally ordered to the good of spouses and the generation and education of children' (2353), as evidence of the preoccupation of the text. Then, masturbation is said to be the 'deliberate stimulation of the genital organs *in order to derive sexual pleasure*' (2352, emphasis added). Two sentences later we read that 'The deliberate use of the sexual faculty, *for whatever reason*, outside of marriage is essentially contrary to its purpose' (ibid., emphasis added). One might ask for a clarification as to whether motive or intention play a role in ethical judgement or not. This is hardly an academic question when one thinks about the need to procure semen for the purpose of a sperm count. Finally, while the reference to rape here is redeemed by the immediate inclusion of the broader perspective of justice and love, I expect that most people are going to ask why the *Catechism* never mentions *sexual harassment* as an offence against chastity.

Quite apart from the list of 'offences against chastity', we encounter an entirely separate subsection that takes up the question of 'Chastity and homosexuality' (2357–2359), begging the question whether this is a case that deserves particular attention or a case that must be understood 'differently'. Those familiar with the dynamics of the issue of homosexuality will likely suggest that in the case of the homosexual relationship one encounters a situation that is difficult to fit into the three varieties of chastity that were listed earlier (2349), despite the fact that 'conjugal chastity' has not yet been defined. Given that homosexuality itself is accepted as a condition of the person over which one has no control and which cannot be fully explained,[19] one might be tempted to interpret the title of this separate subsection to suggest that a 'fourth' application of the virtue of chastity might be in order.

A full reading of the text, of course, makes this interpretation impossible. However, it is interesting to note that the end of the first paragraph (2357) merely 'restates' what the 'Tradition' had taught: that homosexual acts are 'disordered', they oppose natural law because they are not open to procreation, nor do they flow from 'complementarity', and that 'under no circumstances can they be approved'. Conspicuously absent are the words 'sin' and 'immorality', reminding us of the teaching of *Humanae Vitae* (1968) that did not repeat the conclusion of *Casti Connubii* (1930) that contraception was a 'grave sin'. Somewhat surprisingly there are no outright condemnations. On the contrary, we are reminded that homosexual persons are 'called' to chastity and that 'they can and should gradually and resolutely approach Christian perfection'. This states nothing different from the expectations that might be applied to any heterosexual person, whether married or not. If one were to make a distinction between 'approving' certain acts and 'tolerating' certain acts as a form of lesser evil, as has been suggested by one of the authors of *Persona Humana*,[20] and to back this up with the *Catechism*'s own stated position on the factors 'that lessen or even extenuate moral culpability' with respect to masturbation (2352) or reducing imputability with respect to prostitution (2355), one might suggest that the *Catechism* is attempting to open the way more broadly to fully integrating homosexual persons into the Catholic Christian community, even those homosexual persons who are living in lasting relationships. While I believe many will disagree with this interpretation, it occurs to me that if this indeed becomes the case in the future, there will be sufficient room to 'reinterpret' this text to say what we might want it to say. Finally, it is worth taking note of the fact that the text is very explicit to the effect that homosexual persons 'must be accepted with respect, compassion and sensitivity. Every sign of unjust discrimination in their regard should be avoided' (2358).

Presumably coming to the issue of 'conjugal chastity', section III of this article now takes up 'The love of husband and wife' (2360–2379). With very few exceptions, what is said here is to be expected and does not deviate from the recent teaching of the magisterium: sexual union is exclusive to the married state, is characterised by 'unitive' as well as procreative 'meanings', and is a sign of the covenant between the spouses that demands lifelong fidelity. A subsection on 'The fecundity of marriage' (2366–2372) literally repeats the teaching of *Humanae Vitae*, especially as it was repeated and interpreted in *Familiaris Consortio* (1981); while another subsection on 'The gift of a child' literally repeats the teaching of *Donum Vitae* (1987).

The attentive reader might take notice of the wording in the opening paragraph, where it is stated that 'Sexuality is ordered to the conjugal love of man and woman' (2360). There is no mention of procreation at all in this text, which appears to follow more closely the teaching of *Gaudium et Spes* 49 on 'Conjugal love'. Unlike some later texts, the *Catechism* does not attempt to interpret the conciliar teaching as stating that conjugal love is 'fully human, exclusive and open to new life',[21] at least not initially. However, later in the text we do encounter the recurring theme:

> The spouses' union achieves the twofold end of marriage: the good of the spouses themselves, and the transmission of life. These two meanings or values of marriage cannot be separated without altering the couple's spiritual life and compromising the goods of marriage and the future of the family. The conjugal love of man and woman thus stands under the twofold obligation of fidelity and fecundity. (2363)

379

We have already pointed out that the ends/goods of marriage doctrine is not foreign to this text (cf. 2233, 2351, 2353 and 2366). The awkwardness of the language in this particular paragraph, however, indicates the relatively high state of confusion that the current teaching has exhibited. The first sentence speaks of a *twofold end* that is achieved by the *union* of the spouses. The immediate context (2362) leads us to interpret this 'union' as the act of (conjugal) sexual intercourse. Next we are told that this 'twofold end' (of intercourse) is equivalent to *meanings* or *values*[22] which are attached to *marriage*. The phrase 'These two . . .' would lead us to believe that there is an equivalence here, so that the ends/meanings/ values of intercourse and of marriage are the same. Yet, we read that any separation between these ends/meanings/values will compromise the *goods of marriage*. One is left with the question of what the *goods* of marriage are if they are not the twofold ends/meanings/values? If this is not complex enough, we find the introduction of yet another category, 'conjugal love', which is said to require both 'fidelity and fecundity'. Thus we have ends–meanings–values–goods of the (sexual) union–marriage– conjugal love that consist in (1) the goods of spouses, (2) the goods of marriage, (3) the transmission of life, and (4) the family's future. Lastly, we need to add to these lists the possible distinction between the transmission of life and fecundity itself — which are said to be an end of marriage and a requisite of married love respectively.

If a catechism is intended to summarise, encapsulate, clarify, or otherwise explain doctrine, this single paragraph (2363) must stand as a witness to the utter failure of the text. A precise linguistic and scientific interpretation of this teaching would reveal, I propose, that the basic problem stems from nothing more complicated than a failure to sort out the ends of marriage and the ends of conjugal sexual intercourse which has plagued magisterial teaching on this subject since 1930. Unfortunately, what will be communicated to the uninformed reader of this text is the impression that the teaching itself is in a state of confusion.

Section IV of the article endeavours to treat 'Offences against the dignity of marriage' which are listed as adultery (2380–2381), divorce (2382–2386), and 'other offences' such as polygamy (2387), incest (2388), 'free union' (2390), and trial marriage (2391). A thought on the sexual abuse of children or adolescents taking on the additional dimension of scandal hardly interrupts what is an otherwise bland, insensitive, and nearly pastorally ignorant list of sins that adds nothing to our understanding of the complexity of issues facing real people in a real world. When the *Catechism* mentions the particular categories of 'a spouse who has sincerely tried to be faithful to the sacrament of marriage and is unjustly abandoned' (2386) or the 'predicament' of a man with several wives who desires to become a Catholic (2387), one cannot help getting the feeling of being patronised, since the text offers absolutely no solutions, guidelines, or any sort of help for these people or for those who are responsible for their pastoral care.

As usual, this article ends with a series of statements 'In Brief' (2392–2400). Most of the time these summaries are worth ignoring because they are merely repetitious and tend to give the false impression that morality is primarily about a list of propositions: dos and don'ts. In this case, however, it is worth pointing out some curious differences between the text of this article and the 'In Brief' statements.

Two of the lists given here do not match the text exactly. The 'sins seriously contrary to chastity' (2396) reproduces those listed but omits what was called 'lust' (2351) as well as rape (2256). On the other hand, this list includes 'homosexual practices', which the text appeared to treat separately, presenting a different relationship with chastity than merely that of an 'offence' (2357–2359). The list of offences against the dignity of marriage (2400) omits incest (2388–2389). This might be looked upon as an improvement, for incest is a violation of justice that has little or nothing to do with the dignity of marriage, just as rape must be looked upon as much more than simply a sexual act.[23]

Further, while the 'regulation of births' is finally officially condoned, having been part of papal teaching since 1951, we are reminded that 'legitimate intentions . . . do not justify recourse to morally unacceptable means (for example, direct sterilization or contraception)' (2399). As in the text, we are not told why these things are 'morally unacceptable'. The text never even mentioned 'direct sterilization', and the 'In Brief' summary has the audacity to equate the two things, as if they are completely the same. Some people may find this intellectually offensive. If I can believe the statistics, I suspect that most people have already found the teaching on contraception to be irrelevant.

Finally, the differences between the text and the 'In Brief' summary hint at inconsistency and possibly several authors and/or insufficiently edited versions of the article. I suspect that whoever was responsible for this article wanted to have done with it and to move on to other things as quickly as possible. The task of expounding the sixth commandment may have been viewed as a distasteful project, possibly because the author(s) did not feel comfortable writing about sex, certainly because the text as it turned out says very little in a confusing way.

The seventh commandment

This article may not be the longest treatment of a single commandment, but it certainly gives the impression of being the most comprehensive. One gets the impression that any ethical issues that could not be made to 'fit' under a specific commandment found their way to the seventh.[24] In reality, because the prohibition against 'stealing' involves some consideration of things material, anything even remotely connected with 'goods' (including promises and contracts; 2410) is subsumed under this all-encompassing treatment. The bottom line appears to be that the seventh commandment is the place where the *Catechism* chose to discuss *justice*. A somewhat unfortunate side-effect of this choice is that justice is put forth as nearly synonymous with economic issues.

While some applaud the virtual identification of the 'social teaching of the Church' with economic issues, I personally feel a little dismayed at such a prospect. Human rights are not reducible to the economic sphere, nor are issues of discrimination or ecology. In fact, one of the primary events that brought the magisterium to address socio-economic questions in such a solemn manner that it was considered to symbolise the beginnings of the 'social teaching' itself, namely *Rerum Novarum* (1891) and the famous 'workers' question', while ostensibly concerning issues as economic as the 'just wage', ultimately expressed ideas in a realm of human endeavour that has been demonstrated to be vastly more complex. On the ninetieth anniversary of Leo XIII's encyclical, John Paul II (*Laborem Exercens*, 1981) expounded the phenomenon of 'work' as something not merely material but spiritual, aesthetic, caught up in the vocation of every human person to humanise creation and co-operate with the love of God. While economics clearly occupies the thoughts of many concerned persons today, particularly in the light of a world recession, we should resist the temptation to see everything in the light of economics.

Although it is somewhat regrettable to encounter 'The social doctrine of the Church' being subsumed under the seventh commandment (2419–2425), we should be particularly attentive to the sort of restriction that is implied in reading 'The Church makes a moral judgement about economic and social matters "when the fundamental rights of the person and the salvation of souls requires it".[25] In the moral order she bears a mission *distinct from that of political authorities*' (2420). Somewhat later we also read 'It is not the role of the Pastors of the Church to intervene directly in the political structuring and organization of social life' (2442). However, this second statement is aimed at distinguishing the vocation of pastors from that of lay people, and presumably at discouraging the former from pursuing any political involvement. What we miss here is any reference to the statement made by Paul VI in his own anniversary apostolic letter of 1971, *Octogesima Adveniens*:

> In the face of such widely varying situations it is difficult for us to utter a unified message and to put forward a solution which has universal validity. Such is not our ambition, nor is it our mission. It is up to the Christian communities to analyze with objectivity the situation which is proper to their own country, to shed on it the light of the Gospel's unalterable words and to draw principles of reflection, norms of judgment and directives for action from the social teaching of the Church.[26]

Nevertheless, the thrust of the 'social teaching' even here in the *Catechism* is cast in fundamental, basic terms that hesitate to draw concrete conclusions about specific issues. Even the remainder of this section (2421–2425) is composed primarily of quotations from *Gaudium et Spes* and *Centesimus Annus* that address the questions of ideology and the need to find alternatives beyond communism and the market-place mentality. The following section, 'Economic activity and social justice' (2426–2436), while primarily about work and related issues, drawing heavily upon *Laborem Exercens* for its inspiration, takes the position that

'The primordial value of labour stems from man himself, its author and its beneficiary. Work is for man, not man for work' (2428; cf. LE 6). Human rights, personal responsibility, the common good and above all the notion that human persons are 'created in the image of God and called to prolong the work of creation by subduing the earth, both with and for one another' (2427; cf. Gen 1:28; GS 34; CA 31) are themes that inform the text throughout and lie closer to the heart of the social teaching of the Church than mere economic issues.

This, of course, is not to deny the importance of such economic and material issues as may be indicated by the seventh commandment. As might be expected (based upon the previous development of the 'social teaching'), one of the very first issues to surface in the text is that of *private property*. The title of the first section, 'The universal destination and the private ownership of goods' (2404–2406), already indicates the relativisation of the 'right' to private property in service to 'common stewardship' of the earth and its resources (2402). Furthermore, the right 'does not do away with the original gift of the earth to the whole of mankind. The *universal destination of goods* remains primordial, even if the promotion of the common good requires respect for the right to private property and its exercise' (2403). Unless I am mistaken, I seem to detect a change in perspective here from the so-called 'traditional' position. Whereas formerly private property was assumed to be necessary 'for guaranteeing the freedom and dignity of persons . . . helping each of them to meet his basic needs', and so forth (2402), so that any change in this order of things could or would have to be justified by an appeal to the common good, what we see here is a presumption in favour of the universal purpose and common stewardship of all the resources of the earth as the normal (created) order of things so that the 'promotion of the common good' needs to be invoked in order to justify the function of private property (2403). This appears to be substantiated by the reflection in 2408 (see below) that the appropriation of the goods of another may be justified by appealing to the 'universal destination of goods'. Whether this change in perspective was intended is a matter of interpretation. However, it does appear to be reflected in the remainder of the text. 'The ownership of any property *makes* its holder a steward of Providence, with the *task* of making it fruitful and communicating its benefits to others . . .' (2404; emphasis added). Private property, then, rather than being a privilege, is the source of obligations. This is classical moral theology in the sense of Augustine and Thomas Aquinas, not in the sense of *Rerum Novarum* and the moral manuals of the nineteenth and early twentieth century.

What all this entails concretely is then spelled out in the next section, 'Respect for persons and their goods' (2407–2418). This title is somewhat misleading, for the subject area covers the whole of creation, including the animal kingdom. A first subdivision, 'Respect for the goods of others', contains the 'lists' of offences that range from 'simple theft'[27] to speculation, corruption, fiscal fraud, etc. (2408–2409). This is followed with thoughts on contracts (2410–2411), restitution (2412), gambling, cheating (2413), and enslavement or the use of persons as objects (2414). The paragraph on contracts is interrupted with a reflection upon 'commutative justice', which is distinguished from 'legal' and 'distributive' justice (2411). This is a repetition of the, again classic, division of justice into the threefold, triangular relationship; an idea originally put forth by Cajetan that has been far surpassed since the development of the specific notion of 'social justice'. Unfortunately, the author(s) of this text did not or could not combine the textbook version of justice with contemporary thought on the matter.

A second subdivision of this section borrows part of the terminology of the World Council of Churches' programme ('Justice, Peace and the Integrity of Creation'; Vancouver, 1983; Seoul, 1990; Canberra, 1990) by invoking the title 'Respect for the integrity of creation' (2415–2418). Here we find admonitions about maintaining the (human) quality of life, concern for future generations (2415), and three entire paragraphs on humanity's relationship with animals (2416–2418).

More characteristic of contemporary times is the section on 'Justice and solidarity among nations' (2437–2442). This text is extremely brief, and only touches upon a number of important issues that are largely but not exclusively economic in character. Underlying these considerations is the understanding that development is about much more than aid, money and financial systems. The 'obligation in justice' (2439) demands that the well-off peoples of the world contribute to the improvement of human living for every member of the human family. When 2441 states that 'An increased sense of God and increased self-awareness are fundamental to any full development of human society . . .', one hears echoes of the original ideas on the dignity of the human person based upon our creation in God's image (1700–1709).

The final section of this article, on 'Love for the poor' (2443–2449), is apparently the *Catechism*'s manner of introducing the concept of the 'preferential option for the poor'[28] that had been developed by the so-called 'liberation theology'. The fact that the *Catechism* makes no reference, not even a polite nod in the direction of this contemporary movement in Roman Catholic Christian thinking, hints at a kind of parochialism that works only to the detriment of 'official teaching' and does little to increase the credibility of such documents. The fact that there are some excellent ideas contained in this text – here we could single out the extremely important point that giving alms (or international development aid) is not a matter of charity but of justice (2446–2447; cf. 2439–2440) — is in danger of being lost to a wider public because of the general rigidity of the text as a whole, the outdated methodology that is employed, and consequently the diminished communicability of what is contained in these pages.

The eighth commandment

Most people would probably give immediate verbal assent to the idea that 'it is wrong to lie', that it is good to speak the truth, and that in special circumstances putting one's signature to an official document or taking an oath before speaking in a court of law constitutes an act of personal commitment to truth-telling, the violation of which is justifiably punished by almost every legal and moral system or structure. Why, then, one might ask, does the *Catechism* devote over two pages of text (2464–2474) to attempting to 'establish' the basis for the goodness of truth-telling? That attempt reaches all the way back to the nature of God and of the covenant, quotations from Scripture to Thomas Aquinas, not to mention two conciliar documents and two patristic texts; and commits probably the most common error experienced by every parent who asks a child to 'own up' to who was responsible for starting this fight, breaking that object, or otherwise behaving in some irritating manner, knowing that the threat of punishment is hanging over their head: the climax of the argument is that the ultimate in truth-telling results in death by martyrdom (2473–2474)!

With the reader left with the image of being 'food of the beasts, through whom it will be given to me to reach God' (2473), it is no wonder that this whole business of truth-telling is considered somewhat distasteful. The reward for reading this far is to be plunged into a list of 'Offences against truth' (2475–2487) ranging from perjury (2476) through our old friends 'rash judgement, detraction, and calumny' (2477–2479), into an encounter with some perhaps unexpected concepts, 'flattery, adulation or complaisance,[29] boasting and irony' (2480–2481), before we finally get to the heart of the matter: lying. The fact that no fewer than six paragraphs here (2482–2487) and two additional paragraphs in the next section (2488–2489) are needed to deal with the phenomenon of lying may indicate some of the problem.

The truth is, the text is not very clear about what constitutes a lie. It begins with the relatively simple notion that 'a *lie* consists in speaking a falsehood with the intention of deceiving' (2482; actually a quotation from Augustine). The 'intention of deceiving' part protects one from the sophomoric objection that the 'liar' could be in ignorance or that everyone could know what the 'truth' really is (as in the telling of a joke). In the following paragraph we find the next qualification: 'To lie is to speak or act against the truth in order to lead into error someone *who has the right to know the truth*' (2483; emphasis added).[30] There follows a treatise on intention, circumstance, seriousness, culpability, consequences, and the need for restitution (2484–2487). All this said, a new section on 'Respect for the truth' begins with the strikingly paradoxical statement that '*The right to the communication* of the truth is not unconditional' (2488). The text appears to have come full circle, so that we now read that, motivated by the Gospel and 'fraternal love' (2488), we must face the demands presented by 'the good and safety of others, respect for privacy, and the common good' (2489) and balance these considerations with 'respect for truth'. It will be no surprise if the reader feels trapped at this point. The best the *Catechism* has to offer is remaining silent, using discreet language, or 'strict discretion'. There is not even any mention of the classic 'mental reservation' that some of us learned about (and learned to defend as being no more a form of a 'Catholic lie' than annulment was a form of 'Catholic divorce'). Mental reservation is a problem because it is functionally the same thing as a lie: deliberately leading someone to draw a conclusion that we know will be false. Or is it? In this case, do we not need to take into account the 'right to know that truth' (2483)?

A review of the text at this point may lead to the observation that when 2482 spoke of the 'intention of deceiving' it explicitly used the phrase 'speaking a falsehood', whereas when 2483 qualified the idea that when the one led into error may not have the right to know the truth, it was merely talking about 'leading into error', 'speaking or acting *against* the truth', and not necessarily saying what was known to be false. Is this the 'mental reservation'? Did we need to engage in this amount of casuistry to arrive at a 'way out' of the practical dilemmas?

Suppose a different approach had been taken here. Let us suggest that human persons, adequately considered as living in the world with others, are interdependent beings whose mutual sustainability and development is closely tied to open communication and a basic atmosphere of trust and credibility that supports a flow of information that is as open as possible. Whatever disrupts the exchange of information or destroys trustworthiness or credibility is harmful to human persons and their relationships and should therefore be avoided. This approach emphasises the good of persons (which necessarily includes relationships) and the function of information exchange without becoming bogged down in metaphysical questions about 'truth'. Truth questions are largely irrelevant since they miss the point of how truth or falsity function within the parameters of human relationships; one can deceive or be deceived by an exposition of 'truth'. At the same time, human experience testifies to a certain prejudice towards truth-telling: we would rather tell the truth all the time, but we sometimes judge that a greater harm is done by doing so than by deceiving another person. This is conflict. It is real, human, demonstrable, and it pervades the whole of life.

The *Catechism* does not recognise or admit to conflict, and as a result does not speak a language that the average reader will understand. Reading this article, one gets the impression that the principal questions are about fallible human beings attempting to discern, respect, and communicate about the structure of ontological truth. This, however, is not what morality is about, even a morality about 'bearing false witness'. Taking on the issues raised under the eighth commandment is not a question of absolute truth, 'Let what you say be simply "Yes or No"' (2466; cf. Mt 5:37). It occurs to me that this particular saying of Jesus is not about truth but about trust: Christians should have relationships, and by extension should contribute to building a world, in which the love between persons so much supports an atmosphere of trust that they do not *need* to invoke any other source or witness to the truth of their communications.

In defence of the *Catechism,* one could say that what is being taught here is the 'positive side' of the moral dilemma, urging and encouraging us to acquire and practise the virtues of uprightness, truthfulness, sincerity and candour (2468). I suggest, however, that this is only half of the picture, and as long as the other half is not communicated there will remain a gulf of incredulity between this 'teaching' and those whom the *Catechism* is attempting to teach. By refusing to recognise conflict, the *Catechism* is only capable of bringing out the most extreme cases of breaching moral propriety. We have already observed that the treatment of the other commandments lists 'offences' with which few people would disagree.

The same is true in this text. Who will disagree with the condemnation of violating professional confidence (2491) or breaking the seal of confession (2490)? Even the muckrakers (a form of detraction?) will have difficulty getting away from the *Catechism's* (not explicit enough) reference to the so-called tabloid press with the observation that 'interference by the media in the private lives of persons engaged in political or public activity is to be condemned' (2492).

What is missing here is a reference to the daily lives of ordinary people and a reasonable suggestion about how real people can deal with questions of 'truth'. How should we as Christians respond to the 'little white lie'? Do we have a call to perfection that urges us to tell the truth at all times, no matter what; or is the *Catechism* insinuating that perhaps small liberties taken with the 'truth' should not worry us? The point is that the text never states a position on these questions.

What does one say when they have just been served a meal that was really awful by someone they hardly know? How does one answer questions related to their income when they live in a place where tax evasion is considered a national sport? How does one deal with the cultural differences about what constitutes 'truth', especially when circumstances bring several cultural patterns into confrontation? How does one negotiate, for instance, a labour contract or an arms agreement without 'playing with the truth'? These are the kinds of questions about 'truthfulness' that concern most people, but one looks in vain for even the beginnings of an answer in the text of the *Catechism.*

The last two sections of this article deal with 'The use of the social communications media' (2493–2499), and 'Truth, beauty and sacred art' (2500–2503). The latter hangs in the text like an ornament on a Christmas tree; this was as good a place as any to put it! The former, however, constitutes one of the more significant disappointments of the *Catechism.* The phenomenon of mass communication is less than fifty years old. In that short time, the topic has been studied, researched, written and spoken about. The last two Popes have frequently addressed the issue, and there even exists a 'Pontifical Council for Social Communication'. What we find in the *Catechism* is little more than quotations from *Inter Mirifica,* the very first conciliar document

387

promulgated in 1962. One might have expected better.

If the purpose of a catechism is to teach on the practical level, while teaching itself involves the art and science of communication, one might have expected this section to be more directive in addressing what needs to be done and to offer some suggestions about how to begin doing it. This may have been the place to introduce the topic of Catholic Christian educational goals, programmes, and institutions; the vocation of teachers at every level; perhaps even some guidelines on how to interpret, criticise, use and even counteract what is taking place through the communications media. Unfortunately, one finds nothing of the sort.

The ninth and tenth commandments

Attention to the references that are given for the ninth and tenth commandments will reveal that they have their origins in a single verse that appears in two biblical traditions: 'You shall not covet your neighbour's house; you shall not covet your neighbour's wife, or his manservant, or his maidservant, or his ox, or his ass, or anything that is your neighbour's' (Ex 20:17; cf. Dt 5:21). The continuous text of these 'two' commandments at first appears to be one. If that is the case, the number of 'ten' commandments is not necessarily destroyed; for at the same place in either Deuteronomy or Exodus the reader will note that what may be considered two commandments (Ex 20:3 and Dt 5:7; Ex 20:4 and Dt 5:8) have been combined into one.[31] When we read in 2514 that 'In the Catholic catechetical tradition, the ninth commandment . . .', and then continue to read a description of what is forbidden by that commandment, most readers will not notice that the *Catechism* has skipped over a hermeneutical question of some substance, namely that it is precisely the 'Catholic catechetical tradition' that has handed down a certain interpretation that is not easy to reconcile with the scriptural text. While this may not be the place to introduce exegetical or even ecumenical questions, we would be negligent if we failed to point out the importance of the scriptural evidence in attempting to construct a theology of morality. At this particular point, the *Catechism* merely glosses over a problem of exegesis in favour of maintaining a neat, untroubled picture of traditional moral theology.

On the one hand, there may be good reason to maintain the distinction between the ninth and tenth commandments, because to read the scriptural evidence literally may lead one to conclude that there was equivalence between a neighbour's 'house, wife, manservant or maid-servant, ox, or ass' (Ex 20:17). Such an interpretation would imply that a wife or a servant was something equivalent to a possession, a notion that is not far from possible in ancient patriarchal society but is hardly smiled upon today.[32] One could begin to speculate here about the historicity of concrete moral norms. However, that would begin a discussion far beyond the scope of this commentary, and certainly beyond the outlook of the *Catechism* itself.

On the other hand, we should not forget the importance of this (these) commandment(s) as such. Again, the *Catechism* glosses over the obvious question of the repetition, or at least the overlap of the ninth and tenth with the sixth and seventh commandments respectively. The traditional textbooks had little problem with this repetition, usually treating the two sets together so that, for instance, the treatise on sexual morality was entitled *De sexto et nono*, rendering a kind of appropriate onomatopoeia.

If we take the ninth and tenth commandments together, we see how each in its own turn, first directed to human relations and then to things, emphasises the importance of *intention, motivation*, and indeed fundamental or basic *attitude*. To 'covet' is to harbour an attitude that insidiously destroys the integrity of the self and ultimately the integrity of human relationships. Such an attitude is quite complex and must be distinguished from appreciation, admiration, even desire which is not yet committed to action. Further, to 'covet' the spouse of another is not necessarily or exclusively sexual, even though the *Catechism* may entice one to commit the classic mistake of thinking of it in these terms. To 'covet' goods is bound up (and frequently confused) with issues of social justice, especially when confronted with the vast discrepancy between rich and poor, or bombarded with the image-making techniques of the advertising industry.

In a way, one could suggest that this kind of 'double commandment' complements the *materiality* of the previous four commandments in reminding the hearer that bad intentions already constitute a drifting away from the good, even from the ultimate Good, even before these intentions may (or may not) be realised in action. Though the occasion may never arise to possess what one covets, the self-inflicted damage to personal moral integrity is already present. Covetousness itself, whether having to do with partners or goods, will demonstrate its presence in other ways because covetousness is characteristic of an even more general attitude that places the self before others and one's good(s) before the respect for persons. In the end, it destroys community by placing things above persons and possession above use.

The attitude of covetousness is indeed at the root of numerous sins. However, the way in which the *Catechism* attempts to elaborate upon this is extremely vague. The article on the ninth commandment begins with a proof-text from 1 John 2:16, claiming that the threefold 'lust of the flesh, lust of the eyes and pride of life' are typical of those things forbidden by the ninth and tenth commandments. The text immediately follows this with the introduction of the concept of *concupiscence*, a sophisticated and generally misunderstood theological term that serves more to confuse than to clarify the discussion. The *Catechism* accurately observes that concupiscence is not 'in itself an offence', but immediately follows this with the observation that it 'inclines man to commit sins' (2515). Without further explanation, this will merely reinforce the (wrong) impression that many people have concerning human desire. To find something attractive is not equivalent to being 'inclined to sin', nor does the desire for something automatically cast suspicion either upon the thing desired or on the one who desires. This kind of neo-gnosticism helps theological reflection not at all. The subsequent texts on 'a certain struggle of tendencies between "spirit" and "flesh" (2516), the need for a 'purifying of the heart' (2517–2519), and the 'battle for purity' (2520–2527) demonstrate the preoccupation with things sexual that does not rise above the level of the commentary on the sixth commandment. This is unfortunate, for there are a few intriguing ideas in the text, such as those linking 'modesty' with 'privacy' (2521) and 'the intimate centre of the person' (2522). Because of the surrounding context, I doubt that these ideas will ever have any impact.

The commentary on the tenth commandment (2534–2550) is even more explicit in demonstrating how the text fails to make distinctions between attitudes (intentions) and behaviours (actions). The opening paragraph gives hints of being profound, but leaves one with the feeling that the author(s) never really grasped what it is all about:

> The tenth commandment unfolds and completes the ninth, which is concerned with concupiscence of the flesh. It forbids coveting the goods of another, as the root of theft, robbery and fraud, which the seventh commandment forbids. 'Lust of the eyes' leads to the violence and injustice forbidden by the fifth commandment. Avarice, like fornication, originates in the idolatry prohibited by the first three prescriptions of the Law. The tenth commandment concerns the intentions of the heart; with the ninth, it summarizes all the precepts of the Law. (2534)

This attempt to be profound has somehow left out the fourth and eighth commandments. Nor has it clearly demonstrated how the 'lust of the eyes' leads to the violation of the fifth commandment. It is typical of the remainder of the text that bounces from one topic to another without any clear sense of direction. It slides from an exposure of 'covetousness' to a condemnation of 'envy' without pointing out the difference between the two. This apparent identification between covetousness and envy (2538–2540) echoes the former identification of covetousness with lust (2514). One may wonder what has happened to the classical list of capital sins (1866), which has effectively been reduced from seven to five, lust and envy having now been identified merely as variations of covetousness.

I would suggest that the real crux of the matter can be found in the paragraph cited here (2534) that also equates avarice with fornication. This equation is typical of the entire commentary on the Ten Commandments that fails to distinguish between the intentional and the behavioural. Greed is an attitude, a moral direction and a chosen perspective that characterises the moral person. It stands against virtue and the call to moral uprightness, and may correctly be called an obstacle to moral responsibility. Fornication, on the other hand, is a behavioural, descriptive term that can be applied to the activity of human beings regardless of whether these persons are free to act or even aware of what they are doing (foreknowledge). Granted that the term has been invested with a meaning that *implies* moral responsibility, this only highlights a sloppiness of terminology that should have been avoided in a document as 'official' as a catechism for the universal Church.

The distinction between attitudinal, intentional categories and descriptive, behavioural categories is crucial for articulating a comprehensible morality. However, taking these distinctions seriously would necessitate a willingness to speak of things like 'means and ends' as something more than abstract, (de)ontological concepts. It would necessitate an openness to entertaining such ideas as ambiguity, conflict, non-moral evil and proportionality. In short, it would necessitate articulating a type of moral method that the author(s) of the *Catechism* had no intention of even considering.

If the *Catechism* was written to function at least partially as an instrument for teaching, even the most 'traditionalist' (moral handbook) theologian will have to be disappointed by the lack of nuance exhibited by this text. One does not teach by uttering clichés, perpetuating slovenly language and succumbing to popular misunderstanding. The pity is that if well-intentioned persons pick up a text like this, read it attentively, and come away with the feeling that they have not learned anything from what they read, then the text we are speaking of can only be classified as a missed opportunity.

Notes

1 This commentary was originally written several months before the release of the encyclical *Veritatis Splendor*. Therefore, there is no mention of the encyclical and no comparison between that text and the text of *Catechism*. However, the encyclical itself draws attention to the priority of the *Catechism* with respect to moral teaching.

2 John Paul II, '*Fidei Depositum*, the "Apostolic Constitution on the Publication of the Catechism of the Catholic Church"', *Origins* 22 (1993), 525, 527–529, p. 258; cf. J. Ratzinger, 'The Catechism of the Catholic Church in context', *Origins* 22 (1993), 529–532.

3 John Paul II, ibid.

4 Something resembling the 'principle of double effect' can be found at 1789.

5 The text identifies *sunderēsis* at this point as the 'principles of morality'. At another place (1865), but without the designation of the term, we find the more traditional notion of *sunderēsis*: 'Thus sin tends to reproduce and reinforce itself, but it cannot destroy the moral sense at its root.'

6 See Jan Grootaers and J. A. Selling, *The 1980 Synod of Bishops 'On the Role of the Family': An Exposition of the Event of an Analysis of Its Texts* (BETL 64; Louvain: Leuven University Press, 1983), pp. 102–6.

7 Further cross-references are given to 357, 1903, 2032, 2313 and 2420. The original source is (sometimes given to be) actually *Gaudium et Spes* 74 §5. I refer to the arguments as 'unsubstantiated' because the *Catechism* explains neither its sources nor its methodology for proposing a doctrine of human rights.

8   The original English translation used the words 'lawful protest' in this sentence. The 'improved' version of the *Catechism* has considerably watered down the strength of the original statement.

9   'You have heard that it was said to those of ancient times: "You shall not murder" and "whoever murders shall be liable to judgement." But I say to you that if you are angry with a brother or sister, you will be liable to judgement.'

10 Both 'direct and indirect' activities are considered to be subdivisions of voluntary homicide, the concrete example of the latter being drug trafficking.

11 At least one insightful reflection lies buried in the treatment of self-defence, in particular through the use of capital punishment. The second paragraph of 2266 begins: 'The primary effect of *punishment* is to redress the disorder caused by the offence. When his punishment is voluntarily accepted by the offender, it takes on the value of expiation.' This somewhat provocative and more clearly theological idea is unfortunately not further developed.

12 'Instruction on Respect for Human Life and its Origin and on the Dignity of Procreation' (Vatican: Polyglot, 1987); *Origins* 16 (1987), 697, 699–711. This instruction is dedicated to dealing with the questions about medically assisted reproductive techniques.

13 AAS 66 (1974), 730–747; *Origins* 4 (1974), 385, 387–392. This 'Declaration' is very cautious about the question of the personhood of the fertilised ovum, which it refers to as a philosophical problem, and is satisfied with the observation that 'it is objectively a grave sin to dare to risk murder'. Neither *Donum Vitae* nor the *Catechism* apparently considers it necessary to delve into philosophical problems.

14 'Vatican Declaration on Euthanasia', AAS 72 (1980), 542–552; *Origins* 10 (1980), 154–157.

15 One should be careful in identifying the issues here because, as pointed out earlier, language plays a very important role in this area. If we use words like 'murder', 'torture', or 'vengeance', it is clear that we are talking about 'immoralities'. However, these categories of behaviour imply much more than a description of what is happening: they imply foreknowledge, freedom, intention, circumstances, and above all fundamental injustices. It is much less clear when we speak of issues such as self-defence, capital punishment, just war, and even 'mutilation' when it is a case of donating a healthy organ.

16 The concept of 'difference and complementarity' has received some strong criticism from many feminist theologians who observe that women usually end up with the 'smaller half' of the complementarity.

17 The last paragraph of the first section concludes 'The tradition of the Church has understood the sixth commandment as encompassing the whole of human sexuality' (2336). While this may be too obvious to debate, I would personally prefer to interpret the sixth commandment as being about 'right relationships', with 'adultery' being used primarily as an example. In fact, I like to challenge students with the possibility of thinking about 'adultery' being committed without any reference to sex at all: about a spouse having an 'adulterous' relationship with their work, their possessions, their hobby — whatever threatens one's commitment to the marital covenant. By the same token, I suggest that the primary virtue governing marital life, and subsequently the principal topic of conjugal morality, should be not chastity, but justice.

18 As an indication of the difficulty of adapting the entire scheme of moral living to that of the Ten Commandments, one could draw attention to the relationship between the sixth and ninth (as well as the seventh and tenth)

commandments. This is particularly evident at this point since the *Catechism* here (2351) considers 'lust' to be forbidden by the sixth commandment while later (2517) it will identify 'carnal covetousness' against which we are called to struggle according to the ninth commandment. The original translation inserted the word 'lust' in parentheses to identify 'carnal covetousness'.

19 2357 states simply that 'Its [homosexuality's] psychological genesis remains largely unexplained'. This appears to follow the reasoning first hinted in *Persona Humana*, the first document from the magisterium that recognised the reality of the homosexual orientation beyond any 'choice' of the homosexual person. In the time since that document, there appears to have been a tendency to retract that admission, if not explicitly then at least by refusing to take this simple observation as a point of departure in whatever is said about homosexual persons and homosexual behaviour. To substantiate the Church's position on this question, one could add that there is also no consensus about the genesis of the *heterosexual* orientation either. I would suggest that it will not be possible to speak of the origins or genesis of homosexuality until we can more fully understand and explain the origins or genesis of heterosexuality.

20 James McManus, with Sean O'Riordan and Henry Stratton, 'The "Declaration on Certain Questions Concerning Sexual Ethics"', *The Clergy Review* 41 (1976), pp. 231–7. The person referred to here is Jan Visser CSsR, and his position on the pastoral care of homosexual persons is based upon a quotation of an interview with Fr Visser related in this article by Sean O'Riordan (p. 233).

21 Cf. *Humanae Vitae* 9 and 12; Proposition 21 of the 1980 Synod of Bishops; and *Familiaris Consortio* 29.

22 One could, and to be consistent with analysing a viable methodology *should*, ask whether there is a distinction to be made between 'meaning' and 'value'.

23 Experts have pointed out that for the perpetrator rape is primarily an act of power and domination. Its manifestion as a sexual event may serve to cloud the issue that what is happening here is a violation of the person — a violation that the common language is perhaps more apt in describing when it refers to psychological, emotional, or even intellectual 'rape'.

24 Perhaps the best example of this is the enumeration of the spiritual and corporal works of mercy in 2447.

25 Reference here (note 199) is given to GS 76 §5, and other references are given to 2032 and 2246. To these could be added 2237 and 2242, which also mention the 'fundamental rights of the person'.

26 This translation of OA 4 is taken from Joseph Gremillion, *The Gospel of Peace and Justice: Catholic Social Teaching since Pope John* (New York: Orbis Books, 1976), p. 487.

27 The seventh commandment forbids *theft*, that is, usurping another's property against the reasonable will of the owner. There is no theft if consent can be presumed or if refusal is contrary to reason and the universal destination of goods. This is the case in obvious and urgent necessity when the only way to provide for immediate, essential needs (food, shelter, clothing . . .) is to put at one's disposal and use the property of others. (2408; cf. GS 69 §1).

Methodologically, this is an important text, for it underscores the fact that moral judgements cannot be made without consulting a broader range of factors than the mere physical description of what is happening at a given moment. Only in the following paragraph does the text use the word '*unjustly* taking and keeping the property of others . . .', which makes the same point.

28   'Hence, those who are oppressed by poverty are the object of a *preferential love* on the part of the Church . . .' (2448).

29   These three terms appear to be synonymous, although in the text (2480), while *flattery* is not classified, *adulation* is described as a 'grave fault' or a 'venial sin', depending upon circumstances.

30   This observation is strengthened later in the text when we read 'No one is bound to reveal the truth to someone who does not have the right to know it' (2489). This statement carries a footnote reference to Sir 27:16 and Prov 25:9–10, both of which are about *not* disclosing secrets. The references would have been more appropriate in 2491, which is specifically about secrets and confidences, whether implicit (professional) or explicit (personal).

31   In fact, the notion of 'ten' commandments is not even typical of the Old Testament. According to Jewish tradition, there are 613 commandments. The designation of there being only ten was considered wrong, for it would imply that not all the commandments originate in God. See Raymond F. Collins, 'Ten Commandments', *The Anchor Bible Dictionary*, vol. 6 (New York: Doubleday, 1992), pp. 383–7.

32   In what might be an oversight, the *Catechism* itself quotes the 'tenth commandment' including the reference to manservant or maidservant. If those who put forth the *Catechism* consider themselves to be exercising part of the teaching function within the Catholic Christian community, the magisterium, one could rightfully ask whether this function is being exercised responsibly when scriptural references to owning servants are merely reproduced without explanation. If the magisterium is not going to use its self-claimed right and responsibility to interpret Scripture, who will perform this function?

The Encounter Known As Prayer

(Paragraphs 2558–2758)

Philip Endean SJ

Heythrop College, London

Part Four of the *Catechism of the Catholic Church* is about prayer, and opens by recalling the work's overall structure (2558). The whole is about the 'mystery of the faith'. Part One deals with the Apostles' Creed, and sets out the content of Christian belief. The second Part deals with the celebration of this content through the sacraments, while Part Three has outlined the consequences for ethics. But our belief, our celebration, and our moral life make sense only through 'a vital, personal, conscious and responsible relationship with the living and true God'. And this relationship, the paragraph concludes, is prayer.

The Part's first chapter is entitled 'The revelation of Prayer', and draws on biblical sources. The second chapter, 'The tradition of Prayer,' sets out various resources for developing the life of prayer. In the third chapter the focus narrows. While in the first two chapters, prayer is understood as a relationship pervading the whole of the Christian life, we are reminded at the opening of the third that this relationship requires prayer in a narrower sense, prayer as a specific activity at specific times (2697). Various kinds of prayer are expounded, and there is then some brief discussion of difficulties in prayer. The final article is a meditation on the prayer put on Jesus' lips in John 17.

The *Catechism* writes with great eloquence and insistence on prayer, but at the end — *after* doctrine and morals. In doing so, it follows a pattern well established in catechetical tradition and which has had widespread influence on what some people call 'spiritual reading'. But this option has unspoken implications that are both significant and questionable. Prayer occurs *within* a previously established framework. However lyrically prayer is described, it can only be a decoration on a structure that would remain perfectly well in place without it. It would no doubt be sad were no one ever to pray, but the content of Christian doctrine would remain. There is a sense in which prayer is theologically unimportant. Hence, conversely, no one worries too much if 'spiritual' writers fail to satisfy rigorous theological standards.

The *Catechism* thus sends mixed messages about the importance of prayer in the Christian life. My comments, impressionistic though they must be, will suggest an alternative account of the relationship between prayer and theology. A universal catechism must aim to express what is applicable to all situations, and only that. It must therefore allow for the fact that God's self-revelation is a continuing process. This is not to say that doctrine is dispensable or unimportant, but it is to insist that the relationship we call prayer is, in a real sense, essential, indeed foundational to Christianity. There would be no Christian doctrine had people never prayed, and it is only through prayer that one appropriates and understands doctrine properly.

What I have to say falls into three sections. In the first, I document more fully how the authors of the *Catechism* understand the relationship between theology and 'spiritual' (or 'catechetical') writing. In the second and third sections, I argue that the positions formulated in the *Catechism* need to be deepened if the project of a truly universal catechism is to be realised.

I

These three chapters of Part Four reminded me of George Eliot, the classic nineteenth-century English novelist, and her complex relationships with Christianity. She had a deep respect and sympathy for simple rural piety. Chapter 18 of *Adam Bede* includes a description of the village community assembled for a funeral:

> . . . the effect must have been warm and cheering when Mr Irwine was in the desk, looking benignly round on that simple congregation . . . [N]one of the old people held books — why should they? not one of them could read. But they knew a few 'good words' by heart, and their withered lips now and then moved silently, following the service without any very clear comprehension indeed, but with a simple faith in its efficacy to ward off harm and bring blessing.

In chapter 10 of *Silas Marner*, a woman called Dolly Winthrop, wife of Ben, brings Silas, who has just been robbed, some cakes on Christmas morning. On each of them she has marked out the letters 'IHS':

> 'There's letters pricked on 'em . . . I can't read 'em myself, and there's nobody . . . rightly knows what they mean; but they've a good meaning, for they're the same as is on the pulpit-cloth at church . . . [I]t's a stamp as has been in our house, Ben says, ever since he was a little 'un, and his mother used to put it on the cakes, and I've allays put it on too; for if there's any good, we've need of it i' this world . . . Ben's read 'em to me many and many a time, but they slip out o' my mind again; the more's the pity, for they're good letters, else they wouldn't be in the church . . .'

These chapters of the *Catechism* have not been written for illiterates, but they do presume in their readers something of the uncritical, respectful and trusting attitude exemplified by Dolly. Their words are good words; they are the words of the Church, the words of life. They will not do anyone any harm, and memorising some of them may indeed be salutary. But they have not been formulated in such a way as to withstand serious questioning.

Adam Bede is really a story about Hetty, a young farm-girl, who becomes pregnant by the son of the local squire and murders her baby when he abandons her; its greatest and most moving scene comes when Hetty is visited in prison by a Methodist lay-preacher, and finally begins to be able to talk about what she has done. *Silas Marner* is about an isolated miser who is robbed of all his money but, in its place, finds an abandoned baby girl; through her he is integrated into the community and his painful past is healed. In both these novels George Eliot shows a profound imaginative grasp of Christian truth, a deep sense of the potential for reconciliation mediated by Christian tradition. Yet she spent her adult life outside ecclesial Christianity, partly because she was not formally married to her life-partner, partly because, as the translator of D. F. Strauss's pioneer work on the life of Jesus, she found the historical claims made then by mainstream Christians impossibly naive. Her intellectual honesty would not allow her to rest content with Christian convention or with a theology that avoided the difficulties raised by modern discoveries; thus, a woman whose sense of the Christian mystery was profound remained cut off from any Church.

More than a century later, it is not just avant-garde intellectuals who feel keenly the sheer difficulties with the Christian message. The questions raised by historical consciousness, critical scholarship and modern science have penetrated our cultures profoundly, though obviously in unreflective form. We naturally expect any book presenting the Christian faith somehow to engage with these questions. But we will only understand the *Catechism* when we realise that it is not even trying to meet that expectation. Its aim is not to defend or explain Roman Catholic Christianity, but merely to present it.

Let us take the presentation of Abraham and Isaac in 2572. The story is presented as one of a number of points in the Old Testament where prayer is revealed in a special way (2569). There is simply no discussion of the complex moral issue raised by the story: the potential for conflict between divine command and other sources of moral obligation. Why is Abraham's readiness ritually to murder his son seen as a praiseworthy act of faith? 'God told me to do it' would not normally be accepted as an excuse for intended homicide; it would be taken either as evidence of delusion or else as a joke. Again, how would the authors expect a catechist to deal with a twelve-year-old I once had in class, whose reaction to the Exodus story was 'But you're always saying that God loves everybody. What about the Egyptians who got killed then?' Questions of this kind are neither raised nor answered. The *Catechism* deals with difficult biblical material by a policy of unashamed harmonisation, presenting Scripture as serenely and uniformly edifying. Dogmatically, such an approach is certainly necessary and defensible (134), but today's catechists need further help.

Another illustration of the editors' general approach comes with the classification of explicit prayer into three types: vocal, meditative and mental. The text distinguishes the latter two with the following:

> Christian prayer tries above all to meditate on the mysteries of Christ, as in *lectio divina* or the rosary. This form of prayerful reflection is of great value, but Christian prayer should go further: to a knowledge of the love of the Lord Jesus, to union with him. (2708)

This text draws on traditional distinctions which have been widely discussed and, in some quarters, radically criticised. The distinction between vocal and ratiocinative prayer, on the one hand, and a prayer of pure 'love' and 'union' with Christ, on the other, depends on a philosophy of mind that is at least disputable. Can one be united personally without the mind and language somehow being involved? And even if this is possible, how then do we refute the charge that prayer is an irresponsible escape from the world (2727, 2745, 2660)? Moreover, if prayer is really God's gift to be given as God wills, and if it is truly to be the expression of a unique personal relationship between each believer and God (2567), does it really make any sense to talk of 'contemplative' prayer as 'the pre-eminently *intense time [temps fort]* of prayer' (2714)? This kind of bracketing of difficult issues in the *Catechism* indicates its distinctive genre. The authors are content to draw uncritically on a conventional theology. They abstract from what is, in this case, a particularly lively and complicated specialist debate.

The *Catechism of the Catholic Church* is an abstract document in two senses of the word. The Prologue and the Apostolic Constitution placed at the front of the text state clearly that a univeral catechism — such as this one or the Tridentine catechism — abstracts from the particular situations in which catechesis is done (24). What is less clearly stated is that the authors are trying to do catechesis in some kind of abstraction from theology. Two bishops from the editorial commission have published articles which confirm the point. The British bishop, David Konstant, writes of how modern theology, 'quite properly', '. . . has taken on a more critical role and pluralistic character. Hence the systematic exposition of the truths of the faith, then as now primarily the responsibility of the bishops, is less easily delegated to the theologian.'[1] The Archbishop of Tours, Jean Honoré, understands a catechism as a document which presents 'the truths of the faith and the requirements of the moral life in the form of statements more designed for affirmation than demonstration, with the expression aiming for vividness rather than proof'.[2]

If theologians are faced with the charge of reading their own meanings into Scripture, they must refute it. But the problem is not so serious in catechetics, which is 'less concerned with grounding faith than with stating it'.[3]

The Pope, for his part, has expressed himself sharply on the need for catechists not to pay too much attention to contemporary theology. Though the questions posed by modern historical scholarship are real and important, catechists:

must have the wisdom to pick from the field of theological research those points that can provide light for their own reflection and their teaching, drawing, like the theologians, from the true sources, in the light of the Magisterium. They must refuse to trouble the minds of children and young people, at this stage of their catechesis, with outlandish theories, useless questions and unproductive discussions, things that Saint Paul often condemned in his [*sic!*] pastoral letters. (*Catechesi Tradendae* 61)

Moreover, according to Archbishop Honoré, the concern that the *Catechism* be of use in a wide range of catechetical situations demanded theological neutrality. The structure of this new *Catechism* is a variant on a traditional model going back to the second century, and had the advantage of not requiring the modern authors to choose their own theological principle of coherence. The editorial commission was in fact 'very scrupulous in avoiding all espousal of any one school of theology or recent approach to exegesis'.[4] They were trying to address all situations, not just some. Thus the purpose of the book is different from, for example, that of a catechism recently published by the French bishops' conference. This latter 'is more concerned with showing how faith in the Christian mystery apears with regard to the mentalities and situations which human awareness, confronted with unbelief, today encounters'. By contrast:

> The editors of the *Catechism* often had to opt against a style that
> would have been fully up-to-date, but which would have run the risk
> of sacrificing the permanence of the categories of faith to a certain
> contingency of thought and language — which, as one knows
> (particularly in the West), are always changing and vulnerable.[5]

To the critically-minded, what the *Catechism* says about prayer will appear neither interesting nor cogent. But these impressions are largely a consequence of limitations which the editors imposed upon themselves, limitations which they regard as inherent in the genre. One can only read the text fairly if one makes allowance for these. And then some positive features do become apparent. This section of the *Catechism* is best taken as giving us, simply, a list of themes that should be borne in mind when catechesis on prayer is being planned. If we are also given a normative way of treating them, this should be taken as a specimen formulated as neutrally as possible, not as an example to follow. The individual catechist should precisely not repeat what is said in the text, but rather take it as a basis on which to make responsible variations.

The *Catechism of the Catholic Church* is meant, at least on the surface, as a reference point rather than a model, even if the promotion and publicity given to it may imply a different intention. Different people will need different styles of presentation and argument. What the text provides is a starting-point for creativity and discernment. Through that process, our 'vital and personal relationship with the living and true God' — otherwise known as our prayer (2558) — will grow and develop.

II

Growth in the Christian life is inevitably a muddled business; growth in prayer is rarely tidy. Nevertheless, there is a difference between pluralism and anarchy, and one of the concerns behind the *Catechism* is that of establishing and protecting that difference. It will not do simply to say that everything is in process. So Bishop Konstant:

> In preparing the text a major concern has been to avoid an overemphasis on modes of expression, on the historical and cultural conditioning of truth, on process and relationships. These categories, important though they are, can all too easily suggest to the unwary that truth has been relativised; hence the emphasis in the Catechism on a substantial and coherent presentation of the doctrines of the faith.[6]

It is no part of my intention in this essay to question the need for solid doctrine. But it must also be stressed that prayer — at least in the broad sense predominant in the first two chapters of Part Four — is of central and irreplaceable importance in any Christian epistemology, in any Christian account of how we know God. And the *Catechism* may fairly be accused of giving insufficient weight to this point. The remainder of this essay, then, explores the relationship between doctrine and prayer. In this section, I suggest that Thomas Aquinas's teaching on petitionary prayer implies insights of great relevance for the project of a universal catechism — insights which have been missed. In the final section, I argue for a suitably nuanced version of the claim that it is prayer which is foundational in the Christian life, and doctrine which is the superstructure — not the other way round.

The *Catechism* presents petitionary prayer as 'the most usual, because the most spontaneous' form of supplication. Yet from the start the editors seem to regard the petition itself as somehow unworthy, so much so that even by the end of the first paragraph they have effectively collapsed petition into contrition:

> by prayer of petition we express awareness of our relationship with God. We are creatures who are not our own beginning, not the masters of adversity, not our own last end. We are sinners who as Christians know that we have turned away from our Father. Our petition is already a turning back to him. (2629)

There follows a small-print reminder of Paul's text (Rom 8:23–36) on how it is the Spirit himself who supplies for the shortcomings in the way we make our petitions. The main text then speaks of how forgiveness leads to a humility that 'brings us back into the light of communion between the Father and his Son Jesus Christ and with one another, so that "we receive from him whatever we ask" (1 John 3:22)' (2631).

Petition in the ordinary sense of the word is radically relativised. The key paragraph, supported by a wealth of New Testament references, runs as follows:

Christian petition is centred on the desire and search for the Kingdom to come, in keeping with the teaching of Christ. There is a hierarchy in these petitions: we pray first for the Kingdom, then for what is necessary to welcome it and co-operate with its coming. This collaboration with the mission of Christ and the Holy Spirit, which is now that of the Church, is the object of the prayer of the apostolic community. It is the prayer of Paul, the apostle *par excellence*, which reveals to us how the divine solicitude for all the churches ought to inspire Christian prayer. By prayer every baptized person works for the coming of the Kingdom. (2632)

The following paragraph asserts the value of petitionary prayer, but only under the condition that, in making it, 'we share in God's saving love'. The suggestion that it might actually work is avoided. Alluding to John 14:13, the *Catechism* continues: 'Christ, who assumed all things in order to redeem all things, is glorified by what we ask the Father in his name.'

The theme recurs when the *Catechism* deals with difficulties in the life of prayer, in the second article of the third chapter. In tribulation, the major difficulty often concerns 'the prayer of petition, for oneself or for others in intercession' (2734). This observation introduces brief discussions of so-called 'unanswered prayer' and of the ways in which prayer is efficacious. Two main points are made. Firstly, referring to James 4:2–3, the *Catechism* insists that God will only answer the right sort of petitions, those which are made in accord with his 'Spirit of freedom':

> 'You ask and do not receive, because you ask wrongly, in order to spend it on your passions'. If we ask with a divided heart, we are 'adulterers'; God cannot answer us, for he desires our well-being, our life . . . If we enter into the desire of his Spirit we shall be heard. (2737, cf. 2736)

Secondly, the real object of any petitionary prayer is not the gifts but the Giver (2740): 'If our prayer is resolutely united with that of Jesus, in trust and boldness as children, we obtain all that we ask in his name, even more than any particular thing: the Holy Spirit himself, who contains all gifts' (2741).

Let us now set these paragraphs alongside one article from St Thomas's *Summa Theologiae* (II-II, 83, 2).[7] The question discussed runs 'Is prayer useful (*conveniens*)?' As always, Thomas begins by making the case against his own view. A part of this case still finds an echo in modern discussions: there seems little point in telling God about our needs if he knows them anyway and if his will is immutable. Nevertheless, Jesus in Luke 18:1 exhorts us always to pray and not lose heart. Thomas's own position emerges from his more general teaching on how all that exists is caused *both* by God, the first cause, *and* by created, secondary causes:

> When considering the problem of the usefulness of prayer, one must remember that divine providence not only disposes what effects will take place, but also the manner in which they will take place, and

which actions will cause them. Human acts are true causes, and therefore human beings must perform certain actions, not in order to change divine providence, but in order to obtain certain effects in the manner determined by God. What is true of natural causes is true also of prayer, for we do not pray in order to change the decree of divine providence, rather, we pray in order that our asking bring about those things which God has determined would be obtained only through our prayers. In other words, people pray so that 'by asking they might deserve to receive what Almighty God has decreed to give them from all eternity', as Gregory says.

On this basis, Thomas answers the case made against petitionary prayer. Indeed God does not need to be told what we need, but we need to remind ourselves of our dependence on divine help. Indeed we cannot change God's mind, but there are some realities which God has willed to bring about only by means of our prayer.

The comparison reveals three important points. In the first place, it must be noted that the *Catechism*'s editors, despite Archbishop Honoré's disclaimers, have taken a very definite theological option. When we set these two texts together, it becomes clear that we are comparing two theologies. One cannot resolve the differences by saying that the catechetical text is 'merely' catechetical, and abstracts from theology. Any statement about God at least implies a theology of some sort, and the only question is whether the theology is sensible or not. In our case here, the *Catechism*'s editors are making some none too subtle theological moves in order effectively to redefine the whole concept of petitionary prayer.

Secondly, the texts are addressing different kinds of prospective objector, and treating their objections in different ways. The *Catechism* seems to presuppose an objector who has tried praying for something and not received it. This objector is rebuked, on the ground that it is both theologically wrong and morally self-centred to pray for particular intentions. Thomas, by contrast, addresses an objector worried about speculative issues regarding divine immutability and divine agency. Like the *Catechism*, Thomas corrects the objector's theology, but unlike the *Catechism* he acknowledges the legitimate concerns behind the objections, and does his best to incorporate these concerns into his own position. Thomas's pedagogy here goes to the deep and difficult issues, resolving them creatively while showing a courteous respect for his dialogue partners. He is also straightforwardly faithful to the tradition, and does not seek to theologise away the embarrassing questions it raises. Catechists have much to learn from him.

Thirdly and most importantly, it is Thomas's approach that is the more appropriate for a *universal* catechetical text. Petitionary prayer is an uncomfortable topic. How should theologically trained pastoral workers interpret the deep piety of simple people? I think of an old lady I knew who was for many years housebound. Whenever her family worried about her climbing the staircase, her retort was 'Our Lady gets me up the stairs'

— and indeed each step she took was accompanied by loud cries to the Virgin Mary. On the teaching of the *Catechism*, one must probably write this kind of prayer off as superstition, or at least demythologise it out of recognition. On Thomas's theology, matters are left open. He states a general metaphysical principle, but leaves it entirely open how that principle will work out in the concrete. 'We pray in order that our asking bring about those things which God has determined would be obtained only through our prayers.' This formulation avoids *specifying* how God uses our prayers; it leaves space for saying that God can subvert our preconceptions of him, can reveal himself through another person in a way that we would find unfamiliar and challenging. Thomas is far from committing us to saying that simple petitionary prayer is *always* authentic, but he stops properly short of rejecting it altogether. The question raised by such piety is allowed to stand simply as a question, and as a reminder that something is at stake in the spiritual life which cannot be pinned down, cannot be subject to immediate judgement.

Thomas's theology is superior to that of the *Catechism* because, paradoxically, it is more reticent, more sensitive to the mystery of God's working, and less committed to any one account of how that working takes place. It is important to see that Thomas does not exactly contradict the *Catechism*'s account of petitionary prayer. It may indeed be that the good which God brings about through our prayer is a 'transformation of the praying heart' (2739), and also that God does this in and through the 'failure' of our prayer to obtain particular benefits. But that is only one possible application of Thomas's formal principles — an application that might indeed be appropriate in many catechetical situations, but one application among others nevertheless. Scholastic discourse may be dry and unattractive, but, precisely as such, it is also well suited to naming what is universally valid across the whole range of all catechetical situations, both actual and possible.

Underlying the *Catechism* is a worry that academic theology has become needlessly complicated and irrelevant, sapping confidence in the faith. In reaction, the authors of the *Catechism* seek to short-circuit academic theology, and isolate a clear doctrinal foundation somehow immune from theological questioning. The concern is a real and worthy one, and no one would claim that theologians always succeed in avoiding useless difficulty. But equally, the best theology will always be difficult and provisional because it will leave God's options open. A doctrinal foundation can only be a foundation: it must be offered, not as something complete in itself, but as a resource empowering people to discover who God is for them. And the result may well surprise both individual catechists and the Church which sponsors them.

III

The *Catechism* understands prayer primarily as a relationship with God, and only secondarily as an activity occupying some parts of our time as opposed to others (2558). 'Prayer' thus becomes almost a synonym for 'Christian commitment'. Moreover, the *Catechism* presents prayer, correctly, as our response to a divine initiative. Although 'all religions bear witness to men's [*sic*] essential search for God', this only answers God's call to 'every being from nothingness into existence' (2566). As the following paragraph — in needlessly offensive fashion — puts it:

> Man may forget his Creator or hide far from his face; he may run after idols or accuse the deity of having abandoned him; yet the living and true God tirelessly calls each person to that mysterious encounter known as prayer. In prayer, the faithful God's initiative of love always comes first; our own first step is always a response.

Now, if prayer, if the Christian life, is always a response to God's initiative, and if this initiative is continuing to unfold in a 'covenant drama engaging the heart', then it is in principle unpredictable. Though new believers certainly need to be instructed in the Church's tradition, it is God's free call which is central to their commitment — a call which may be leading them, like Abraham, along hitherto unexplored ways.

Moreover, though Christian commitment certainly involves assent to doctrinal content, it is surely only some sort of experiential conviction of God's presence in prayer that makes this content plausible. Faith involves going beyond demonstrable evidence, a sense of being led by one whom we do not comprehend. One of Karl Rahner's most famous sayings ran: 'tomorrow's believer will either be a "mystic" — someone who has "experienced" something — or else they will not be a believer at all.'[8] A disciple of Rahner's tells a story which testifies to the personal conviction lying behind that statement. They were arguing about whether it is possible to prove the existence of God, with no ground being given on either side: 'Once the discussion became hopeless, he brought the conversation to an end with the words, "I believe because I pray".'[9]

Taken to their logical conclusion, such ideas would lead to a *Catechism* in which prayer, instead of coming in Part Four as a response to doctrinal and moral material, would come at the beginning. The doctrinal material would flow out of what could be said about prayer, not vice versa. And that which is common to all catechetical processes would be in the form of a set of rules for spiritual discernment and spiritual guidance.

In this final section, I want to look at the considerations which led the editors of the *Catechism* to adopt a more conventional strategy, and suggest that this strategy, though fine for many particular situations, is inappropriate for a text purporting to set out what should be common to *all* catechesis. I shall then try to illustrate what an alternative approach might look like by showing how it would generate an account of difficulties in prayer rather different from that in the *Catechism*.

The *Catechism*'s structure presents prayer as the response to a message preached, not the source of the message itself. The underlying concern was clearly articulated by Pope John Paul in *Catechesi Tradendae* 60:

> Certain contemporary philosophical schools . . . like to emphasize that the fundamental human attitude is that of seeking the infinite, a seeking that never attains its object. In theology, this view of things will state very categorically that faith is not certainty but questioning, not clarity but a leap in the dark.
>
> These currents of thought certainly have the advantage of reminding us that faith concerns things not yet in our possession, since they are hoped for . . . They help us to make the Christian faith not the attitude of one who has already arrived, but a journey forward as with Abraham . . .
>
> However, we must not fall into the opposite extreme, as too often happens . . . Although we are not in full possession, we do have an assurance and a conviction. When educating children, adolescents and young people, let us not give them too negative an idea of faith — as if it were absolute non-knowing, a kind of blindness, a world of darkness — but let us show them that the humble yet courageous seeking of the believer . . . is based on the word of God who cannot deceive or be deceived . . . It is . . . one of the aims of catechesis to give young catechumens the simple but solid certainties that will help them to seek to know the Lord more and better.

This passage acknowledges the pilgrim, provisional status of all we can say about God, but cautions against emphasising this in catechetics. Two concerns motivate this caution. The first is a desire not to complicate matters unduly for simple catechumens. The second is a worry that a stress on God's freedom and unpredictability can all too easily encourage an anarchically subjectivist understanding of Christianity, lacking cognitive content or solid certainty.

The first of these concerns should certainly be operative when one is devising a particular catechetical programme, but surely not in a text purporting to articulate *general* principles for *all* catechetical programmes. The second might be answered by a more careful reflection on the relationship between experience and doctrine, and on the complex concept of certainty. There is a long-standing tradition of contrasting approaches to religion based on doctrines and institutions with those centring on the free experience of the Spirit. This tradition influences classic texts such as William James's *The Varieties of Religious Experience* or Rudolf Otto's *The Idea of the Holy*, and it runs through much contemporary popular writing aiming to synthesise Christian teaching with Hindu or Buddhist ways of prayer. Similarly, pre-conciliar Roman Catholic theology often distinguished the life of the ordinary believer, dependent on words and liturgy, from that of the mystic, who was favoured with a direct experience of God — a distinction which is still, ironically, influencing what the *Catechism* says about mental prayer. But a moment's reflection is enough to show, minimally, that the relationship between language and experience is at once much closer and more complicated. Though our experiences in prayer will often lead us along unknown paths, we could not understand and identify them (even mistakenly) as experiences coming from God unless we had been socialised in certain ways, and taught the use of a language.

Though this theoretical point can and should be developed much further, here I simply offer an ancient text to show how the Christian life, while dependent on biblical tradition, nevertheless consists in an unpredictable mystery of freedom. The text is by St Ephrem the Syrian, and is found in the Divine Office (Office of Readings: Sunday, week 6 of the year):

> Lord, who can grasp the wealth of just one of your words? What we understand is much less than what we leave behind, like thirsty people who drink from a fountain. For your word, Lord, has many shades of meaning just as those who study it have many different points of view. The Lord has coloured his words with many hues so that each person who studies it can see in it what they love. He has hidden many treasures in his word so that each of us is enriched as we meditate on it . . .
>
> The one who comes into contact with some share of its treasure should not think that the only thing contained in the word is what they themselves have found. They should realize that they have only been able to find that one thing from among many others . . . Be glad that you were overcome, and do not be sad that it overcame you. The thirsty person rejoices when they drink, and they are not downcast because they cannot empty the fountain. Rather let the fountain quench your thirst than have your thirst quench the fountain. Because if your thirst is quenched and the fountain is not exhausted you can drink from it again whenever you are thirsty . . . Do not have the presumption to try and take in at one draught what cannot be taken in at one draught, and do not abandon out of laziness what you may consume only little by little.

The word of God, in the Scriptures or in catechesis, is essential and unnegotiable, but the process of drawing out its meaning is never ending. Christian faith is permanently provisional and uncertain, not because doctrine is somehow unreliable, but rather because the lived realisation of that doctrine is an interplay of God's freedom and our own.

Ignatius Loyola describes a retreat-giver as 'the one who gives to another the way and ordering of meditating and contemplating' (*Exercises*, 2). The description could apply also to catechists. We cannot hand on to another the truth for their lives, but we can give them resources for finding that truth, under God's grace, for themselves. Catechesis must involve a sensitivity to the unpredictable; we cannot foresee, and should not try to control, how God will reveal himself in the experience of the one being catechised. What we have that is of universal validity is a set of ground rules, to be applied in an inexhaustible variety of ways.

The point being made here chiefly concerns the structure and genre of the *Catechism*. But it also has some implications for the content, particularly as regards negative experiences in prayer. 2728–2733 of the *Catechism* presents these as 'obstacles'; to overcome them, 'we must battle to gain humility, trust and perseverance'. In face of distraction, we must 'turn back to our heart: for a distraction reveals to us what we are attached to, and this humble awareness before the Lord should awaken our preferential love for him and lead us resolutely to offer him our heart to be purified'. The struggle against distraction is the expression of a more fundamental conflict between God and Mammon, of 'the battle against the possessive and dominating self'. Dryness is described as 'the moment of sheer faith clinging faithfully to Jesus in his agony and in his tomb . . . If dryness is due to the lack of roots, because the word has fallen on rocky soil (Luke 8:6, 13), the battle requires conversion.' There follow paragraphs on lack of faith and on *acedia* — rendered in the first English translation as 'apathy or sloth'.

The article from which these quotations come is entitled 'The battle of prayer'. It opens by stating that prayer is 'both a gift of grace and a determined response on our part. It always presupposes effort.' The tradition teaches us that 'prayer is a battle. Against whom? Against ourselves and against the wiles of the Tempter who does all he can to turn man [*sic*] away from prayer, away from union with God' (2725). There is certainly an acknowledgement here that God is at work in our prayer, but this acknowledgement has had no decisive influence on the way the article is formulated. We have already noticed a general nervousness on the part of the editors regarding God's free action in our experience, and the influence this has had on the structure and genre of the *Catechism*. Here this nervousness influences the content of the *Catechism*'s teaching. Nothing that is said here is false in itself, but an obvious truth has been left unstated, namely that *God* might be communicating something through what feel like negative experiences of prayer. The stress on how these reflect our shortcomings has the real, if unintended, effect of implying that the life of prayer will be unproblematic if only one has the 'right' dispositions and prays in the 'right' way. Yet this is obviously false. Consolation in prayer is God's gift. It is not something we can turn on by good behaviour, nor does our sinfulness (mercifully) prevent its occurrence. Rather, it is through the interplay of consolations and desolations that God continues his saving self-revelation, the drama of salvation history (cf. 2567).

It follows that one should not be too quick to interpret psychologically negative experiences in prayer as a sign of one's own selfishness. They may indeed be that, but even then the question arises: Why is it now that God is stirring me to face this particular need for conversion whereas (perhaps) for many years he has been prepared to go along with my repression of it? The more general and deeper point is that nothing happens in prayer — and 'prayer' here means a person's whole life as seen in relationship to God — without God's having a purpose for it. This purpose must proceed from God's gratuitous love, independent of our merits. One should not, however, be too quick to decide what that purpose is, else one may fail to perceive the signals that God is sending. Distraction in prayer may be a sign of a distracted heart, but it may also be a sign that God is leading us to pray in a new way, or to face constructively the issue which is, perhaps very indirectly, obtruding itself on us.

I have already suggested that catechesis, especially in the area of prayer, has much to learn from the Church's inherited wisdom about spiritual direction. Let me end by recalling one point from the Ignatian tradition. Though Ignatius Loyola seems to have insisted that no one should give the Spiritual Exercises without having gone through the process themselves, he also held that there could be no greater error in spiritual matters than that of wanting to direct others along the lines of one's own experience. One of Ignatius's most distinguished early followers, an Italian Jesuit called Achille Gagliardi, wrote in the same vein. If a retreat-giver, or any pastoral worker, tries to impose on the other what they themselves have found helpful:

> this is to tie God and impose on him a law whereby he must do to this soul what he has done to one's own. In fact very often, because of the soul's capacity and the divine good pleasure, a very different procedure is appropriate for it from that which one has experienced in oneself. Therefore one must take distance from oneself.[10]

In pastoral care, we know that God is working for the salvation of the other, but we must remain quite agnostic about how. Church life must therefore look chaotically diverse, as chaotically diverse as the reality of God's people. There is indeed a certainty in the process, because we build on God's word, and God is faithful. But the role of theology, of spiritual direction and of catechesis is to keep us open to the mystery of God, not to anticipate or foreclose its working. The relationship we call prayer is central to theological epistemology, central to the proper understanding of doctrine, and central to catechetics — especially universal catechetics. It will be a pity if the placing of these chapters, and their lack of theological rigour, obscure this point.

Notes

1 David Konstant, 'A Catechism for the times', *The Tablet* 246 (1992), pp. 1528–32; the citation occurs on p. 1528.
2 Jean Honoré, 'Le Catéchisme de l'église catholique', *Nouvelle Revue Théologique* 115 (1993), pp. 3–18; the citation occurs on p. 6.
3 Ibid., p. 14.
4 Ibid., p. 7.
5 Ibid., pp. 17–18.
6 Konstant, 'Catechism for the times', p. 1530.
7 The quotations from Aquinas are taken from the translation of the *Summa Theologiae*, Blackfriars edition, vol. 39, Kevin D. O'Rourke (ed.), *Religion and Worship (2a 2ae 80–91)* (London: Eyre & Spottiswoode, 1964).

8   Karl Rahner, *Theological Investigations*, vol. 7 (London: Darton, Longman & Todd, 1971), p. 15 (translation corrected).
9   Karl-Heinz Weger, 'Ich glaube weil ich bete: Für Karl Rahner zum 80. Geburtstag', *Geist und Leben*, 57 (1984), pp. 48–52; the citation occurs on p. 51.
10   Ignacio Iparraguirre, *Historia de los Ejercicios de San Ignacio*, vol. II (Bilbao–Rome, 1955), p. 384.

The Lord's Prayer

(Paragraphs 2759–2865)

Noel D. O'Donoghue ODC

New College, Edinburgh (Emeritus)

The Section on the Lord's Prayer in the 1994 *Catechism of the Catholic Church* is at once complete and compendious and also carries a current of enthusiasm and a sense of new beginnings. It is an excellent teacher's manual that may yet be perused with profit by all 'even Christians' and all men and women of goodwill everywhere. Yet it *is* a manual, a teacher's presentation that does not explore those horizons through which it travels. It is the purpose of the following annotations to do just this, and so to open the mind and heart to some of the pathways and vistas of the Christian tradition. I have chosen ten topics for exploration and will say a little about each of them, it being understood that the *Catechism* text is being taken as the background from which our exploration sets forth and to which it returns.

1. The Lucan text (2759)

It must be said that although the theme of prayer has an important place in all the books of the New Testament, it is especially and uniquely important in the Gospel according to St Luke, so much so that the Lucan version of the Lord's Prayer (henceforth 'the Our Father') is of particular importance especially as bearing on the theme of personal prayer. In a sense it acts as a balance to the communal and liturgical emphasis in St Matthew's longer version. As it comes to us in the eleventh chapter of the Gospel, we see Jesus himself at solitary prayer in the presence or proximity of his apostles, and we hear their request that he should teach them to pray as John the Baptist, the solitary ascetic, taught *his* disciples to pray.

At first sight it looks as if the Lucan text is but a truncated version of the Matthaean inasmuch as it omits two of the seven petitions that we find in Matthew: 'Thy will be done' and 'Deliver us from evil'; yet the petition 'Thy will be done' is given its full depth and amplitude in the account of the agony-prayer on the Mount of Olives (Luke 22:42), where deliverance from the testing by the evil one is also emphasised; besides, some important ancient texts and witnesses include at this point an invocation of the Holy Spirit ('the Holy Spirit come upon us and cleanse us') that seems necessary to explain v. 13 of Luke 11.[1]

2. The prayer of Jesus (2765)

The statements that Jesus is 'our teacher of prayer' and 'the model of our prayer' must be stressed and deepened and extended to their full dimensions by opening up the Scriptures as they tell us, in the four Gospels especially, of the coming of Jesus, his style of life and the inner drama of his redemptive death. Jesus is cradled in prayer: the priestly prayer of Zechariah at the hour of incense 'while the whole congregation was praying' (Lk 1:10), the prayer of Mary, his mother, who is twice presented in deep meditation as the mystery of his coming unfolds (Lk 2.19, 51), the prayer of the heavenly host, the lifelong prayer of expectation of Simeon and Anna, the *Magnificat* and *Benedictus*.

Jesus is presented in all four Gospels not only as a teacher who commends prayers and who gives time to prayer, but who is, first and last, and through and through, and night and day, a man of prayer. We see him at prayer in the great epiphanies of his life: at his baptism (most clearly in the Lucan account), at the transfiguration (again Luke is explicit, 'as he prayed, the aspect of his face was changed' JB), at the Last Supper, in Gethsemane, on the cross. The place of prayer in the everyday style of life of Jesus is well expressed in the Jerusalem Bible version of Luke 5:15–16: 'He would always go off to some place where he could be alone and pray.' And the first chapter of Mark at v. 35 presents us with an unforgettable picture. After a day in which his work of healing and exorcism goes on well into the night, we read that 'in the morning, long before dawn, he got up and left the house, and went off to a lonely place and prayed there'. Clearly not only Luke and Mark but Matthew and John as well, and Paul too, will with varying degrees of emphasis have us see Jesus as a man of prayer, a being in the depths of whose being the gold and jewels of prayer are being constantly and laboriously mined.

The mining metaphor is helpful only because the labour was real and very great, as great indeed as the 'dark and driven' passion itself. For the passion of Jesus was not passive; it was not only freely accepted and that in the terrible prayer-freedom of Gethsemane, but it was activated at every moment by the prayer of Jesus as far indeed and *through* the *lama sabachthani* of utter dereliction.

The final cry of Jesus on the cross, that 'great cry' named by all four evangelists, that cry in which he yields his spirit to the Father, becomes a calling down into the darkness of earth and the deeper darkness of the estranged hearts of men and women the power of the Holy Spirit. It is only the human being who has entered this intolerable darkness who can call the Spirit into it, and so Jesus had to descend into the depths in order that he should reach the ground of all human beseeching. It is in and with and through him and in union with his life-giving sacrifice present in the Mass that we can fully 'make bold to say' the Lord's Prayer.

3. The sacrificial dimension

The section in the *Catechism* text entitled 'The prayer of the Church' (2767–2771) represents a triumph of brevity and comprehensiveness, and repays long and careful study. It firmly places the Our Father at the centre of the continuing traditional Christian luturgy as prayer and sacrament, though some Catholics may wish that there were more explicit recognition of the sacrificial aspect of the eucharistic liturgy implicit in the first three Father-centred petitions. For these petitions are not simply a calling forth of the divine presence, the heavenly kingdom and the all-holy will of the Father; they have no real meaning unless they express piercingly that sacrificial cost of discipleship shown forth in the life and death of Jesus. Part of what the Catholic understanding of the Our Father has to affirm for Catholics *and for other Christians* is that the sacrificial dimension of the prayer of the Church must be kept in mind and deeply felt.

We must therefore look carefully at what is said about the eschatological character of the Lord's Prayer. The word eschatology (literally: the study of the last things or of what is called the 'end-time') has perhaps been over-used in modern Catholic and Reformed theology, and sometimes only serves the purpose of taking the edge off the sharp sacrificial sayings of Jesus, as if they could be seen hazily within a never-never land. The consciousness of this has pushed some theologians to speak of 'realised eschatology', a phrase that barely escapes contradiction, but at least affirms that the Christian must live within the difficulties and ambiguities of the here and now, and that Christian hope is not escapist, but realistic.

Fortunately our *Catechism* provides a definition of eschatology (2771) as having to do with the end-time as 'the time of salvation that began with the outpouring of the Holy Spirit and will be fulfilled with the Lord's return'. Now it must be said firmly that for Catholic doctrine, nobody has the least idea of 'the time of the Lord's return'. We are therefore forced to see eschatology as having to do with the time after Pentecost, in which time we now live as men and women have always lived, seeking happiness and a better world, but surrounded by all kinds of sufferings and calamities in our own lives and the lives of those around us. It is in this situation that we re-enact the sacrifice of the cross and say that great prayer in which we not only ask for bread and forgiveness and protection, but place ourselves sacrificially as Jesus did at the service of the will of the Father and the coming of the kingdom. What distinguishes the 'end-time' from all other times is that through the sacrificial death, the resurrection and the ascension of the incarnate Son we are given access to that outpouring of the Holy Spirit which can enter the humble and contrite heart that reflects the glorious heights and depths of the heart of Jesus. It may be added that some Catholics find themselves drawn to some of those devotional byways of Catholic devotion in which the heart of Mary is seen to reflect and mediate that sacrificial love which marvellously animates the heart of Jesus Christ. For some Catholics, and for most non-Catholics, this world of Marian devotion is without sufficient foundation in Scripture; what *is* solidly founded in Scripture is the call to sacrificial love and loving sacrifice addressed to all men and women of goodwill.[2]

4.　The fatherhood of God

The image of fatherhood is taken from the order of human relationship and is affirmed of the divine source by denying or negating all human limitations and seeing what is affirmed as present *eminenter*, that is in a way beyond all images, a way which can be grasped spiritually by men and women under the deep inner guidance of the Holy Spirit of God (2777, 2778). Because we are here in the world of Spirit, there can be no question of retaining the gender limitations of the image of fatherhood, nor is there any gain in the switching of gender from masculine to feminine and speaking of 'Our Mother who art in heaven': this simply emphasises the limitations of the sense image against the free flight of that imagination which can keep the concreteness of human perceiving while shedding all that could hold down the Spirit as it 'thinks of many things'. We can, of course, speak with real metaphorical truth of 'the mother-face of God' as showing forth the divine mercy and compassion. It is true, however, that the Lord's Prayer, for many people, first and foremost shows forth what may be called the masculine face of that being which is 'nearer to me than my own self' (*intimior intimo meo*, says St Augustine), and this may bring up negative or even cruel images from the past and lead me to use the image of mother or bridegroom (or bride) as a way towards meeting with that being who is forever beautiful, truthful and loving.

We are dealing here with a very large question that has come to the fore only in recent times, sometimes angrily and confusingly, but always poignantly, and with the kind of challenge that has to be met by both men and women. It seems at first reading that the authors of the *Catechism* have simply ignored this whole problem or range of problems. Yet by sagacity or by that divine guidance which we all need today more than ever, they have, it seems to me, dealt with the problem of the feminine and 'the motherhood of God' by bringing forward, at this point especially, the ancient and ever new horizons of the Holy Spirit as the royal road from the depths of the human heart to the glory of the divine countenance as we are taken across the 'threshold of the divine holiness' (2777) by the human–divine bridegroom who calls each of us by name. We are here being strongly invited to think deeply about the Holy Trinity not as a theological treatise but, as in the Celtic spiritual tradition, as the very

413

house in which we dwell. It is through the presence and power of the Spirit that we are given that 'freedom of speech', that *parrhēsia*, that 'boldness' of the little way of St Thérèse of Lisieux by which she walked foolishly childish into that very place on the Mount of Olives where the great *peirasmos* of the Lord's Prayer was faced in all its terror and undoing.

The Abba-experience in which we share the prayer of Jesus in its depths is no mere active 'lifting up' of the mind and heart to the source, though it involves this as well as a 'knocking at the door'. Most profoundly, it is a being lifted up by way of the Holy Spirit praying the Abba-prayer within us (2776). This is the full meaning of that 'ask and you shall receive' that runs like a refrain through the teaching of Jesus on prayer; it is in the earnestness of the asking that a great receptivity opens up within us, a receptivity filled by the Holy Spirit with the all-fathering all-mothering love of the Father and the Son. It is in the eucharist and the Divine Office especially that all are invited to enter this ambience of prayer in togetherness and in personal intimacy.

5. Prayer and 'exteriority'

The *Catechism* tells us that the *our* of the Our Father expresses 'an entirely new relationship with God' and that 'this new relationship is the gift of belonging to each other'. This gift is also a deep need to share and to communicate, yet this is balanced and sometimes negated by a refusal to emerge from the seeming safety of the self-in-and-for-itself. If I relate to God as *my* God, I can remain within the self; if I relate to the God of others as the common fathering–mothering source of all of us, I am taken out of myself, beyond myself, and in this experience I am discovering that basic dimension within myself named 'exteriority' by a contemporary philosopher, Emmanuel Levinas.[3]

This dimension of 'exteriority' releases the margins of my ego, not to dissipate the self in superficial relationship, but in that 'new relationship with God' by which I begin to understand that dimension of belonging which has its highest expression in the cross of Christ. This is easily said; it can be achieved only very imperfectly and by way of constant prayer. This mutual love is the very atmosphere of 'the heavens' in which the Father dwells. It is very near, very present for those who truly strive after the charity of Christ of which St Paul speaks (1 Cor 13).

In all this there is a 'letting go' of the self as possessive, of things, of persons, of itself and its own desires. In this 'letting go' there is an ever-deepening understanding of the self as an image of the Father as total self-giving in the mystery of the Trinity. In the recitation of the Our Father there is a constant affirmation of the passage from self-love to universal love. And this is the ethical centre of Christianity.

6. The contemplative dimension: St Teresa of Avila

Article 3 of the Section on the Our Father in the *Catechism* deals with the seven petitions and the request for seven blessings, which together form the movement or dynamic of all Christian prayer as the voice of man seeking the presence of God. The first three of these petitions are called theological in the rather *special* sense that they link us directly to God (*Theos*); in a *general* sense, all seven petitions and all that has to do with prayer is matter for theological study and meditation. Indeed this whole exposition of 'The seven petitions' is an admirably clear and complete exemplar of theological writing; and a commentary should begin by pointing this out lest it runs the risk of trying to illumine the greater light by means of the lesser.

This is especially true of the three theological petitions: 'Hallowed be thy name', 'Thy kingdom come', 'Thy will be done'. Here the recovery or rediscovery of the idea of *glory* associated with the theology of Balthasar and others (including Karl Barth) is used to good effect, and serves to connect the text of the Lord's Prayer with that of the so-called 'priestly prayer of Jesus' of John 17.

In all this, our text is tending to break through the limits of vocal and community prayer into the world of contemplative prayer, active and passive (or receptive), and our commentary has to do mainly with this.

St Teresa of Avila, who was named a Doctor of the Church in 1967, devotes a remarkable section in her book *The Way of Perfection* to a presentation of the Our Father as a contemplative or, to use her own terminology, a 'supernatural' prayer. Supernatural prayer, as is clearly shown in her earlier book, the *Life*, in the image of the four waters or four waterings (*Life*, chs 11–22), is that prayer which comes by earnest and even laborious asking to an ever increasing receptivity in which, in the fourth watering, God fills the human heart and mind abundantly with his presence like 'the blessed rain from heaven'. The asking has led, entirely by divine favour, but only because one is ready for it, to an abundance of receiving, 'for everyone who asks receives'. This is what Teresa and the sixteenth-century Carmelite mystics term 'supernatural' prayer, even though *all* prayer, however natural and laborious, is primarily the work of God.

One of the central controversies in Catholic mystical theology in the twentieth century, a controversy with roots much further back, has had to do with the question whether all active prayer, all 'natural' prayer, has its proper completion in the mystical or 'supernatural', or whether there is a pathway of active contemplation that goes all the way to the heights of Christian perfection. Teresa has been claimed by both sides of the controversy, and there is no doubt but that she felt that some of the women who joined her convents were not at all suited to truly supernatural prayer. It is well to bear this in mind as we read what she has to say in *The Way of Perfection* on the Our Father as a contemplative prayer, yet we must bear in mind also that she is facing the strong and clamorous opposition of those who were strongly opposed to the higher flights of prayer as open to all kinds of delusion and exaggerations. Her approach to these opponents is a subtle one. She takes the fact, admitted by all Christians, that it is good and right and indeed essential to say the Our Father as a vocal prayer, and she presses hard on the obvious and universally admitted consideration that vocal prayer must have meaning, and that all genuine praying must stress and deepen this meaning; if I pray that God's kingdom should come and his will be done, I must *mean* this in all its consequences, and so with the other petitions. It becomes clear as we read these chapters in *The Way of Perfection* (ch. 27ff.) that the emphasis soon passes over from meaning to willing, so much so that everything is centred on God as the focus or object of the will and that the distractions of the intellect are to be ignored (see esp. ch. 31, para. 8).

In other words, the petitions of the Our Father transcend the meaning or content of the petitions, so that there arises a steady quiet gazing on the source that is a kind of total self-giving. This is 'the general and loving attention' of St John of the Cross, and echoes that 'naked intent of the will' which the English mystic who wrote the *Cloud of the Unknowing* spoke of two centuries before Teresa's time. In more recent times the popularity of the Jesus prayer and other mantra-type ways of prayer are within the same general 'elevation of the soul to God' (to quote the words of an older Catechism) by willing and loving.

Typically, St Teresa, in opening up the mystical dimension of the Our Father, does not lose touch with the actual words heard and spoken, said or sung, alone or in community. As in her attitude to the physical manhood of Jesus Christ, so in relation to the prayer Christ taught us she is thoroughly incarnational. That delicate balance of body and spirit central to the way of St Teresa is shown very clearly in the following excerpt from chapter 30, paragraph 7, of *The Way of Perfection*, which because of the importance of this equilibrium is worth quoting in full. She is talking of an elderly nun who came to her:

> I know a person who was never able to pray any way but vocally, and though she was tied to this form of prayer she experienced everything else. And if she didn't recite vocal prayer her mind wandered so much that she couldn't bear it. Would that our mental prayer were as good! She spent several hours reciting a certain number of Our Fathers, in memory of the times our Lord shed His blood, as well as a few other vocal prayers. Once she came to me very afflicted because she didn't know how to practise mental prayer nor could she contemplate; she could only pray vocally. I asked her how she was praying, and I saw that though she was tied to the Our Father she experienced pure contemplation and that the Lord was raising her up and joining her with Himself in union. And from her deeds it seemed truly that she was receiving such great favours, for she was living a very good life. So I praised the Lord and envied her for her vocal prayer.

7.   Our daily bread

This seemingly simple petition is not without its difficulties and ambiguities, and the scriptural commentaries *in loco* should be consulted, or, best of all, the relevant chapter in Ernst Lohmeyer's *The Lord's Prayer*, available in most theology libraries.[4] The text of the *Catechism* is very clear, and it makes some notable points, especially as regards the sharing of both material and spiritual goods and as regards the link between daily bread and daily Eucharist. Through it all there runs the analogy and duality of the physical and spiritual orders of sustenance, and it is well to bring this more fully into the open.

The story of Jesus is not only the story of a man who taught and prayed and healed the sick and cast out devils and offered his life for others. It is not only the story of a charismatic leader who attracted disciples and formed a world-wide and enduring community of followers. Above and beyond all this, Jesus was and is the 'living bread that came down from Heaven' (John 6:51) who calls men and women to 'eat his flesh and drink his blood', and by so doing receive eternal life (John 6:54). The physicality of the language alerts us to the fact that in some way, at once physical and infinitely more than physical, the Jesus-Emmanuel who 'came in the flesh' is not just a teacher and miracle-worker who *does* great deeds, but a being who has somehow entered *incorruptibly* into the *physical* texture of the earth. In other words, we are forced, in order to find room for the living bread of the Eucharist, to find again that 'lost category' of the incorruptible physical, a region of being that is at once spatial and trans-spatial, being, in the words of T. S. Eliot, 'the point of intersection of the timeless with time', the world of another poet's vision of 'orient and immortal wheat', which can take us into itself, visibly as in the multiplication of the loaves and fishes, invisibly as in the multiplication of the one body of Christ in the Holy Eucharist. This is near to the world of the resurrection and the 'spiritual body' of the resurrection (1 Cor 15:44), a 'super-substantial' world opened up by that eucharistic bread which is '*super*-substantial' inasmuch as it has all the reality of physical bread yet in another, 'higher' way. From this perspective, the word *epiousios*, which appears in both the Matthaean and Lucan texts of the Our Father, and which our English versions simply avoid, is perhaps a key that opens the door to an inner world.[5]

8.   The community of forgiveness

I find the section of the *Catechism* that deals with the fifth petition of the Our Father ('forgive us our trespasses', etc.) especially noteworthy, and indeed especially fresh and original, from the very first statement which frankly asks us to be 'astonished', right to the final linking of the unity and community of forgiveness with the unity of the Holy Eucharist. At the centre of an exposition rich in traditional Christian symbolism is the image of the open heart, the heart 'opened by grace', yet not by unconditional grace — here as elsewhere evangelical 'fundamentalism' is carefully avoided — but by meeting the condition of confessing our own need to forgive as we are forgiven (2840). In the development of this image of the open heart, the central Catholic symbol of the deeply wounded heart of Jesus Christ, glowing with a fire that burns up all sentimentality in its cleansing and creative power, begins to radiate through the words (2843, 2844). We are not far here from the symbolism of the burning bush chosen by the Reformed Church of Scotland as its symbol.

A point that needs perhaps to be stressed more strongly than we find in the text of the *Catechism* is that forgiveness, to be fully real, must not only be given, but must also be asked for and received. Jesus forgave his enemies even as far as those who nailed him to the cross of pain and derision, but his whole preaching had to do with *metanoia*, a change of heart, and he had stern and terrible words to say to those who persisted in hardness of heart and in opposition to his gospel of conversion of heart. There is a kind of supine or 'idiot' forgiveness that allows evil to flourish and is too cowardly to face the hurt of confrontation. This has never been the Christian way, nor does it have a place in a living community of forgiveness, which is never without honest confrontation.

'There is no limit or measure to . . . divine forgiveness' (2845), yet it is, nevertheless — indeed *because* it is unlimited — totally realistic to the last detail. All this means is that forgiveness, in order to be truly given, must be truly received into 'a contrite and humble heart'. It is only thus that the truth of forgiveness is established; it is only thus that the divine forgiveness can find an opening through which it flows into the human heart. God's forgiveness is unconditional, but it *is* forgiveness, and can only be real when it is really and truly received freely by free human persons. In this, human persons are accorded enormous dignity. At the human level I do not accord any dignity by ignoring personal responsibility in myself or in the other. If I am to live the Our Father in this central petition, I can never under any circumstances turn my back finally on the other, but there are times when I have to wait in prayer for a change of heart, and this prayer must be self-transforming as well as other-transforming in its intent. Only thus do I fulfil that one essential condition of all Christian prayer.

No Christian community, even if it be a monastery or convent — indeed most of all if it is — should be seen as shrouded in the peace of a dead tranquillity. If it is a community of true Christian forgiveness, it will be vibrant with confrontation and altercation, with recurrent crises and precious moments of transformation. The way of forgiveness is a way of constant crisis and of all the holy travail of human living.

9. The mystery of temptation

People are often puzzled or even scandalised by the usual version of the sixth petition of the Our Father: lead us not into temptation. What kind of father (or mother) has to be asked not to *lead* children into temptation?

Surely the God of love and protection will not only *not* lead but will indeed *prevent*, will not allow any of us to enter into temptation. It is thus that the *Catechism* interprets it and appeals to a text from Matthew 26, but only, be it noted, by way of a comparison: the footnote says 'Cf.', i.e. *conferre*, compare; for one cannot really equate the Greek of Matthew 26:41 with the Our Father text of Matthew 6:13. In this the *Catechism* is following a long tradition of 'softening' the original text, which finds its best ground in the quotation from James 1:13 which says that 'God tempts no one'. Yet Christ himself was 'tempted' (e.g., Luke 11:2), and that rigorously and deeply, and we cannot deny a certain rightness to John Milton, who in his *Paradise Regained* makes everything depend on the outcome of that testing time. It must be noted that the 'test' and the victory in the desert was only temporary (Lk 4:13), to be resumed in its full terror in Gethsemane, so terrible indeed that the disciples are urged to pray not to be drawn into it (Mt 26:41; Mk 14:38; Lk 22:40). Jesus himself had prayed in extreme agony that he should be spared this final intolerable testing (Lk 22:43, 44).

We are here, as in the seventh petition, in full view of the mystical dimension of the Our Father; we are with the authors of Job and Jonah and the Psalms of the depths; we are also with 'the dark night of spirit' of St John of the Cross, with the last temptations of St Thérèse of Lisieux, with the later poems of G. M. Hopkins. Something of this begins to appear in 2848 and 2849 of the *Catechism*.

There is a verse to be found in all Catholic versions of St Luke's account of the agony of Jesus in Gethsemane, including the Jerusalem Bible, which is often excluded from non-Catholic versions, including the Revised Standard Version. This text has been accepted as authentic by the standard Nestle–Aland edition of the *Novum Testamentum Graece*, though with brackets and a note to say that some ancient manuscripts omit it while most accept it. The text in the Jerusalem Bible reads: 'Then an angel appeared to him, coming from heaven to give him strength.' This ministry of angels, and the fact that Jesus stood in need of it, has obviously been found unacceptable to some, but it is elsewhere clearly stated or implied in the New Testament (as in the account of the temptations in the desert). In the Catholic tradition Jesus is without sin but not without human limits, and the whole tradition of reparation and *Imitatio Christi* emphasises the need to 'complete what is lacking in Christ's afflictions' (Col 1:24 RSV). Jesus is, of course, far higher than the angels in dignity and as reflecting the glory of God (Heb 1:3, 4). Yet he has taken on himself the sin of the world (Jn 1:29) and all this means of agony and vulnerability, all this means of *peirasmos*; and in his subjection to all this the 'angels of heaven' are always available with heavenly help (Mt 26:53, 54). The angels belong to that *ouranos* in which the Father dwells, and which is involved in the very first invocation of the Our Father, and which is set over against the *kosmos* in the 'priestly prayer' of Jesus in John 17.

All this is in head-on confrontation with the programme of 'demythologisation' of Rudolf Bultmann and his followers, and is, rather, appealing to that lost category of the 'physical incorruptible' already spoken of. However one understands the matter, there can be no doubt but that this acceptance of the very real presence of the angels is part of the Catholic tradition, especially in its understanding of prayer and the eucharistic liturgy. It gives its full charge of transcendence to the first invocation of the Our Father as reaching towards the higher regions (*ouranoi*, not *ouranos*: in the heaven*s*).

10. The great adversary

The *Catechism* sees that evil, the *ponēros*, against which the seventh petition of the Our Father prays for protection, as powerful and personal. Moreover, this petition places the Christian in that *ouranos* world where the great war of the angels, of Revelation 12, takes place. This war is not a detail or appendix to what is revealed in the Christian gospel. Rather, it is at the very centre of the story from first to last, for the whole world into which Jesus comes 'lies under the power of the evil one', *keitai*: not just 'lies under' but 'lies within' this power, lies prone and helpless (1 Jn 5:18, 19).

And so we ask for protection, and not only protection but deliverance from what already holds us in its power through our own connivance. This connivance has accepted and reinforced that original connivance which we name the fall of man. This deep mystery of iniquity relates back to an even deeper mystery of that 'fall of the angels' which is always exercising on us a kind of gravitational pull from which we pray to be delivered: the original Greek word (we do not have the original Aramaic, if it existed) is very strong, and it is not far from some such English word as 'snatch'. Each of us *belongs* to that cosmos that lies prone in the power of the Evil One.

As Luficer, the adversary shines with a false light, a glamour that counterfeits that glory that is full of grace and truth; as Satan this same adversary lies across our path (2851) in another form as bringing death and disease (Lk 16:13) and the bondage of decay that lies across the whole of the physical creation (Rom 8:19–24). The final petition of the Our Father is a 'cry without ceasing' to be released from this bondage. In the Catholic tradition Mary the Virgin-Mother is free of this bondage, both in her coming into this world (the Immaculate Conception) and in her release from it (the Assumption). So it is that the invocation of Mary has come to accompany the Our Father in Catholic piety and liturgy. In the Reformed tradition, a glory-prayer, or doxology, has come to be added as a final invocation after the seventh petition. This is not in the original text, but comes from very early sources (2760), and it gives a hint of the resurrection following on the passion and death of Jesus Christ, who yielded his spirit to the Father 'with loud cries and tears' (Heb 5:7).

The 'Amen' that ratifies the central Christian prayer (2856) must feel deeply the sorrows of 'the world of this death' while looking beyond them 'in joyful hope' (1041, 2632).

Notes

1   See B. M. Metzger, *A Textual Commentary on the Greek New Testament* (London: United Bible Societies, 1990).
2   On 'eschatology' see the article under that title by Karl Rahner in *Sacramentum Mundi* (London: Burns & Oates, 1968).
3   Emmanuel Levinas, *Totalité et Infini* (The Hague, 1971).
4   Ernst Lohmeyer, *The Lord's Prayer* (ET London: Collins, 1965).
5   N. O'Donoghue, 'The awakening of the dead', *Irish Theological Quarterly* 42 (1991), pp. 435–43.

CONTRIBUTORS

Lisa Sowle Cahill is Professor of Theology at Boston College, and Past President of the Catholic Theological Society of America. She is author of *Between the Sexes: Toward a Christian Ethics of Sexuality* (1985) and *Ethics of Sex and Gender: Challenges for Roman Catholicism* (forthcoming from Cambridge University Press).

Brian E. Daley SJ is Associate Professor of Historical Theology at the Weston School of Theology, Cambridge, Massachusetts. He studied theology in Frankfurt, and holds a doctorate from Oxford University. In addition to a number of articles on patristic and theological subjects and the sections on biblical soteriology and patristic eschatology in the *Handbuch der Dogmengeschichte*, he has published *The Hope of the Early Church: A Handbook of Patristic Eschatology* (1991). He has translated Hans Urs von Balthasar's *Kosmische Liturgie* (a study of Maximus Confessor), and has edited the works of Leontius of Byzantium for the Corpus Christianorum series, both of which should be published in the near future.

Gabriel Daly OSA has degrees from the Gregorian University, Oxford University, and the University of Hull. He is Lecturer in Systematic and Historical Theology at Trinity College, Dublin, and also lectures at the Irish School of Ecumenics. His writings include *Transcendence and Immanence: A Study in Catholic Modernism and Integralism* (1980) and *Creation and Redemption* (1988). He is a former chairman of the Irish Theological Association.

Brian Davies OP is Regent of Studies at the Dominican house in Oxford, where he teaches philosophy and philosophical theology. He is also tutor in theology at St Benet's Hall, Oxford, and a member of the Faculty of Theology of Oxford University. He is review editor of *New Blackfriars*, associate editor of the *International Philosophical Quarterly* and series editor of 'Outstanding Christian Thinkers', published by Geoffrey Chapman. He has recently published *The Thought of Thomas Aquinas*

(1992) and a revised edition of his *Introduction to the Philosophy of Religion* (1993).

Kevin Donovan SJ read classics at Oxford and went on to study liturgy at the Institut Catholique in Paris, where he was assistant choirmaster under Joseph Gelineau SJ. He now divides his time beween teaching at Heythrop College, University of London, and pastoral work in a busy London parish.

Regis A. Duffy OFM studied in the United States and at the Institut Catholique in Paris, before returning to teach in the States at Washington Theological Union. He is now a Professor at the University of Notre Dame. His publications include *A Roman Catholic Theology of Pastoral Care* (1983) and *On Becoming a Catholic: The Challenge of Christian Initiation* (1984).

Jacques Dupuis SJ was born in Belgium in 1923, and has a doctorate in theology from the Gregorian University, where he now holds a professorship. From 1948 to 1984 he lived in India, and taught theology there for twenty-five years. He is the author of several books and many articles, mainly on Christology, the theology of religions, and the theology of mission. He is the co-editor of *The Christian Faith*, which has run to five editions in the United Kingdom and in India, and is editor of the quarterly *Gregorianum*. He is a Consultor for the Pontifical Council for Inter-religious Dialogue.

James L. Empereur SJ was for many years Professor of Liturgical and Systematic Theology at the Jesuit School of Theology at Berkeley, and at the Graduate Theological Union in Berkeley, California. He is the founder of the Institute for Spirituality and Worship. He has written numerous articles, and among his books are *Prophetic Anointing* and *The Liturgy That Does Justice*. His present work is concentrating in three areas: liturgical inculturation, art and theology, and non-Western forms of spirituality.

Philip Endean SJ studied at Heythrop College, University of London, Oxford University and most recently at Innsbruck, where he made a special study of the works of Karl Rahner. He is now based at Campion Hall, Oxford, lectures at Heythrop in Systematic Theology, and has a special interest both in the writings of Rahner and in the Ignatian spiritual tradition.

Bernhard Häring CSsR has a doctorate in theology from the University of Tübingen, and was Professor of Moral Theology at the Academia Alfonsiana (Graduate School) at the Lateran University, Rome from 1957 to 1988. He has held guest professorships at a number of universities in Europe and the United States. He has published over eighty books, mainly on moral theology, in a number of languages, including his three-volume *The Law of Christ* (English translation 1963–66) and most recently *No Way Out? Pastoral Care for the Divorced* (1989) and *My Witness for the Church* (1992). Since his retirement he has lived at the Redemptorist house at Gars am Inn, Germany.

Monika K. Hellwig is Landegger Distinguished University Professor of Theology at Georgetown University in Washington. She has published widely in a number of theological fields. Among her recent works are *Jesus, the Compassion of God*, and a series of reflections on the readings of the liturgy. Other publications include *Understanding Catholicism* (1981) and *The Role of the Theologian* (1987).

Gerard J. Hughes SJ is chair of the Department of Philosophy at Heythrop College, University of London. He read Greats at Oxford and obtained his PhD in philosophy from the University of Michigan. He has published books and articles on a variety of topics in ethics and in the philosophy of religion, and is at present completing a book on the nature of God.

Catherine Mowry LaCugna is Professor of Theology at the University of Notre Dame (Indiana USA). She is the author of numerous articles on the Trinity in various theological, pastoral and liturgical journals, and recently of *God For Us: The Trinity and Christian Life* (1991). She is a past member of the Board of directors of the Catholic Theological Society of America, and is also a member of the College Theological Society, Societas Liturgica and the North American Academy of Ecumenists.

Dermot A. Lane is a priest of the Archdiocese of Dublin. He has been teaching theology full-time in the Mater Dei Institute of Education and the diocesan seminary of Holy Cross College for the last twenty years. He was recently appointed parish priest of Balally in Dublin. He is the author of *Christ at the Centre* (1990) and editor of *Religion and Culture in Dialogue: A Challenge for the Next Millennium* (1993).

John McDade SJ has a doctorate in theology from the University of Edinburgh and now lectures in Systematic Theology at Heythrop College, University of London. He has been editor of the Jesuit journal *The Month* since 1986. Previous publications include 'Catholic theology in the post-conciliar period' in *Modern Catholicism: Vatican II and After*, edited by Adrian Hastings (1991), and a number of articles on contemporary trinitarian theology, Christian–Jewish relations, creation and salvation, and aspects of contemporary culture.

Raymond Moloney SJ studied in Ireland and at the Gregorian University, Rome, where his doctorate was on 'The theology of worship in the writings of Oscar Cullmann'. He is currently teaching at Milltown Park, Dublin, and is preparing for publication a study of the presence of Christ in the Eucharist.

Robert Murray SJ gained a doctorate in theology (ecclesiology) from the Gregorian University, Rome, in 1964. He has taught theology at Heythrop College since 1963: first ecclesiology and revelation, later biblical studies (both Testaments) and languages, including Aramaic and Syriac. He has served on church commissions for theology, inter-church dialogue and Jewish–Christian relations, and has published books and articles on all the areas of study mentioned, including *Symbols of Church and Kingdom: A Study in Early Syriac Tradition* (1975) and *The Cosmic Covenant* (1992).

John O'Donnell SJ is an American Jesuit who has taught at Heythrop College, University of London, and at the Gregorian University, and is now at Weston School of Theology, Cambridge, Massachusetts. He has studied in the United States, England and Germany. His doctoral thesis was published as *Trinity and Temporality: The Christian Doctrine of God in the Light of Process Theology and the Theology of Hope* (1983). Most recently (1992) he produced a study of the theology of Hans Urs von Balthasar, and an introduction to the study of dogmatic theology has recently appeared in Italian.

Noel Dermot O'Donoghue ODC is a Carmelite priest who has taught philosophy at Maynooth College, Ireland, and philosophical theology in the Divinity Faculty of Edinburgh University. He retired in 1988. He has published, among other books and articles, *Heaven in Ordinarie* (1979) and *The Holy Mountain: Approaches to the Mystery of Prayer* (1983).

Gerard O'Hanlon SJ is Dean of Theology and Lecturer in Systematic Theology at the Milltown Institute of Theology and Philosophy, Dublin. He is author of *The Immutability of God in the Theology of Hans Urs von Balthasar* (1990), and co-authored *Solidarity: The Missing Link in Irish Society* (1991). He has contributed numerous articles to theological journals, is editorial advisor to the journal *Studies*, and a consulting editor for the journal *Communio*. He is a member of the Department of Theological Questions of the Irish Inter-Church Meeting, and a member of the Irish Theological Association. His area of research is the development of social theology within the context of Ireland.

Philip J. Rosato SJ studied theology at Woodstock College, then in New York, and at Tübingen. His doctoral dissertation, published in 1981, was on the pneumatology of Karl Barth. More recently he has published in Italian an 'Introduction to Sacramental Theology', which is shortly to be translated into English. He taught at St Joseph's College, Philadelphia, before being summoned to Rome in 1979 to teach at the Gregorian University.

Joseph A. Selling is Professor and Chairperson of the Department of Moral Theology in the Faculty of Theology of the Katholieke Universiteit Leuven, Belgium. He teaches fundamental, as well as sexual and conjugal, morality and has recently been involved in ecumenical dialogue through the 'Conciliar Process for Justice, Peace and the Integrity of Creation' (Basel, 1989). His publications include numerous studies on conjugal morality, as well as on topics ranging from just war to suffering. Among his more recent articles are 'Magisterial teaching on marriage, 1880–1968' in *Studia Moralia* (1990), and 'Reflections on the "conciliar process": from Basel to Seoul . . . and back' in *Bijdragen: Tijdschrift voor filosofie en theologie* (1990).

Jean-Marie Tillard OP was born in France, but entered the Dominicans in Canada. He is Professor of Dogma at the Dominican Faculty of Theology in Ottawa, but teaches in a number of universities, including for one term a year at Fribourg. He was a *peritus* at Vatican II, and a member of the International Theological Commission. He has long been involved in ecumenism, both as a member of the Anglican–Roman Catholic International Commission (ARCIC) and as Vice-President of the Faith and Order Commission of the World Council of Churches. He is the author of numerous studies mainly on ecclesiological topics, including most recently *Chair de l'Eglise, chair du Christ*.

Michael J. Walsh, a former member of the Society of Jesus, is now Librarian at Heythrop College, University of London. He has degreees from Heythrop itself, Oxford University and University College, London. He has written a number of books and articles, both bibliographical and historical, and has a special interest in modern church history and in hagiography. His most recent book is *A Dictionary of Devotions* (1993), and he is currently working on a study of Pope John Paul II.

Edward Yarnold SJ studied philosophy and theology at Heythrop College and classics at Oxford University, where he later received a Doctorate of Divinity. He has taught theology at Campion Hall, Oxford, since 1964, and since 1982 he has been a visiting professor at the University of Notre Dame. His books include *The Awe-inspiring Rites of Initiation* (1972) and *The Second Gift* (1974). He was joint editor of *The Study of Liturgy* (1978) and *The Study of Spirituality* (1986). He was a member of ARCIC from 1970 to 1991.

SCRIPTURE INDEX

Genesis

1 – 3	94–5
1	243
1:1	58
1:26	174
1:28	383
2:7	21
3	105, 324
5:24	209
7 – 8	243
9:8–16	87
12:2	209
22:2	244

Exodus

3	56
4:22	68
12	265
14	243
19:5–6	251
20	361
20:4	388
20:13	361
20:17	371, 388
24:8	148
25:17–22	148
33:19	154

Leviticus

25:10	170

Numbers

11:29	30 n. 24

Deuteronomy

5	361
5:8	388

5:21	361, 388
6:1–3	359
32:6	67
32:8	79

Joshua

3	243

1 Samuel

28:6–25	209

2 Samuel

2	23
4	23
7:14	68

2 Kings

2:1–18	209

2 Maccabees

7:9–29	209

Job

38:4–5	87

Psalms

2:7	116
6:5	209
8:6	87
21	263
22:1	122
22:9–10	79
45:7	253
51:7	243–4

68:5–6	68
69:1–2	175
73:24	209
88:12	209
94:17	209
110:1	117
115:17	209
118:22	147
123:2	79
131:1–2	79
131:2	68
139:8	153
139:15	354

Proverbs

4:6–8	79
9:1–6	79
10:7	209
25:9–10	394 n. 28

Ecclesiastes

9:10	209

Wisdom

2:12ff.	147
5:1ff.	148
7:25 – 8:2	79

Ecclesiasticus

15:2	79
24:5–7	158
27:16	394 n. 28

Isaiah

11:2–3	254
11:2	168, 252

26:19	209	13:40	219	2:11	117
38:18	209	13:42	219	2:19	411
42:1–4	244	15:24	165 n. 2	2:21–22	163
42:1	117	16	135	2:51	411
42:6	358	16:16	114, 116	2:52	136
46:3–4	79	16:17	114	4:1	244
49:14–15	79	17:5	117	4:13	419
52:13ff.	145	18	135	4:14	244
53:11	148	19:9	324	4:16–19	244
61	169	19:16–19	337	4:16	262
61:1–3	244, 252	19:24–28	139	4:18–21	252
61:1	247	20:28	146	5:15–16	411
65:16	222	21:34	116	5:17	241 n. 12
66:12–13	79	22:41–46	117	6:19	241 n. 12
66:13	68	24:36	116	6:36	359
		25	138	8:6	407
Jeremiah		25:40	210	8:13	407
		25:41	219	8:46	241 n. 12
1:5	354	25:45	210	8:48	296
31:33	164	26:28	242	9:2	114
32:20	79	26:41	419	9:31	265
		26:53–54	419	10:34	253
Ezekiel		26:64	125 n. 5	11:13	411
		27:25	163	12:50	176, 244
10:1ff.	158	27:54	125 n. 5	15:11–32	277
14:14	30 n. 16	28:19	66, 247	16:13	420
36:25–27	252	28:20	268	17:19	296
				18:1	401
Daniel		**Mark**		22	135
				22:40	419
12:2	209	1:11	117, 244	22:42	411
		1:35	411	22:43–44	419
Joel		1:4	244	22:70	125 n. 5
		3:27	152	23:43	216
2:28–29	252	5:34	296	23:46	170
		7:6–8	354 n. 10	23:47	125 n. 5
Habakkuk		8:29	114	24:13	158
		8:31	121, 144	24:32	158
2:3	158	8:38	210	24:44ff.	144
		9:31	121	24:45	158
Malachi		9:43–48	219		
		10:11–12	325	**John**	
2:10	67	10:14	246, 248		
		10:33–34	121	1:1–18	117–18
Matthew		10:38	244	1:9	243
		10:45	145, 148	1:11	117
1:20	123, 124	10:52	296	1:14	119, 159 n. 1, 169
1:23	124	12:10	147	1:29	159 n. 1, 419
3:10–12	219	12:24–27	210	3:5–8	243
3:15	244	13:32	121	3:5–6	247, 249, 251
3:17	117	14:22ff.	146	3:5	118
5:17–46	359	14:24	148	3:9	176
5:17	164	14:36	117	3:14	159 n. 1
5:21–22	372	14:38	419	3:16	117, 118, 244
5:31–32	366	14:61	125 n. 5	3:18	117, 244
5:32	324	15:34	122	3:19–21	216
5:37	366, 386	15:39	125 n. 5	4:10	118
6:13	419	16:16	248	4:14	118
9:22	296			4:24	62
10:16	138	**Luke**		5:22–24	216
11	169			5:25–26	157
11:4–5	210	1:10	411	5:25	152
11:27	68, 116	1:28	123	6	20
12:28	210	1:35	124, 169	6:27	254
13:31	158	1:43	117	6:31ff.	159 n. 1

6:51–58	270, 272	6:11	176, 243, 251	13:14	69
6:51	417	7	106		
6:54	417	8:3	148	**Galatians**	
7:37–39	170	8:11	157, 205, 250		
7:38–39	159 n. 1	8:15–17	250	1:4	145
8:12	243	8:18ff.	157	2:10	197
10:10	272	8:19–24	420	2:20	145
11:24	210	8:22–24	176	3:28	132, 133
12:24	158	8:23–36	400	4:4	163
12:31–32	16	8:23	157		
13 – 17	272	8:24–25	205–6	**Ephesians**	
13:1–20	139	8:32	149		
14:9	359, 365	9:4	163	1:3–14	70
14:13	401	9:5	117	1:3–6	228–9
14:16	234	12 – 15	337	1:8–10	118
15	337	12:1	251	1:15–23	118
15:11ff.	158	12:6	24	2:10	118
16:8	172	15:8	163	2:13ff.	150
16:13	243			2:14ff.	148
17	366, 395, 415, 419	**1 Corinthians**		2:15	158
				2:21	158
17:3	365	1:18ff.	144	4 – 6	337
17:6	366	1:24	132	5:21 – 6:9	354 n. 2
17:24	62	2:9	206	5:25	320
18:38ff.	163	3:15	218	5:26	245, 250
19:14ff.	163	5:7	148	19:1	155
19:28	171	6:11	250		
19:30	170	6:19	250	**Philippians**	
19:34	159 n. 1, 245	7:3–5	320		
20:19	158	7:7	320	1:21–23	214
20:22–23	274	7:8	320	1:23	216
20:22	21	7:10–12	324	2:6–11	119
20:23	158, 283	7:13–14	320	2:6	118
20:26ff.	158	7:15	324	2:9–11	118
20:28	117	10:3–4	25	2:9–10	116
21	135	10:16–17	242	2:11	116
21:7	117	10:17	247	5:6–7	169
		11:22–29	270		
		11:25	145		
Acts of the Apostles		12 – 13	337	**Colossians**	
		12:13	251		
2:22	117	13	414	1:15–20	118
2:23	145	14	30 n. 24	1:15	174
2:34–35	117	15	212	1:24	419
2:36	116	15:3	145	1:27	205
2:38	250, 252	15:20ff.	213	2:9	123
7:51ff.	163	15:21–23	210	2:11–12	242
8:27	118	15:22ff.	156	3 – 4	337
9:1ff.	158	15:28	168	3:1–3	212
10:37–38	244, 247	15:44	417	3:18 – 4:1	354 n. 2
10:38	253	15:45	210		
10:47–48	245	15:51	209		
13:32–33	116	15:57	210	**1 Thessalonians**	
23:6	210				
				4:13–18	157
		2 Corinthians			
Romans		1:18–21	222	**1 Timothy**	
		1:20	155		
1:3–4	117	1:21	253	2:4	249
3:5	148	1:22	254	2:6	145
4:16–18	205	2:15	253	3:16	119
4:25	145	3:18	157		
5	105–6	5:17	173, 250	**2 Timothy**	
5:5	205	5:18	281, 283		
5:6	145	5:21	148	1:12	391
6:2–3	250				
6:4	176, 243, 251				

Titus

2:13	117
2:14	145
3:5	243

Hebrews

1:3–4	419
1:13	117
2:10	32 n. 46
2:15	149
2:18	151
4:15	123, 164
5:5–6	159 n. 1
5:7	420
6:2	243, 251
7:14	159 n. 1
9:12ff.	148
9:14	171
10:5–7	119
11	27
11:40	38
12:1–2	40
12:2	32 n. 46

James

1:13	419
4: 2–3	401
5:13–16	296
5:14–15	291

1 Peter

1:19	148
1:23	245
2:5	251
2:9	251
2:21ff.	145
3:18	145

2 Peter

1:4	119, 250

1 John

1:3–4	358
1:5	62
2:16	389

2:20–27	253
2:26–27	20
2:27	251
3:1–2	208
3:2	207
3:9	176
3:22	400
4:2	119
4:8	62
4:9–10	62
4:9	118
5:18	420
5:19	420
5:20	117

Revelation

3:14	222
12	420
19:9	247
22:2	158

INDEX TO THE DOCUMENTS OF VATICAN II

(Some more general references will be found in the Subject Index.)

Ad Gentes
(Decree on the Church's Missionary Activity)

3	30 n. 15
11	30 n. 15
48	247

Dei Verbum
(Dogmatic Constitution on Divine Revelation)

1–2	45
1	11
2	10
3	10, 12, 45
4	10, 12
5	10, 12, 30 n. 19
6	10, 12
7–10	14
7–8	13
7, 1	10
7, 2	11
8, 1	11, 14, 15, 19
8, 2	11, 14, 15, 19, 30 n. 19
8, 3	11, 14, 17
9–10	16, 20
9	11, 15, 17, 20
10, 1	11, 14ff., 17, 19, 24
11	21
12	22–3, 24–5, 32 n. 54
13	20, 32 n. 43
14–15	26
16	25, 27
17–20	26
18	115
19	27
21–26	28
21	20–1
24	20, 28

Gaudium et Spes
(Pastoral Constitution on the Church in the Modern World)

1	45
3–4	46
3	45
4–5	45
5	45
10	106
11	9, 45
13	102, 105–6
16	348, 368
18	39, 213
19	39, 362
20	361
22	29 n. 6, 39, 113, 120, 174, 177, 249, 332
24	355 n. 17
26	29 n. 6
32	113
33	45
34	83
36	85
37	109
38	131, 177
45	113
48	322
49	322, 379
50	322
57–58	29 n. 6
62	45
69	393 n. 25
74	391 n. 6

Lumen Gentium
(Dogmatic Constitution on the Church)

7	175
8	9, 79, 193
11	255, 260, 266, 278, 288, 306

12	12, 14–15, 31 n. 38
13	39
15–16	29 n. 7
16	30 n. 15, 310
21	312
22	193, 195
23	45, 195–6
25	15, 18
27	198
28	313–14
29	313
34	332
40	332
50	231
52	124
56	124
57	124

Nostra Aetate
(Declaration on Non-Christian Religions)

2	30 n. 15, 310

Optatam Totius
(Decree on Priestly Formation)

16	357

Presbyterorum Ordinis
(Decree on the Ministry and Life of Priests)

4–6	309
5	269, 252
6	306
18	269

Sacrosanctum Concilium
(Constitution on the Sacred Liturgy)

7	231, 267
8	231
47	259
71	242

Unitatis Redintegratio
(Decree on Ecumenism)

2	188
3	251
11	18, 45, 112
21–23	20

SUBJECT INDEX

(Only general references to the documents of Vatican II are listed below.
For detailed references see separate index.)

Aaron, priesthood of 309
Abba 117, 132, 136–7, 366, 414
Abelard *see* Peter Abelard
abortion 373–4
Abraham 10, 37, 38–9, 40, 164, 397, 404
absolution 279, 281–2, 285
abuse, sexual *see* sexual abuse
acedia 407
Ad Gentes 190
Adam and Eve 97ff., 152
Adam Bede 396
Addai and Mari 229
adultery 325, 351, 380, 390–1
Advocate *see* Holy Spirit
Alberigo, Giuseppe, quoted 109
Albert the Great, St 183
Alexander III, Pope 320
allegory *see* Scripture, senses of
Alleluia 223
almsgiving 281
Alphonsus de Liguori, St 202, 338, 348
Ambrose, St 218, 220
Amen 222–3
anamnesis 232
angels 30 n. 16, 91, 106, 419–20
anger 372
Anglican Communion 18
animals 93, 371–2, 384
Anna 411
annulment of marriage *see* marriage,
  annulment of
anointing of the sick 288–302
anonymous Christians 250
Anselm of Canterbury, St 51–2, 108, 144
  on the nature of God 54
Apollinaris of Laodicaea 119
apologetics 38, 46
Apostles' Creed 37, 42–3
Apostolic Tradition 229
Aquinas *see* Thomas Aquinas
Aristotle 75, 93

Arius 69, 73, 77, 119–20
Assumption 155–6, 420
  see also Mary
Athanasius, St 73, 119, 167, 213
atheism 361–2
Athenagoras 210
atonement 18, 31 n. 40, 143ff., 206
auctor 21, 32 n. 46
Augustine of Hippo, St 9, 20–1, 53, 74,
  99–100, 179, 183, 218, 227, 251, 358,
  363, 413
  on faith 39
  on freedom 343
  on heaven 223, 224 n. 22
  on lying 385
  on ministry 195, 228
  on private property 383
  on the eucharist 267
  on the Holy Spirit 172–3, 175
  on the nature of God 54
  on the problem of evil 88ff.
  on the resurrection of the body 209
Auschwitz 90
authority 135–6, 139–40, 368ff.
  in morals 353

Balthasar, Hans Urs von 129–30, 133–4,
  153–4, 173, 415
  on the atonement 149–50
  on the incarnation 168–9
Baltimore Catechism 72
baptism 66–7, 175–6, 243–52, 276, 297
Barfield, Owen 147
Barlaam 75
Barr, James 56
Barth, Karl 64–5 n. 29, 80 n. 15, 89, 130,
  415
Barton, John 165
Basil, St 73, 91, 167
beatific vision 217–18
beatitudes 336ff., 353, 358, 360

Benedict XII, Pope   216ff.
Benedict XV, Pope   31 n. 31
Benedictus   411
berakah   228–9
Biblical Commission   34
bishops   140, 196ff.
blasphemy   362
Blondel, Maurice   83
Boethius   51
Bonaventure, St   183
brothers   293
Brown, Raymond E.   62, 172, 262, 335 n. 1
Buckley, Francis J.   300–1
Buddhism   405
Bultmann, R.   419
Byzantine liturgy   285

Caesarius of Arles   218
Calvin, Jean   63 n. 3
Cana, wedding feast at   324
canon law   3, 200, 275, 278, 319, 321–4,
   331
canon of Scripture *see* Scripture, canon of
capital punishment   371ff., 392 n. 9, 392 n.
   13
Cappadocians   77, 167
   see also Basil; Gregory of Nazianzus;
   Gregory of Nyssa
Carthage, Council of   99
Casti Connubii   322, 378
Catechesi Tradendae   3, 399, 405
Catechism *see* Baltimore Catechism; Dutch
   Catechism
   of the Council of Trent *see* Roman
   Catechism
catechisms   46–7
catechists   398–9
Celan, Paul   146
celibacy   315–16, 320, 364
Centesimus Annus   382
Chalcedon, Council of   120, 121, 130, 155
chastity   377ff.
children   326, 369
Childs, Brevard   229–30
chrism   247, 253–4
   see also oil
chrism Mass   296
Christ, as title   116
Christ
   baptism   135
   crucifixion   411
   death   143–54, 170–1
      and the Jews   162–5
   descent among the dead   152–4
   heart of *see* Sacred Heart
   incarnation   112–26, 150–1
      see also Christology
   infancy narrative   133–4
   life   127–42
   passion   297
   presence in the eucharist   267ff.
   public life   135–40
   resurrection   154–9, 208–13
   titles   115–18
Christifideles Laici   131
Christmas narrative   133

Christology   39, 69, 71, 114–22, 129ff., 155
   see also Christ, incarnation
Church   175ff., 178–204
Cicero   240
circumcision   242
circumincessio   70
citizenship   369
civil authority   369–70
Clement of Alexandria   218
Clinton, President   50
Cloud of Unknowing   416
Coleridge, Samuel Taylor   155
collegiality   192, 194ff., 199
commandments   336ff., 341, 351, 358, 363
   1–3   358–66
   4   368–71
   5   371–75
   6   376–81
   7   381–4
   8   385–8
   9 and 10   388–91
common good   345, 352, 383
communion, holy   270–3
   under both kinds   271
communion of saints   180–1, 217, 266
communion *see also* Church; Rome, Church
   of
concupiscence   389–90
confession   272, 274–87
confirmation   252–6
Congregation for the Doctrine of the
   Faith   206–7, 211, 216, 248, 374
conscience   348ff., 353, 368
conscience, examination of   282–3
consoler   172
   see also Holy Spirit
Constantinople I, Council of   68, 69, 125
   n. 8, 166–7
Constantinople II, Council of   120, 125 n.
   11, 126 n. 15
Constantinople III, Council of   121–2
Constantinople V, Council of   220
Constantinople, Synod of (543)   220
contraception   318, 377ff.
contract, marital   320
contrition   282
Cooke, Bernard   323
Copleston, Frederick   58
corruption   352
Council for Culture   49 n. 18
   see also culture
Council of Trent *see* Trent, Council of
counsels, evangelical   354 n. 10
covenant   164
covenant, marital   321–2
creation   82–96
creation spirituality   84, 97
credo *see* creeds
Creed, Apostles' *see* Apostles' Creed
Creed, Niceno-Constantinopolitan *see*
   Nicene Creed
creeds   42–3
culture   46, 225–6, 230, 232, 238ff., 341
Cunningham, Lawrence S.   301
Cyprian, St   257 n. 13
Cyril and Methodius, Sts   196

Cyril of Alexandria   125 n. 11, 150
Cyril of Jerusalem, St   222

Daly, Gabriel   4, 149
Damasus, Pope   125 n. 8
damnation *see* hell
Daniel   30 n. 16
Dante   154
Darwin, Charles   84
Davies, Brian   4
Davies, W. D.   163–4
De Mello, Anthony   48, 49 n. 22
deaconesses   308, 315
deacons   293
dead, prayers for   218, 267
death   151, 205, 213–15, 292, 294
Decalogue *see* commandments
Dei Filius   9, 64 n. 20, 184, 340
Dei Verbum   6–31 *passim*
Deism   87
Democratic Party   50
demythologisation   419–20
deposit of faith   1, 234, 363–4
Descartes, René   94
devil *see* Satan
diaconate   314
  see also deaconesses; deacons
Didache   229
discrimination   352
Divinae Consortium   242, 252, 254–5
Divino Afflante Spiritu   8, 20, 22–4, 338
divorce   324, 325–6, 328, 366, 380
Docetism   119
Dodd, C. H.   62
Dominic, St   179
Dominum et Vivificantem   29 n. 6, 171–2
Doms, Herbert   321
Donum Vitae   374, 379
double effect   373, 375, 391 n. 3
drugs   374
drunkenness   374
du Bay, Michel   100
Dutch Catechism   2, 46–7, 72, 103–4, 107

Easter Vigil   83, 243, 245–6, 249
Eastern Church(es)   68–9, 73, 166, 233, 271
  see also Orthodox Church
ecofeminism   86
ecology   36, 82, 85ff., 355 n. 17, 382, 384
economy   381ff.
  of redemption   67
ecumenism   4, 18–19, 364
  see also Unitatis Redintegratio
Eden, Garden of *see* Adam and Eve; fall
education *see* moral education
Egypt, monks of   274
Eliot, George   396–7
Eliot, T. S.   417
Elizabeth of the Trinity   70
employers/employees   369
ends of marriage *see* marriage; sexual intercourse
Ephesus, Council of   120
Ephrem the Syrian, St   32 n. 43
epiclesis   233, 246, 254

Erikson, Eric   137
eschatology   205–24, 232, 273, 412–13
Essenes   244
eternal life   212–13, 215–22
  see also heaven; hell; purgatory
ethics   78, 336–55
  method in   338ff.
Eucharist   78, 92, 182, 217–18, 259–73, 280, 293, 417
Eucharistic devotion   269
Eunomius   73
Eusebius   354 n. 10
euthanasia   373–4
Evangelii Nuntiandi   30 n. 15, 233–4, 239
Eve *see* Adam and Eve
everlasting life *see* eternal life
evil   89–90
ex opere operato   236
excommunication   282
Exodus narrative   230, 397
exorcism   246, 333
extreme unction   292

faith   36–49
  and reason   40
fall   104–5, 106
Familiaris Consortio   322–3, 379
families   369–70
Family, Synod on the (1980)   369
fascism   50
fasting   281
fatherhood of God *see* God, fatherhood of
Faustus of Riez   255
feminism *see* women
Fidei Depositum   95
filioque   68–9, 73
financial offences   383–4
Fitzmyer, Joseph   147
Florence, Council of   68ff., 218, 250
forgiveness   417–18
forgiveness of sin *see* sin, forgiveness of
fornication   390–1
Forster, E. M.   151
fortitude   350
Fowler, J.   44
Francis of Assisi, St   86
fraud   352
freedom   154, 343ff., 355 n. 18
free-will *see* freedom
fundamentalism   84
funerals   217

Gagliardi, Achille   408
Galileo   84, 140
gambling   383
Gaudet Mater Ecclesiae   1
Gaudium et Spes   6, 9, 45, 98, 100–1, 109–10, 275
Geach, Peter   59
gender *see* sexism; women
Genesis, exegesis of   84, 87, 94
Gethsemane   411, 419
Gnosticism   119
God
  fatherhood of   68, 413–14
  motherhood of   68, 79 n. 5, 413–14

name of 56, 366
nature of 50–65
Goethe, quoted 92
good, common *see* common good
Good Friday 274
grace, prevenient 39
grace and law 337ff.
grace and nature 337ff.
Gratian 320
Grayston, Kenneth 62
Greatrex, Joan 4
greed 390
Greeley, Andrew 228
Gregory I, St 178, 218, 402
Gregory of Nazianzus, St 73, 144, 167–8, 316
Gregory of Nyssa, St 73, 118, 213, 218, 220
Gregory Palamas 75
Greinacher, Norbert 329
Gutiérrez, Gustavo 138

Haight, Roger 335 n. 3
Hallett, Garth 354 n. 4
harassment, sexual *see* sexual harassment
Häring, B. 364–5
Hartshorne, Charles 52
healing 296ff.
heaven 216–17
Hebblethwaite, Peter 5 n. 2
hell 153, 218–20
Hengel, Martin 159–60 n. 5
hesychasm 75
hierarchy 193ff.
hierarchy of truths 45, 17, 67, 91, 104, 112
Hildebrand, Dietrich von 321
Hinduism 405
Hippolytus 229, 245, 248
Hitler, Adolf 50, 363
Holy Office 321
Holy Spirit 166–77, 205, 232–4, 297 and *passim*
Holy Trinity 66–79, 230 and *passim*
homilies 228
homosexuality 318, 378–9, 393 nn. 17–18
Honoré, Archbishop Jean 398–9, 402
Hopkins, Gerard Manley 148–9, 419
Hughes, Gerard J. 156
Huizing, Peter 323
human reason 10
  and faith 128
  in ethics 340–1
human rights *see* rights, human; women
Humanae Vitae 322, 378–9
Humani Generis 9, 15, 29 nn. 3 and 14, 101, 340

idolatry 50
Ignatius of Antioch, St 154, 198, 214
Ignatius of Loyola, St 134, 140, 406, 408
images, cult of 122, 365
Immaculate Conception 29 n. 13, 123–4, 420
  see also Mary
immigrants *see* migrants
incarnation 118–19, 168–9
  see also Christ

incest 380
India 239
indulgences 278, 284–5, 300
Indulgentiarum Doctrina 284
infallibility, papal 197–8
injustice *see* justice
Innocent I, Pope 257 n. 19
insurrection 370–1
integralism 104
Inter Mirifica 387–8
International Theological Commission 2–3, 159 n. 5
Interpretation of the Bible in the Church 35
intrinsic evil 368
Irenaeus, St 29 nn. 10 and 12, 42, 118, 128, 166–7, 196, 210, 213, 363
Isaac 397

James, William 404
Jansenism 100
Janssens, Cornelius 100
Jantzen, Grace 52
Jeremias, J. 248
Jesus, as title 115–16
Jesus Christ *see* Christ
Jewish liturgy 228–9, 233, 260–1, 265
Jews 143
  and the death of Christ 162–5
Joan of Arc, St 179, 204 n. 3
John XXIII, Pope 1–2, 8, 45, 101, 107, 109, 361
John Chrysostom, St 20, 253, 324
John of the Cross, St 12, 216, 416, 419
John Paul II, Pope 1–2, 6, 35 n. 7, 83, 95, 130–1, 139, 178, 190, 196, 201, 239, 367, 398, 406
  on marriage 322
  on the Holy Spirit 171–2
  on the Jews 162–3
  quoted 46
John the Baptist 174, 244ff.
Johnson, Elisabeth 130
Josephus 244
jubilee, year of 170
Judaism 4, 12, 22
  see also Jews
judgement, particular 216
Jüngel, Eberhard 150, 160 n. 18
just war 370–1, 374–5
justice 352, 381ff., 384
justification 236
Justin Martyr 263, 358

Karamazov, Ivan 90
Kasper, Walter 173
Kavanagh, Patrick 134
Kelly, Kevin 142 n. 29
kidnapping 374
killing 351, 372ff.
  see also murder; suicide
Kilmartin, Edward 226, 237, 241 n. 21
kingdom of God 137ff.
Klein, Charlotte 163
Konstant, David 3, 398, 400
Küng, Hans 223 n. 5, 354 n. 5

Laborem Exercens 369
Lactantius 218
LaCugna, Catherine 226–7
laity 199ff.
Langland, William 145
language, inclusive/non-inclusive 68, 127–8, 133, 141, 319, 404
Laplace, Pierre de 88
Last Supper 171, 261ff., 411
last things *see* eschatology
Lateran Council (649) 126 nn. 14–15
Lateran IV, Council of 51, 55, 61, 91, 93, 105, 275
law and grace *see* grace and law
Lazarus 156
Leibniz 89
Leo I, Pope 126 n. 15, 234, 307
Leo XIII, Pope *see Rerum Novarum*
Levinas, Emmanuel 414
Levites 309
liberation theology 345, 361, 384
liberty, religious 362
Lies, Lothar 226
life everlasting *see* eternal life
Lima document on the Eucharist 92
limbo 207, 249
liturgy 42, 225–41, 412
Lohmeyer, Ernst 417
Lord, as title of Christ 117–18
Lord's Prayer 274, 276, 279, 358, 360, 410–26
Lubac, Henri de 29 n. 5, 272, 339
Lucas, J. R. 52–3
Lucifer 420
Lumen Gentium 7, 11, 178–9, 192–3, 195, 197–8, 200, 219, 275, 331–2, 334
Luther, Martin 216
quoted 99
lying 347, 351, 385ff.
Lynch, Maura 134

Mackin, Theodore 320
magisterium 11, 15–20, 29 n. 14, 30 n. 27, 34–5, 197, 360, 376, 394 nn. 30 and 46
on marriage 328
Magnificat 411
Manicheanism 99, 109–10
Marcel, Gabriel 174
Marcion 26, 32 n. 46
Marialis Cultus 39, 124
Marian devotion 413, 420
marital fidelity 325
marital love 319, 325, 379–80
marriage 318–29
marriage, annulment of 323
marriage, second *see* remarriage
Marxism 361
Mary, Blessed Virgin 12, 30 n. 17, 37, 39, 40, 123–4, 202–3, 403
see also Immaculate Conception
symbol of the Church 124
virginity 124, 126 n. 16
masturbation 378–9
Maundy Thursday 254
Maximus the Confessor 150, 185–6, 188, 218

media 386ff.
Mediator Dei 266
Meouchi, Paul, Maronite Patriarch 31 n. 34
Metz, J. B. 90
Meyer, Ben F. 160 n. 6
migrants 371
Milton, John 419
ministry 193ff., 237
see also priesthood
mission of the Church *see Redemptoris Missio*
Modernism 7
Moltmann, Jürgen 150, 160 n. 18, 169–70
monasticism, Celtic 274
monks of Egypt 274
Monophysitism 120, 130
moral education 349ff.
moral theology 336–94
Mosaic law 337
Moses 10–11, 56, 164, 265
motherhood of God *see* God, motherhood of
Mount of Olives 414
Mühlen, Heribert 175
Mulieris Dignitatem 131
murder 371ff.
Murray, John Courtney 130
Murray, Robert 3
myron 253
Mysterium Ecclesiae 178
Mysterium Fidei 267
mystery 128–9
mystical theology 415–16

Napoleon 88
national security 346
natural law 340–1
nature and grace *see* grace and nature
neo-scholasticism 41–2, 83, 100, 129–30
Nestorianism 120
Nestorius 125 n. 11
Newman, John Henry 21, 23, 32 n. 51
newspapers 387
Newton, Isaac 88
Nicaea, Council of 68, 73, 119–20, 167–8
Nicaea II, Council of 122
Nicene (Niceno-Constantinopolitan) Creed 37, 42–3, 167
Nicetas 204 n. 6
Nicodemus 243, 247, 250
Noah, covenant with 116
Nostra Aetate 26, 138, 143, 162–3
nouvelle théologie 101
nuns 293

oaths 347, 366
obedience 134–5, 363
obedience of faith 37–8, 360
O'Collins, Gerald 5 n. 1, 13
Octagesimo Adveniens 382
O'Fiaich, Cardinal Tomas 131
oil 246
see also chrism
option for the poor 385
Orange II, Council of 99
Orders, sacrament of 303–17

ordination of women   413
organ transplants   373
Origen   153, 218, 220
original sin *see* sin, original
Orthodox Church   18, 246–7, 31 n. 38,
  152–3, 218, 256, 365
  see also Eastern Church(es)
Otto, Rudolf   405
Our Father *see* Lord's Prayer
ownership, private   383–4

Paraclete *see* Holy Spirit
parenthood   326, 369
Pascal, Blaise   98, 100
paschal mystery   234–5
  see also liturgy
passion of Christ   297
'passion psalms'   159 n. 4
passover   261–2, 265
Pastoralis Actio   248–9
Paul, St   6, 185, 196, 399
  on marriage   325
Paul VI, Pope   30 n. 15, 39, 103, 124, 131,
  178, 185, 196, 202, 233–4, 239, 267, 278,
  284, 322, 370, 374, 382
  *see also Divinae Consortium; Humanae
  Vitae; Mysterium Fidei*
Paulinus of Nola, St   218
Péguy, Charles   140
Pelagianism   100, 108, 338
Pelagius I, Pope   126 n. 15
penance, sacrament of   274–87
  see also sin, forgiveness of
People of God   181ff.
perichoresis   70
Persona Humana   376, 379, 393 n. 17
Peter, St   116, 125, 136, 187–8, 192–3, 196
Peter Abelard   91–2
Peter Lombard   71
petitionary prayer   400
Pieris, Aloysius   138
Pius IV, Pope   126 n. 15
Pius IX, Pope   28 n. 2, 101, 123, 321
Pius X, Pope   101, 285
Pius XII, Pope   8, 22, 101, 122, 201, 266,
  340
  see also *Divino Afflante Spiritu*
Plantinga, Alvin   53–4, 55
Platonism   93
plenary indulgence *see* indulgences
pneumatology *see* Holy Spirit
Polanyi, Michael, quoted   93
politics   345
  see also social teaching
polygamy   324, 280
pontiff, Roman *see* Rome, bishop of
Pope *see* Rome, bishop of
Populorum Progressio   370, 374
pornography   378
poverty   371
Power, David   324
prayer   281, 395–409
  types of   398
  see also Lord's Prayer
priesthood   234–5, 237
  see also Orders

priesthood of the baptised   182
priests, shortage of   364–5
primacy, papal *see* Rome, bishop of
process theology   52
procreation *see* sexual intercourse
prodigal son   281
prostitution   378–9
Protestantism   218, 264–5, 281–2
prudence   350, 356 n. 27
psychology   344–5
Puebla   331
pupils   369
purgatory   153, 206, 216, 218, 250

Qumran   244

racism   352
Rahner, Karl   29 n. 5, 44, 76, 130, 134, 226,
  250, 332, 335 n. 3
  on angels   91
  on eschatology   206
  on grace and nature   339
  on mystery   129
  on the atonement   149
  on the Holy Spirit   173
  on the sacraments   236
  quoted   103, 107, 404
rape   378, 381
Ratzinger, Cardinal Joseph   3, 5 nn. 5 and
  9, 30 n. 25, 31 n. 32, 35 n. 7, 46–7
  quoted   102, 105, 106, 142 n. 29
RCIA   79 n. 1, 245–6, 252, 256
reason, human *see* human reason
reconciliation, sacrament of   274–87
redemption   67, 108
Redemptor Hominis   130
Redemptoris Missio   190ff.
refugees   352, 371
religious life   201–2
remarriage   325–6
Rerum Novarum   382–3
resurrection of Christ *see* Christ,
  resurrection
resurrection of the body   208–13
revelation   6–33, 116, 355 n. 16
  and ethics   341ff., 353
  personal   13
Ricoeur, Paul   89, 147
  quoted   95
rights, human   345–6, 352, 370, 382
Rilke, Rainer Maria   158
Roman Catechism   2, 72, 82, 109, 143, 180,
  183, 279, 363, 368, 398
Rome, bishop of   192, 195–6, 198, 266, 364
Rome, Church of   184ff.
Rosato, Philip   4
Rus   196
Russell, Bertrand   50, 58

sabbath   91–2, 170, 230
  see also Sunday observance
sacraments   78, 182, 225–41
  effects of   257 n. 18
Sacred Heart   122
sacrifice, eucharistic   263ff.
Sacrosanctum Concilium   278, 331–2

saints 208, 266
  see also communion of saints
salvation 206ff., 226–7
  see also atonement
Samaritan woman 132, 277
Sarah 37
Satan 105–6, 108, 109, 420
Scheeben, Matthias 149
Schillebeeckx, Edward 264
Schleiermacher, F. 63 n. 3
Schnackenburg, R. 114, 125 n. 2
Schoonenberg, Piet 107
Schutz, Roger 13, 15
Schweitzer, A. 140
science 84–5, 87, 93
Scotists 118
Scripture
  canon of 25–6, 234
  related to Tradition 14–20
  senses of 24–5
secrets 394 n. 28
Segundo, Juan 130, 140
self-defence 373–4, 392 n. 13
sensus fidelium 18, 251
Sermon on the Mount 337, 342, 354 n. 9,
  358
sexism 131ff.
sexual abuse 380
sexual harassment 378
sexual intercourse 320–1
sexuality 78, 318
Shannon, Mgr William 4, 5 n. 11
sick, anointing of *see* anointing of the sick
signs of the times 46
Silas Marner 396
Simeon 411
sin 213–14, 350–1
  forgiveness of 272
    see also confession
  mortal 351
  original 2, 97–110, 276, 279, 364
sisters 293
Skelley, Michael 335 n. 3
slavery 384, 394 n. 32
Snow, C. P. 85
social justice 301
social teaching 138–9, 351–2, 318ff.
sociology 344–5
Son of God 116–17
soteriology 71, 76
Spirit, Holy *see* Holy Spirit
spirituality 78
  creation *see* creation spirituality
Stalin 363
Staniloe, Dumitru 150
sterilisation 373, 381
stewardship of creation 86
stipends 267
Strauss, D. F. 397
subsidiarity 352, 369
suffering 89, 143
Suffering Servant 145–6, 148
suicide 373–4
Sunday observance 347–8, 361, 364
sunderēsis 368, 391 n. 4
Swinburne, Richard 52–3

symbols 237–9
Synod of Bishops (1985) 3
synods 196, 199

Taizé 13
tax 370, 383
teachers 369
Teilhard de Chardin, Pierre 221–2
  quoted 98, 102
temperance 350, 377
Teresa of Avila, St 415–16
terrorism 374
Tertullian 97, 209, 210–11, 248
theology, nature of 67
Thérèse of Lisieux, St 414, 419
Thomas Aquinas, St 6, 40–1, 51, 59–60,
  71, 74–5, 93, 119, 159 n. 2, 179, 183, 252,
  255, 373
  on ethics 341ff.
  on prayer 400ff.
  on private property 383
  on the atonement 144–5, 149
  on the Eucharist 259–60
  on the nature of God 54
  on the resurrection of the body 212
Thomists 118
  see also neo-scholasticism
Thurian, Max 13, 15
Tillard, Jean-Marie 3, 4, 5 n. 6
Tincq, Henri 5 n. 5
Toledo XVI, Council of 68–9, 126 n. 15
Tomos Agapēs 178
Torah 163ff.
Tradition, related to Scripture 14–20
transplants, organ *see* organ transplants
Trent, Council of 1, 26, 34, 94, 99, 104,
  108, 182, 214, 218, 264, 354 n. 6
  on anointing of the sick 291, 293
  on confession 275, 278, 282
  on grace 339
  on holy communion 271
  on marriage 320
  on purgatory 206
Trinity, Holy *see* Holy Trinity
  see also Holy Spirit
truths, hierarchy of *see* hierarchy of truths
typology 27–8

Unitatis Redintegratio 17, 20, 178, 183,
  187, 189–90
US Catholic Bishops Conference 86

Vandervelde, G. 107
Vatican I, Council of 1, 6–18, 39–40, 61–2,
  64 n. 20, 64 n. 29, 128–9, 184, 340, 355 n.
  12, 362
Vatican II, Council of 1–3, 39–40, 45–6,
  83, 91, 100, 104, 105, 109–10, 115, 162,
  176–7, 179, 196, 221, 237, 239, 242, 245,
  247–8, 275, 303ff., 313–14, 357, 362, 368
  and *passim*
  on anointing of the sick 291
  on marriage 321ff.
  on the Eucharist 264, 267ff., 272
Veritatis Splendor 348, 351, 391
viaticum 299–300

Vienne, Council of   93
Vigilius, Pope   125 n. 11, 126 n. 15
Vincent of Lérins, St   30 n. 25
virginity   320, 325
virtues   350
Vorgrimler, H.   241 n. 20

warfare   373ff.
   see also insurrection; just war
washing of feet   227
Weil, Simone   137
Westcott, B. F.   62
Wittgenstein, Ludwig   59–60
women   30 n. 17, 88, 131, 319, 324, 326–7,
   352, 361

women, ordination of *see* ordination of
   women
work   382–3
World Council of Churches   384
world religions   167, 177
worship   50
   see also liturgy

Yhwh   56–7, 64 n. 23, 117, 366

Zacchaeus   277
Zaïre   239
Zechariah   411